BECOMING A PHYSICIAN

Becoming a Physician

Medical Education in Britain, France, Germany, and the United States, 1750–1945

THOMAS NEVILLE BONNER

New York   Oxford
OXFORD UNIVERSITY PRESS
1995

Oxford University Press

Oxford   New York
Athens   Auckland   Bangkok   Bombay
Calcutta   Cape Town   Dar es Salaam   Delhi
Florence   Hong Kong   Istanbul   Karachi
Kuala Lumpur   Madras   Madrid   Melbourne
Mexico City   Nairobi   Paris   Singapore
Taipei   Tokyo   Toronto

and associated companies in
Berlin   Ibadan

Copyright © 1995 by Thomas Neville Bonner

Published by Oxford University Press, Inc.,
198 Madison Avenue, New York, New York, 10016

Oxford is a registered trademark of Oxford University Press

Library of Congress Cataloging-in-Publication Data
Bonner, Thomas Neville.
Becoming a physician : medical education in Britain, France, Germany, and the United States,
1750–1945 / Thomas Neville Bonner.
p.   cm.
Includes bibliographical references and index.
ISBN 0-19-506298-1
1. Medical education—History.   I. Title.
R735.B66   1995
610'.71'1—dc20   94-42800

9 8 7 6 5 4 3 2 1

Printed in the United States of America on acid-free paper

For Lucille Maitland, Jane Lutz,
Betty Spaulding, Pat Tappa, and Annette Riley,
who know how much I owe them

Acknowledgments

I am happy to acknowledge the many debts gathered in the making of this book. Nearly a decade ago, when I began my preliminary study, the National Library of Medicine made possible a year of background reading as Visiting Historical Scholar at its superb facility in Bethesda, Maryland. The National Endowment for the Humanities, through its Division of Research Programs, was responsible for a three-year grant that enabled me to make four lengthy trips to archives and libraries abroad. A memorable five weeks at the Rockefeller International Conference Center at Bellagio, Italy, in 1992 gave me an unrivaled opportunity to think through the outlines of the whole project. And Wayne State University, finally, by awarding me a Charles Gershenson Distinguished Faculty Fellowship, made much easier the completion of the task of writing this book.

Along the way, literally scores of colleagues, scholars, and friends have given invaluable assistance. At the outset, W. F. Bynum, Dora B. Weiner, Robert G. Frank Jr., Michael Kater, George Weisz, Richard Kremer, and James Albisetti all provided generous guidance to sources in the countries of their expertise. While abroad, I found helpful colleagues in every country. Special mention must be made of Bynum in London, John Pickstone in Manchester, Elisabeth Leedham-Green in Cambridge, Michael Barfoot in Edinburgh, Michael Moss in Glasgow, and Jack Lyons in Dublin. In France, I received much help from Andre Cornét, Gabriel Richet, Jean Imbert, Jean-Charles Sournia, Anne Marie Moulin, and Donna Evleth, all of Paris; Jacques Heran of Strasbourg; Louis Dulieu of Montpellier;

and Maurice Boucher of Lyon. German and Austrian scholars who provided helpful local assistance included Karl Holubar (Vienna); Ulrich Tröhler (Göttingen); Gerhard Fichtner (Tübingen); Johanna Bleker and Peter Schneck (Berlin); Dieter Jetter and Axel Karenberg (Cologne); Gundolf Keil (Würzburg); Achim Thom and Cornelia Becker (Leipzig); Paul Unschuld (Munich); Max Otto (Heidelberg); Hans Renschler (Bonn); Hendrik van den Bussche (Hamburg); and Eduard Seidler (Freiburg). Countless others have tracked down dissertations, checked references, and made available copies of their unpublished work.

Librarians and archivists in more than a hundred institutions gave me crucial help in finding materials. At Wayne State University, in particular, Candice Williams and her colleagues in the Inter-Library Loan Department went far beyond their duty in finding rare books and articles.

In the last stages, a number of friends and colleagues did yeoman service in reading all or parts of the manuscript. I hope that others will pardon me if I single out John Burnham, whose sharp eye and sharper pencil were extraordinarily helpful at a critical stage. Others who provided detailed and unusually helpful commentaries were W. F. Bynum, William G. Rothstein, Gert H. Brieger, Dora B. Weiner, Gerald Grob, Gabriel Richet, Kenneth Ludmerer, and George Weisz. Valuable, too, in shaping the final form of the work were the advice and suggestions offered by Johanna Bleker, Axel Karenberg, Edward Lurie, Daniel M. Fox, Russell C. Maulitz, and John Harley Warner. None of them, needless to say, is to any degree responsible for errors of fact or interpretation in the present book.

Appreciation is due, too, to the Harvard University Press for allowing me to use small portions of my recently published study: *To the Ends of the Earth: Women's Search for Education in Medicine* (1992), and to the *Bulletin of the History of Medicine and Medical History* for the use of several paragraphs from recently published articles in these journals.

Finally, I want to thank John Stewart, for his research assistance over these past four years, and Annette I. Riley, coworker, counselor, and friend, without whom I could not have found my way through the new age of computers and word processing.

Contents

BECOMING A PHYSICIAN

Introduction

In the following pages, I argue for a new way of looking at the history of medical education. The growth of medical training, I believe, has too long been viewed in almost exclusively national terms. Changes in medical teaching seem to have come only when creative individuals or powerful centers of innovation in a single country—Leyden, Vienna, Edinburgh, Paris, Giessen, Leipzig, or perhaps Baltimore—have discovered new ideas and techniques and radiated them outward to peripheral training centers in less advanced cities and towns. Strong personalities have put their stamp on new methods of imparting medical knowledge. The periodization of historical development is marked by important discontinuities that center on large historical events.

The historical focus is understandably on dramatic change, new schemes of conveying learning, the advance of science in medicine, or the travels of foreign physicians to centers of innovation. Students appear in standard accounts, if at all, only as passive and voiceless participants in an impersonal process. History becomes a tale of successive national centers of influence that wax and wane in their importance to medicine. Rarely is it clear why these centers climb suddenly to historical prominence or why they later decline. And almost always, in even the best writing on medical education, a teleological thread is visible in which nineteenth-century and earlier patterns are followed largely to reveal how they helped shape twentieth-century realities. In short, medical education, like medicine itself, is often portrayed as a story of steady and sometimes heroic progress.

In this book, I seek further answers to the reasons for change in med-

ical teaching in the social, industrial, political, and educational transformations of Europe and North America that took place between the Enlightenment and World War II. Especially important, I believe, was the
differential impact on individual nations of such major shifts in Western
thought and society as the eighteenth-century Enlightenment, the rapid
bursts of population and explosion of cities in the Industrial Revolution,
the expansion of the market for health practitioners due to educational
and urban growth, the rise of an entrepreneurial spirit in education, the
widespread transformation of secondary and higher education in the
nineteenth century, advances in the explanatory power of observational
and experimental science, and the differing roles played by nation-states,
as well as by the students themselves, in matters of health and education.

Because of the need for limits, I have chosen for study those nations—
Great Britain, France, Germany, and the United States—that were most
populous and exerted the greatest influence on their neighbors in the
past two centuries. In the case of the German states, I have necessarily included sections on Austria and Switzerland, especially before 1871, in
tracing developments in central Europe, and in North America I have
taken some notice of developments in Canada, which although they differed at times from those south of the border, largely paralleled trends in
the United States. For reasons of space, I have also concentrated on the
basic academic and practical education of practitioners, including the
"practical year" or internship, and taken less notice of the extensive
growth of postgraduate and specialized training in the twentieth century,
especially after World War II.

Although it has long been known that education in medicine followed
different paths in the principal countries, with important effects on world
medicine, the attempt here is not only to describe these differences but also,
wherever possible, to explain the reasons for national divergence. Existing
studies of medical education are usually rooted in a single time or place and
do not allow for wider cross-national or cross-cultural comparisons. As Fritz
Ringer, the chronicler of the decline of Germany's academic mandarins,
wrote about national systems of education in general, "one must be able to
separate characteristics unique to this or that national system" in order to
find at least tentative explanations "and not just descriptions of change."[1]

Modern scholars such as Ringer, Joseph Ben-David, Charles McClelland,
Konrad Jarausch, and Kenneth Ludmerer have increasingly viewed the education of physicians as a part of the general history of higher education. In
his presidential address to the American Association for the History of Medicine, Gert Brieger argued persuasively for medical education to be seen as
"a part of the history of education, not merely of the history of medicine."[2]
Nonetheless, despite such exhortations, changes in historical explanation

1. Fritz K. Ringer, *Education and Society in Modern Europe* (Bloomington: Indiana University Press, 1979), 1.
2. Gert H. Brieger, "'Fit to Study Medicine': Notes for a History of Pre-medical Education in America," *Bulletin of the History of Medicine* 57 (1983): 6.

have been slow, and in many studies, the persistence of national differences is rarely noticed. By presenting the major characteristics and interactions of several national systems of educating doctors, I believe that it may be possible to understand better the developments in a single state. Often when writing this book I was struck by how familiar events in a single country simply "looked different" when viewed against a wider canvas.

Historians have given surprisingly little attention to the general subject of medical education. Useful national histories exist for only a few countries, and almost no modern work compares developments in more than one country. The only comprehensive history of medical education, that of the Viennese historian Theodor Puschmann, was written more than a century ago. When it was republished in 1966, Erwin Ackerknecht, a leading historian of the time, declared in the introduction that it was "most surprising and disturbing" that it was still "the only serious treatise in the field up to this day."[3] Since that time, only the loosely organized (but still useful) symposia led by C. D. O'Malley in 1968 and Teizo Ogawa in 1982—neither of which attempted to move beyond descriptions of medical education in single nations—have tried to deal systematically with the subject.[4] Surprisingly, Abraham Flexner's comparative studies, written three-quarters of a century ago, remain among the most useful sources for the study of comparative medical education.[5]

In the case of the United States, a number of recent books, especially those by William Rothstein and Kenneth Ludmerer, do deal both comprehensively and analytically with the growth of medical study in a single nation. The study by Rothstein, stressing the continuity of development in American medical schools and questioning the heavy emphasis on laboratory and scientific work as defining elements in modern medical pedagogy, covers the entire span of American medical study. Ludmerer, concentrating on changes after 1870, emphasizes the new institutional framework of universities, secondary schools, and foundations, as well as the role of an academic elite, in furnishing the ingredients for reform in the United States.[6]

Few such comprehensive studies have been made in recent years of the British, French, or German experience in educating physicians. Still the

3. Theodor Puschmann, *A History of Medical Education* (New York: Hafner, 1966), 1.

4. C. D. O'Malley, ed., *The History of Medical Education* (Berkeley and Los Angeles: University of California Press, 1970); and Teizo Ogawa, ed., *History of Medical Education* (Tokyo: Saikon, 1983).

5. See Abraham Flexner's *Medical Education: A Comparative Study* (New York: Macmillan, 1925); *Medical Education in Europe* (New York: Carnegie Foundation for the Advancement of Teaching, 1912); and *Medical Education in the United States and Canada* (New York: Carnegie Foundation for the Advancement of Education, 1910). See, too, Flexner's "Medical Education, 1905–1924," *Educational Record*, April 1924, pp. 3–17; and *Universities: American, English, German* (New York: Oxford University Press, 1930).

6. See William G. Rothstein, *American Medical Schools and the Practice of Medicine: A History* (New York: Oxford University Press, 1987); and Kenneth M. Ludmerer, *Learning to Heal: The Development of American Medical Education* (New York: Basic Books, 1985).

only general survey of the subject in Great Britain, by Charles Newman, is now nearly forty years old.[7] In the case of France, the pioneering survey by Charles Coury remains the only broad treatment, although a number of recent scholars have brought fresh insights into limited periods of medical training.[8] Most of the studies that put German medical education in a larger perspective are older. The best known is the now classic history by Theodor Billroth, written in 1876 and translated into English fifty years later, but it has limited use for the modern reader.[9]

After nearly a decade of intensive study of the subject and a lifetime of reflection, what have I learned that is at all new or useful about the shaping of modern medical education? What is the value of comparative history in seeking new perspectives in medical education? Some of this book's major themes are the following:

1. Viewed from a comparative perspective, the late eighteenth century seems to be a more critical watershed in the development of medical education than has hitherto been realized. The old medieval order and structure of medical studies, long weakened by new ideas in education and science, collapsed completely after 1750. New subjects from the scientific revolution of the preceding century found their way into the curriculum in every country; a movement toward practical training was gathering momentum everywhere; hospital reform, critical to medical teaching, was spreading through the major cities of Britain and the Continent; medicine and surgery, divided by centuries of tradition, were drawing closer together in a number of places; the old separation between physicians and

7. Charles Newman, *The Evolution of Medical Education in the Nineteenth Century* (Oxford: Oxford University Press, 1957).

8. See Charles Coury, *Enseignement de la médecine en France des origines à nos jours* (Paris: Expansion scientifique française, 1968). Some of Georges Weisz's work, especially his essay "Reform and Conflict in French Medical Education, 1870–1914," in *The Organization of Science and Technology in France, 1808–1914,* ed. Robert Fox and George Weisz (Cambridge: Cambridge University Press, 1980), is particularly suggestive and useful, as are studies by Toby Gelfand, Mathew Ramsay, Dora Weiner, Jacques Léonard, and Jean-Pierre Goubert.

9. See Theodor Billroth, *The Medical Sciences in the German Universities* (New York: Macmillan, 1924). This edition contains an introduction by William Henry Welch. More recently, such scholars as Thomas Broman, Arleen Tuchman, Robert Frank Jr., William Coleman, Frederic L. Holmes, and a group of recent scholars in Germany have made detailed, analytical studies of aspects of German medical education in the eighteenth and nineteenth centuries, but they have not ventured far from a national framework. See Thomas H. Broman, "The Transformation of Academic Medicine in Germany, 1780–1820" (Ph.D. diss., Princeton University, 1987); Arleen M. Tuchman, *Science, Medicine, and the State in Germany: The Case of Baden, 1815–1871* (New York: Oxford University Press, 1993); and William Coleman and Frederic L. Holmes, eds., *The Investigative Enterprise: Experimental Physiology in Nineteenth-Century Medicine* (Berkeley and Los Angeles: University of California Press, 1988). The last contains essays by Coleman, Holmes, Tuchman, and Frank, as well as by John E. Lesch, Timothy Lenoir, and Kathryn M. Olesko. Among German historians, the work of Johanna Bleker, especially her *Die Naturhistorische Schule, 1825–1845: Ein Beitrag zur Geschichte der klinischen Medizin in Deutschland* (Stuttgart: Gustav Fischer, 1981), is outstanding.

apothecaries was breaking down in several countries; and several of the absolutist states were beginning to set new standards of medical study and practice.

National differences in training doctors that were important to the future were becoming increasingly evident in these years. From a broader perspective, the most turbulent or creative period in the history of medical training in the West was the closing decades of the eighteenth century.

2. The variety of healing programs that developed after 1780 was immense, with the traditional university losing importance everywhere except Germany as the principal site of medical learning. Special schools for training practical healers needed by the growing populations sprang up in every country. Indeed, until the late nineteenth century, most medical training in the English-speaking countries took place outside universities, and a considerable portion of healers on the Continent were also educated in such schools.

Among such nonuniversity institutions, only the American "proprietary" school has received much attention from historians. The quality of medical instruction in the practical schools of Britain and the "secondary" and "medical–surgical" academies of France and Germany was similar to that of the United States and sometimes remarkably good by contemporary standards. By 1820, for example, the curriculum of the continental practical schools included many of the courses being taught in the university; the classes were often small and individual teaching was possible; the teaching faculty was sometimes as large as that of the universities; and students and teachers moved back and forth with surprising ease from these schools to university schools of medicine.

The sharp division between such schools and the university training in medicine portrayed by later writers, moreover, was never as sharp in the minds of contemporaries. Among freestanding schools lacking any university connection, military schools of medicine, in particular, offered for nearly a century the best medical instruction available in Europe. And when physician-entrepreneurs organized courses for profit in the hospitals, especially in Great Britain, they too began to attract some of the most able students interested in medicine. Well before 1800, the mixed patterns of medical training familiar to educators in the nineteenth century were clearly visible in all the Western countries, and virtually all the questions that would plague reformers for decades to come had already been raised.

3. Despite the great variety of schools and learning opportunities, the students in every country were themselves the organizers of their own education, and this remained true for much of the nineteenth century.

The lives and experiences of students in general and their impact on medical education have been too little studied. Many of the medical students of the late eighteenth and early nineteenth century, I have found, were extremely young. While still in their teens, many worked ten to twelve hours per day as apprentices; some entered the university at age fifteen or sixteen; and others at a similar age walked the wards of hospitals or served as assistant surgeons in the army. Many completed their education before they were twenty or twenty-one years old. In fact, the age requirement of twenty-one for graduation or licensing in medicine was sometimes seen as a radical reform preventing those who had completed their education from earning a living.

In this book I describe the daily lives of the students; their varied and changing social backgrounds; the religious, gender, class, and racial restrictions imposed on them; the deep concerns they had about the preparation they received; the reasons for their often rowdy behavior; and the universal demand for more practical opportunities and the role they played in the shaping of their own medical education.

4. The importance of practical, hands-on training at the bedside as the best method of teaching medicine was all but universally recognized well before 1800. What was argued in the following decades was how best to carry out this kind of training, not whether it was necessary or desirable. Was it best carried out through an apprenticeship, one on one, with an experienced practitioner, in a large hospital with impromptu lectures at the bedside, or in a small infirmary or clinic under the control of a teacher?

The wide variations and controversies that marked the introduction of the teaching clinic into Western medicine have been too little noticed. France, as is well known, was the first country to open its hospitals to large numbers of students and to organize a national plan for teaching at the bedside. But according to many contemporaries, it was the small German *policlinic*, or academic hospital run by the faculty, that offered students actual experience in managing patients. In the university clinic, wrote Christoph Hufeland around 1800, students were more than the "simple spectators" that they were in the overcrowded and understaffed hospitals of Paris.

The assignment of responsibilities to students for patient care in Germany, described by the Dubliner Robert Graves in 1821 as the best way to learn medicine, became the central feature of the system of clinical clerkships later adopted in Britain and America. In France, by contrast, the great advances in scientific discovery and new technology of the first half of the nineteenth century overshadowed and often concealed the severe strains on well-intentioned plans for the hands-on teaching of medicine.

5. The powerful role of differing political and cultural structures in shaping the national outcomes in medical education has also been given too little attention. The state's authority over medical education was overwhelming in France after the Revolution, only slightly less powerful in the German states, and largely absent in Britain and America. The entrepreneurial spirit in private education in the English-speaking countries stimulated the creation of a great number of practical schools that differed in important ways from the state-run schools of the Continent. This

difference in national control had enormous consequences in setting standards for graduation and licensing, gaining control over hospitals for teaching purposes, fostering innovations in teaching, and opening medical schools to women.

In the case of women, for example, the state-sponsored medical schools of France and Switzerland and, later, those of Germany were educating more medical women in universities by the early twentieth century than were any in the English-speaking countries. In Britain and the United States, although the laissez-faire tradition of private control permitted early experimentation in educating women, it delayed the full acceptance of coeducation in medicine until well into the twentieth century.

6. Scholars working in American medicine have overstated the weaknesses of medical schools in the nineteenth-century United States. Not only in America but also in Britain and on the Continent, commercial motives were strong in the many private schools and private courses. Neither the "proprietary" school nor teaching for private gain was ever exclusive to North America. A carefully graded curriculum, too, was as unusual in Britain as it was in America for much of the nineteenth century, and the repetition of courses by students in both countries was not uncommon. In Germany, the students' vaunted *Lernfreiheit* made certain that there would be no required order of studies in that country.

Opportunities for bedside instruction (as opposed to clinical lectures), furthermore, were frequently as lacking in Europe as in America. Apprenticeship remained a central feature of British and American medical training until well past the middle of the century.

Perhaps most serious is the absence of any comparison between the much-maligned independent or "proprietary" schools that educated most American physicians in the nineteenth century and the large number of "practical" or non-degree-granting schools of Britain and Europe at which practitioners were prepared—as they were in the United States—for service in rural areas. In comparing the rural, proprietary schools of backwoods America in 1840 with the Paris medical faculty or perhaps that of Edinburgh or Vienna, contemporary reformers confused some very small apples with some very large oranges.

A comparison of the Ohio Medical College in Cincinnati with the practical school at Bamberg in Bavaria, for example, as suggested in Chapter 6, or with the Anderson Medical College in Glasgow, would have yielded far less striking contrasts. The American experience in medical education, in short, simply looks different when viewed in a larger, transatlantic perspective.

7. Further thought is needed, too, regarding the concept of radical change in medical education, whether in revolutionary France, mid-nineteenth-century Germany, or America after 1870. The modern clinical method of educating physicians did not arise de novo in the France of 1789–1815, and other major shifts in medical teaching—the introduc-

tion of laboratory teaching in medicine in midcentury Germany, the fusion of clinical and laboratory study at the end of the nineteenth century in America, and the reemergence of the university as the site of most medical training in several countries around 1900—all developed less spontaneously and against far greater resistance than is commonly portrayed.

The impulse to try to make medicine an experimental science by means of the laboratory, for example, was felt throughout the transatlantic world. But it was the resistance to its introduction into teaching because of national factors that explains the paths followed in the different countries. Even in the German states—where universities had early forged an uneasy alliance with the practical study of medicine—the transition to laboratory instruction came only gradually after overcoming powerful obstacles, and it was ultimately justified only by its practical or clinical uses. The teaching laboratory in medicine was finally shaped by the historical, educational, and political circumstances peculiar to each country. Throughout this book, I have tried to remember that past history has nearly always been written by the victors in the ongoing fight over the direction of change.

8. Unlike some researchers, I consider the changes in scientific knowledge and medical effectiveness in the nineteenth century as being critical to the transformation of medical education. Any account that fails to consider the practical achievements of laboratory science in the late nineteenth century in changing the perception of medicine, I believe, is incomplete. The deep skepticism among students, faculty, and the public toward the utility of laboratory study that persisted in many places until at least 1890 finally gave way to the sweeping achievements in bacteriology and germ theory. To question now whether this fin-de-siécle spirit of optimism about scientific medicine was misguided in the light of later events is to indulge in a kind of reverse Whiggism that distorts the picture of what actually happened. By 1910, in any case, few educators or practitioners in any country questioned the need for serious scientific study and laboratory experience as indispensable parts of a medical education.

9. The persistence of national differences in shaping the outcome of social and scientific movements in medical teaching is a constant refrain of this book. Although all Western countries experienced many of the same broad impulses toward change in teaching, each dealt with them in quite different ways. Differences in social structure, the pace of industrialism, the level of state intervention, national prosperity, the market economy, better educational systems, and the impact of different styles of leadership and personality had an important and sometimes decisive impact on both the spread of change and the forms of institutional life in the various countries. Despite the internationalism of science at the end of the nineteenth century and the parallel revolution in communications, these differences were in some ways sharper in 1900 than they had been in 1800. And in our own century, despite the growing uniformity of standards and

curricula, striking differences in the teaching of medicine still persist among the Western nations.

In summary, what I have attempted here is a study of medical education that is comparative throughout, broadly based, more continuous than discontinuous in organization, focused to a considerable degree on students, and as attentive to the periphery as to the great medical centers; that looks to political and economic factors as well as scientific and social ones to understand change; and one that may help explain current differences in the approach to teaching medical students.

I know that the answers given to long-standing issues of interpretation in medical education can be only partial and must rest to considerable degree on previous work. Whatever is new in this book comes from my effort to see medical education as a larger whole and to infuse new sources of information into the discussion. I have been mindful throughout of the words of James H. Billington when he was appointed librarian of Congress, that "the kind of scholarship we need more of is providing tentative answers to important questions rather than definitive answers to secondary ones. . . . We need to put things together, not just take them apart."[10]

This is a modest effort to put a few things together.

10. *Washington Post*, April 18, 1987.

1

An Uncertain Enterprise: Learning to Heal in the Enlightenment

There was no more turbulent yet creative time in the history of medical study than the latter years of the eighteenth century. During this troubled era, familiar landmarks in medicine were fast disappearing; new ideas about medical training were gaining favor; the sites of medical education were rapidly expanding; and the variety of healers was growing in every country. Student populations, too, were undergoing important changes; governments were shifting their role in medicine, especially in the continental nations; and national differences in educating doctors were becoming more pronounced. These transformations are the subject of the opening chapters of this book.

These changes in medical education were a reflection of the general transformation of European society, education, and politics. By the century's end, the whole transatlantic world was in the grip of profound social and political movement. Like other institutions, universities and medical schools were caught up in a "period of major institutional restructuring" as new expectations were placed on teachers and students.[1] Contemporaries spoke of an apocalyptic sense of an older order falling and new institutions fighting for birth, and inevitably the practice of healing was also affected.

From the middle of the century, the nations of Europe and their New World offspring had undergone a quickening transformation in their eco-

1. Björn Wittrock, "The Modern University: The Three Transformations," in *The European and American University Since 1800: Historical and Sociological Essays*, ed. Sheldon Rothblatt and Björn Wittrock (Cambridge: Cambridge University Press, 1993), 312.

nomic activity, educational ideas, and political outlook. By 1800, in the island kingdom of Great Britain, the unprecedented advance of agricultural and industrial change had pushed that nation into world leadership in manufacturing, agricultural productivity, trade, and shipping. Its population growth exceeded that of any continental state, and in addition, nearly three-fourths of all new urban growth in Europe was occurring in the British Isles.[2] The effects on higher education were to create a demand for more practical subjects, modern languages, and increased attention to the needs of the thriving middle classes. Although Oxford and Cambridge, the only universities in England, were largely untouched by the currents of change, the Scottish universities, by contrast, were beginning to teach modern subjects, to bring practical experience into the medical curriculum, and to open their doors to a wider spectrum of students. "No longer did a single kind of learning or a privileged path," writes Joseph Ben-David, "lead through the ancient universities of Oxford and Cambridge to the learned professions."[3]

Across the Channel, France—the most populous nation west of the Urals and long a power in scientific and medical discovery and now the leader in Enlightenment ideas—was erupting in violent revolution against the old order of society and sending its citizen armies against a succession of enemies in Austria, Britain, Prussia, and Russia. Early in the Revolution, the old universities and their faculties were abolished as symbols of privilege, and specialized schools of engineering, medicine, and military science rose to take their place. At the height of their power, the armies of Napoleon carried French concepts, French culture, and French ideas about education and medicine across much of central and southern Europe. Many of the famous medical and university centers of the Continent were now in French hands, including many in Germany, Italy, and the Low Countries.

In the middle of Europe, what was to become modern Germany was still a jumbled congeries of principalities, small kingdoms, a loose confederation of Rhenish states, and a Prussia humbled by Napoleon's *grande armée*—all together a vast arena that was deeply affected by the storms sweeping across the Continent. German reformers, who were resisting the tide of French influence, reorganized their universities to accommodate new ideas about science and professional education while at the same time retaining the humanistic core of liberal study.

The violent shake-up of old institutions and habits in these countries and also in an independent America profoundly affected the training of physicians, surgeons, and other healers, for the teaching of medical students, like the practice of medicine, was and is deeply embedded in its so-

2. E. A. Wrigley, *Continuity, Chance and Change: The Character of the Industrial Revolution in England* (Cambridge: Cambridge University Press, 1988), 12–13.

3. Joseph Ben-David, *Centers of Learning: Britain, France, Germany, United States* (New York: McGraw-Hill, 1977), 18.

cial surroundings. Unlike experimental science, in which relationships to the outer world are sometimes complicated by isolation and the need for privacy, medical teaching has been unambiguously a social enterprise. What students learn, how they learn it, where they study, and who is permitted to learn are rooted in particular historical and cultural circumstances that have varied from country to country.

The Breakdown of the Medieval Order

For the generation of medical students who lived in the latter half of the eighteenth century, the practice of medical healing was clearly in turmoil. For five hundred years, after all, the education of physicians had been more or less stable and similar from country to country. Everywhere the learned study of medicine was limited to a small minority whose families met the social and class tests for university study. For the most part, their patients were likewise drawn from the landed and monied classes with whom they shared a measure of social status.

As viewed by the established classes, medicine was a learned occupation studied principally in universities, based on the classics of medicine and literature, rooted in the universal language of Latin, and divorced from the practical, hands-on work of the surgeons, the pharmacists, and other healers. The medical curriculum, classical texts, and Latin language were equally familiar to a German visitor in Padua or Paris or to a Frenchman at Edinburgh or Halle. Likewise, the few Americans who took formal instruction in medicine did so in schools modeled closely on that of Edinburgh, which in turn closely resembled the medical schools of the Continent.

Now, however, the old synthesis was breaking up in every country. New subjects arising out of the scientific revolution of the preceding century—notably chemistry, botany, and physiology—were rapidly finding a place in the university curriculum. Interest in natural science was accelerating, too, in the ways in which such traditional subjects as anatomy, materia medica, and legal medicine were taught. The works of Hippocrates and Galen, though still assiduously studied, were no longer the heart and soul of the medical curriculum. In medical teaching, the movement toward practical training was gathering momentum in nearly every country. National languages were beginning to be used alongside Latin as the medium of instruction. Hospital reform was spreading throughout the major cities of Britain and the Continent. And a new interest in *nosology*, or the effort to classify diseases by characteristics or symptoms, was a further indication of change.

Moreover, medical practice itself was changing. Medicine and surgery were drawing closer together in a number of locations. The therapeutic division among physicians, surgeons, and apothecaries was likewise breaking down in many places. Spurred by Enlightenment concerns for the people's health, the absolutist states were setting definitive standards for medical teaching and practice. And in many places the demand for trained medical care, though still limited, was showing signs of expanding to new populations and new regions.

As the medieval synthesis finally disintegrated, national differences affected the directions of medical education. This change was most radical in France, where the restraints of an older social structure and governing traditions were swept away in the violence of revolution. In central Europe, a powerful surge of statism and nationalism, stimulated in part by the continuing threat of French expansion, gave a new direction to the medical curriculum. In Great Britain, where the forces of liberal constitutionalism and social conservatism were least disturbed by the currents of nationalism and revolutionary change flowing in Europe, old practices and arrangements in medicine lingered much longer, especially in the English universities. As late as 1889, the critical Viennese historian Theodor Puschmann wrote of the old universities that "the customs of the middle ages in regard to medical teaching have been preserved longest in England."[4]

In the case of England's overseas colonies in North America, the sense of isolation, independence, and new conditions and needs pushed American medical education into variations of traditional British practices. In an age of nationalism, national factors took on growing significance in explaining the directions that the education of doctors took after 1750.

Much that happened later in medical education had its roots in the disordered world of the late eighteenth century. In the German states, for example, the universities were undergoing an important transformation that put them in a favorable position to benefit from the intellectual and scientific shifts in the years ahead. A new emphasis on freedom for both students and teachers, together with a growing humanistic and scientific orientation and the increasing use of the German language, brought an important change in university teaching throughout German-speaking Europe.[5] The principle of uniting teaching and research in the person of the university professor had already been established in many places, and the first specialized chairs had already been created.[6] But medical teaching remained in the revitalized German universities, even as elsewhere it found new roots outside the university.

For many centuries the teaching of traditional medicine had been a university activity everywhere, but now the changed conditions encouraged new experiments in training physicians in hospitals, military schools, academies, and private enterprises.

By 1800 in Britain, for example, a growing sense of chaos in medical training had produced, in the words of Irvine Loudon, an "extraordinary

4. Theodor Puschmann, *A History of Medical Education* (New York Hafner, , 1966), 498. This work was originally published in 1889.

5. Friedrich Paulsen, *Geschichte des gelehrten Unterrichts* (Berlin: Walter de Gruyter, 1921), 147–48.

6. Hans-Heinz Eulner, *Die Entwicklung der medizinischen Spezialfächer an den Universitäten des deutschen Sprachgebietes* (Stuttgart: Ferdinand Enke, 1970), 22.

degree of hostility and bitterness" between an elite of university-educated physicians and a growing number of apprentice and hospital-trained practitioners.[7] The latter group was now demanding recognition and an end to special privileges and restrictions in medicine. By the end of the century, preparation for medical practice in Great Britain was increasingly confused: a mixture of old traditions, new initiatives, and privileged corporations in a murky stew of established universities, hospital medical training, private courses, apprenticeships, and separate licensing authorities for physicians, surgeons, and apothecaries. Even before 1800, English medical education had embarked on a course that, in addition to its traditionalism, set it apart from the continental schools.

Similarly, in France, a highly trained elite of physicians and first-rank surgeons who had enjoyed the benefit of a university education, was being increasingly challenged by a much larger group of practically trained practitioners who treated the health problems of the great mass of the population.[8] As they were in Britain, practical surgeons, apothecaries, and midwifes were expanding their practice and clamoring for a larger place in the hierarchy of healers. At the same time, the education of academic physicians and surgeons was being altered by such changes as the creation in Paris of the Ecole pratique de dissection (1750), and the establishment of the Royal Society of Medicine for leading physicians.[9] Well before the Revolution in France, a demand for new methods of teaching, more practical instruction, and a leveling of distinctions in health training was widely reported throughout the country.

Varieties of Healers

In the waning years of the eighteenth century, it was not at all clear which varieties of healers would prevail in the fierce struggle for position and dominance. Later historians have understandably emphasized the role of the university-educated elite, who are rightly seen as the forerunners of the scientifically trained physicians and surgeons of our own time. But in the heated political atmosphere of the years of Enlightenment, other options seemed possible. The failure of regular physicians to offer their patients much more than uncertain drugs and frequent bleeding, as

---

7. Irvine Loudon, *Medical Care and the General Practitioner, 1750–1850* (Oxford: Clarendon Press, 1986), 129.

8. See the full discussion in Matthew Ramsey, *Professional and Popular Medicine in France, 1770–1830* (Cambridge: Cambridge University Press, 1988), 17–38.

9. For the Ecole pratique, see Marie-José Imbault-Huart, "L'Ecole pratique de dissection de Paris de 1750 à 1822 ou l'influence du concept de médecine d'observation dans l'enseignement medico–chirurgical au XVIIIème siècle et du debut du XIXème siècle" (Ph.D. diss, University of Paris, 1973); for the Royal Society, see Caroline Hannaway, "Medicine, Public Welfare and the State in Eighteenth-Century France: The Societé Royale de Médecine de Paris (1776–1793)" (Ph.D. diss., Johns Hopkins University, 1974).

well as their inability to recognize with certainty the origins of a single human disease, made even those who could afford the best medical care skeptical of traditional medicine's authority and power.

One of the early actions of the revolutionary government in France was to destroy the university and corporate structure of medical teaching and to declare a universal freedom to practice medicine. In the German states, too, although the practice of medicine here was more closely regulated than it was elsewhere, a large body of alternative healers provided health care for the vast majority of their populations. In Great Britain, a vast "pluralist medical scene" embraced a wide spectrum of medical and surgical options as well as practices that included midwifery, bonesetting, drugselling, and other forms of healing.[10] Similarly, no clear boundary between university-trained and lesser practitioners was evident in the widely spread settlements of North America. Not until the Civil War, at least, was the line of demarcation clearly drawn between professionally trained practitioners and popular healers in the United States.[11]

The Practice of Healing in Great Britain

In both Britain and America, the limited regulation of private activity made even richer than on the Continent the mixture of practitioners of all sorts. Cries for reform from university physicians in late-eighteenth-century Britain were more shrill than in either Germany or prerevolutionary France. By this time, a number of surgeons and apothecaries, having acquired hospital training in the London and provincial hospitals, were creating a new class of general practitioners that resented the archaic controls over practice exercised by the royal corporations and their university-trained members. The surgeon-apothecaries also faced a growing army of competitors from below in their struggle for a larger share of the medical market. These included female midwives, many of them skilled and experienced, a swiftly growing number of apprentice-trained druggists, itinerant healers and peddlers of nostrums, and even members of the Anglican and dissenting clergy. In Scotland, the term *mediciner* was coined to embrace a wide variety of practitioners that included doctors of medicine, surgeons, apothecaries, and druggists.[12]

A representative survey of health practitioners in rural Lancashire at the beginning of the nineteenth century showed that graduate physicians made up only 2 percent of all healers, surgeons and apothecaries 9 percent, druggists 16 percent, and irregular practitioners and midwives 73

---

10. Dorothy Porter and Roy Porter, *Patient's Progress: Doctors and Doctoring in Eighteenth-Century England* (Stanford, CA: Stanford University Press, 1989), 18–27.

11. Lamar R. Murphy, *Enter the Physician: The Transformation of Domestic Medicine, 1760–1860* (Tuscaloosa: University of Alabama Press, 1991), xviii.

12. Anderson's College Minutes, undated, 1796, University of Strathclyde Archive. In John Anderson's will, one category of trustees provided for nine "mediciners," which he defined as including the categories listed.

percent of all those in practice. "At present," concluded the author gloomily, "physicians without degrees ... surgeons and apothecaries without instruction, and apothecaries and druggists without having served an apprenticeship, have intruded themselves ... into almost every market town in England."[13]

In a revealing study of eighteenth-century Bristol, Mary Fissell uncovered the surprisingly large role played by women in the care of the sick. Not only did they serve as midwives and family healers in many instances, but some pursued careers as barber-surgeons and apothecaries as well. In rural areas, it was not uncommon for the widows of physicians to replace their husbands in treating patients. Midwives, too, often did more than deliver babies. The case of Nanny Holland, who inoculated patients against smallpox and set bones, in addition to attending women in childbirth, is particularly striking.[14] A similar range of practice could be found among American midwives, notably that of Martha Ballard, who dispensed drugs, performed minor surgery, nursed neighbors in her home, and assisted physicians in her hometown of Augusta, Maine.[15] In addition, the wives of ministers in both America and Britain were frequently important attendants in childbirth and family illness.[16]

Although midwifery and other popular healing arts were largely uncontrolled by government in Britain and America, efforts were made from time to time by professional groups, especially in the larger British cities, to give them instruction and to license their practice. In Glasgow, for example, the Faculty of Physicians and Surgeons, which enjoyed a regional monopoly over the licensing of physicians and surgeons, instituted an examination for midwives in 1740. "Having considered the many dismal effects of the Ignorance of midwives, we enact that ... any midwife who shall pretend as such to practise ... without a license from the Faculty shall be fined the sum of forty pounds"—but the fine would be canceled if she submitted to an examination. The records of the Faculty suggest that almost all who took the examination subsequently passed.[17] Later in the century, British midwives protested vehemently the intrusion of male practitioners into a domain they considered their own. A pioneer obste-

13. Edward Harrison, *Remarks on the Ineffective State of the Practice of Physic in Great Britain, with Proposals for Its Future Regulation and Improvement* (London: R. Bickerstaff, 1806), 1–2, 38–39.

14. Mary E. Fissell, *Patients, Power, and the Poor in Eighteenth-Century Bristol* (Cambridge: Cambridge University Press, 1991), 59.

15. Laurel T. Ulrich, *A Midwife's Tale: The Life of Martha Ballard, Based on Her Diary, 1785–1812* (New York: Knopf, 1990).

16. Patricia A. Watson, "The 'Hidden Ones': Women and Healing in Colonial New England," in *Medicine and Healing: The Dublin Seminar for New England Folklife, Annual Proceedings, 1990*, ed. Peter Benes (Boston: Boston University Press, 1992), 26–27.

17. Alexander Duncan, *Memorials of the Faculty of Physicians and Surgeons of Glasgow* (Glasgow: Maclehose, 1896), 101; Royal College of Physicians and Surgeons of Glasgow, Faculty Minutes.

trician, William Smellie, was described by one midwife as "a great-horse-God-mother of a he-midwife."[18]

Efforts to control the training and licensing of surgeons were more stringent than was the case with midwives. In London, Edinburgh, and Glasgow, in particular, local surgeons kept a close watch on those aspiring to practice, but their effectiveness did not extend into the countryside. All the royal corporations were constantly battling against the steady encroachment of unlicensed and unexamined practitioners inside and outside the cities. The Royal College of Physicians and Surgeons of Glasgow, for example, repeatedly sought to ban the practice of unlicensed surgeons in both the region surrounding the city and the Royal Infirmary, urging magistrates to protect "the poor classes who are most apt to be imposed on by presumptuous ignorance." The magistrates, responding soothingly to one such request in 1812, explained that they were very sympathetic but urged the college to relax its "exclusive privilege, so far as to allow young men, who may not be able to contribute the sums requisite for their admission as members of the Faculty, to practice in the City." To prosecute all such unqualified medical practitioners, they chided the college, "would be a measure without precedent in the judicial annals of the country."[19]

The large number of English apothecaries was also under intermittent scrutiny by magistrates and corporate bodies of physicians and surgeons intent on limiting their role to preparing and dispensing drugs. Their right to visit patients and to prescribe for them had been clear since 1703, but they were under legal restraints not to charge for their professional visits or advice. One writer advised them in 1789 to guard against "the impropriety of letting the word 'visits' constitute a part of your charges, instead of the more modest term of 'journey' or 'attendance.'"[20]

Along with the surgeons, apothecaries were clearly ignoring these historic limitations by the middle of the eighteenth century and taking on a larger role as general practitioners of medicine. By the 1770s, their education was beginning to resemble that of university graduates in medicine. An apothecary, according to a widely used guidebook, should be "tolerably well acquainted" with Latin; have a good understanding of his own language; be acquainted with botany, chemistry, and pharmacy; and have studied anatomy and physiology (though "the minutiae of anatomy are not necessary") so as to "know what perfect life and health are." He should avoid the growing practice of rushing to London to attend the hospitals and their surgical operations, since "as an apothecary, he must in the course of his practise have twenty medical cases for one that is

18. Herbert R. Spencer, *The History of British Midwifery from 1650 to 1800* (London: John Bale, 1927), 148.

19. Royal College of Physicians and Surgeons of Glasgow, Faculty Minutes, November 7, 1807, and January 1, 1812.

20. [William Taplin,] *A Dose for the Doctors, or the Aesculapian Labrynth Explored*, 3rd. ed. (London: G. Kearsley, 1789), 59.

chirurgical." His training, normally with an experienced practitioner, according to the author, should last at least three years.[21]

In actual practice, the line of demarcation between apothecary and surgeon was steadily erased in the towns and villages of the English countryside. According to a medical register compiled in 1783, more than 80 percent of all medical practitioners in provincial England called themselves surgeon-apothecaries, and the remaining number was split among those describing themselves as physicians, surgeons, or apothecaries.[22]

North American Practitioners

In Britain's North American colonies, the range of health practitioners was similar to that in the mother country but lacked a sizable cadre of university-educated physicians at the peak of the social pyramid. In both Canadian and American settlements, practically trained midwives, druggists, and lay practitioners, as well as others calling themselves doctors, met the health needs of the population. Very few medical graduates of European universities embarked on the adventure of starting a new life across the ocean, and the few educated physicians who had studied in Edinburgh or London confined their practices to urban centers.

Even after the first American medical schools were founded in Philadelphia and New York in the 1760s, the bulk of those calling themselves doctors were still trained by apprenticeship to an experienced practitioner. Few heeded the call of John Morgan in 1765 to renounce the apprenticeship system in favor of a systematic study of the learned branches of medicine. Indeed, in the opening decades of the nineteenth century, only 31 percent of even the prominent medical practitioners held a medical degree.[23] The decision in the American colonies to recognize a medical degree of any sort as a *prima facie* license to practice, quite different from the custom in Canada or Britain, had a profound impact on later efforts to control medical training in the United States.[24]

Healers on the Continent

The variety of healers was no less striking on the European continent. In every country, the healing of the sick was largely the work of trained and un-

21. James Makittrick, *Commentaries on the Principles and Practise of Physic, being an Attempt, on a New Plan, to connect the several Branches of Medicine, and to plan the Practise of it on a rational and solid Foundation* (London: T. Becket, 1772), xvii–xxxv.

22. Cited in Joan Lane, "The Medical Practitioners of Provincial England in 1783," *Medical History* 28 (1984): 355.

23. Robert F. Hudson, "Patterns of Medical Education in Nineteenth Century America" (master's thesis, Johns Hopkins University, 1966), 51. "Even the most marginal practitioner," writes Eric Christianson, "thought of himself as a doctor." See Christianson, "The Emergence of Medical Communities in Massachusetts, 1790–1794: The Demographic Factors," *Bulletin of the History of Medicine* 54 (1980): 65.

24. Joseph F. Kett, "American and Canadian Medical Institutions, 1800–1870," *Journal of the History of Medicine and Allied Sciences* 22 (1967): 345–46.

trained practitioners who had never attended a university. In the rural, preindustrial Germanic kingdoms and principalities, for example, a range of practical surgeons, apothecaries, lay healers, and indifferently trained midwives practiced their crafts with few restrictions. At the top of the social ladder among German practitioners was the relatively homogeneous group of academic physicians, akin to the elite physicians of France and Britain, whose education, speech, and dress set them apart from the vast majority of healers.

Surgeons, who gained a foothold in the German universities during the eighteenth century, ranked next in importance, followed by the far more numerous practical surgeons (*Wundärzte*) who, like the British surgeon-apothecaries, treated the great majority of the rural sick. Then came the apothecaries, bathkeepers, midwives, and other healers, all of whom possessed less formal educational credentials. In the kingdom of Bavaria, a distinctive hierarchy of medical practitioners was early recognized by the government: physicians at the top, first-class surgeons, practical surgeons, country doctors (*Landärzte*), and midwives.[25]

According to one estimate, for every university graduate in medicine in late-eighteenth-century Germany, twelve practical surgeons were in practice, along with an undetermined number of other healers.[26] In the countryside, a large number of practical healers (*Heilpraktikanten*) dispensed herbs, teas, and salves to thousands of patients.[27] By the late eighteenth century, unlicensed practitioners of all sorts were so numerous in the city-state of Hamburg that it was described in one local journal as "the battleground of quacks and sham-physicians of all sorts . . . who sacrifice thousands of inhabitants each year without exciting the slightest scandal."[28]

Unlike the Anglo-American nations, special schools to train the subordinate ranks of healers were common in the German states. By the end of the eighteenth century in almost every state, specialized institutions for the practical training of *Wundärzte*, *Landpraktikanten* (country practitioners), midwives, or *Bader* (bath keepers who administered mineral baths and performed such minor procedures as bleeding) could be found. At least seventeen such schools were in existence throughout Germany by 1786.[29] The Austrian state founded schools for midwives in Vienna and

---

25. Christiane Scherg-Zeisner, "Die ärztliche Ausbilding an der Königlich-bayerischen Julius-Maximilians Universität in Würzburg, 1814–1872" (Ph.D. diss., University of Würzburg, 1973), 22.

26. Alfons Fischer, *Geschichte des deutschen Gesundheitswesen*, 2 vols. (Berlin: Hildesheim, 1965), 2:64.

27. Claudia Huerkamp, *Der Aufstieg der Arzte im 19.Jahrhundert: Vom gelehrten Stand zum professionellen Experten: Das Beispiel Preussens* (Göttingen: Vandenhoeck & Ruprecht, 1985), 36.

28. Hansjörg Reupke, "Zur Geschichte der Ausüburg der Heilkunde durch nichtapprobierte Personen in Hamburg, von den Anfängen bis zum Erlass des 'Heilpraktikergesetzes' im Jahre 1939" (med. diss., University of Aachen, 1987), 69.

29. List compiled by Axel Karenberg, Cologne, and sent to me on March 27, 1993. See also Hans Killian, *Meister der Chirurgie und die Chirurgenschulen im gesamten deutschen Sprachraum*, 2nd ed. (Stuttgart: Georg Thieme, 1980).

Graz in 1748 and 1758 as well as a lyceum for practical surgery in the latter city in 1782, and Bavaria offered instruction to both bath keepers and barber-surgeons in its schools of military surgery in Munich and Bamberg.[30] In the German-speaking canton of Zurich, a surgical institute providing training for scores of second-class surgeons or "country doctors," as well as aspiring physicians, served the educational needs of much of the canton.[31]

Midwives were trained in special courses in more than twenty German cities before 1800, including Berlin, Mannheim, Dresden, Hannover, and Breslau.[32] A school for Bavarian midwives, for example, offering semi-weekly lectures and demonstrations over a period of four years, was founded in Würzburg in 1739.[33] In the state of Württemberg, midwives had been required to undergo instruction and examination since the sixteenth century.[34] One historian compiled a list of more than two hundred German teaching enterprises conducted outside universities for midwives, surgeons, and bath keepers before 1826.[35]

Serving the Rural Population

Despite all the efforts to train nonuniversity practitioners in the German states, dissatisfaction was widespread because of the poor preparation of many of them. How best to serve the needs of the rural population, who lacked access to well-trained physicians and surgeons, was a recurring question in Germany, just as it was in France, Britain, and North America in these years. During much of the eighteenth and early nineteenth centuries, schools of practical surgery came to supply the greater part of trained general practitioners for the towns and countryside of France and

30. Tilman J. Elliger, *Die Medizinerausbildung in Österreich* (Munich: Profil, 1986), 22–24; Anna D. von Rüden, "Medecina Graecensis: Das medizinisch–chirurgische Studium in Graz (1782–1862)" (med. diss., Technical University of Munich, 1978), 4; Erhard Grunwald, "Das niedere Medizinalpersonal im Bayern des 19.Jahrhunderts" (med. diss., University of Munich, 1950), 11, 33.

31. Moritz Leisibach, *Das medizinisch–chirurgische Institut in Zurich, 1782–1833* (Zurich: Hans Rohr, 1982), 52–53. See also Ernst Bezel, ed., *Johann Jakob Steger: Beispel eines Medizinstudenten im frühen 19.Jahrhundert nach den Briefen an seine Eltern* (Zurich: Juris Druck & Verlag, 1981), 11–14.

32. Axel Karenberg, "Lernen am Bett der Schwangeren: Zur Typologie des Entbindungshauses in Deutschland (1728–1840)," *Zentralblatt für Gynäkologie* 113 (1991): 904, table 1.

33. Franz J. Schmitt, *Anfänge und Entwicklung der Hebammen-Kunst, des geburtshilflichen Lehrstuhles und der Universitäts-Frauenklinik in Würzburg* (Würzburg: Memminger, 1934), 5–6.

34. Manfred Becht, "Das Dekanatsbuch der Tübingen medizinischen Fakultät, 1808–1858 (Teil 6: 1829–1833)" (med. diss., University of Tübingen, 1982), 45.

35. E. Th. Nauck, "Uber die anatomischen, chirurgischen und geburtshilflichen Lehranstalten vornehmlich ausserhalb der Universitäten im 16.–19.Jahrhundert," *Anatomischen Anzeiger* 113 (1963): 193–213, and 116 (1965): 202–16.

German-speaking Europe. These practical schools, as described later, resembled the independent or "proprietary" medical schools of Britain and North America.

What kind of training was possible or suitable in the eighteenth or early nineteenth century for a country practitioner, who at best earned only a meager living and who lacked a first-class education? The Bavarian *Landarzt*, the French *officier de santé*, the Austrian *Landwundarzt*, the English surgeon-apothecary, and the American "country doctor" all were responses at various times to this universal problem. The reformer Johann Peter Frank, who spent much of his life trying to improve medical education, despaired of ever solving the problem and suggested that rural pastors be trained to fill the population's health needs.[36]

In the German city of Erfurt, a prize essay entry of 1791 asked the central question, "How can practical surgeons, entrusted with the care of the country population, be afforded a better and more purposeful education at low cost?" The winning contestant wrote that under existing conditions, it was simply not possible to prepare good physicians for the countryside. Country surgeons, as he described them, were raw youngsters, neglected by the lower schools, who could barely read or write. After an indifferent apprenticeship, they found themselves in a surgical school in which as few as two teachers and a prosector struggled with the task of teaching anatomy, physiology, pathology, therapy, and surgery to forty or fifty listless and ignorant students. To remedy the situation, the author recommended—in terms reminiscent of the English guidebook for apothecaries—that a practical surgeon be able to understand enough Latin to read a book, have a reasonably good general education, know the elements of anatomy and surgery, and hear lectures on simple surgery, midwifery, and medicine.[37]

In Prussia, the well-known reformer Johann Christian Reil of Halle proposed a more ambitious plan to train routine medical practitioners (*Routiniers*) for the better care of poor and rural communities. The state had no less an obligation, he argued in good Enlightenment fashion, to found useful schools for *Routiniers* than to establish universities to educate physicians for the well-to-do. The education of such practitioners, he insisted, similar to those advocating the creation of *officiers de santé* in France, should be limited to what was practical and useful. The period of study should be three to five years; special textbooks in ordinary language were needed; both medicine and surgery should be brought into the curriculum; and a hospital should be part of the educational program. The graduates of such a course, Reil explained, should serve as secondary or

---

36. Johann Peter Frank, "Akademische Rede über die Priesterärzte," *Wiener Universitäts Taschenbuch*, 1804, i–lx.

37. Georg Adam Keyser, *Beantwortung der Frage: Wie kann man auf eine leichte, nicht allzukostspielige Art den Wundärzten, denen das Landvolk anvertrauet ist, und auf der leidenden Menschheit oft sehr schädlich, als nützlich sind, einen bessern und zweckmässigern Unterricht beybringen* (Erfurt, 1791), 7–8, 44-45.

auxiliary physicians to the university-educated medical men. In time, they would replace the practical surgeons, barber surgeons, and apothecaries who had failed to meet the health needs of the Prussian people.[38]

Similar schemes for improving medical care for less-favored groups in the population, especially in the countryside, were commonplace in pre-revolutionary France as well. There, too, a growing level of frustration was occasioned by the wide gap separating the medicine of the poor from the care of the privileged. As in Germany and Britain, the range of practitioners was immense and showed little sign of diminishing. In words reminiscent of Irvine Loudon's work in England and Claudia Huerkamp's portrayal of German practice, the French historian Jean-Pierre Goubert wrote that "the French population practiced self-medication; it consulted quacks, bonesetters, and matrons, listened to ambulant charlatans, and followed the course of treatment prescribed by the sorcerer-healer of the village."[39] No clear line of demarcation, then, separated learned and popular medicine in France any more than it did elsewhere in Europe or North America.

Efforts were made in France, as they were in Germany, to create schools of surgery and midwifery to provide a minimal standard of training for popular practitioners. The results, however, were similarly uneven. As early as the fourteenth century, French surgeons had organized themselves into guilds that influenced strongly the training of future surgeons. After 1731, they were operating the prestigious Academy of Surgery in Paris that served as a center of teaching and research and a professional organization. Large numbers of students, both French and foreign, flocked to its courses.[40]

Quite differently from Germany, the Paris surgeons were generally well educated, possessed a master of arts degree, knew the Latin language, and enjoyed a status approaching or sometimes surpassing that of the university-trained physicians. In the provinces, however, the standards for surgical practice were much lower and less strictly enforced, especially in small towns and settlements. And on the fringes of the surgical establishment was a large group of marginal practitioners who treated surface wounds, set bones, removed stones, extracted cataracts, pulled teeth, or bled patients.[41] This group resembled in many ways the *Wundärzte* of

38. Johann Christian Reil, *Pepinièren zum Unterricht ärztlicher Routiniers als Bedürfnis des Staats* (Halle: Curtsche Buchhandlung, 1804). See also Robert Heller, "Johann Christian Reil's Training Scheme for Medical Auxiliaries," *Medical History* 19 (1975): 321–32.

39. Jean-Pierre Goubert, "The Art of Healing: Learned Medicine and Popular Medicine in the France of 1790," in *Medicine and Society in France: Selections from the Annales, Economies, Sociétés, Civilisations*, vol. 6, ed. Robert Forster and Orest Ranum (Baltimore: Johns Hopkins University Press, 1980), 1.

40. Charles Coury, "Medical Education in France from the Beginning of the 17th Century to Our Day," unpublished manuscript, 1968, 13–14, Institute of the History of Medicine, Vienna, doc. 36.547. This account differs somewhat from the published version of his work.

41. Ramsey, *Professional and Popular Medicine*, 22–24.

the German states and the apprentice-trained practitioners of Britain and North America.

When practiced by men, midwifery in France was normally a surgical subspecialty. Women practitioners were intermittently tested and approved by surgical groups, especially in cities, as was true in Great Britain and Germany. We know that midwives were being trained at Strasbourg in the 1720s and that a lying-in course was created for them in Nancy after 1773. In the latter city, the course was taught in 1776 by the famous midwife Madame du Coudray.[42] Another renowned midwife, Marguérite le Boursier, who devised a mannequin for obstetrical teaching, was charged by Louis XV in 1763 with organizing courses in midwifery throughout the country. According to one account, she taught more than four thousand pupils during her long career.[43] In Lyon, a free school of midwifery was established by the Collège des médecins in 1786 that provided three years of instruction.[44] Despite these and other efforts to improve the education of midwives, however, the continuing lack of sufficient opportunities for their instruction became a major grievance reported in the *cahiers* addressed to the Estates General in 1789.[45]

It is small wonder that in the chaotic conditions of the late eighteenth century, the future preparation of medical practitioners seemed cloudy and uncertain in every country. University graduates in medicine especially felt besieged by the mushrooming ranks of lesser-educated practitioners. A state of undeclared war existed in some countries between academic physicians and the "irregular," "unlicensed," or "unapproved" healers who were extending the range of their services. Already there were sharp national and regional differences in the range and distribution of practitioners and in the degree of government protection and control.

Fundamental questions about the education of practitioners had still not been answered. Who would practice medicine in the future on which groups in the population? How much knowledge of anatomy and physiology and other scientific subjects should be required of a general practitioner? What kind of practical indoctrination was needed by physicians, surgeons, and other healers? Were specialized schools necessary for training each variety of practitioner? Where should medicine be studied? In universities? In specialized schools? In hospitals? In apprenticeship to an

---

42. Agnes Wang, "L'enseignement de la médecine à Nancy de 1789 à 1822" (med. diss., University of Nancy, 1971), 64. Two good recent studies of French midwifery are those by Jacques Gélis, *La sage-femme ou le médecin* (Paris: Fayard, 1988), esp. 109–94; and Sigrid Hader, "Geburtshilfe in Frankreich im Spiegel ihrer Einrichtungen (1500–1800)" (med. diss., University of Cologne, 1988), esp. 16–18.

43. Wolfgang Gubalke, *Die Hebamme im Wandel der Zeiten* (Hannover: Elwin Staude, 1964), 88.

44. Henri Hermann, "Histoire de la faculté de médecine," *Revue lyonnaise de médecine*, special issue, 1958, 223.

45. Jean-Charles Sournia, *La médecine révolutionnaire 1789–1799* (Paris: Payot, 1989), 20.

older practitioner? What was the students' responsibility for planning and organizing their own medical education? And what was the role of the state, if any, in providing for the training and licensing of health practitioners?

The Role of the State

By the end of the eighteenth century, these questions were being answered differently throughout Europe and North America. Each nation responded to the growing sense of crisis in ways dictated by the special circumstances in each country. As the old medieval synthesis of medical studies came apart, a variety of new approaches were tried in an effort to bring order to the training of health practitioners.

The spirit of the Enlightenment, which had spread widely but unevenly over the transatlantic world, affected medical as well as educational and political thought in its questioning of the old arrangements, in its insistence on the power of reason to solve human problems, and in its quest for utilitarian answers to ancient problems of social organization. Physicians and surgeons became involved as never before in studying the condition of the masses of their compatriots, in the treatment of the sick in the crowded hospitals, in the growing questioning of the neglect of the insane, and in the care of the casualties of war.[46] Articulate and concerned citizens were becoming convinced that life could be more hopeful and happy if sickness, along with poverty and ignorance, could be given universal treatment and preventive care. The role of physicians was consequently seen to be more vital than that of their university-educated colleagues. "The doctor of laws may be bad, that hurts the public little," the Old Testament scholar Johann Michaelis told his Göttingen colleagues in 1776; "the doctor of theology does even less harm . . . but the doctor of medicine goes directly to [matters] of life and death."[47]

As national differences grew, the Enlightenment took very different forms in its effects on medicine in the cultural and political milieus of individual nations.[48] The impact of new ideas and agendas for social action was bound to weigh differently in an inefficiently despotic France, a liberal and industrializing Britain, an enlightened but feudalistic Germany, and a libertarian but primitive North America. In particular, state power was not the central focus of the reformers' efforts in America or England that it was in France and the German states.[49]

46. Antonie M. Luyendijk-Elshout, "The Medical World of the Nineteenth Century: Its Impact upon Medical Education," unpublished manuscript, 1990, 2. I am indebted to Prof. Luyendijk-Elshout for sending me a copy of his chapter for a forthcoming book.

47. Johann D. Michaelis, *Räsonnement über die protestantischen Universitäten in Deutschland*, 4 vols. (Frankfurt: Andreä, 1768–76), 4:116–17.

48. See Roy Porter and Mikulas Teich, eds., *The Enlightenment in National Context* (Cambridge: Cambridge University Press, 1981), vii–viii.

49. Ibid., 16.

In the German-language areas especially, the concept of "medical police"—meaning the vigorous use of the state's police power to regulate and control medical practice and public health—was marked by a strongly paternalistic and authoritarian tone that had no counterpart in the Anglo-American nations.[50] In the absolutist German state, the enlightened ruler was considered responsible for his people and their health and safety. A healthy population meant a strong and growing population and was best promoted by strict controls over the conditions that promoted disease and by effective regulation of the training and licensing of practitioners.

In France, by contrast, the establishment of a state system of medical education came only haltingly in the years of revolutionary ferment and was held back by the enduring image of rank and privilege associated with the physicians and surgeons of the Old Regime. But it did come. The strongly paternalistic tendencies of the French monarchy, moreover, made easier the acceptance of a powerful governmental role in French medicine and public health during the Revolution. Well before 1800, as a number of modern students of social welfare policies have emphasized, the two major powers of continental Europe had already taken important steps to establish national standards of social policy and medical training that would set them sharply apart from British and American practices for nearly two centuries.[51]

No state went further than Prussia in the eighteenth century in exercising close control over the preparation and licensing of its medical practitioners. Early in the century, the rulers of Prussia began to distinguish physicians from other healers and to bring the licensing of all practitioners under the direct control of the state. In the name of the people's health, the state began in 1725 to take away the power of issuing licenses to practice from the universities and move it to Berlin.[52] Qualifications for physicians, practical surgeons, apothecaries, midwives, and barbers were now set with precision and in great detail by a central authority. A state system of examinations and requirements for medical practice followed. Course offerings by medical faculties had to be approved in advance; failing students had to be reported to Berlin; and students had to

50. George Rosen, "The Fate of the Concept of Medical Police, 1780–1890," *Centaurus* 5 (1957): 99.

51. See, for example, Arnold J. Heidenheimer, "Professional Knowledge and State Policy in Comparative Historical Perspective: Law and Medicine in Britain, Germany, and the United States," *International Social Science Journal* 41 (1989): 529–53; Daniel Levine, *Poverty and Society: The Growth of the American Welfare State in International Comparison* (New Brunswick, NJ: Rutgers University Press, 1988), esp. 261–85; and Allan Mitchell, *The Divided Path: The German Influence on Social Reform in France After 1870* (Chapel Hill: University of North Carolina Press, 1991), esp. xi–xii.

52. Johannes Steudel, "Medizinische Ausbilding in Deutschland 1600–1850," in *Et Multum et Multa: Festgabe für Kurt Lindner*, ed. Sigrid Schwenk, Gunnar Tilander, and Carl Anderson Willemsen (Berlin: Gruyter, 1971), 416.

demonstrate practical experience in diagnosis and therapy.[53] Practical surgeons were required to serve seven years of apprenticeship and enroll for anatomical and surgical courses at a special anatomical school established in Berlin. Apothecaries, too, had to study with a licensed master for seven years and then complete a practical course in pharmacy and chemistry. Nor were midwives exempted from the requirement to take formal training and undergo examinations on their knowledge and skill.[54]

The demand for clinical or practical training among all grades of practitioners rose steadily throughout the century. By 1800, the Prussian state had extended its authority into virtually every aspect of medicine and public health.[55] No other function of the state, noted Christoph Wilhelm Hufeland, was more urgent than its control over those who were given the *jus vitae et mortis* over millions of their fellow human beings.[56]

Other German rulers likewise sought to bring medical and public health matters under the aegis of a benevolent state. Nearly all German states, including the Hapsburg monarchy, made medical practice a subject of intense governmental scrutiny and control. In the Hapsburg lands, the reforms of Gerard van Swieten, supported by the power of Maria Theresa and her successors, launched a "revolution from above" starting in 1749 as he destroyed the privileges of established physicians, began a system of state examinations, and insisted on clinical experience as an integral part of a medical education.[57] As happened in Prussia, the autonomy of the universities was ended, and new courses, new methods of teaching, and more professorial appointments were directed from Vienna. To serve better the population in the countryside, higher educational standards and licensing controls were imposed on surgeons, midwives, and apothecaries, which resembled in many ways those of the Prussian law of 1725.[58]

The neighboring kingdom of Bavaria likewise moved to establish a series of schools for "country doctors" in Munich, Bamberg, and Inns-

53. Hans-Heinz Eulner, "Historische Aspekte zu aktuellen Fragen des Medizinstudiums," *Medizinhistorisches Journal* 3 (1968): 186–87.

54. Rolf Winau, *Medizin in Berlin* (Berlin: Gruyter, 1987), 68–71.

55. For an example of the immensely detailed rules for different types of health personnel in Prussia, see "Neues Prüfungsreglement für sämtliche Medizinal-personnen des preussischen Staates," GSPK, Merseburg, 76, VIII, A535, Bd. I. See also the royal edict of 1791 requiring "skilled physicians and practical surgeons" to prove their clinical experience or to attend the government's clinical institute in Berlin: 51, 1a, Nr. 1, edict of February 4, 1791.

56. C. W. Hufeland, "Zweck und Einrichtung des medicinisches Cursus zu Berlin und Nachricht von den im Jahre 1802 daselbst öffentich geprüften Arzten und Wunderärzten," *Journal der practischen Arzneykunde und Wunderarzneykunde* 14 (1802): 6.

57. Paul P. Bernard, "The Limits of Absolutism: Joseph II and the Allgemeines Krankenhaus," *Eighteenth-Century Studies* 9 (1975): 204. See also Erna Lesky and Adam Wandruszka, eds., *Gerard van Swieten und seine Zeit* (Vienna: Hermann Böhlaus, 1973).

58. Herbert H. Egglmaier, "Das medizinisch–chirurgische Studium in Graz" (med. diss., University of Graz, 1980), 21–37.

bruck to bring medicine to the unserved countryside and to improve the educational preparation of the "people's practitioners."[59] In the state of Württemberg, similar efforts were under way to redefine the legal requirements for practitioners and to improve their training.[60]

In the tightly controlled world of the absolute monarchs, no figure of the Enlightenment exerted more influence on medical education than Johann Peter Frank. Born and brought up in the borderlands along the Rhine River, Frank and his son Joseph reflected the influence of both German and French reformers as they served the most powerful rulers of central Europe.[61] In 1779, Johann Frank launched a massive study of public health and medical study whose advocacy of a strong "medical police" was widely influential throughout the Hapsburg domain, the German states, Russia, and beyond.[62]

For the next forty years, under the aegis of strong rulers, Frank organized new curricula of medical study, pushed for more bedside study in hospitals and clinics, brought the study of surgery closer to that of medicine, introduced courses in public health into the universities, and in a multitude of articles and public speeches preached the doctrines of rational living. In the very first sentence of his six-volume study, he struck the note that would guide his life's work: "The internal security of the state is the subject of general police science."[63]

But the concept of a powerful role for the state in medical and health affairs in the late eighteenth century found only an uncertain echo west of the Rhine. In France only in the lower Rhine valley where German influences were strong was there an important early interest in the kind of health measures and governmental control of medicine that marked the Enlightenment in Germany.[64] Joseph Frank himself recognized that national differences made impossible the simple transfer of ideas from one country to another. Following a trip to Paris and London, he wrote that the teaching of medicine depended on distinctive local traditions, "national character," and "the spirit of the times."[65]

Under the Old Regime, controls over medical training and licensing in France were uneven and widely dispersed. Although reformers sought the

---

59. Johannes M. Hautmann, "Die ärztliche Ausbildung im Königreich und im Freistaat Bayern, 1808–1980" (med. diss., Technical University of Munich, 1982), 4.

60. Mary Wessling, "Medicine and Government in Early Modern Württemburg" (Ph.D. diss., University of Michigan, 1988), 105–39.

61. Ramúnas A. Kondratas wrote an excellent study of Joseph Frank and his influence: "Joseph Frank (1771–1842) and the Development of Clinical Medicine" (Ph.D. diss., Harvard University, 1977), esp. 235–42.

62. Johann Peter Frank, *A System of Complete Medical Police*, ed. Erna Lesky (Baltimore: Johns Hopkins University Press, 1970).

63. Ibid., 12.

64. Matthew Ramsey, "Medical Power and Popular Medicine: Illegal Healers in Nineteenth-Century France," *Journal of Social History* 10 (1976–77): 560.

65. Joseph Frank, *Reise nach Paris, London, und einem grossen Theile des übrigen Englands und Schottlands*, 2 vols. (Vienna: Camesinaische Buchhandlung, 1804), 1:iii–iv.

same broad goals of improving the people's health and bringing greater order to the practice of the healing arts as their German contemporaries did, they found only wavering support from the French government. At times, the royal authorities might be responsive to pressures to create more effective national medical institutions, as when Louis XVI founded the Academy of Surgery or his successor launched the progressive Royal Society of Medicine, but more often the government seemed lethargic or unresponsive to the mounting problems.

When the Revolution came, the old institutions were largely swept away, and power became highly centralized in the government at Paris. Some of the old institutions and personalities survived in new forms, however, armed now with the power of the revolutionary state.[66] Some members of the Royal Society of Medicine—Fourcroy, Vicq d'Azyr, Cabanis—became, in Martin Staum's words, "shock troops of enlightenment and virtue" in the medical revolution.[67] By the century's end, the role of a powerful government in health and medical matters was firmly established both in France and across the Rhine.

The drive to sweep away the barriers in the Old Regime to change in health and medical policies, according to a recent study, was due to a new "mentality of intervention" that had been growing in France since 1750. A pivotal figure in this transformation of thought was S. A. D. Tissot, a French–Swiss physician, friend of the *philosophes*, and close disciple of the activist Montpellier school, who campaigned much of his life for a public role in matters of health and medical care. He was an early critic of malnutrition and overwork among the poor, wrote poignantly about the special health risks of women and children, pleaded for new protective laws for factory workers, and argued for a new conception of the hospital as a place to heal rather than a place to die. His was an important voice, too, in the reform of medical studies, especially in placing more emphasis on practical training.[68]

Like other of his contemporaries, Tissot sought a middle way between the strong authoritarianism of the German conception of medical police and the laissez-faire individualism of the British Manchester school. In his unpublished manuscript, "Medical Police," he argued for a larger role for physicians in investigating the causes of poor health and recommending public measures to overcome them.[69] What is not clear from Tissot's writings is how the liberal state he favored could carry out the detailed

66. George Weisz, "Constructing the Medical Elite in France: The Creation of the Royal Academy of Medicine 1814–20," *Medical History* 30 (1986): 419–23.

67. Martin S. Staum, *Cabanis: Enlightenment and Medical Philosophy in the French Revolution* (Princeton, NJ: Princeton University Press, 1980), 109.

68. Antoinette S. Emsch-Deriaz, *Tissot: Physician of the Enlightenment* (New York: Peter Lang, 1992). See also Emsch-Deriaz, "Towards a Social Conception of Health in the Second Half of the Eighteenth Century: Tissot (1728–1797) and the New Preoccupation with Health and Well-being" (Ph.D. diss., University of Rochester, 1984).

69. Emsch-Deriaz, "Towards a Social Conception of Health," 308–60.

controls he advocated over so much of daily life without interfering with the personal liberties of its citizens. Viewed critically, the logical outcome of Tissot's views was much closer to the absolutist state of Johann Peter Frank than to the libertarian doctrines espoused by British reformers.

The idea of a strong "medical police" supervising health and medicine found almost no resonance in Britain and North America. For nearly a hundred years the training of medical practitioners reflected the liberal, laissez-faire environment of the Anglo-American political world, remarkably little influenced in its tolerance of diversity and competing health and pedagogical ideas by the example of German or French statism. The state was simply not a crucial factor in medical education in either Britain or North America until late in the nineteenth century. The state in Britain, wrote Peter Alter, was always a "reluctant patron" of science and professional training.[70] As late as 1897, the American medical education reformer Nathan Smith Davis attributed the century-long diversity and confusion in medical training in the United States to its having developed "under no general supervision, nor in accordance with any uniform systems of laws."[71]

In the British and American context, the term *medical police* came to mean voluntary or local efforts to improve sanitation, provide better housing, protect communities from disease, and instruct the public on matters of diet and health. Rarely was it invoked to justify state controls of the education or licensing of practitioners. In Enlightenment Scotland, where the term first appeared in Great Britain, Andrew Duncan was lecturing at the University of Edinburgh on the subject of medical police in the 1790s, and a colleague, John Roberton, published a book on medical police in 1809, but neither advocated a vigorous role for the state in improving public health, nor did they suggest a system of governmental controls over the chaotic licensing and educational situation in Britain.[72] "The importance of a proper medical police," wrote William Buchan in his *Domestic Medicine* of 1769, "is either not understood or very little regarded."[73] In London, a mushrooming site of medical teaching by 1780, the organization and control of education were almost entirely in the hands of "medical entrepreneurs," who were developing a hospital sys-

---

70. Peter Alter, *The Reluctant Patron: Science and the State in Britain, 1859–1920* (Oxford: Berg, 1987).

71. Nathan S. Davis, "A Brief History of the Origin of the American Medical Association," *Janus* 2 (1897): 31.

72. Rosen, "Fate of Concept of Medical Police," 107–9; John Roberton, *Medical Police: or, the Causes of Disease, with the Means of Prevention; and Rules for Diet, Regimen, etc. adopted particularly to the Cities of London and Edinburgh, and generally to all large Towns* (Edinburgh, 1809). See also the article by Brenda M. White suggesting that Roberton was somewhat closer to the European position than Duncan was: "Medical Police, Politics and Police: The Fate of John Roberton," *Medical History* 27 (1983): 407–22.

73. Quoted in David Hamiltion, *The Healers: A History of Medicine in Scotland* (Edinburgh: Canongate, 1981), 133.

tem of training independent of both universities and governmental authority.[74]

Likewise, in the United States and Canada, the power of the government over matters of education and health was severely circumscribed by a political ideology that praised "republican virtue" and suspected centralized power.[75] Nowhere in the transatlantic world were there fewer restrictions over health practitioners and fewer efforts to use the power of the state in behalf of the people's health than in North America.

If the national cultures differed sharply in the role played by government in the years of Enlightenment, as well as in their patronage and tolerance of unproven healers, they were nearly unanimous in encouraging the practical side of medical training. No current of the medical Enlightenment met with more universal response than the humane and utilitarian impulse to prepare practitioners more practically for their service to the people's health. By the middle of the eighteenth century, movements to bind the traditional learned study of medicine to hands-on experience at the bedside were under way in every country. But the academic education of physicians was also in flux, and the outcome of the struggle over the shape of medical education was by no means a foregone conclusion. Particularly striking at the close of the century was the great diversity of locations and the types of institutions offering instruction in medicine. It is to a closer look at these locations, and the kind of education they offered, that we turn in the following chapter.

74. Susan C. Lawrence, "Science and Medicine at the London Hospitals: The Development of Teaching and Research, 1750–1815" (Ph.D. diss., University of Toronto, 1985), i.

75. See the essay by J. R. Pole, "Enlightenment and the Politics of American Nature," in *The Enlightenment in National Context*, ed. Roy Porter and Mikulas Teich (Cambridge: Cambridge University Press, 1981), 192–214.

2

Changing Patterns of Medical Study Before 1800

For the traditional physician of the eighteenth century, medicine was above all a humane study, mastered largely through books and the careful examination of medicine's past and leavened now by a growing concern to know something firsthand of the feel of the human body in sickness and in health. To be a French or German or British physician in these years was to be a member of a cultural elite who, like other university graduates, found the truth in the rich treasures of ancient Greek and Latin writings.

A degree in medicine was a testament of higher learning, not merely a professional qualification, and Latin was the visible symbol of that learning. Medicine was valued not so much for its efficacy in curing patients as for the knowledge it implied about the universe and humankind. Such notable figures as Quesnay, who had a medical degree, and Diderot, Voltaire, and Rousseau studied medicine as an integral part of a broad, humanistic culture.[1] The character of a physician, wrote an English practitioner in 1794, "ought to be that of a gentleman, which cannot be maintained . . . but by a man of literature. He is much in the world, and mixes in society with men of every description."[2]

Students were easily converted to the idea of the centrality of classical study in their lives. A young man in Edinburgh, for example, ridiculed his

1. Jean-Charles Sournia, *La médecine révolutionnaire, 1789–1799* (Paris: Editions Payot, 1989), 15–16.
2. Thomas Withers, *A Treatise on the Errors and Defects of Medical Education: in which are contained Observations on the Means of correcting Them* (London: C. Dilly, 1794), 31. Withers was physician to the York County Hospital and Public Dispensary.

medical professors in 1797 for their ignorance and that of their students, who "could not translate the easiest passage in Latin."[3] On the Continent, a Munich professor offered at about the same time to instruct a whole class of medical students in liberal studies, since "their knowledge of the Latin language, philosophy, logic, and other general branches of education" brought "shame" to the faculty.[4] Such complaints were frequent by 1800, revealing the growing tension between the ideal and the real in the classical training of students and professors.

Medicine as University Study

What kind of education, then, was suitable for a late-eighteenth-century physician? The mastery of ancient literature and medical texts was still essential to one's status as a gentleman but was no longer regarded as the sole qualification for success as a physician. Some knowledge of clinical practice and the newer academic subjects was increasingly sought by would-be physicians.

To some degree, of course, experience in practical medicine before seeing patients had been expected of physicians since the late Middle Ages. As early as the twelfth century, Emperor Frederick II had ruled that graduates in medicine must undertake an apprenticeship before starting a practice. Likewise, the teachers of Padua, who brought students to the bedsides of patients in the sixteenth century, attracted hundreds of students from all over Europe.[5] At Vienna and Prague, students had long written dissertations on practical subjects and often spent a year or two in practical service before starting their own practice.[6] In Leyden, Hermann Boerhaave conducted a famous clinic for students in 1714. His pupils, John Rutherford and Gerard van Swieten, offered clinical courses in Edinburgh and Vienna. By the 1780s, as described more fully in Chapter 4, clinical or hospital training was considered an important part of every physician's education, whether required by a university, as in the German states and in Edinburgh, or sought outside the university by individual practitioners, as in France, England, and America.

The Uniqueness of the German University

The German commitment by the 1790s to clinical study within the university was striking. Whereas revolutionary reformers in France were moving to create a practical kind of training outside the universities and

3. Francisco S. Constancio, *An Appeal to the Gentlemen Studying Medicine at the University of Edinburgh* (Edinburgh: privately printed, 1797), 7.

4. Protokolle congregatae facultatis Medicinae, NI 4, folder 13, November 13, 1804, September 30, 1805, University of Munich Archive.

5. C. D. O'Malley, "Medical Education During the Renaissance," in *The History of Medical Education*, ed. C. D. O'Malley (Berkeley and Los Angeles: University of California Press, 1970), 95–97.

6. Alois Krobot, "Zur Geschichte der medizinischen Ausbildung an der Prager Karlsuniversität von 1650 bis 1800" (med. diss., University of Zurich, 1985), 24–28.

hospital surgeons in London were building practical schools of medicine far removed from the British universities, in Germany academic leaders were struggling to bring the clinic into the university. Since few university towns in Germany could sustain the costs of a local hospital and such large cities as Berlin, Hamburg, and Munich had no university, a solution was found in the small university clinic of a dozen or so beds that catered to the poor of the surrounding area.

The movement to shape a more useful education for academic physicians in Germany, as demanded by the utilitarian spirit of the times, met strong resistance from those who, as in Britain and France, believed that such vocational training had no place in a university. The reformers, however, led by such figures as Johann Christian Reil and later Wilhelm von Humboldt, argued that the practical study of medicine in universities would have a scholarly and scientific character that set it wholly apart from the practical schools outside.[7] In their view, medicine was a learned study that must also use empirical means to establish new truths and educate practitioners.

By the early 1800s, both the professorial clinic and the academic teaching of medicine were lodged together in the German university, with consequences of enormous importance for nineteenth-century medical pedagogy and science. Earlier than the teachers of other nations did, German university teachers proclaimed a "unity of theory and practice" that made it possible to educate physicians in academic and practical subjects in the same institution.[8]

By 1800, the academic study of medicine itself was undergoing changes as significant as the search for practical knowledge. In nearly every country, the medical curriculum was in ferment. The list of medical courses was expanding; new scientific subjects were being added; and old subjects were being taught in new ways. More terms of study were being added to the requirements for graduation. In all the German universities by the end of the eighteenth century, medical study required three and sometimes four years and included courses in anatomy, chemistry, botany, medical practice, obstetrics, hygiene, surgery and ophthalmology, and occasionally even psychiatry. Most required the completion of a university education in liberal arts before commencing medical study. All had anatomical theaters complete with prosectors and preparation rooms, many of them dating from the seventeenth century.

Physiology, not yet an experimental science, was taught descriptively as a part of anatomy, although a special chair in the subject was created as early as 1774 in Freiburg. Sometimes it was taught as a separate course

7. Thomas Broman, "University Reform in Medical Thought at the End of the Eighteenth Century," *Osiris* 5 (1989): 37–48. See also his "The Transformation of Academic Medicine in Germany, 1780–1820" (Ph.D. diss., Princeton University, 1987), esp. 3–13.

8. Johanna Bleker, "Die Idee der Einheit von Theorie und Praxis in der Medizin und ihr Einfluss auf den klinischen Unterricht im 19.Jahrhundert," *Arzt und Krankenhaus* 6 (1982): 232–36.

within anatomy, and it was not unusual for "demonstrations" to be announced as a part of the instruction.[9] "Without physiology," declared Friedrich Wetzel in 1805, "anatomy remains dead and incomprehensible."[10] The teaching of physiology was particularly innovative at the newer universities in Halle and Göttingen, founded in 1694 and 1733, whose medical faculty "monopolized the teaching of the new sciences of chemistry, botany, and physiology."[11] At his inaugural lecture at Göttingen as early as 1736, Albrecht von Haller, a student of Boerhaave, referred to not a single classical author when he established a program of direct observation and animal experimentation as the foundation of future physiological and medical study.[12] At the Hapsburg-controlled university at Freiburg, the most popular center for medical study in western Germany, the curriculum of 1765 included not only physiology as a separate course but also "demonstrative" lectures in botany and chemistry.[13]

Similarly, the University of Munich, then located in Ingolstadt, announced a series of new courses in 1799 that included the "physiological part of chemistry," mineralogy, zoology, and anthropology.[14] Heidelberg listed sixteen different courses in medicine in such subjects as human physiology, general pathology and therapy, zoology and comparative anatomy, and botany.[15] Although they reflected the growing diversity of the curriculum, such courses were still linked to the older descriptive studies that had preceded them.

Still other combinations of courses were offered in the yeasty medical curriculum around 1800. At Tübingen, the professor of pathology taught semiotics as well as pathology; the anatomy professor lectured on physiology and osteology; and the teacher of botany and chemistry also taught pharmacology and materia medica.[16] Differences among the curricula of

9. Hans-Heinz Eulner, *Die Entwicklung der medizinischen Spezialfächer an den Universitäten des deutschen Sprachgebietes* (Stuttgart: Ferdinand Enke, 1970), 42–45, 65.

10. Friedrich G. Wetzel, *Briefe über das Studium der Medizin für Jünglinge, die sich ihr widmen wollen* (Leipzig: C. G. Weigel, 1805), 28.

11. R. Steven Turner, "The Prussian Universities and the Research Imperative, 1806 to 1848" (Ph.D. diss., Princeton University, 1973), 124.

12. Ulrich Tröhler, "250 Jahre Göttinger Medizin," *Göttinger Universitätsschriften* 13 (1988): 15–16.

13. Hans Böhner, "Die Geschichte des medizinischen Ausbildungs—und Prüfungswesen in Deutschland von etwa 1240 n. Chr. bis Heute" (med. diss., University of Cologne, 1962), 24.

14. Heinz Goerke, "Die medizinischen Fakultät von 1472 bis zur Gegenwart," *Die Ludwig—Maximilians—Universität in ihren Fakultäten*, ed. Laetitia Boehm and Johannes Spörl, 2 vols. (Berlin: Duncker & Humblot, 1972), 2:205.

15. Akten der medizinischen Fakultät, June 1, 1807, III, 4a, 50, p. 28, University of Heidelberg Archive.

16. Martina Beese, "Die medizinischen Promotionen in Tübingen, 1750–1799" (med. diss., University of Tübingen, 1977), 8.

the twenty-odd medical faculties of the German states were already enormous and remained so for the next half-century and more.[17]

At those universities influenced by Johann Peter Frank, the changes in medical education were even more pronounced. At Göttingen in 1784, Pavia in 1786, Vienna in 1798, and Vilnius in 1804, Frank's reforms were aimed directly at narrowing the gap between academic and practical teaching. The professor of anatomy, he insisted, should combine practical dissection with lectures on the purposes and functions of parts of the body; the physiologist should join discussion of normal body functioning to lessons on diseased organs; and the pathologist must not only lecture on particular diseases but also demonstrate them whenever possible at the bedside.

Before starting medicine, every student should spend at least a year of preparation, Frank advised, in learning the rudiments of natural science, since medicine was now "the daughter of natural science." Comparative anatomy, too, was a new and useful tool for understanding both human and animal functions. The sciences of botany and chemistry, crucial to understanding medicine, should be taught by specialists and not by medical professors. In the four- or five-year medical curriculum that Frank planned and partially realized, study began with general anatomy in the first year, proceeded to physiology and pathological anatomy in the second, and then turned to special pathology and therapy in the third- and fourth-year medical and surgical clinics. Medicine and surgery, he declared, must be equally stressed in the university clinics.[18]

Diversity in the French University Before 1789

By the 1780s not only in the German states but also in other parts of Europe, the academic course in medicine was showing wide variations. The spur of scientific discovery, a growing interest in the possibilities of experimental medicine, and a new emphasis on utility all affected university study in different ways. Even within these countries, differences among medical schools could be as great as those separating them from the schools of other nations. Under the Old Regime in France, for example, the contrast in medical teaching at a small university such as Nantes with the instruction given at Strasbourg or Paris was more pronounced than the differences between Strasbourg and Heidelberg. Despite a royal edict in 1707 that sought to standardize the curricula and examinations of the

17. See also the range of medical lectures given at Erlangen after 1792, in Axel Paetzke, "Die Lehrer der Heilkunde der Universität Erlangen, 1792–1818" (med. diss., University of Erlangen–Nuremberg, 1966), 81–98.

18. Ramúnas Kondratas, "Joseph Frank (1771–1842) and the Development of Clinical Medicine" (Ph.D. diss., Harvard University, 1977), 22–36. See also Erna Lesky, "Johann Peter Frank als Organisator des medizinischen Unterrichts," *Sudhoffs Archiv* 39 (1955): 1–29.

French universities, nothing approaching uniformity in medical teaching was achieved. Of the sixteen faculties of medicine offering courses and degrees at the time of the revolutionary convention, no two were alike in the range of subjects taught, the amount of practical instruction offered, or the length and difficulty of examinations.[19]

The principal characteristic of the prerevolutionary faculties in France, writes a modern scholar, was their independence. Only half of them had any students enrolled at all in the doctor's degree program in medicine, and the other half trained students for the lesser baccalaureate degree or the intermediate licentiate in medicine.[20] Most teaching programs required three years of study to complete, but two additional years of practical experience in a hospital were demanded by the Paris faculty. Other faculties required as little as three to six months of such practical study.

Whereas Parisian students of medicine were expected to have completed a program of liberal study at the university before enrolling in medicine, provincial schools often asked for no more than a year or two of preliminary preparation.[21] Anatomy was taught well in Paris and Montpellier—and perhaps also in Strasbourg—but a lack of anatomical theaters, too few cadavers, and traditional formal teaching methods were typical of many of the provincial cities. Botany, too, was indifferently taught at the smaller universities, and instruction in chemistry was given at only seven of the French medical schools during the Old Regime.[22]

Clinical experience was gained largely, if at all, outside the medical school, in contrast with the growing importance of bedside instruction in the German universities. Among the exceptions were the school at Strasbourg, where an obstetrical clinic had been created in 1728 and a chair in clinical medicine in 1754, and at the progressive school at Angers, where the local hospital had become, according to one account, "a veritable arm of the faculty."[23] The school at Montpellier, the oldest in France, also sought to provide clinical training and to integrate the teaching of surgery into that of medicine. A degree in surgical medicine had been introduced there as early as 1732, and students at the school presented a formal demand for even more practical instruction at the bedside in

19. See the detailed descriptions of each medical faculty in André Finot, *Les facultés de médecine de province avant la révolution* (Paris, 1958).

20. Germaine Picard, "La réglementation des études médicale en France: Son évolution de la révolution a nos jours" (med. diss., University of Paris, 1967), 2–3. See also Pierre Huard, "L'enseignement medico–chirurgical," in *Enseignement et diffusion des sciences en France au XXVIIIe siècle*, ed. René Taton (Paris: Hermann, 1964), 172–76.

21. Charles Coury, "Medical Education in France from the Beginning of the 17th Century to Our Day," unpublished manuscript, 1968, Institut für Geschichte der Medizin, Vienna, 8.

22. L. W. B. Brockliss, *French Higher Education in the Seventeenth and Eighteenth Centuries: A Cultural History* (Oxford: Clarendon Press, 1987), 394.

23. George J. Granger, "Recherches sur l'enseignement de la médecine militaires à Strasbourg au XVIIIe siècle" (med. diss., University of Strasbourg, 1967), 37; Huard, "L'enseignement medico–chirurgical," 183.

1762.[24] By 1789, the medical faculties at Toulouse and Caen were listing courses in practical medicine, although the extent of the students' involvement in patient care is not clear.[25]

On the eve of the Revolution, the faculty in Paris comprised five medical chairs (anatomy, botany, pathology and physiology, pharmacy, and materia medica) and two chairs in surgery (one in the Latin language and the other in French for the more practically minded surgeons). Pressures were building, as they were elsewhere in France, to abandon the formal medieval-style lecture (*lectio*) altogether, to equalize instruction in medicine and surgery, and to introduce a larger practical element into the teaching program. Even without a revolution, in other words, the future of medical education in France promised to be quite different by the closing years of the century.[26]

Academic Medicine in Great Britain

The future course of academic medicine in Britain seemed far from clear in the late eighteenth century. As was the case on the Continent, the numbers of those enrolled in medical study at the universities were but a handful of all those planning to be practitioners. Between 1751 and 1800, the English universities graduated only 246 men in medicine, or an average of about 5 per year.[27] By the 1780s, the hospitals in London were already becoming a center of medical teaching that rivaled Paris, Vienna, and Edinburgh, although no university appeared in the city for another half-century. At Oxford and Cambridge, the only two degree-granting schools in England, the course in medicine was long, formal, and inflexible. It could take as long as fourteen years, beginning with a master's degree in liberal arts, and proceeding, as on the Continent, through the licentiate and then the doctorate in medicine.[28]

Unlike the universities on the Continent, however, especially those in Germany, the English universities "held aloof from the professions requiring specific training" and continued to teach medicine as a series of discreet scholarly subjects within the classical confines of the residential colleges.[29] A typical university degree at Cambridge in 1748, for example,

24. Paul Delmas, "Les étapes de l'enseignement clinique a Montpellier," *L'Informateur médical* 5 (1926): 2.

25. Brockliss, *French Higher Education*, 396, note.

26. See especially the pioneering work of Toby Gelfand in reinterpreting eighteenth-century French medicine, *Professionalizing Modern Medicine: Paris Surgeons and Medical Science and Institutions in the 18th Century* (Westport, CT: Greenwood Press, 1980).

27. A. H. T. Robb-Smith, "Medical Education at Oxford and Cambridge Prior to 1850," in *The Evolution of Medical Education in Britain*, ed. F. N. L. Poynter (London: Pitman, 1966), 49.

28. Arnold Chaplin, "The History of Medical Education in the Universities of Oxford and Cambridge, 1500–1850," unpublished manuscript, 1920, 11, Royal College of Physicians, London.

29. Michael Sanderson, ed., *The Universities in the Nineteenth Century* (London: Routledge & Kegan Paul, 1975), 3.

was voted by the "venerable Senate" on the petition of a faculty member of Queens College to admit a fellow of that college to "the Benefit of . . . the Degree of Doctor of Physick."[30]

Sometimes, it was said, a Cambridge graduate could "take a Doctorate in Medicine without attending any lectures on medicine, or any hospital practice, and without examination in medicine."[31] So little demand was there for medical lectures there that the Regius Professor of Medicine had not taught a regular course for more than a hundred years.[32] At both Oxford and Cambridge, a dissertation was required in order to be awarded a degree, as was true in France and Germany. The dissertation became the subject of a formal, institutionalized exchange of views in Latin known as a *disputation*. It is not surprising that under these conditions, many who seriously intended to pursue the study of medicine in the late eighteenth century went to Scotland or to the Continent for their training.

The small number of English physicians who took their entire course of study at the English universities, however, exercised a disproportionate influence on the course of medical education in Britain. Unquestionably broadly trained in the classics of medicine and literature and having the benefit of "years of leisure and reading within a close intellectual community," many were motivated to further study of the natural sciences and clinical medicine.[33] Although not required to attend lectures in anatomy at Oxford until 1767 and only then to prove having attended just one dissection, many students did much more to improve their scientific educations and readiness for practice. Private courses in anatomy, chemistry, and botany were freely available at both universities by the latter half of the century, and medical students were prominent among those who took advantage of them. Clinical experience was gained through apprenticeship to a local or university physician or by spending a period in London. The education thus received, it has been suggested, was often far better than the system that produced it.[34]

By far the largest number of university physicians in Great Britain was educated in Edinburgh and Glasgow. During the half-century after 1750, 2,600 students received their degrees in the Scottish universities, or more than ten times the number from Oxford and Cambridge.[35] Already, Scot-

---

30. "Medicine: Memoranda, Reports, Correspondence, 1694–1926," University of Cambridge Archive, CUR 28.4.1.

31. Charles Newman, *The Evolution of Medical Education in the Nineteenth Century* (Oxford: Oxford University Press, 1957), 10.

32. D. A. Winstanley, *Early Victorian Cambridge* (Cambridge: Cambridge University Press, 1940), 3.

33. Robert G. Frank Jr., "Science, Medicine and the Universities of Early Modern England: Background and Sources," *History of Science* 11 (1973): 207.

34. Ibid., 207–11, 264.

35. L. R. C. Agnew, "Scottish Medical Education," in *The History of Medical Education*, ed. C. D. O'Malley (Berkeley and Los Angeles: University of California Press, 1970), 260.

tish graduates comprised half or more of all university-educated physicians practicing in London. By the time of the American Revolution, more than 400 students were enrolled in medicine each year at Edinburgh alone.[36]

A Scottish degree in medicine required three years of study, at least one of them in Edinburgh or Glasgow, and an examination—conducted in Latin át the house of one of the professors—on anatomy and surgery, chemistry, botany, materia medica and pharmacy, and the theory and practice of medicine. The courses resembled those on the Continent, especially in the German universities, and included clinical lectures in a local infirmary.[37] Dissertations were written on such broad topics as smallpox, alimentation, respiration, "malignant angina," rheumatism, and pneumonia.[38]

The student body at Edinburgh included a number of persons with previous study or practice of medicine. The great appeal of the university lay in its willingness to instruct students in various stages of preparation. A guide published in 1792 pointed out that among the students enrolled were some who had served an apprenticeship or practiced medicine, others who held a medical degree from another university, some who were just starting, and still others who intended to complete their educations in London or Paris.[39] At Glasgow, the records of the University Senate reveal that a number of the candidates for the medical degree had studied previously in Paris, Leyden, or Dublin for one or two years.[40]

What was unique about Edinburgh and Glasgow was that they attempted to provide a full range of medical courses, including surgery and midwifery, and to integrate them into the practical work of the clinic while still offering a university degree. They also pioneered in Britain in efforts to relate the new sciences of chemistry and botany to the practice of pharmacy and medicine. The redoubtable William Cullen persuaded the authorities in Glasgow to equip a chemistry laboratory in 1747 and stressed its usefulness for medical study. A year later he introduced the first course in botany.[41] In 1753, one of his students, Joseph Black, wrote his father that "I find every day that Chemistry is a branch of natural philosophy of the most extensive and solid use in all the arts but particularly

36. Minutes of Senatus, December 8, 1783, University of Edinburgh Archive.

37. Ibid.; Records of University of Glasgow Senate, March 30, 1802, University of Glasgow Archive.

38. Minutes of Medical Faculty, 1792, University of Edinburgh Archive.

39. J. Johnson, *A Guide for Gentlemen Studying Medicine at the University of Edinburgh* (London: Robinson, 1792), 54–55.

40. Records of University of Glasgow Senate, March 9, 1787, March 10, 1796, June 10, 1796. One candidate for a medical degree at Glasgow had practiced medicine in England for eighteen years (May 2, 1791).

41. Alexander Duncan, *Memorials of the Faculty of Physicians and Surgeons of Glasgow* (Glasgow: Maclehose, 1896), 127–28.

in Medicine."[42] Later, when he followed Cullen to a post in Edinburgh, he reported that four of the Edinburgh professors were regularly attending his lectures in chemistry.[43]

The teaching in the Scottish schools threatened, as Christopher Lawrence argues, to hasten the breakdown of the rigid social structure of British medicine. Both Edinburgh and Glasgow, as well as Aberdeen, appealed to a class of students that was largely excluded from the ancient universities of England. At the Edinburgh Medical School, founded in 1726, for example, the first Alexander Monro not only included surgical apprentices in his classes but also took the bold step of lecturing in the English language. A new utilitarian emphasis on practical training and surgery reflected the Scottish Enlightenment ideology of "cultural improvement" for a broad spectrum of the population.[44] Both future physicians and surgeons found a place in the flexible curriculum.

Unlike the continental practice of establishing separate schools of surgery, the surgeons of Scotland sought to adapt the academic courses of the university to their own use. Many entered the medical classes at Edinburgh or Glasgow with little or no training in the traditional liberal subjects and graduated at an early age, some still in their teens. Not until 1824 was a two-year program of study in Latin, Greek, and mathematics recommended for admission to medicine at Edinburgh.[45] Established physicians in London looked askance at medical men who "were shaky in Latin and . . . knew no Greek," who were not members of the established church, and who were well versed in surgery and man-midwifery.[46] In addition, a number of needy Scottish students were admitted free to the lectures, breaking down still further the rigid division of social classes in medical healing.

Creating Medical Doctors in America

The loose and informal Edinburgh system appealed to students in North America, who found little in England or on the Continent to satisfy their need for both a practical and an academic education. Lacking universities of the European type, without medical schools of any kind of their own,

42. Joseph Black to George Black, March 10, 1753, Joseph Black Correspondence, University of Edinburgh Archive.

43. Ibid., June 30, 1766.

44. Christopher Lawrence, "Ornate Physicians and Learned Artisans: Edinburgh Medical Men, 1726–1776," in *William Hunter and the Eighteenth-Century Medical World*, ed. W. F. Bynum and Roy Porter (Cambridge: Cambridge University Press, 1985), 157–58, 173–75. See also Lawrence, "Medicine as Culture: Edinburgh and the Scottish Enlightenment" (Ph.D. diss., University College London, 1984).

45. David B. Horn, *A Short History of the University of Edinburgh, 1556–1889* (Edinburgh: University of Edinburgh Press, 1967), 107.

46. David Hamilton, *The Healers: A History of Medicine in Scotland* (Edinburgh: Canongate, 1981), 142.

and often as "shaky" in Latin and Greek as were the youth of Scotland, the American students turned in considerable numbers to the medical school in Edinburgh as the best place to learn their calling. More than a hundred Americans took their medical degrees in Edinburgh before 1800, and many more enrolled for shorter periods of study.[47]

When the first medical schools were created in the United States and Canada, it was the Edinburgh graduates who planned and taught in them. "Edinburgh's reputation," declared John Morgan in his address launching the medical school at Philadelphia, "is raised to such a height . . . that it already rivals, if not surpasses that of every other school of Physic in Europe."[48] The school founded on Morgan's plan in 1765 reflected the Scottish university's openness to students with different academic needs and also its pattern of courses, clinical teaching, textbooks, and examinations. It followed also the example of Edinburgh in its dependence on student fees for professorial income. The Philadelphia school accommodated itself, too, to the extensive American system of apprenticeship, just as Edinburgh enrolled hundreds of medical apprentices in its program of formal study.[49]

When a similar effort to begin medical teaching was started at King's College in New York in 1767, the model for the new institution was again Edinburgh. By the end of the century, according to Frederick Waite's careful compilation, 312 persons had qualified for a medical degree in the United States, almost two-thirds of them in Philadelphia and the rest in New York or in the new Edinburgh-influenced schools at Harvard and Dartmouth.[50] The existence of four such schools connected to academic institutions by 1800 put the United States far ahead of England (but not Scotland) in the production of academic degrees in medicine.

Other Sites of Medical Study

Important though university study was to the medical reputation and authority of physicians, it represented in the eighteenth century only a small segment of the organized teaching of medicine. The site of most medical

---

47. Samuel Lewis, "List of the American Graduates in Medicine in the University at Edinburgh," *New-England Historical and Genealogical Register* 42 (1888): 159–65.

48. John Morgan, *A Discourse upon the Institution of Medical Schools in America* (New York: Arno Press, 1975), 29. This work was first published in Philadelphia in 1765 by W. Bradford.

49. Lisa Rosner, "Thistle on the Delaware: Edinburgh Medical Education and Philadelphia Practice, 1800–1825," *Social History of Medicine* 5 (1991): 24–25. See also Deborah C. Brunton, "The Transfer of Medical Education: Teaching at the Edinburgh and Philadelphia Medical Schools," in *Scotland and America in the Age of Enlightenment*, ed. R. B. Shor and J. R. Smith (Princeton, NJ: Princeton University Press, 1990), 241–58.

50. Frederick C. Waite, "Medical Degrees Conferred in the American Colonies and in the United States in the Eighteenth Century," *Annals of Medical History* 9 (1937): 317–19.

study in 1800 was outside the university, and except for Germany, the proportion of nonuniversity study was growing swiftly in every country. Indeed, for much of the next century, the principal sites of medical teaching remained outside the walls of academe. In Britain and France, the rise of hospital medicine in the closing decades of the eighteenth century accounted for an ever larger share of medical training, and the independent American medical school, unrelated to any university, claimed a far larger proportion of medical graduates than did the academic colleges. Indeed, many students of the early nineteenth century came to question the need or utility of the academic study of medicine altogether.

By the late eighteenth century, then, the study of medicine and surgery was pursued less in academic surroundings than in private courses, in contractual relationships with a practitioner, in state-run practical schools, in military courses of study, in private medical colleges, and in hospitals. To a very large degree, the students were the organizers of their own education, putting together a combination of experiences through serving a master, walking the wards of a hospital, perhaps taking a course in a private home or hospital, serving in the army or navy, attending a school of surgery or military medicine, and sometimes following lectures at a university. Only one in every five students who took courses in Edinburgh between 1765 and 1825 went on to graduate, and fewer than two of five students in Philadelphia completed their medical studies at the college.[51] All of them, almost without exception, attended medical lectures only as a supplement to other, more vital, experiences in practical medicine. In America, as in Europe, it was not uncommon for students to pursue their premedical, scientific, and clinical training at the same time.

The Role of Apprenticeship

The defining experience for most eighteenth-century medical practitioners in Great Britain and America, and to a lesser extent for those on the Continent, was the formal apprenticeship in medicine. Lacking the specialized schools for surgeons and country practitioners found on the Continent, those seeking such training in the English-speaking countries often had no recourse other than to a private teacher. Even those who took academic courses in Philadelphia or Glasgow or even Oxford almost certainly gained further practical experience and guidance from a preceptor or "master" in his private practice or at a hospital.

The laws governing apprenticeship in Great Britain, because they concerned boys as young as fourteen, were extremely strict and cast the master in the role of in loco parentis in guiding his young charges. Lengthy contracts spelled out in great detail the duties of the preceptor to supply food and clothing and discipline, as well as to provide books and to instruct the apprentice in the technical skills of his calling. The Leeds prac-

---

51. Rosner, "Thistle on the Delaware," 22–24.

titioner William Dawson, for example, contracted in 1750 to instruct a fourteen-year-old apprentice, William Hay, "in the Arts Trades or Mysteries of an Apothecary and Surgeon" and to provide him with meat, drink, lodging, and "two shirts weekly" in exchange for Hay's pledge to "well and faithfully" serve his master, keep his secrets, and refrain from fornication or adultery and from frequenting taverns or alehouses.[52]

By the end of the third year of service, according to a contemporary treatise on medical teaching, a good apprentice might "be able to attend his master to the patient's bedside."[53] Another guidebook for masters and apprentices suggested an intricate system of fines for dereliction of duty, such as a sixpence fine for an apprentice "for not being out of bed and dressed when the clock strikes seven" and a two-shilling fine for the master "for omitting to say how often a medicine is to be taken."[54]

The contract itself was a binding public document certifying the education received. The charge for such a tutelage was high, ranging from £50 to £200 or more, increasing with the reputation of the master, especially one with a hospital appointment. Although the term of service of an apprentice varied widely, more than 67 percent of them in early-eighteenth-century England were bound to periods of seven or more years.[55]

The trials and frustrations of such young pupils, many of them unhappy with their choice of career or master, are evident in the diaries and other records they left behind. The young Scot Alexander Hamilton, for example, who was apprenticed to a physician he disliked intensely, made desperate attempts to get out of his bondage. "My courage fails me," he wrote in his diary, "oh fortune, after all my struggles wilt thou at last prove treacherous . . . my case is desperate . . . I shall go to the bottom."[56] In London, an apprentice to the noted Percivall Pott complained of his constant weariness and frustration at studying the "obsolete ancient authors in Surgery to whom Mr. Pott introduced me." He was released from his contract, however, when "a courtship of one fortnight terminated the virginity of Miss Pott [his daughter]."[57]

In America, the demanding Charles Caldwell found his experience as apprentice to a North Carolina physician "sad and mortifying," especially

52. S. T. Anning and W. K. Walls, *A History of the Leeds School of Medicine* (Leeds: Leeds University Press, 1982), 1–2.

53. James Makittrick, *Commentaries on the Principles and Practise of Physic, being an Attempt, on a New Plan, to connect the several Branches of Medicine, and to plan the Practise of it on a rational and solid Foundation* (London: T. Becket, 1772), xxxiii.

54. William Chamberlaine, *Tirocinium Medicum; or a Dissertation on the Duties of Youth apprenticed to the Medical Profession* (London: privately printed, 1812), 208–9.

55. Joan Lane, "The Role of Apprenticeship in Eighteenth-Century Medical Education in England," in *William Hunter and the Eighteenth-Century Medical World*, ed. W. F. Bynum and Roy Porter (Cambridge: Cambridge University Press, 1985), 73.

56. Alexander Hamilton diary, March 6, 1805, Royal College of Physicians of Edinburgh.

57. Diary and autobiographical notes of Ludford Harvey, 1777, St. Bartholomew Hospital Archive, London.

when he discovered that his preceptor had "no library, no apparatus, no provision for improvement in practical anatomy, nor any other efficient means of instruction in medicine."[58] Another student apprenticed to a Louisville doctor wrote his father that "I might as well read by myself, as with Doctor Ferguson for he now never pretends to examine me on what I have read, nor has he since I came down in the spring."[59] By the turn of the century, such complaints were common among both British and American students, but nonetheless many others treasured the practical instruction they received and the opportunity to engage, at whatever distance, in the actual practice of medicine.

In contrast with the long period of indenture in England and Scotland, the contract to a preceptor in America, especially by the late eighteenth century, had shrunk to about three years.[60] Unlike the practice in Great Britain, the apprenticeship was not closely tied to the legal right to practice medicine or surgery, and a large number of American practitioners lacked either apprenticeship or classroom training. Of more than two hundred "doctors" who began their practice in Massachusetts in the 1770s, for example, less than half, according to one study, had served any kind of apprenticeship.[61]

In any case, by this time the apprenticeship system was growing rapidly as more and more trained practitioners became available and saw in the system a means of augmenting their own incomes and carrying out menial tasks. The normal price paid by an American student was $100 per year, which was a considerable sum for a colonial family. Some highly successful physicians, notably John Redman and Benjamin Rush of Philadelphia, attracted a large number of apprentices and endeavored to teach them in group sessions, using skeletons, charts, and other teaching devices.[62]

Private Teaching

By the 1780s, the advantages of such group teaching were apparent to most medical teachers and students. All during the century, individual efforts to organize private courses for both apprentices and medical stu-

58. Harriot W. Warner, ed., *Autobiography of Charles Caldwell, M.D.* (Philadelphia: Lippincott, 1855), 77.

59. William L. Sutton to his father, December 17, 1810, William Loftis Sutton Papers, Kornhauser Library Historical Collections, University of Louisville.

60. William D. Postell, "Medical Education and Medical Schools in Colonial America," *International Record of Medicine* 171 (1958): 365; William F. Norwood, "Medical Education in the United States Before 1900," in *The History of Medical Education*, ed. C. D. O'-Malley (Berkeley and Los Angeles: University of California Press, 1970), 474. In French Canada, according to N. Tait McPhedran, the period of apprenticeship was normally from five to seven years. See his *Canadian Medical Schools: Two Centuries of Medical History, 1822 to 1992* (Montreal: Harvest House, 1993), 2.

61. Eric Christianson, "The Emergence of Medical Communities in Massachusetts, 1790–1794: The Demographic Factors," *Bulletin of the History of Medicine* 54 (1980): 69.

62. William G. Rothstein, *American Medical Schools and the Practice of Medicine: A History* (New York: Oxford University Press, 1987), 21.

dents had been growing in nearly every country. The teaching enterprise was sometimes centered in a local hospital or dispensary while at other times it was carried on in a separate building or in the teacher's home.

In those countries where medical training was closely controlled by the state, especially in Germany and Austria, such private endeavors were fewer in number than in the looser political climate of the Anglo-American nations. In Great Britain, especially, a sizable teaching industry was being created by ambitious surgeons and physicians in the latter part of the century. The city of London, in particular, despite the lack of any academic institution for teaching medicine, became a world center for medical learning by virtue of its many crowded hospitals, famous teachers, and private schools of anatomy.

Throughout the century, teaching medicine as a private enterprise was common in France as well as Great Britain. Early on, Parisian surgeons attracted scores of students to their private courses in surgery and midwifery. In 1727, the Swiss surgeon Johannes Gessner, for example, joined his Leyden classmate Albrecht von Haller in seeking practical experience in dissecting and operating in Paris. In his diary Gessner wrote about the "hundreds" of surgeons in the capital and described his own experience in operating on cadavers, being allowed to repeat procedures under the guiding hand of the surgeon, examining pregnant women, and performing deliveries under a teacher's supervision. Such hands-on training was given only in private courses, he wrote his old teacher Boerhaave, and was available "only for large sums of money."[63]

By midcentury, dozens of such private courses, usually on subjects that were new or undergoing change, were offered in Paris and other cities. Because of the opposition of the medical corporations and many of the faculty, they were conducted quietly in homes, rented dwellings, or even barns.[64] Many of the best-known names in French medicine—Fourcroy, Portal, Vicq d'Azyr, Pelletan, Desault, Chomel, Laplanche—took part in these courses. Fourcroy, for example, gave numerous lectures on chemistry and natural history in his private laboratory, later in a rented house, and finally to large crowds in the Jardin du roi.[65] In Strasbourg, private courses flourished so extensively that a royal minister complained as early as 1736 that "the professors are not conducting all their public courses, doubtless because their private lessons are well paid and they find this method more lucrative."[66] When the revolutionary government finally proclaimed "freedom of teaching" in 1791, it was only recognizing a growing reality among teachers of medicine in France.

63. *Johannes Gessners Pariser Tagebuch 1727*, ed. Urs Boschung (Bern: Hans Huber, 1985), entries for September 4, 11, and November 14, 1727, pp. 201–6, 246. See also pp. 127, 130–31, 151–52.

64. Coury, "Medical Education," 15.

65. W. A. Smeaton, *Fourcroy: Chemist and Revolutionary, 1755–1809* (Cambridge: W. Heffer, 1962), 7–12.

66. Daniel J.-C. Amzalac "Reflexions sur l'enseignement de la médicine en France des origines à la révolution" (med. diss., University of Paris, 1967), 60.

Both hospital and private teaching, as Toby Gelfand wrote, took place in the eighteenth century "within a common fee-for-educational-service nexus."[67] Even in the German states, where government and university officials kept a tight lid on extramural teaching, the professors themselves and *dozenten* (private instructors judged qualified by the faculty to teach classes) were free to offer courses for pay within the university framework. The new university at Berlin, for example, reported in the early nineteenth century that at least four courses in medicine offered privately by faculty members were attracting more than one hundred students each.[68]

The distinction between courses offered for payment outside academic or legal requirements by a private teacher in a German medical school and courses given on the same basis in a French hospital was often difficult to draw. In practice, they became indistinguishable. In the early decades of the century, the practice had grown up in Paris—as well as in London, Philadelphia, and other cities—that a private student or "pupil," as well as apprentices, might "walk the wards" with his teacher as he visited a hospital on his daily rounds. What defined him as a pupil was the private arrangement for teaching with a teacher to whom he paid a fee.

The New Hospital Teaching

Records of the early hospitals in London show a slow, steady evolution of medical teaching over more than two centuries. At St. Thomas's Hospital, for example, a student apprenticed to a surgeon was mentioned as early as 1561. Another century passed, however, before students were numerous enough to be the subject of hospital regulation.[69] A complaint in 1713 charged that one of the hospital surgeons had been visiting the hospital with more than the three apprentices allowed under hospital rules. The hearing revealed that the additional student "does not live with him but attends him only in the nature of a pupil."[70] Such private pupils, who were not bound by apprenticeship, were common by the 1720s, and the fees they paid went directly to the teacher. Later, they were divided among all those teaching students and providing them ac-

---

67. Toby Gelfand, "'Invite the Philosopher as well as the Charitable': Hospital Teaching as Private Enterprise in Hunterian London," in *William Hunter and the Eighteenth-Century Medical World*, ed. W. F. Bynum and Roy Porter (Cambridge: Cambridge University Press, 1985), 145.

68. Rudolf Köpke, *Die Gründung der Königlichen Friedrich-Wilhelms-Universität zu Berlin* (Berlin: Gustav Schade, 1860), 130–31.

69. "Extract from Mr. Whitfield's MSS on the history of St. Thomas Hospital, September, 1873," St. Thomas Medical School papers, HI/ST/K/O/27, Greater London Record Office. In 1699 the Grand Committee "ordered that no Surgeons Cubs or persons in that nature do keep their Hats on before the Physicians and Surgeons of this house when they are in the wards of this Hospital." Ibid., Governors' Minutes, Grand Committee, January 18, 1697.

70. Governors' Minutes, Grand Committee, September 30, 1713, St. Thomas Medical School folder, ibid.

cess to their patients. An arrangement with Guy's Hospital, which was founded in the vicinity of St. Thomas in 1724, made it possible for St. Thomas students to attend lectures on medicine and chemistry at that institution. By 1730, a dissecting room for students had been added to St. Thomas's Hospital.[71]

Similar developments were under way at other London hospitals. At St. Bartholomew's Hospital, Percivall Pott, a famous medical teacher of the 1740s, was giving lectures to pupils in a private house in 1741 while also serving as surgeon to the hospital.[72] Within a few years, Pott and others had obtained permission to use the hospital itself for their teaching. Likewise, the medical attendants at the new London Hospital, opened in the city's east end in 1740, were teaching private pupils almost from the start. Disputes broke out at this hospital over the responsibility for the young pupils who "lounged around" on the premises in the absence of their teachers and who sometimes brought their friends to the wards or the operating room "to see the show." A resolution by the hospital governors in 1758 ordered that "all the pupils shall be under the directions of all . . . the surgeons" and that teaching fees should henceforth be divided equally among them.[73]

It was at this hospital that William Blizard proposed in 1783 a full range of medical lectures to accompany the experience of "walking the wards." Hospital attendance was indispensable to a would-be practitioner, he wrote, but to ensure a real education, it must be joined to regular classes in such subjects as chemistry, materia medica, anatomy, and surgery "as in every part of Europe, and in America."[74] His success in persuading the hospital to support his plan to build a lecture theater caused some writers to describe his venture as "England's first medical school." For the next half-century, the school at the London Hospital, like other such ventures, was run independently of the hospital by the surgeons and physicians, with the fees of students going directly to them.[75]

The lucrative trade in medical teaching was not confined to such hospital centers as London and Paris. Dozens of examples of similar enterprises can be found in the provincial towns of Europe and America. Lyon, for example, had its "superb" Hôtel-Dieu, as Mathew Baillie described it,

71. F. G. Parsons, *The History of St. Thomas's Hospital*, 3 vols. (London: Methuen, 1932–36), 2:184–86.

72. Victor C. Medvei and John L. Thornton, eds., *The Royal Hospital of Saint Bartholomew, 1123–1973* (London: Royal Hospital of Saint Bartholomew, 1974), 46.

73. Minutes of Board of Governors, March 14, 1758, London Hospital Archives, LH/X/B/8.

74. James Maddocks and William Blizard, *Expediency and Utility of Teaching the Several Branches of Physic and Surgery, by Lectures at the London Hospital; and for Erecting Theatres for that Purpose* (London, 1783), 5–6. Copy in London Hospital Archives.

75. John Ellis, *LHMC 1785–1985: The Story of the London Hospital Medical College, England's First Medical School* (London: London Hospital Medical Club, 1986), 12.

where private pupils were given instruction in operative surgery, bandaging, and midwifery.[76] In Edinburgh and Glasgow, extramural teaching sometimes attracted more students than did the courses listed formally by the universities.[77] At Manchester, Bristol, Liverpool, Leeds, Bath, Exeter, and other provincial centers, apprentices and pupils turned to attending medical men at local hospitals for medical teaching.

By the close of the eighteenth century, a "growing network of hospitals in the provinces" was offering new opportunities for teachers and students throughout the country.[78] The infirmary at Bristol, for example, was "a microcosm of London" in its range of surgical apprenticeships, ward walking by private pupils, and abundance of lecture courses.[79] In Manchester, students were admitted to the Royal Infirmary in the 1780s in exchange for fees, and they also enjoyed access to lectures on anatomy and chemistry at the Manchester Literary and Philosophical Society.[80]

Similarly, before 1800 in the new American republic, despite the scarcity of hospitals and the lack of towns and cities of any size, private lecture courses on anatomy, midwifery, surgery, and medicine were available in Philadelphia, New York, Boston, Baltimore, and other cities.[81] As early as 1730 or 1731, Thomas Cadwalader, who had studied under William Cheselden in London, was giving anatomical demonstrations and performing dissections for students in Philadelphia.[82] Throughout the century, a range of courses and bedside teaching was offered in the early hospitals, notably in Philadelphia, as well as in almshouses, private dwellings, apothecary shops, dispensaries, and army hospitals. As was true in Europe, most of these courses were taught by medical entrepreneurs who found in them an important source of additional income. The American hospital, writes Charles Rosenberg, "was from its very origins inextricably linked to the careers of successful and ambitious medical men."[83]

76. Pierre Huard, "Les échanges medicaux franco-anglais au XVIII siècle," *Clio Medica* 3 (1968): 47. See also Alain Horvilleur, *L'enseignement médical à Lyon de 1789 à 1821* (Lyon: Bosc, 1965), 17–23.

77. Christopher Lawrence, "The Edinburgh Medical School and the End of the `Old Thing' 1790–1830," *History of Universities* 1 (1988): 264–67.

78. Joan Lane, "The Medical Practitioners of Provincial England in 1783," *Medical History* 28 (1984): 357.

79. Mary E. Fissell, *Patients, Power, and the Poor in Eighteenth-Century Bristol* (Cambridge: Cambridge University Press, 1991), 129.

80. Notes by W. Brockbank in Manchester Collection, John Rylands Library, Manchester, F3a; Katherine A. Webb, "The Development of the Medical Profession in Manchester, 1750–1860" (Ph.D. diss., University of Manchester, 1988), 425–27.

81. Dale C. Smith, "The Emergence of Organized Clinical Instruction in the Nineteenth Century American Cities of Boston, New York and Philadelphia" (Ph.D. diss., University of Minnesota, 1979), 11–36. See also David Riesman, "Clinical Teaching in America, with Some Remarks on Early Medical Schools," *Transactions of the College of Physicians of Philadelphia* 41 (1938): 89–110.

82. F. R. Packard, "Cadwalader, Thomas," in *Dictionary of American Biography*, 10 vols., ed. Allen Johnson and Dumas Malone (New York: Scribner, 1927–36), 2:400.

83. Charles E. Rosenberg, *The Care of Strangers: The Rise of America's Hospital System* (New York: Basic Books, 1987), 20.

The spread of hospitals across Europe and, to a lesser extent, North America had a forceful impact on the locus of medical teaching. Hospitals themselves were undergoing an important transformation of purpose. Under the spur of the Enlightenment and new attitudes toward the poor, the hospital was becoming an important outlet for charitable and philanthropic endeavor, as well as a favorite reform of enlightened despots. New ideas about public health and national strength were changing the traditional hospital that had once served only humanitarian and religious ends. In France, Germany, and the Anglo-American nations, an effort was under way to transform the hospital from a *mourier* into a *machine à guérir*.[84] For such reformers as Tenon and Tissot, the "new" hospital was a place of healing and teaching, not just a place of custody and a vestibule to death. A hospital should have a bed for every patient and separate wards for different diseases, allow students and teachers at the sickbed, and concentrate on healing patients.[85]

In France alone, nearly two thousand hospitals, ranging from giant *hôtels-Dieus* that cared for thousands of the sick poor to small hospices meeting special needs, had been created in cities and towns before the Revolution.[86] In the states of central Europe, too, progressive monarchs created hospitals in such cities as Vienna, Berlin, Mainz, Munich, and Karlsruhe while the prosperous cities of Hamburg and Stuttgart built their own municipal hospitals.[87] In making the decision to build a great general hospital in Vienna, Emperor Joseph II insisted on the centrality of healing and teaching in the new enterprise in order to "end the eternal confusion of medical services with poor relief."[88]

A major shift was also taking place in the character of British hospitals, especially in the endowed institutions of London, where teaching and a growing interest in science and research were creating a new role for hos-

84. This expression, first used by Jacques Tenon, was revived by Michel Foucault et al., *Les machines à guerir* (Paris: Institut de l'environment, 1975).

85. Jacques Tenon, *Memoires sur les hôpitaux de Paris* (Paris: P. H. Pierres, 1788); and Antoinette S. Emsch-Deriaz, "Towards a Social Conception of Health in the Second Half of the Eighteenth Century: Tissot (1728–1797) and the new Preoccupation with Health and Well-being" (Ph.D. diss., University of Rochester, 1984), esp. 272–88. See also Louis S. Greenbaum, "'Measure of Civilization': The Hospital Thought of Jacques Tenon on the Eve of the French Revolution," *Bulletin of the History of Medicine* 40 (1975): 43–56. A translation of Tenon's important work, with an introduction by Dora B. Weiner, is currently in press under the auspices of the National Library of Medicine.

86. Muriel Joerger, "The Structure of the Hospital System in France in the Ancien Regime," in *Medicine and Society in France: Selections from the Annales, Economies, Societés, Civilisations*, vol. 6, ed. Robert Forster and Orest Ranum (Baltimore: Johns Hopkins University Press, 1980), 108.

87. Axel H. Murken, *Das Bild des deutschen Krankenhauses im 19.Jahrhundert* (Münster: Murken-Altrogge, 1978), 9–10.

88. Paul P. Bernard, "The Limits of Absolutism: Joseph II and the Allgemeine Krankenhaus," *Eighteenth-Century Studies* 9 (1975): 7.

pitals as "nature's schools."[89] During the eighteenth century, nearly every British hospital made clear its interest in teaching as part of its function. The building of a small hospital in Exeter, for example, was supported in 1741 by the dean of the local cathedral because, among other reasons, it was "as serviceable to the Rich as to the Poor by furnishing the Physicians and Surgeons with more experience in one year, than they could have in ten without it."[90] Contrary to later accounts, a remarkable range of agreement existed well before 1800 on the importance of the hospital or clinic to medical education.

The Private Medical School

Still another site of medical teaching that lay outside both the university and the hospital was the private medical school. The most famous of these eighteenth-century schools was that organized on Great Windmill Street in London by William Hunter in 1767. Here Hunter built a large auditorium, a library, several rooms for dissecting, and a museum, all of which gave the school facilities well beyond those of most hospitals and universities. He and others gave lectures on anatomy, physiology, surgery, and midwifery, often accompanied by demonstrations, and provided every student with opportunity to dissect a human body.[91] In a surprisingly short time, the Hunter school became a center for anatomical teaching and investigation in the city. As a private enterprise separate from the hospitals, Hunter enjoyed a "freedom from meddling governors or quarrelsome and greedy surgical colleagues" that gave him unusual opportunities to try new methods of teaching.[92]

Other such ventures, though none so renowned, flourished in London and other cities by the early years of the nineteenth century. In Glasgow alone, three such private schools were teaching medicine and surgery by the 1820s.[93] One of them, opened as a part of "Anderson's University" in 1800, eventually attracted more students than did the University of Glasgow.[94] In many respects, these privately organized ventures in Britain, separated as they were from both hospitals and universities, resembled the later proprietary colleges of an expanding America, though

89. See Robert L. Kilpatrick, "Nature's Schools: The Hunterian Revolution in London Hospital Medicine 1780–1825" (Ph.D. diss., Cambridge University, 1988).

90. William B. Howie, *Medical Education in 18th Century Hospitals* (Scottish Society of the History of Medicine, 1970), 3.

91. Stuart C. Thompson, "The Great Windmill Street School," *Bulletin of the History of Medicine* 12 (1942): 383–85.

92. Kilpatrick, "Nature's Schools," 108.

93. Derek Dow and Michael Moss, "The Medical Curriculum at Glasgow in the Early Nineteenth Century," *History of Universities* 1 (1988): 250, n. 3. For information on the College Street Medical School, founded in the late eighteenth century, see F. L. M. Pattison, *Greenville Sharp Pattison: Anatomist and Antagonist, 1791–1851* (Tuscaloosa: University of Alabama Press, 1987), 20–25.

94. Hamilton, *The Healers*, 150.

they never gained the power to confer medical degrees, as did those in the United States.

Government Schools of Practical Medicine

If all but the elite of British and American practitioners were forced by 1800 to seek a helter-skelter education in apprenticeships, private courses, and hospitals, quite a different situation prevailed on the Continent. In France and Germany, as well as elsewhere, specialized schools of surgery and practical medicine were available to a sizable number of students throughout the century. It was from such schools that a large number of the medical practitioners in central and western Europe were trained until well into the nineteenth century. Frequently they were combined with training programs for military surgeons, whose services were in steady demand in the incessant warfare of the period.

The practice of surgery in France, which had gained a measure of independence and status since 1700, was taught in separate schools that sometimes required a preparation rivaling that of physicians. At the Royal Academy of Surgery in Paris, which was teaching seven hundred to eight hundred students a year by the 1750s, and also at fourteen provincial colleges and a dozen military, naval, and ecclesiastical schools, students were offered a program of study in anatomy, operative surgery, pharmacy, medical therapeutics, and botany.[95] The level of instruction at these schools varied by region and type of school, but some of them, especially the royal colleges, provided a four-year course in surgery and practical medicine unsurpassed in Europe. At the school in Grenoble, for example, where instruction was given in the acclaimed military hospital, a remarkable range of practical and theoretical courses was given in all branches of medicine and surgery. As the principal medical training institution of the region, its leaders made available several scholarships to needy students, and other applicants vied for competitive awards of free tuition.[96]

On the German side of the Rhine, many states also created separate schools for surgeon-practitioners, who were becoming the healers of choice in much of the German countryside. In Hannover, Berlin, Dresden, Salzburg, Bamberg, Munich, Innsbruck, and other cities, such schools were founded between 1716 and 1808. The state of Prussia, which had long offered courses in anatomy to military surgeons, built an anatomical theater in Berlin in 1713 that was subsequently enlarged to accommodate 150 army and civilian surgical students, as well as those studying academic medicine and midwifery. Eleven years after its founding, the theater was made part of the new four-year Collegium

---

95. Willem Frijhoff, "L'école de chirurgie de Paris et les Pays-Bas: Analyse d'un recrutement, 1752–1791," *Lias* 17 (1990): 194; Huard, "L'enseignement medico–chirurgical," 198–99.

96. Huard, "L'enseignement medico–chirurgical," 200.

Medico–Chirurgicum, one of the best known schools for *Wundärzte* in Europe.[97]

In Saxony, a medical–surgical institute was established at Dresden in 1748 to put the practice of surgery on a stronger footing. Open to both military and civilian surgeons, it offered a wide selection of practical courses in both medicine and surgery and taught as many as 200 students at a time in the German language. In all, more than 2,400 practical surgeons were given training at the school before 1813.[98] The lecture notes of one of the school's surgeons of 1754 show that the surgical course was divided into a theoretical section, with lectures on general surgery, wound healing, inflammation, swellings, abscesses, eye ailments, and fractures; and a practical portion was devoted to joints, intestinal obstructions, catheterization, stone removal, tracheotomy, amputations, midwifery, and bandaging.[99]

Some schools boasted an impressive array of faculty members. The number of teachers at the institute in Zurich was set at sixteen, and the Alpine school in Salzburg, then part of Bavaria, taught practical surgery and midwifery with a faculty of seven, still equal to the size of a university school of medicine.[100]

The Military School of Medicine

Perhaps the most underrated site of medical teaching in the eighteenth century was the continental military medical school. In the famous Josephinum of Vienna, the military school of Val-de-Grâce in Paris, the Pepinière in Berlin, the Mediko–khirurgicheskaya Akademiya in St. Petersburg, and the similar schools of Spain, Italy, and the Low Countries, some of the best medical instruction of the century was to be found. The training in these schools, which embraced both medicine and surgery, was eminently practical yet included academic courses in such auxiliary sciences as chemistry and botany. The use of clinical methods in teaching was an important feature of these institutions. At the school in Berlin, for example, students spent the greater part of two years in practical instruction and supervised care of patients at the Charité hospital, following a two-year academic program in mathematics, botany, chemistry, pathology, physiology, and pharmacy.[101]

97. Wilhelm Tasche, "Die anatomischen Theater und Institute der deutschsprachigen Unterrichtsstätten" (med. diss., University of Cologne, 1989), 25–30.

98. V. Klimpel, "Zur chirurgischen Ausbildung am ehemaligen Dresdner Collegium medico–chirurgicum," *Zentralblatt für Chirurgie* 115 (1990): 181.

99. Staatsarchiv Dresden, Archiv für alte Militärakten, Nr. 1503, Bl. 14–17, cited in ibid., 183.

100. Moritz Leisibach, *Das medizinisch–chirurgische Institut in Zürich, 1782–1833* (Zurich: Hans Rohr, 1982), 64; Anton E. Mai, "Die niederärztliche Ausbildung zu Salzburg im 19.Jahrhundert" (med. diss., University of Erlangen–Nuremberg, n.d.), 11.

101. Dr. Schickert, *Die militärärztlichen Bildungsanstalten von ihrer Gründung bis zur Gegenwart* (Berlin: Ernst Siegfried Mittler, 1895), 33–36.

In many instances, civilian students sought to gain access to their superior resources. Unlike civilian hospitals, in which most practitioners got whatever clinical training they could, the military hospitals did not depend on charity patients for teaching purposes.[102] Many well-known medical leaders were trained in such schools, including the French surgeons Pierre Desault, Antoine Louis, and Raphael Sabatier, and such German savants as Hermann von Helmholtz, Rudolf Virchow, and Emil Behring. Some of these schools had teaching faculties that surpassed in size those of the universities. The school of military surgery in Munich, for example, had nine full-time teachers in 1799.[103]

By the close of the century, more than a dozen centers of military and naval medical teaching had emerged in France and the German states. As early as 1747, a royal ordinance in France required that courses in medicine, anatomy, and operative surgery be offered in every military hospital. Teaching amphitheaters were built for the education of army and navy surgeons in such places as Lille, Metz, Strasbourg, Rochefort, Brest, and Toulon. The teaching in these schools was spread over a period of three to six years, depending on the student's previous study or apprenticeship training.[104] In most such institutions, courses were given in the French language. At Strasbourg, surgical study was divided into three parts, beginning with the study of osteology and myology in the first year, proceeding to a course in operations and fractures in the second year, and concluding in the third year with supervised operations and courses in neurology, physiology, and pathology. Clinical teaching was heavily stressed throughout the medical and surgical phases of the curriculum. In 1779, a school of midwifery was added to the military hospital to prepare women in the region for obstetrical service.[105]

Similar schools were founded in Prussia and throughout the German states. The Prussian schools of military medicine, in the view of Richard Kremer, were "the training institutions of highest quality" among those educating physicians in the eighteenth century.[106] Especially outstanding was the school in Berlin, many of whose professors later constituted the first faculty of the University of Berlin.

102. Antonie M. Luyendijk-Elshout, "The Medical World of the Nineteenth Century: Its Impact upon Medical Education," unpublished manuscript, 1990, 21. I am indebted to Professor Luyendijk-Elshout for sending me a copy of this paper.

103. Erhard Grunwald, "Das niedere Medizinalpersonal im Bayern des 19.Jahrhunderts" (med. diss., University of Munich, 1950), 24.

104. David M. Vess, *Medical Revolution in France, 1789–1796* (Gainesville: University Presses of Florida, 1975), 27. See also Danièle Voldman, "Les hôpitaux militaires dans l'espace sanitaire français, 1708–1789" (med. diss., University of Paris, n.d.).

105. Christian Wolff, "Facultés, écoles de médecine et hôpitaux militaires à Strasbourg sous la révolution et l'empire (1789–1815)" (med. diss., University of Strasbourg, 1986), 79–81.

106. Richard L. Kremer, "Between Wissenschaft und Praxis: Experimental Medicine and the Prussian State, 1807–1848," in *"Einsamkeit und Freiheit" neu besichtigt*, ed. Gert Schubring (Stuttgart: Franz Steiner, 1991), 156.

Rapprochement of Medicine and Surgery

The movement to draw medicine and surgery more closely together,
which was evident everywhere after 1750, was pronounced in these military schools. By the very nature of military service, distinctions on the
battlefield between surgical and medical therapies were blurred and often
nonexistent. "The military surgeons of all countries," writes one modern
student, "made a vital contribution to the coming together of both healing professions in the course of the 18th century."[107]
Many of the military faculties were required by governments to train
surgical practitioners for the civilian population, who increasingly took on
the role of general practitioners of medicine and surgery. Authorities in
Bavaria, Prussia, and Austria demanded at various times a knowledge of
both medicine and surgery for both civilian and military practitioners. In
Vienna, for example, Joseph II decreed in 1785 that "if someone wants
to be a physician or surgeon, he must in both cases become familiar with
the entire range of the healing arts."[108] At about the same time, the military and naval schools of medicine in France were making provision for
further training in medicine as well as surgery for their graduates. At
Rochefort, Toulon, and Brest, writes Marie-José Imbault-Huart, the
teaching program encompassed "the two branches of the art of healing."[109]
Until recently, the conventional historical view, resting heavily on the
testimony of university-educated physicians, described a deep divide between eighteenth-century medical and surgical teaching. It now appears
that physicians' fears of losing status caused them to exaggerate their descriptions of the actual conditions. For not only in the centers of military
and naval medicine but also in virtually every stratum of medical education, the rapprochement between medicine and surgery was well under
way by 1789. In a recent international symposium in Berlin, scholars
from seven countries agreed on the radical transformation of
medical–surgical relationships in the latter eighteenth century. In France,
it was reported, a definite "tendency toward the equalization" of medical
and surgical teaching was growing in the schools while rapprochement at
the practice level in small towns and rural areas "was already realized." In
the case of the United States, the testimony of an American practitioner
of 1775 was cited, who had written that the "invidious distinction" be-

107. Grunwald, "Das niedere Medizinalpersonal," 143–44.
108. Manfred Skopec, "Das Ringen um die Einheit von Medizin and Chirurgie am
Beispiel des Wiener Josephinums," in *Chirurgische Ausbildung im 18.Jahrhundert, in Abhandlungen zur Geschichte der Medizin und der Naturwissenschaften, 57,* ed. Georg Harig
(Husum: Matthiesen, 1990), 144.
109. Marie-José Imbault-Haunt, "La formation chirurgicale en France au XVIIIème siècle, composante essentielle d'une nouvelle chirurgie," in *Chirurgische Ausbildung im
18.Jahrhundert, in Abhandlungen zur Geschichte der Medizin und der Naturwissenschaften,
57,* ed. Georg Harig (Husum: Matthiesen, 1990), 82.

tween medicine and surgery common in Europe was lacking in America and that the two skills were "so intimately connected, as not to admit of absolute separation."[110]

In Great Britain, despite a deep public animosity between physicians and surgeons, the split between them showed signs of breaking down by the end of the century. "The most striking characteristic" of these years, writes Susan Lawrence in regard to hospital pupils in London, "is the increase in the number following both the physicians and surgeons on their rounds, or mixing their apothecary's studies with one or the other experience." The sharp distinctions of earlier years in surgical, medical, and apothecary education had almost disappeared with "the rise of the de facto general practitioner . . . well before 1780."[111]

Physicians and apothecaries in London were now routinely studying pathology and anatomy and witnessing operations, and surgeons were spending more time learning materia medica and therapeutics. The immensely popular teaching of John Hunter, who pioneered in Britain in the physiological teaching of anatomy and medicine, furnished a powerful argument against the separation of medical and surgical teaching.[112] In the English countryside, the old distinctions were increasingly ignored in any case as more and more practitioners described themselves as surgeon-apothecaries.

Only the power and influence of the royal corporations, especially in the cities, slowed the rapprochement of the healing professions in Britain. No cataclysmic change as in France forced the final reunion of medical and surgical teaching. Despite the growing protest from surgeons in Scotland against restrictionist policies, the Royal College of Physicians in Edinburgh reiterated in 1765 its firm intention to admit no person from the "lower arts . . . whose common business it is either to practice Surgery in general, or Midwifery, Lithotomy, Innoculation [*sic*], or any other branch of it."[113] The battle to keep surgery and medicine separate raged on into the nineteenth century. As late as 1821, the respected Dublin teacher Robert Graves told his students that "the absurd idea that the education of a surgeon should differ from that of a physician [has] not been altogether abandoned."[114]

In the continental countries after 1750, surgery began to enter the medical curriculum of universities with increasing frequency. In the

110. Ibid., 88, 160, 115. The participants cited are Imbault-Huart and Gert H. Brieger.

111. Susan C. Lawrence, "Science and Medicine at the London Hospitals: The Development of Teaching and Research, 1750–1815" (Ph.D. diss., University of Toronto, 1985), 334, 428.

112. Kilpatrick, "Nature's Schools," 225.

113. Royal College of Physicians of Edinburgh Minutes, May 7, 1765, in Richard Poole Papers, Royal College of Physicians of Edinburgh Library.

114. Robert J. Graves, "On Clinical Instruction," *London Medical Gazette* 10 (1832): 402–3, note. As Graves reports, this article was taken from a lecture he gave at Meath Hospital in 1821.

words of Imbault-Huart, surgery was "the advancing wing of medical science . . . equipped with scientific methodology, structures and practice." As in Hunterian London, the "closed [medical] systems of explanations of man and his illnesses" were under mounting attack in both the French and German universities.[115] Nearly every German university by the closing decades of the century offered courses in clinical as well as theoretical surgery. The old distinction between the "medical surgery" of the universities and the "practical surgery" outside them was beginning to fade.[116] In 1797, in answer to a prize essay question of whether or not it was "necessary and possible" to unite medicine and surgery in all medical teaching, fourteen of the fifteen competitors at Erfurt argued in the affirmative on both issues.[117] In the Hapsburg monarchy, the teaching of surgery was formally declared equal to that of medicine a decade earlier.[118]

In Old Regime France, on the other hand, the teaching of surgery, though enjoying an increasingly respectable status, was nonetheless fully accepted by educators only in the colleges of surgery and in military medicine. Like its counterpart in England, the medical establishment of Paris was strongly opposed to admitting to medical study those with a bent toward surgery. Outside Paris, however, provincial universities were willing to award a degree in medicine to some surgical students. The faculties at Montpellier and Grenoble, in fact, had introduced surgery into their curricula, and by the early 1790s, the former could count more than six hundred graduates in its combined medical–surgical program. The academic physicians of France were thus moving steadily, if slowly, toward accepting the surgical viewpoint in disease. Beneath the surface of academic quarrels in France, in the words of Toby Gelfand, a "*de facto* unification already existed."[119]

The Shape of Things to Come

A prescient observer viewing the wide variety of training sites in medicine about 1790 would certainly have remarked on the fluidity of the medical curriculum, the growing closeness of medicine and surgery, the drawing

115. Marie-José Imbault-Huart, "The Teaching of Medicine in France and More Particularly in Paris in the 19th Century (1794–1892)," in *History of Medical Education*, ed. Teizo Ogawa (Tokyo: Saikon, 1983), 58.

116. Owsei Temkin, "The Role of Surgery in the Rise of Modern Medical Thought," *Bulletin of the History of Medicine* 25 (1951): 249.

117. J. H. Jugler, *Gekrönte Preisschrift über die von der Churfürstlichen Akademie nützlicher Wissenschaften zu Erfurt aufgegebene Frage: Ist es notwendig, u. ist es möglich, beide Theile der Heilkunst, die Medicin u. die Chirurgie, sowohl in ihrer Erlernung als Ausübung wieder zu vereinigen?* (Erfurt, 1799).

118. Krobot, "Zur Geschichte der medizinischen Ausbildung," 90–91.

119. Gelfand, *Professionalizing Modern Medicine*, 151–53.

together of practical and theoretical study, and the ambiguous place of classical learning in the new age of science. Whether in the hospital training centers of London, the military medical schools of France, the universities of Germany, or the young medical colleges of America, a nearly universal impulse to unite the empirical spirit of science with the practical skills and knowledge of the bedside was evident.

In a hundred different institutions from Dresden to Philadelphia, students of medicine were looking for better ways to prepare themselves to treat disease and promote healing. The newer subjects—particularly chemistry, botany, pathological anatomy, and, increasingly, physiology— were being taught outside the universities as well as within them. Chemistry was now as important to the drug-dispensing physician as anatomy was to the operating surgeon. Experiments, sometimes quite elegant, were commonplace in the classroom and were occasionally performed by the students themselves. Human corpses, live patients, teaching models, mannequins, skeletons, anatomical specimens, live animals, and class demonstrations were frequently as important to teaching as were textbooks or formal lectures. Hospital pupils were asked to keep records and to perform simple tasks at the bedside. The search for hands-on experience was a feature of student life in every country.

None of the important questions about medical learning of the decades ahead went unasked in the fin-de-siècle years. How does a student actually learn how to become a good practitioner of medicine? Should medical knowledge and surgical skills be taught routinely to every practitioner? What scientific subjects were essential or desirable for one seeking a career in healing? How long can the period of medical study be without excluding the great majority of potential students? What kind of premedical education adequately prepares a would-be physician to learn medicine? How important are classical literature and languages? Should the teaching of medicine be centered in the hospital, the clinic, the apprenticeship, or the university? Should all practitioners be forced to undergo a period of practical experience? Does the state have a role in protecting the people's health, or is the training of doctors best left to competitive enterprise?

In the dynamic, whirling cycle of change through which medical training was passing, it was impossible to foresee the period just ahead. Who would be the medical practitioners of the future? Would it be in France the numerous surgeon-practitioners of the *écoles de chirurgie* and the *écoles militaires*, with their superior knowledge of the human body, or the tiny band of academic physicians who, even in 1790, were still powerful and influential in the French medical world? Which of the seven classes of medical practitioners sanctioned by Prussia, ranging from university graduates in medicine to licensed apothecaries, would best adapt to the changing circumstances of the new century? Could an academically based education ever hope to prevail in Great Britain over the hospital-centered practical teaching that already dominated the training of medical practitioners? And what about North America? Was the apprenticeship training that was so important in the New World, supplemented as it was by short periods of college lectures, likely to prevail over other systems of medical education?

What is perhaps most striking about the condition of medical education at the close of the eighteenth century was the sharply different patterns of national response. Only in Germany and France had the state begun to play a critical role in controlling the educational choices of doctors. In an industrializing Britain, where the state played almost no role, the surgeon-apothecaries were emerging as the most numerous, most useful, and most adaptable of all practitioners. The pattern of diffused power over and responsibility for medical education that marked Britain in the nineteenth century was already in place.

In North America, the same uncertainty of medical polity prevailed as it did in Britain. The lack of training institutions and especially hospitals put far more emphasis than in Britain on simple apprenticeship as the main route to medical practice. The federal system of government made each state a law unto itself in chartering medical schools and opening its boundaries to a range of practitioners. Conditions were set for the unprecedented expansion and competition among degree-granting medical schools that marked a westward-expanding America.

In Europe, the French monarchy, powerful but inefficient, had permitted the growth of alternative healing institutions that offered a considerable range of choice to French medical students. In the turbulent France of 1790, it was the reforming hospitals and the well-regarded surgical schools that seemed to be the sites of greatest promise for the future. And farther east, a peculiarly German pattern of medical teaching was emerging in the changing universities and the many-tiered schools for practical and military surgeons and apothecaries.

To the medical student, often starting his study at age fourteen, the need for guidance through the maze of choices was clear. Students wrote in their diaries and letters about the agonizing choices that confronted them. "I was enabled to take my education very much upon myself," wrote Benjamin Brodie, who, more than others, saw the anarchy of choice as an opportunity. "No rules were laid down," he continued, and "I was acquiring knowledge in [many] ways."[120]

The experience of students by the end of the century was very different from that of a century before and bore little resemblance to that of students a century hence. An enormous burden of responsibility was placed on them, and the effect on their lives, as suggested in the next chapter, was often powerful.

---

120. Charles Hawkins, "Works of Sir Benjamin Brodie with an Autobiography," *Dublin Quarterly Journal of Medical Science* 40 (1865): 138.

3

The Lives of Medical Students and Their Teachers (Late Eighteenth and Early Nineteenth Century)

The lives of students in all periods of history are difficult to recapture. Only scattered correspondence and occasional diaries can normally be found to give us a firsthand look at their experiences. Less satisfactory but still useful are the accounts of teachers, often written long after the events they describe, as well as the memoirs of former students, usually composed with nostalgia toward the close of their careers. Enough evidence does exist, however, to provide at least some glimpses into the student culture of past eras. In this chapter, we trace the social origins of medical students from about 1780 to 1820 and describe something of their lives in and out of the classroom as well as give some account of medical teachers and teaching of the same period.

No more uncertain time in the life of a medical student can be imagined than the unsettled years after 1780. Both Europe and America were convulsed by war during much of the period and by fears of the spreading revolution in France. Students everywhere were being pressed into military service; academic enrollments dropped on both continents; and demands for military surgeons had become desperate. Deans and directors of medical schools pleaded with governments to spare their students from army service. In 1799, for example, the director of the French school at Montpellier asked his counterpart in Paris to join him in a last effort to save students from the huge call to arms of that year.[1]

Some medical schools were suddenly closed during the years of war;

1. Letters of 22 Fructidor, 21 Vendemiare, 1799, Archives nationales, Paris, AJ[16] 6685.

61

others were reorganized; and everywhere standards fell rapidly. Most of the small number of American schools were forced to shut down during the War for Independence and were then slow to reopen. In Great Britain, the hope of recruiting more medical students needed for war service was dashed by "the reality of low pay, lack of respect and the physical dangers facing most recruits."[2] In revolutionary France, the medical schools were officially closed early in the Revolution; the title of doctor was disdained by equalitarian reformers; and near chaos prevailed in the hospitals. More than a hundred French physicians and surgeons were condemned to death during the Terror, and by the mid-1790s, another five hundred were lost on the battlefield.[3] In the German states, over half of all universities disappeared in the Napoleonic maelstrom, and others were reorganized or closed for extended periods.

Ideas about the training of doctors were strongly affected by the prolonged period of peril. The demand for trained men put new pressures on the curriculum and duration of study. In response to the demand, more and more of the London hospitals began to organize practical "schools" of instruction around the work of the wards. In the new "schools of health" created by the revolutionary government in France, pragmatic considerations of military needs dictated a reunion of medicine and surgery, an acceptance of practical training, and a new emphasis on the hospital as the principal training ground for practitioners. In 1803, the authorities in Paris also created a second class of medical men, known as *officiers de santé*, to meet the critical needs of the army and civilian population, and they planned new medical schools in the conquered cities of Mainz, Genoa, and Turin.[4]

In the German universities, too, medical training was transformed by the scourge of war. Reformers in Prussia, stirred by the loss of half its territory and stung by strong resentments against the French, laid plans for a new medical school in the university to be built in Berlin. The highly regarded university at Halle, recently conquered by the French, was to be eclipsed, predicted a Scottish journal, by the powerful amalgam of teaching and hospital facilities in the Prussian capital. Medical education in Germany, "like a wax nose," wrote the Scottish editor, "is to be moulded and fashioned into a new form to attract . . . students to the banks of the Spree."[5]

2. Susan C. Lawrence, "Science and Medicine at the London Hospitals: The Development of Teaching and Research, 1750–1815" (Ph.D. diss., University of Toronto, 1985), 262.

3. Jean-Charles Sournia, *La médecine révolutionnaire, 1789–1799* (Paris: Editions Payot, 1989), 43; Jean Imbert, "La crise économique des hôpitaux français sous la révolution," in *Nouvelles frontières des défenses sanitaire et sociales*, ed. Maurice Gueniot (Paris: Université René Descartes, 1990), 25–28.

4. Robert Heller, "Officiers de Santé: The Second-Class Doctors of Nineteenth-Century France," *Medical History* 22 (1978): 27–28.

5. *Edinburgh Medical Journal* 8 (1812): 251.

The old problem of providing skilled practitioners for the bulk of a nation's population was accentuated by the military demands of wartime. In the four decades between 1780 and 1820, new ventures were launched across Europe and America to educate general practitioners for an expanding medical market.

Social Class and Medical Study

These were the years of rapid growth in the ranks of secondary practitioners in France (*officiers de santé*), practical surgeons in Germany (*Wundärzte*), surgeon-apothecaries in Britain, and "country doctors" in the United States. All of them drew on the humanitarian or democratic urge to provide better health care for the rank and file of citizens, and enterprising teachers found in them a new and profitable market for their services. The growth in numbers of such lesser-trained practitioners met resistance from elite physicians, who fought hard to defend their special rights and to keep high the standards of educational training. The line of demarcation between physicians and surgeons and lesser grades of practitioners became more rigid, even in France after 1800, and was increasingly fixed in law. No question in the nineteenth century was more agitated than the precise formulation of the educational and practice requirements for becoming a doctor of any grade.

The class divisions separating university physicians (the German *medici puri*) from other healers were nowhere clearer than in Great Britain. The swelling ranks of the surgeon-apothecaries, who served the same clientele as did the second-class practitioners of France and Germany, contained almost no graduates of the old English universities. Only the well-to-do could afford the prolonged and expensive study of medicine at Oxford or Cambridge. Yet the graduates of these schools wielded enormous influence over the licensing corporations and blocked efforts at reform. The Royal College of Physicians, for example, which until 1820 conducted its examinations for licensure wholly in Latin, continued its barrage of scorn against the apothecaries and surgeons who practiced medicine without a thorough liberal education. Said the college's Christopher Merrett of them late in the eighteenth century: "They are wholly ignorant of all Philosophy [i.e., natural philosophy or science] and the very elements of the Arts and therefore unskilled in Knowing diseases and more surely their causes."[6] Members of a medical society in Lancashire went so far in 1804 as to assail the lack of classical knowledge of their own apprentices, complaining that "only a small number . . . [are] of respectable parentage."[7] The country practitioner, the backbone of the English effort to treat the

6. Paul K. Underhill, "Science, Professionalism and the Development of Medical Education in England: An Historical Sociology" (Ph.D. diss., University of London, 1987), 79.

7. Edward Harrison, *Remarks on the Ineffective State of the Practise of Physic in Great Britain* (London: R. Bickerstaff, 1806), 30. The discussion took place in 1804.

sick of the nation, was indeed a "marginal man" in the established society of the years around 1800.[8]

Not only were those of modest means barred from the academic pathway to medicine, but also nonconforming Protestants and all Roman Catholics were refused admittance at the English universities. As described in Chapter 8, women were banned completely from medicine in Britain, the rest of Europe, and America until the second half of the century. Social class was all-important in the universities of England. Between 1752 and 1886, no fewer than nine of every ten Oxford students came from "a gentry, clergy, or military background."[9] Teaching at Oxford and Cambridge, unlike Scotland, the Continent, or North America, was centered on the residential college, which drove even higher the costs of a complete education. Scholarships for needy students, common in Scotland and Germany, were comparatively rare in the English schools. German critics described Oxford and Cambridge as *Fürstenschulen*, likening them to socially exclusive German secondary schools that closely regulated the daily lives of their pupils.

The Scottish Exception

Only in Scotland, where the "culture of improvement" was flourishing, could a less affluent or non-Anglican student hope to win a place in a university. No rigorous entrance requirements screened out those who lacked a strong background in Latin, Greek, or mathematics. The cost of instruction was much lower than in England, and students could live in cheap rooming houses at a fraction of the cost of living in an English college. Young men from families of marginal economic means were thus accommodated in the Scottish medical schools. When Dr. John Leyden took courses in Edinburgh at the turn of the century, for example, he recalled that "it was a time when poor students were encouraged, and frequently allowed to attend without paying a fee."[10] Another contemporary remarked that the Scottish universities were "good for imparting general knowledge to the middle and lower classes . . . but they are not calculated to educate gentlemen."[11] The universities of Scotland prided themselves on their mixture of students from different social classes. Many lived frugally, as an Edinburgh official testified, citing cases of stu-

8. See Ian Inkster, "Marginal Men: Aspects of the Social Role of the Medical Community in Sheffield, 1790–1850," in *Health Care and Popular Medicine in Nineteenth Century England*, ed. John Woodward and David Richards (New York: Holmes & Meier, 1977), 128.

9. Michael Sanderson, ed., *The Universities in the Nineteenth Century* (London: Routledge & Kegan Paul, 1975), 17.

10. Douglas Guthrie, "Dr. John Leyden, 1775–1811," *University of Edinburgh Journal* 23 (1967–68): 164–65.

11. John Hamilton Gray, *Autobiography of a Scottish Country Gentleman* (privately printed, 1868), 69.

dents who could not afford even candles for study and others who lived on as little as £1 per month (less than U.S.$5 at that time).[12]

The royal colleges of London and other privileged groups understandably questioned the soundness of such a lax and equalitarian system of education. When Scottish and other reformers petitioned the colleges for a hearing in 1809 in an effort to ease the sharp restrictions on medical practice in England, the colleges, according to the *Edinburgh Medical Journal*, "behaved in a rude and selfish manner" and made no official response at all.[13] A few years later, a prominent Oxford professor, attacking the medical teaching at Edinburgh as "too elementary," singled out for special attention "the rabble attending the anatomy class." Degrees at Edinburgh, the professor declared, were awarded "to beardless youths or striplings" rather than to those of mature age. The Edinburgh editor responded that the harsh criticism from Oxford was due only to the fact that the Edinburgh degree was "not sufficiently expensive to prevent all but the wealthy from obtaining it."[14]

The cost of teaching in the several private medical schools of Scotland was even cheaper than in the universities. The extramural school at Anderson's University in Glasgow, for example, which offered classes in anatomy and surgery as early as 1800, was especially popular among the artisan classes for its low fees. Chemistry was taught there soon after its opening because of its "indispensable utility" to the whole community. Some courses were offered in the evening for the convenience of working students.[15] By the early 1820s, two other inexpensive private institutions, the College Street School and the Portland Street School, were teaching an assortment of medical courses in Glasgow to several hundred students.[16]

In London, the private and hospital schools, though much cheaper than the English universities, were still more expensive than the private schools of Scotland. A student attending lectures, walking the wards of a hospital with a mentor, and perhaps serving as a dresser or clerk might easily pay £100 to £200 a year for his instruction. For the most part, only those from professional or relatively wealthy families could afford such high expenses. The surgeon Henry Cline wrote the father of an interested pupil in 1802 that "being a dresser for one year is an expense of fifty pounds. . . . My lectures and the privilege of dissecting is fifteen guineas

12. John D. Comrie, *History of Scottish Medicine*, 2 vols. (London: Wellcome Historical Medical Museum, 1932), 1:341–42. Lisa Rosner wrote an excellent recent study of Edinburgh's flexible admissions policies: *Medical Education in the Age of Improvement: Edinburgh Students and Apprentices, 1760–1826* (Edinburgh: University of Edinburgh Press, 1991).

13. *Edinburgh Medical Journal* 6 (1810): 487.

14. *Edinburgh Medical Journal* 13 (1817): 226–28.

15. Anderson's College minutes, October 1, 1807, University of Strathclyde Archive.

16. Alexander Duncan, *Memorials of the Faculty of Physicians and Surgeons of Glasgow* (Glasgow, 1896), 178–86.

for a winter. There are also other lectures on chymistry, the practice of physic, and on midwifery; all of which are subscribed to separately."[17]

In addition, of course, the student had to provide his board and lodging, books, and other expenses while away from home. In the opinion of Sir John Ellis, medical education in London in about 1800 "was relatively more expensive in terms of what the English student or his parents had to pay, than at any time since."[18] These high costs in London were an important factor in the establishment of provincial medical schools in the years after 1815.

Class Differences on the Continent

On the Continent, the class system of medical practice was often endowed with the force of law. By the early nineteenth century, even revolutionary France—bending to its failure to train enough physicians for either the army or the civilian population—created an official class of secondary practitioners, who were clearly the educational and social inferiors of established physicians. Whereas students in the prestigious schools of medicine at Paris, Montpellier, and Strasbourg came principally from professional (especially medical) and middle-class families, the *officiers de santé* were chiefly the sons of farmers, artisans, and shopkeepers.

The cost of instruction for the second-class doctor was about a fourth of those for a physician, which, in turn, had been markedly reduced for French students since 1789. The length of study for an *officier* was three years, compared with four for regular physicians, and could be replaced by sufficient hospital and apprenticeship experience.[19] Less was demanded of them, too, in knowledge of Latin and other preparatory subjects. And most significantly, in their subsequent careers, the second-class practitioner was restricted by law to working in small towns and was supposed to consult physicians, when feasible, in important operations and cases of serious illness.

In the reformed hospitals of Paris, the privileged students were the externs and especially the small number of interns from the academic faculties of medicine. The continuation of this Old Regime practice, according to Laurence Brockliss, guaranteed "the perpetuation of a privileged elite" in the French medical profession, though for some it was an important avenue of social mobility.[20]

17. F. G. Parsons, *The History of St. Thomas's Hospital*, 3 vols. (London: Methuen, 1932–36), 3:9.

18. John Ellis, *LHMC, 1785–1985: The Story of the London Hospital Medical College* (London: London Hospital Medical Club, 1986), 13.

19. Jacques Léonard, *La vie quotidienne du médecin de province au XIXe siècle* (Paris: Hachette, 1977), 16–22.

20. Laurence Brockliss, "L'enseignement médical et la révolution," *Histoire de l'education* 42 (1989): 105. In a letter to me (April 4, 1994), Gabriel Richet, great-grandson of the illustrious nineteenth-century physiologist, argues that Brockliss's statement underestimates the significance of these competitions for many "in the lower social classes."

The social and educational differences among practitioners were also sharply defined in Prussia and the other German states. Among the officially recognized practitioner ranks of Prussia—each with its own educational requirements and restrictions on practice—were graduate physicians who could practice anywhere in the state; graduate physicians with surgical training who were likewise free to treat patients everywhere; practical surgeons who practiced in cities of six thousand or more people; country practical surgeons who were confined to rural areas; military physicians educated at army schools who were allowed a limited practice on leaving the army; specialized practitioners such as dentists, oculists, and midwives, whose work was closely regulated; and apothecaries who were trained to dispense drugs in both small towns and cities.[21]

The state of Württemberg similarly provided for four classes of surgeons, ranging from university-graduated men to those who had served only a simple apprenticeship. A survey of 1819 showed 134 of the first class, 278 of the second, 338 of the third, and 426 of the fourth class in practice in the state.[22] Unlike its neighbors, Württemberg made clear provision for a "lower" surgeon to move up to the rank of "higher" surgeon through additional academic training.[23] In that state, according to a recent study, those choosing a career in practical surgery were by no means drawn wholly from the lower social ranks. Further research in other states, the study's author suggests, may reveal that the educational background and training of many of these students often approached that of university students.[24]

Bavaria, too, offered both an academic and a nonacademic pathway to the practice of surgery. In a royal edict of 1808, a careful distinction was drawn between university surgeons and so-called (*sogenannten*) surgeons or country doctors who were trained in practical schools.[25] The latter, whose education was subsidized fully by the state, would, by their "speech, habits, and education," more closely relate to the "less educated class of people" in the rural areas.[26] In the Hapsburg monarchy, too, a

21. Edict of February 4, 1791, GSPK Merseburg, 511 a, Nr. 1; "Neues Prüfungsreglement für sämtliche medizinal-personnen des preussischen Staates," Merseburg, 76, VIII, A535, Bd. I; Heinrich O. Meisner and Georg Winter, *Ubersicht über die Bestände des geheimen Staatsarchivs zu Berlin-Dahlem,* 2 vols. (Leipzig: S. Hirzel, 1934–35), 2:43. See also Hans G. Wenig, "Medizinische Ausbildung im 19.Jahrhundert" (med. diss., University of Bonn, 1969), 6–7.

22. Edgar Niklas, "Das Dekanatsbuch der Tübinger medizinischen Fakultät, 1808–1858 (Teil 3: 1818–1822)" (med. diss., University of Tübingen, 1985), 25.

23. Brigitte Niklas, "Das Dekanatsbuch der Tübinger medizinischen Fakultät, 1808–1858 (Teil 2: 1816–1818)" (med. diss., University of Tübingen 1985), 42.

24. Sabine Sander, *Handwerkchirurgen: Sozialgeschichte einer verdrängten Berufsgruppe* (Göttingen: Vandenhoeck & Ruprecht, 1989), esp. 133–34, 149–51, 183, 233–35.

25. Christiane Scherg-Zeisner, "Die ärztliche Ausbildung an der Königlich-bayerischen Julius-Maximilians-Universität in Würzburg, 1814–1872" (med. diss., University of Würzburg, 1973), 22.

26. Erhard Grunwald, "Das niedere Medizinalpersonal in Bayern des 19.Jahrhunderts" (med. diss., University of Munich, 1990), 57–58.

like social distinction was drawn between academically educated physicians and surgeons and "the surgeons of lower grade . . . so-called civilian or country practicing surgeons." Even the costs of the lower grades of surgical education in the Hapsburg lands were beyond the reach of many. The director of the surgical academy at Graz petitioned the government in 1789 to shorten the two-year course because "few surgical students [are] in a position to pay for their board, lodging, laundry, clothes, and the necessary books."[27]

Some university professors warned against the sharp legal distinctions being made between medical education inside the university and the practical training received outside. Most German universities, as described earlier, had already introduced surgery into their teaching programs and had started practical training in their own clinics. In the view of the Berlin anatomist Carl Rudolphi, the education of a medical practitioner must always be a learned (*wissenschaftlich*) study, and everyone, whether physician or practical surgeon, "must be given access to the sources of knowledge." Were he to be asked to teach anatomy to a group of second-class students, he observed, "I would not know what to leave out." Although students did not necessarily have to know any ancient languages, it was imperative that they be able to understand modern medical terms and descriptions. "I favor therefore [the proposition] that no half-physician should be educated in special institutions."[28]

Rudolphi's colleague Christoph Hufeland, with the support of Wilhelm von Humboldt, sought to end the separation of military and civilian surgical teaching in Berlin and to create a single practical school that would teach enough of the academic subjects to make it a first-rate institution. In Rudolphi's view, university physicians would still be distinguished from the rest by their *wissenschaftlich* obligation "to investigate nature, deciphering its secrets and piecing together the laws of health and disease."[29] Such reform efforts, however, gained little support from the authorities.

Studies of the social origins of German medical students date chiefly from the later nineteenth century, but some data are available for the earlier years. A study of 144 medical graduates of the University of Tübingen in the last half of the eighteenth century, for example, reveals that almost all of them came from middle-class (*bürgerliche*) families, more than half of them the sons of university graduates. A small number of them

27. Anna D. von Rüden, "Medicina Graecensis: Das medizinisch–chirurgische Studium in Graz (1782–1862)" (med. diss., University of Munich, 1978), 14.

28. Statement by Carl Rudolphi to the medical faculty at the University of Berlin, January 23, 1811, GSPK Merseburg, 76, VIII, A535, Bd. l.

29. Thomas Broman, "University Reform in Medical Thought at the End of the Eighteenth Century," *Osiris* 5 (1989): 45. See also Manfred Stürzbecher, "Zur Geschichte der Ausbildung von Wundärzten in Berlin in der 1. Hälfte des 19.Jahrhunderts," *Forschung und Fortschritte* 33 (1959): esp. 144–45.

were classified as "handicraft workers," which at least suggests the possibility of a broader range of students.[30]

A later study of the years from 1800 to 1814 in Tübingen shows similar results, including a group of students whose fathers' occupations were given as "shoemaker," "innkeeper," "glazier," "baker," "farmer," and the like. Forty-eight tuition scholarships were awarded to approximately half of the class; of those given help, thirty-two students were said to be from the "middle and lower classes [*Mittel- und Unterschichten*]." But most of these, it can be assumed, came from the middle levels of society.[31]

At other universities, less complete data indicate comparable results. Berlin, for example, counted 46 percent of its students with university-educated fathers in 1810, and Halle reported a like proportion.[32] In the case of Halle, we know that no more than 3 percent of the students came from farm families (*Bauernfamilien*).[33] Although the small number of poorer students in German universities was hardly enough to give alarm, it was sufficient to cause the critic Johann Michaelis to deplore their impact on the discipline, deportment, and social atmosphere of university towns.[34]

The Social Origins of American Practitioners

The class lines among grades of medical students in Europe, though less sharply drawn in the more primitive circumstances of North America, were nevertheless evident there as well. Americans who attended medical school before 1800 were clearly from families comparable to those who sent their sons to medical school in Europe. To support a son in Edinburgh or London, or later in the medical schools of Philadelphia or New York, was an expense comparable to, or perhaps greater than, that of European families with similar obligations. In about 1800, of forty-four physicians in America's largest city, Philadelphia, fully three-fourths were the sons of professional men, merchants, or large landowners. Many had benefited from private tutors, academies, or study abroad. "On the whole," writes a knowledgeable student, "a physician's claim to social recognition depended as much on his birth as it did on his skill and intelligence."[35]

30. Martina Beese, "Die medizinischen Promotionen in Tübingen, 1750–1799" (med. diss., University of Tübingen, 1977), 57–58.

31. Uta Peschel-Kudernatsch, "Die medizinischen Promotionen in Tübingen, 1800–1814" (med. diss., University of Tübingen, 1985), 58.

32. Hellmuth Rössler and Günther Franz, eds., *Universität und Gelehrtenstand, 1400–1800* (Limburg/Lahn: C. A. Starke, 1970), 264–65, table III.

33. Franz Eulenburg, *Die Frequenz der deutschen Universitäten von ihrer Gründung bis zur Gegenwart* (Leipzig: B. G. Teubner, 1904), 67–68.

34. Johann D. Michaelis, *Räsonnement über die protestantischen Universitäten in Deutschland*, 4 vols. (Frankfurt: Andreä, 1768–76), 3:157–68, 237.

35. Leo J. O'Hara, "An Emerging Profession: Philadelphia Medicine 1860–1900" (Ph.D. diss., University of Pennsylvania, 1976), 28–29.

The unsettled nature of New World conditions, along with the push westward after the American Revolution, created the same kind of demand as in Europe for less refined practitioners whose "speech, habits, and education" would fit them to serve the thinly populated regions beyond the eastern cities. A new kind of training institution, the "country medical school," was organized early in the century by enterprising practitioners to meet the need for doctors in such places as Hanover, New Hampshire; Lexington, Kentucky; Fairfield, New York; Castleton, Vermont; and Cincinnati, Ohio.[36] Like their counterparts in Europe, these early schools were not connected to either universities or hospitals and were intended to supplement the training gained by apprenticeship. Although data are scarce, the students who attended them—as surely as those at the Scottish private schools and the "lower" surgical schools in Germany—came from a broader spectrum of the population than was true of the collegiate schools of the eastern cities.

The Chorus of Advice

Such a diversity of pathways to medical study brought a plethora of guidance and warnings from friends, family, and commercial guidebooks. Students were the targets of well-meaning counsel concerning costs, living conditions, personal conduct, and preparatory study. Eighteenth-century fathers wrote long, serious, and detailed letters of instruction to their sons ready to commence a medical career: "Keep yourself from bad habits and bad company[,] for your manners will be counted," wrote Sir John Clerk earlier in the century to his fifteen-year-old son, who was leaving home for an apprenticeship, "and never spend your time in trifling . . . or acts of intemperance." In his leisure time, the boy was told to "read the best written books in your own language." He should "neglect no opportunity for studying anatomy" but "beware of the barbarity of raising dead bodies." He would never understand medicine "without a perfect knowledge of the Latine [*sic*]," and without Greek, he "will never have the honour of being reputed as a Scholar."[37]

Another Scottish father, this time a lord, called on a physician friend in 1796 to advise him about his son who was likewise interested in medicine. The physician told him that "a short apprenticeship with some respectable country surgeon" would be best, followed by "a winter or spring [in London] to dissect, and study anatomy," and then a summer of "lectures and experiments in chemistry," all the while walking the wards of a hospital and gaining further experience in midwifery. With

36. Frederick C. Waite, *The Story of a Country Medical College* (Montpelier: Vermont Historical Society, 1945), 15–17.

37. Sir John Clerk to his son John, April 16, 1745, clerk of Penecuik papers, Scottish Record Office, G D 18.

these preparations, the lord was told, the young man might "obtain a situation in the army, or in the navy, or in some residence."[38]

At least two dozen guidebooks for medical study were published in France, Germany, and Great Britain between 1794 and 1817. After the chaos of the revolutionary years in France, when advice was difficult to come by, the handbook by T. V. Vaïdy was especially valued. Vaïdy described carefully in 1816 the legal requirements for medical practice and the best way to prepare for either the *écoles secondaires* of medicine or the major schools in Paris, Montpellier, and Strasbourg. This book, like others of the early nineteenth century, stressed the importance of good character and a strong liberal education as prerequisites to medical study. Among the necessary studies for a premedical student were Latin, logic, physics, and chemistry, whereas such subjects as mathematics, Greek, German, English, zoology, and botany were described as "useful." Among strictly medical subjects, Vaïdy listed physiology, dissection, anatomy, and the medical and surgical clinics as "indispensable," but clinics for venereal diseases, sick children, women's diseases, and chronic illnesses, as well as those for pharmacy and materia medica, were only "necessary."[39]

In Germany, Wilhelm Plouquet, a medical professor at Tübingen, addressing only those seeking a degree at a university, stressed the importance of social graces to a gentleman entering the highest ranks of the profession. Personal appearance, behavior, gait, speech, and clothing all were critical to the successful physician, and he recommended dancing instruction, music, painting and sketching, and horsemanship. In his preparatory studies, the future student of medicine must master Greek, Latin, French, mathematics, natural science, and philosophy.[40]

Plouquet's countryman Friedrich Wetzel warned beginning students in 1805 against thinking of medicine as a finished study at a time when it was undergoing "perpetual transformation" at the hands of science. "Medicine is truly a natural science," he wrote, and students can have no better preparation than "the thorough study of anatomy, tied to physiology."[41] In Berlin, another voice, that of Ludewig Formey, urged more attention by students to practical education, charging that "despite all the riches of science and all the great discoveries of the last decades, many of our present educational institutions produce fewer useful students than before."[42] Full of such conflicting advice and often written in a dense,

---

38. Letter from Dr. A. Marshall, February 16, 1796, Leven and Melville papers, Scottish Record Office, G D 26.

39. T. V. Vaïdy, *Plan de l'étude, à l'usage des aspirans* (Paris, 1816), 35–36.

40. D. Wilhelm G. Plouquet, *Der Arzt, oder über die Ausbildung, die Studien, Pflichten, Sitten, und die Klugheit des Arztes* (Tübingen: J. G. Cotta, 1797), 23–30.

41. Friedrich G. Wetzel, *Briefe über das Studium der Medizin für Jünglinge, die sich ihr widmen wollen* (Leipzig: C. G. Weigel, 1805), 7, 17, 28.

42. D Ludewig Formey, *Uber den gegenwärtigen Zustand der Medicin in Hinsicht auf die Bildung künftiger Arzte* (Berlin: Karl Friedrich Amelang, 1809), 31.

academic style, such treatises could hardly have brought much enlightenment to the young student seeking practical advice on his future.

The British manuals, on the other hand, were both more numerous
and more practical. Complete with detailed, homely suggestions, they
were clearly directed to a younger group of readers than those in France
or Germany. Most of the books were written for the expanding market in
surgical and apothecary study. As one of them put it, "the physician seldom obtains bread by his profession until he has no teeth left to eat it,"
whereas surgeons and apothecaries, on the other hand, "have it easier."[43]
Although most British writers recommended the traditional apprenticeship as essential, one, a London surgeon, thought it "absurd" to spend so
many years in repetitious labor.[44] Almost all urged the careful study of
Latin, "the universal language of science," and a strong preparation in
anatomy, "the very alphabet of physiology."[45] Every student, advised
William Chamberlaine, a surgeon, in 1812, should undertake his own
dissection, for even "the clumsiest dissection by his own hands" is superior to "the neatest dissection executed by another." No person, he
warned in a typically homely illustration, can "repair a Watch without
being first acquainted with the structure of it."[46] A provincial writer in
York agreed with his London colleagues in urging students to get both a
classical and a scientific education before commencing medical study. In
addition to botany, chemistry, anatomy, materia medica, and clinical
medicine, a practitioner should know Latin and Greek thoroughly, possess some knowledge of history and the belles lettres, and have "a moder-
ate knowledge of mathematics" in order to win "the character of a gentleman."[47]

A Portrait of a Student of Medicine

What is most striking about the young men who studied medicine two
centuries ago is their extreme youth. While still in their teens, many of
them labored ten to twelve hours per day as apprentices, entered universities, served as assistant surgeons in the army, traveled to distant places, or
walked the wards of a hospital. Most practitioners had completed their
medical education by age twenty-one or twenty-two. Although fourteen
was the normal age to begin an apprenticeship in Britain, some started as
early as twelve or thirteen. University students in Scotland were usually

43. James Parkinson, *The Hospital Pupil; or an Essay intended to facilitate the Study of
Medicine and Surgery in four Letters* (London: H. D. Symonds, 1800), 26.

44. Ibid., 29–30.

45. Ibid., 12, 42–43.

46. William Chamberlaine, *Tirocinium Medicum; or a Dissertation on the Duties of Youth
apprenticed to the Medical Profession* (London: privately printed, 1812), 65.

47. Thomas Withers, *A Treatise on the Errors and Defects of Medical Education: in which
are contained Observations on the Means of correcting them* (London: C. Dilly, 1794),
38–58.

fifteen or sixteen when they began their studies, although John Hamilton Gray was only thirteen when he enrolled at Glasgow.[48] By starting their studies so young, it was possible for them to become full-fledged practitioners, depending on the length of their apprenticeship, by the age of eighteen or nineteen, which was an embarrassment to many in the profession. But not until 1802 did Glasgow authorities move to require the age of twenty-one as a condition for a medical degree.[49]

A similar situation existed in the United States, where it was not uncommon for medical graduates to be younger than twenty-one years of age. In his study of the patterns of medical education in the nineteenth century, Robert Hudson found a surprising number of physicians who had graduated at eighteen or nineteen (one was seventeen) from some of America's leading medical schools.[50] At least nine underaged students graduated from the medical school at Woodstock, Vermont, where one of the professors, Jerome Smith, had received his own medical degree from Brown University at age eighteen.[51]

On the continent of Europe, even in the university schools, graduation before the age of twenty-one was also not uncommon. At the University of Tübingen, nearly half the future physicians in the late eighteenth century had entered medical school between the ages of fifteen and nineteen, and one in eight earned a medical degree by the age of twenty-one. Johann Steger was only eighteen when he graduated there in 1816.[52] In Zurich, nearly half the students entering the practical school in that city were seventeen or younger (two were fourteen).[53] In France, some fifteen- and sixteen-year-old students were studying medicine in revolutionary Paris, even though the government had set a minimum age of seventeen.[54]

At the opposite end of the scale, a large number of older students could be found in the medical schools and hospitals of Europe and America. A French Canadian student who had studied in Paris entered the Harvard Medical School in 1789 at the age of forty-one.[55] Almost 10

48. W. M. Mathew, "The Origins and Occupations of Glasgow Students, 1740–1839," *Past and Present* 33 (1966): 74–94.

49. Records of University of Glasgow Senate, May 3, 1824, University of Glasgow Archive. This account recalls past admission policy.

50. Robert P. Hudson, "Patterns of Medical Education in Nineteenth Century America" (master's thesis, Johns Hopkins University, 1966), 57–59.

51. Waite, *Story of a Country Medical College*, 49, 124.

52. Beese, "Die medizinische Promotionen," 58–59; Ernst Bezel, ed., *Johann Jakob Steger, 1798–1857: Beispiel eines Medizinstudenten im frühen 19.Jahrhundert nach den Briefen an seine Eltern* (Zurich: Juris Druck & Verlag, 1981), 1.

53. Moritz Leisibach, *Das medizinisch–chirurgische Institut in Zürich* (Zurich: Hans Rohr, 1982), 112, table 6.

54. Mireille Wiriot, "L'enseignement clinique dans les hôpitaux de Paris entre 1794 et 1848" (med. diss., University of Paris, 1970), 45.

55. Reginald Fitz, "The Surprising Career of Peter la Terrière, Bachelor in Medicine," *Annals of Medical History* 3 (1941): 402.

percent of all the graduates of the Woodstock school in the early nineteenth century were over thirty years of age, and some were more than forty.[56] At Dartmouth, William Tully wrote in his journal in 1808 that "the majority of us, undoubtedly, [are] on the wrong side of thirty."[57] In Germany, the records at Tübingen for 1818 show the case of a former military surgeon who earned his M.D. degree at age forty-eight.[58] In both America and Europe, many of these older students were already practitioners who had returned to school in order to earn a degree to upgrade their status and ability to attract patients.

A Reputation for Rowdiness

The youth of many of the students, together with the harsh circumstances of their lives, often produced in them noisy, boisterous behavior that was decried by authorities and the general public alike. "It was axiomatic," writes John Duffy, "that [American] medical students, even in the better schools, were a coarse, crude, uncouth lot."[59] The English medical student of the period was said to be loathed for his "foulmouthedness, indecency, callousness and cynicism." The sensitive Henry Acland, encountering the hospital students of London for the first time, described them as "low men, of low habits . . . the most bearish I have ever beheld."[60] Richard Bright complained that he was shocked by their drunkenness, their ribaldry in the dissecting room, and their casual attire.[61]

At Montpellier, according to one account, students were "turbulent, licentious, aficianados of individual and group violence," and the preparatory medical school at Nantes, in the words of a contemporary, was the site of "scandalous profanations and disrespect for human remains."[62] In Berlin, following an outburst of fighting in the anatomical theater in 1812, the rector of the university, the philosopher J. G. Fichte, decried the "barbarism" of student life, which "every profound observer of our

56. Waite, *Story of a Country Medical College*, 125.

57. Oliver S. Hayward and Elizabeth H. Thomson, eds., *The Journal of William Tully, Medical Student at Dartmouth, 1808–1809* (New York: Science History Publications, 1977), 51.

58. E. Niklas, "Dekanatsbuch," entry for December 29, 1818, p. 84.

59. John Duffy, *From Humors to Medical Science: A History of American Medicine*, 2nd ed. (Urbana: University of Illinois Press, 1993), 144.

60. Charles Newman, *The Evolution of Medical Education in the Nineteenth Century* (Oxford: Oxford University Press, 1957), 41–42.

61. Pamela Bright, *Dr Richard Bright (1789–1858)* (London: Bodley Head, 1983), 75.

62. Colin Jones, "Montpellier Medical Students and the Medicalization of 18th-Century France," in *Problems and Methods in the History of Medicine*, ed. Roy Porter and Andrew Wear (London: Croom Helm, 1987), 63; Daniel Geoffrey, "La vie d'un étudiant en médecine à Nantes en 1820," *Archives médicales de l'ouest* 14 (1982): 280.

students recognizes."[63] It was everywhere an adolescent or young man's world. Coarse expressions and sexual innuendo were as common in the lecture hall as they were in the dissecting room.

No contemporary account of life in the medical schools of the time fails to mention the importance of stern discipline in curbing the excesses of student behavior. More than other students, would-be physicians were the target of state and university regulations. Reports of hissing, booing, fighting, raucous arguments, shouted obscenities, and even shooting pistols in the classroom were not infrequent at the University of Edinburgh. A medical student there was expelled in 1801 for "producing a pistol" and threatening to shoot it in the anatomy room, whereupon the university senate warned all medical students that it was "determined to put a stop to [these] disgraceful practices."[64]

On the Continent, medical students were more likely to be involved in political, often radical, movements that brought down the wrath of governments on them. Prussian authorities passed law after law to force students to observe higher standards of behavior, but the thick files of discipline cases, many of them involving medical students, suggest that, in the words of one report, "the administration of academic discipline and police power has not reached the hoped-for success."[65] A dozen or more medical students at Berlin were punished between 1810 and 1821 for offenses ranging from rowdy public behavior to "immorality."[66] A serious academic offense, according to a royal proclamation of 1819, could be defined as "damage to property; disturbance of the peace in public places; insulting a public official; insults to teachers; provocation; gang behavior . . . and participation in secret or unauthorized organizations."[67]

French students at the turn of the century were likewise charged with everything from "counterrevolutionary attitudes" to provoking duels to creating public disturbances. Even police with fixed bayonets were unable for several days to quell a bloody student riot over admission to a local theater in Montpellier in 1819. The dean of the medical school was relieved of his duties as a result, and several professors were suspended for failing to control the students.[68]

---

63. Fichte to the Cultural Ministry, February 14, 1812, in Rudolf Köpke, *Die Gründung der Königlichen Friedrich-Wilhelms-Universität zu Berlin* (Berlin: Gustav Schade, 1860), 231.

64. Minutes of Senatus, December 7, 1801, University of Edinburgh Archive.

65. *Reglement für die künftige Verwaltung der akademischen Disziplin und Polizei-Gewalt* (Berlin, 1819), 3–6, copy in GSPK, Meiseburg, 51, 1a, Nr. 1.

66. "Die Disziplin u. die Exzesse auf der Universität Berlin, 1810–1821," GSPK, Merseburg, 76, Va, Sekt. 2, Tit. 12, Nr. 1. See also "Instruktion für die ausserordentlichen Regierungsbevollmächtigten bei den Universitäten," GSPK, Metseburg, 51, 1a, Nr. 1; and "Massregeln wegen der überhand nehmenden Unsittlichkeiten unter den Studenten, 1820–21," Akten der Universitäts-Kurator in Berlin, Humboldt University Archive, Berlin, 522, Litt. U 9.

67. *Reglement*, 6.

68. File F[17] 4451, "Student Disorders," Archives nationales, Paris.

Daily Life

Sensational and numerous as such reports were, the daily life of the average student was far more preoccupied with the dreary, exhausting routine
of life—endless hours of lecture, continual study, frequent examinations,
and scurrying from classroom to hospital to dissecting room. It was a
harsh and strenuous life. A typical student at Strasbourg before the Revolution enrolled for nine separate courses each day from six o'clock in the
morning to seven o'clock at night.[69] "During my time in London," recalled William Savory, "I was never at leisure."[70] Richard Bright's father
was told that his son "runs to the lectures, in the afternoon he runs to the
dissecting room . . . in the evening he runs back to his dinner, often eating alone, reading as he cuts his meat and drinks his beer."[71] The American Daniel Drake wrote his parents from Philadelphia in 1805 that "I try
not to lose a single moment, seeing I have to pay so dear . . . I only sleep
six hours in the twenty-four."[72]

Many rose daily before sunrise and worked on into the night. The
Swiss Elias Haffter, according to his diary, frequently began his day at 4
a.m. by reading for several hours before going to his first lecture, and
only then eating his first meal of the day.[73] Lectures began at a very early
hour, especially in the continental universities. A course in medical history at Bonn, for example, was offered at 6 a.m.![74]

Many attempted to describe what a typical day was like. "You are so
anxious to know what I do every hour," wrote a St. Thomas student to
his parents in the mid-1790s:

> I must begin before I am out of my slippers . . . almost before I am
> awake, I go to the Midwifery Lecture; next I breakfast and put on
> my boots, then to a lecture on Chemistry or Physic, till eleven, at this
> hour the business of the hospital commences and I go round with
> the dressers.

In the early afternoon, there were more lectures and then an hour or two
of dissection until "our appetites begin to crave for dinner, after which . . .
I look over some books, write down cases and observations, or . . .

---

69. Christian Wolff, "Faculté, écoles de médecine et hôpitaux militaires à Strasbourg
sous la révolution et l'empire (1789–1815)" (med. diss., University of Strasbourg, 1986),
24.

70. Quoted in introduction to John M. T. Ford, ed., *A Medical Student at St. Thomas's
Hospital, 1801–1802: The Weekes Family Letters, supplement to Medical History* (London:
Wellcome Institute for the History of Medicine, 1987), 27.

71. Bright, *Dr Richard Bright*, 52.

72. Cited in Emmet F. Horine, *Daniel Drake (1785–1852): Pioneer Physician of the
Midwest* (Philadelphia: University of Pennsylvania Press, 1961), 81.

73. Carl Haffter, ed., *Tagebuch des Zürcher Medizinstudenten Elias Haffter aus dem
Jahre 1823* (Zurich: Hans Rohr, 1976).

74. Karl Schmiz, *Die medizinische Fakultät der Universität Bonn, 1818–1918* (Bonn: R.
Marcus and E. Weber, 1920), 64.

[write] to a friend." On Saturday evening, he added in a postscript, "there is an assembly in the theatre at Guy's, to read and debate on a Medical paper."[75]

Students frequently organized medical societies to supplement the work of classroom and clinic. At Glasgow, a group of students formed the Medico–Chirurgical Society in 1801 that created its own library of books.[76] The medical libraries of this period, we should note, were normally for the professors and not the students. The purpose of the Glasgow students, members of the society wrote later, was "to keep pace with the present advancing state of the science."[77] Within a few years they began to present papers and invite professors to address them.

By 1800, a number of the London hospitals were also the site of student organizations. The pupils of the United Hospitals (Guy's and St. Thomas's) had organized their Physical Society as early as 1771.[78] Students were also encouraged to join the staff medical societies that existed in a number of hospitals. Sometimes pupils even made up a majority of those attending the numerous meetings. In the years between 1795 and 1806, more than three hundred papers were presented at Guy's and St. Bartholomew's alone.[79] At the latter hospital, for example, the surgeon John Abernethy led a discussion before a large gathering of pupils and surgeons in 1800 on the new technique of vaccination.[80] Similar societies, though less numerous, were found on the Continent and in the United States. Students in New York, it is known, formed a medical and surgical society in 1807, and by the 1820s, those at Harvard were meeting every Friday evening "for Medical Discussion and improvement."[81]

Outside the residential enclaves of Oxford and Cambridge, virtually every student of medicine was forced to make his own arrangements for meals and lodging. Although many had left homes of relative comfort, few were given allowances large enough to free them from financial worry. Students were expected to live frugally and to expect little help

---

75. Parsons, *History of St. Thomas's Hospital*, 2:250–51.

76. Derek Dow and Kenneth C. Calman, eds., *The Royal Medico–Chirurgical Society of Glasgow: A History, 1814–1989* (Glasgow: Royal Medico–Chirurgical Society, 1989), 2.

77. Glasgow University Medico–Chirurgical Society Minutes, January 10, 1827, Special Collections, University of Glasgow Library. In 1820 the students were compelled to merge their collection with that of the university library.

78. Parsons, *History of St. Thomas's Hospital*, 2:228.

79. Susan C. Lawrence, "'Desirous of Improvements in Medicine': Pupils and Practitioners in the Medical Societies at Guy's and St. Bartholomew's Hospitals, 1795–1815," *Bulletin of the History of Medicine* 59 (1985): 97, table 1.

80. Abernethian Society minutes, October 14, 1800, St. Bartholomew's Hospital Archive. The society was then called the Medical and Philosophical Society of St. Bartholomew's Hospital.

81. Byron Stookey, *A History of Colonial Medical Education in the Province of New York, with Its Subsequent Development (1767–1830)* (Springfield, IL: Thomas, 1962), 186; Anna C. Holt, ed., "A Medical Student in Boston, 1825–26," *Harvard Library Bulletin* 6 (1952): 364.

from home. The management of one's own financial affairs was a new and trying experience for many. A surprising number made a full and regular accounting to their parents for every penny spent. While a student at Bonn, Jakob Henle reported regularly to his parents on his expenses and pleaded with them for more: "Money! Money! Money! I have no more and owe 10 dollars [*Taler*] to my friend. My tuition costs [*Kollegiengelder*] alone were 46 dollars, four for books and 20 dollars for household expense."[82]

Some lived a marginal existence, scrimping on food, staying in the cheapest rooming houses, and spending very little if anything on entertainment. While a student in London, the reformer Thomas Wakley spent about two shillings a day for his meals, which was very close to the minimum.[83] A country apprentice in the same city, who had saved barely enough to come to the capital, reported that he had sold his surgical instruments for food and was freezing in the raw weather. "It's the vilest thing in the world," he said, "to have but one coat."[84] Enough poor students, many from the medical school, were studying in Leipzig about 1800 that a local convent provided 220 meals a day to students at little or no cost.[85] In revolutionary Paris, to which scores of impecunious students from the provinces flocked, the candidates for *officier de santé* were especially visible in the memory of one Paris physician, who recalled them as extremely poor and some being forced to work as barbers' or wigmakers' helpers to make ends meet.[86]

For any young student, away from home and family for the first time and often limited by funds, the weight of independence was often heavy. Frequent reports of illness, homesickness, and self-doubt are found in the letters and diaries of the period. The fifteen-year-old Johann Steger wrote his parents from Zurich:

> In rereading my letter, I notice that I did not report on my home-sickness. —I am no longer letting it get the upper hand for I get up at 5:30 in the morning and don't go to bed until 11 or 11:30, so I sleep the entire night and have no time to think about it.[87]

In Vienna, about the same time, a student of practical surgery wrote in his diary that his long hours and meager meals had made him "haggard,

82. Hermann Hoepke, "Studentisches Leben aus Jakob Henles Bonner Zeit," *Heidelberger Jahrbücher* 13 (1969): 24.

83. Newman, *Evolution of Medical Education*, 47.

84. Joan Lane, "The Role of Apprenticeship in Eighteenth-Century Medical Education in England," in *William Hunter and the Eighteenth-Century Medical World*, ed. W. F. Bynum and Roy Porter (Cambridge: Cambridge University Press, 1985), 84.

85. A. G. F. Rebmann, *Der Leipziger Student vor hundert Jahren* (Leipzig: J. C. Hinrichs, 1897), 34.

86. Poumiès de la Siboutie, *Souvenirs d'un médecine de Paris* (Paris: Plon-Nourrit, 1910), 92.

87. Steger to parents, April 25, 1813, in Bezel, *Johann Jakob Steger*, 46.

pale, wasted, and gloomy."[88] The young Henle admonished his parents, "Just think how I sit here all day with nothing to do but [work]. What a nice change it would be to get a letter from you occasionally!"[89]

Mortality was surprisingly high. In the eight years after 1796, sixteen Harvard medical students died, most of them from tuberculosis.[90] Among French students of medicine a few years later, one student in every fifty succumbed before graduating.[91] Undoubtedly, the students' unprotected contact with infectious patients, many of them suffering from tuberculosis, played a part in the high mortality rate in every nation.

Except for revolutionary France, most European nations still used a religious test to screen prospective students. The English universities, as we have seen, barred Catholics, Jews, and nonconforming Protestants from the student body. In the German states, many of the universities were denominated as "Protestant" or "Catholic," depending on the religion of a particular state. Jewish students were widely discriminated against, and reports of anti-Semitic outbursts were not uncommon. Until the late eighteenth century, Jewish graduates in surgery in central Europe were required to take an oath that they would not treat Christians. Only in Italy and Holland was admission relatively open to them. Not until 1721 was any Jewish student awarded a medical degree in a German university. In Prussia until 1784, the law forbade the granting of degrees to Jews, except by royal permission.

As state policies grew more tolerant in the years of the Enlightenment, a small number of Jews were admitted to German schools. Their promotions, however, were conducted in private without the usual public ceremony.[92] By the end of the eighteenth century, several hundred Jews were enrolled in medicine in German universities, and more than sixty had earned degrees at Halle alone.[93] The atmosphere, however, remained suspicious and often difficult for them. "The tolerance of Jews is a real nuisance for the Göttingen students," wrote Wilhelm Mackensen in 1791, "it is totally irresponsible that they are allowed so much latitude."[94]

88. Gottfried Roth, ed., *Vom Baderlehrling zum Wundarzt: Carl Rabl, ein Mediziner im Biedermeir* (Vienna: Oberösterreichischer Landesverlag, n.d.), 41.

89. Hoepke, "Studentisches Leben," 24.

90. Henry K. Beecher and Mark D. Altschule, *Medicine at Harvard: The First Three Hundred Years* (Hanover, NH: University Press of New England, 1977), 44.

91. Léonard, *Vie quotidienne*, 35. In the case of law students in the same period, only one in eighty perished.

92. Moses A Spira, "Meilensteine zur Geschichte der jüdischen Arzte in Deutschland," in *Melemata: Festschrift für Werner Leibbrand zum siebzigsten Geburtstag*, ed. Joseph Schumacher (Mannheim: Grossdruckerei, 1967), 153–54.

93. Wolfram Kaiser and Arina Völker, "Die Geschichte der halleschen Ars medica Judaica. II: Die Anfänge des jüdischen Medizinstudiums," *Zeitschrift für die gesamte innere Medizin* 44 (1989): 30.

94. Wilhelm F. A. Mackensen, *Letztes Wort über Göttingen und seine Lehrer* (Leipzig, 1791), 12. Republished by Vandenhoeck & Ruprecht, Göttingen, 1987.

Almost as striking as their youth and varied living experiences was the high degree of mobility among students in pursuing a medical education. In this largely preindustrial period, when travel was difficult and expensive, a large proportion of those preparing to practice medicine studied in two, three, or more locations before they were finished. Frederick Waite wrote about the "migratory students" of early nineteenth-century America, who took advantage of the varying calendars of early medical colleges to attend two different schools in the same year and thereby to meet quickly the requirement of two terms of study to qualify for a degree.[95] Since the schools were ungraded and each term was a repetition of the last, such movement gave American students a practical means of introducing some variety into their studies.

English students, as described earlier, commonly joined a period of local hospital or apprenticeship study to a sojourn in London, where various lecture courses and hospital experiences were available. French students were similarly peripatetic. Among those who applied at Paris in the years from 1803 to 1808 was a François Noël, who had already studied medicine for three years at the secondary school in Angers, been pressed into army medical duty, and then decided to come to Paris; a François Barré, who after a period as extern in Rouen, served as an assistant surgeon in the army and was now working in Paris; and a "Monsieur Barroillset," a former navy surgeon who was now employed at the military hospital at Val-de-Grâce.[96] In the German university of Württemberg, many medical students had likewise studied in two or three other places previously; some had trained as apothecaries or military surgeons; and a surprising number had already worked as practical surgeons before coming to the university.[97]

Classroom and Hospital

Students' reactions to medical teaching varied from warm appreciation to sharp criticism. Motivated chiefly by career concerns, they valued most those teachers who prepared them best for the practical trials that lay ahead. Teachers of anatomy and surgery were particularly favored for their directness and practicality. The famous teachers of London, like those in Edinburgh and on the Continent, all had sizable followings of students. "Heard a surgical lecture by that droll man Abernethy," wrote John Green Crosse in his diary, about the whimsical and caustic surgeon at St. Bartholomew's Hospital.[98] "He kept up our attention so that it never flagged," said Benjamin Brodie of the same teacher, and "what he

95. Waite, *Story of a Country Medical College*, 27.
96. Archives nationales, AJ6375, AJ886.
97. E. Niklas, "Dekanatsbuch."
98. V. Mary Crosse, *A Surgeon in the Early Nineteenth Century: The Life and Times of John Green Crosse, 1790–1850* (Edinburgh: E. & S. Livingstone, 1968), 35.

told us could not be forgotten."[99] In reference to the demonstrative teaching of John Hunter, Henry Cline noted that "he was so far superior to anything I had conceived . . . that there seemed no comparison."[100] At Guy's Hospital, the deft skills and flamboyant style of Astley Cooper brought him overflowing classes and the praise that "he rarely endeavoured to tell us more than he knew from his own personal work and knowledge."[101]

Across the Channel, in France and Germany, similar instances of the attraction of powerful teachers for fledgling practitioners were evident in a number of places. "Great audiences of all classes and nations," it was said of the pioneering chemist and revolutionary Antoine Fourcroy, "spent hours, tightly packed, almost fearing to breathe, their eyes fixed on his. He could see those who were not convinced, or did not understand, and he would go over the subject [until] the whole audience was equally satisfied."[102]

But such adulation, it must be said, was the exception in medical teaching at the turn of the century. Students were often critical of their teachers and of the way in which medical studies were carried out. There was as yet no fixed order of studies, and students in every country encountered uncertainty and conflicting advice on how to arrange their instruction. John Greene Crosse, visiting Paris in 1815, found students bewildered and "at a loss for persons to direct them." Bodies were too cheap and freely available, he wrote, "and consequently most of them are rather cut up than dissected."[103] Most authorities agreed that anatomical study was crucial to understanding other subjects and should therefore come early—but when and in what order should one learn pathological anatomy, the principles of medicine, pharmacy, chemistry, or clinical practice? Contrary to the impression left by some writers, the lack of agreement on the curriculum and the ordering of medical studies in the early nineteenth century was widespread and not simply an American phenomenon.

Vexations of Academic Life

Students everywhere complained about the lack of order and repetition in their courses. The medical classes at Glasgow, for example, "bore something of a resemblance to a merry-go-round." Students took classes in

99. "The Works of Sir Benjamin Brodie," *Dublin Quarterly Journal of Medical Science* 40 (1865): 134.

100. Robert L. Kilpatrick, "Nature's Schools: The Hunterian Revolution in London Hospital Medicine, 1780–1825" (Ph.D. diss., Cambridge University, 1988), 208.

101. H. C. Cameron, *Mr. Guy's Hospital, 1726–1948* (London: Longmans, Green, 1954), 150.

102. W. A. Smeaton, *Fourcroy: Chemist and Revolutionary, 1755–1809* (Cambridge: privately printed, 1962), 12.

103. John Green Crosse, *Sketches of the Medical Schools in Paris* (London: J. Callow, 1815), 49.

different order; not all took the same courses; and some enrolled only "to gain some smattering of medical knowledge."[104] As late as 1826, the medical dean at Edinburgh testified that "no order is prescribed" for the study of medicine.[105] Medical study in London was a helter-skelter mixture of private and hospital courses sandwiched between periods of clinical study. By 1800, thirty-five different courses in seven subjects were being offered across the city by individual lecturers.[106]

The medical faculties of Germany, too, were reluctant to impose any firm order on their curricula because of the vaunted *Lernfreiheit* which put the entire responsibility for choice upon the student. Typically, a faculty did list a series of recommended courses or divided the university's offerings into those that were considered either "necessary" or "useful." Among the "necessary" courses at the school in Landshut (later moved to Munich) in 1806 were human anatomy, physiology, pathological anatomy, pharmacy, materia medica, general and special pathology, and the history of medical literature, whereas semiotics, gynecology, ophthalmology, hygiene, and bone diseases were listed as merely "useful."[107] Although some medical teachers protested that such anarchy was confusing to young students and some encouraged students to take their studies in a particular order, no specific requirements were set in any university.

Only in revolutionary France, where a strong centralized government prescribed in great detail the courses to be taken each year, was there less confusion about requirements, but even there most students found it necessary to take private classes in order to fill the gaps in their education. The young René Simon-Bailly, a student at both Strasbourg and Paris, for example, wrote that "a student who is content to take only the [prescribed] courses does not acquire a sound knowledge." "Most of the professors," he reported, urged their students to "come, come to my house, to my private course" if they really wanted to learn.[108]

How confusing and disappointing this was to most students can only be imagined. Not many followed the example of Benjamin Brodie in welcoming the opportunity to create his own pattern of instruction. When Simon-Bailly arrived in Strasbourg in 1795, he explained that he had "no plan of instruction . . . no guide to direct my studies, no elementary texts,

104. Derek Dow and Michael Moss, "The Medical Curriculum at Glasgow in the Early Nineteenth Century," *History of Universities* 7 (1988): 228, 240.

105. Royal Commission, *Evidence, Oral and Documentary, taken and received by the Commissioners appointed by His Majesty George IV, July 23, 1826; and re-appointed by His Majesty William IV, October 12, 1830; for visiting the Universities of Scotland*, 4 vols. (London: His Majesty's Stationery Office, 1837), 1:193.

106. Susan C. Lawrence, "Private Enterprise and Public Interests: Medical Education and the Apothecaries' Act, 1780–1825," in *British Medicine in an Age of Reform*, ed. Roger French and Andrew Wear (London: Routledge, 1991), 48.

107. Protocolle congregatae facultatis Medicinae, December 6, 1806, NI 3 1/2–4, University of Munich Archive.

108. René Simon-Bailly, *Souvenirs d'un élève des écoles de santé de Strasbourg et de Paris* (Strasbourg: Strasbourg médical, 1924), 19.

not knowing my own language very well . . . and not knowing enough Latin to understand the simplest author."[109]

The hawking of private offerings by medical school professors particularly confused students. Complaints were especially harsh in such university centers as Edinburgh, Vienna, Montpellier, and Paris. Students in Montpellier, for example, harshly attacked those professors who expended more energy on private instruction than on their public lectures. But the professors insisted that their low salaries made this necessary and that such courses "were the prime means of instruction in all the top medical schools of Enlightened Europe." It was in such small groups, they argued, rather than in huge lecture halls, "that the best teaching was done."[110]

Students in the French capital, stirred by the equalitarian spirit of 1789, complained about the large number of paying auditors, especially foreigners, in the large clinical courses of the noted surgeon Pierre Desault. In a petition to the National Assembly, they charged that Desault was demanding unreasonable fees from students when he was already being "paid by the government." A furious Desault responded that he had sacrificed for twenty-five years to give students instruction in surgery yet was now publicly denounced as "immoral, impolitic, odious, and meretricious." He denied that he was paid for teaching by the government. "For a modest sum" given to him for patient care, he complained, "I am separated from my family [and] obliged to live in the [hospital]." Those who had brought charges against him, he said, were not real students of surgery, anyway, but "a class apart, all or nearly all of them wigmakers"—a demeaning reference to the second-class surgical students described earlier.[111]

By 1800, not just in France but almost universally, students were turning a critical eye on their courses and their teachers. Voices were raised in dozens of schools against the remoteness of professors, the continued use of Latin, the systems of examination, the stress on academic knowledge, the chronic shortage of human bodies, the lack of practical training, and the crowding of clinics. The tone of protest was often irreverent and sometimes bitter. Many complained of the cold and formal style of some of the lectures, unaltered in some cases from the medieval *lectio*, as professors read in Latin for an hour without interruption or humor from a manuscript or perhaps a printed book. The students' strong reactions were critical factors in bringing change to medical teaching.

109. Ibid., 10.

110. Jones, "Montpellier Medical Students," 68–69.

111. Réclamation de M. De Sault, chirurgien en chef de l'Hôtel-Dieu de Paris, contre une pétition presenteé à l'assemblée nationale par des éléves en chirurgie, Archives nationales, D XXXVIII, 3, XLVII, 1–3. This seven-page statement was rediscovered by Toby Gelfand in 1970 and published, with a commentary, as "A Confrontation over Clinical Instruction at the Hôtel-Dieu of Paris During the French Revolution," *Journal of the History of Medicine and Allied Sciences* 28 (1973): 268–82.

Scottish students, perhaps because of their young age, were particularly known for their impatience and shrill reactions. The hapless Alexander Monro III was sometimes booed or hissed in anatomy class (as were other professors at Edinburgh), and according to a contemporary, even the venerable William Cullen was described by students as "the Oraclete" because "he generally uses pompous language."[112] In America, William Shippen, a senior member of the faculty at Philadelphia, was called "dull, cold, and monotonous" by students, and at Harvard the "right learned professors", according to another source, made annually "very little improvements in their old stories."[113]

German students—by reputation more sedate—could also be demonstrative as well as highly critical. The students at Freiburg greeted a new professor in the 1770s with shouts and catcalls and threatened to storm his house because he had the temerity to urge the reunion of medical and surgical teaching.[114]

The weakness of medical teaching in the eighteenth and early nineteenth centuries that was most pronounced in the eyes of students was the disproportionate stress on theoretical or classroom teaching over practical instruction. In place after place, students clamored, often vainly, for more classroom demonstrations, more opportunities for dissection, more teaching in the clinic or hospital, and especially more hands-on experience at the bedside. Especially valued by students but very difficult to obtain was direct experience in midwifery. In Paris, the gates of the huge Maternité Hospital were long closed to medical students, who were forced to pay private teachers to observe childbirth outside the hospital. It was only through such private courses that most European and American students around 1800 were able to get a modicum of practical instruction. By choosing such courses, they gave direction to changes in medical education.

Students often found clinical lectures in obstetrics, surgery, or medicine—unless they were accompanied by clear demonstrations—to lack practical value. Regarding the lectures on obstetrics in Zurich, young Johann Steger opined that "it would be better if [they] were not given at all . . . there is not the shadow of a good clinic" in the city.[115] French students of the 1780s were likewise dissatisfied with "the incongruity of a professor who lecture[s] on chemical theory but scorn[s] the drudgery of

112. David B. Horn, *A Short History of the University of Edinburgh, 1556–1889* (Edinburgh: University of Edinburgh Press, 1967), 138; "Letter of Thomas Ismay, Student of Medicine at Edinburgh, 1771, to His Father," *University of Edinburgh Journal* 8 (1936–37): 59.

113. Charles Caldwell, *Autobiography* (Philadelphia: Lippincott, 1855), 115; Holt, "Medical Student in Boston," 385.

114. Hans G. Wenig, "Medizinische Ausbildung im 19.Jahrhundert" (med. diss., University of Bonn, 1969), 69.

115. Bezel, *Johann Jakob Steger*, 77.

. . . soiling his hands with chemicals."[116] "In practice," writes Lisa Rosner in regard to teaching in Edinburgh, "students' clinical experience came from studying written case histories" and not from direct observation.[117]

Crowding in the hospital wards in the large cities of Britain and the Continent as the physician or surgeon made his way through his rounds was a nearly universal complaint. "There is always such a Crowd of Students about the Physician and Surgeon," wrote an eighteenth-century Edinburgh student, "that there is nothing either to be seen or heard . . . a few superficial questions are asked and some Medicines are prescribed without saying why."[118] The students of Montpellier petitioned authorities "to complain of the speed with which the hospital doctor conducted his rounds, and the lack of consideration he showed toward medical students."[119] In Boston, too, a student who had come to the Massachusetts General Hospital to witness an operation, remarked sarcastically that "Dr. Warren had only Seventeen Assistants with him in the Area . . . we should not have known what was going on had we not been told beforehand."[120] Where a hospital was not at hand, as at Dartmouth, students, upon hearing of a proposed operation at home, would often "hire horses and post off, break-fastless, to the patient's house."[121] Even when an attempt was made to give more time and attention to students, it was rare, outside Germany, that they were given any direct responsibility for patients. Only in some of the small German university clinics were some students regularly asked to examine and treat patients.

In no country could a medical student of 1800 be certain of having a chance to practice dissection on a human body. Although Paris and London, with their large numbers of sick poor, offered opportunities far beyond those of other places, lingering legal restrictions and religious taboos continued to limit the availability of unclaimed bodies. Once procured, bodies were treasured by students as long as they lasted. "I must now spend most of my time on anatomy," Steger wrote his parents in 1813, "so that my cadaver does not decay completely without having been used."[122] Where bodies were relatively more available, as in the French and English capitals, private courses in anatomy flourished outside the normal channels of medical education. John Hunter claimed to have introduced into London the "Paris manner of dissection," meaning

116. David M. Vess, *Medical Revolution in France, 1789–96* (Gainesville: University Presses of Florida, 1975), 16.

117. Lisa Rosner, "Eighteenth-Century Medical Education and the Didactic Model of Experiment," in *The Literary Structure of Scientific Argument: Historical Studies*, ed. Peter Dear (Philadelphia: University of Pennsylvania Press, 1991), 191.

118. Christopher Lawrence, "Medicine as Culture: Edinburgh and the Scottish Enlightenment" (Ph.D. diss., University of London, 1984), 79.

119. Jones, "Montpellier Medical Students," 69.

120. Holt, "Medical Student in Boston," 360.

121. Hayward and Thomson, *Journal of William Tully*, 48.

122. Bezel, *Johann Jakob Steger*, 70.

the dissection of a whole body by a single student, which was a great attraction to most students.[123]

Students in every country were involved to a greater or lesser degree in robbing graves in order to procure bodies for anatomical study. At the time of the American Revolution, those in New York and Philadelphia, for example, finding that they were only long-range spectators in the formal classes in anatomy, were forced to find their own bodies if they wanted firsthand experience in dissection. Harvard students formed a society of "Spunkers" in 1771 that sought out "corpses of friendless derelicts and criminals."[124] Valentine Mott, a young demonstrator of anatomy at Columbia, described in 1806 carrying the heavy body of an exhumed criminal, its "white robes flying," to a waiting carriage so that it could be used for teaching.[125]

At Montpellier, the courses in anatomy and surgery were interrupted in 1799 by a lack of cadavers, and the authorities were implored to make them more freely available.[126] In London, about the same time, a student wrote that "we have of late been froze out of the Dissecting Room . . . subjects are very scarce . . . and they charge a most exorbitant price."[127] Almost all London visitors in this period commented on the bizarre practices of the "resurrection men."[128] In Scotland a Glasgow student complained in 1812 that "the Anatomical Schools of Scotland are in a most deplorable state for the want of subjects, it now being quite impossible to procure more than two or three bodies in the course of a year by exhumation."[129] And in Berlin, the anatomist Rudolphi told the Education Ministry in 1816 that a lack of corpses had forced one of his colleagues to cancel classes eight days in a row.[130]

Teachers were caught up in the public controversies over body snatching. The anatomist Granville Sharp Pattison, for example, was put on trial

123. Toby Gelfand, "The 'Paris Manner' of Dissection: Student Anatomical Dissection in Early Eighteenth-Century Paris," *Bulletin of the History of Medicine* 46 (1972): 99–130.

124. James T. Goodrich, "The Colonial American Medical Student: 1750–1776," *Connecticut Medicine* 40 (1976): 841. Still one of the best studies of the subject is that by Frederick C. Waite, "Grave Robbing in New England," *Medical Library Association Bulletin* 33 (1945): 272–87.

125. Valentine Mott, *An Address introductory to a Course of Lectures at the College of Physicians and Surgeons* (New York: Joseph Jennings, 1850), 13.

126. Faculty minutes, 12 Vendose [1799], S. 110, Archives, Faculty of Medicine, Montpellier.

127. Letter of January 2, 1797 in Ford, *Medical Student at St. Thomas's Hospital*, 35.

128. See, for example, Eckart Buchholz, "Grossbrittanische Reiseeindrücke deutscher und österreichischer Ärzte von 1750 bis 1810" (med. diss., University of Frankfurt am Main, 1960), 92–93.

129. Thomas Lyle, "University Reminiscences," cited in L. R. C. Agnew, "Scottish Medical Education," in *The History of Medical Education*, ed. C. D. O'Malley (Berkeley and Los Angeles: University of California Press, 1970), 256.

130. Carl Rudolphi to ministry, February 20, 1816, GSPK, Merseburg, 76, Va, Sekt 2, Tit X, Nr. 3, Bd. 2.

in Scotland in 1814 for encouraging his students to take bodies from a local churchyard. "Had seen a body on Patterson's Table," testified one witness, according to a judge's notes, "and knew that students were in the practice of raising bodies for dissection."[131] In Manchester, the pioneer teacher Joseph Jordan boasted of his part in local grave robbing, as he endeavored to provide bodies for his students.[132] And again in Berlin, Rudolphi, in his letter to the ministry, complained about a new government policy of burying the poor "in a coffin with a heavy lid."[133]

Most magistrates, understanding the pressing need for bodies in instruction, sought to minimize the penalties applied to those who were caught. As the nations of Europe, led by France, passed legislation making easier the assignment of unclaimed bodies to medical schools, the situation gradually eased on the Continent, but in Britain and America, the search for bodies remained a nagging concern for decades. By the late 1820s, before Great Britain finally passed its Anatomy Act, British students were paying on the average thirty times as much for a body as their counterparts in France were.[134] This helps explain the great popularity of studying in Paris in the years after the Napoleonic wars.

The continued insistence by most faculties on using Latin, especially in the formal examinations and in the writing of the dissertation, was another source of irritation to the students. To many, it seemed an archaic requirement preserved only for its value in screening out those without a "gentlemanly" education. Although declining as the language of instruction by 1800, Latin was nevertheless still used in some medical courses. At Prague, for example, the lectures on materia medica and clinical medicine were still given in Latin, as were a number of the medical courses in Heidelberg.[135] The medical faculty at Greifswald taught some of its "necessary" courses in Latin until the 1820s and, in the case of the medical clinic, until the 1830s.[136] A student applying for admission to medicine at the University of Berlin in 1813 was promptly rejected when it was found that "he knows practically nothing about the Latin language" and was

---

131. Transcript of Notes taken by one of the Judges at the Trial of Granville Sharp Pattison et alia on June 6 and 7, 1814, Library, Royal College of Physicians and Surgeons of Glasgow.

132. Katherine A. Webb, "The Development of the Medical Profession in Manchester, 1750–1860" (Ph.D. diss., University of Manchester, 1988), 475.

133. Rudolphi to ministry, 20 February 1816.

134. Russell C. Maulitz, *Morbid Appearances: The Anatomy of Pathology in the Early Nineteenth Century* (Cambridge: Cambridge University Press, 1987), 142, figure 6.2. See also Ruth Richardson, *Death, Dissection and the Destitute* (London: Routledge & Kegan Paul, 1987).

135. Alois Krobot, "Zur Geschichte der medizinischen Ausbildung an der Prager Karlsuniversität von 1650 bis 1800" (med. diss., University of Zurich, 1985), 94; Richard A. Keller, *Geschichte der Universität Heidelberg im ersten Jahrzehnt nach der Reorganization durch Karl Friedrich (1803–1813)* (Heidelberg: Carl Winter, 1913), 233.

136. Paul Grawitz, *Geschichte der medizinischen Fakultät Greifswald, 1806–1906* (Greifswald: Julius Abel, 1906), 7.

therefore "only suited to the Pépinière (a practical military school of medicine)."[137]

Final examinations in most continental and British universities were conducted in Latin until at least the 1830s. Students in Paris, although they now wrote their theses in French, still had to respond orally in Latin to questions concerning their written responses to clinical questions on the examinations.[138] At Edinburgh, where graduate examinations were described by the dean as "really stringent," Latin was required until 1833.[139]

Disputes between students and teachers over a thesis or a dissertation, especially regarding the quality of its Latin or over the conduct of an examination, were a common feature of academic life in the early nineteenth century. At the Scottish and other universities, it was often the practice for students weak in Latin to buy their theses from a resourceful entrepreneur.[140] Controversy followed whenever plagiarism was suspected. A dispute over a medical thesis at Montpellier in 1802, for example, brought an angry confrontation and a challenge from the student involved to a duel with his professor.[141] In Berlin, an acrimonious quarrel broke out in the 1820s between the medical faculty and the ministry over the poor Latin found by authorities in some of the dissertations.[142]

At the medical school in Philadelphia, where Latin was not required after 1789, examinations were noted for their length and frequent controversy. Notes taken at one examination in the late eighteenth century reveal that scores of very specific questions were asked—"Where do the nerves arise?" "What sort of a membrane is the pleura?" "How many perforations are there through the diaphragm?" "Where does the pancreatic juice come from?" "Is there any peristaltic motion in the arteries?" "How do you dissolve iron in vitriolic acid?" "What calcareous substances are used as astringents?" "Is opium useful in all pain?" "How are the purgative virtues of rhubarb increased?"—to which the student was expected to respond "quickly and briefly."[143] At the examination of the strongly opinionated Charles Caldwell in 1796, Benjamin Rush challenged his

137. Carl Rudolphi to medical faculty, March 1813, medical faculty files, University Archive, 58, M1, Bd. 1, Humboldt University, Berlin.

138. René Roche, "An Account of the Origin, Progress, and present State of the Medical School of Paris," *American Journal of the Medical Sciences* 9 (1828): 362.

139. Royal Commission, *Evidence, Oral and Documentary*, 203; R. D. Lobban, *Edinburgh and the Medical Revolution* (Cambridge: Cambridge University Press, 1980), 42.

140. Francisco S. Constancio, *An Appeal to the Gentlemen studying Medicine at the University of Edinburgh* (Edinburgh: privately printed, 1797), 7.

141. F17 4451, Archives nationales, Paris.

142. "Streitigkeiten zwischen dem Ministerium u. der med. Facultät über die Disssertationen von Piper u. v. Persyn wegen schlechten lateinischen Formulierungen," medical faculty files, University Archive, 312, Q51, P8, Humboldt University, Berlin.

143. From the notes of Thomas Parke in Whitfield J. Bell Jr., "Medical Students and Their Examiners in Eighteenth Century America," *Transactions of the College of Physicians of Philadelphia* 21 (1953): 18–22.

thesis on children's diseases, waving a copy of it as he spoke, whereupon Caldwell grabbed the document from his hand and declared it to be a fraudulent copy and known by Rush to be spurious. Rush thereupon refused to approve the thesis.[144] Professors at Philadelphia often accused one another of favoritism toward particular students, which led to a requirement in 1810 that students sit behind a large green screen ("the green box") to shield their identity while answering questions.[145]

The Medical Teacher

Teachers of medicine in the late eighteenth and early nineteenth century were largely drawn, like their students, from the broad ranks of the middle classes. A few were wealthy; some were well connected in European or American society; and others came from modest economic circumstances. Most saw in teaching a source of further income and opportunity as well as an enhancement of their social status. Those who taught apprentices in Britain and America, especially outside the cities, were often hardworking general practitioners who lacked academic training or access to the wards of a hospital. Their resources for teaching were therefore limited, and the instruction they gave was informal, sporadic, and practical. Not a few saw it as a burdensome economic necessity to be added to the principal business of attending patients and mixing drugs.

The London hospital teacher, by contrast, was far more likely to have attended a university and to aspire to the standing of a gentleman. Frequently he had grown up in a professional or aspiring middle-class family. Outside the large hospitals, in the private medical schools of Britain and America, the typical teacher was more likely to be drawn, in Stella Butler's phrase, from the "unconnected but talented."[146] In such cases, the private medical teacher was seldom eligible for membership in the select royal colleges.

In the rural medical colleges of America, which most resembled the British private schools, the supply of even "unconnected" teachers was often too small to teach a full curriculum. By an ingenious juggling of teaching schedules, such a college might attract enterprising teachers from other schools as "visiting professors" during vacation periods at home. Some of these teachers taught in two, three, or even four or five medical schools, by traveling constantly from place to place. By 1820, these marginal schools, academically weak but often profitable and clearly meeting a need, flourished in both Britain and America.

---

144. Bell, "Medical Students," 24.

145. John L. Atlee, "The Education of a Physician in Early 19th Century," *Journal of the Lancaster Co. Historical Society* 91 (1987–88): 83.

146. Stella V. F. Butler, "Science and the Education of Doctors in the Nineteenth Century: A Study of British Medical Schools with Particular Reference to the Development and Uses of Physiology" (Ph.D. diss., University of Manchester, 1981), 22.

Many of the London teachers were socially prominent surgeons or physicians, graduates of Oxford or Cambridge or perhaps Edinburgh, and members of a royal college. By 1800 all the metropolitan hospitals, especially St. Bartholomew's, Guy's, St. Thomas's, St. George's, and the London Hospital, were thriving as teaching enterprises. Their lectures were crowded; students flocked around the teachers in the wards; and many took private courses from the more famous men. It could be a very lucrative business, and by 1814, fifty courses were being advertised each year.[147]

By this time, a surgeon of the popularity of Benjamin Brodie could realize an income of more than £1,500 (perhaps $7,500, a very large sum in the American currency of that time) from his teaching and practice.[148] Teachers were paid directly by the students who came to their lectures. A course in medicine or materia medica brought as much as ten guineas from each student, and a single apprentice in surgery might pay five hundred or a thousand guineas to his teacher for several years of tutelage. A dresser paid the surgeon fifty guineas for a year of instruction. Simply accompanying the physician or surgeon on his rounds cost a student twenty-four guineas a year.[149] By recent tradition, the fees for "walking the wards" were divided equally among all the attending medical men, but this was occasionally challenged, as did John Hunter at St. George's Hospital in 1792, on the ground that some teachers brought a disproportionate share of pupils to the hospital.[150]

The university teachers of Edinburgh and Glasgow likewise relied on student fees as the main source of their income. Since the salaries paid them by the town councils were exceedingly small, they depended almost entirely for their livelihood on the amounts paid in advance by each student for a course of lectures. If multiplied by a large number of students, the three guineas paid by a student for each class, such as anatomy or chemistry, could become a sizable income for the professor. A student in the class of the anatomist Alexander Monro II, for example, wrote his father in 1771 that "he has about 300 Pupils which pay him 3 guineas each, so you may judge of his Yearly Income."[151] Competition for student fees led to bitter quarrels among the professors and resistance to the introduction of new courses. One such quarrel in 1792 resulted in an Edinburgh professor's striking another with his walking cane.[152] As happened later in Germany, the fee system in Scotland discouraged specialized teaching by encouraging the continuation of large classes in broad fields of study. Extramural teaching flourished precisely in those areas of

147. Lawrence, "Science and Medicine at the London Hospitals," 349.
148. "Works of Sir Benjamin Brodie," 140.
149. Cameron, *Mr. Guy's Hospital*, 146–48.
150. Lawrence, "Science and Medicine at the London Hospitals," 284.
151. "Letter from Thomas Ismay," 57.
152. Horn, *Short History*, 108.

the curriculum, in Scotland as elsewhere, in which change was thwarted by the system or the teaching was known to be poor.

The Edinburgh fee system was closely followed at Philadelphia and other early American schools. As they did in the Scottish city, medical teachers in Philadelphia relied on course and examination fees, as well as their income from practice, to earn a livelihood. Since the operating costs for a building and equipment were fixed, each additional student beyond a certain minimum brought more income to the faculty. Some of the teachers did exceedingly well, even by later standards. Those teaching at the medical college in Baltimore by the 1820s, for example, were earning as much as $4,000 a year. If income from private practice were included, "a popular and enterprising faculty member at a successful urban school could expect to earn at least ten thousand dollars in a good year, and his less popular colleagues well over five thousand annually."[153]

In both America and Britain, such a large financial stake in the teaching enterprise helps explain the intense and often bitter conflict among schools of medicine in the early nineteenth century. Almost no one advocated a system of fixed salaries for medical teaching of the continental European type. Indeed, when such a system was suggested at the College of Physicians and Surgeons in New York in the 1820s, a committee of the New York Board of Regents promptly advised that it "would damp the ardor of literary pursuit in the professors; would take from individuals the proportionate rewards due to their celebrity, and might endanger the ultimate prosperity and success of the institution."[154]

Everywhere teachers fought to gain more access for their students to the hospitals and infirmaries of the larger cities. Not only in London but in many other cities in Britain and North America as well, the right to give lectures to students in a hospital and to take them through the wards was a highly prized advantage. On the wards of a hospital, students were at first tolerated but seldom welcomed.

By the end of the eighteenth century, however, students were given more encouragement because of the many tasks they performed for free in the hospital. Authorities were still reluctant, nevertheless, to convert their hospitals into places of medical teaching. In both Edinburgh and Glasgow, for example, the faculties had to struggle for many years to hold a foothold for teaching in the royal infirmaries of these cities. Opposition came not only from the governing boards of the infirmaries but also from the staff physicians and surgeons, who feared the competition of faculties in offering instruction to their own pupils. The Royal College of Physicians and Surgeons of Glasgow repeatedly underscored its opposition to having the lectures at the Royal Infirmary "solely in the hands of

153. William G. Rothstein, *American Physicians in the Nineteenth Century: From Sects to Science* (Baltimore: Johns Hopkins University Press, 1972), 95.

154. David L. Cowen, *Medical Education: The Queen's–Rutgers Experience, 1792–1830* (New Brunswick, NJ: State University Bicentennial Commission, 1966), 23.

the medical Professors."[155] In response, the faculty argued that the infirmary's attitude was driving "many advanced students to go to another
university."[156]

The prolonged and bitter struggle over hospital teaching in the largely
private hospitals of Anglo-America, which continued well into the twentieth century, contrasted sharply with the much swifter evolution of the
"teaching hospital" in the publicly controlled institutions of France and
Germany.

Indeed, the highly competitive, business-oriented teaching of medicine
in much of Britain and America stood in sharp relief to the continental
system of medical education in the years around 1800. Teachers in
France and Germany were selected differently, paid differently, and followed different career patterns from those in Britain or North America.
They were much more likely to work in a government-sponsored institution, to have easy access to a hospital or clinic, and to regard medical
teaching as a lifelong career. In general, they also taught more than their
contemporaries in Britain or America. Although medical professors on
the Continent, like those in Anglo-America, carried on a private practice
and taught private courses, their appointments as professors carried far
more prestige and demanded more of their time. Furthermore, medical
investigation and scholarly publication were beginning to play a role in
their hiring and promotion. Not a few, especially in Germany, were called
from one university to another—at an increase in rank or emoluments—
because of their scholarly accomplishments. Many of their career moves
at century's end, with the accompanying deliberations and drawn-out negotiations, would seem familiar two centuries later.

The German universities were clearly changing rapidly by the turn of
the eighteenth century. They had become, in the words of Friedrich
Paulsen, "state institutions . . . founded and administered by the government."[157] Professors were state employees; their teaching was supervised
by the state; and their duty was to train young men for service to the
state, the church, or the school. Although faculties were normally consulted about teaching vacancies and often made formal recommendations, the power of appointment lay clearly with the government. Salaries
were paid by the state for the "public" courses they taught, although
many turned increasingly to *privata* teaching, sanctioned by the government, which brought them a share of the student fees paid for such
courses. In their teaching, professors were expected to use a textbook
listed in the university catalog and to follow it closely in their teaching.
The professors at Heidelberg, for example, were criticized by the authori-

155. Faculty Minutes, Royal College of Physicians and Surgeons of Glasgow, September
7, 1812.
156. Minutes, Royal Infirmary of Glasgow, August 1812, Special Collections, University
of Glasgow Library.
157. Friedrich Paulsen, *Geschichte des gelehrten Unterrichts auf den deutschen Schulen
und Universitäten vom Ausgang des Mittelatters bis zur Gegenwart*, 2 vols. (Berlin and
Leipzig: Vereinigung wissenschaftlicher Verlager, 1921), 2:127.

ties in 1807 for not basing their lectures on textbooks but, rather, "on their own notes."[158]

Teaching loads in Germany were heavy by comparison with those in Britain or America, doubtless because their primary responsibility was to teach students. A Prussian regulation of 1768 required that professors teach from five to seven hours daily. Many were in the classroom more than twenty-five hours a week as the century ended. When Rudolphi was called to Berlin in 1810, he began his teaching with sixteen hours of lectures each week, in addition to eighteen hours spent guiding students in the anatomy room.[159] His colleague Johann Christian Reil complained that "no teacher can teach more than two hours a day if he intends to keep up with his subject and not sink to the level of a mechanic."[160]

The Size of Medical Faculties

The medical faculties of Germany and France were generally much larger than those in the English-speaking countries. A considerably wider selection of courses was available to students than in either Britain or America. A Scottish editor wrote in 1807 about the "formidable" size of the German faculties.[161] At this time, Edinburgh was offering eleven lecture and practical courses in medicine, and Glasgow listed a total of seven.[162] A review of the medical curricula at the German universities in this period, on the other hand, shows Heidelberg with thirty-six courses, Berlin twenty-nine, Göttingen twenty-two, Würzburg twenty-one; Munich (then in Landshut) seventeen, Erfurt sixteen, and Marburg thirteen.[163] Even a

158. Akten der medizinischen Fakultät, 1743–1914, University of Heidelberg Archive, III, 4a, 50.

159. Peter Schneck, "Zum Wirken von Karl Asmund Rudolphi in Berlin," *Wissenschaftliche Zeitung Ernst-Moritz-Arndt-Universität Greifswald* 34 (1985): 73.

160. Wolfram Kaiser and Reinhard Mocek, *Johann Christian Reil* (Leipzig: B. G. Teubner, 1979), 90.

161. *Edinburgh Medical Journal* 3 (1807): 123.

162. *Edinburgh Medical Journal* 4 (1808): 506, 509.

163. Akten der medizinischen Fakultät, University of Heidelberg Archive, III, 4a, 50, 51; *Anzeige der Vorlesungen welche im Sommerhalbenjahre 1810 auf der Grossherzöglich Badischen Ruprecht–Karolinischen Universität zu Heidelberg gehalten werden* (Heidelberg: Gutmeir, 1810), 8–13; "Vorbereitung für die Herausgabe der Vorlesungverzeichnisse," Akten der medizinischen Fakältat zu Berlin, Humboldt University Archive, Berlin, 137, E1, L1; *Vorlesungs-Verzeichnis und Index Lectionum der Universität Berlin für das erste Semester ihres Bestehens, 1810/11* (Berlin, 1810); *Catalogus Praelectionum in Academia Georgia Augusta* (Göttingen: Henrici Dietrich, 1810); *Ordnung der Vorlesungen an der Grossherzöglichen Universität zu Würzburg für das Sommer-Semester 1810* (Würzburg: 1810); Christiane Scherg-Zeisner, "Die ärztliche Ausbildung an der Königlich-bayerischen Julius-Maximilians-Universität in Würzburg, 1814–1872" (med. diss., University of Würzburg, 1973), 24–25; *Verzeichnis der Vorlesungen, welche an der Königlichen Ludwig-Maximilians-Universität zu Landshut im Wintersemester MDCCCIX–MDCCCX gehalten werden* (Landshut: Joseph Thomann, 1809), 13–16; *Universitatis Literarum Erfordiensis Catalogum Praelectionum* (Erfurt: Goerling, 1810); *Indices Lectionum in Academia Marburgensi* (Marburg, 1810). Many of these catalogs may be found in "Bericht Uhdens über die Bereisung mehrerer Universitäten Deutschlands," GSPK, Merseburg, 76, Va, Sekt. 2, Tit. 1, Nr. 5.

medium-size university such as Munich advertised in 1810 such as yet uncommon courses as pathological anatomy, anatomy and the natural history of worms, physiology of the fetus and the senses, physiological and pathological semiotics, hygiene, and medical police.[164]

In the same year, the faculty at Heidelberg were teaching separate courses in such subjects as fevers, chronic illnesses, women's diseases, syphilitic diseases, pediatrics, and "psychological anthropology."[165] At Göttingen, Friedrich Stromeyer offered a course in *chemiam theoreticam experimentis,* in addition to his teaching of chemistry and chemical analysis.[166] Halle listed a course in "experimental pharmacology" in its catalog.[167] Psychiatry was taught by a full-time professor at Leipzig in 1811.[168] By this time, the German medical faculties ranged in size from that of Berlin, which listed fourteen professors and lecturers, to tiny Wittenberg, which could still count seven instructors of all ranks.[169]

In Napoleonic France, the teachers of medicine struggled to find a secure place in the emerging order. Despite the abrupt closing of the universities in 1792, a number of medical faculties had continued their efforts to teach students and to bring new ones into their classes. Throughout the country, some teaching continued, even in the most turbulent period, in the hospitals and schools of surgery.[170] The medical school at Caen was expressly given the right to continue teaching and was later exempted from the decree closing the universities.[171] At Montpellier, the professors of medicine, sometimes at the risk of imprisonment, continued to teach their classes, hold examinations, and admit new pupils, describing themselves as "perhaps the only [faculty] in the republic that did not interrupt its useful work." Later they petitioned for indemnification for the years in which they had served without pay, but without much success. "The government," according to faculty minutes in 1801, "has absolutely abandoned us."[172]

164. *Verzeichnis der Vorlesungen zu Landshut,* 14–15.

165. *Anzeige der Vorlesungen,* 10-11; Akten der medizinischen Fakultät, University of Heidelberg Archive, III, 49, 51, 89-90.

166. *Catalogus Praelectionum in Academia Georgia Augusta.*

167. *Catalogus Praelectionum in Academia Friedrichiana Halensi* (Halle, 1810).

168. Ingrid Kästner and Achim Thom, *575 Jahre der Universität Leipzig* (Leipzig: Barth, 1990), 24.

169. *Vorlesungs-Verzeichnis . . . der Universität Berlin; Catalogus Lectionum in Academia Vitebergensi* (Wittenberg: Graessleri, 1810).

170. Marie-José Imbault-Huart, "L'école pratique de dissection de Paris de 1750 à 1822 ou l'influence du concept de médecine pratique et de médecine d'observation dans l'enseignement medico–chirurgical au XVIIIe siècle et au debut du XIXe siècle" (med. diss., University of Paris, 1973), 58–59.

171. "Note, sur l'existence de l'école de médecine de Caen, [1801]" Archives nationales, Paris, F17 2455.

172. Montpellier medical professors to Committee of Public Instruction, 25 Frimaire, 1795, Archives nationales, Paris, DXXXVIII; Faculty Minutes, series 5, no. 110, April 23, An 8, Medical School Archive, Montpellier. See also Louis Dulieu, "La vie médicale et chirurgicale à Montpellier du 12 Août 1792 au 14 Frimaire an III," *Revue d'histoire des sciences et de leurs applications* 8 (1955): 38–51, 146–69.

It was an agonizingly difficult time for all teachers of medicine. Even after the opening of the "Schools of Health" at Paris, Montpellier, and Strasbourg in 1795, the professors fought against constant government interference, charges of monarchism, overlapping directives, shortages of supplies and funds, and chronic failure to pay their salaries. In the school at Montpellier, students and faculty were ominously warned in 1795 that those "whose conduct is contrary to . . . the principles of Republicanism will be denounced in the Council of the School, which will recommend punishment."[173] From Strasbourg came complaints that only six of the fourteen positions needed to teach the entire curriculum had been filled by 1798 and that there was a shortage of equipment. Particularly resented in Strasbourg was the favored treatment given to Paris and the larger number of professors authorized at Montpellier. Instruction in chemistry and clinical medicine, the Strasbourg professors charged, could not yet be carried out because of the lack of a chemistry laboratory and a satisfactory hospital.[174]

Professors at Montpellier protested against the reduction in their number from the prerevolutionary period and pleaded, as did their colleagues in Strasbourg, for remuneration for their services.[175] The Paris faculty likewise claimed that the government had failed to honor its commitments for faculty and adjunct positions.[176] Complaints from all the schools about unpaid salaries abound in the correspondence of the period.[177]

The revolutionary decree of December 4, 1794, put an end to the three years of medical *brigandage*, to use the term of Marie-José Imbault-Huart, when every citizen enjoyed "the [legal] right to care for his fellow-citizens."[178] The three new schools established by the decree, as well as the preparatory courses in medicine subsequently authorized in a score of provincial hospitals, were closely regulated by the Committee of Public Instruction, which set the curriculum, professors' salaries, the size of the student body, graduate requirements, admissions standards, and even the dress code for professors.[179] The former schools of surgery were gradually

173. University of Montpellier School of Medicine Archive, 25 Ventôse, 1795, series S, nos. 107, 30.

174. *Observations sur le rapport fait au nom de la commission d'instruction publique et d'institutions républicaines réunies, par le citoyen Hardy, membre du Conseil des Cinq-Cents, sur l'organisation des écoles de médecine* (Strasbourg: Dannbach, [1798]), 5–16.

175. Montpellier medical professors to Committee of Public Instruction.

176. L'organisation de l'école de médecine, 1810, Archives nationales, AJ16 6357.

177. See, for example, Archives nationales, AJ16 6685.

178. Marie-José Imbault-Huart, "The Teaching of Medicine in France and More Particularly in Paris in the 19th Century (1794–1892)," in *History of Medical Education*, ed. Teizo Ogawa (Tokyo: Saikon, 1983), 59.

179. Rapport et décret de la convention nationale sur les écoles de santé de Paris, Montpellier et Strasbourg, 14 Frimaire, 1795, Archives nationales, AJ16 6226; P. Huard and M. J. Imbault-Huart, "Concepts et réalités de l'education et de la profession medico–chirurgicales pendant la révolution," *Journal des savants*, 1973, 135.

incorporated into the new schools, and many faculty members—indeed, two of every three at Paris—were recruited from their ranks. The Paris school was housed in the same buildings as the old Academy of Surgery. At Montpellier, the old faculty was restored intact to teaching.

Salaries were fixed initially for all professors at 6,000 francs (roughly $1,100 in contemporary terms) and 5,000 for adjunct professors. This figure was subsequently raised to 10,000 francs for professors and was supplemented by other emoluments.[180] As they did in Germany and Britain, many professors taught private courses that brought them additional income. Indeed, by 1810, the official courses offered by the medical faculties were attracting fewer students than were the private courses held in professors' homes or in the hospitals. Anatomy and surgery, as was true everywhere, brought the largest number of clients.[181] As conditions improved, a number of the medical professors became very prosperous, so much so that by 1820, 70 percent of a sample group left substantial estates valued at 100,000 francs or more.[182]

Teaching schedules, as in Germany, were often heavy, especially for clinical teachers in the hospitals. Desault, according to one estimate, spent fourteen hours a day in teaching. A typical day for the noted surgeon was described as follows:[183]

> It is my duty to counsel and supervise one hundred young people. I visit each day the sick and I do myself, or with me present if done by others, all operations and important bandaging. I am busy every day, in all seasons, on this task, starting at 6 a.m. up to 9 a.m. and pass the next two hours consulting freely and instructing students in the amphitheater. In the evening, I make a new visit from 4 to 5 p.m. and thereafter, with my students, I consult free of change, and [teach] a second lesson up to 7 p.m. Often I make a further visit at 10 p.m. when I have seriously ill patients.

After 1810, the French method of selecting professors was by means of a public competition known as a *concours*. The revolutionary generation wrote this Old Regime custom into the law of the new republic. (Later it was abolished in the Restoration but restored in 1823).[184] In a *concours*, the candidate was forced to appear before a jury of seven or eight mem-

180. Charles Coury, "The Teaching of Medicine in France from the Beginning of the Seventeenth Century," in *The History of Medical Education*, ed. C. D. O'Malley (Berkeley and Los Angeles: University of California Press, 1970), 149.

181. Pierre Huard and Marie-José Imbault-Huart, "L'enseignement libre de la médecine à Paris au XIXe siècle," *Revue d'histoire des sciences* 27 (1974): 48–49.

182. George Weisz, "The Medical Elite in France in the Early Nineteenth Century," *Minerva* 25 (1987): 161, table IV.

183. Marie-José Imbault-Huart, "Concepts and Realities of the Beginning of Clinical Teaching in France in the Late 18th and Early 19th Centuries," *Clio Medica* 21 (1987–88): 61.

184. Germaine Picard, "La réglementation des études médicales en France: Son évolution de la révolution a nos jours" (med. diss., University of Paris, 1967), 16.

bers after having written detailed examinations and delivering several public lectures. It was a lengthy and grueling process intended to promote openness and fairness but one that put a high premium on memory, verbal dexterity, and public performance. A number of the best-known medical men of France failed in the *concours*, and others refused to appear before such a public tribunal.

A candidate for a teaching post at Montpellier in 1812 was advised beforehand to "practice your spoken Latin . . . until it is possible to deliver impromptu half-hour lectures." His leading rival, he found upon arriving in Montpellier, was a man of formidably icy composure, whose knowledge of surgery "came from his mouth like a torrent" and reinforced his notable "polish" and "eloquence" in speaking. The rival was chosen, and the defeated candidate returned home with "sadness and regret."[185]

The concentration of advanced medical teaching in Paris produced a breadth of offerings that was surpassed by only a few of the German universities. In Germany, the dispersion of authority permitted a higher degree of latitude in arranging courses than in the tightly controlled French system. But by the early nineteenth century, the depth of French teaching, especially in the clinics of Paris, exceeded that of Germany. The three schools of health (*écoles de santé*) had been established in 1795, with twenty-four teachers (twelve professors and twelve adjuncts) assigned to Paris, sixteen to Montpellier, and twelve to Strasbourg. Surgery was made an integral part of the curriculum, and hospital training was given a new and striking emphasis. By the early 1820s, the number of professorial chairs had doubled, and an additional teaching position of "*agregé*" or lecturer had been created.[186]

But outside the major schools, medical teaching in France entered a long period of uncertainty and decline. Cries from such important provincial centers as Lyon for a school of medicine were repeatedly ignored.[187] For three-quarters of a century, no additional medical school was created, and the overwhelming superiority of Paris became ever more pronounced. Time and time again, critics pointed to such foreign cities as Heidelberg, Göttingen, Philadelphia, or Glasgow, where important medical schools were flourishing in small towns, and asked why French training must be so concentrated in Paris. For example, John Crosse, an English visitor, following a trip in 1815, described France as "the only country where such grave inconvenience exists."[188]

185. Jean Olivier, "Un concours à Montpellier in 1812," *Le Progrés Médical* 6 (1952): 141–42.
186. Charles Coury, "Medical Education in France from the Beginning of the 17th Century to Our Day," unpublished manuscript, Institute of the History of Medicine, Vienna, 1968, 17–19.
187. See A. M., Sénateur, Grand-maître de l'université impériale à prefecture du Rhône, Lyon, May 29, 1811, Archives nationales, F[17] 2107.
188. John Crosse, *Paris et Montpellier, ou tableau de la médecine dans deux écoles* (Paris: Plancher, 1820), 154–55. Crosse asked, in particular, why the venerable school at Montpellier was being neglected in favor of Paris. The physicians of Paris, he said, "treat [Montpellier] with a revolting injustice" (p. 156).

But in Paris the range of teaching, compared with that of the prerevolutionary period, was remarkable. Clinical teaching was now officially promoted as the government converted the great hospitals of the city into major centers of teaching. In their very first semester, students were required to follow patients in the hospitals, as well as to hear clinical lectures and to begin work in dissection. One-fourth of all the professorial chairs and adjunct appointments were committed to clinical teaching. In all, twelve formal courses in medicine, one for each chair, were offered in Paris, including anatomy and physiology (still joined in 1795), medical chemistry, hygiene, legal medicine, external and internal pathology, and four hospital clinics.[189] The number of students, which had begun with three hundred in 1795, climbed to more than twelve hundred in the first three years. By 1798, a faculty report boasted of the great advances in Parisian teaching that "should serve as a model for all of Europe."[190]

The schools at Montpellier and Strasbourg—which were allocated half the number of students as Paris and a smaller proportion of faculty members—were required to follow the same basic curriculum as Paris had.[191] By 1798, Strasbourg was offering a separate course in physiology for first-year students, but such departures from the prescribed pattern were rare.[192] At Montpellier, whose teaching plan was the first to be accepted by the National Convention, the emphasis on bedside instruction was clear from the start. "The clinic is taught at the sickbed," read its report of March 31, 1795; "it is nothing more than the application of Theory to Practice."[193]

Across National Boundaries

The impact of the revolutionary upheaval on teachers and students of medicine all over Europe was profound. It was "practical necessity rather than theory," argues one scholar, that "determined the form and content of medical education" in the long years of crisis.[194] The urgent military necessities of the period demanded a practical mindedness and a willingness to experiment that hurried trends that had been long in the making.

189. August Corlieu, *Centenaire de la faculté de médecine de Paris (1794–1894)* (Paris: Imprimerie nationale, 1896), 10. Detailed descriptions of these courses are found on pp. 31–56.

190. De l'état actuel de l'école de santé de Paris, Archives nationales, AJ[16] 6357, 4, 24–25.

191. See *Plan général de l'enseignement dans l'école de médecine de Strasbourg* (Strasbourg: Levrault, 1798); and *Programmes des cours d'enseignement dans l'école de santé de Montpellier* (Paris: Committee of Public Instruction, 1795).

192. *Plan général*, "Cours de physiologie."

193. *Programmes des cours d'enseignement*, 58.

194. David M. Vess, "The Collapse and Revival of Medical Education in France: A Consequence of Revolution and War, 1789–1815," *History of Education Quarterly* 7 (1967): 89.

The eighteenth-century faith in science, measurement, and close observation as well as the Enlightenment belief in the practical benefits of bedside experience to students were given new life in the turbulent years of revolution and war. "We live in a time of innovation and transformation," wrote the influential Hufeland from beleaguered Jena, "and medicine has felt the influence of this overriding spirit in the most lively manner."[195]

Everywhere medical curricula became a swiftly changing mixture of the old and the new and bore the imprint of different national conditions. Courses in chemistry, botany, and anatomical dissection were now all but universal, but they existed side by side in many countries with traditional courses in materia medica, disputations in Latin, and lectures on the aphorisms of Hippocrates. Strikingly new courses in hygiene, legal medicine, and pathological anatomy were available to students in only a fraction of the established schools.

Clinical teaching was being introduced in more and more of the medical schools of Europe and America, but hands-on experience at the bedside, in which the student was more than a passive observer, was still the exception rather than the rule. Despite the drastic efforts to reform traditional medical education in France and elsewhere, most practitioners were still trained in 1810 in such practical schools as the Wundarzt institutions of Germany, the secondary medical schools of France, the hospital schools of Great Britain, and the apprenticeship programs of Anglo-America. Such non-degree-granting programs continued to place a heavy premium on useful information and hands-on instruction for students in anatomy, surgery, clinical medicine, midwifery, and drug dispensing. At the Bavarian Landarzt schools, for example, the teaching of chemistry, zoology, and natural science was expressly forbidden.[196] Efforts in several countries to unite the teaching of all grades of medical practice through a legal *Einheitsstand*, or a "single port of entry" to medicine, were still viewed skeptically by the great majority of practitioners and citizens alike.

National differences in educating students were accentuated as medicine underwent its season of change. Old distinctions in the training of physicians, surgeons, and apothecaries, which had never taken hold in America, faded rapidly in revolutionary France but weakened more slowly in the German states and persisted strongly in Great Britain. The university as a principal site of medical study, though declining sharply in France and Britain, was growing more important in Germany. Professional training was more and more relegated to specialized schools in every country, except for those areas under German influence.

New scientific subjects were introduced at a faster rate in the government-run systems of France and Germany than in the entrepreneurial

195. Christoph W. Hufeland, *System der practischen Heilkunde* (Jena, 1800), foreword.

196. Johannes M. Hautmann, "Die ärztiche Ausbildung im Königreich und im Freistaat Bayern, 1808–1980" (med. diss., Technical University of Munich, 1982), 93.

schools of Britain and America. Latin as the language of instruction in medicine—even though it was disappearing in every country—clung to life much longer in Europe than in America. Control over medical teaching by a centralized authority, stringent in Napoleonic France, remained rigid but dispersed in the German nations and scarcely existed at all in Britain or America. The radical example of France in attacking the importance of academic study in medical education and in separating the study of basic sciences from clinical study was followed at a distance by Great Britain and the United States but had the least impact on the German states.

The size of the teaching enterprise in medicine at the turn of the century cannot be determined with any degree of exactness. The numbers of students pursuing a medical degree in each country can to some extent be recovered, but data are lacking on the large numbers who studied in the secondary medical schools of France and Germany or in the hospital and apprenticeship programs of Britain and America. Of those enrolled in a degree-granting institution around 1800, the German universities as a whole educated the largest number. Including the German-speaking medical schools of Austria and Switzerland, no fewer than 4,000 students were studying medicine in a German university.[197] Enrollments at individual universities ranged from the 491 at Göttingen to the 18 students listed in the Erlangen catalog of 1800.[198]

Across the Rhine, a total of two thousand students, over half of them in Paris, were pursuing their studies in the three French schools of medicine. The twelve hundred students registered in Paris made it the largest school of medicine in the world. But even these numbers underestimate the concentration of teaching in the French capital, for, according to Pierre Cabanis, at least five thousand students and practitioners of all grades had flocked to Paris by the early nineteenth century.[199]

In Great Britain and North America, those studying medicine at an academic institution were a smaller proportion of those preparing to practice. The Scottish universities, together with Oxford and Cambridge,

197. Based on E. Th. Nauck, "Die Zahl der Medizinstudenten der deutschen Hochschulen im 14.–18.Jahrhundert," *Sudhoffs Archiv* 38 (1954): 182. The numbers not listed in Nauck are estimated. For a discussion of the literature on student numbers, see Johanna Geyer-Kordesch, "German Medical Education in the Eighteenth Century: The Prussian Context and Its Influence," in *William Hunter and the Eighteenth-Century Medical World*, ed. W. F. Bynum and Roy Porter (Cambridge: Cambridge University Press, 1985), 181, note.

198. Nauck, "Die Zahl," 182; University of Erlangen, *Personalstand der Friedrich-Alexanders Universität Erlangen in ihrem ersten Jahrhundert* (Erlangen: C. H. Kunstmann, 1843), 149–53.

199. Cited in Pierre Darmon, *La vie quotidienne du médecin Parisien en 1900* (Paris: Hachette, 1988), 30.

accounted for about 600 matriculants in 1800.[200] Of this number, Edinburgh was responsible for three-fourths of all those who registered. As in Paris, the number of unmatriculated and short-term students in Edinburgh and Glasgow was very large. In the case of the London hospitals, we know that about 150 pupils were following a nondegree program at the end of the century.[201] Finally, the four medical schools of the young United States, it can be estimated, were educating fewer than 150 students at this time, over half of them in Philadelphia.[202]

The large numbers of medical students in the German lands meant also a larger corps of professional teachers. Franz Eulenberg counted 159 full professors (*ordinaria*) of medicine spread among thirty-four universities in 1796, which suggests a total teaching body of 300 or more, or an average of 9 per institution.[203] Despite their heavy enrollments, the three schools of France were authorized to have only 52 professors and adjuncts, although additional classes were taught in the hospitals and scientific institutions. In Great Britain, according to an account of 1806, medical students were instructed by no more than 25 men in the universities and another 46 in the London hospitals.[204] The medical schools of the United States could scarcely have counted 20 teachers in 1800.

These figures fail to take into account, of course, the large group of medical teachers in the secondary hospital programs of France, the many practical schools of surgery in Germany, and the extensive teaching offered in Britain and America outside the universities and the hospitals. What is surprising, nevertheless, is the size of the early lead taken by the German states in the development of an academically oriented, increasingly specialized, and largely full-time cadre of medical teachers.

Of more significance in the short run, however, was the forceful shift of medical instruction in France at the end of the century to the large

200. This estimate is based on the following: Lisa Rosner, "Students and Apprentices: Medical Education at Edinburgh University, 1760–1810" (Ph.D. diss., Johns Hopkins University, 1985), 390, app. I, table 1; Minutes of Senatus, University of Edinburgh Archive, December 8, 1783, March 28, 1812; Alexander Duncan, *Memorial of the Faculty of Physicians and Surgeons of Glasgow* (Glasgow: Maclehose, 1896), 172; John B. Hay, ed., *Inaugural Addresses by Lords Rectors of the University of Glasgow* (Glasgow: University of Glasgow, 1839), 187; and Arnold Chaplin, "The History of Medical Education in the Universities of Oxford and Cambridge, 1500–1850," unpublished manuscript, Royal College of Physicians of London, 22.

201. Lawrence, "Science and Medicine at the London Hospitals," 294, Graph 8.1.

202. Student data on early American medical schools, according to those who have studied them, are notoriously rare. My estimate is based on scattered reports from individual schools and on the references to student numbers in William F. Norwood, *Medical Education in the United States Before the Civil War* (Philadelphia: University of Pennsylvania Press, 1944).

203. Eulenburg, *Frequenz der deutschen Universitäten*, 319.

204. *Edinburgh Medical Journal* 2 (1806): 506–9.

teaching hospitals and the specialized clinics. Other nations—likewise
stirred by the growing impulse to see medicine as a practical science and
seeking to respond to student pressures—began to transform their systems of medical education as well, with consequences that are the subject
of the next chapter.

4

The Clinical Impulse and
the National Response, 1780–1830

As the previous chapters have suggested, striking changes in medical education had occurred by 1800 in nearly every Western country. In particular, the movement toward practical training in medical teaching had gathered momentum toward the end of the eighteenth century. Not only in
Vienna, Paris, Edinburgh, and Leyden but also in scores of universities,
hospitals, military schools, dispensaries, lying-in clinics, and private courses
spread across Europe and North America, students were finding new opportunities to practice dissection; see patients at the bedside; take case histories; practice surgical, obstetrical, and other procedures; and even diagnose and treat patients under a teacher's supervision. It is this sea change
in attitudes toward practical training that we explore in this chapter.

Spurred by Enlightenment concerns for public health and utilitarian
concepts of practical training, new clinical experiences were becoming
available in many places. Although in some countries, notably France and
Germany, the state played a decisive role in fostering the new development, in others, especially Britain and America, students were left largely
on their own to gather practical experience, choosing from a variety of
lecture-demonstration courses, hospital training, apprenticeship opportunities, experience in outpatient dispensaries, and private classes.

National differences in social and political development channeled the
strong pressures for utilitarian education into new forms of clinical training. Differing concepts of what constituted a "teaching clinic" came to
exist side by side, especially in Europe. In unsettled France, the clinical
impulse, which had early centered on surgical practice in urban hospitals

and was now promoted by an all-powerful revolutionary government, found its primary outlet in large hospitals. In the German states, on the other hand, politically divided and lacking large hospitals in most university towns, clinics developed largely as small appendages to university programs in medicine.

British clinical training, as described in earlier chapters, was centered haphazardly in the London hospitals away from the nation's universities and was growing also in provincial hospitals and dispensaries. In North America, the search for clinical experience was spread over a great variety of small infirmaries, dispensaries, and private courses, and apprenticeship training remained the dominant mode of getting hands-on practice. These differences, already wide in 1800, intensified in the opening decades of the nineteenth century, so that by 1830 distinctive national differences in clinical training were well established in the Western world.

What Is a Clinic?

By 1800, praise for the clinic as the ideal site for medical training, even when it was not fully developed or clearly defined, was all but universal. As early as 1759, the Cambridge fellow Richard Davies was calling for compulsory attendance by British students "at some public hospital, which ought to be the finishing school of the clinical physician."[1] By the early nineteenth century, a total of eleven thousand pupils had had the experience of walking the wards of London's hospitals alone.[2] The Apothecaries' Act of 1815 only made mandatory what was already commonplace in Britain—a six-month attendance or more at a hospital, infirmary, or dispensary.

Meanwhile, in France before the Revolution, Vicq d'Azyr and the leaders of the Royal Society of Medicine had called for a "new plan" of medical teaching, in which professors of "clinical medicine" would take all students to the bedside and conduct classes immediately afterward in what they had seen.[3] Johann Peter Frank's description of clinical teaching at his "academic hospital" in Pavia was available the same year in a French edition.[4] Early in the Revolution, the reformer Cabanis called for the establishment of distinctive clinical schools of medicine modeled on the practical marine schools of Brest and Toulon.[5] Similarly, in Germany, the

1. Quoted in J. Ellis, "Medical Education in the UK and Europe," *Oxford Companion to Medicine*, ed. J. N. Walton et al. (New York: Oxford University Press, 1986), 716.

2. This figure is taken from Chapter 4 (p. 2) of Susan Lawrence's revised dissertation. I am grateful to her for sending me a copy.

3. Société royale de médecine, *Nouveau plan de constitution pour la médecine en France présenté à l'assemblée nationale* (Paris, 1790), 94–95.

4. Jean Pierre Frank, *Plan d'école clinique, ou méthode d'enseigner la pratique de la médecine dans un hôpital académique* (Vienna: Chrétien Wapples, 1790).

5. P. G. J. Cabanis, *Coup d'oeil sur les révolutions et sur la réforme de la médecine* (Paris, 1804), 356–59.

Würzburg professor Philipp Horsch, like others before him, told an audience of the early nineteenth century that "the true school of medical training is the clinic." Only there, he observed, "can the whole body of medical knowledge be brought to a practical use."[6] Even among American physicians and in their medical schools—despite the scarcity of hospitals and teaching clinics—the need for clinical instruction was widely acknowledged before 1800.[7]

But such widespread agreement did not extend to the best means or the feasibility of achieving a practical education in medicine. The questions are familiar. Where should practical teaching and learning take place? Was experience with patients best acquired in a crowded hospital, where a great array of human afflictions could be viewed side by side, or given the choice, was a small infirmary or clinic under close control of a teacher a better way to impart useful knowledge? Should patients used in demonstrative teaching be segregated in special wards from the rest of the sick? How useful were the clinical lectures in large hospitals that were becoming common by 1800? Was the student's responsibility only to follow his teacher, to observe, and to listen? Should he also have a role in examining the patient, taking a history, or suggesting a treatment? Under what circumstances, if any, should students be allowed to "touch" the patient? Was it useful or practicable for them to see patients in their homes and thus acquire a knowledge of the circumstances of their lives? How was the theoretical learning of textbook and lecture to be incorporated into teaching at the bedside? How did students learn medical practice, anyway? And how could any future physician or surgeon, now that practical education was possible, perform an operation or deliver a baby or detect signs of disease unless given the chance while still a student, or immediately thereafter, to learn these procedures?

Such questions brought a surprising range of answers in the half-century after 1780. Too little attention has been given to the wide variations and controversies that marked the introduction of the teaching clinic into Western medicine. Even the word *clinic*, derived from a Greek word meaning "bed" (*kline*) and long used to describe any form of practical teaching, was employed to portray very different efforts to unite medical theory and practice at the bedside.

In France, according to Jean-Charles Sournia, the word *clinic* itself was used variously around 1800 to describe a practical lesson, a place, a school, or a whole hospital, as well as a method of learning. The more common term of the late eighteenth century to describe what later was called *clinical medicine* was *practical medicine* or *the method of observation*.[8]

---

6. Phillipp J. Horsch, *Uber die Bildung des Arztes als Klinikers und als Staatsdiener* (Würzburg: Joseph Stahel, 1807), 12, 14.

7. Dale C. Smith, "The Emergence of Organized Clinical Instruction in the Nineteenth Century American Cities of Boston, New York and Philadelphia" (Ph.D. diss., University of Minnesota, 1979), 22.

8. Jean-Charles Sournia, *La médecine révolutionnaire (1789–1799)* (Paris: Payot, 1989), 155–56.

The Revolutionary Changes in France

The revolutionary government in France, desperate for trained doctors
after a period of anarchy, suddenly in 1795 instituted a series of practical
changes in the teaching of medicine that had been long in the making.
Only the many years of preparation during the Old Regime can explain
the swiftness with which ideas for change were now converted into action.[9] Three practical courses in medicine were established in the Paris
hospitals, where interesting cases of disease, especially those common to
the revolutionary armies, were to be grouped together for teaching purposes and where students were to be given a progressively larger role in
examining patients, preparing them for surgery, and keeping records of
individual cases.[10] Unlike Strasbourg or Montpellier, where the move to
establish teaching in the hospitals met with serious problems and inter-
minable delays, a wide measure of agreement existed at first in Paris on
the new hospital role in teaching. Midwives, too, were to be given more
practical training. A new school for them in Paris, according to John
Green Crosse, was preparing "five hundred well-educated women . . . to
practise midwifery in different parts of France."[11]

Philippe Pinel, one of the professors in the new School of Health,
found little disagreement with his declaration that "the healing art should
be taught only in hospitals . . . [where] one can follow the evolution and
progress of several illnesses at the same time."[12] His colleague in the same
school, Antoine Fourcroy, likewise found little dissent when he told the
National Convention that in the future students "will do . . . dissections,
operations, and bandaging" and when he gave the new pedagogy its
most memorable slogan: "little reading, much seeing, and much
doing."[13]

9. For prerevolutionary calls for practical training in medicine, see the plan of Claude-
François Duchanoy and Jean-Baptiste Jumelin, "Memoire sur l'utilité d'une école clinique
en médecine," *Observations sur la physique, sur l'histoire naturelle et les arts* 13 (1778) (supplement): 227–86. Other suggestions for reform can be found in G. C. Wurtz, *Mémoire sur
l'établissement des écoles de médecine pratique à former dans les principaux hôpitaux civils de
la France* (Paris: Didot and Barrois, 1784); Nicolas Chambon de Montaux, *Moyens de rendre les hôpitaux plus utiles à la nation* (Paris, 1787); and François Thiery, *Voeux d'un patriote sur la médecine en France* (Paris: Garney, 1789).

10. Mireille Wiriot, "L'enseignement clinique dans les hôpitaux de Paris entre 1794 et
1848" (med. diss., University of Paris, 1970), 30–32.

11. John Greene Crosse, *Sketches of the Medical School of Paris* (London: J. Callow,
1815), 186–88.

12. Philippe Pinel, *The Clinical Training of Doctors: An Essay of 1793*, ed. Dora B.
Weiner (Baltimore: Johns Hopkins University Press, 1980), 67. For a later and more ex-
plicit description of Pinel's ideas on clinical teaching, see his *La médecine clinique rendue
plus précise et plus exacte par l'application de l'analyse, ou recueil et résultat d'observations sur
les maladies aiguës, faite à la salpêtrière*, 3rd ed. (Paris: J. A. Brosson, 1815).

13. M. J. Guilaume, ed., *Procès-verbaux du comité d'instruction publique de la convention
nationale*, 6 vols. (Paris: Imprimerie nationale, 1891–1904), 4:980.

But how much did the students actually see and do in the hospitals of revolutionary France? Was their clinical experience confined to watching what their teachers did at the bedside, or did the students actually perform, under supervision, the medical procedures themselves? According to the course announcements at Montpellier, the clinical professor was to "examine each patient with great care, having placed the pupils conveniently around the bed."[14] Nothing was said about allowing students to examine the patient. As the number of students doubled and tripled, the intention to give practical instruction to each student at the bedside foundered on the rock of sheer numbers. Even after dividing the practical classes into smaller groups, the "multitude of pupils" around each professor, according to Cabanis, "makes their instruction impossible." "How can one conduct one hundred fifty, or two hundred pupils to a sickbed?" he asked. "How do you permit them to observe and to touch in a leisurely way? It cannot be done. The pupils see nothing, learn nothing, and the patients are terribly disturbed and exhausted." The need for more teachers and more sections, especially in Paris, Cabanis told the Council of Five Hundred in 1798, was acute.[15]

In Montpellier and Strasbourg as well as in Paris, the schools and hospitals were in reality ill prepared for the momentous changes ordered by the government. The terrible disorganization and dislocations of wartime made impossible the smooth functioning of the new clinics. A shortage of beds at the Hôtel-Dieu in Paris continued to force some patients into the same bed; teaching at the Charité could not be reorganized until 1799; and students were often too "disoriented" or poorly prepared to take advantage of the new opportunities. "No program or direction [for students] existed," according to one account, "the medical courses were not approved, the students [were] abandoned to their inexperience, following lectures without order, without method, at the mercy of fancy or caprice."[16] By the turn of the century, writes Laurence Brockliss, "the program continued to offer no real practical instruction in medicine . . . [without] resorting to private courses for . . . direct contact with patients."[17]

But the new teaching had some striking successes, especially in the private courses that sprang up everywhere after 1795, and also in the *externat* and *internat* programs offered after 1803 to selected students in the hospitals. In the small bedside *conférence* of advanced students and their teacher, in which the aspiring physician could try out his own ideas about diagnosis and treatment, the French system of clinical medicine reached

14. *Programmes des cours d'enseignement dans l'école de santé de Montpellier* (Paris: Imprimerie des sciences et arts, [1796]), 46–47.

15. P. G. J. Cabanis, "Rapport fait au conseil des cinq-cents sur l'organisation des écoles de médecine," in *Oeuvres completes* (Paris: Bossanges, 1823), 380–82.

16. Wiriot, "L'enseignement clinique," 34–35.

17. Laurence Brockliss, "L'enseignement médical et la révolution," *Histoire de l'education* 42 (1989): 102.

its apogee.[18] Here were brought together the new anatomical conceptualization of disease, the brilliant techniques of percussion and auscultation pioneered in France after 1800, the varied resources of a large hospital, and Enlightenment ideas about learning by doing. Desault had brought students of surgery into the care and treatment of patients as early as the 1780s; Corvisart now taught them the better use of the senses in physical examination; and Pinel, through his private courses at the Salpêtrière, involved students in the search for effective diagnosis and treatment. All three organized their teaching around the hospital bed, the teaching auditorium, and the deadhouse. None of the teaching was completely new, but the revolutionary authorities' emphasis on the new pedagogy, especially the opening of the great hospitals to student teaching, made Paris after 1815 the most sought-after center for practical training in the medical world.[19]

A key issue from the outset was the relationship between the medical faculty and the hospital clinic. The Paris school sought repeatedly to control the teaching in the hospitals, arguing that "the Clinics can only be made useful for education by making them independent of any administration other than the School." Clinics should be organized as in Holland and the German schools as part of the educational structure, the professors asserted, for they were "the laboratory of a clinical teacher." But in the ensuing battle between the faculty and the newly created hospital administration of Paris, the absence of funds to create a separate set of clinics for the medical school and the continuing distrust of academic authority caused the Paris school, in the words of one authority, to "lose the struggle and France never had its university clinics."[20] It also widened the breach in clinical teaching between France and Germany that had been opened in the eighteenth century by the creation of small clinics under faculty control in the German universities.

The French system of teaching medicine, now anchored in the hospitals of Paris, came to resemble more and more the hospital instruction of contemporary London. In both cases, the academic authorities exercised

18. L. S. Jacyna, "Au Lit des Malades: A. F. Chomel's Clinic at the Charité, 1828–9," *Medical History* 33 (1989): 422.

19. Much of this discussion is based on an unpublished paper by Gabriel Richet, to whom I am indebted for his kindness: "Le sens de la responsabilité médicale: Son acquisition par la pedagogie clinique"; and on Marie-José Imbault-Huart, "Concepts and Realities of the Beginning of Clinical Teaching in France in the Late 18th and Early 19th Centuries," in *Clinical Teaching, Past and Present*, vol. 21, ed. H. Beukers and J. Moll (Amsterdam: *Clio Medica*, 1987–1988), esp. 61–67. Good contemporary descriptions of teaching in the French clinics can be found in S. G. B. Bruté, *Essai sur l'histoire et les avantages des institutions cliniques* (Paris: Belin, 1803), esp. 75–92; and F. S. Ratier, "Coup d'oeil sur les cliniques médicales de la faculté de médecine de Paris," *Archives générales de médecine* 13 (1827): 321–34; 14 (1827): 161–85, 559–86; 15 (1827): 247–66; 16 (1828): 215–32; 17 (1827): 37–54. Ratier's articles describe the clinics of Laennec, Chomel, Recamier, Cullerier, and Baron.

20. Imbault-Huart, "Concepts and Realities of Clinical Teaching," 64.

little control over clinical teaching, especially when compared with those in Vienna or Berlin. On both sides of the English Channel, a heavy emphasis was placed on practical learning over purely academic instruction. The small group of interns and externs who gained most from the openness of the Paris hospitals (only the former lived in the hospitals) was matched in London by the handful of dressers, clerks, and house officers who learned their crafts in the larger hospitals. Both systems were elitist and benefited most a small portion of all students of medicine in the two capitals. Indeed, as George Weisz wrote, "formal clinical instruction was, to all intents and purposes, non-existent for those not fortunate enough to be appointed interns and externs."[21]

In Britain also, the principal means of instruction for most students remained the didactic lecture with greater or fewer demonstrations in the hospital amphitheater, and hands-on experience in dealing with patients was obtained for the most part privately and on the student's own initiative.

Hospital or Policlinic?

The development of the clinical lecture in the hospital amphitheater, in the view of a modern authority, was a deadly blow to bedside teaching.[22] It quickly became a central feature of French clinical teaching (*la leçon*), and by 1816 André Duméril was praising the medical "amphitheater as being for us what the school of the city of Ptolemy was to the ancient world."[23] The growing numbers of students flocking to Paris made largely impracticable the kind of personal bedside-teaching that the reformers of 1794 envisioned, so that the demonstrative lecture became the principal source of instruction for many. "Three-fourths of the pupils" in the large clinics of Paris, charged the Strasbourg lecturer Victor Stoeber in a prize-winning essay of 1829, "find it impossible to follow the professor." More schools of medicine, more faculty members, and fewer students would be required if French teaching were to be effective.

In such foreign cities as Edinburgh, Berlin, and Halle, wrote Stoeber, a form of clinical teaching unknown in France was far more effective in introducing students to the practice of medicine. The *policlinic* (ambulatory clinic) of the German university, and later the small inpatient clinic, gave students more hands-on experience with patients, he declared, than

21. George Weisz, "Reform and Conflict in French Medical Education, 1870–1914," in *The Organization of Science and Technology in France, 1808–1914*, ed. Robert Fox and George Weisz (Cambridge: Cambridge University Press, 1980), 64.

22. Hans E. Renschler, *Die Praxisphase im Medizinstudium* (Berlin: Springer, 1987), 10, 31.

23. Cited in *Progrès médical* 15 (1938): 8.

was possible in the overcrowded hospitals of France. The student in the German clinic, said Stoeber, thus came face to face with the daily run-of-the-mill afflictions that he would later meet in practice and was not distracted by the bewildering numbers of patients in a hospital ward.[24]

A description of the practical training given German students after 1815 in the twenty-eight-bed clinic at Heidelberg was provided by its director, Johann Wilhelm Conradi. Students accepted for clinical teaching, he wrote, had to be "decent, serious, not callous but friendly, patient, and sympathetic to the sick." They were then given responsibility for certain patients, examined them, made a diagnosis and a prognosis, and determined the treatment to be given. They wrote the prescriptions, showed them to the director, and kept a daily record of changes in the patient. They had also to see that prescribed treatments—mineral baths, massages, injections, bloodletting, or catheterization—were carried out. Finally, if the patient died, they had to perform the autopsy in the presence of the director or his assistant.[25]

The French pioneers in clinical medicine, especially in Paris—d'Azyr, Pinel, Cabanis, Corvisart—all paid tribute to their forerunners in Germany—as well as in Italy, Holland, and Great Britain—as they sought to create manageable academically based units of practical teaching for an entire country. Before the Revolution, C. G. Wurtz had praised Vienna, in particular, for its teaching clinics in which "teaching is not by words but by deeds."[26] In his influential report of 1790, d'Azyr, citing the pressing need in France for practical training, argued that such teaching already existed in the clinics at Göttingen, Leyden, and Edinburgh.[27] But in preparing a plan to give trained medical care to twenty million "citizen-patients," as Dora Weiner reminds us, d'Azyr was not free to copy the personalized methods of the small German or Dutch clinic.[28] A true clinical school, nevertheless, declared Cabanis, must be an integral part of a university, as it was in Vienna and Edinburgh.[29] Pinel, too, cited these cities when setting the ideal size of a teaching ward at no more than fifteen or twenty—the size of a German university clinic—and even this

24. Victor Stoeber, *De l'organisation médicale en France* (Paris: Levrault, 1830), 44–47. For an early example of an ambulatory clinic for the poor, where teaching was carried out for medical students as well as practical surgeons and midwives, see Christian Gottlieb Hofmann, *Erste Nachicht von der Anstalt für arme Kranke zu Altdorf im Nürnbergischen* (Altdorf: George Peter Monath, 1787), 9; and the further annual reports.

25. Johann Wilhelm Conradi, *Uber das medicinisch–klinische Institut in dem akademischen Hospitale in Heidelberg* (Heidelberg: Mohr and Winter, 1817), 10–14. A similar contemporary description of clinical teaching in Germany can be found in D. Nasse, *Von dem Krankenhause für Bildung angehender Artzte zu Halle* (Halle: Rengerschen Buchhandlung, 1816), 25–34.

26. Wurtz, *Memoire*, 6.

27. *Nouveau plan*, 16.

28. Dora B. Weiner to me, March 21, 1994.

29. Cabanis, *Coup d'oeil*, 356–59.

number was "very demanding."[30] But by the early nineteenth century, clinics of so small a size were largely unknown in Paris, if not in the provinces, and the *leçon* was delivered before increasing numbers of students.

Outside the official clinics, a considerable amount of hands-on training was given privately in such hospitals as the Saltpêtrière, where Pinel taught in a thirty-bed ward, the Enfants malades, the Maternité, and the Pitié. Courses were also held in anatomical theaters, the Collège de France, the Academy of Sciences, and in dispensaries and special sessions organized by the students themselves. It was these largely private courses that attracted so many students, including visitors from Britain, Germany, and America.

In the German-speaking nations, where clinics were generally much smaller, the emphasis from the beginning was on the pedagogical advantage of hands-on experience at the bedside. "What I understand by a surgical and ophthalmological clinic," explained the Prussian educational minister, Johann Rust, in 1817, "is a place of practical teaching, where the student not only sees and observes how the patient is treated, but where he also treats every surgical and ophthalmological case himself [and] makes up the prescriptions."[31]

By this time, a divergence in practical teaching had opened in the German states between the southern, largely Catholic states, where a tradition of charity in large hospitals had led to the creation of hospital clinics in such university cities as Vienna, Prague, Bamberg, and Würzburg, and in the north German Protestant states, where universities located in small towns such as Halle, Jena, and Göttingen, had organized a system of outpatient visits (*Polikliniken*) and then stationary clinics with six to twelve beds. Since hospital administrators in Germany, as in France and Britain, often resisted the spread of hospital teaching, the university clinic or *Poliklinik* was the favored site for clinical instruction among German medical professors. With the founding of the University of Berlin in 1810, academic authorities sought to combine both methods of instruction by creating their own stationary clinics and policlinics and also using, as far as possible, the rich resources of the giant Charité hospital.[32]

30. Pinel, *Clinical Training of Doctors*, 78. See also Johann V. von Hildenbrand, *Discours preliminaire sur l'histoire des cliniques* (Paris, 1830), esp. 55–77; Johann V. von Hildenbrand, *Médecine pratique* (Paris: Gabon, 1828), 57–67; and the article by Moreau de la Sarthe, "Médecine," *Encyclopédie methodique* 7 (1816): 53–70.

31. Johann Rust, "Uber den Zweck und die Einrichtung ärztlich-praktischer Lehranstalten," *Aufsätze und Abhandlungen aus dem Gebiete der Medicin, Chirurgie und Staatsarzneikunde,* 3 vols. (Berlin, 1840), 3:426.

32. I am grateful to both Axel Karenberg and Johanna Bleker for sending me helpful materials. Karenberg provided a summary of his forthcoming *Habilitationsschrift* on the subject, as well as his article "Osterreichische und deutsche Einflüsse während der Gründung der ersten Hochschulkliniken in Breslau (1810–1850)," *Würzburger medizinhistorische Mitteilungen* 10 (1992): 433–41; and Bleker sent an important paper, "'Der einzig Wahre Weg, brauchbare Männer zu bilden'—Der medizinisch–klinische Unterricht an der Berliner Universität, 1810–1850," to be published in *Abhandlungen der Geschichte der Medizin und der Naturwissenschaften.*

By the early nineteenth century, the advantages and disadvantages of both types of clinic were under intense scrutiny in the German medical world. A good hospital, wrote Philipp Horsch of Würzburg in 1807, can offer to students a wide variety of patients' illnesses and close control over the patients' diet and medications, whereas a university clinic, on the other hand, enabled the students to know their patients better and to see common illnesses on a daily basis.[33]

For Christoph Hufeland, a leader of the policlinic movement, what was important was the nature of the teaching, not whether it took place in a hospital or a small clinic. The advantage of the university clinic lay in its intimate size and personalized teaching, in which the students were more than "simply spectators." For the young practitioner, Hufeland explained, the critical need was for hands-on experience with a few patients, not a mere glimpse of a large number of diseases and procedures in a hospital. Too often, the hospital-trained student had his head filled with a "chaos of sense impressions" that lacked any connection or meaning.

In the small clinic at Jena, Hufeland told his readers, the student could see patients as individuals, perhaps visit them in their homes, and not see them merely as "objects" of instruction, as they did in the hospitals. The student cared for these people as though they were his own patients. At its best the small clinic was a moral institution that taught the young physician respect and caring for others, even the most poverty stricken, as it guided him in learning the art and science of medicine.[34]

Like Hufeland, many German physicians insisted on the pedagogical superiority of the small clinic to the hospital medicine of Paris and to the commercial hospitals of London. Many of the German universities, of course, had no financial means to support a larger enterprise. In a number of them, bedside teaching was still "non-existent, chaotic, or suffering from severe drawbacks." Why did German clinical experience develop as it did? Primarily because, wrote Axel Karenberg in an unpublished study, of "the chronic lack of capital in the German states" and the low priority given to "academic hospitals" by state authorities, which made it necessary for university clinicians to begin slowly and improvise wherever possible.[35] Whatever the reason, the relatively large amount of attention given to the individual student in a number of the universities created a model that was the envy of students elsewhere.

Streams of German visitors to Paris, London, and other places returned to write about their surprise and disappointment in finding how small a

---

33. Horsch, *Uber die Bildung des Arztes und des Klinikers*, 36–43.

34. Christoph W. Hufeland, "Nachrichten von der medizinisch–chirurgischen Krankenanstalt zu Jena, nebst einer Vergleichung der klinischen und Hospitalanstalten überhaupt," *Journal der practischen Heilkunde* 3 (1797): 528–66.

35. Axel Karenberg, "Die Kliniken an den Universitäten der deutschen Kleinstaaten," unpublished manuscript, 1991, 92–93.

role students played in the large hospitals.[36] Many recognized, of course, that it was the small size of the German medical school that made possible the more intensive education at the bedside and the close contacts between teachers and students that they valued.

"The French have no idea of a clinic," declared the Halle surgeon Carl Dzondi, who was commissioned by the Prussian government to survey French and British schools in 1821, "there is a huge difference between a hospital and a clinic. Only the former is found in Paris, nowhere the latter." In the larger hospitals, such as the Hôtel-Dieu, according to Dzondi, one would search in vain for a small teaching clinic of the sort found in Vienna. "When the physician must see 100, 200, 300 patients in a period of 1–2–3 hours and order food and medicines for them, how is it possible that he can spend time at the bedside and give instruction?"

Particularly noticeable to Dzondi was the absence in Paris of opportunity for the average student to take any part in examining patients and performing minor procedures. Even in the clinical lecture the student was usually too far away to see anything, let alone closely observe. As for obstetrics, the French medical student, unlike the French midwife, received no practical instruction at all in the official curriculum. Only in the school at Strasbourg, which Dzondi found to be more like German than French schools, did he find "clinical institutions [where] the professor teaches, in part, at the bedside."[37]

A German-trained practitioner from Copenhagen left a similar description of the clinical training of students in the hospitals of Paris. His account of the clinic of the surgeon Joseph Claude Récamier furnishes an insight into the actual sequence of teaching in a well-known clinic of the mid-1820s:[38]

> The students do not learn very much at the bedside from [Récamier]: for he moves too fast from one bed to another, making no comment as he goes, and examines and prescribes in so low a voice that no one can hear a word if not close by. Afterward, however, everyone gathers in the conference room, adorned with the portraits of Bichat, Desault, and others, and here Récamier conducts the real clinic; i.e., describing, with the ward book in his hands, the most re-

---

36. See Ursula Geigenmüller, "Aussagen über die französische Medizin der Jahre 1820–1847 in Reiseberichten deutscher Ärzte" (dental diss., Free University of Berlin, 1985), 39–43; Eckart Buchholz, "Grossbritannische Reiseeindrücke deutscher und österreichischer Ärzte von 1750 bis 1810" (med. diss., University of Frankfurt am Main, 1960), 82–92; and Friedrich-Wilhelm Bayer, "Reisen deutscher Ärzte ins Ausland (1750–1850)," *Abhandlungen zur Geschichte der Medizin und der Naturwissenschaften* 20 (1937): esp. 16–23.

37. Although I used the Dzondi report in the GSPK, Merseburg (Rep. 76 V f Lit. D Nr. 2), I relied here on Hans-Theodor Koch, "Zwei Studienreisen des halleschen Chirurgen Carl Heinrich Dzondi (1770–1835) nach Paris (1821) und nach Holland, England, Schottland und Irland (1822), *Acta Historica Leopoldina* 2 (1905): 148–51, 159.

38. D. C. Otto, *Reise durch die Schweiz, Italien, Grossbrittanien und Holland,* 2 vols. (Hamburg: August Campe, 1825), 1:49–50.

markable cases and speaks of the most important and striking pathological and therapeutic indications. This is very instructive[,] for Récamier's lecture is not only lively and informed but interesting and
fascinating. But this method has the disadvantage that the attention
of the audience is not as concentrated as it is at the bedside, since
one can often not remember the patients, nor see for himself on the
spot.

Clinical Teaching in Britain and America

The clinical teaching of Great Britain in the early nineteenth century was
criticized even more by German educators than was that of France. "The
form and manner in which the clinic [at Edinburgh] is held," said the
Jena visitor Johann Albers, "I do not like at all; for example, the professor
examines the patient himself, dictating in English to the surrounding students, who write down what he says with the greatest scrupulousness,
without perhaps even looking at the patient." How much better was the
practice in Vienna or Jena, he declared, in which "the beginning physician not only examines the patient, but makes a diagnosis and suggests a
remedy."[39] Joseph Frank expressed a similar reaction in remarking on the
"too small part" played by Edinburgh students in their own education.[40]

A German physician living in London in 1827 likewise complained of
the remote and impersonal teaching he found in the British capital. He
found London teaching "entirely wanting in the close supervision of students' activity, the bedside interchanges between teacher and students,
and the responsibility given to students for individual patients."[41]

In 1821, Robert Graves, just returned to Dublin from lengthy studies
in Göttingen and Berlin, advocated the adoption of the German system
of clinical teaching in Britain. The teaching in Paris, he told his students,
though better than in Great Britain, was still "expostulatory" rather than
practical and was characterized too much by "long harangues" and little
learning by the students.[42] Instruction at Edinburgh was likewise lacking
because the learner "is never obliged to exercise his own judgment in distinguishing diseases, and has no opportunity of trying his skill in their
care." Both the French and British systems, Graves charged, resulted in
"a practitioner who has never practiced." The German system, by con-

39. Johann A. Albers, "Die Krankenanstalten und Lehrschulen der Arzneykunde zu
London, Edinburgh, Bath und Wien betreffend," in William Blizard, *Vorschläge zur
Verbesserung der Hospitäler und anderer mildthätigen Anstalten*, trans. from English (Jena,
1799), 108.

40. Joseph Frank, *Reise nach Paris, London, und einem grossen Theile des übrigen Englands und Schottlands*, 2 vols. (Vienna: Camesinaische Buchhandlung, 1804), 2:224–27.

41. C. M. Kind, "On Medical Education in the German Universities," *Lancet* 1 (1827):
252–57.

42. David Riesman, "The Dublin Medical School and Its Influence upon Medicine in
America," *Annals of Medical History* 4 (1922): 88.

trast, which he introduced at Meath Hospital in Dublin in 1821, was aimed at giving the student maximum freedom, under reasonable supervision, to learn the actual techniques as well as the theory of medicine.[43]

Most British teachers, admiring what little they knew about the German clinic, did not believe that it could take root in British soil. In testimony before a royal commission in 1826, the Edinburgh professor Andrew Duncan Jr., after describing the bedside teaching of "the celebrated Dr. Frank in Vienna," remarked that "such a plan of instruction is quite incompatible with the circumstances of this school, and I very much doubt if the managers of our Infirmary would permit it." In central Europe, he told the commission, the professor controlled everything relating to clinical instruction, but "we could not do that here." For one thing, the size of the clinical classes in Scotland made them "unwieldy" for bedside training, and so he advised students to pick out a few patients and attempt to follow them.[44]

A former student testified at the same hearing that "I attended two courses of clinical medicine at [Edinburgh] and I really profited very little by them." Clinical visits, he pointed out, were limited to one hour; few questions were ever put to the patients; and the time "might as well be [spent] in the lecture-room as by the bedside of the patient."[45] Students at Glasgow likewise complained of the acute need for more hours of hospital attendance and more contact with patients, but as they were in Ed-

43. Robert J. Graves, "On Clinical Instruction, with a Comparative Estimate of the Mode in which it is conducted in the British and Continental Schools," *London Medical Gazette* 10 (1832): 404–6. Although this article was published in 1832, Graves makes clear that the lectures were first given at Meath Hospital in 1821. Graves continued for many decades to call for fundamental reform in British clinical teaching but regarded his campaign as a failure. See his *Clinical Lectures on the Practice of Medicine*, 2 vols. (London: Sydenham Society, 1884), 1:13. An American doctor in Berlin in 1823 was likewise impressed by the clinical training there: "At a regular hour daily, each [clinical] professor meets his pupils in the class-room, where they place themselves around a large table, leaving a seat for the patients, who are introduced separately from an antichamber. . . . When the patient is seated, the professor calls upon any one pupil to examine him, and ascertain the disease, which being done, the pupil declares aloud, in the Latin tongue, his diagnostic, prognostic, and methodus curandi, when the professor, if necessary, interrogates both the patient and pupil, and explains the disease in all its bearings; after which, the pupil writes the prescription, reads it to the class, and hands it to the professor for his signature, who gives it to the patient to carry to the apothecary. . . . All the pupils take a patient in rotation, and are expected to attend every morning . . . to report the state of the patient under his [*sic*] charge. . . . Every student must have passed through the above clinical discipline, before he can become a candidate for graduation. . . . It is obvious . . . that no physician of the University of Berlin can be ignorant of the practical part of his profession." T. F. Andrews, "An Account of the Medical Institutions of Berlin," *American Medical Record* 6 (1823): 475–76.

44. Royal Commission, *Evidence, Oral and Documentary, taken and received by the Commissioners appointed by His Majesty George IV, July 23d, 1826; and re-appointed by His Majesty William IV, October 12th, 1830; for visiting the Universities of Scotland*, 4 vols. (London: His Majesty's Stationery Office, 1837), 1:224–25.

45. Ibid., 358.

inburgh, the authorities were reluctant to risk antagonizing the public by increasing the presence and responsibility of students.[46]

These constraints on the student role in British hospitals, writes Guenter Risse, were "perhaps the most serious flaw of clinical instruction."[47] Although they did not prevent Edinburgh from becoming a leading medical school in the eighteenth century, they did become an increasing handicap in the face of new alternatives in Paris and central Europe.

In London, which was the principal site of clinical teaching in Britain, the student's place in the hospital was undergoing important changes but was not overseen by any educational authority. The teaching program of 1800, according to Susan Lawrence, "had a loose overlying structure . . . far more dispersed than [in] the universities at Edinburgh or Paris."[48] Sporadic clinical lectures supplementing the walks on the wards did not provide students with the kind of correlation among academic teaching, clinical lectures, and ward visits that the Edinburgh and continental systems did. Each London student made his own decisions concerning his studies, subject only to the limitations of his previous training, the availability of courses, and the size of his purse.

The portrait of a medical student randomly walking the wards, spending a few hours in dissection, rushing to an operation or postmortem, and sandwiching in lectures in dispersed locations left little room for organized academic study. "If I were speaking to students in Edinburgh, Paris, Vienna, or Pavia," Alexander Marcet told Guy's Hospital students in 1818, "it would not be necessary to discuss the Clinical department as the most important part of medical education." But in London, he continued, because of the overriding emphasis on surgery and anatomical studies and the infrequent visits by physicians to the hospitals, "it is nearly impossible to explain at the bedside the particulars of a case."[49]

Clinical instruction of the kind commonplace on the continent, noted Marcet, was "scarcely known" in London. Whereas students in London and elsewhere were allowed in some circumstances to "touch the patient," this did not play the role in educating students that it did in France or Germany. Before Graves came to Dublin, said his colleague William Stokes, the student was "unassisted, undirected, left to grope his way as best he could . . . no one cared to instruct him, to show him how to teach himself, [or] to

46. Royal Infirmary of Glasgow, Minutes, May 9 and August 1, 1831, Special Collections, University of Glasgow Library.

47. Guenter B. Risse, *Hospital Life in Enlightenment Scotland: Care and Teaching at the Royal Infirmary of Edinburgh* (Cambridge: Cambridge University Press, 1986), 273.

48. Susan C. Lawrence, "Science and Medicine at the London Hospitals: The Development of Teaching and Research, 1750–1815" (Ph.D. diss., University of Toronto, 1985), 405.

49. Alexander Marcet, *Some Remarks on Clinical Lectures, being the Substance of an Introductory Lecture delivered at Guy's Hospital, on the 27th of January 1818* (London: G. Woodfall, 1818), 5–6.

make him familiar with bedside medicine."[50] A Hannover physician visiting London as late as 1838 wrote that "the examinations of patients are brief, and afford little instruction to the pupil . . . little regard is had for him; at least not so much as . . . [occurs] at the bedside in German practice."[51]

If the German student of the early nineteenth century was afforded in some cases the greatest amount of contact with patients and the French student was limited only by the large size of his classes, the British student was frequently barred altogether from close contact with patients out of concern for control of the hospital and the patients' privacy.

The British and American outpatient dispensary of the late eighteenth century, in which students could gain some direct experience in treating patients, was an alternative to the hospital. It resembled in many ways the ambulatory or outpatient program of the German clinics. Such clinics (*ambulanten Kliniken*) had been known for decades in the university towns of Germany. A report of 1764, for example, showed that Rudolf Vogel of Göttingen was holding clinics for the poor on Wednesday and Sunday evenings, at which students took part in the examination and treatment of patients. Similar arrangements existed in such university communities as Tübingen, Erlangen, Marburg, and Heidelberg. Students not only assisted in the treatment of ambulatory patients but also accompanied the professor to the homes of patients.[52]

In Britain, where the first general dispensary was started in London in 1770, concern for teaching students was likewise from the beginning an important part of the plan. Indeed, the founder of the venture, the Quaker John Coakley Lettsom, argued that a much closer student–teacher relationship was possible in a dispensary than in a hospital. The dispensary, he wrote, offered the student "an opportunity of watching a disease from the moment of its commencement" and not only, as in the hospital, when "it is considerably advanced" and "in an artificial situation."[53] At least forty such dispensaries, many of them providing clinical teaching to students, were in existence by the end of the century, and by the early 1830s one in every six general practitioners (apothecaries) in Britain was being trained in a dispensary.[54]

50. William Stokes, *Studies in Physiology and Medicine by the Late Robert James Graves, F.R.S.* (London: John Churchill, 1863), xxiii.

51. Adolph Muehry, *Observations on the Comparative State of Medicine in France, England, and Germany* (Philadelphia: A. Waldie, 1838), 26.

52. Dieter Jetter, "Die ersten Universitätskliniken westdeutscher Staaten," *Deutsche medizinische Wochenschrift* 87 (1962): 2038–41. "Almost always," writes Professor Jetter, "the poor house and practice among the poor are the crystallization points of practical medical education" (p. 2038).

53. Ulrich Tröhler, "The Doctor as Naturalist: The Idea and Practice of Clinical Teaching and Research in British Policlinics, 1770–1850," *Clinical Teaching, Past and Present*, vol. 21, ed. H. Beukers and J. Moll (Amsterdam: *Clio Medica*, 1987–88), 23–27.

54. I. S. Loudon, "The Origins and Growth of the Dispensary Movement in England," *Bulletin of the History of Medicine* 55 (1981): 424–25; Tröhler, "Doctor as Naturalist," 26. See also I. S. Loudon, "Historical Importance of Outpatients," *British Medical Journal* (1978): 974–77.

Clinical education in North America was as haphazard and separated from medical schools as it was in England. Apprenticeship, which had grown steadily in the years since the Revolution, remained the dominant path to practical training, but a host of new dispensaries, outpatient clinics, private courses, and small urban hospitals were becoming available by the 1820s. By this time, a number of new medical schools, some loosely tied to a liberal arts college, were offering lectures to supplement the apprenticeship and other practical training that were seen as the real heart of medical teaching. The education of doctors was only partly their responsibility, and most were quite satisfied with their limited role.

By 1832, according to the *American Almanac,* twenty medical schools had spread along the Atlantic seaboard from Maine to Georgia.[55] A number of them, especially in the rural areas, operated dispensaries or outpatient clinics as a means of providing a modicum of supervised clinical experience. "The great value of the dispensary," writes Dale Smith, "was never the major [cases] but rather the daily contact with injuries and diseases seen by the general practitioner."[56] For a number of decades, the outpatient dispensary, serving primarily the poor but sometimes the faculty's own patients, was a distinctive feature of the American medical college.

Where urban hospitals existed, as in Philadelphia and New York (and later Boston), the same nagging problems of control and resistance to the students' participation in treating patients plagued educators as they did in Great Britain. The authorities at the College of Philadelphia, for example, who early required students to attend lectures and visit wards at the Pennsylvania Hospital, dropped the requirement as unworkable in 1789 and were only intermittently able thereafter to demand hospital attendance before graduation. Some students were allowed to observe procedures at the bedside in the Philadelphia Almshouse, where "students of good character" were allowed to be present at cases of labor.[57] In 1817, a pioneering effort to establish a teaching unit in the wards of the Pennsylvania Hospital was turned down, the first defeat "in a long struggle by American medical schools to gain control of teaching facilities in hospitals."[58] In New York, where clinical teaching remained optional for a medical degree, some lectures were given at first in the presence of patients in the wards. As the number of students grew larger after 1810, however, the lectures were given in large amphitheaters similar to those in Europe.

---

55. *American Almanac and Repository of Useful Knowledge, 1832* (Boston: Charles Bowen, 1832), 167.

56. Smith, "Emergence of Organized Clinical Instruction," 168. I am indebted to Professor Smith's work for much of the material on which this and the following two paragraphs are based.

57. Joseph Carson, *A History of the Medical Department of the University of Pennsylvania from Its Founding in 1765* (Philadelphia: Lindsay and Blackston, 1869), 196.

58. George W. Corner, *Two Centuries of Medicine: A History of the School of Medicine, University of Pennsylvania* (Philadelphia: Lippincott, 1965), 89.

Clinical training outside the medical school thus became the rule in North America as it was in the former mother country. In Philadelphia, a private school was founded in 1817 to give students clinical and didactic instruction not available in the medical schools. Similar private schools were flourishing in Boston and New York a decade later. All in all, an "amazing range" of clinical opportunities, according to Smith, existed in North America by 1830, spread over hospitals, dispensaries, private schools, almshouses, and physicians' homes but, as they were in Britain and France, only loosely tied to the academic instruction given in medical schools.[59] Even in America's "grandest schools," complained the Philadelphia physician Reynell Coates in 1835, with some exaggeration, the catch and catch-can arrangements of clinical and academic study were more "chaotic" than "in any other country."[60]

Outside the Walls of Academe

Much of what was regarded by 1820 as the most important part of medical training in Europe and America was thus taking place apart from formal medical education. An uneasy truce marked the relationship of the newer practical courses to the academic learning that had so long dominated the medical curriculum. To create a more flexible structure to accommodate the practical impulse in medicine, new clinical forms outside academic institutions were devised that often stood in tense relationship to the theoretical instruction of the classroom.

In Germany, because of the special circumstances in small university towns, this tension was markedly less because of the professors' role in running the clinics. A "deliberately aggressive orientation toward practical medicine," to use Thomas Broman's phrase, marked the new University of Berlin (1810), and a loose equilibrium between theory and practice was reached in most of the German schools.[61] Outside Germany, however, a sharp divide separated the increasingly scientific teaching of the classroom and the more practical instruction of the clinic, sparking frequent antagonisms between academically schooled physicians and those trained in practical medicine. "Those branches of Med Science, wh. are improved only by observation of facts, have been much advanced of late years—Experimental Physiology, Pharmacy, Morbid Anatomy, Diagnosis of morbid lesions," wrote the Edinburgh practitioner W. P. Allison in his travel diary in 1825, "but the knowledge of them goes but little way, in promoting useful *practise*."[62] In Britain, as in France and Amer-

59. Smith, "Emergence of Organized Clinical Instruction," 176.

60. Reynell Coates, *Oration on the Defects of the Present System of Medical Instruction in the United States* (Philadelphia: James Kay, 1835), 26.

61. Thomas Broman, "University Reform in Medical Thought at the End of the Eighteenth Century," *Osiris* 5 (1989): 47.

62. W. P. Allison, Travel diary, London and France, 1825, Allison Papers, Royal College of Physicians of Edinburgh. Emphasis in original.

ica, the small, private classes in practical medicine, making frequent use of patients and cadavers, drove many students away from the theoretical lectures of the medical professors.

Academic teachers of medicine in every country understandably tried to put as much distance as possible between their own programs for physicians and the practical courses that lacked theoretical or scientific content. More and more, they staked their claims of superiority on the scientific understanding of disease. Studies in "morbid anatomy," experimental physiology, and medical chemistry, all based on careful observation and the growing use of measurement, stimulated the conviction that disease was best studied (and taught) by relating what was seen or felt in the patient to the pathological changes found at autopsy. The close observation of physical signs, made more acute by auscultation and (after 1816) the stethoscope, was replacing, especially in France, the patient's own complaints as the principal source of bedside diagnosis. French savants, like their colleagues in Germany, taught that only a knowledge of underlying medical science could enable the physician to understand the physical changes in the body.

In Britain and America, however, the slow development of the academic component in medical education made it difficult to insist on such study as crucial to all medical practice. The continental distinction between the "pure physician" of the academy and the "general practitioner" outside was never as sharp in Anglo-America.

In both Germany and France, on the other hand, clear provision was being made by 1803 for training second-class practitioners outside the walls of academe. By this time, every German state, including the Hapsburg dominions, had created practical training schools for *Wundärzte* or *Landarzte* and also for midwives. In Württemberg, for example, practical surgeons outnumbered university physicians in 1806 by a ratio of three to one in one key district.[63] The curriculum at the three Bavarian *Landarzt* schools (Munich, Bamberg, Innsbruck) of 1809, which may serve as an example, stretched over six semesters and offered ten courses in anatomy, diagnosis, pharmacy, obstetrics, diet, medicine, and operative surgery. The teaching of surgery and medicine was formally fused. Each school, according to a royal edict, was "to create a special class of physicians who are trained exclusively in those things that concern application at the sickbed." Graduates must "acquire mechanical skill," be able to recognize "the commonly occurring diseases," and be kept away from "all contact with mere speculation and . . . scientific lectures."

On completion of his studies, the Bavarian practical student then had to spend two years in apprentice-type work (*biennium practicum*) "under the direction of an older physician." Every public hospital in the Bavarian cities affected was to set aside at least five beds for teaching the students,

63. Sabine Sander, *Handwerkchirurgen: Sozialgeschichte einer verdrängten Berufsgruppe* (Göttingen: Vandenhoeck & Ruprecht, 1989), p. 182, table 19.

with the teachers allowed to select the patients to fill them. As they did in the other German states, students of practical surgery shared classes in midwifery with the midwives in the hospitals or lying-in clinics. By 1810, more than three hundred students of practical medicine—a larger number than all those studying medicine in London or at the Bavarian universities of the time—were enrolled in these three schools.[64]

Other German states, even in these years of Romantic medicine, made similar provisions for practically trained doctors. The Saxon school at Dresden, for example, which attracted over a hundred students in 1810, was educating a number of well-known future physicians and surgeons in the early nineteenth century, including Carl Ferdinand von Graefe and Karl August Weinhold.[65] The Hapsburg rulers, too, supported five-year secondary schools for surgeon-practitioners in five cities throughout their domain.[66] In Prussia, practical surgeons, both civilian and military, and midwives were trained in the Charité hospital and at the Collegium Medico–Chirurgicum in Berlin, and in the 1820s four more practical schools were built in Münster, Breslau, Magdeburg, and Greifswald. These latter schools offered two to three years of intensely practical training to those preparing to serve rural communities or the army.[67]

All practical surgeons in Prussia, according to an ordinance of 1825, were required to complete a three-year course (or two years of practical experience in place of the third year), to know enough Latin to understand the pharmacopia, and to pass a series of demanding, weeks-long clinical examinations involving, among other things, the performance of operations on a cadaver and the diagnosis and treatment of two medical patients at the Charité.[68] A similar practical examination was required for licensure in Bavaria and other German states. In the case of midwives, thirty-one schools for their instruction were organized across Germany before 1820.[69]

64. Johannes M. Hautmann, "Die ärztliche Ausbildung im Königreich und im Freistaat Bayern, 1808–1980" (med. diss., Technical University of Munich, 1982), 4–5, 93. See also Carlos Lehmann, "Uber die Medizin an der Academia Ottoniana und Universitas Ottoniano–Fridericiana Bambergensis, 1735–1803" (med. diss., University of Erlangen–Nuremberg, 1967); Paul Böhmer, "Die medizinischen Schulen Bambergs in der ersten Hälfte des 19.Jahrhunderts" (med. diss., University of Erlangen–Nuremberg, 1970); and Erhard Grunwald, *Das niedere Medizinalpersonal im Bayern des 19.Jahrhunderts* (Munich: Demeter Verlag, 1990), 64–65, 80, 85.

65. V. Klimpel, "Zur chirurgischen Ausbildung am ehemaligen Dresdner Collegium Medico–Chirurgicum," *Zentralblatt für Chirurgie* 115 (1990): 181–84.

66. William Mackenzie, "Sketches of the Medical School of Vienna," *Quarterly Journal of Foreign Medicine and Surgery* 1 (1818–19): 34–35.

67. Rolf Winau, *Medizin in Berlin* (Berlin: Gruyter, 1987), 155.

68. *Reglement für die Staats-Prüfungen der Medicinal-Personen* (Berlin, 1825). A copy of these regulations is in GSPK, Merseburg, Akten der medizinischen Fakultät, 1502, N5, P5, Bd. 1.

69. Axel Karenberg, "Lernen am Bett der Schwangeren: Zur Typologie des Entbindungshauses in Deutschland (1728–1840)," *Zentralblatt für Gynäkologie* 113 (1991): 899–912.

Many of the students in these practical schools praised the close relationships they found between teachers and students, and also the opportunities for practical experience. A Swiss student at the medical–surgical institute in Zurich, for example, described in 1823 how he had been assigned to a sickroom in the local hospital, where he was given responsibility for reporting each day on the progress of his patients.[70] In Vienna, a student of practical surgery spent seven weeks in a private course in midwifery with the famous Johann Lucas Boër, where he examined pregnant women, was counseled by Boër at the bedside, and assisted in delivering babies.[71] Another of Boër's students wrote about how "extremely instructive" the teacher had been in personal talks, not only with the university and practical students, but "also with the student-midwives."[72]

In both Germany and France, the quality of medical training in these secondary schools, contrary to some later accounts, was often quite good. By 1820 the curriculum included most of the courses taught in the university; classes were kept small; the teaching cadre was often as large as at the universities; and students and teachers moved back and forth with surprising ease to university medical schools. "It is an open question," writes Claudia Huerkamp in reference to the German schools, "whether the education in the medical–surgical schools, as most physicians asserted, was really inferior to that of the universities."[73]

Similarly, with the exception of the minority of French students who enjoyed the benefit of private courses and hospital appointments, the education given in the *écoles secondaires* was not always inferior to that of the *écoles de médecine*. After all, the many large hospitals outside Paris offered practical students the same pedagogical advantages in learning medicine as those of the capital. "Young pupils will learn anatomy by dissecting," said Cabanis of the planned secondary schools for the provinces, "pharmacy by preparing remedies, [and] the practice of medicine by caring for the sick," all in the hospitals of every French city.[74]

At Bordeaux, for example, the *école secondaire* had a student body of sixty in 1815 and a faculty of eight professors, who taught anatomy and physiology, medical chemistry, pathology, obstetrics, natural history, hygiene, and legal medicine, as well as providing clinical instruction at the local hospital.[75] At Rennes, the secondary school of medicine listed a fac-

---

70. Carl Haffter, ed., *Tagebuch des Zürcher Medizinstudenten Elias Haffter aus dem Jahre 1823* (Zurich: Hans Rohr, 1976), 19.

71. Gottfried Roth, ed., *Vom Baderlehrling zum Wundarzt: Carl Rabl, ein Mediziner im Biedermeier* (Vienna: Oberösterreichischer Landesverlag, n.d.), 60.

72. J. V. d'Outrepont, "Erinnerungen aus den Studienzeiten," in *Die Wiener medizinische Schule im Vormärz*, ed. Max Neuburger (Vienna: Rikola, 1921), 36.

73. Claudia Huerkamp, *Der Aufstieg der Ärzte im 19. Jahrhundert: Vom gelehrten Stand zum professionellen Experten: Das Beispiel Preussens* (Göttingen: Vandenhoeck & Ruprecht, 1985), 56.

74. Cabanis, "Rapport fait au Conseil des Cinq-Cents," 386.

75. G. Pery, *Histoire de la faculté de médecine de Bordeaux et de l'enseignement médical dans cette ville, 1441–1888* (Paris: O. Doin, 1888), 258, 301.

ulty of seven and about the same number of students as Bordeaux had.[76] In Lyons, which boasted a large hospital and excellent clinicians, more than two hundred students were enrolled in the secondary school of that city by the middle 1820s.[77] As they were in the German states, midwives were frequently trained in the same clinics, although not in the same classes, as the *officiers de santé*.

In all, eighteen such schools existed in France by 1820 in such cities as Amiens, Caen, Dijon, Marseilles, and Nancy.[78] Supported largely by municipal funds but supervised by educational authorities in Paris, the schools reached their peak of influence at the close of the Napoleonic era. Although under constant attack from academically trained physicians, as were their counterparts in Germany, the *officiers* continued to outnumber physicians in France until the early 1830s.[79] Further investigation of these little-known schools will doubtless modify further the traditional portrait of medical teaching during these years.

Military Medicine and the Clinic

Much better known and respected than the practical schools were the institutions for training of military doctors. The huge scale of land conflict stretching over two decades heightened the already steep demand for military surgeons. Governments poured large sums into military hospitals and the training of army surgeons. Schools in Paris, Berlin, Vienna, and St. Petersburg achieved so high a reputation that civilian students clamored to share in their training.

In Berlin, for example, the Charité hospital, which was largely controlled by the military, became a fiercely disputed locus of conflict with the medical faculty of the University of Berlin. In a letter to the Education Ministry in 1811, the surgeon Graefe compared the great teaching resources in Paris, London, and Vienna unfavorably with those open to teachers in Berlin, where "military medical authorities" blocked efforts to make greater use of the Charité.[80] Other Berlin professors, notably Hufeland and Rudolphi, contended that what was needed was more teaching

76. E. Perrin de la Touche, *L'enseignement médical à Rennes (1800–1896)* (Rennes: Oberthur, 1896), 16–22.

77. Gab. Despierres, *Histoire de l'enseignement médical à Lyon* (Lyon: ACEML, 1984), 87.

78. For a list of these schools, see Jacques Léonard, "Les études médicales en France entre 1815 et 1848," *Revue d'histoire moderne et contemporaine* 13 (1966): 89, note. See also Léonard, *La médecine entre les savoirs et les pouvoirs* (Paris: Aubier Montaigne, 1981), esp. 46–54.

79. Matthew Ramsey, *Professional and Popular Medicine in France, 1770–1830: The Social World of Medical Practice* (Cambridge: Cambridge University Press, 1988), 116.

80. Graefe to ministry, February 4, 1811, in "Das medizinische und chirurgische Klinikum bei der Universität zu Berlin," Bd. 1, 1811–14, GSPK, Merseburg, 76 Va, Sekt. 2, Tit. X, Nr. 3.

opportunities at the hospital.[81] In view of the huge numbers of civilian and military students in the city, wrote Rudolphi in 1823, the government must somehow "make it possible in the future for not just the [military] students but also those from the University to take part in the work of the Charité."[82] In 1828, the Berlin physician Johann Ludwig Casper publicly charged that the Prussian authorities were discriminating in favor of military over civilian physicians in training.[83] In the state of Bavaria, by contrast, authorities required that all civilian medical students serve a *Praktikum* in the well-regarded military hospital in Munich.[84]

The education offered at the Pepinière, the elite military school founded in Berlin in 1795, was the envy of many university graduates. Its curriculum combined instruction in medicine and surgery, courses in science and basic medical subjects, clinical teaching in the amphitheater, and bedside learning at the Charité. Among the course requirements were not only medical and surgical subjects but also French and Latin, history and geography, mathematics and philosophy. A typical student of the early nineteenth century spent four years in formal study, beginning with such classes as anatomy, botany, chemistry, Latin, and mathematics; proceeding to physiology, pathology, pharmacy, and logic; then semiotics, materia medica, obstetrics, surgery, and bandaging; and concluding with intensive clinical work at the Charité in the fourth year. Students were carefully selected, given full support by the state, and paid a small stipend. The teachers were well paid and included a number of the early professors at the university.[85] No university of the time could offer more to a student of medicine.

In the same year that Prussia launched the Pepinière, the French government founded its school of military medicine at Val-de-Grâce. With a faculty headed by the inspector of military hospitals, Jean Coste, and including the surgeons Dominique Larrey and Nicolas Desgenettes, the school quickly became a favored institution of the revolutionary leaders.[86] Additional military schools were created at Lille, Metz, Toulon, and Strasbourg. The course of study at these schools was similar to that in the civilian secondary schools but with a heavier emphasis on military hygiene and battlefield diseases. As they were in Germany, the teachers at these

81. See, for example, the letter from Hufeland, April 12, 1814, and others from Rudolphi, in "Verhandlungen der medicinischen Fakultät mit dem Ministerium über die Gewährung einer Krankenanstalt und Benutzung der Charité zu Lehrzwecken," Akten der medizinischen Fakultät zu Berlin, 211, F10, C3, Humboldt University Archive, Berlin.

82. Rudolphi to ministry, October 27, 1823, GSPK, Merseburg, 76 Va, Sekt. l, Tit. VII, Nr. 9.

83. Johann Ludwig Casper, "Blick auf die Fortschritte der Kgl. Preuss. Medicinal-Verfassung bei ihrem hundertjahrigan Jubiläum," *Hufelands Journal* 66 (1828): H. 1.

84. Wolf Bachmann, "Die Gründung der ersten medizinischen Fakultät in München 1823," *Münchener medizinische Wochenschrift* 110 (1968): 2569.

85. Winau, *Medizin in Berlin*, 100–4.

86. David M. Vess, *Medical Revolution in France, 1789–1796* (Gainesville: University Presses of Florida, 1975), 176.

schools—who included physicians and pharmacists as well as surgeons—were paid as well as those in the schools of medicine. At Strasbourg, for example, which, like Paris was the site of both a civilian and a military school, the military faculty numbered three physicians, three surgeons, and three pharmacists in 1816.[87]

There was no comparable development of military medicine in the English-speaking world. Both the British and American governments, opposed to large standing armies, depended on civilian-trained practitioners in the conflicts of the late eighteenth and early nineteenth century. Both countries tried in wartime to expedite the training of surgeons for combat, but the steps taken were often unavailing. In Great Britain, the military hospitals at Chatham and Plymouth were overburdened in wartime and did not instruct future practitioners in peacetime. Following the War of 1812, an effort to create a naval medical course in Philadelphia foundered for lack of student and governmental interest.[88] Returning military surgeons found few opportunities in either country for continuing their study of military medicine. At Edinburgh, the university did establish a controversial chair in military surgery, with the support of the government in 1806, that attracted upward of two hundred students by 1815.

But efforts to expand such teaching in the civilian colleges met with stiff opposition. Such ventures, in the words of a holder of the Edinburgh chair, Sir George Ballingall, met in Britain with "little sympathy in the public mind." Ballingall, who visited the continental schools and was "much struck" by them, especially the "truly imperial establishment" in Vienna, campaigned for many years without success for a chair of military medicine in London.[89]

Glimpses of Clinical Teaching

Whether in military classes, practical schools, private courses, dispensaries, hospitals, or policlinics, by 1820 clinical teaching had come to occupy a secure place in medical pedagogy. Even where practical training was not readily available, as in most of the American schools, the search for bedside experience was a part of every student's introduction into medicine.

---

87. Christian Wolff, "Faculté, écoles de médecine et hôpitaux militaires à Strasbourg sous la révolution et l'empire (1789–1815)" (med. diss., University of Strasbourg, 1986), 87–97. See also H. Beaunis, *L'école du service de santé militaire de Strasbourg et la faculté de médecine de Strasbourg de 1856 à 1870* (Nancy: Berger-Levrault, 1888), 4.

88. Harold D. Langley, "The Navy's Medical School in Philadelphia: An Experiment in 19th Century Medical Education," paper presented at the annual meeting of the American Association for the History of Medicine in Louisville, KY, May 1993. I am grateful to Dr. Langley for sending me a copy of his interesting paper.

89. George Ballingall, *Remarks on Schools of Instruction for Military and Naval Surgeons* (Edinburgh: Balfour and Jack, 1843), 3–15.

Nor were most students content with the minimal requirements of the statutes in the nations where these existed. Typically, as many contemporary letters and diary entries poignantly reveal, a young student in training was fearful of the awful responsibilities about to fall on him and availed himself of every opportunity to shore up his shortcomings.

Although pecuniary motives drove many teachers to offer these additional opportunities to learn, it was a sense of responsibility, or a fear of failure in many cases, that brought students under their tutelage. "How little are the labours and hardships of a student known," wrote John Metcalf in his Boston diary of 1826, for he "must find during his pupillage, many hardships and many perplexities . . . he is not dealing with romance or fiction, but with all the grave and responsible realities of Life and death."[90] To prepare to meet these "realities" was for most students much more than a matter of meeting minimal educational or state requirements.

Students understandably treasured most those teachers and opportunities that enabled them to see and do most. The clinics of Germany clearly afforded to some students a greater chance to "practice" medicine than did the hospitals of France but gave them far less opportunity to see a great variety of diseases. French students, in contrast, benefited greatly from the enormous resources of the Paris hospitals, but except for a few, they were largely passive learners. In Britain and America, private hospitals were less hospitable to students than were the publicly controlled hospitals of Europe, and medical schools made at most only limited provision for clinical instruction. Even in London—the city most like Paris in the number of its sickbeds—only a minority of students were able to get hands-on experience at the bedside.

What must have seemed ideal to a would-be practitioner of these years was a small teaching clinic located in a large hospital population. "One of the best Clinical Institutions I have ever seen," testified the Scot John Thomson before a royal commission in 1826, "was in the Clinicum attached to the Great Hospital at Vienna, where there is an immense number of patients, [but] each of the Clinical wards receives only 12 or 14."[91] The popularity of such teaching centers as the Pepinière, the Val-de-Grâce in Paris, the Julius Hospital in Würzburg, and the clinics of the Allgemeine Krankenhaus of Vienna lay precisely in this combination of small teaching clinics in a large hospital. It could occur only in places where a powerful government put a small number of teaching beds under the direct control of an effective teacher. In the hands of a Schönlein at Würzburg, a Skoda in Vienna, or a Larrey in Paris, the clinic of the early nineteenth century found its most effective expression.

To take the less familiar example of Würzburg, the medical clinic at the Julius Hospital, which came under the direction of Johann Lucas Schön-

90. Anna C. Holt, ed., "A Medical Student in Boston, 1825–26," *Harvard Library Bulletin* 6 (1952): 372–73.

91. Royal Commission, *Evidence, Oral and Documentary*, 1:468.

lein in 1819, was for a time the most favored of central Europe. The large hospital in the city had long been a training ground for *Wundärzte* as well as physicians.[92] From the beginning of his tenure, Schönlein used the hospital both to acquaint his students with the symptoms of a large variety of illnesses and to teach them in small groups at the patient's bedside. Standing near the patient's bed, he led a cluster of students in a discussion of the peculiar features of the patient's disease. The students themselves were required to examine the patient in Schönlein's presence and to suggest a plan of treatment. On successive days they reviewed together the changes in the patient's condition.[93] The teaching clinic, Schönlein insisted, "is not a form of lecture with demonstration . . . but [is] intended for the practical guidance of the learning physician." He pioneered in Germany, although well behind France, in the teaching of percussion and auscultation to students, and in the use of the microscope. Stools, urine, and sputum were chemically and microscopically examined before the class.[94] Schönlein's towering reputation as a teacher, although he published no textbook or other notable work, is testimony to the high value that students placed on this kind of informal, practical education.

But outside Würzburg and the large cities of Vienna, Prague, Leipzig, and Berlin, no German university of the early nineteenth century was housed in a city with a large hospital. The Bavarian university of Landshut had not yet been moved to Munich, and the municipal hospital in the entrepôt of Hamburg had no local university to exploit its resources. More typical of clinical teaching in Germany than Würzburg was the small clinic at Göttingen, where authorities tried a variety of means to attract a range of patients to its "academic hospital." If such a clinic was seen by German educators as superior for teaching, the lack of patients from which to select examples for teaching often worried them. When Karl August Himly arrived in Göttingen in 1803, for example, he found "not a single [suitable] medical case" among the chronically ill and surgical patients in the "hospital."

Himly forged an alliance with the city clinic to increase the number of cases seen by students, and he was determined "to fill the few beds only with selected teaching patients."[95] Beginning students in the clinic (called *Auscultanten*) were allowed to look on and ask questions at the bedside, and the remaining students (*Praktikanten*) were required to engage in in-

92. Horsch, *Uber die Bildung des Arztes*, 49.

93. Johanna Bleker, "Die Idee der Einheit von Theorie und Praxis in der Medizin und ihr Einfluss auf den klinischen Unterricht im 19.Jahrhundert," *Artz und Krankenhaus* 6 (1982): 234. See also Bleker, *Die naturhistorische Schule, 1825–1845: Ein Beitrag zur Geschichte der klinischen Medizin in Deutschland* (Stuttgart: Gustav Fischer, 1981), 40–42.

94. Christiane Scherg-Zeisner, "Die ärztliche Ausbildung an der königlich–bayerischen Julius-Maximilians-Universität in Würzburg, 1814–1872" (med. diss., University of Würzburg, 1973), 39.

95. Heike Winkelmann, "Das akademische Hospital in Göttingen von 1781 bis 1850" (med. diss., University of Göttingen, 1981), 175.

creasingly active patient care. Outpatients at the city clinic, as well as hospital patients, were assigned to the care of a *Praktikant*. All students were given assignments. Two or three of the older of them were given responsibility for medical visits to each of three surrounding towns. In one of these towns, Weende, 165 sick were cared for by two students in one winter alone.[96] The university hospital was enlarged to twenty-five beds in 1825, and a surgical clinic of thirty beds was built for Conrad Johann Langenbeck.[97] By the middle 1820s, the hospital was treating 1,500 inpatients a year.[98]

All over Germany during this time, the policlinics were being converted into small teaching hospitals of twenty-five or more beds, and ambulatory patient care and home visits were used by teachers to supplement the students' practical experience. Such arrangements, said Peter Krukenberg of Halle in 1820, enabled many of his students "to care for 3 to 400 patients" in the course of their studies.[99]

Contrasts in French Clinical Training

The German pedagogical emphasis on hands-on experience was equally favored in theory by contemporary French clinicians. Pinel, Cabanis, and Corvisart all believed that a small class at the bedside, with the students actually learning on patients, was essential to effective clinical teaching. The teaching ward at Vienna, wrote Pinel, "holds only 12 patients," whereas that at Edinburgh, with its thirty-two beds, was already too large.[100] At Montpellier, according to the founders of the new School of Health in 1795, the number of patients in a clinic should not exceed twenty-five, since "no clinical school in Europe provides a larger number."[101] When Auguste-François Chomel, the successor of Laennec, taught his clinic of forty patients in 1828, he told his students that even this number was still "of more benefit to them . . . than to be exposed to a multiplicity of patients."[102]

But for all the good intentions and plans, the disorganization of war and revolution, together with rapidly growing numbers of students and the sharp separation of authority between schools and hospitals, made the ideal difficult to realize. Corvisart, whose teaching ward was limited to

96. Wilhelm Ebstein, "Uber die Entwickelung des klinischen Unterrichts an der Göttinger Hochschule und über die heutigen Aufgaben der medizinischen Klinik," *Klinisches Jahrbuch* 1 (1889): 77.

97. File 4 IVe 2, University of Göttingen Archive.

98. Ebstein, "Uber die Entwickelung des klinischen Unterrichts," 79.

99. Peter Krukenberg, "Entstehung, Einrichtung und Fortgang der ambulatorischen Klinik zu Halle," *Jahrbuch der ambulatorischen Klinik zu Halle* 1 (1820): 16.

100. Pinel, *Clinical Training of Doctors*, 78.

101. *Programmes des cours d'enseignement*, 55–56.

102. Jacyna, "Au Lit des Malades," 423–24.

forty beds, was forced in 1801 to take in 385 students. To combat the disorder of so large a number, he encouraged students to seek their own means of gaining experience.[103]

Large clinical classes and a growing dependence on the amphitheater lecture became the general rule in Paris. Two hundred or three hundred students in a teaching ward were not unusual by the 1820s. "You can form no idea how crowded the medical lectures are here," wrote the Englishman George Paget in 1833:

> I have discontinued attending the public ones. . . . In the same way, there are about 200 students going round every morning with each of the best physicians . . . so that you are tolerably lucky if you get in a third row round the bed of a patient: the light by which you see the patient being moreover only that of a candle, because it is so early in the morning.[104]

Under these conditions, bedside teaching for the masses of students was becoming more and more impracticable, and the hospital was largely "reserved for a medical aristocracy, which excluded the simple practitioner, who [was] kept at the ground-floor, as it were."[105]

The Concours and the Internship

For the "aristocracy" who were appointed interns after 1803, however, following a fiercely contested *concours*, the way was cleared to a lifelong career as teacher, specialist, or medical official. Only one in every twenty medical students, on the average, had this experience of spending four years in the hospitals of Paris, working with some of the great figures of French medicine. The *internat*, or internship, was called the *grand école* of medicine, selecting out those who would form the aristocracy of the French profession. With roots in the surgical apprenticeship of the Old Regime, the internship revolved around an intensive examination conducted among the more numerous *externs* in the student body. If the extern was like the German *Auscultant* in the limited range of experience he acquired—the observation of patients, unskilled hospital duties, perhaps some record keeping—the intern was an enlarged and extended version of the *Praktikant*, who had real responsibility for patients. The *Praktikant*, in turn, was an early version of the later Anglo-American clerkship for undergraduate medical students, whereas the internship, with its longer period of training and intensive indoctrination in the culture of

103. Imbault-Huart, "Concepts and Realities of Clinical Teaching," 62–63.

104. Stephen Paget, ed., *Memoirs and Letters of Sir James Paget* (London: Longmans, Green, 1902), 96.

105. Marie-José Imbault-Huart, "The Teaching of Medicine in France and More Particularly in Paris in the 19th Century (1794–1892)," in *History of Medical Education*, ed. Teizo Ogawa (Tokyo: Saikon, 1983), 64–65.

the hospital, led to the Anglo-American house officer or twentieth-century medical or surgical resident.[106]

The *concours* itself did as much to shape the student's experience in medical school as did the long years spent in the hospital. The examinations, lasting for two months but sometimes requiring a year or more in preparation, were a grueling, public, and largely oral testing of the candidate's encyclopedic knowledge of medical and surgical theory, as well as his ability to speak extemporaneously and fluently on randomly chosen subjects. One candidate later described the

> terror [as] I entered the amphitheater more dead than alive. As if through a cloud, I saw the jury on the podium. . . . I walked forward with legs of jelly [and] climbed the scaffold . . . the usher pushed the trigger of the clock, which rang, and which would ring again, a few minutes later to cut off my words.

Becoming hopelessly confused, the candidate lost his balance, "grabbed the drape, carried it and the clock down with him, and left the amphitheater amid explosions of mad laughter."[107] Each year, Leonard Groopman tells us, "between five-sixths and six-sevenths of those competing" in the *concours* failed.

Once past this fearful hurdle, the French intern's experience in practical medicine was unparalleled in the nineteenth century. These years, in Groopman's words, "were a continuous, undifferentiated period, outside historical time, bracketed off from real life. They would be remembered . . . as beautiful, carefree years of security and illusion, as life's honeymoon."[108] The intern, truly a physician-in-waiting, performed all the duties of a physician or surgeon yet still had the technical status of a student. He was, noted William Osler later, "about the best hospital product with which I am acquainted, and it is no wonder that as a body the 'Internat' is looked on as the special glory of French medicine."[109]

For the run-of-the-mill student at the Paris school of medicine, however, it was often both difficult and expensive even to get the kind of practical experience that marked the German clinic at its best. A vast array of clinical tours, an elitist practical school, private courses, and numerous specialty hospitals shored up the structural weaknesses of Parisian clinical training for the majority of students. It was these opportunities offered outside the school of medicine that brought so many from so far to the

106. The best account of the development of the French internship is by Leonard C. Groopman, "The Internat des Hôpitaux de Paris: The Shaping and Transformation of the French Medical Elite, 1802–1914" (Ph.D. diss., Harvard University, 1986). The account in this and the following two paragraphs is based heavily on pp. 1–25 of this work.

107. Paul Legendre, *Du quartier latin à l'académie* (Paris, 1930), 135–38, quoted in Groopman, "Internat," 14–15.

108. Groopman, "Internat," 16, 49.

109. William Osler, "Impressions of Paris: Teachers and Students," *Journal of the American Medical Association* 52 (1909): 773.

Paris of the 1820s and 1830s. "It is not the teaching methods which attract so large a crowd of foreigners each year to the French hospitals," wrote Friedrich Ammon of Dresden in 1823, "nor is it the high level of science . . . it is the confluence of the most unusual cases of disease in a Hôtel-Dieu, in a Charité, in a Hôpital St. Louis."[110] In the French capital, noted his fellow countryman Johann Kopp, the bewildered beginning student "sees too much and does himself too little."[111] And the Englishman John Green Crosse said that only interns and externs "take any share in the practical duties of the hospital."[112] It was the graduate physician and the student with a hospital appointment, almost all observers agreed, who benefited most from the vaunted hospital medicine of Paris.

Far better for the average student was the situation in the secondary schools and in the smaller medical schools of Montpellier and Strasbourg. Although far behind Paris in their scientific achievements and lacking in the career opportunities of the capital, the smaller institutions gave a more thorough introduction to practical medicine. Frequent interference from Paris made it difficult for provincial schools to experiment or deviate from national requirements, but their smaller size made possible a more personalized instruction.

Faculty leaders at Strasbourg continually tried to break away from the Paris model of clinical instruction. "Not Paris, but Göttingen should be our model," one professor had written at the time of reorganization.[113] Time and time again, such professors as Stoeber and Schützenberger pleaded for greater autonomy for Strasbourg and other faculties. In his 1829 essay, Stoeber argued for more degree-granting schools of medicine in France, comparing unfavorably the three French schools with the twenty-one in the German states. He praised Hufeland's clinic in Berlin for the individualized training it gave students and urged its adoption in France.[114] For the next quarter-century, the faculty at Strasbourg regularly petitioned the authorities in Paris to permit a trial of the policlinic at their school.[115] All such entreaties, however, proved futile, and control over the provincial schools was little relaxed until late in the century.

A glimpse of Parisian clinical teaching at its best is found in the memoirs of Poumiès de la Siboutie, a student at the Ecole de médecine in 1812. "I was named intern of the hospitals of Paris," he recalled, "it is

110. Friedrich A. Ammon, *Parallele der französischen und deutschen Chirurgie nach Resultaten einer in den Jahren 1821 und 1822 gemachter Reise* (Leipzig: C. H. F. Hartmann, 1823), 46.

111. Johann H. Kopp, *Ärztliche Bemerkungen, veranlasst durch eine Reise in Deutschland und Frankreich im Frühjahr und Sommer 1824* (Frankfurt am Main: Hermann, 1825), 21.

112. Crosse, *Sketches of the Medical Schools of Paris*, 61–62.

113. Otto Lenel, *Die Universität Strassburg, 1621–1921* (Freiburg: Julius Boltze, 1921), 11.

114. Stoeber, *De l'organisation médicale*, 8, 44–45.

115. See, for example, the report of December 7, 1855, on adopting the German educational institution of the policlinic, F[17] 4453, Archives nationales.

the marshal's baton of a medical student." One of only 18 chosen that year from 120 candidates, he found "the advantages of the internship [to be] immense." As an intern, he examined patients on their arrival at the hospital, took responsibility for their routine care, reported to his supervisors on their condition, supervised the less advanced externs in their work, and conducted the evening visits to the patients. By comparison with the rest of his four years of education, he said, the internship was "an immense source of instruction."[116]

Another view, a decade and a half later, is afforded by the notes of the Scot Allen Thomson, who attended Chomel's clinic in 1828. What impressed Thomson most about the clinic was *la conférence* that followed Chomel's tour of the teaching ward and his lecture in the amphitheater. In this meeting, reports were given by a few senior students selected to examine the patients, which Chomel then criticized. In these small conferences, writes L. S. Jacyna, "the distance between the student and the patient . . . [as well as] the distance between professor and student" were markedly reduced. This kind of personalized instruction, he concludes, "can . . . be regarded as the most significant aspect of Chomel's clinical teaching."[117]

Still another teaching technique was used by the surgeon Guillaume Depuytren, who followed his crowded ward visits and amphitheater lectures with consultations with his patients in the amphitheater in the presence of students. There he interrogated the patients, at times brutally, and made remarks to the students about his impressions.[118]

Practical Teaching in Anglo-America

Conditions in Great Britain and America understandably made for a very different kind of practical teaching than in the French hospital or the German clinic. Nowhere in either country were hospitals organized for clinical teaching on the scale of France, nor were students normally able to get the kind of hands-on education available in the German clinic. "More time must be allowed for professional intercourse between the student and the preceptor," wrote David David to the council of the new University of London in 1826, "the very reverse of the system which has hitherto prevailed in London."[119] It was imperative in the new venture, added the pharmacist Anthony Thomson, "that the teacher not be

---

116. Poumiès de la Siboutie, *Souvenirs d'un médecin de Paris* (Paris: Plon-Nourrit, 1910), 111–12. These memoirs were published by his daughters after his death.

117. Jacyna, "Au Lit des Malades," 425–26.

118. Russell M. Jones, ed., *The Parisian Education of an American Surgeon: Letters of Jonathan Mason Warren (1832–1835)* (Philadelphia: American Philosophical Society, 1978), 27.

119. David D. David to Council of University, December 17, 1827, University College London Archive, Science Library, college correspondence 312.

thronged with students. Everyone should stand close to the patient or corpse." Classes much be kept small and under professorial direction, as they were on the Continent, although the examination of patients by students would be in Britain "injurious to the interests of the University."[120]

For the average hospital pupil in London, teaching was casual, episodic, and uneven. Lectures were rarely systematically presented or illustrated by cases from the wards. "There was very little active practical teaching in the wards or by clinical lectures," recalled James Paget regarding his studies in the 1830s; "it was customary to think it sufficient to give opportunities for learning to those who could learn by looking-on and by occasional rather casual talking about the cases." For the "great majority of students," he wrote, "work at that time had to be self-determined and nearly all self-guided."[121]

Most students had had some experience as apprentices, which made their passive role in the hospital less harmful to their education. The medical lectures that were given, wrote a student to the *Lancet* in 1826, were "written compositions read over to the students." To be of value, he said, such lectures had to be made "as *clinical* as possible."[122] Another student complained as late as 1842 that although he had been in London for six weeks, he had not heard a single clinical lecture.[123]

The overwhelming majority of students in London were interested primarily in surgery and eagerly looked for chances to see every operation possible. In the recollection of Robert Christison, several hundred surgical pupils were studying at St. Bartholomew's Hospital in the early 1820s, whereas only three students were preparing for medicine.[124]

The best examples of effective teaching under these circumstances were those arising from a personal relationship between a teacher and an advanced student. For a clerk or dresser who worked under the direction of a hospital teacher, the opportunities for direct experience with patients, as with the externs and interns of France, were considerable. At Guy's Hospital, for example, Richard Bright was privileged at the very beginning of his studies to enter the wards as a physician's clerk for a fee of £10 and to live in the house of the hospital apothecary. With these advantages, he was able to visit patients daily, to record the features of each case, to carry out the orders of his mentor, and to be present at autopsy. His continual search for new experience enabled him to gain a wealth of practical instruction. "Nobody stopped to teach much at the bedside," wrote his biographer, "it was largely his own observations that gave him his great skill in doctoring."[125]

120. Anthony Todd Thomson, December 19, 1827, ibid.

121. Paget, *Memoirs*, 40, 60.

122. *Lancet* 10 (1826): 78–79. The emphasis is that of the student-author.

123. *Lancet* 26 (1842): 504.

124. Victor C. Medvei and John L. Thornton, eds., *The Royal Hospital of Saint Bartholomew, 1123–1973* (London: Royal Hospital of Saint Bartholomew, 1974), 51.

125. Pamela Bright, *Dr Richard Bright (1789–1858)* (London: Bodley Head, 1983), 69–70.

The American system of clinical education was, if anything, less organized and more limited than that of Great Britain. "For a long time," Edward Atwater wrote, "there were too few hospitals, too few patients, and
too many students to provide sufficient clinical experience." As the apprenticeship system of training began to deteriorate after 1820, students
were left with fewer means to prepare themselves for practice. "The student often finished his formal education," says Atwater, "without ever
having been alone with, much less touched a patient."[126]

Clinical training had only a small place in the many rural medical
schools that sprang up after 1800. Only in Philadelphia, New York, and
Boston were serious efforts made before 1830 to emulate the organized
clinical training available to medical students in Europe. Even in these
cities, however, teaching suffered from the lack of sickbeds, the small
number of clinically trained teachers, the failure of cooperation by hospitals, and the destructive competition among medical schools. The absence of a hospital caused Benjamin Waterhouse of Boston to plead with
authorities of the United States Marine Hospital in 1803 to open its
wards to Harvard students, since "most of them never saw an amputa-
tion, the operation of trepanning, and some not even the reduction of a
broken or dislocated bone."[127] It was the scarcity of hospital patients in
Cambridge that drove the medical school to Boston in 1810. Even the
opening of the Massachusetts General Hospital in 1821 did not solve the
problem for long. The managers of the new institution severely limited
the freedom of students, warning that "they are not to converse with the
patients or nurses" and that "in all cases, in which it will be proper for the
pupils to make any personal examination of a patient, such as feeling the
pulse, examining a tumor, etc. an intimation to that effect will be given
them by the physician or surgeon."[128]

Similar difficulties and restrictions were reported in Philadelphia and
New York. In the former city, tensions with the managers of the Pennsylvania Hospital over the extent of clinical teaching in the hospital in 1829
caused professors to arrange lectures and ward visits at the Philadelphia
Almshouse.[129] The practical Medical Institute in the city, with a staff of
seven by 1823 and a longer school term than the University of Pennsylvania had, served as an effective arm of the medical faculty.[130]

Although almost all teachers deplored the severe limitations on patient
contact in the American setting, they urged their students, as their British

126. Edward C. Atwater, "'Making Fewer Mistakes': A History of Students and Patients," *Bulletin of the History of Medicine* 57 (1983): 168–171.
127. Benjamin Waterhouse to General Lincoln, February 9, 1803, in Thomas F. Harrington, *The Harvard Medical School: A History, Narrative and Documentary, 1782–1905*, 3
vols. (New York: Lewis, 1905), 1:442–43.
128. Ibid., 2:582–83.
129. Carson, *History of the Medical Department of the University of Pennsylvania*, 200.
130. Langley, "The Navy's Medical School in Philadelphia," 5.

contemporaries did, to seize every chance for practice. Even where hospitals were lacking or were only a future prospect, educators stressed their importance to the townspeople and students. "It is [only] in hospitals," Daniel Drake told those attending the opening ceremony of the Medical College of Ohio in 1820, "that the lectures on practical or clinical medicine must be delivered."[131] In Louisville, James Cross contended in 1834 that regardless of the shortage of hospitals, every teacher should involve himself in clinical instruction, so that

> every student . . . be enabled to hear and see all that he could wish. . . . At every visit the professor should spend two or three hours, and even longer if necessary. . . . Every pupil should be presented with a stethoscope . . . and the professor should patiently stand by the bedside while he is listening.[132]

Such personalized instruction at the bedside, it must be said, was rarely realized in the first three decades of the century. The great majority of students continued to get their practical experience from a private preceptor, and a small number gained experience in the outpatient dispensaries run by some of the colleges.

We can get a glimpse of what clinical teaching in a hospital was like in these years through the students' accounts of their experiences in such cities as New York and Philadelphia. When Asa Fitch left his studies at the rural school in Castleton, Vermont, in 1828 to study at Rutgers Medical College, he was determined to take full advantage of the hospital's opportunities in the city. "Seven hours of the day are taken up in hearing lectures and one more in attending the hospital," he wrote in his diary. One winter he saw demonstrations of lithotomy, amputations, and cataract removal, and an operation for cancer of the lip—but no mention is made of any role in examining or caring for patients.[133]

A student at Philadelphia recalled that it was only through family connections that students were able to get a coveted position as house-pupil, which brought a flood of opportunities for contact with patients. One such fortunate student, a nephew of Professor Benjamin Smith Barton, was able after serving a term at the Pennsylvania Hospital to secure a position as attending surgeon.[134] But such opportunities were rare and rep-

131. Daniel Drake, *An Inaugural Discourse on Medical Education delivered at the Opening of the Medical College of Ohio in Cincinnati, 11 November 1820* (New York: Henry Schuman, 1951), 17.

132. Edward C. Atwater, "Internal Medicine," in *The Education of American Physicians: Historical Essays,* ed. Ronald L. Numbers (Berkeley and Los Angeles: University of California Press, 1980), 162.

133. Samuel Rezneck, "A Course of Medical Education in New York City in 1828–29: The Journal of Asa Fitch," *Bulletin of the History of Medicine* 42 (1968): 560–61.

134. John L. Atlee, "The Education of a Physician in Early 19th Century," *Journal of the Lancaster County Historical Society* 91 (1987–88): 85.

resented "the first step in an elite medical career."[135] Not one in a thousand won such an appointment in the nineteenth century.[136]

Paris, the Clinic, and History

For those Americans who went abroad to get the kind of education denied them at home, their principal destination was Paris. Why did they go? Most Americans, like those who came from Germany and Great Britain, reported that it was not French teaching methods or even French science but the unwonted freedom of the hospitals that brought them to Paris. The revolutionary opening of the great hospitals to students set Paris apart from London, Edinburgh, Berlin, and even Vienna. The surprisingly easy access to hospitals for foreigners, the unfamiliar (and at first shocking) disdain for patients' privacy, the seemingly limitless supply of dead bodies for surgical training as well as routine dissection, the absence or very low official fees, and the friendly reception given graduate physicians by noted clinicians and surgeons made an indelible impression on visitors from all countries.

Here, too, they could learn, usually in private tutelage, the practical uses of the stethoscope and of percussion, including the correlation of internal signals with postmortem findings. For many, even with good training, it was their first contact with "scientific medicine," in which anatomical knowledge of underlying disease conditions informed the discussion of living patients. Compared with conditions at home, whether in the sharply restricted hospitals of Britain and America or the small hospital clinics of Germany, Paris offered a richness of experience that was unmatched.

So powerful were these impressions on a whole generation of physicians that they became fixed in historical imagination. What they saw and experienced in Paris was seen as a radical innovation in both pedagogy and medical science. Historians have endlessly repeated travelers' vivid reactions to the remarkable accessibility of the hospitals and the work of the great clinicians who taught in them. The creation on a new scale of an anatomoclinical method of investigating disease, the clinical method of teaching itself and especially bedside instruction, and the "medicalization" of patient care all have been variously attributed to the Paris clinic.

Such a rendering of history ignores how much it depends on the later testimony of the leaders of French medicine themselves and on their admiring followers. It fails to take into account the widespread criticism, inside and outside France, of the pedagogical weaknesses of the teaching system. It leaves out altogether the numerous sites of medical training

135. Charles E. Rosenberg, *The Care of Strangers: The Rise of America's Hospital System* (New York: Basic Books, 1987), 63.
136. Atwater, "'Making Fewer Mistakes'," 172.

outside the schools that contributed so much to the triumph of the clinic. It takes no account of the destructive effects of centralization on French medical pedagogy. It passes over the forced separation of academic studies from the clinical side of medicine, with all its long-term consequences. It leaves out the well-known fact that practical teaching was well under way before the Revolution and found its most effective expression outside France. And it neglects the testimony of careful observers of the time, such as Robert Graves and Carl Dzondi, who completely discounted the Parisian hospital as a model for teaching in their own countries.

The first wave of reformers and students in France were keenly aware that the chaos and disorganization of the revolutionary era were preventing them from achieving the kind of teaching clinic that was flourishing in Vienna, Edinburgh, and the German universities. "The general hospital at Vienna . . . is . . . similar to what [we] hoped for and has not been completely executed in France," wrote Jean-François Coste in the classic *Dictionnaire des sciences médicales* in 1817.[137] A young Parisian physician just graduated in 1818 complained of the lack of a real clinic anywhere in the capital. "Nothing resembles less a clinical school," he wrote, "than the mob of young people who frequent at will the wards of medicine and surgery." Only in "the immediate presence of illness"—an experience denied to most Parisian students—could they "ask questions, palpate, hear the patient's story."[138]

For some foreign visitors, especially those from Germany, the French hospital of 1820 seemed to be a *pseudoclinic*, as Friedrich Ammon called it, that differed from normal hospitals "only in the permission given young physicians to enter freely."[139] In the costly private courses monopolized by young British and American physicians, visitors "were well aware," John Harley Warner writes, "that their experience of the Paris School was very different from that of its French students." During the crowded ward visits and lectures, he continues, visitors, like the French students, relished "an underlying sense of clinical instruction as spectacle"—and enjoyed "the theatricality of seeing the medical lions perform" but looked for effective teaching elsewhere.[140]

The teaching clinic of the early nineteenth century, it seems fair to say, owed its origins to impulses far more diffuse than those of revolutionary

137. Quoted in Othmar Keel, "The Politics of Health and the Institutionalisation of Clinical Practices in Europe in the second Half of the Eighteenth Century," in *William Hunter and the Eighteenth-Century Medical World*, ed. W. F. Bynum and Roy Porter (Cambridge: Cambridge University Press, 1985), 244.

138. G. T. M., *De l'enseignement clinique dans les écoles de Paris* (Paris: A. Egron, 1818), 12.

139. Ammon, *Parallele der französischen und deutschen Chirurgie*, 23.

140. I am indebted to Prof. Warner for sending me a copy of his paper, "Paradigm Lost or Paradise Declining? American Physicians and the `Dead End' of the Paris Clinical School," prepared for discussion at the conference, "History of Scientific Medicine in Paris, 1790–1850: A Reinterpretation," Wood Institute for the History of Medicine, College of Physicians of Philadelphia, February 1992.

France, and it achieved its most notable triumphs in places far removed from Paris. Bedside teaching flourished in France only outside the famous clinics of Paris.[141] The French contribution to medicine as an emerging practical science is, of course, another matter altogether and will be considered in the next chapter.

By locating the beginnings of "hospital medicine" and "the birth of the clinic" exclusively in early-nineteenth-century Paris, it has been possible for some scholars to trace such modern ills as "medical dehumanization," object-centered patient care, and the patient's loss of identity to events set loose in Paris nearly two centuries ago.[142] In a kind of reverse Whiggism, much that is impersonal, bureaucratic, insensitive, and technological in modern patient care can be ascribed to choices made necessary by the exceptional conditions in France in that unsettled era.

In the years before the French Revolution, such writers seem to suggest, the patient was treated more humanely, felt less powerless, and was more likely to be seen as a person by the physician than merely as a case of disease. But any familiarity with the treatment of the twenty thousand paupers in Paris who sought medical care before 1789 hardly supports this view. For Jacques Tenon and his study commission, the indescribable cruelty and neglect of those in the prerevolutionary hospitals could be remedied only by making it a place of curing and of teaching.[143] A Lyon physician of 1791, keenly aware of conditions in the large hospitals, lauded the effort to see the sick person as a whole in the German clinic and urged that France adopt a similar plan.[144] Pinel himself said that the aim of the new teaching hospital in France was to make it possible for "patients [to] be cared for as if they were at home."[145]

Although the reorganized hospital gave the physician more direct control over patients' lives—including their diet, medications, and daily routine—and thus limited their freedom, the purpose of Pinel and others was

141. For revisionist views of the French role in the "birth of the clinic," see Othmar Keel, "La problématique institutionnelle de la clinique en France et à l'étranger de la fin du XVIIIe siècle à la période de la restauration," *Bulletin canadienne d'histoire de médecine* 2 (1985): 183–204; 3 (1985): 1–30; Laurence Brockliss, "L'enseignement médical et la révolution: Essai de réévaluation," *Histoire de l'education* 42 (1989): 79–110; and Pierre Huard and Marie-José Imbault-Huart, "Quelques réflexions sur les origines de la clinique parisienne," *Bulletin de l'academie de médecine* 159 (1975): 583–88.

142. The classic studies of this genre are those by Erwin H. Ackerknecht, *Medicine at the Paris Hospital, 1794–1848* (Baltimore: Johns Hopkins University Press, 1967); Michel Foucault, *Naissance de la clinique*, 2nd ed. (Paris: Presses universitaires, 1972); and N. D. Jewson, "The Disappearance of the Sick-Man from Medical Cosmology, 1770–1870," *Sociology* 10 (1974): 225–44. Dora Weiner has quite rightly advised me that Ackerknecht would not have been happy at being included in this group.

143. Jacques Tenon, *Mémoires sur les hôpitaux de Paris* (Paris: Pierres, 1788). An English translation of this important book, with an introduction by Dora B. Weiner, is currently in press under the translation program of the National Endowment for the Humanities.

144. P. Parat, *Mémoire sur les moyens de perfectionner les études de l'art de guérir* (Lyon, 1791), 11.

145. Pinel, *Clinical Training of Doctors*, 79.

clearly to promote their healing and not just facilitate the scientific observation of their diseases.[146] The subsequent failure to conquer the problem of numbers in the rejuvenated hospitals of Paris and to find a solution to the tense division of authority between medical school and hospital came as a severe disappointment to reformers and as a shock to foreigners.

Scarcely a visitor to Paris returned home without commenting on the callous disregard of patients in the overcrowded clinics and their invisibility as human beings. The classification of diseases, not the healing of patients, it was said, was the principal concern of the busy doctors. "The French physician," declared Adolph Muehry in a comparative study, "thinks more of the disease than the patient."[147] British and American travelers reported similar reactions.[148] But these criticisms, a close reading makes clear, were inspired more by the chronic overcrowding and the confusion of teaching authority in the Paris hospital than by any condemnation of the new anatomoclinical method of teaching. Outside Paris and, in any case, at the numerous *écoles secondaires* and military schools, as well as in the schools of Montpellier and Strasbourg—where the new "hospital medicine" was also practiced—such reactions were not reported by native or foreign observers.

Hospital conditions and the care of patients generally, whether in France or elsewhere, were almost certainly better in 1830 than in 1800, and consequently there was markedly less public criticism of hospitals everywhere than in the late eighteenth century. Certainly the paying patient, whether or not in a hospital, as Christopher Lawrence observed, was little affected by the presumed disappearance of the sick person from the "scientific" physician's field of vision.

In any case, most ordinary practitioners continued to believe, as did the reformer Thomas Beddoes, that the patient's account of his own illness was a central feature of his diagnosis and treatment.[149] The very purpose of clinical teaching, explained a German handbook of 1815, was to demonstrate to students the best ways of enlisting the patient's cooperation in making a diagnosis. "The physician listens quietly to their stories," reads the manual, "looks for the meaning in what is being said, and tries to find the truth."[150] Similarly at Edinburgh, according to Guenter Risse, the managers of the infirmary "earnestly tried to keep the patients' inter-

---

146. I am grateful to Dora Weiner for sharing with me her extensive knowledge of Pinel to clarify this point. Letter to me, January 16, 1993.

147. Muehry, *Observations*, 126. Muehry was a practicing physician and surgeon in Hannover.

148. See, for example, John Harley Warner, "The Selective Transport of Medical Knowledge: Antebellum American Physicians and Parisian Medical Therapeutics," *Bulletin of the History of Medicine* 59 (1985): 213–31.

149. Christopher Lawrence, "The Meaning of Histories," *Bulletin of the History of Medicine* 66 (1992): 638–39.

150. Quoted in Fritz Hartmann, "Erziehung zum Arzt: Diachronische und interkulturelle Vergleiche der Formen und Inhalte," in *Krankheit, Heilkunst, Heilung*, ed. Eduard Seidler and Paul U. Unschuld (Freiburg/Munich: Karl Alber, 1978), 598.

ests ahead of other considerations."[151] In London, Richard Bright recalled that teacher William Babington "gave the impression of being in league with the patient" and insisted that students wash their hands, clean their nails, take off their hats, and act courteously whenever entering the rooms of patients.[152]

Dozens of such reports from hospitals and clinics across Europe and America, especially when students and teaching were involved, seem to belie accounts of a widespread transformation of patient–doctor relationships in the early nineteenth century. Certainly the argument for such a transformation is weakened once the spotlight is turned away from Paris to a military hospital in provincial France, to a German policlinic, or to a dispensary in a Scottish or American medical school. Paris, it cannot be emphasized too strongly, was not France and certainly not Europe and did not embody all the characteristics of early-nineteenth-century teaching.

By the end of the period under review, the locus of medical teaching had clearly shifted to the urban hospital in France and in Great Britain while remaining fixed in the university in the German states. In the United States, it could not be said to be lodged in either place, since most of the new medical schools had no ties to either a hospital or a college. The key issues in medical education by 1830 no longer concerned the place of practical training in a physician's preparation for medicine. For better or worse, the French hospital system of joining lectures to ward visits, often with little direct contact with patients, was firmly in place; the German clinic attached to a university medical school had everywhere become a small hospital; the informal British hospital school had replaced the university as the principal training ground of future practitioners in that country; and the American practice of supplementing apprenticeship training with freestanding medical schools was entering its period of greatest growth.

The typical clinical teacher of 1830 was variously a university professor in Germany, with responsibility for a definite ward of a hospital under university control; a hospital teacher in France holding his appointment from a hospital with similar responsibility for a teaching ward; a hospital lecturer in Great Britain, whose teaching was subordinate to patient care and to the physician's convenience; and an American practitioner who taught students in his own private practice or perhaps in a local hospital or dispensary.

The issues of greatest concern by the end of the 1820s now revolved around the relationship of the fast-growing academic studies in pathological anatomy, medical chemistry, and physiology to the practical training being given widely at the bedside. How should such science be taught at the bedside? How much science was necessary or desirable, anyway, for

---

151. Risse, *Hospital Life*, 283.
152. Bright, *Dr Richard Bright*, 72.

the physician-in-training? What about the second order of practitioners who were schooled principally in the practical aspects of medicine? Should they be taught any science? And if the practical physician were to be given more training in science, as was happening in many places, and the academic physician were to be given more training at the bedside, how long could the distinction between them be kept up? These are some of the questions to be taken up in the next two chapters.

5

Science and Medical Study: Early Nineteenth Century

The strong utilitarian impulse to make medical training more practical—the subject of the last chapter—coincided in time with a growing understanding of the human body. Indeed, the remarkable advances in anatomical knowledge of the eighteenth century were crucial to the adoption of the surgical model of teaching students in the nineteenth century. Medical educators now accepted without question the anatomical basis of disease and put increasing emphasis on anatomical studies and personal experience in dissecting the human body in their teaching. Whether in a university course, a hospital clinic, a school for practical physicians, a program for midwives, or private classes, by the early nineteenth century the study of anatomy, both theoretical and practical, was seen as the cornerstone of all medical teaching.

It was by means of the study of anatomy and the routine performance of autopsy, the famed French clinicians taught, that a real understanding of disease could be ultimately gained. In their zeal to discover new means of diagnosing illness in the living body, they searched for ways to determine the presence of telltale lesions or faulty functioning in the body that were not visible to the human eye. To "see" inside the body, to "feel" the presence of disease, to hear the sounds of irregular function would enable the physician to understand the course of the disease before it was found at autopsy.

If disease were local and lodged in the organs and tissues, as Morgagni and Bichat had demonstrated, then the new French technology of measurement, percussion, and auscultation would enable the physician to locate it and, conceivably, to arrest or extirpate it. The practical impulse in teaching and the new anatomical science of pathology thus worked together to create a new, more hopeful approach to the ancient riddle of how illness began, spread, and worked its mischief. The French achievement in creating a science of pathological anatomy out of the study of diseased tissue, declared the German clinician Karl Pfeufer, brought to medicine a "hitherto unknown sharpness of diagnosis."[1]

For the student of medicine, however, whether in a university or a practical school, it was an extraordinarily difficult and confusing time of changing concepts of disease, conflicting theories of causation, new scientific courses of study, and nagging doubts about the best preparation for a medical career. "The beginning student," advised the head of a practical medical school in Magdeburg in 1833, was now faced with the "massive size" of every medical science and "driven to despair" at the thought of mastering even a single subject.[2] How best to prepare oneself—and the student must normally make his own decisions—for a calling so greatly in flux? How much academic or scientific study did he actually need, and how much practical learning must he acquire in order to practice?

If serious anatomical study were now indispensable to medicine, what about such growing sciences as organic chemistry, physiology, or the study of pathological conditions in the laboratory? And how important were the traditional materia medica, the continuing lectures on the practice of medicine, the study of Latin, or a knowledge of the classical writers? If clinical training were best carried out in a hospital, as everyone now believed, and the systematic study of underlying science belonged in a school or university, how were the two to be combined, and in what proportion? How important was didactic training in the sciences, anyway, when it was the practical breakthroughs in surgery and pathological anatomy that promised most to the future practitioner? These are some of the questions to be considered in this and the following chapter.

Just as the teaching clinic took different forms in differing national and institutional settings, so the new sciences developed quite differently across national boundaries. New scientific ideas spread rapidly but unevenly from country to country and were then filtered through quite different educational and political structures. The special advantages of the Paris clinic—the close control under governmental authority of immense numbers of patients in specialized wards and hospitals—gave an important stimulus to the systematic observation and study of both living and dead patients. French studies of anatomy and pathological conditions, aided by the new technology of monitoring internal sounds, developed swiftly in the post-Napoleonic clinic, whereas those sciences dependent

1. Karl von Pfeufer, "Uber den gegenwärtigen Zustand der Medicin," *Annalen der städtischen Allgemeinen Krankenhäusern in München* 1 (1878): 395–406. The paper by Pfeufer was originally given at his installation as a professor in Zurich in 1840.

2. Friedrich Fritze, *Uber die Schwierigkeiten und Annehmlichkeiten des medizinischen und chirurgischen Studiums* (Magdeburg: Faber, 1833), 6.

on closely studying healthy organisms and making use of animal experiments, notably physiology, were pursued independently in special scientific institutes that often had little connection with a clinic or a school of medicine. The postrevolutionary cleavage of hospital from academic authority seemed to make inevitable a growing split in France between theoretical and practical science.

In Germany, by contrast, the eighteenth-century movement to incorporate clinics into the university had kept the tension between theory and practice within the same institution. Professors of chemistry and professors of surgery might have their separate institutes or laboratories, but they held equal status in the faculty that shaped the medical education of students. British and American clinics, on the other hand, still further removed from systematic academic and scientific study, remained the most practical of all in their reactions to the new sciences.

London teachers, in particular, who now dominated much of the medical teaching in Britain, were quick to seize on the practical uses of the anatomoclinical science of pathology but were slow to become interested in such theoretical studies as physiology. "The indicators are," writes Pauline Mazumdar in regard to London physiology in these years, "that little weight was placed on it."[3] Professional education in Britain and America, as in France, thus tended to follow the path of practical schooling, the lawyer learning his trade from another lawyer, the engineer from another engineer, and the doctor from another doctor, usually in a hospital following a short period of general education. Science was of value only insofar as it had a practical application to the training of a doctor.

The tension between theory and practice in medical teaching in the early nineteenth century was palpable in nearly every country. Even in the German states, the practical (or military) school of medicine, still the dominant site for preparing practitioners, was viewed with skepticism by university teachers because of its presumed scientific shortcomings, but the university school, despite its policlinics, was criticized as too theoretical and too far removed from actual practice to produce good practitioners.[4]

Likewise in Britain, when the new University of London tried in the 1830s to join the theoretical study of science to the practical work of the clinic, as was done in Germany, the hospital teachers at St. Bartholomew's objected strenuously that the new school was superior "in no respect" and that it was "much inferior" to others in its practical instruction.[5] In France, there was constant tension between hospital and

3. Pauline M. H. Mazumdar, "Anatomy, Physiology, and Surgery: Physiology Teaching in Early Nineteenth-Century London," *Canadian Bulletin of Medical History* 4 (1987): 122. See also Russell C. Maulitz, *Morbid Appearances: The Anatomy of Pathology in the Early Nineteenth Century* (Cambridge: Cambridge University Press, 1987).

4. Johanna Bleker, "Medical Students—To the Bed-Side or to the Laboratory? The Emergence of Laboratory-Training in German Medical Education, 1870–1900," in *Clinical Teaching, Past and Present*, vol. 21, ed. H. Beukers and J. Moll (Amsterdam: *Clio Medica*, 1987–88), 35.

5. Minutes, medical college, March 9, 1835, St. Bartholomew's Hospital Archive, London.

medical school teachers. A study commission of 1817 in Paris lamented the emphasis on theory for all students of medicine, declaring that what was most needed was "a class of enlightened practitioners, without being learned scientists, who will look for their clientele in the rural areas."[6] In the United States, too, in the early years of the century, many students and teachers were well aware "of a potential inconsistency between the demands of science and those of clinical practice."[7]

The New Sciences and the Old Curriculum

The shape of the emerging medical curriculum was as varied as the educational and political systems that set the framework for medical teaching. Medical teachers everywhere sought to strike some kind of balance between the growing number of theoretical courses in medicine, embodying new findings about the body and its ailments, and the clinical teaching of surgery, medicine, and obstetrics, but it was at best a shifting and uncertain equilibrium. As described earlier, the curriculum was most closely regulated by external authority in France and somewhat less so in Germany, and it was subject to the fewest restrictions in Britain and America. Whatever the external framework, teachers endeavored to instruct their pupils in the new practical methods of examination and diagnosis as best they could and to instill in them at the same time a sense of the growing authority of medicine as a practical science.

By 1840, a prospective student of medicine, whatever his country, could expect to be schooled in anatomy, including dissection, physiology, morbid anatomy, medical chemistry, materia medica or pharmacy, and the theory and practice of medicine, and also to be introduced to the actual practice of medicine, surgery, and midwifery in a hospital or under the tutelage of a preceptor. He might also reasonably expect to be required to study botany and natural history and perhaps medical jurisprudence as well. But the range of options, the methods of teaching, the selection of teachers, the periods of study, and the requirements for graduation varied considerably, even within the same country.

The core of the new practical science was the study of *morbid anatomy*, as it was then called. Whether taught by a surgeon such as Depuytren or a physician such as Laënnec, its goal was, in Laënnec's words, "to arrange the morbid appearance[s] in a nosological order" in the minds of students, so as to "render the classification of disease more exact."[8] This had

6. Rapport à la faculté de médecine sur les examens, leur ordre et leurs époques, 1817, AJ[16] 6358, Archives nationales.

7. Charles E. Rosenberg, "The Therapeutic Revolution: Medicine, Meaning, and Social Change in Nineteenth-Century America," in *The Therapeutic Revolution: Essays in the Social History of American Medicine*, ed. Morris J. Vogel and Charles E. Rosenberg (Philadelphia: University of Pennsylvania Press, 1979), 20.

8. Cited in Maulitz, *Morbid Appearances*, 74.

the practical effect of teaching the student to be more precise in both diagnosis and prognosis and to enable him to consider such limited therapies as removing serum from affected body cavities or performing surgery
to relieve symptoms. In describing an autopsy performed before a hundred Parisian students in 1815, the Englishman John Crosse remarked,
wonderingly, that "nothing is more useful than . . . these *demonstrations*
of morbid parts." He praised, in particular, the clarity with which the diseased patient's symptoms were correlated with the observed "cavity of
the abscess . . . under Poupart's ligament, along the course of the psoas
muscle, and its connection . . . with disease of the vertebrae."[9]

Medical students in France learned this "new language of the body"
for the most part in hospital clinics and private courses held outside the
official curriculum. An academic chair in the subject was established as
early as 1819 in the medical school at Strasbourg, but not until 1836 was
an official appointment in pathological anatomy made in the Paris faculty
as a result of a gift by Depuytren.[10] The intensive study of morbid
anatomy was thus a pedagogical means of bridging the gap between the
practical work of the clinic and the scientific understanding of disease.

The Spread of "Morbid Anatomy"

Across the Channel, the study of morbid anatomy developed quite differently in the entrepreneurial, loosely structured, and laissez-faire environment of early-nineteenth-century Britain. The continued resistance by
elite professional groups to combine surgery and medicine in medical
training made difficult the adoption of a common approach to the
pathology and physical diagnosis of disease. "Surgery is taught [in
Britain] without reference to medicine, and medicine is taught empiri-
cally," wrote the London editor of the *Medical Intelligencer* in 1822. Although students "are taught dead anatomy to a certain point, [teachers]
give little or no demonstrative information on morbid anatomy."[11] Long
after the Continent had moved from symptoms to physical signs as the
most important markers of serious internal illness, many British teachers
continued to urge the importance of painfully detailed patient histories
while neglecting to examine the patient at all. Not until the late 1830s,
concluded Charles Newman after examining ward case-notes at Guy's
Hospital, did physical examinations of incoming patients become routine.
"It is little short of astonishing," he observed, "how completely physical

9. John Greene Crosse, *Sketches of the Medical Schools of Paris* (London: J. Callow,
1815), 43. Emphasis in original.

10. Maulitz, *Morbid Appearances*, 75, 101; Johannes Steudel, "Medizinische Ausbildung in Deutschland, 1600–1850," in *Et Multum et Multa: Festgabe für Kurt Lindner*, ed.
Sigrid Schwenk et al. (Berlin: Walter de Gruyter, 1971), 412.

11. *Medical Intelligencer: or Monthly Compendium of Medical Knowledge* 3 (1822): ix.

examination was disregarded."[12] Students' experience in dissection and instruction in morbid anatomy as qualifications for practice were not made mandatory for apothecaries until 1835. Instead it was the teaching of normal anatomy and materia medica that constituted what Russell Maulitz called "the linchpins of a medical education."[13]

But many British students sought in Paris what they could not easily find at home. The chronic shortage of cadavers in Britain, noted earlier, sent hundreds of young English and Scottish students to the French capital after 1815 to practice dissection and pursue the study of anatomy and the new science of pathology. French laws enabled a steady flow of dead bodies to go to teachers of anatomy and surgery, whereas British legal practice still restricted dissection for the most part to postmortem examinations of the causes of death. By 1828, according to testimony before a parliamentary commission, two hundred British students were studying anatomy in Paris. Another two hundred entrepreneurs were at home trying to satisfy the huge domestic demand for bodies by exhuming them from British cemeteries.[14]

Many of those who went to Paris, like their American contemporaries, organized their own courses by hiring private instructors, much as a later generation of Anglo-Americans did in Vienna. One audacious Englishman, James Richard Bennett, taught a course to English students, using French cadavers, at the Hôpital de la Pitié.[15] The venture was quickly denied recognition by the Royal College of Surgeons in London, which argued that it would put the instruction of British youth in the hands of the mercurial French and destroy the hard-pressed British schools of anatomy.[16] The faculty in Glasgow likewise repeated its concern about the growing dependence on France for anatomical study, which could only lead to "dreadful and incalculable evils."[17]

Despite the flow of students to France, the teaching of anatomy in Britain at first was little changed. The great majority of students, of course, as was true of North America, received their training entirely at home. Doubts were widely expressed about the value of French study and whether or not the study of pathological anatomy had any real practical use. Resistance to the French method of teaching anatomy, fueled

12. Charles Newman, *The Evolution of Medical Education in the Nineteenth Century* (Oxford: Oxford University Press, 1957), 86–88.

13. Russell C. Maulitz, "Intellectual Migration: The Case of Pathological Anatomy," paper delivered at joint meeting of the British History of Science and History of Science societies, Manchester, July 13, 1988, p. 4.

14. House of Commons, Select Committee on Anatomy, *Report* (London: House of Commons, 1828), 7–8.

15. Russell C. Maulitz, "Channel Crossing: The Lure of French Pathology for English Medical Students, 1816–36," *Bulletin of the History of Medicine* 55 (1981): 492.

16. House of Commons, Select Committee on Medical Education, *Report*, 3 vols. (London: House of Commons, 1834), 2:80.

17. Senate Records, April 26, 1830, University of Glasgow Archive.

by chronic Francophobia, was strong among medical teachers, the royal corporations, and established practitioners. When the progressive Town Council of Edinburgh proposed establishing a chair in pathological anatomy in 1831, a university senate committee objected strongly on the ground that the subject was "inseparable" from teaching the practice of medicine.[18] A German visitor to Britain in 1825 remarked that he could find "no general pathology" being taught anywhere in the country.[19] In London, when Robert Carswell did begin teaching the subject at University College in 1830, he found only a tiny fraction of the medical students in his class. Two years later, only 9 of the 129 students enrolled in the medical school were taking his course.[20] The professor of the practice of medicine complained publicly about Carswell's course, charging that "morbid anatomy . . . cannot be taught . . . by anyone but the teacher of the practice of medicine." To do otherwise, he charged, would only "increase the expense" of students and "waste the[ir] time."[21]

But an important minority of British teachers did try to introduce the new methods of clinical diagnosis and pathological anatomy to their students. Matthew Bailie had published a pioneering textbook, *Morbid Anatomy*, as early as 1793, in which he urged the importance of studying postmortem changes "to detect some marked difference, by which the disease may be distinguished in the living body."[22] Students of both medicine and surgery, he insisted, could profit greatly from performing numerous dissections. By the early nineteenth century, other London teachers were guiding their students toward the pathological viewpoint in studying disease. Still others, notably in obstetrics, were recommending that students "feel" as well as listen to patients' complaints when making a difficult diagnosis. By the 1820s and 1830s, a number of popular teachers, many of whom had spent considerable time on the Continent—Robert Graves and William Stokes in Dublin and Robert Carswell, Richard Bright, Thomas Addison, and Thomas Hodgkin in London—were systematically teaching and carrying on research in morbid anatomy. Bright was lecturing three times a week on the subject in the early 1820s at Guy's Hospital as well as giving practical training to students in palpation and percussion and taking specimens from

18. Minutes of Senatus, October 4, 1831, University of Edinburgh Archive.

19. Wilhelm Wagner, *Uber die medizinal-Anstalten und den jetzigen Zustand der Heilkunde in Grossbritannien und Irland* (Berlin: G. Reimer, 1825), 4.

20. List of Students in the Medical Classes, Session 1, 1832–33, medical faculty correspondence, student registers, etc., University Archive, Science Library, University College London.

21. Robert Carswell to dean of Faculty of Medicine, February 20, 1838, ibid., File 90-111. Carswell complains in this letter about Prof. Elliotson's communication to the *Lancet*, which he cites.

22. Quoted in Susan C. Lawrence, "Science and Medicine at the London Hospitals: The Development of Teaching and Research, 1750–1815" (Ph.D. diss., University of Toronto, 1985), 446.

patients.[23] In 1827 Carswell was insisting on a separate course in morbid anatomy at the planned University of London, telling the council that "morbid anatomy will receive ere long in England that consideration which it deserves, and Professors [will] be appointed in British universities, whose special objective shall be to investigate and teach this, one of the most important branches of an elementary medical education."[24]

By the end of the decade in the provinces as well, courses in pathology—often taught with few clinical resources—were given in the new regional medical schools. A Manchester surgeon told his students in 1831 that it had been his practice for several years "to devote a large share of attention to Morbid Anatomy . . . [because] it is only by an accurate and careful comparison of what you have noted at the bedside, with what is disclosed (anatomically speaking) after death, that you can ever hope to become good Pathologists."[25]

In both France and Germany, an Edinburgh professor reported in 1831, separate classes in pathology were now being widely offered. Citing the lectures on pathology given in Berlin, Jena, Göttingen, and Heidelberg, he warned that the Scottish university was falling far behind Germany as well as France in teaching the new science.[26] In fact, Johann Friedrich Meckel, whom the University of London sought to attract to its first faculty, had been giving lectures on pathological anatomy at Halle as early as 1796.[27] The University of Bonn, opened as a showcase university by Prussia in 1818, offered courses in the subject from the beginning, including instruction for students in the preparation of pathological specimens.[28]

Elsewhere, private teachers (*privatdozenten*) had begun teaching separate courses in pathology at a number of the universities by 1820, and established professors combined teaching in pathology with courses in physiology or clinical medicine. The "innovation time" for making this and other sciences a requirement for German students of medicine, however, often lasted several decades.[29] As late as 1850, only Vienna,

23. Diana Berry and Campbell Mackenzie, *Richard Bright, 1789–1858: Physician in an Age of Revolution and Reform* (London: Royal Society of London, 1992), 118.

24. Robert Carswell to Council of University of London, December 21, 1827, college correspondence file 300-311, University Archive, Science Library, University College London.

25. Thomas Fawdington, *A Catalogue descriptive chiefly of the Morbid Preparations contained in the Museum of the Manchester Theatre of Anatomy and Medicine, Marsden Street* (Manchester: Harrison and Crosfield, 1833), iii–iv, Manchester Collection, Rylands Library, University of Manchester.

26. John Thomson to George Aitchison, October 29, 1831, Royal College of Physicians of Edinburgh.

27. Steudel, "Medizinische Ausbildung," 412.

28. Karl Schmiz, *Die medizinische Fakultät der Universität Bonn, 1818–1918* (Bonn: R. Marcus and E. Weber, 1920), 81.

29. See Wolf-Ingo Steudel, "Die Innovationszeit von Prüfungsfächern in der medizinischen Ausbildung in Deutschland" (med. diss., University of Kiel, 1973).

Würzburg, and Prague had established full chairs of pathology, although all the universities offered some teaching in the subject.[30]

Although the study of pathological anatomy in America suffered from an acute need for clinical facilities, it was not hampered by the rigid separation of medical and surgical training that plagued British efforts to introduce the new science. The theoretical teaching of the subject was undertaken in America long before clinical resources permitted the student to gain practical experience in applying it at the bedside. In a number of the eastern schools, as well as in such western centers as New Orleans, Cincinnati, Lexington, and Louisville, the academic study of pathology was begun early in the century.

Elsewhere, a number of peripatetic medical teachers carried the word of advances in the new science to the many rural schools in the United States.[31] When dedicating a clinical amphitheater in Louisville in 1840, for example, Daniel Drake stressed the importance of both the academic study of pathology and its applications in the clinic. "Every physician who is not a pathologist," he told the assembled students, "is a routinist. . . . The morbid appearances are the internal manifestations [of disease] revealed to us after death," he explained, and "the pathological anatomist sits judge on the Clinical practitioner. . . . Pathological anatomy is the *new* tribunal of practical medicine."[32]

Contrary to a widespread belief, the classroom teaching of such subjects as pathological anatomy in the United States and Canada was not markedly dissimilar to that of Britain and much of Europe, especially in the practical schools, during the first half of the nineteenth century. The British editor of the *Medical Intelligencer*, after describing the "fanciful hypotheses" about medical science growing in Europe, remarked that "the Americans have apparently deviated little from their parent country in their mode of studying medicine. They are great collectors of facts, although they do not proceed on a very scientific principle."[33]

What made American teaching different was the dearth of hospitals and teaching clinics, the lack of full-time teachers, and especially the absence of centralized control over what was taught and who could practice medicine. In both Britain and America, the medical teacher was almost always a busy practitioner and rarely a full-time instructor, as he was on the Continent. The typical curriculum of an American medical college encom-

30. Johannes Pantel and Axel Bauer, "Die Institutionalisierung der pathologischen Anatomie im 19.Jahrhundert an den Universitäten Deutschlands, der deutschen Schweiz und Osterreichs," *Gesnerus* 47 (1990): 316, table 6.

31. Russell C. Maulitz, "Pathology," in *The Education of American Physicians: Historical Essays*, ed. Ronald L. Numbers (Berkeley and Los Angeles: University of California Press, 1980), 128–29.

32. Daniel Drake, *An Introductory Discourse to a Course of Lectures on Clinical Medicine and Pathological Anatomy* (Louisville: Prentice and Weissinger, 1840), 9–10. Emphasis in original.

33. *Medical Intelligencer* 3 (1822): xvii.

passed virtually the same subjects being taught in Great Britain, including pathology, anatomy and physiology, chemistry, materia medica, botany and natural history, therapeutics, and lectures, sometimes with demonstrations, on surgery, medicine, and obstetrics. As in England and frequently on the Continent, anatomy and surgery were taught by the same person; pathological anatomy was often combined with the teaching of medicine or perhaps anatomy; and medical jurisprudence was added as teaching resources permitted. Medical faculties varied in size from five to seven professors, as did most of the British schools and the practical schools on the Continent at that time.

The textbooks used in American schools were often British publications or else translations, especially from French, of continental works. The terms of study were usually short, and the courses were not graded, as they normally were not in Great Britain. The preceptorship remained the principal method of acquiring practical experience in both countries. Both nations relied, as did France, on an abundance of private courses to supplement the medical school curriculum. American schools were later denounced as "proprietary" because they depended on student fees and lacked any connection with a university, but this was also true of most British schools and many private continental schools. In comparing the rural, proprietary schools of backwoods America with the Paris medical faculty, or perhaps that of Vienna, the reformers of the antebellum years, anxious to provoke change, were comparing some very small apples with some very large oranges. A comparison of the Ohio Medical College in Cincinnati with the practical school at Bamberg in Bavaria or Anderson's Medical College in Glasgow, by contrast, would have yielded a far less striking contrast.

The Beginnings of Physiology as a Medical Subject

In the classroom teaching of the new science of physiology, just as in the teaching of pathological anatomy and chemistry, the American teacher often used the same textbooks and teaching methods as did his contemporaries in England, In neither country before 1850 was physiology seen to be a practical or laboratory course. "Whether a student learned physiology by reading a textbook from his preceptor's library [or by] listening to lectures in a proprietary medical school," writes John Warner, "he was made constantly aware that a knowledge of bodily functions was important to an understanding of disease."[34] Although the clinical value of this physiological teaching was often questioned, it was rarely omitted from

34. John Harley Warner, "Physiology," in *The Education of American Physicians: Historical Essays*, ed. Ronald L. Numbers (Berkeley and Los Angeles: University of California Press, 1980), 48. Much of the following discussion of American physiology follows Warner's treatment of the subject on pp. 50–59.

the medical school curriculum, in the belief that it somehow strengthened the preparation and authority of the future practitioner. As early as
1765, John Morgan had urged its inclusion in America's first medical
school. Many early professors of anatomy included a discussion of bodily
functions in their courses, as did the professors of medicine. As they were
in England, most American courses in physiology in the early nineteenth
century were confined to some treatment of body chemistry, along with a
survey of knowledge about digestion, respiration, blood circulation, and
other functions.

The amount of physiology taught varied in both America and Britain
with the interests of the professor, but under the tutelage of a man such
as the Edinburgh-trained Robley Dunglison, it might rank with some of
the best teaching in Europe. Physiology, Dunglison told students in
1837, "is the real foundation of medical knowledge." The great weakness
of British teaching, he added, was "that they teach anatomy as if a knowledge of the dead body were the sole foundation of medical study," rather
than "knowledge of the *living* body."[35] His textbook in physiology sold
nearly 100,000 copies over the next quarter-century. In a few cases, notably at the University of Pennsylvania, students even carried on crude
physiological experiments using live animals for the medical thesis that
was required for their graduation.[36]

The teaching of physiology in Britain in the early nineteenth century
was much closer to that of America than to that of the Continent. Physiological instruction remained a part of anatomy much longer than it did
in either France or Germany, and it eschewed the kind of routine animal
experimentation that later provoked such a wave of antivivisection sentiment in England. In the London hospitals and the Scottish universities,
as well as in the private anatomy schools, the teaching of physiology was
at best a small part of the instruction. James Paget recalled that the
"physiological portion" of the combined lectures in anatomy and physiology he had heard at Guy's in 1834 "was, even for that time, feeble."
When he was named the first lecturer in the subject at Guy's a decade
later, his appointment was not opposed, he said, because "no one had seriously studied it."[37] A long British review of new works in physiology in
1839, dominated by a discussion of the works of Johannes Müller, defended the slow practicality and commonsense empiricism of the "English school" and its rejection of experimentation, arguing that "physiology, being a physical science, is [not] to be advanced by experiment and
observation alone."[38]

By this time, the first separate appointments in physiology were being

35. Robley Dunglison, *The Medical Student; or, Aids to the Study of Medicine* (Philadelphia: Carey, Lea & Blanchard, 1837), 157–58. Emphasis in original.

36. Edward C. Atwater, "'Squeezing Mother Nature': Experimental Physiology in the
United States Before 1870," *Bulletin of the History of Medicine* 52 (1978): 321–22.

37. James Paget, *Memoirs and Letters* (London: Longmans, Green, 1902), 46, 120–21.

38. *British and Foreign Medical Review* 5 (1839): 87, 99.

made in the London hospitals and also in Edinburgh. Only the University of London tried seriously to break the traditional pattern of physiological teaching when it appointed the German-trained William Sharpey in 1836.[39] Sharpey introduced concepts of experimental investigation into his combined course with anatomy. He was a pioneer in Britain in performing experiments on animals before his classes.[40] Although never an original investigator, he stimulated in others an abiding interest in physiology, so much so that he was later called the "Father of Modern Physiology in Britain" by such scientists as E. A. Schäfer.[41] "As a student at University College," Joseph Lister later wrote, "I was greatly attracted by Dr. Sharpey's lectures which inspired me with a love of physiology, that has never left me."[42] But however inspirational, Sharpey's teaching, the most important in Britain before 1850, was described by others as wholly didactic with "no attempt whatever at any practical teaching."[43]

The teaching of physiology on the Continent, meanwhile, had veered sharply away from the uncertain, didactic teaching of the subject in Britain and America. In both France and Germany, the study of physiology had taken on a more independent and experimental character. The movement to free the study of organic functions in all living creatures from the dominance of normal anatomy and its practical uses was well under way by the 1820s. Unlike the British and the Americans, continental researchers were not held back by the "yoke of utility," in Gerald Geison's phrase, and did not worry so much about the lack of useful applications of the new physiology.[44] At the French Academy of Science, the Collège de France, the Museum of Natural History, veterinary schools, and hospitals, and in private courses outside the *écoles de médecine*, physiology achieved a degree of support and recognition that gave France an early lead in physiological investigation. Experiments on living animals, sometimes shocking to foreign visitors, were common by 1820. "The taste of Bichat for experiments," wrote the Englishman John Crosse, "has produced [a] mania of vivisection."[45] An impressive list of seventeen

39. See his letter to the Council of the University of London, July 29, 1836, for a full recitation of his accomplishments and his preparations for teaching a different kind of course. William Sharpey Papers, University College London Archive, college correspondence, Medical Faculty, 3678-94.

40. L. S. Jacyna, ed., *A Tale of Three Cities: The Correspondence of William Sharpey and Allen Thomson* (London: *Medical History* supplement, Wellcome Institute for the History of Medicine, 1989), xix.

41. D. W. Taylor, "The Life and Teaching of William Sharpey (1802–1880): 'Father of Modern Physiology' in Britain," *Medical History* 15 (1971): 126.

42. Ibid., 141.

43. Henry Sewell, "Henry Newell Martin," *Johns Hopkins University Bulletin* 22 (1911): 329.

44. Gerald L. Geison, "Social and Institutional Factors in the Stagnancy of English Physiology, 1840–1870," *Bulletin of the History of Medicine* 46 (1972): 41.

45. Quoted in John E. Lesch, *Science and Medicine in France: The Emergence of Experimental Physiology, 1790–1855* (Cambridge, MA: Harvard University Press, 1984), 80.

persons doing experimental work in the subject in France by 1820 was compiled by the historian John Lesch.[46]

But the teaching of the new physiology seeped only slowly into the formal classes in medicine. Professors in France could count on, at best, only a small working space for their experimental interests, and ordinary medical students were seldom found there. Financial support and laboratory assistance were generally not available to medical teachers. "The proper course of physiology is that taught by experiment," a British surgeon told a parliamentary committee in 1834, "but although the Paris school of medicine has a distinct professor of physiology . . . they have no experimental physiology."[47] Much of the French achievements in the new science, then, came outside the official structure of medical education.

François Magendie, himself a product of the Paris medical school and the acknowledged leader in the field, taught his pioneering courses privately or at the Collège de France and rarely came into contact with run-of-the-mill medical students. The sharp division between scientific investigation, on the one hand, and the teaching of medicine, on the other, a heritage of the Revolution, caused France to suffer from, in the opinion of some scholars, the lack of opportunity to "introduce new students to scientific inquiry."[48]

Historians have long debated why the science of physiology developed so differently on the other side of the Rhine, but pedagogically it seems clear that the early amalgamation of the teaching clinic into the German university made far easier the task of curricular change than in France or Britain. Although the tensions there were sometimes severe as new subjects pushed for more resources and more space in the German medical curriculum, the interests of both clinicians and scientifically oriented teachers were usually accommodated. In Prussia, for example, the responsible ministry worked hard to reconcile practical and theoretical interests in medical education.[49] In the early 1820s, the Czech physiologist Jan Purkyne, with the knowledge of the ministry, was conducting experiments for medical students at the University of Breslau.[50] Even earlier, at Bonn, Professor A. C. Mayer, according to the 1821 university catalog, was teaching a course in human physiology to medical students, in which

46. Ibid., 84.

47. House of Commons, Select Committee, *Report*, 2:216.

48. William Coleman and Frederic L. Holmes, eds., *The Investigative Enterprise: Experimental Physiology in Nineteenth-Century Medicine* (Berkeley and Los Angeles: University of California Press, 1988), 13.

49. Richard L. Kremer, "Between Wissenschaft und Praxis: Experimental Medicine and the Prussian State, 1807–1848," in *"Einsamkeit und Freiheit" neu besichtigt: Universitätsreformen und Disziplinenbildung in Preussen als Modell für Wissenschaftspolitik im Europa des 19.Jahrhunderts*, ed. Gert Schubring (Stuttgart: Franz Steiner, 1991), 156.

50. Jan Purkyne, "A Brief Report on the Origin and Present Condition of the Institute of Physiology in Breslau, 30 August 1841," in Vladislav Kruta, "J. E. Purkyne's Account of the Origin and Early History of the Institute of Physiology in Breslau (1841)," *Scripta Medica* 39 (1966): 3.

"students have the opportunity, under supervision of the director, to take part in experiments on animals and to witness a series of remarkable demonstrations."[51] In Freiburg, about the same time, a similar innovation was being introduced by Carl Schultze.[52] The Bavarian university at Würzburg also made provision in 1825 for "the necessary vivisections of animals for the lectures in physiology."[53]

By the late 1820s, a considerable number of the German universities were teaching physiology as an "experimental" discipline.[54] The tempo of change increased during the 1830s as Johannes Müller began teaching physiology in Berlin, and Purkyne sent his first request for a separate physiological institute to the Prussian government, asking for a place where medical students, as well as advanced researchers, could do microscopic and chemical studies. Only in such a teaching laboratory, Purkyne argued in 1836, could physiology "create its own disciplinary boundaries."[55] What was happening in Germany by this time, as described more fully in Chapter 9, was the beginning of the laboratory teaching of medical students and the first attempts to portray medicine to them as an experimental science.[56]

Although other sciences, notably chemistry, were helping reshape the understanding of medicine, their impact on the curriculum was as yet insignificant in comparison with that of pathology and physiology. Since medicines were the major weapon in the physician's armamentarium, their chemical composition had long been the subject of study in most medical schools. By 1810, courses in medical chemistry, taught by descriptive lectures and sometimes accompanied by simple demonstrations, were a staple in medical education. Interest was growing, too, in the applications of chemistry to such organic functions as digestion, respiration, and excretion, as well as in the chemical analysis of blood, urine, saliva, and other body fluids.[57] In the early nineteenth century in a number of

51. *Jahrbuch der preussischen Rhein-Universität* (Bonn, 1821), 434 ff. See also *Vorlesungen auf der königlich preussischen Rhein-Universität Bonn im Sommerhalbjahr 1822* (Bonn, 1822), 4.

52. E. Th. Nauck, "Bemerkungen zur Geschichte des physiologischen Instituts Freiburg i. Br.: Paul Hoffmann zum 65. Geburtstag," *Bericht der naturforschungs Gesellschaft zu Freiburg in Br.* 40 (1950): 148–49; Eduard Seidler, *Die medizinische Fakultät der Albert-Ludwigs-Universität Freiburg im Breisgau* (Berlin: Springer, 1991), 119–20.

53. Instruction für die anatomischen Anstalten an der Universität zu Würzburg, 1825, Anatomisches Institut Papers, Universität Würzburg, Bayerisches Hauptstaatsarchiv, Munich, Bd. I, MS., MK 11401.

54. See Hermann F. Kilian, *Die Universitaeten Deutschlands in medicinisch-naturwissenschaftlicher Hinsicht* (Amsterdam: B. M. Israël, 1966). This work was originally published in 1828.

55. Kremer, "Between Wissenschaft und Praxis," 165.

56. For a full discussion of the introduction of physiology into the German medical curriculum, see Hans-Heinz Eulner, *Die Entwicklung der medizinischen Spezialfächer an den Universitäten des deutschen Sprachgebietes* (Stuttgart: Ferdinand Enke, 1970), 46–65.

57. André Bescher, "L'enseignement de la chimie en médecine au début du XIXe siècle" (med. diss., University of Lyon, 1959).

the French scientific institutes and in the German universities, chemical laboratories were being added, and courses in "animal chemistry" were offered to medical and nonmedical students alike. But it was not until the 1840s, with some exceptions, that chemistry began to have the same kind of effect on medical teaching that had marked the advent of pathological anatomy and physiology. Similarly, although botany continued to be taught in most medical schools because of its importance to pharmacy, it did not provoke the kind of interest among students that the newer sciences did.

Medical Study and National Differences

The differences in medical education caused earlier by the advent of clinical teaching had thus been widened by 1830 through the introduction of the new medical sciences. A careful observer traveling in Europe and North America in these years would certainly have been struck by the many changes in the curriculum since 1800 and by the growing divergence among nations in training doctors. Medical education, on the whole, was becoming both more practical and scientific in every country. It was studied less and less in the universities, with the important exception of Germany, and more and more outside the classroom. Flourishing schools of medicine could now be found in many small towns in Germany and the United States but were located almost wholly in cities in France and Great Britain. The apprenticeship system, which was dying on the Continent, still remained a principal means of gaining practical experience in the English-speaking countries. Although medical and surgical teaching were growing steadily together nearly everywhere, the pace of change was much slower in Great Britain. And research in the new sciences, which was carried out informally in Great Britain, was pursued in hospitals and specialized institutes in France by 1830, in universities in Germany, and scarcely at all in North America.

In Great Britain, a traveler would have noticed a major shift in medical teaching toward the hospital and private schools of London, which were quickly moving to meet the rising demand for both scientific and especially practical education in medicine. The old center of medical training in Britain, the University of Edinburgh, was declining in relative importance, and a number of provincial cities had begun to organize their own schools of medicine. A new university school of medicine, the first in England to stress the new sciences, was established in London in the late 1820s. And the British state had taken its first hesitant step toward requiring uniform standards of education for apothecary-practitioners.

Crossing the Channel, the visitor would have found that the postrevolutionary settlement in medicine had left intact most of the reforms of the revolutionary generation. To the cross-channel visitor, the *Medical Gazette* reported, the French system of training physicians seemed too centralized, too unstable, too lacking in the *elements de durée* to be effective in producing good doctors.[58] Although a highly structured educational and scientific program, under the direction of a powerful state, had made Paris a principal site of research in the medical sciences and a world center for private training and experience in anatomy, the education of ordinary physicians, it seemed to Britons, was neglected. "The Sciences of France," wrote the visiting Englishman W. P. Allison in his diary, contrasting what he saw with his own country, "are *forced* in Paris as in a hotbed, by the schools—by the Institute, by ambition & emulation—not looking for its reward in useful arts and consequent wealth, it is disjoined from the industry of the country & adds little to its resources."[59]

The old centers of Montpellier and Strasbourg, meanwhile, like the school at Edinburgh, had lost much of their luster for students, and a score of practical medical schools were now filling the need for general practitioners. An effort to elevate these secondary schools of medicine into regional universities, to replace the single University of France created by Napoleon, had failed in 1817.[60]

Farther east, by contrast, a still disunited Germany benefited from the large number of its universities spread across central Europe. Long used to a powerful role for government in setting standards for medical practice and structured to provide scientific and practical instruction in medicine, the German states by 1830 were experiencing a rise in medical enrollment and in interest in the study of natural science. As in France, the practical medical schools of Germany continued to supply much of the demand for practitioners outside the large cities.

In North America, finally, a medical traveler would have been impressed by the wave of entrepreneurial enterprise that was creating medical schools at a rate faster than that of any other country. Both state and national governments in the United States showed less interest in regulating medicine than did any government of western Europe. But the teaching of academic medicine in America was closely patterned after European schools, even if the term of study was shorter, and the drive to acquire clinical experience, though diffuse and scattered, was as strong and evident as it was anywhere in Europe.

58. *Medical Gazette* 13 (1833–34): 724.

59. W. P. Allison, Travel diary, London and France, 1825, Allison Papers, 11/53, Royal College of Physicians of Edinburgh. Emphasis in original.

60. Robert Fox, "Scientific Enterprise and the Patronage of Research in France, 1800–70," *Minerva* 11 (1973): 450.

6

A Bird's Eye View of
Medical Education in 1830

The changes under way in medical training in the transatlantic world by 1830 owed much to the political and social transformations of the preceding half-century. The political revolutions of the old century, which ushered in a long period of turmoil and conflict, had been followed by a period in the early nineteenth century of reaction and consolidation, new industrial growth and the spread of cities, commercial expansion and rising prosperity, and a high degree of political turbulence in every country. No nation escaped the impact of rapid population changes, of buoyant capitalistic enterprise, of the spreading democratic tide, or of the efforts of reformers to help those most adversely affected by the urban-industrial revolution.

The training of doctors was inevitably influenced by the rising power of the middle classes in Europe and America as they demanded more medical services and a higher standard of medical competence. The continued growth of industrial cities, notably in Britain, posed serious problems of public health and the medical care of the poor. By 1831, London's population was already approaching a million and a half, and nearly half the remaining population were now living in towns of more than five thousand.[1]

The doctors most in demand in these conditions were those who joined a skill in practical medicine with a knowledge of the new practical sciences. The new studies of science, it was increasingly believed by laypeople, gave the physician a surer command of diagnosis and a better

1. R. D. Lobban, *Edinburgh and the Medical Revolution* (Cambridge: Cambridge University Press, 1980), 26.

understanding of the disease process, and his practical skills assured the patient of the best possible treatment. Medicine as a practical science, in short, was seen by the public as an important advance over both the old humanistic medicine of the universities and the crude empiricism of the earlier practical schools.

The triumph of the clinic and the rise of the new sciences together created a new confidence in medical education. The schools themselves were becoming more alike. University medical faculties now insisted as a matter of course on a large measure of practical experience in a clinic or hospital, or at least a supervised apprenticeship, before allowing graduates to practice, and the practical schools in every country were adding course after course in those sciences deemed most useful for general practice. Some were beginning even to question the need for different levels of medical training altogether and to urge the adoption of a common educational standard for all who treated the public. The new ideal of a physician in Britain, writes Irvine Loudon, was an "all-rounder," a "general Practitioner . . . who could officiate in all departments of the profession and dispense medicines as well as prescribe."[2]

The years after 1830 were thus a critical turning point in the movement in Britain and elsewhere to create a more systematic and uniform approach to training doctors. Before looking at these efforts at change, however, we take a closer look in this chapter at the actual state of medical education in each of the major countries in about 1830.

The German Enterprise in Medical Education

In sheer size, the German enterprise in medical teaching, if considered as a whole, dwarfed that of any other nation. A reasonable estimate of the number of medical students formally enrolled in 1830 in German-speaking universities, practical schools of medicine, and military schools would be in excess of six thousand. Of these, more than half were now studying in universities.[3] A course of study in a university was becoming more and more the standard route to licensure and practice. The requirements for a university degree in medicine and for a license to practice were close to those in France. As it was in France, a diploma from a humanistic *gymnasium* (university preparatory school) was required everywhere for admission to a university.

2. Irvine Loudon, *Medical Care and the General Practitioner, 1750–1850* (Oxford: Clarendon Press, 1986), 194–95.

3. This estimate is based on a number of sources, especially the following: Franz Eulenburg, *Die Frequenz der deutschen Universitäten von ihrer Gründung bis zur Gegenwart* (Leipzig: B. G. Teubner, 1904), 255, figure 8; "Zusammenfassung über die Anzahl der Studenten auf den Universitäten pro Sommer-Semester 1824," manuscript, Nachlass Altenstein, GSPK, Merseburg 92, A VI, b, Nr. 21; and incomplete statistics for individual universities and practical schools.

The medical course of study in Germany by 1830 generally took four years, beginning with botany, chemistry, physics, zoology, and anatomy in the first year; physiology, pharmacy, pathology, and pathological anatomy in the second; and concluding in the last two years with advanced pathology, surgery, midwifery, ophthalmology, and practical clinics in the university hospital. Unlike the French system, however, the student was given a great deal of freedom in choosing his courses, subject only to his need to prepare for the state licensing examinations after the fourth year.

For the academic degree of doctor of medicine, which the university student (unlike the situation in France) did not need to take in order to practice, a series of further examinations, still conducted in Latin at many universities, was required, followed by a dissertation written and defended in Latin. The state examinations for licensure, on the other hand, included tests of practical skill and assumed a sound classical education by the candidates so that, in the words of the Prussian law, "they are not only practically [trained] but perfectly literary men."[4]

Prussia was increasingly the model for other German states in organizing their systems of medical education. Two new universities at Berlin and Bonn, founded in 1810 and 1818, were given particular support by the new minister of education and culture, Karl zum Altenstein, an ardent proponent of the natural sciences in medicine. The older Prussian universities—Halle, Breslau, and Königsberg—though declining in relative importance, were still among the leading schools of continental Europe. Elsewhere, Bavaria supported three medical schools in its universities at Würzburg, Erlangen, and (after 1826) Munich. The state of Baden could boast the oldest German medical school outside the Hapsburg dominions in Heidelberg, as well as the flourishing western outpost of German medicine at Freiburg.

Other medical schools of varying quality could be found in Leipzig, Jena, Tübingen, Marburg, Kiel, and Rostock and in German-language universities in Switzerland, and especially Vienna and Prague. All in all, by the early 1830s twenty-four university medical schools and thirty practical schools of medicine were spread across German Europe.[5]

Well before 1830, a number of observers noted an important transformation occurring in the German universities in favor of the scientific and scholarly grounding of medicine. A French survey of European universities in 1808, for example, described the "magnificent establishments" to

---

4. This paragraph is based on the summary in Joseph Leo-Wolf, "Medical Education in Germany," *American Medical Recorder* 13 (1828): 481–90. Leo-Wolf was an immigrant-physician from Hamburg.

5. See Hermann F. Kilian, *Die Universitaeten Deutschlands in medicinisch-naturwissenschaftlicher Hinsicht* (Amsterdam: B. M. Israël, 1966), originally published in 1828, for descriptions of all these universities except Bern and Zurich, which were founded in the 1830s. Another contemporary description of the distribution of students in the German universities is in Anonymous, *The University of Göttingen at the Beginning of the Year 1835* (London: Robert Boswell, 1836), 18–22.

be found across the Rhine and praised their range of scientific offerings, the "profound erudition" of their "mandarin" professors, the "genius" of their educational organization, all of which, said the author, made them "destined to become . . . the institutions to which other nations will pay tribute."[6] Other accounts pointed to the growing importance of professorial research, the rapid differentiation of subject matter in the medical curriculum, and the increasing mobility of students and professors as governments competed for outstanding talent to serve their own ends. "University education must excel in comprehensive thoroughness and scientific content," read a typical German handbook for medical students of the early 1830s.[7]

Strong ministers such as Altenstein ignored the objections of medical faculties in their zeal to attract builders of scientific strength in medicine. "The high officials," wrote Jacob Henle concerning the Berlin appointment over faculty protest of Johannes Müller to a post in physiology, "hope for a violent shake-up in academic life, particularly in the study of medicine."[8] In the same year, Friedrich Fritze of Magdeburg, leader of a medical–surgical academy at which presumably practical studies were emphasized, told the students in almost lyrical fashion that a new scientific spirit was sweeping through Germany and that it had become even for practical physicians "a blessed goddess, comforter, and helper of the sick and weak."[9]

Of all the universities in Germany, reported the widely traveled Hermann Kilian in 1828, Berlin was by far the most comprehensive and richest in scientific study. Its twenty-nine medical faculty members included the venerable clinician Christoph Hufeland, the ophthalmologist Carl Friedrich Graefe, the obstetrician Elias von Siebold, the anatomist Carl Rudolphi, and the botanist and physiologist C. H. Schultz. The last, according to Kilian, was "a remarkably experienced observer" in the use of the microscope.[10] A four-year plan of study was presented to the authorities by Dean Rudolphi in 1820, following a long and heated debate by members of the faculty over the relative weight to be given to scientific and practical courses.[11] The twenty-five courses offered in 1828 included new offerings in pediatrics, psychiatry, and venereal diseases.[12]

When the Prussian government opened a new university at Bonn in

6. Charles Villiers, *Coup d'oeil sur les universités* (Cassell, 1808), 12–24, 109–10.

7. Johann W. Arnold, *Hodegetik für Medicin-Studirende oder Anleitung zum Studium der Medicin* (Heidelberg: Karl Gerold, 1832), 38.

8. Quoted in R. Steven Turner, "The Growth of Professorial Research in Prussia, 1818 to 1848—Causes and Context," *Historical Studies in the Physical Sciences* 3 (1971): 175.

9. Friedrich Fritze, *Uber die Schwierigkeiten und Annehmlichkeiten des medizinischen und chirurgischen Studiums* (Magdeburg: Faber, 1833), 17.

10. Kilian, *Die Universitaeten Deutschlands*, 27–48.

11. Akten der medizinischen Fakultät zu Berlin, "Diskussion über einen 4-jährige Studienplan für Medizinstudenten," 73, E60, February 22, 1820, October 28, 1820, Humboldt University Archive, Berlin.

12. Ibid., "Tabellarische Uebersicht der zur gesamten Medicin gehörigen Lehrvorträge," 1828, 137, E1, L1.

1818 to serve its newly acquired Rhine provinces, Berlin was its model. From the beginning, the University of Bonn stressed natural science and the "need to root out French influences (i.e., the professional and practical emphasis in medical training)," which was best done "in a small university town."[13] Next to Berlin, wrote Kilian, Bonn ranked highest in the fields of science and medicine.[14]

Although smaller than Berlin in its medical faculty, the new university attracted such promising scholars as Johannes Müller in physiology, Friedrich Nasse in medicine, and A. C. Mayer in anatomy. From its earliest years, courses were offered in such still uncommon subjects as "medical science and student learning," pathological anatomy, human and comparative physiology, physiology of the senses in man and animal, and sleep and its disorders.[15] In physiology alone, as many as five different courses were being given in the same semester by clinicians, anatomists, gynecologists, and pharmacologists alike.[16] As in other German universities, practical work in the clinics was prescribed, too, as a necessary part of the curriculum. Nasse used his popular medical clinic at Bonn to give hands-on instruction to students in auscultation, percussion, and the use of the microscope and to assign them direct responsibility for diagnosing and treating patients.[17]

Much was made later by reformers and historians alike of the philosophical cast of scientific thought in early nineteenth-century Germany and its effects on medicine. To a later generation, the *naturphilosophie* of Friedrich Schelling, Johann Fichte, and their followers seemed the very epitome of the vague and speculative reasoning that had held back the progress of scientific medicine. The emphasis by the Romantic philosophers, including some physicians, on the polarity between spirit and matter, and the search for analogies between the makeup of the human organism and the structure of the natural world appeared to be the antithesis of the rational, empirical nature of science. But in the view of a number of recent scholars, as well as contemporary medical figures, the conflict between philosophical speculation and medical teaching was more apparent than real.

The widespread interest of medical men in *naturphilosophie*, in fact, had surprisingly little direct impact on their teaching of either scientific or practical subjects. A close look at the medical curriculum of German universities during these years shows remarkably few traces of the raging intellectual debate between Schelling's supporters and his critics. At Freiburg, for example— except for Johann Schaffroth's proselytizing for

13. "Die Einrichtung der Universität zu Bonn," manuscript, Bd.1, GSPK, Merseburg, 76 Va, Sekt. 3, Tit. 1, Nr. 2.

14. Kilian, *Die Universitäten Deutschlands*, 169–72.

15. *Vorlesungen auf der Königlich Preussischen Rhein-Universität im Winterhalbjahre 1820–21* (Bonn, 1820).

16. Karl Schmiz, *Die medizinische Fakultät der Universität Bonn, 1818–1918* (Bonn: R. Marcus and E. Weber, 1920), 62.

17. Ibid., 8–9, 75–78.

Schelling's ideas in his lectures on special pathology and therapeutics—the debate left little enduring effect on medical teaching, whereas at Heidelberg—again excepting Karl August Himly—the impact was even less.[18] The medical faculty of the University of Göttingen, according to Ulrich Tröhler, was "untouched" by the wave of romantic-speculative medicine.[19] And in his comprehensive survey of scientific and medical teaching in the German universities, Kilian, while stressing that science had struck deeper roots in Germany than in any other country, makes no mention at all of philosophical differences or conflicts in the institutions he surveyed.[20]

The early developments in pathological anatomy, experimental physiology, and other sciences that have already been recounted, moreover, took place during the heyday of the *naturphilosophie* influence in Germany. In some ways, this speculative reasoning about the fundamental nature of things may well have been a positive stimulus to scientific development, by promoting serious examination of the roots of scientific thinking and by freeing medical professors to become independent scholars and thinkers and not merely teachers of practical medicine.[21]

The French System: Comparisons and Contrasts

To compare the French system of medical education around 1830 with that of Germany is to be struck by both the many similarities and the many differences between them. For all the contrasts, the two systems were in fact far closer to each other than either was to medical teaching in Britain or North America. In both nations, natural science had come to play a much stronger role in training doctors than was true in Anglo-America. Both continued to make a sharp distinction in training between academically schooled physicians and those educated in the practical schools serving the countryside. Both made far less use of the apprenticeship as a means of acquiring practical experience than did either Britain or America. Both valued highly the teaching clinic—even though it took different forms—as a central focus of medical learning. Both had overcome the centuries-old separation of surgery from medicine in teaching. And fi-

18. See the discussion in Ernst G. Kürz, *Die Freiburger medizinische Fakultät und die Romantik* (Munich: Münchener Beiträge zur Geschichte und Literatur der Naturwissenschaften und Medizin, Nr. 17, 1929), 43–85; and Eduard Seidler, "Entwicklung naturwissenschaftlichen Denkens in der Medizin zur Zeit der Heidelberger Romantik," *Sudhoffs Archiv für Geschichte der Medizin* 47 (1963): 47–53.

19. Ulrich Tröhler, "250 Jahre Göttinger Medizin: Begründung-Folgen-Folgerungen," *Göttinger Universitätsschriften* 13 (1988): 21.

20. Kilian, *Die Universitäten Deutschlands*, esp. 1–26.

21. Thomas Broman, "University Reform in Medical Thought at the End of the Eighteenth Century," *Osiris* 5 (1989): 52–53. See also Timothy Lenoir, "The Göttingen School and the Development of Transcendental Naturphilosophie in the Romantic Era," *Studies in the History of Biology* 5 (1981): 111–12.

nally, both systems owed much to strong and interventionist governments over the preceding half-century.

The size of the teaching enterprise in France, furthermore, was second only to that of the combined German states. Probably more than 3,500 students were enrolled in 1830 in the three medical faculties, twenty-two *écoles secondaires,* and nine military and naval medical schools of France.[22] Beyond the matriculated students, moreover, hundreds—at times thousands—of students and graduate physicians flocked to Paris in the 1820s and 1830s. Already it was being hailed, as described earlier, as the first postgraduate medical school of the world.

The contrasts between the two systems lay in the differences that had grown out of the eighteenth century. The three degree-granting medical schools of Paris, Montpellier, and Strasbourg that had survived the Revolution were greatly outnumbered by the twenty-four university schools that awarded degrees in the German-language states. The German schools were more widely spread across the territory they served, were smaller in size, often provided more personalized training, and competed fiercely with one another for academic talent. In France, on the other hand, the huge school of Paris with its score of teaching hospitals was the uncontested heart and soul of French science and French medical teaching.

The definitive division between educational and hospital authority in Paris, furthermore, had no real counterpart by 1830 in the German universities. As courses in the natural sciences, especially those requiring laboratories and animal experimentation, became increasingly important to medical study, the isolation of much of French science from ordinary medical students made it far more difficult than in Germany to introduce such courses into the medical curriculum.

By 1830, as in Germany, a growing proportion of would-be practitioners in France were enrolled in faculties of medicine rather than in practical schools. By the 1840s, the tide turned even more sharply as three of every five French practitioners of medicine were trained in faculties of medicine.[23] The requirements for a medical degree—which gave its possessor the right to practice medicine—were a diploma from a humanistic secondary school and four years of study in a medical faculty. After 1836, a student also had to earn a bachelor's degree in the sciences in a secondary school before entering medical study.

Little choice was given to the French student in the tightly prescribed curriculum that covered sixteen courses of study, although attendance

22. There is no single source of data, so far as I have been able to find, for the numbers of medical students in the secondary or military schools. My estimate, based on fragmentary sources, is that approximately two thousand students were enrolled in the three medical faculties in 1830, another nine hundred or more in the *écoles secondaires,* and at least four hundred in the schools for the armed forces.

23. George D. Sussman, "The Glut of Doctors in Mid-Nineteenth-Century France," *Comparative Studies in Society and History* 19 (1977): 293–98.

was not normally taken in classes and the student was free to supplement the official curriculum with private courses. The order of studies proceeded much as it did in Germany, from anatomy, physiology, chemistry, botany, hygiene, and surgical pathology in the first year; to more courses in these subjects in the second year, with the addition of clinical and operative surgery; then to medical and surgical clinics, pathological anatomy, and materia medica in the third year; and concluding with still more clinics, now including midwifery, in the final year. Unlike their counterparts in Germany, French students spent their mornings in the hospital from the beginning of their first year. A total of five demanding examinations, some of them in Latin and including practical exercises, began at the end of the second year, which was followed after the last examination of the fourth year by a thesis in French or Latin, which was then published (140 copies!) at the student's own expense.[24]

When the Napoleonic empire collapsed in 1815, a flurry of reaction against the radical changes of the revolutionary era had broken out in France, but it was largely spent by 1830. For a period around 1820, however, there was a sense of exhilaration and "intellectual liberation" as many hoped to loosen the bonds of Parisian control, to resuscitate the provincial universities, or to create research facilities for professors and advanced students, as was beginning to happen across the Rhine.

In contrast with Germany, French scientists lacked space in which to carry out their work. The "little closet" at the Collège de France, where François Magendie, like other research-minded colleagues, found a modest home for his pioneering work was, in Robert Fox's description, not only "unsuitable for the purposes of research, but it was also damp and unhealthy."[25] Many would-be investigators lacked even Magendie's small space. Hopes for change, however, were dashed in the continuing political turmoil of the 1820s and 1830s that pitted radicals against conservatives, rebellious students against conservative ministries, and old-time surgeons against the medical faculties. For several months in 1822, the entire school of medicine in Paris was shut down by a series of student disorders, and eleven professors lost their posts in the resulting crackdown.[26]

In France, much of the reformers' energy was spent beating back the threat of those who wanted to restore the separate schools of surgery and other institutions of the Old Regime. The old Paris College of Surgery, according to the conservative surgeon J. C. Caron, had been "invaded" and "overrun" in the revolutionary years by the medical faculty, who had

24. This summary of requirements is based on René La Roche, "An Account of the Origin, Progress, and Present State of the Medical School of Paris," *American Journal of the Medical Sciences* 9 (1832): 355–63; and S. J. Otterburg, *Das medizinische Paris* (Carlsbad: Bielefeld, 1841), 6–9.

25. Robert Fox, "Scientific Enterprise and the Patronage of Research in France, 1800–70," *Minerva* 11 (1973): 449, 459.

26. See the very full files on "l'affaire Bertin" in the Archives nationales, AJ[16] 21.

proved to be "of little use" in teaching students either practical medicine or the new medical sciences.[27] A report prepared for the restored king by a royal favorite, J. T. Marquais, decried the anarchy and destruction of the Revolution and urged the restoration of both the Paris College of Surgery and the Royal Academy of Surgery. The three medical faculties, he charged, were "helpless" before the huge number of students now seeking instruction, especially in Paris, and they did not have enough teachers, laboratories, or clinical facilities to teach them. Only the king, Marquais asserted, could save French medicine and surgery from the intolerable confusion into which they had been plunged for twenty-one years.[28]

But the campaign to restore the medical "glories" of the Old Regime, like the efforts at new reform, met with little success in the years after 1815. The Paris Faculty of Medicine, besieged and under continuing criticism, at times reeling from inward and outward pressures, nevertheless survived the onslaughts to become by 1830 the strongest medical institution in France. Indeed, writes George Weisz, "a professorship in the faculty of medicine seems to have been closely associated with ennoblement," by that time.[29]

An Overview of Medical Education in Great Britain

At the same time that the Paris faculty triumphed over its adversaries and new universities and natural science were appearing in Germany, the island kingdom of Great Britain was likewise undergoing important changes in its system of training doctors. By the early 1830s, the national government had passed its first general law regulating the education of apothecaries; a new university medical school, modeled after those on the Continent, had been started in London; a dozen provincial medical schools had been launched across England; and the Scottish universities were experiencing a period of intense reexamination and governmental scrutiny.

Somewhat more than three thousand students were enrolled in medicine in universities, hospital medical schools, and private institutions

27. Jean Charles Caron, *Démonstration rigoureuse du peu d'utilité de l'école de médecine* (Paris: Pillet, 1818).

28. J. Th. Marquais, *Rapport au roi sur l'état actuel de la médecine en France, et sur la necessité d'une réforme dans l'étude et l'exercise de cette science* (Paris: privately printed, 1814), 4–19.

29. See two articles by George Weisz, "The Medical Elite in France in the Early Nineteenth Century," *Minerva* 25 (1987): 150–70, esp. 159; and "Constructing the Medical Elite in France: The Creation of the Royal Academy of Medicine, 1814–20," *Medical History* 30 (1986): 419–43. For a very detailed account of the political events affecting medicine in these years, see Paul Delauney, "Les médecines, la restauration et la révolution de 1830," *Médecine internationale illustrée* supplements, January 1931 to May 1932 (16 installments).

across Britain and Ireland in 1830.[30] Contrary to the trend on the Continent, the proportion of students enrolled in university medical schools was declining, not rising. The period of formal medical study in Great Britain was generally much shorter than it was in Europe, and the requirements for licensure more uncertain and varied. The preliminary education required for medicine ranged from a smattering of Latin and natural science to a bachelor's degree from Oxford or Cambridge.

By the mid-1830s the period of formal study had reached two and a half years for apothecaries, who made up the bulk of Britain's general practitioners. The Apothecaries Act of 1815, passed by Parliament amidst conflicting pressures for change, set minimum requirements in anatomy, physiology, chemistry, materia medica, and the practice of medicine and demanded six months of hospital attendance. The most distinctive mark of British (and American) medical education of these years, however, was the continued heavy reliance on private apprenticeship. Although the amount of time spent in service to a master of surgery or an apothecary was dropping in favor of organized clinical training, a period of apprenticeship was still indispensable to most in acquiring the experience needed to begin a practice. Indeed, the Apothecaries Act required a period of five years of apprenticeship for a license to practice.

A unique feature of the British system of licensing practitioners and apothecaries of medicine and surgery was the wide range of regional and professional bodies empowered to grant licenses to practice. Nineteen such agencies, many of them overlapping in jurisdiction and varying in requirements, existed in Britain and Ireland, including nine medical corporations, such as the Royal College of Physicians of London, and ten universities spread over Scotland, England, and Ireland. According to Jeanne Peterson, "medicine men practiced with university degrees, various forms of medical licenses, sometimes a combination of these, and sometimes with none at all." The training of a practitioner in Britain in 1830 could vary all the way from classical university study at Oxford and Cambridge to a series of courses in a provincial hospital to "broom-and-apron apprenticeship in an apothecary's shop."[31]

The old divisions among surgeons, physicians, and apothecaries, still insisted on by the royal corporations, were in fact disappearing in actual

---

30. This estimate is based on a number of sources, including the following: Minutes of Senatus, December 12, 1835, University of Edinburgh Archive; John B. Hay, ed.; *Inaugural Addresses by Lords Rector of the University of Glasgow* (Glasgow, 1839), 187; William Brockbank, Notes on size of provincial schools, 1836, Manchester Collection, F4c, Rylands Library, University of Manchester; *Manchester Guardian* clipping, October 5, 1836, Manchester Collection, ibid.; Susan C. Lawrence, "Private Enterprise and Public Interests: Medical Education and the Apothecaries' Act, 1780–1825," in *British Medicine in an Age of Reform,* ed. Roger French and Andrew Wear (London: Routledge, 1991), 61, figure 2.2; and a letter from Susan Lawrence to me, July 1, 1993.

31. M. Jeanne Peterson, *The Medical Profession in Mid-Victorian London* (Berkeley and Los Angeles: University of California Press, 1978), 5.

practice. Most apothecaries now sought qualifications in surgery, and surgeons likewise sought experience in medicine. The president of the Royal College of Surgeons of London, describing the situation in the early 1830s, estimated that not more than two hundred surgeons confined themselves to surgery alone and that 70 percent of these were in London.[32] "It is now the custom in most parts of the British Empire," reads a report of a faculty discussion in Edinburgh, "to practice both branches of the Profession; a majority of persons who take a degree in medicine find it advisable to take the Surgical Diploma also."[33]

In Scotland, particularly, where apothecaries were rare, "the service of the public has demanded & has created . . . general Medical Practitioners, who practice the healing art in all its branches." Scots were much disturbed by the workings of the Apothecaries Act, which gave the Society of Apothecaries in London "a monopoly on the education of general practitioners," most of whom were being educated in Scotland.[34] The requirement by the society of five years of apprenticeship was especially a hardship, since the Scottish universities had long incorporated a period of practical training into their academic curriculum.

Whatever the weaknesses of the new legislation, however—and critics have perhaps highlighted its failures too strongly in dealing with the anomalies and class divisions of British medicine—the Apothecaries Act did, in fact, represent an important change in British medical training.[35] For the first time, the British Parliament had intervened in the training of the nation's general practitioners. With further support by government, the society moved steadily after 1815 to raise the educational requirements for such practitioners and to regulate the order of their medical courses and clinical experience.

New teaching enterprises were founded after 1815 to meet the standards of the apothecary legislation. By 1830, seven medical schools had already been opened in English provincial cities.[36] The new faculties bombarded the examining bodies with applications for recognition of their teaching. An early victory was won by Joseph Jordan in Manchester when the Society of Apothecaries voted to "receive his certificate of the attendance of pupils upon his Anatomical Lectures, in the same manner as they do those of public teachers of Anatomy in [London]."[37] By 1828, the secretary of the society was praising the training being given in Man-

32. House of Commons, Select Committee on Medical Education, *Report*, 3 vols. (London: House of Commons, 1834), 2:11.

33. Minutes of Senatus, April 24, 1830, University of Edinburgh Archive.

34. Ibid., April 23, 1825.

35. See Lawrence, "Private Enterprise and Public Interests," 47.

36. Stella V. F. Butler, "Science and the Education of Doctors in the Nineteenth Century: A Study of British Medical Schools with Particular Reference to the Development and Uses of Physiology" (Ph.D. diss., University of Manchester, 1981), 17, table II.

37. Secretary, Society of Apothecaries, to Dr. Hull, April 24, 1821, Manchester Collection, F492, Rylands Library, University of Manchester.

chester, saying that "no young man came before the Court better qualified in every respect, than those who have been entirely educated at Manchester."[38] Soon the Manchester school was also offering clinical lectures,
in a variety of subjects at the Royal Infirmary in the city.[39]

Other provincial schools were successful in building approved programs and breaking the monopoly of London on practical medical education. A typical venture in Leeds began with the announcement by a
group of enterprising physicians in 1831 that they intended to establish
"a course of lectures as will qualify for examination at the College of Surgeons and Apothecaries Hall."[40]

It was these provincial and private medical schools in Britain that,
along with the London hospital schools, supplied—in far less organized
fashion than on the Continent—the general practitioners who served the
majority of the British people. Not only were there thirteen provincial
medical schools in England by 1834, but the city of Glasgow alone could
also count an additional five medical schools within its limits, and the
London student had his choice of lectures at nine hospital and six private
schools of medicine.[41] The requirements at these practical schools corre-
sponded broadly to those of the secondary medical schools of the Continent and, except for clinical training, to the "country medical schools"
then spreading throughout the United States. As in America and on the
Continent, the British practical schools required little premedical education beyond the rudiments of Latin, grammar, and natural science. They
offered such standard lecture courses as anatomy, physiology, chemistry,
materia medica, practice of medicine, surgery, and sometimes obstetrics.

A comparison of the practical school at Leeds, for example, with similar
schools in Lyon, Salzburg, and Cincinnati about 1830 shows surprisingly
few differences. In 1831, the seven faculty members at the new school in
Leeds taught all the courses just listed, claiming that they were only following the example of "every great town on the Continent of Europe,
and in the United States of America."[42] Two courses of lectures were
given at a local dispensary, but the student was expected to get most of

38. Report of Secretary, Apothecaries Hall, May 14, 1828, copy in Manchester Collection, F3a.
39. Edward Carbutt, *Clinical Lectures in the Manchester Royal Infirmary* (Manchester:
Thomas Sowler, 1834), xix, copy in Manchester Collection, F4.
40. Leeds School of Medicine, Minutes of Council, June 6, 1831, Leeds University
Archives.
41. Butler, "Science and the Education of Doctors," 17, table II; "Account of the Metropolitan Hospitals, Medical Schools, and Lectures" *Lancet* (1832-22): 3–11; Anderson's
University, Board of Managers, Minutes, June 7, 1834, University of Strathclyde, Glasgow.
Aside from the University of Glasgow and Anderson's University, these minutes list the
Portland Street School, the College Street Medical School, and the Clinical School of Glas-
gow Royal Infirmary in Glasgow.
42. Leeds School of Medicine, Minutes of Council, June 6, 1831, Leeds University
Archives; Leeds Mercury, August 27, 1831, quoted in S. T. Anning and W. K. J. Walls, *A
History of the Leeds School of Medicine* (Leeds: Leeds University Press, 1982), 14.

his clinical experience, as he was in America, during his years as an apprentice. At Lyon, where the faculty sometimes acted as if it were teaching at a full-fledged medical school, clinical training was an important part of the three-year course at the *école secondaire*, but the academic offerings of the eight professors were identical to those of Leeds, with the exception of separate courses in physiology and pathology.[43] The practical school at Salzburg likewise listed a faculty of seven full-time professors teaching essentially the same courses over three years as those given in Lyon and Leeds.[44] Finally, the school at Cincinnati, though similar to Leeds in its lack of clinical training and the brevity of its terms (four months, compared with nine or ten on the Continent), was comparable to all of them in its range of offerings and size of faculty.[45]

In short, all the practical schools were about the same size, offered similar courses, had many of the same problems (especially procuring bodies for anatomy classes), trained an important part of the rural and small-town practitioners in Europe and America, and were looked down on by university-trained physicians. The political influence of the latter and their share of the medical market were on the rise, especially in Europe. Only the greater dependence on private arrangements for clinical experience separated the British and American schools from the others. One reason for the shorter academic terms in Britain and America indeed was the expectation that the student would get his bedside or hospital training during the rest of the year.

In London, the number of hospital schools offering systematic instruction to students tripled between 1800 and 1830. More and more hospitals provided lecture rooms and classrooms to accommodate the growing numbers of pupils and their teachers. For the first time, teaching became an important responsibility of the hospitals' boards of governors. The instruction given, however, varied immensely in quality, and most students continued to take courses at more than one hospital. The organization of studies in London, in the words of a recent scholar, was still "inchoate, unstructured and predominantly anatomo-chirurgical in character."[46]

The largest of the metropolitan schools, St. Bartholomew's, announced a program in the early 1830s that emphasized the practical char-

43. Christian Roche, "L'enseignement médical à Lyon de 1821 à 1877" (med. diss., University of Lyon, 1975), 21–22.

44. Anton E. Maier, "Die niederärztliche Ausbildung zu Salzburg im 19.Jahrhundert" (med. diss., University of Erlangen—Nuremberg, n.d.), 23–25. At another practical school, this time in Greifswald, seven faculty members were joined part time by four others from the University of Greifswald to teach about forty students each year. See Dietrich Forstmann, "Die medizinisch–chirurgische Lehranstalt zu Greifswald" (med. diss., University of Berlin, 1938), 23–26.

45. William F. Norwood, *Medical Education in the United States Before the Civil War* (Philadelphia: University of Pennsylvania Press, 1944), 310.

46. Paul K. Underhill, "Science, Professionalism and the Development of Medical Education in England: An Historical Sociology" (Ph.D. diss., University of Edinburgh, 1987), 463.

acter of its teaching. According to the 1835 catalog, the lectures of Dr. Clement Hue in medicine, for example, were to be "illustrated by clinical observations on the cases of patients in the hospital," and surgery was to be taught by William Lawrence in lectures "illustrated clinically, as far as cases in Hospital allow." The professor of midwifery likewise announced that "students when qualified will have ample opportunity of attending labours, without additional expense." Mention was even made of a chemical laboratory "for the preparation and repetition of experiments" and "an extensive apparatus" for the course in "medical physics."[47] New accommodations were added in 1834 for work in anatomy and chemistry, along with a "pathological theatre."[48]

At Guy's, the noted triumvirate of Bright, Addison, and Hodgkin was attracting a large following. Bright was endeavoring to teach his students percussion and auscultation and to take specimens of blood and urine from patients. Those who accompanied him on his rounds, according to his biographers, "were to see and do, rather than to trail dutifully along behind."[49] Courses offered at Guy's included all the standard offerings of the period and, in addition, a course in "experimental philosophy" and a separate course in physiology.[50] The close connection between Guy's and St. Thomas's was broken in 1825, and the latter now competed vigorously for new students.[51]

The effort to create a university-type medical school in London, modeled principally after Edinburgh and the German universities, was the most innovative change of the period. It was aimed at the overwhelmingly practical nature of English medical education. The need to unite theory and practice in British medicine, as was occurring on the Continent, was cited as an urgent requirement in the early announcements. "The whole ordinary practice of medicine in England," read a statement of 1827, lay in the hands "of those who are called general practitioners, who take no Degree, [and] confine themselves to no single branch of the profession." Oxford and Cambridge, readers were reminded, were still closed to all but Anglicans, were beyond the financial means of most students, and did not offer a truly professional course in medicine in any case.[52] In London, on the other hand, "the education to be obtained at

47. St. Bartholomew's Hospital, *Medical School session 1835–36* (London: Adland, 1835).

48. House of Commons, Select Committee, *Report*, 3:54, pt. VI.

49. Diana Berry and Campbell Mackenzie, *Richard Bright, 1789–1858: Physician in an Age of Revolution and Reform* (London: Royal Society of Medicine, 1992), 118.

50. See, for example, Terms of Attendance on the Lectures, etc. in the Medical and Chirurgical School of Guy's Hospital for the Session of 1824–25, manuscript, Greater London Record Office, H9/GY/A209/2.

51. See Terms of Attendance on the Lectures and Practice of the Medical and Surgical School, St. Thomas's Hospital, for the Session of 1836 and 1837, ibid., H9/GY/A209/5.

52. *Statement by the Council of the University of London, explanatory of the Nature and Objects of the Institution* (London: Longman, Rees, 1827), 7–8, 37.

the different Medical Schools . . . is most defective."[53] What was needed, argued the founders, was a high standard of preliminary education, a curriculum offering the most advanced of medical science, and a hospital under faculty control.

Germany rather than France was clearly the model in the founders' eyes as they contrasted the teaching of anatomy, physiology, and pathology in that country with the stumbling uncertainty of the courses being taught in London. The prominent comparative anatomist at Halle, Johann Friedrich Meckel, was ardently courted for the London faculty but ultimately declined, and the anatomist Granville Pattison was sent to Frankfurt and Halle to examine their anatomical collections.[54] Morbid anatomy was to be taught by Robert Carswell, who was doing advanced study in Paris, and physiology was assigned to the experimentally minded Charles Bell, who would teach the subject, according to the 1830 catalog, "in a form somewhat different" from that usually found in Britain.[55] Surgery and medicine, furthermore, were to have equal attention in the new venture. Professors at the new school, it was promised, would spend 50 percent more time on their teaching duties than did their contemporaries in the hospital schools.[56]

Unlike Edinburgh—at which planners claimed that only a small number of students reached the patients' bedside—every student of the new university was to be given a chance to observe and occasionally treat the patient in the hospital. "It is a scene of the most disgraceful confusion," Pattison said of the Edinburgh of the late 1820s, "for if an able-bodied and zealous [student] does by dint of muscular exertion succeed in getting near enough to the bed-side . . . the probabilities are that he will not again be equally successful, until the interest of the case has been terminated."[57] London clearly intended to be different.

But the grandiose plans envisioned by the university's creators were impossible to realize so quickly. Although nearly three hundred students did enroll by the second year of operation, complaints were frequent of the inadequate facilities, overlapping teaching assignments, friction among the professors, high course fees, the Spartan character of student life, and especially the lack of a teaching hospital. "We can hold no rank among medical schools" without such a hospital, complained Professor John Elliotson in 1832, if we are "to present actual symptoms to [the

53. University College London, medical faculty minutes, March 5, 1828, College Record Office, University College London.

54. University of London, Council minutes, July 12, 1827, College Record Office, University College London.

55. University of London, *Medical Classes, 1830–31* (London: University of London, 1830), 1.

56. *Second Statement by the Council of the University of London, explanatory of the Plan of Instruction* (London: Longman, Rees, 1828), 24.

57. Pattison to Council of University, December 18, 1827, University College of London Archive, college correspondence 312.

student's] touch, his hearing, and his sight."[58] With no hospital of its own, the faculty was forced to rely for the first six years on the scanty resources of a college dispensary and a loose arrangement with Middlesex Hospital. Some professors, advising the council that it was better to operate with no hospital at all than one that "is not wholly under your government," offered to waive their own remuneration until a hospital could be built.[59]

But opposition to an academic hospital on the German model was intense in many quarters. The creation of such a hospital, warned one council member, would "excite much animadversion," for "it is the first instance [in this country] of a hospital being rendered subservient to and secondary to the purposes of medical and surgical education, instead of the reverse." Some feared, Eliotson pointed out, "that it will be a theatre for experiments and operations."[60] Under the threat of faculty resignations and student withdrawals, a university hospital of one hundred beds, built with public subscriptions, was opened across the street from the university in 1834. For the first time, control of a British hospital was in the hands of academic authorities, and the teaching was wholly the responsibility of a medical faculty.[61]

The Scottish universities, meanwhile, confronted with the rising competition of both the London schools and those in the provinces, faced additional threats to their reputation and their autonomy. Edinburgh, in particular, lost its earlier eminence as one of the leading medical schools of Europe. More and more, the city's town council, which was influenced by local political conditions, pressured the medical faculty to enlarge its course of study and to recognize the many extraacademical lecturers who attracted students to the city. For half a century, the council charged in 1824, no real change had been made in the required curriculum of the school of medicine.[62] Many of the famed teachers who had made Edinburgh's reputation were now gone; dissatisfaction was growing at the lack of premedical requirements and the short length of medical studies vis-à-vis the Continent; clinical lectures were restricted to a "ward set aside from the rest of the hospital";[63] the division between medical and surgical teaching was still painfully evident; the reliance on student fees

58. John Elliotson, *Address, delivered at the Opening of the Medical Session in the University of London* (London: Longman, Rees, 1832), 8.

59. Memorial drawn by Dr. Pattison respecting the Hospital, 1828, University College London Archive, college correspondence, medical faculty file, 1–4; medical faculty minutes, October 26, 1827, College Record Office, University College London.

60. William Tooke to Council, March 10, 1828, University College London Archive.

61. Committee of Management Report, July 2, 1832; Inquiries relating to Hospital, November 3, 1834, college correspondence, medical faculty, file 51–74, University College London Archive.

62. Remarks on the Memorial of the Town-Council of Edinburgh to the Right Honorable Lord John Russell, [1824], Royal College of Physicians of Edinburgh.

63. Christopher Lawrence, "The Edinburgh Medical School and the End of the 'Old Thing' 1790–1830," *History of Universities* 7 (1988): 277.

from large classes reinforced the faculty members' resistance to change; and unfavorable comparisons of Edinburgh's teaching with the changing curriculum of France and Germany were becoming commonplace.

It was a fight over the town council's insistence on making midwifery a required subject for medical students that sparked what Robert Christison called the final episode of "irritating intermeddling" by the town in university affairs.[64] The council told the faculty that although "it will at all times be disposed to pay the most respectful deference" to its opinion, it was its duty to give paramount attention to "the interests of the public and of the Medical Students."[65] The university's granitic resistance to direction on the issue led, at the faculty's initiative, to the establishment of a royal commission by the British government in 1826.

Even before the commission's recommendations could be published, however, the faculty had moved part of the way to meet the demands for reform. Between 1824 and 1833 the Edinburgh faculty voted to make medicine a four-year study, to require six months of hospital attendance, to substitute English for Latin as the language of examinations, and to begin grading the medical curriculum. The new order of studies would begin with such basic studies as chemistry, botany, and anatomy and then proceed to medical, surgical, obstetrical, and clinical courses.[66] Resistance to other changes suggested by the commission, however, was strong, particularly to creating a new chair of pathology, setting stricter requirements for admission, and giving formal recognition to the extramural lecturers.[67]

By this time, the city's "leadership in the medical world had been lost."[68] Critics were writing openly of "the declining reputation of the Medical Faculty of the University of Edinburgh."[69] Similar criticisms were directed at the teaching in Glasgow and other Scottish schools. When asked by the royal commissioners in 1827 why Glasgow required no clinical lectures of its students, the rector responded that it was "be-

---

64. Robert Christison, *Graduation Under the Medical and Scottish Universities Act* (Edinburgh: Black, 1861), 28.

65. Cited in Minutes of Senatus, May 19, 1824, University of Edinburgh Archive.

66. Ibid., December 18, 1824; Lobban, *Edinburgh and the Medical Revolution*, 42–43.

67. Some Remarks on a Communication from the Senatus Academicus to the Patrons at the University of Edinburgh, October 29, 1831, Royal College of Physicians of Edinburgh; Lisa Rosner, *Medical Education in the Age of Improvement: Edinburgh Students and Apprentices, 1760–1826* (Edinburgh: University of Edinburgh Press, 1991), 190–96.

68. Lawrence, "Edinburgh Medical School," 278.

69. See Anonymous, *An Examination into the Causes of the Declining Reputation of the Medical Faculty of the University of Edinburgh and the Origin of another Class of Medical Professors, commonly called "Private Lecturers"* (Edinburgh: W. Burness, 1834). A copy of this pamphlet is in the Library of the Royal College of Physicians of Edinburgh. The author attributed the decline to the appointment of unqualified persons to professorships, the character of examinations, the writing of student dissertations by hired "grinders," and the fact that students were "overwhelmed" by the uncertainties of the curriculum.

cause there are no clinical lectures . . . on the efficiency of which we can repose confidence."[70]

North American Medical Training in 1830

The medical scene in the North America of 1830 was strikingly similar to that in Great Britain. In the United States, apprenticeship training continued as the principal route to practical learning; new medical schools were proliferating in the United States at a rate even faster than in Britain; the requirements for practice were as varied as in the former mother country; the proportion of practitioners being trained in schools apart from universities and colleges, as in Britain, was growing swiftly; teaching was offered in both countries almost wholly on a fee-for-instruction basis; and the new clinical science of France and the experimental studies of the Continent found little echo outside a few institutions, largely in the east.

Medical education in the English-speaking countries, in short, was alike in its grafting of newly organized lecture courses in practical science onto a program of apprenticeship or hospital training undertaken at the student's own initiative. It differed from the practical schools on the European continent in its essentially commercial character and in the limited role played by government in its support or control. Reynell Coates, who had seen the birth of America's first medical school, attributed the divergence from Europe in his lifetime to "the obvious and natural connection between the character of government and medical institutions."[71]

Conditions in America, of course, were not identical to those in Great Britain. Here could be found no hospital-crowded cities such as London, no new university as in the British capital, nor even a medical school like Edinburgh with a long tradition of medical teaching—although many had tried to adapt the Edinburgh system to American circumstances. By 1830, the continued movement of the American population, the thinness of settlement in many areas, the scarcity of hospitals of the European type, and the hands-off posture of the government had combined to force a rapid growth of small, independent medical schools, many of them in rural areas, that generally offered fewer clinical opportunities than did the provincial schools of Britain and less full-time faculty instruction than on the European continent.

70. Royal Commission, *Evidence, Oral and Documentary, taken and received by the Commission appointed by His Majesty George IV, July 23d, 1826; and re-appointed by His Majesty William IV, October 12th, 1830; for visiting the Universities of Scotland*, 4 vols. (London: His Majesty's Stationery Office, 1837), 2:166. The graduation requirements at Glasgow in medicine were similar to those in Edinburgh: See Records of Senate, November 15, 1833, University of Glasgow Archive.

71. Reynell Coates, *Oration on the Defects in the present System of Medical Instruction in the United States* (Philadelphia: James Kay, 1835), 11.

The ties that bound the early medical schools of America to academic institutions, such as the College of Philadelphia or Harvard College, had grown much looser by 1830, and for the most part the newer schools had but the most ephemeral ties to either a college or a hospital. Unlike the practical schools abroad, moreover, the graduates of American schools, upon receiving their medical degrees, were able to practice medicine almost immediately without further examination.

The competition for students and the decline or absence of public authority over degrees or licensing in Jacksonian America worked to keep down the demands made on medical graduates, even in the more established eastern schools. As a result, the bulk of America's training programs continued, as they did in Britain, to be brief, to be run by busy physicians, to demand little preliminary education, and to be more difficult to change than even the schools of Great Britain. They owed their origin after all, as in Britain, to an effort to supplement the practical experience of apprenticeship and not to supplant it by a system of organized instruction. The majority of practitioners in 1830, it is important to remember, had not attended even a single course of medical lectures.[72]

By this time, the nation had established twenty-five medical colleges, including two early sectarian schools, a number roughly equal to that of the largest European countries, with a population less than half the size of France. These colleges were giving instruction to about 2,200 students in 1830, a fraction of those studying by apprenticeship alone.[73] Joseph Kett graphically described these proliferating schools as "operating without outside restraint, quickly [taking] on molecular characteristics, bouncing about at random, smacking into each other, forming chance alliances, and breaking into still smaller particles."[74]

Scholars working on American medicine, aware of developments to come, understandably describe the many weaknesses of these early-nineteenth-century medical schools: They were poorly organized; they served commercial ends; they refused few applicants; they required students to pay twice for the same four-month course of lectures; they made no effort to measure the apprenticeship training that was normally required; they offered little clinical instruction of the kind common in Europe; they graduated students without examination; and they served as both advocate and jury in deciding who should practice medicine. This harsh indictment, it should now be clear, needs to be softened in the light of a more realistic comparison with conditions in Europe.

Why did nineteenth-century reformers, whose writing has carried so

72. Frederick C. Waite, *The Story of a Country Medical School: A History of the Clinical School of Medicine and the Vermont Medical College, Woodstock, Vermont, 1827–1856* (Montpelier: Vermont Historical Society, 1945), 22.

73. The data on schools and enrollment are taken from Robley Dunglison, *The Medical Student; or, Aids to the Study of Medicine* (Philadelphia: Carey, Lea & Blanchard, 1837), 292–306; and *Edinburgh Medical Journal* 26 (1826): 210–11.

74. Joseph F. Kett, *The Formation of the American Medical Profession: The Role of Institutions, 1780–1860* (New Haven, CT: Yale University Press, 1968), 65.

much weight in later accounts, depict so harshly the conditions in American medical education? In part, it may simply have been the strategy of reformers in all countries, who pointed to a very high standard elsewhere in order to spur changes at home. It doubtless reflected, too, the widely shared view of Americans that things were somehow more sophisticated and developed in Europe and that American institutions were inferior by comparison. But most of all, the negative and often unfair comparisons of the general state of American medical education vis-à-vis that of Europe came from widespread ignorance of the great variety of medical schools outside their own country. Those who had been to Paris or London or Vienna were not likely to have taken much notice of the numerous practical schools, hospital programs, and apprenticeship systems that most resembled those they had left behind.

The American schools of 1830, then, were not so radically different in concept and structure from the practical British and continental schools, and they served a population that was in the midst of one of the great movements of peoples in modern history. The first schools of medicine, after all, were so recent in origin that some of their founders were still alive. The demand for doctors in so vast and thinly settled a country was real. The abbreviated curriculum and the loose requirements, as well as the dependence on practical experience, reflected the political and social circumstances of a republic only four decades old.

Nearly all the American schools, nonetheless, no matter how small or isolated, tried to offer the same basic courses as did their counterparts in Europe. If the sequence of studies in America was ungraded and students repeated the same courses in the second year, it should be remembered than this practice was not unique to the United States. In later years, William Henry Welch, in decrying the backwardness of the American system of preparing doctors during most of its history, admitted that it produced physicians "who were better than the system," but perhaps the system, for all its stresses and shortcomings, was not so markedly different from its actual British and European counterparts, at least in the opening decades of the century.

American medical education has always had its critics. Physicians of the early nineteenth century at various times complained, pleaded, protested, or defended the system of training practitioners. "There is good reason to believe," the aging Benjamin Rush told the trustees of the University of Pennsylvania in 1813,

> that some young men have obtained degrees in our university who did not know how to spread a common plaster, to dress a sore, or to perform the operation of bleeding. . . . Would you cross the ocean in a ship built by a carpenter who had heard lectures only on shipbuilding for two years, without ever having handled an ax or hammer in the course of his life?[75]

75. Quoted in George W. Corner, *Two Centuries of Medicine: A History of the School of Medicine, University of Pennsylvania* (Philadelphia: Lippincott, 1965), 63.

But Rush's complaint, it needs to be made clear, was based on the fact that graduates in medicine—as was true of Britain and some of the continental countries as well—were expected, indeed required, to serve an apprenticeship or work in a hospital before actually starting practice. Rush, in fact, proposed as the solution to the problems at his school that the medical course be extended to three years, so that students would then have more time between lectures to spend with their preceptors in learning the practical side of medicine.

Not all preceptors, of course, could be skilled in bedside teaching, have learned the new techniques of physical diagnosis, or be knowledgeable about the new medical sciences. Often they had had no opportunity to upgrade their skills since their own apprenticeships. Students seeking such up-to-date training were forced to go to the few places in America offering such instruction or, more likely, to travel abroad. More than two hundred Americans went to Paris in the 1830s alone.[76]

Proposals for change came thick and fast after 1820. In Cincinnati, the reformer Daniel Drake offered a five-month term of instruction at his new "Medical College of the West" and planned a hospital at which training in clinical medicine could be given.[77] In Northampton, Massachusetts, a convention of medical men in 1827 sought to agree on minimal requirements for medical practice but, because of competing interests, could not. The Philadelphian Reynell Coates, ignoring the many restrictions on medical teaching in hospitals in Britain, contrasted the openness of European hospitals to students with the situation in America, where the "very laws . . . are made to interdict the ingress of the student."

Coates also assailed the lack of premedical requirements in America and the absence of university-level courses in science, without which, he said, "the medical schools, not only of this country, but of Great Britain also, must forever remain as they are now—secondary schools!"[78] Yet in Scotland, at about the very same time, Professor John Thomson was arguing almost the reverse, that preliminary educational requirements for medicine were actually lower in that country than in the United States.[79] To a considerable extent, as suggested earlier, orators in every country made selective use of data and impressions of other countries in order to bolster movements for reform at home.

The country medical schools of America, located in very small towns, had no real counterpart in Europe but were nevertheless a significant part of the medical teaching enterprise. These schools, which made up nearly

76. Russell M. Jones, "American Doctors and the Parisian Medical World, 1830–1840," *Bulletin of the History of Medicine* 47 (1970): 42.

77. Daniel Drake, *An Inaugural Discourse on Medical Education delivered at the opening of the Medical College of Ohio* (Cincinnati: Looker, Palmer, and Reynolds, 1820), 16–19.

78. Coates, *Oration*, 7, 19, 24.

79. See the reference to Thomson's views in a review article on medical education in the *Edinburgh Medical Journal* 27 (1827): 366.

half of all medical schools by 1830, gave access to some systematic medical training to thousands of rural youth in the first half of the nineteenth century. The school at Transylvania in Kentucky, for example, numbered 235 students in 1826.[80] By 1834, two of the largest three medical colleges in the country were in small western towns.[81]

All these schools were empowered by law to grant medical degrees, which in turn exempted their recipients from the licensing examinations that a few of the states, especially New York, still required. They also drew students away from the eastern cities as town after town in the expanding country opened schools far from the Atlantic seaboard. In quick succession, new ventures were started in such places as Fairfield, New York (1812); Lexington, Kentucky (1817); Cincinnati (1819); Richmond (1825); and Auburn, New York (1825). At the same time, the first of the sectarian schools, which eventually found such fertile soil in the United States, were established in New York (1825) and Worthington, Ohio (1830).[82]

Across the northern border, British Canada had undertaken its first attempts at medical education in Montreal and Toronto in 1824. As in the United States, these early ventures were led by Edinburgh graduates and closely followed the pattern of education in the Scottish city. Before this time, many Canadians had come south to American schools to get their medical training. "It is melancholy to think," wrote a Toronto physician in 1826, "that more than three-fourths of the present practitioners have been educated or attended lectures in the United States."[83]

From the beginning, the Canadian schools differed from American schools in the degree of governmental control exerted over their graduates. Boards of licensure made up of appointed physicians had been established in all parts of Canada by the early nineteenth century, and Canada did not experience the wholesale abandonment of licensing that occurred in America. The province of Ontario, for example, had effective legislation limiting the practice of doctors as early as 1795.[84] Many Canadians feared, not unjustly, that "the lax enforcement of licensing laws would invite a descent on Canada by battalions of American quacks armed with republicanism as well as charlatanism."[85]

Canada followed the example of the mother country in distinguishing freestanding medical schools, such as those common in Britain and the

80. Otto Juettner, "Rise of Medical Colleges in the Ohio Valley," *Ohio Historical and Archaeological Quarterly* 22 (1913): 486.

81. Waite, *Story of a Country Medical College*, 10.

82. Frederick C. Waite, "American Sectarian Medical Colleges Before the Civil War," *Bulletin of the History of Medicine* 19 (1946): 150–52.

83. John J. Heagerty, *Four Centuries of Medical History in Canada*, 2 vols. (Toronto: Macmillan, 1928), 2:55–75.

84. J. T. H. Connor, "'A Sort of Felo-de-Se': Eclecticism, Related Medical Sects, and Their Decline in Victorian Ontario," *Bulletin of the History of Medicine* 65 (1991): 524.

85. Joseph F. Kett, "American and Canadian Medical Institutions, 1800–1870," *Journal of the History of Medicine and Allied Sciences* 22 (1967): 348–49.

United States, from medical schools connected with universities that were empowered to grant medical degrees. Although independent schools similar to those that developed on the American side of the border were established in a number of Canadian cities, they were not able to offer degrees as they could in America and were thus more readily brought under control by governmental and professional authority. As a result, the intense rivalries and fierce competition among medical schools so often remarked in the United States were far less severe in Canada. Later, Canada moved more quickly than did either Britain or the United States toward uniform standards of education and qualifications for practice.[86]

As in Britain, medical training was also available in North America in extramural schools that aimed only at supplementing the courses given in an existing medical school. Much of the organized clinical instruction in North America during the nineteenth century, in fact, came from such schools. For example, at the Medical Institute in Philadelphia, founded in 1817, William Gerhard, returning from Paris in the early 1830s, offered courses in clinical medicine. By 1834, more than a hundred students were pursuing courses at the institute. In the same city, Joseph Warrington started a "school of obstetrics" at the Philadelphia Dispensary in 1828, at which a future practitioner was able to get more hands-on experience in observing and assisting in live births than anywhere in the nation.

In the 1820s, farther north, James Jackson began teaching the new techniques of auscultation to students at the Boston Private Medical School. Anatomy and surgery were added to the school's offerings following the enactment of an anatomy law in Massachusetts in 1831. In addition to clinical and anatomical teaching, these and other extramural schools advertised lectures and quiz classes on a wide range of medical subjects. By the middle 1830s, Boston was enrolling 129 students in its extramural courses. It was in such courses, especially in Boston, Philadelphia, and New York, according to Dale Smith, that "the ideas and practices of French hospital medicine" were first introduced into the United States.[87] The role of private enterprise in meeting needs not met in any medical school was thus as important in America as it was in Britain and France.

By 1830, the differences in medical preparation among the various grades of practitioner were pronounced in every country. Not only did the national systems differ in organization, goals, and degree of govern-

86. Ibid., 351–54; Connor, "'A Sort of Felo-de-Se'," 524–25. See also N. Tait McPhedran, *Canadian Medical Schools: Two Centuries of Medical History 1822 to 1992* (Montreal: Harvest House, 1993), 4.

87. Dale C. Smith, "The Emergence of Organized Clinical Instruction in the Nineteenth Century American Cities of Boston, New York and Philadelphia" (Ph.D. diss., University of Minnesota, 1979), 123, table II. These paragraphs are based heavily on pp. 112–48 of Smith's useful study.

mental control, as suggested in this chapter, but the range of studies within each country also was enormous. Efforts were under way in all the transatlantic nations—to greater or lesser degree—to bring the education of medical practitioners under some kind of common standard. Normally the goal, though it varied by individual country, was to make medicine more practical and more scientific and also more useful to the enterprising classes. One of the major questions of the preceding century—whether medicine was a learned study or a practical art—had now been answered: It was both. The new questions had more to do with how such combined training could best be organized and carried out in different national circumstances. Who should decide? And what was the role of government in making such decisions?

7

Toward New Goals for Medical Education, 1830–1850

The years around 1830, as just described, were a turning point in the movement to create a more systematic and uniform approach to the training of doctors. For the next quarter-century, a battle royal raged in the transatlantic countries between those seeking to create a common standard of medical training for all practitioners and those who defended the many-tiered systems of preparing healers that prevailed in most of them. At stake were such important issues as the care of the rural populations, largely unserved by university-trained physicians, the ever larger role claimed for science and academic study in educating doctors, the place of organized medical groups in decision making about professional training, and the role to be played by government in setting standards of medical education.

The Struggle for Change in Britain and America

In Great Britain, the conflict over change centered on the efforts of reformers, mainly liberal Whigs, apothecary-surgeons, and Scottish teachers and practitioners, to gain a larger measure of recognition for the rights of general practitioners to ply their trade freely throughout the nation. Ranged against them were the royal colleges, the traditional universities, and other defenders of the status quo. Particularly sensitive in Britain was the entrenched power of the royal colleges of medicine and surgery—"the most conservative bodies in the medical world," S. W. F. Holloway called them—which continued to defend the importance of a liberal, gentlemanly education for medicine, as well as their right to approve the qualifications for practice of all other practitioners except apothecaries.[1]

Members of the Royal College of Physicians of London, the most elite of all the British medical bodies, were divided by class into a small number of fellows, almost all graduates of Oxford and Cambridge, and a larger number of licentiates, who, though permitted to practice, took no part in serious policy discussions and could not even use such college facilities as the library or the museum. "The Fellows," claimed a petition signed by forty-nine London physicians in 1833, "have usurped all the corporate power, offices, privileges, and emoluments attached to the College."[2] Asked why a member of the college could not also be a member of the Company of Apothecaries or the College of Surgeons, its president replied at a parliamentary hearing in 1834 that "we think it would diminish somewhat the high respectability of men of education, who stand on the same ground as members of the English Universities."[3]

Such high-handed pronouncements infuriated the swelling army of general practitioners, whose demands for equal treatment grew ever louder. Their readiness for practice, they argued, was at least the equal and often greater than that of academic physicians. "The chief qualification for eminence in the healing art," read a scathing editorial in the reform journal *Lancet*, "is ignorance of one or the other half of it."[4] Why were apothecaries, so widely welcomed as exemplars of the new breed of general practitioner, so roundly condemned as inferior by the academic physicians? It was, in the opinion of a leading scholar, because they were a constant and unpleasant reminder "of the old-style apothecary, and . . . blurred the distinction between the druggist and the general practitioner."[5] Even if licensed by both surgeons and apothecaries, as most were, the status of general practitioners was still anomalous, and there was no professional body to speak for them. Some wanted to establish a new governmental corporation or college for general practitioners, similar to those of other groups, but most looked instead to a common governmental registry of all practitioners that would give them practice rights equal to those of physicians and surgeons.

Medical writings of the period and records of faculty discussions confirm a widespread sense of outrage at the corporations and a growing anger at the "supine indifference" of the British government.[6] The Royal

1. S. W. F. Holloway, "Medical Education in England, 1830–1858: A Sociological Analysis," *History* 49 (1964): 323.

2. Petition of the Undersigned Physicians, Practicing in London, manuscript, W. P. Allison Papers, Royal College of Physicians of Edinburgh Library.

3. House of Commons, Select Committee on Medical Education, *Report*, 3 vols. (London: House of Commons, 1834) 1:18.

4. *Lancet* 7 (1842–43): 721.

5. Irvine Loudon, *Medical Care and the General Practitioner, 1750–1850* (Oxford: Clarendon Press, 1986), 196.

6. *Lancet* 2 (1837): 507.

College of Physicians of London, wrote the naval surgeon William Barrett Marshall while still a student, was marked by its "infamous discipline" and "odious by-laws."[7] The sharp-tongued *Lancet* editor Thomas Wakley charged the government with "criminal" neglect of its duties in not pushing for change.[8] In 1839, all the professional bodies in Edinburgh, including the medical faculty of the university, asked the national government to fix a minimum course of study for licensure that would lead to "the right of acting as General Medical Practitioners and of dispensing medicines in all parts of the British domains."[9] In Glasgow, too, the city's medical society likewise petitioned Parliament the following year for "a uniform and responsible system of Medical Government, invested with full powers to regulate all matters relating to Medical Jurisprudence, Education and Practice."[10]

The problem was growing. By the 1840s, more than 80 percent of all those in active practice in Britain were engaged in general medicine.[11] Beneath the travail of these years, a whole new structure of practitioner relationships, not yet recognized by any professional group, was beginning to take shape. Doctors were starting to divide along lines of general practice and hospital consultants. The more academically trained physicians and surgeons, usually members of the royal colleges, were concentrating their practices more and more in and around the hospital centers of London. Their teaching emoluments and consultants' fees, when added to a select private practice, enabled them to continue as members of an elite. The everyday care of patients outside the hospitals was left to the far larger number of general practitioners.[12] A similar division was under way in the regional centers and rural areas of the country. By their successful efforts to delay change and to hold in check the aspirations of their rivals, the

7. William B. Marshall, *An Essay on Medical Education* (London: Burgess and Hill, 1827), 74.

8. *Lancet* 2 (1837): 508.

9. Propositions relative to the Education and Privileges of Practitioners in the several Branches of Medicine . . . agreed on by the Medical and Surgical Professors in the University, the Royal College of Physicians, and the Royal College of Surgeons of Edinburgh, March 1839, in Minutes of Senatus, April 2, 1839, University of Edinburgh Archive. The convenor of the Edinburgh group, William Wood, sought the support of the medical faculty of the University of London, but I could find no record of a response. See William Wood to William Rothman, registrar, November 15, 1838, in Faculty of Medicine minutes, November 21, 1838, Department of Paleography, University of London Library.

10. Minutes, March 6, 1840, Glasgow Faculty of Medicine, Royal Society of Physicians of Glasgow Archive.

11. Paul K. Underhill, "Science, Professionalism and the Development of Medical Education in England: An Historical Sociology" (Ph.D. diss., University of Edinburgh, 1987), 151.

12. Ivan Waddington, "General Practitioners and Consultants in Early Nineteenth-Century England: The Sociology of an Intra-Professional Conflict," in *Health Care and Popular Medicine*, eds. John Woodward and David Richards (New York: Holmes & Meier, 1977), 164–88. See also Noel Parry and José Parry, *The Rise of the Medical Profession: A Study of Collective Social Mobility* (London: Croom Helms, 1976), 104–30.

royal colleges were thus able to maintain an unshakable foothold on the high slopes of British medicine. At midcentury, the "main structure of the present medical profession" in Britain, according to Irvine Loudon, was already in place.[13]

Across the Atlantic, efforts to move toward a common standard gained ground only very slowly. American doctors, answering to many of the same forces pushing for a "single portal" in Britain or an *Einheitsstand* in Germany, especially in the eastern cities, were desperately seeking ways to change the system of creating new doctors. But the rapid shifts in the American population, the continual appearance of more and more schools, the raw competition among them, and the laissez-faire attitude of government made agreement on any kind of uniform standard extraordinarily difficult, even in comparison with the situation in Great Britain.

If concern about the willingness of better-educated doctors to go to rural areas slowed major change in Europe, it virtually stopped it in a country where settlement continued to move farther and farther west. Indeed, many of the earlier licensing laws, enacted in a period of much slower growth, were repealed by the states in the heyday of expansion and unregulated enterprise of the 1830s and 1840s. The terms of study were actually shortened in some schools in deference to the stiff competition while admission standards, if anything, were less restrictive than they were a quarter-century before.

The Aims of Reformers on the Continent

To create a common standard of medical education embracing both academic and professional training was also the aim of continental reformers. The same forces that drove the movement in Britain—the growing number of general practitioners, the new hopefulness awakened by changes in medicine, the spread of cities and population, the bitter rivalry among competing medical groups, and the rising demand for physicians' services—all were felt in France and Germany. Unlike Britain, however, the continental states had created a whole class of practical schools that were supplying a significant proportion of general practitioners. Could the education in these schools be made more complete, more scientific, in order to increase their usefulness to a growing population? Or should the university physicians, now more broadly trained, be relied on to serve the countryside as well as the city? Would this latter group, after so heavy an investment in education, be likely to go to small towns and rural areas where the need was greatest? Quite differently from Britain (or America), these questions were undeniably the responsibility of government in the continental countries.

---

13. Loudon, *Medical Care and the General Practitioner*, 3.

In both Germany and France, voices were raised as early as the 1820s in favor of abolishing the lower ranks of healers. Pressures were growing for the government to unify the medical profession by doing away with the distinctions among licensed practitioners. If the tendency of reform in the English-speaking countries was downward in the face of governmental inaction, the continental movements for change were aimed at forcing a much higher common level of training. Critics of the practical schools in France and Germany argued that the acceptance by these schools of lesser-educated students and their generally lower standards were dragging down the economic and social status of the entire profession.

But the practical schools had their vigorous defenders. Some of these schools were clearly becoming stronger in their academic offerings and aspirations. Not a few, notably Lyon, Bordeaux, Graz, and Munich, were pushing for university status and the right to grant medical degrees. In the debates in Prussia in 1825, as elsewhere on the Continent, the government continued to insist on the continued segregation of practitioners by qualification, preliminary education, and the places where they were allowed to practice. The time was not yet ready, declared the Ministry of Health and Education in Prussia, to replace the country doctors with university-trained men.

The competition among different types of practitioner to meet the rising demand for doctors' services began to spill over into the smaller cities and towns of France and Germany. University physicians in Germany were now being routinely trained in surgery and obstetrics, as well as in medicine, as required by law in many of the German states, which gave them a much broader range of usefulness. The goal of medical education in the German universities was thus no longer merely to prepare students for entrance into the service of the privileged classes but now included giving them the capacity to serve a larger spectrum of patients. "The new physician," writes Claudia Huerkamp, "was defined more by his practical actions and not by adherence to the world of privilege and its associated lifestyle."[14]

The years from 1830 to 1850 were marked on the Continent by increasingly sharp agitation of the question of how to regulate medical training. Only the nagging uncertainty whether university-educated men—now more broadly trained, with their higher social background and their long periods of study—would move in sufficient numbers to the rural areas held back the movement for change. "A doctor in a village," contended a French senator, "would be just as much out of place as a graduate of the Sorbonne as a village priest, or a member of the Academy

---

14. For much of this and the preceding paragraph, I have depended on Claudia Huerkamp, *Der Aufstieg der Ärzte im 19. Jahrhundert: Vom gelehrten Stand zum professionellen Experten: Das Beispiel Preussens* (Göttingen: Vandenhoeck & Ruprecht, 1985), 22–59.

of Sciences as a village schoolmaster."[15] In 1840, as a partial compromise, some of the French secondary schools of medicine were turned into "preparatory schools," offering three years of study to students planning to transfer to a degree-granting faculty, while still maintaining their programs for *officiers de santé*.[16]

Meanwhile, in both Europe and America, students were finding medicine an increasingly attractive field of study. The great leaps in population in the industrializing countries, together with advances in wealth and education, swifter transportation, and a rising faith in medicine's power to diagnose and sometimes to palliate or heal, brought a marked expansion in the demand for trained medical care. "Within the last half century," declared a committee of the American Medical Association in 1849, in recognizing the growth of the medical market, "no one acquainted with the progress of medicine can hesitate to recognize its rapid expansion into a science. . . . It is now far more certain in [its] judgments and opinions . . . than are the law, theology, or the moral sciences."[17] This increased faith in medicine's usefulness and future potential, which was shared by the better-educated public, brought in turn renewed pressures on governments and educators to raise requirements and to shrink the ranks of the purely practically trained. The economic self-interest of the practitioners themselves in reducing competition for patients understandably spurred the interest in reform. The movement to restrict entrance to medicine, which took different forms and was led by different groups in each country, was most successful by midcentury in the German states, less so in France and Britain, and had as yet minimal impact in the United States.

Germany Advances the Single Standard

In the German states, especially during the political turbulence of the 1840s, the drive for a single standard of medical training achieved its greatest victories. By 1850, the old hierarchy of healers had largely been abolished, and the university had become the "single portal" through which all future practitioners had to pass.[18] During the Prussian debates on education in the 1840s, the reformer Rudolph Virchow—citing advances in German science and the need for better-trained physicians to serve the nation's population—declared that institutions of advanced education "must stop being merely places for

15. Robert Heller, "Officiers de Santé: The Second-Class Doctors of Nineteenth-Century France," *Medical History* 22 (1978): 32.
16. Jacques Léonard, *La vie quotidienne du médecin de province au XIXe siècle* (Paris: Hachette, 1977), 33.
17. "Report of Committee on Education," *Transactions of the American Medical Association* 2 (1849): 361.
18. Huerkamp, *Aufstieg der Ärzte*, 58.

bread and butter studies" and that "the training of future physicians must be given entirely to universities."[19] Other German states adopted the same policy of "leveling upward" in ending the two-tiered system of medical instruction.

As early as 1842, Bavaria had finally closed its practical schools in Bamberg and Landshut. Three years later, the government of Saxony decreed that the education of all future physicians must be in the hands of the universities.[20] The two largest German states, Austria and Prussia, also passed legislation by the early 1850s that ended summarily the training of most second-order practitioners. Three of the Hapsburg practical schools were closed in 1848; three others lingered on for a period; and the school in Graz was converted into a university school.[21] In Prussia, the medical–surgical schools in Breslau, Greifswald, Münster, and Magdeburg all were closed between 1849 and 1852.

Nowhere at midcentury was the new faith in science as the basis for medical education, mastered through experiment and the use of the laboratory, more advanced than in Germany. The early differences between German medical teaching and that of France and Great Britain, which had become apparent at the time of the French Revolution and had grown wider with changes after 1800, now became wider still. As the practical schools of Germany disappeared, universities added to their scientific offerings in medicine, built research institutes, and began to make provision for teaching students in laboratories. "Whoever undergoes clinical instruction without a thorough acquaintance with the natural sciences," especially chemistry and physics, declared the pharmacologist Philipp Phoebus in 1849, "is grasping the husk rather than the grain itself."[22]

Although much of the scientific revolution in German medicine, described more fully in Chapter 9, was yet to come, it was already clear in 1850 that medical education was following a very different path from that in other European nations. By this time, Johannes Müller and Johannes Schönlein had pioneered a new science-based approach to medical teaching in Berlin; such formerly theoretical subjects as physiology, pathology, and pharmacology were being made into practical, experimental studies there and elsewhere; and scarcely a university in Germany had not made some start in developing laboratory courses in medicine. In

19. Rudolph Virchow, "Der medicinische Unterricht," *Die medicinische Reform*, no. 12, 1848: 77–79.

20. Carl Bock, *Auch ein Votum in Betreff der Medicinalreform in Sachsen* (Leipzig: Reclam, 1846), n.p., in Akten der medizinischen Facultät, VI, 59a, University of Leipzig Archive.

21. Anna D. von Rüden, "Medicina Graecensis: Das medizinisch–chirurgische Studium in Graz (1782–1862)" (med. diss., Technical University of Munich, 1978), 29–30.

22. Philipp Phoebus, *Uber die Naturwissenschaften als Gegenstand des Studiums, des Unterrichts und der Prüfung angehender Ärzte* (Nordhausen: Adolph Büchting, 1849), 4.

Baden, work in the laboratory was being required for a medical license as early as 1858.[23]

Dozens of voices, among them those of Schönlein, Henle, Müller, Ludwig Choulant, Carl Wunderlich, and Wilhelm Roser, expressed the conviction that medicine was on its way to becoming an exact, more reliable, scientific study. Practical studies alone, wrote Choulant in his guidebook for students as early as 1829, were no longer enough for a well-prepared practitioner. "Since medicine is a science," he told his students, "it can only be learned and taught in a university."[24] "Medicine as an empirical and inductive science," wrote Wunderlich and Roser in their opening manifesto in the *Archive for Physiological Medicine* in 1842, "must be subject to the same methods as the exact, physical sciences."[25] So widespread was the change in viewpoint among medical educators that the Leipzig professor Carl Bock complained in 1846 that his colleagues were ignorant of "the physiological point of view" being taught in other German medical schools and that they still continued to teach students "to hand out prescriptions blindly" in treating all illness.[26]

The size of the German teaching enterprise in medicine, though smaller than it had been a quarter-century before, was still the largest in Europe. A conservative estimate of the number of those studying medicine in the German-language universities and the remaining practical and military schools in 1850 is about 4,500 students.[27] Enrollment in medicine was falling, however, not only because of the phasing out of the practical schools but also because of political turbulence, economic unrest, rising scientific requirements, and the conviction that too many doctors were being produced.[28]

Classes throughout the German medical world remained generally smaller than those in France and Britain, where large urban schools accounted for much of the medical enrollment. At Halle, for example, still a well-regarded university at midcentury, classes in 1845 numbered from twelve to thirty-four students in anatomy, from thirty-six to forty in phys-

---

23. Arleen Tuchman, "Experimental Physiology, Medical Reform, and the Politics of Education at the University of Heidelberg: A Case Study," *Bulletin of the History of Medicine* 61 (1987): 203.

24. Albert Steiner, *Ludwig Choulant und seine "Anleitung zu dem Studium der Medicin" (1829)* (Zurich: Juris Druck & Verlag, 1987), 32.

25. Carl Wunderlich and Wilhelm Roser, "Über die Mängel der heutigen deutschen Medicin und über die Nothwendigkeit einer entschieden wissenschaftlichen Richtung in derselben," *Archiv für physiologische Heilkunde* 1 (1842): ii.

26. Bock, *Auch ein Votum*.

27. This estimate is based on the following: For the German states outside Austria and Switzerland, W. Lexis, *Die deutschen Universitäten*, 2 vols. (Berlin: A. Asher, 1893), 1:121, table 1; for Austria, Johannes Conrad, *The German Universities for the Last Fifty Years*, trans. John Hutchinson (Glasgow: David Bryce, 1885); and for Switzerland and the practical and military schools, my own estimates.

28. Georg Heinemann, "Die Studierenden der Medizin in Deutschland am Anfange des 20.Jahrhunderts," *Klinisches Jahrbuch* 10 (1903): 223–24.

iology, and from eighteen to sixty-seven in pathology.[29] Only Vienna, Berlin, and Munich enrolled more than two hundred students in their faculties of medicine, whereas most universities could count fewer than a hundred.[30]

In France, by contrast, the Paris faculty was teaching twelve hundred students in 1850; several hundred others were studying in Montpellier and Strasbourg; and thirty-one secondary and military schools were dividing another thousand students among them.[31] The figures for Great Britain, more elusive and unreliable, suggest that fourteen hundred young men were studying medicine in the thirteen medical schools of Scotland and Ireland around 1850, perhaps another thousand in the eleven London schools, and not more than three hundred or four hundred in the thirteen provincial schools and older universities.[32]

The Reform Movement in France

Educators in France for the most part paid remarkably little heed to the changes in medical education occurring beyond the Rhine. French clinical teaching, now at the peak of its popularity, was still, in the words of Joy Harvey, "faithful to its old traditions."[33] Little had changed since 1830, with the possible exception of Strasbourg, in the courses being offered, the requirements for a degree, and the organization of the curriculum. Laboratory teaching was not yet an integral part of the curriculum at any French medical school. At Strasbourg, with its border culture, faculty members did repeatedly seek in the 1830s and 1840s to reorganize clinical teaching along German lines and to introduce courses in "chemical pathology," histology, and other scientific studies, as well as to keep close relationships to German colleagues. "The faculty at Strasbourg," explained the noted internist Charles Schuetzenberger in 1867, "has always been . . . an experimental school, a practical school, a school of positive science."[34] But elsewhere the French, at least to outsiders, seemed indifferent to reports of educational change in Germany. After a stay in

29. Verzeichnis der auf der königlichen vereinten Friedrichs-Universität Halle-Wittenberg für das Winter Semester 1845/46 nach dem Lections-Cataloge angekündigten und wirklich zu Stande gekommenen Vorlesungen, manuscript, GSPK, Merseburg, 76, Va, Sekt. 8, Tit. 7, No. 2, vol. X.

30. Lexis, *Die deutschen Universitäten*, 1:120–21, table 1.

31. "Report of Committee on Medical Education," *Transactions of the American Medical Association* 2 (1849): 265; George Weisz, *The Emergence of Modern Universities in France, 1863– 1914* (Princeton, NJ: Princeton University Press, 1983), 49, table 1.6; F. H. Arneth, *Über Geburtshilfe und Gynaekologie* (Vienna: Wilhelm Braumüller, 1853), 21.

32. "Report of Committee on Medical Education," 262; and my own estimates.

33. I am indebted to Dr. Harvey for sending me her manuscript "`Faithful to Its Old Traditions': Paris Clinical Medicine from the late 1840s to the Third Republic."

34. See Christian Sifferlen, "Contributions à l'histoire de la faculté de médecine" (med. diss., University of Strasbourg, 1968), 11.

Paris in 1840, Carl Wunderlich wrote about the "isolation" of French medicine and the lack of attention to natural science in deepening students' understanding of what they had seen in the clinic.[35]

At a time when laboratory instruction and exposure to research were fast becoming an important part of German medical teaching, the French schools seemed more intent on retaining a "rigid distinction between the conveying of established truths and the acquisition of new knowledge." This was all the more remarkable because German science itself was built in such large measure on the work of French scientists. A number of German savants, including Wunderlich, Justus von Liebig, and Alexander Humboldt, had learned much of their science in Paris. When Liebig opened his chemistry teaching laboratory in Giessen following a stay in Paris and attracted scores of students from all over Europe and America, only a handful of French students, most of them from Alsace, came across the Rhine.[36] By the early 1850s, an Erlangen professor was likening French medical schools to the earlier practical schools of provincial Germany in their narrow professionalism and was charging that "university medical education for physicians never found a foothold in France."[37]

Yet the hold of Paris on the medical imagination remained powerful at midcentury. Graduate physicians from Britain and North America, in particular, continued to pour into Paris to experience the welcoming wards, the lectures on the emerging clinical specialties, the numerous private courses, and the virtually unlimited opportunities for dissection that eluded them at home. More American doctors were studying in Paris in the early 1850s, in fact, than ever before. "It was overwhelmingly the promise of practical experience that drew them to Paris," writes John Harley Warner in words that apply also to other visitors, "not its intellectual vigor or the chance to witness the cutting edge of medical science."[38]

German physicians were turning more and more to Vienna for practical, postgraduate training by 1850, whereas those from other lands continued to go to Paris. "There were only five Americans in Vienna last winter," wrote the New Jersey physician George Doan in 1853, "while Paris could boast of between three and four hundred. These latter crowded every private lecture-room, and clinique in the 'Quartier Latin' to their own discomfort . . . while in Vienna the same, and in many cases greater facilities exist, unknown and unimproved."

Vienna, Doan continued, offered not only all the practical advantages of Paris but also the chance to "listen to the lucid diagnoses of Skoda and

---

35. Carl A. Wunderlich, *Wien und Paris: Ein Beitrag zur Geschichte und Beurteilung der gegenwärtigen Heilkunde in Deutschland und Frankreich, 1841*, ed. H. M. Koelbing (Stuttgart: Hans Huber, 1974), 37.

36. Robert Fox, "Scientific Enterprise and the Patronage of Research in France, 1800–70," *Minerva* 11 (1973): 464.

37. J. M. Leupoldt, *Uber ärztliche Bildung und Bildungsanstalten* (Frankfurt am Main: Heyder & Zimmer, 1853), 26.

38. I am indebted to Prof. Warner for a copy of his paper "Paradigm Lost or Paradise Declining? American Physicians and the 'Dead End' of the Paris Clinical School," 5.

Oppolzer [which] give the student confidence in the science of medicine."[39] The Danube city became more popular after 1855 when the
dean of the Paris faculty suddenly decreed the end of private teaching by
interns in the hospitals. This had been a principal attraction to visitors.
Thereafter, as a contemporary Philadelphia surgeon accurately predicted,
Vienna began swiftly to replace Paris as "the great centre of medical attraction."[40]

French medical educators, lacking the claim to scientific authority used
so effectively by German reformers, failed in their effort to create a single
standard of medical education. For more than twenty years, the struggle
to eliminate the secondary schools because of their allegedly inferior
training and the general overcrowding in the profession was beaten back
by rural legislators, the Catholic Church, the corps of *officiers*, and those
who feared for the health of the rural poor. A proposal to create salaried
positions for medical doctors in the countryside as a way of spreading
employment for physicians and eliminating the need for lesser-trained
practitioners likewise met with defeat. In 1838, a government commission recommended abolishing the *officiers* and lengthening the medical
curriculum to five years, but its report was never acted on. Medical students in Paris joined the campaign to abolish the second-class schools in
1843 by presenting a petition to the government signed by nearly all of
them.[41]

Those who resisted the move to a common standard in France used
the same arguments employed elsewhere, namely, that it would deprive
thousands of medical treatment and deny the poor any chance to enter
the practice of medicine. The inspector general of medical education in
France, Alfred Donné, stated the case simply: "There are two categories
of sick people, the rich and the poor: there must be two grades of doctors
to meet the needs of one and the other." A mass meeting of physicians in
1845, sanctioned by the government, led to further proposals to suppress
the provincial schools, but again the results were negligible.[42] By this
time, about 40 percent of medical students were enrolled in the secondary schools.[43]

39. George H. Doane, "Comparative Advantages of Vienna and Paris, as Places for
Medical Study, with some Remarks on the Operation of Extraction for the Removal of
Cataract," *New Jersey Medical Reporter* 7 (1854): 18.

40. Cited in Warner, "Paradigm Lost," 41.

41. Robert Heller, "Officiers de Santé: The Second-Class Doctors of Nineteenth-Century France," *Medical History* 22 (1978): 30; Paul Broca, *Correspondance, 1841–1857*, 2
vols. (Paris: privately printed, 1886), 1:129. I am grateful to Paul Broca's great-grandson,
Professor P. Monad-Broca, for lending me a copy of this correspondence.

42. Jacques Léonard, *La médecine entre les savoirs et les pouvoirs* (Paris: Aubier, 1981),
85–86, 213–17.

43. E. Perrin de la Touche, *L'enseignement médical à Rennes (1800–1896)* (Rennes,
1896), 37. Many of those now enrolled in the secondary schools were planning to finish
their studies at one of the three medical schools.

In the meantime, twenty-one of the secondary schools had been converted into "preparatory schools" empowered to instruct those readying themselves to enter a full-fledged medical school. Two years of secondary training would be measured as equivalent to one year at a medical school.[44] Some of the renovated schools, given additional faculty positions and facilities, achieved a respectable standard in the eyes of much of the medical community after 1850. The school at Rennes, for example, listed a faculty of sixteen in 1854, enrolled 111 students, and was moved into new quarters adjoining the school of science.[45] By this time, in the opinion of a French authority, teaching in the preparatory schools "approached that given to future physicians," although the sharp division in the ranks of practitioners remained.[46]

Creating a Safe, General Practitioner in Great Britain

The drive for reform in liberal Britain, though marginally more successful than in France, fell far short of realizing the sweeping changes in Germany. The Medical Registration Act, finally realized in 1858, made mandatory the registration of all licensed medical practitioners—apothecaries, surgeons, physicians, and combinations of these—and created the General Medical Council to set minimal standards. The legislation was the climax of a half-century of effort to bring order and some measure of legal equality out of the chaos of British practice. Whereas once a number of the old licensing bodies—the royal colleges and universities, in particular—had been unable to grant permission for more than a limited range of practice, a medical license was now valid throughout the kingdom.

The new council set a recommended minimum standard for general practice that included an examination in general education before starting medicine, four years of medical and surgical study, and the age of twenty-one.[47] These were as yet only general and somewhat vague recommendations, however, and they were difficult to enforce. What was meant by an adequate general education? What constituted four years of study? Did four years mean, the council asked itself, "four winter and four summer semesters?—or, as the Edinburgh ordinances make them, four sessions of six months, or two years in all?" Under pressure to clarify these and other

---

44. *Almanach général de médecine pour la ville de Paris* (Paris, 1853), 127–41.

45. Touche, *L'enseignement médical à Rennes*, 38–43.

46. Charles Coury, *L'enseignement de la médecine en France des origines a nos jour* (Paris: Expansion scientifique français, 1968), 124. On the struggle to eliminate the officiers, see also George Weisz, "The Politics of Medical Professionalization in France, 1845–1848," *Journal of Social History* 12 (1978): 3–30; and George D. Sussman, "The Glut of Doctors in Mid-Nineteenth-Century France," *Comparative Studies in Society and History* 19 (1977): 287–304.

47. J. N. L. Poynter, "Education and the General Medical Council," in *The Evolution of Medical Education in Britain*, ed. F. N. L. Poynter (London: Pitman, 1966), 197.

matters, the council, according to its own minutes, "seemed to regard it inexpedient so to do." Never in history, complained the council, "did Act of Parliament constitute a body with more of the semblance and less of the reality of power."[48] For the next twenty years, in the view of an editor of the *British Medical Journal*, the examining bodies "almost without exception . . . simply defied the Council. Each examining body in turn has said to the Council, 'That is your opinion; it is not ours.'"[49] The act of 1858 thus stood for a careful and cautious coordination of requirements in order to assure a minimum level of competence.

A license to practice in midcentury Britain could still come only from one of the nineteen licensing bodies whose requirements remained as various as ever. At the University of Edinburgh, for example, the medical degree, which brought with it the right to practice, required in the 1850s the "proper certificates" of having studied "literature and philosophy," a knowledge of Latin, four terms of six months each of medical study, including one term at a hospital, and a dissertation in Latin or English.[50]

The University of London had demanded since 1837 a bachelor of arts degree or its equivalent before commencing four years of graded medical study in basic science, anatomy and physiology, and then clinical instruction ("the whole of Science to be taught before the Practical division"), followed by two years of practice in a hospital or dispensary.[51]

The curriculum of the Society of Apothecaries, on the other hand, which was responsible for most of the licenses awarded in England, made mandatory a preliminary examination in Greek, Latin, and mathematics by 1850, along with five years of apprenticeship and three winter and two summer sessions of medical study.[52]

The range of studies in the London schools alone was immense. By the 1850s, five of the schools taught courses in clinical medicine and surgery but six did not; midwifery was offered as a clinical subject only at Guy's; histology and the use of the microscope were listed in only five schools; and pathology or morbid anatomy was now taught in all but one school.[53] The most common route to general practice at mid-century was still a license from both the Society of Apothecaries and the College of Surgeons. By this time, the old terms of *apothecary* and *apothecary-sur-*

---

48. "Minutes of the General Council of Medical Education and Registration, June 1861," *Edinburgh Medical Journal 7* (1861): 163, 171.

49. House of Commons, Select Committee on Medical Act, *Special Report from the Select Committee on Medical Act (1858) . . . together with the Proceedings of the Committee, Minutes of Evidence, Appendix, and Index* (London: House of Commons, 1879), testimony of Ernest Hart, 265.

50. "Regulations of Universities, Colleges, and Examining Boards, in Scotland and Ireland," *Lancet 2* (1856): 345.

51. Minutes, Committee of the Faculty of Medicine, May 30, July 4 and November 27, 1837, University of London Library, paleography room.

52. Charles Newman, *The Evolution of Medical Education in the Nineteenth Century* (Oxford: Oxford University Press, 1957), 107–8.

53. Ibid., 108–9.

geon had fallen into disuse, and most practitioners were now simply called *doctor* or *general practitioner.*

Apprenticeship as a means of acquiring practical training was under heavy fire by 1850, as it was in America. Almost all educators agreed by this time that five years was much too long a time for so routine and limited an experience. Many stressed that the relationship of a student with a preceptor was often haphazard and undependable and that it always took place outside the view of licensing authorities. "I think that requiring an apprenticeship from an individual who has attained his majority," testified the London teacher John Rideout, who had himself served an apprenticeship, "is altogether inexpedient; and . . . making [it] compulsory has made it less popular."[54] Still others resented the trade and class associations of the apprenticeship.

Resentment was high, too, at the demeaning view of the apprenticeship held by university graduates and continental visitors, for whom medicine was normally a university study. In describing his impressions of English general practitioners in 1840, for example, the clinician Karl von Pfeufer pictured them as "handicraft workers," more technicians than scientists, "who do no regular study."[55] By failing to include apprenticeship in the requirements of the 1858 act, the reformers effectively put the practice on the road to extinction, although it lingered on for a number of years.

Striving for Change in the United States

To read the reports of the American Medical Association (AMA) at mid-century is to be reminded of how similar the goals of the reformers were in all the transatlantic nations. Despite the social and political contrasts with Europe and the raw, unsettled nature of the country, American reformers, like their counterparts in Europe, were urging a common standard of medical instruction that would put an end to apprenticeship training, demand more preliminary education and longer periods of study, add more science to the curriculum, and require a period of hospital training.

Over the vehement opposition of critics, who regarded the reformers as unrealistic, they pressed constantly for change. Opponents dwelled on the great differences in American circumstances from those in Europe and contended that America was not yet ready for anything approaching a single standard. "We have not the means, we have not the leisure to fol-

54. House of Commons, Select Committee on Medical Registration and Medical Law Amendments, *First and Second Reports; together with the Minutes of Evidence and Appendix* (London: House of Commons, 1848), 45.

55. Karl von Pfeufer, "Uber den gegenwärtigen Zustand der Medicin," *Annalen der städtischen Allgemeinen Krankenhäuser in München* 1 (1878): 404. This is a reprint of his 1840 inaugural address at Zurich.

low the standard of European . . . legislation," protested Martyn Paine in 1843. The American student must make his way "under the frigid discipline of poverty" in the hope "that his career may not be arrested by insane exactions . . . borrowed from the overgrown wealth of Europe, and her old and rich institutions."[56]

Even in its very first reports, however, the AMA resolved to push for six-month terms of lectures, three courses of study, at least seven professors at each college, mandatory dissection, and attendance at a clinic or hospital as minimal requirements for graduation.[57] The new association pleaded with hospitals in 1848 to open their wards to students to end "an obsolete system of training"; a year later it resolved that "much might be gained" by grading the curriculum and that college clinics were no substitute for hospital experience. By the 1850s, the education committee was urging the abolition of the "radically wrong" preceptorship system, the adoption of the French competitive method of appointing professors, and the requirement of "instruction in physiology, pathology, and microscopy."[58]

The leaders of the reform effort, many of them young medical teachers, recognized that change would be much more difficult here than on the other side of the Atlantic. Here, after all, there was no tradition of strong government protecting the people's health as there was in Europe, or a unitary state as there was in Britain, which could be nudged, albeit slowly, toward a national standard of medical training. "European governments, their institutions, and the genius of the people are different from [those] of the United States," wrote Dr. Pliny Earle in the 1848 report of the AMA; "political ethics and the control and direction of instruction are there vested in the same hands . . . [but] here the establishment and direction are left to private enterprise."[59]

How was it possible even to contemplate a common standard for training doctors in so unsettled a land where each of thirty sovereign states made its own determinations regarding legislation? An AMA survey of state laws in 1849 produced such responses as "the law was repealed, and the field is now open to all" (Maine); "no law in force at the present time" (Massachusetts); "no restrictions since 1844, when the law was repealed" (New York); and "there have never been any laws regulating the practice of medicine and surgery" (Pennsylvania).[60] The great need for doctors in sparsely settled areas, along with the proliferation of medical schools, had almost completely wiped out earlier efforts to license practitioners. Change in American medical education, it was increasingly rec-

56. Martyn Paine, "Medical Education in the United States," *Boston Medical and Surgical Journal* 29 (1843): 332.

57. Summary in *Boston Medical and Surgical Journal* 40 (1859): 303.

58. *Transactions of the American Medical Association* 1 (1848): 246; 2 (1849): 341, 351; 4 (1851): 17; 7 (1854): 60; 9 (1856): 254.

59. Ibid., 1 (1848): 236.

60. Ibid., 2 (1849): 326–28.

ognized, would come only through voluntary agreement among medical schools and medical societies, or it would not come at all.

Appeal after appeal was directed by the AMA at individual medical faculties to unite in imposing a minimal standard of training. But the schools themselves were undergoing so rapid a multiplication and the competition among them had become so murderous that it seemed impossible for a single school or even a handful to lift their requirements. Even the Harvard Medical School, now virtually an independent college, publicly opposed any effort to extend the school term from four to six months. "The length of a course of lectures," read a faculty response to the AMA in 1849, "is not the measure of its value," and four months of imparting "elementary principles" and "practical truths," if supplemented by individual work in private schools such as those in Boston, was enough to satisfy students' "curiosity . . . [and] pecuniary ability to attend."[61] The school at Harvard, by this time, had become to all intents and purposes a year-round institution through its interlocking relationships with such private schools as the Tremont and Boylston Medical Schools.[62]

Harvard's opposition to change, like that of other schools, owed far more to fears of ruinous competition than any preference for the limited, didactic teaching in American medical classrooms.[63] When in response to the AMA's urging, the University of Pennsylvania did adopt the six-month standard, it lost students immediately and was quickly forced to retreat. If at this moment in history, American schools had been successful in raising their standards, argued the historian Joseph Kett, "no more than a fraction of the actual practitioners" would have bothered to attend a medical school at all.[64] A single standard in America, then, as was true in Britain, would have to await the building of enough cohesion among the parties affected to bring about change and could not come, as in continental Europe, from the protective action of government.

The situation in America at midcentury, recalled the Detroit surgeon Theodore McGraw, who had studied abroad, was "precisely similar" to what he had seen in Great Britain. In both countries, he said, the apprenticeship system still flourished "in a degenerative form"; medical schools

61. "Practical Views on Medical Education submitted to the Members of the American Medical Association by the Medical Faculty of Harvard University," *Boston Medical and Surgical Journal* 42 (1850): 481–84. The report was signed by Jacob Bigelow, Walter Channing, John Ware, John B. S. Jackson, Oliver Wendell Holmes, Henry J. Bigelow, and E. N. Horsford.

62. Thomas F. Harrington, *The Harvard Medical School: A History, Narrative and Documentary*, 3 vols. (New York: Lewis, 1905), 2:498.

63. See Thomas S. Huddle, "Looking Backward: The 1871 Reforms at Harvard Medical School Reconsidered," *Bulletin of the History of Medicine* 65 (1991): 343–51; and Huddle, "Science, Practice, and the Reform of American Medical Education" (Ph.D. diss., University of Illinois, 1988), 25–48.

64. Joseph F. Kett, *The Formation of the American Medical Profession: The Role of Institutions, 1780–1860* (New Haven, CT: Yale University Press, 1968), 69.

in both places were "practically private schools, attached to hospitals"; and the governments of both countries treated medical education with "supreme neglect."[65] That the British system of training doctors was like the American in its weak premedical requirements, brief period of study, lack of training in science, and preference for practical education was the view of many contemporaries.

It was the practitioners themselves in Britain, said Alfred Stillé, who were organizing and leading the fight for change in that country, and this was the only route that improvement could take in America.[66] If Americans were suffering from "defective early education," observed the New York professor John Revere, then "the remark applies with quite as much force to the mass of practitioners in Great Britain." Even though the period of formal study was shorter in America than in Britain, Revere noted, "probably a majority of [American] candidates have [taken] a much longer time" than the minimum required to complete their studies.[67] In American practice, lecture courses were often free after the second term, and a considerable number of American students were able to take three full terms of study. "You should attend three courses of lectures before you attempt to graduate," Daniel Drake told students at Louisville in 1844; "I regard it as most unfortunate that all our schools [are] not organized on the principle of three courses for graduation, two only being paid for."[68] In New York, according to the surgeon John Watson, "the annual term of public teaching has, in effect, been extended of late years to between seven and eight months."[69] In Philadelphia, by the end of the 1850s, seven of every ten physicians entering practice had spent at least three years in study, and four of them had taken four years to prepare themselves.[70] Similarly, as we have seen, by 1850 Harvard had become to some extent a year-round institution.

The new and struggling schools of the American west and south were forced to adapt their ambitions to the less settled conditions in those regions. A number of them, however, did provide free instruction after the second year, just as in the east, and some also offered "preliminary"

65. Theodore A. McGraw, "The Medical Schools of the Last Half-Century," *Journal of the Michigan State Medical Society* 14 (1915): 515.

66. Alfred Stillé, *Medical Education in the United States: An Address delivered to the Students of the Philadelphia Association for Medical Instruction* (Philadelphia: Isaac Ashmead, 1846), 18–27.

67. John Revere, *An Introductory Lecture on the Comparative State of the Profession of Medicine, and of Medical Education, in the United States and Europe* (New York: University of the City of New York, 1846), 7–14.

68. Daniel Drake, *An Introductory Lecture on the Means of Promoting the Intellectual Improvement of the Students and Physicians of the Valley of the Mississippi* (Louisville: Prentice and Weissinger, 1844), 9.

69. John Watson, *A Lecture on Practical Education in Medicine, and on the Course of Instruction at the N.Y. Hospital* (New York: J. and H. G. Langley, 1846), 9.

70. Leo J. O'Hara, "An Emerging Profession: Philadelphia Medicine, 1860–1900" (Ph.D. diss., University of Pennsylvania, 1976), 97–98.

courses at lower rates before the fall term as a way of attracting students. The little college in Willoughby, Ohio, for example, advertised a preliminary course of thirteen weeks in 1845, during which one lecture and one recitation were to be held daily on the nervous system and the physical diagnosis of diseases of the chest.[71] Farther west, at the Rush Medical College in Chicago, discussions were started soon after its founding in 1843 on the possibility of a three-year graded course that would put Rush ahead of eastern schools. When the deliberations finally broke down in 1858, the reformer Nathan Smith Davis, a member of the faculty for ten years, led a group of faculty members into a new collegiate venture that promptly initiated the change.[72] Rush thereupon announced a sixteen-week "Preparatory School of Medicine" to ensure "a longer and more complete course of instruction."[73]

Another example of western initiative came at the State University of Michigan. When a medical department was begun there in 1850, it was made an integral part of the university. Teachers were paid a fixed salary by the university; a separate chemistry building was erected for medical students; and a clinical program under university direction was later started in Detroit.[74]

By the middle of the century, forty-nine medical schools of all kinds were open to students in the United States, and another eight had been opened in Canada.[75] In Canada by this time, three years of study in a medical school, plus a year of hospital practice and six months of preceptorship, had become the standard course of study.[76] In the United States, the size of the enterprise in medical teaching approached that of Britain and France combined. Eleven of the American schools, many of them short lived, were botanic, eclectic, or homeopathic in character. In Philadelphia, six of the eight schools founded around 1850 were sectar-

71. *Annual Announcement of the Willoughby Medical College*, 1845–46, 5.

72. According to the Rush faculty minutes of February 1858, the faculty voted, with President Daniel Brainard absent, to extend the term to nine months and divide the students into a junior and a senior class. Basic academic studies were to be pursued by the junior class, and clinical subjects and hospital practice were reserved for the second. On Brainard's return, the action was rescinded. Faculty Minutes, Rush Medical College, Rush–Presbyterian–St. Luke's Medical Center Archive.

73. Ernest E. Irons, *The Story of Rush Medical College* (Chicago: Rush Medical College, 1953), 15–20; Nathan S. Davis, *Inaugural Address delivered at the Opening of the Medical Department of Lind University* (Chicago, 1859), 17.

74. Horace W. Davenport, *Doctor Dock: Teaching and Learning Medicine at the Turn of the Century* (New Brunswick, NJ: Rutgers University Press, 1987), 4–13.

75. *Transactions of the American Medical Association* 2 (1849): 281; Frederick C. Waite, "American Sectarian Medical Colleges Before the Civil War," *Bulletin of the History of Medicine* 19 (1946): 148–66; John J. Heagarty, *Four Centuries of Medical History in Canada*, 2 vols. (Toronto: Macmillan, 1928), 2:55.

76. R. D. Gidney and W. P. J. Millar, "The Reorientation of Medical Education in Late Nineteenth-Century Ontario: The Proprietary Medical School and the Founding of the Faculty of Medicine at the University of Toronto," *Journal of the History of Medicine and Allied Sciences* 49 (1994): 53–54.

ian, and in Cincinnati three such schools were in operation by midcentury.[77] At all the schools, regular or irregular, the size of the faculty was normally about seven. The AMA complained in 1849 that European schools, by comparison, had "more than double, and, in some instances, four or five times more teachers than in the United States."[78]

Medical Teachers at Midcentury

But this was true only of the university schools on the Continent and not the many practical schools in Britain and France—which were the real counterparts to the American enterprise. In the case of the German universities, excluding Austria and Switzerland, a reliable compilation for 1850 puts the number of medical teachers in universities at 315, or an average of 15 per school, but the practical schools had only half that number.[79] In the French schools, including both degree-granting and secondary schools, those teaching medicine, even in 1865, barely exceeded 180, or an average of 6 per school.[80] Those offering formal medical instruction in Great Britain, in my estimate, did not exceed 150, and perhaps 250—assuming an average of 7 per school and allowing for some duplication—were teaching medicine in the United States.

Professors at British and American schools were much more likely than those on the Continent were to hold more than one teaching position. It was still possible in Britain at midcentury for an instructor to teach in more than one school, and in America it was common for a teacher to move from one school to another according to the calendar. In London, for example, William Carpenter taught a course in medical jurisprudence at the University of London in 1850 while simultaneously teaching physiology at the London Hospital Medical College. In the United States, the well-known John Delameter—admittedly unusual in his zeal—held teaching positions in five different medical schools in 1837![81]

77. Martha Tracy, untitled manuscript on medical education in Philadelphia, 1931, Archives and Special Collections on Women in Medicine, Medical College of Pennsylvania, C-4; "Nineteenth Century Medical Colleges in Cincinnati," list compiled by Cincinnati Historical Society.

78. *Transactions of the American Medical Association* 2 (1849): 277.

79. Conrad, *The German Universities*, 193.

80. George Weisz, *The Emergence of Modern Universities in France, 1863–1914* (Princeton, NJ: Princeton University Press, 1983), 28. The number of faculty members at the preparatory medical schools was set by law in 1840 at six, with two additional adjunct appointments. *Almanach général*, 27–28.

81. Minutes of Medical Council, London Hospital Medical School, June 4, 1850, London Hospital Medical School Archive; Jonathan Forman, "A Brief Historical Sketch of the College of Medicine of the Ohio State University," *The Ohio State University College of Medicine: A Collection of Source Material Covering a Century of Medical Progress* (Blanchester, OH: Brown Publishing, 1934), 506. The schools were Willoughby, Dartmouth, Fairfield, Franklin, and Geneva.

Support for faculty salaries, paid by the state in France and Germany, still came almost wholly from student fees in the English-speaking countries. Debates were frequent in British and American faculty meetings about how the fees were to be divided. "The money is not divided and will not be," wrote a Rush professor in 1849, "they say they pay debts . . . with the matriculation and graduation fees—but the debts are usually going to themselves."[82] At Liverpool the same year the faculty agreed that each lecturer would contribute one shilling out of every guinea received from students to meet common expenses; teachers at the London Hospital meanwhile decided on a general fee from which lecturers would be paid £25 a year; and the faculty at Leeds, on discovering that it had a surplus in 1860, declared a "dividend" with each participant to receive £30.[83] Such decisions and deliberations were common in both British and American schools at midcentury.

Sometimes, especially in London, the combination of teaching and consultation could be very lucrative. The account books of James Paget, which were very carefully kept, show that he received £100 a year for being an attending surgeon at St. Bartholomew's, another £20 for teaching at the Royal College of Surgeons, £50 and the use of a house for being warden, £100 for serving as an examiner, 7 guineas for each private student, and £30 or more from consulting practice. By his own reckoning, his income averaged £425 a year—a very large sum—for more than half a century.[84]

The status of the medical teacher at midcentury reflected the growing differences between the continental and Anglo-American systems of medical education. Although the continental teacher, usually a well-paid civil servant with additional opportunities for earning income, saw himself as a full-time professional whose duties included teaching, research, and consultation, the British or American teacher, by contrast, was more likely to regard his practice as his major concern and to have little time or interest for research or teaching students outside the classroom.

Differences were growing, too, in the content and method of what was taught. The earlier consensus on the centrality of the clinic in teaching augmented by training in "auxiliary" sciences useful at the bedside was clearly giving way in German Europe to a new view that medicine was at bottom an experimental science best learned in the laboratory. So far, the conflict between clinic and laboratory, between medicine as practical science and medicine as natural science, was muted even in Germany. The

82. Graham N. Fitch to John McLean, January 29, 1849, Society of Medical History of Chicago manuscripts, John Crerar Collection, University of Chicago.

83. Minutes, Royal Infirmary School of Medicine, February 24, 1849, University of Liverpool Archive; Minutes of Medical Council, May 31, 1847, London Hospital Medical School Archive; Minutes of Council, Leeds School of Medicine, July 30, 1860, Leeds University Archive.

84. James Paget, autobiographical notes, Western Manuscript Collection, Wellcome Institute for the History of Medicine Library, London.

transformation just ahead in medical teaching came as a surprise to many in the medical world and created new controversies reminiscent of the shift to clinical teaching a half-century before. The German type of university education in medicine, so long subservient in the medical imagination to the French hospital model, created a new mystique of an all-conquering, irresistible science that would enable physicians to tear down the last barriers to understanding and treating disease.

But before examining the introduction and spread of laboratory teaching in greater detail, we turn once more to the lives and experiences of students of medicine, this time at midcentury.

8

Between Clinic and Laboratory: Students and Teaching at Midcentury

Despite the gathering momentum for a single standard of medical education, the portals of access to medicine remained remarkably open at the middle of the nineteenth century. From this time forward, governments and professional associations—in the name of science and clinical knowledge and the protection of the public's health—steadily limited further entrance to medicine to those with extensive preparatory education and the capacity to bear the financial and other burdens of ever longer periods of study.

But in 1850, alternative (and cheaper) paths to medicine, such as training in a practical school or learning medicine with a preceptor, were still available in the transatlantic nations. Not only were the *écoles secondaires* (or *écoles préparatoires*) and the medical–surgical academies still widely open to those on the European continent without a university-preparatory education, but British and American training schools for general practitioners, offering schooling well below the university level, were also widely available to students and growing at a rapid pace. "The establishment of provincial medical schools," for those of modest means, declared Joseph Jordan of Manchester in 1854, was an event "of national importance. . . . Indeed there has not been so great a movement [in Britain] since the College of Surgeons was established."[1] A decade before, probably unknown to Jordan, a New York professor, Martyn Paine, had voiced

---

1. Speech at distribution of prizes at the School of Medicine, Chatham St., March 1854, in Manchester Collection, F3a, Rylands Library, University of Manchester.

similar views about America's rural colleges when he told students that
"no institutions [are] more important than the *country* medical schools,
since these are adapted to the means of a large class of students . . . [of]
humble attainments."[2] In both Britain and America, according to Paine's
New York contemporary John Revere, the bulk of practitioners "are generally taken from the humbler conditions in society, and have few opportunities of intellectual improvement."[3]

Social Distinctions in Preparation for Medicine

The social differences between those who followed the university and the
practical routes to medicine were nearly as sharp as they had been a half-
century before. Even when a medical degree was awarded after what was
essentially a nonuniversity education, as it was in the United States, Paine
distinguished between graduates of country schools, "where lectures and
board are low," and "the aristocrats of our profession, made so through
the difference of a few dollars."[4] The latter group, like the university-educated physicians of Europe, had enjoyed a more thorough preliminary education, sometimes acquired at a liberal arts college, and were graduates
of well-established medical schools in the eastern cities. "For the ambitious and/or wealthy," writes a student of Philadelphia medicine at midcentury, "the educational resources of the city were considerable." As late
as 1860, over half of all those entering the Philadelphia profession were
"from the upper stratum," although this represented a decline from fifty
years earlier. In the leading hospitals of the city, moreover, physicians
were drawn as in London from prominent families headed by physicians,
clergymen, and members of the professional and commercial classes generally.[5]

At the other end of the spectrum, only one in fifty students attending
the rural medical college in Burlington, Vermont, had a college degree
on beginning medical study, and the dean boasted that the school had
"no scholastic barriers to attendance." A later official remarked in regard
to the preparation of the school's medical students that "a large number . . . are quite illiterate."[6] For the nation as a whole, a study of the social origins of prominent physicians of the 1850s reveals that a high pro-

2. Martyn Paine, "Medical Education in the United States," *Boston Medical and Surgical Journal* 29 (1843): 333. Emphasis in original.

3. John Revere, *An Introductory Lecture on the Comparative State of the Profession of
Medicine, and of Medical Education, in the United States and Europe* (New York: University
of the City of New York, 1846–47), 7.

4. Paine, "Medical Education," 332–33.

5. Leo J. O'Hara, "An Emerging Profession: Philadelphia Medicine, 1860–1900"
(Ph.D. diss., University of Pennsylvania, 1976), 41, 49, 321, table 7.

6. Martin Kaufman, "How Prospective Doctors Spent Their Days: Medical Student Life
at the University of Vermont, 1854–1900," *Vermont History* 43 (1975): 274–75.

portion of them came from professional, business, or landed families. Nearly two of five of this favored group had earned a bachelor's degree at a liberal arts college.[7] It was from this group, too, that the several hundred Americans who studied in Paris were largely drawn.

Those without a liberal or classical education were sensitive to the charge that they were less competent as physicians. "I hold it to be a fact that almost any young man may become, at least, a respectable physician," declared a Rush Medical College graduate in 1849, "even though he never were to see a College." He cited his own experience of studying medicine "without either education, knowledge of the world, a faithful preceptor, good books . . . without money or influential friends"—yet "in less than two years I had a more complete training than half of the physicians with whom I was acquainted."[8]

A liberal education, then, was still a principal mark of rank of physicians in the English-speaking nations, in which no sharp line was otherwise drawn between those whose qualifications for practice had been acquired in a university or in a practical school. Leading physicians in Britain and America continued to insist on the importance of a classical education, good manners, and the ability to relate to the privileged classes for those who sought eminence in their work. Increasingly, too, they argued for a broad education in the natural sciences, in addition to liberal studies, as a means of understanding better the processes of health and disease. In the United States, the chairman of the education committee of the new American Medical Association told his colleagues in 1853 that "polished language, delicate manners, and fastidious taste" were indispensable to the aspiring doctor. These could best be acquired, he said, by studying the classics in a good academy or college, and he urged his colleagues to "enlarge the rules on this subject, so as to include the Humanities of the schools, and the natural sciences in medical requirements."[9] Such study, it was frequently asserted, would make the student not only a better physician but a better citizen as well.

Across the Atlantic, the "silvery orator" Thomas Addison—as one of his students described him in 1849—told his class that "the best course of medical studies" must always include "the great utility of a classical education in Latin and Greek to pore over the writings of the ancient authors and reap an enviable advantage" over those to whom such riches were forever closed.[10] Even more than in America, the mark of a liberal education stamped a man as a leader and a member of a higher social

7. Robert P. Hudson, "Patterns of Medical Education in Nineteenth Century America" (master's thesis, Johns Hopkins University, 1966), 183, table 37.

8. William Mathews to John McLean, March 1, 1849, Society of the History of Medicine of Chicago Collection, Joseph Regenstein Library, University of Chicago.

9. Zina Pitcher, "Report of the Committee on Medical Education," *Transactions of the American Medical Association* 6 (1853): 93–95.

10. Notebook of George Newport Pickstock, October 1, 1849, Wills Medical Library, Guy's Hospital, London.

class. "Send the boy to Oxford, and let him pay there no attention to his future profession, but do as he would if he were going into Parliament," Benjamin Brodie advised the father of young Henry Acland; "when he has taken his degree, send him to me and I will tell him what next."[11] The most respected class of medical men in both Britain and America, wrote the American Revere, were those "connected with respectable families, and possessed of some private fortune, whose early education has been good."[12]

On the European continent, an even sharper line divided practitioners of the second class from university-educated physicians. By 1850, a strong campaign to eliminate the second-class *officiers* and *Wundärzte*, as described in the last chapter, was under way in France and Germany. A "crisis of identity," it was said, was afflicting medical practitioners on the Continent.[13] After making a survey of French secondary schools in the late 1830s, the dean of the medical faculty of Paris spoke for many university physicians when he declared that "it was not necessary to have but one class of physicians."[14] Students in the provincial schools continued to be looked down on for their lack of literary skill, poor scientific preparation, bad manners, and lower-class speech. For the most part, they were still drawn from the countryside and small villages, the sons of poor farmers, artisans, or shopkeepers. As late as 1849, they made up nearly 40 percent of all those enrolled in medical school in France, although many were now planning to continue their studies at one or another of the degree-granting schools.[15] At the medical center in Strasbourg, where both medical and secondary school students were enrolled together, a faculty report of 1858 noted "with satisfaction" that the number of *officiers* was rapidly declining.[16]

Those being trained in universities in France and Germany, on the other hand, were treated by governments and public alike as a leadership elite. Like their counterparts in Britain, their family backgrounds were chiefly upper middle class, although a large number were now coming from the middle and even lower levels of society. At the University of Halle, for example, although 51 percent of those studying medicine in 1852 were the children of high government officials, professors, clergymen, physicians, and army officers, at least a quarter were the sons of

11. James B. Atlay, *Sir Henry Wentworth Acland* (London: Smith, Elder, 1903), 76.

12. Revere, *Introductory Lecture*, 8.

13. Jacques Léonard, *La médecine entre les savoirs et les pouvoirs* (Paris: Aubier Montaigne, 1981), 84.

14. Christian Roche, "L'enseignement médical à Lyon de 1821 à 1877" (med. diss., University of Lyon, 1975), 13.

15. Jacques Léonard, *La vie quotidienne du médecin du province au XIXe siècle* (Paris: Hachette, 1977), 32.

16. Report on Work of Faculty at Strasbourg, 1858–59, manuscript, Archives nationales F^{17} 4453.

lower officials, farmers (*bauern*), or artisans.[17] At Göttingen, in the same year, a like proportion of medical students came from the families of farmers, teachers, and officials "without an academic education."[18] A somewhat higher number of students from the ranks of lesser officials and "handworkers" (tanners, clockmakers, rope makers, cartwrights) was reported at the medical school at Tübingen.[19] Across the Rhine, the range of family backgrounds of medical students was similar. About 25 percent of French medical students in 1865 gave their fathers' occupations as government employees, artisans, shopkeepers, or agricultural workers.[20]

The use of Latin in medical instruction, always a badge of liberal learning, persisted much longer in the continental universities than anywhere except Oxford and Cambridge in the English-speaking world. A number of lectures were still being delivered in Latin in the 1840s, and some catalogs were printed in that language for another quarter-century.[21] In Berlin, the popular Johannes Schönlein was forced to negotiate with university authorities in 1840 to allow him to lecture in German.[22] Dissertations could be written in either Latin or German at Göttingen in 1856, but Latin was still the "recommended" language.[23] Even as late as 1860, oral examinations of candidates for degrees in medicine at Heidelberg could be held in either language,[24] and in France, examinations in Latin were not formally discontinued until 1862.[25]

Women and Medical Education Circa 1850

Beyond the barriers of social class and inadequate schooling, many were excluded altogether from medical education by reason of religion, sex, or color. In England, nonconforming Protestants and Roman Catholics had

17. Fritz K. Ringer, *Education and Society in Modern Europe* (Bloomington: Indiana University Press, 1979), 301, table VI.

18. Claudia Huerkamp, *Der Aufstieg der Ärzte im 19.Jahrhundert: Vom gelehrten Stand zum professionellen Experten: Das Beispiel Preussens* (Göttingen: Vandenhoeck & Ruprecht, 1985), 68, table 4.

19. Dieter Grossman, "Die medizinischen Promotionen in Tübingen, 1850–1869" (med. diss., University of Tübingen, 1976), 69.

20. George Weisz, *The Emergence of Modern Universities in France, 1863–1914* (Princeton, NJ: Princeton University Press, 1983), 24, table 1.2.

21. See official medical course notices of 1867, for example, in GSPK, Merseburg, 76 Va Sekt. 2, Tit. VII, Nr. 1.

22. I owe this information about Schönlein to Prof. Johanna Bleker of Berlin. Letter to me, April 18, 1994.

23. "Bekanntmachung betreffend einige Änderungen in der Vornahme der medizinischen Facultätsprüfungen," 1856, Kuratorial Registratur, University of Göttingen Archive, med. 6.

24. Akten der medizinischen Fakultät, 1860, University of Heidelberg Archive, III, 4a, 103, p. 16.

25. Charles Coury, "Medical Education in France from the Beginning of the 17th Century to Our Day," 23, unpublished manuscript, Institut für die Geschichte der Medizin, University of Vienna.

long been prevented from attending the leading universities. A number of nations, including Russia and the German states, discriminated sharply against Jews. In Prussia, for example, throughout the nineteenth century, intense discussions were held on the potential "threat" of large numbers of Jewish students and teachers in medicine and other fields of study.[26] A Prussian edict of 1822, which barred Jews from teaching positions, was gradually relaxed and was finally rescinded in 1847, although sporadic opposition to Jewish students and faculty members at Vienna and other leading universities continued.

In the United States, African Americans, even those freed from slavery, were seldom able to obtain even a modicum of formal training. Among the slave population, most turned to fellow bondsmen in times of sickness, some of whom gained a reputation for special skills and knowledge of folk remedies. Sometimes a black healer was given responsibility by a plantation owner for the medical care of other slaves, and some even treated whites. Black women often assisted both slave and white women in childbirth.[27] Among the free black population a small number succeeded in learning medicine through self-study or by means of an apprenticeship to an abolitionist or Quaker physician. Not more than fifteen or twenty free blacks were admitted to American medical schools in the years before 1850, and a tiny number, probably not more than half a dozen, managed to study in Paris, Glasgow, or some other European center.[28] A poignant letter of 1852 in the files of the Liverpool medical faculty asks for free tuition for a young African American on the ground that "he was prevented from being educated at the colleges in America on account of his colour" and explains that it was for this reason that the family had immigrated to Britain "to secure . . . those opportunities for a livelihood, and a respectable position in society to which as human beings they are entitled."[29]

If those of lesser means, as well as members of some religious and racial groups, were more likely to be barred from the ranks of university physicians, it was the lot of women of whatever means or educational attain-

26. See files on "Die Vorkehrungen gegen den grossen Andrang junger Leute zu dem Universitäts-Studium, respektive zum Staatsdienste, sowie gegen das Überwiegen des Judentums," GSPK, Merseburg, 76, Ia, Sekt. 1, Tit. I, Nr. 7; and "Zulassung von Juden zu akademischen Lehrämtern," Akten der medizinischen Fakultät zu Berlin, University Archive, Humboldt University, 1411, D 14.

27. Todd L. Savitt, *Medicine and Slavery: The Diseases and Health Care of Blacks in Antebellum Virginia* (Urbana: University of Illinois Press, 1978), 171–84.

28. Harold E. Farmer, "An Account of the Earliest Colored Gentlemen in Medical Science in the United States," *Bulletin of the History of Medicine* 8 (1940): 604–12; M. O. Bousfield, "An Account of Physicians of Color in the United States," *Bulletin of the History of Medicine* 17 (1945): 64–66. See also Herbert M. Morais, *The History of the Negro in Medicine* (New York: Association for the Study of Negro Life and History, 1967).

29. William P. Powell to medical faculty, May 5, 1852, Royal Infirmary School of Medicine Records, University of Liverpool Archive. The faculty granted the request (by a three-to-two vote) at its meeting of May 29, 1852.

ments to be denied a career in medicine. In all the world in 1850, no regularly established medical school anywhere consistently opened its doors
to women.[30] Other than the schools for midwives on the European continent, some of which provided as much as two years of classroom and
practical instruction, no formal educational program in the health field
was open to them. As noted earlier, an occasional woman in Britain or
America was able to take over her husband's practice on his death, but
this custom was becoming more rare. A very few women, such as Margaret Cannon Osborn of Michigan, learned medicine from a preceptor,
in her case a physician-teacher in a ladies' seminary, but records of such
occurrences are scarce.[31] The country medical school in Geneva, New
York, which gained international fame for allowing Elizabeth Blackwell
to enter in 1847, slammed its doors shut once she had graduated. A
woman who had long been practicing medicine in Boston without formal
medical training was refused entrance at Harvard in 1850 because, she
was told, "the faculty feared the students would leave . . . and go to
Yale."[32]

The midcentury reaction to the idea of women doctors, in short, was
one of shock and disbelief. The presence of a woman in a hospital, a
clinic, or, even worse, a lecture on male anatomy or women's diseases vi-
olated every precept of the prevailing social code for the conduct of females. "Woman was obviously designed to move in another sphere, to
discharge other duties," declared the editor of America's leading medical
journal in 1849, in denouncing Elizabeth Blackwell's graduation as a
"farce." "It is much to be regretted," he wrote, "that she has been . . .
led to aspire to honors and duties which by the order of nature and the
common consent of the world devolve upon men."[33]

Despite the economic revolution in Europe and America that was
transforming the traditional relationship of women to the family and the
world of work, the early attempts by women to obtain medical training
were more roundly condemned than was their pursuit of any other career. Did women possess the intellectual capacity to master a learned profession? Were they physically strong enough to carry on a strenuous practice? Were pregnancy and menstruation not insuperable barriers to a
profession in which constant attention to duty was an indispensable requirement? Would not the study of anatomy and the dissection of the
human body destroy the special sensibilities of women? Would their presence in mixed classes inhibit the medical teacher from freely discussing

30. This section on women is a much abbreviated version of my *To the Ends of the Earth:
Women's Search for Education in Medicine* (Cambridge, MA: Harvard University Press,
1992), 6–27.
31. For Osborn, see Frances A. Rutherford, "Women Physicians of Michigan," *Michigan State Medical Society Journal* 9 (1913): 483–84.
32. Harriot K. Hunt, *Glimpses and Glances; or Fifty Years Social, including Twenty Years
Professional Life* (Boston: John P. Jewett, 1856), 265–69.
33. *Boston Medical and Surgical Journal* 40 (1849): 1.

sensitive subjects and keep students from raising questions that might be embarrassing to women? For the next three-quarters of a century and more, these all-too-familiar questions were raised over and over again in debates that raged from Moscow to Edinburgh and from Boston to San Francisco.

Medicine, after all, had long acquired the reputation of being the coarsest and most degrading of academic studies. The extreme youth of many of the students, together with the harsh circumstances of their lives, their involvement in grave robbing, and their frequent irreverence toward the human body, had produced a rowdy, boisterous behavior that was decried by authorities and the public alike. Coarse expressions and sexual innuendo were as common in the lecture hall as they were in the dissection room. Indeed, professors used ribald mnemonic verses to tutor their charges in anatomical parts.

To imagine a woman of the early Victorian age thrust into this brutalizing environment is to understand the fear and loathing that ran through the families of young women contemplating the study of medicine. "If you were a young man," the father of the pioneer woman physician in Boston, Marie Zakrzewska, wrote her from Berlin, "I could not find words in which to express my satisfaction and pride . . . but you are a woman, a weak woman; and all that I can do for you now is to grieve and to weep. O my daughter! return from this unhappy path."[34] When told that his daughter wanted to become a doctor, the New York publisher George P. Putnam responded that he thought medicine "a repulsive pursuit" for a woman.[35] In Britain, the industrialist father of the young Elizabeth Garrett, confronted with the same question, burst out that "the whole idea is so disgusting. I could not entertain it for a moment."[36] Almost no woman in these years, whether in Europe or America, was encouraged to take up so shameless and dehumanizing a profession.

And yet despite the crushing opposition of families, the public, and the medical profession, a surprising number of women in the United States were able to study medicine by the end of the 1850s. Elizabeth Blackwell estimated in 1859 that three hundred women had managed, in her words, "to graduate somewhere in medicine."[37] Who were these early women doctors, and how were they able to prepare themselves for practice? What had driven them to so unpromising a career? The large majority of those for whom records are available, both in America and later in Europe, were daughters of the prosperous middle class. They were keenly sensitive to the economic changes taking place around them and the chal-

34. Agnes C. Vietor, ed., *A Woman's Quest: The Life of Marie E. Zakrzewska, M.D.* (New York: D. Appleton, 1924), 140.

35. Ruth Putnam, ed., *Life and Letters of Mary Putnam Jacobi* (New York: Putnam, 1925), 121.

36. Jo Manton, *Elizabeth Garrett Anderson* (New York: Dutton, 1965), 73.

37. Cited in Mary Putnam Jacobi, "Women in Medicine," in *What America Owes to Women*, ed. Lydia Hoyt Farmer (Buffalo: National Exposition Souvenir, 1893), 384.

lenges and opportunities they represented. Many were deeply religious and active in reform movements to abolish slavery, intemperance, and other evils that surrounded them. Almost all were conscious of the growing movement to extend women's rights, and some were involved for much of their lives in the women's movement. Some had attended the convention of women activists at Seneca Falls, New York, in 1848, where a declaration of independence for women was approved.

For many, the opening of medical training was a dramatic test case of their crusade to create new opportunities for women. Nearly all were interested in problems of women's health and hygiene and believed that women doctors could help lift the curtain of ignorance and superstition that surrounded the physiology of women. "I would like to be employed at something that will benefit the part of the human family that has been oppressed and suffered wrongfully," wrote a thirty-year-old woman medical student in Cincinnati in 1854, "to wit women."[38]

Even so, how was it possible for these women to find a place to study medicine? The explanation lies in the American political climate at mid-century and in two institutions that were largely, and at times wholly, American: the sectarian school of medicine and the women's medical college. Any group of citizens with sufficient reason and political support could hope to gain a charter in the laissez-faire, enterprising environment of nineteenth-century America. The same laxness of governmental policy that was so often criticized by reformers for holding back efforts to raise educational standards also made it possible to carry on such social experiments as educating women (and later African Americans) in separate schools.

The sectarian school of medicine, teaching such doctrines as homeopathy, eclectic medicine, hydropathy, and natural remedies, along with providing training in the practical sciences, was fully entitled by its charter to grant medical degrees. Although despised by much of the profession, such schools, though fewer in number than the regular schools and vulnerable to the cutthroat competition among them all, were often associated with popular health reforms of interest to women and tended from the first to be more open to them than their rivals were. The separate colleges for women doctors, on the other hand, gave women a legal means of gaining access to a regular education, a possibility not yet open to any woman in Europe. American women, as well as men, could thus practice medicine with training that, when joined to clinical experience or an apprenticeship to a teacher or woman graduate, approached that of the practical schools of Britain and the Continent.

Four medical colleges for women were founded in major American cities between 1850 and 1870. They found important support among influential men in their argument that the modesty of women required that

---

38. Mary Wright Pierson to correspondent, December 11, 1854, "Physicians, U.S." box, folder 35, Sophia Smith Collection, Smith College, Northampton, MA.

a woman attend them in childbirth and in sickness. "There is no country in the world," wrote Samuel Gregory, the controversial founder of a women's school in Boston, "where females are so dependent upon the opposite sex for assistance on [medical] occasions."[39] He urged the revival of midwifery in America and deplored the practice of obstetrics by male physicians. His school, established in 1848, was confined at first to teaching hygiene, physiology, midwifery, and the diseases of women. A full medical course was not attempted until 1852, and the first medical degrees were not given to women for another two years.

Meanwhile, in Philadelphia, a complete medical course for women was offered in 1850. A far stronger venture than Gregory's school, the Woman's Medical College of Pennsylvania was supported by Quaker benevolence and the strong women's movement in the city. Some of the school's early faculty members, particularly Quakers, had already taken women students as apprentices. "Our object," said the trustees in a public statement, "is not merely to qualify females as Practitioners of Medicine, but to teach 'woman to know herself,' to understand her organism, and . . . to throw open to them those Avenues of Science, from which they have been so long excluded."[40] The remaining schools for women in this period were started in New York (1865) and Chicago (1870).

Although the pioneer women doctors in America continued to plead for women's acceptance into the established colleges, they meanwhile sought to strengthen the women's schools and urged their students, when possible, to go abroad. By the 1860s, a few European clinics and hospitals were allowing graduate women doctors from America to spend brief periods in advanced study while continuing to bar women of their own countries from a medical education. The forced segregation of women into separate schools and hospitals at home—if they were to get any training at all—left a residue of bitter pride in several generations of American medical women. Unable to study in the stronger medical colleges or to gain clinical experience in the larger hospitals, many women exaggerated the benefits of separate institutions and drew closer together for protection against a hostile world. For the early interns at the New England Hospital for Women and children, writes Virginia Drachman, separatism "shaped almost every aspect of their professional lives" even after they had completed their training.[41]

Twenty years after Blackwell's entrance into the Geneva Medical College, it seemed that the United States, thanks to the freedom of its institutions, had moved far to the forefront in the medical education of

39. Samuel Gregory, *Letter to Ladies, in Favor of Female Physicians for their own Sex* (Boston: Female Medical Education Society, 1850), 37.

40. Gulielma F. Alsop, *History of the Woman's Medical College, Philadelphia, Pennsylvania* (Philadelphia: Lippincott, 1950), 19.

41. Virginia G. Drachman, *Hospital with a Heart: Women Doctors and the Paradox of Separatism at the New England Hospital, 1862–1969* (Ithaca, NY: Cornell University Press, 1984), 66–67.

women. As yet no European university or practical school had graduated a single woman in medicine. The sectarian and women's colleges in America, on the other hand, had produced several hundred women doctors. The very success of the growing number of women graduates kept constant the pressure on the medical profession. Women now competed with male physicians for patients; they committed few of the predicted medical blunders; they won friends who were prominent in public life; they fought for admission to medical societies; they petitioned constantly for hospital privileges; and they continually demanded of educational leaders and male faculty members why they would not allow women to matriculate in their schools. The combined effect of all these efforts was to open a sizable breach in the wall of opposition to women.

In Europe, however, medical teachers and physicians continued their exclusion of women and deplored the standards in America that made it possible to create sectarian and women's schools. "Most of these women doctors in America," wrote Professor Wilhelm von Zehender of Rostock in 1875, after corresponding with physicians in America and Europe, "do not stand in very high regard." The government in America, he said, took "no responsibility for the education and licensing of its physicians," which explained "the large number of miserable medical schools and so-called colleges" that gave diplomas to both sexes after a short period of lectures. A few schools, such as Harvard, did try for a higher standard, he added, "but at this university women are absolutely prohibited."[42]

The Lives of Medical Students

Student life in the women's colleges was understandably more disciplined and less boisterous than it was in the rowdy environs of the normal medical school. At the school in Geneva, for example, Elizabeth Blackwell's effect on the male students, even according to the journal that criticized her admission so harshly, "has been good, and great decorum is preserved when she is present."[43] Similar reactions were reported later from Zurich, Paris, and other schools pioneering in women's education. Not only were women generally more mature and better controlled; they were almost universally believed to need protection against the hazards of single life and the crude atmosphere of the dissecting room and the hospital amphitheater. Many shared living quarters in boarding houses close to the college under the watchful eye of members of the faculty. Sometimes a family member was dispatched to care for the student during her months of training. Women students were rarely admitted to the clinics

---

42. Wilhelm von Zehender, *Uber den Beruf der Frauen zum Studium und zur praktischen Ausbildung der Heilwissenschaft* (Rostock: Stiller'sche Hof-und Universitätsbuchhandlung, 1875), 18–19.

43. *Boston Medical and Surgical Journal* 37 (1847): 405.

and hospitals of the cities attended by men but were instead dependent on occasional visits to private sickrooms at the discretion of their preceptor-teachers.

Some well-connected women, such as Elizabeth Blackwell and her sister Emily, were able to get a modest amount of clinical experience by going abroad. Students attended the school in Philadelphia—where a women's hospital was not added until 1862—for twelve years, according to Mary Putnam Jacobi, a graduate, "with almost no chance to see sick people"—a situation, she said, that "would have been considered outrageous in any country but the United States."[44] When women students did encounter men, as in public ceremonies or later in clinics, they were often jeered or mocked. Five hundred male students and their friends crowded into an auditorium in Philadelphia when the first women were graduated, forcing the mayor of the city to summon fifty policemen to cordon off the hall and maintain the peace.[45]

By 1850 the lives of all students were changing. Compared with a half-century before, the average student in Europe and America was older, had studied more science and less Latin, had faced rising costs of tuition and board, had spent a longer period in study, and had undergone stricter examinations but was still regarded by many contemporaries as a marginal social being. Women students, often older than their male counterparts, were more likely to be married and to have had previous job experience, especially in teaching school, before beginning to study medicine. A surprising number of both men and women students were middle aged when they began their formal study. A member of the McGill class of 1850 recalled "a large proportion of the students . . . verging on, or who had passed, middle age. Indeed several of them were married men and the heads of families."[46]

Almost all medical schools now required a student to be at least twenty-one years of age before receiving a degree. The average age at graduation of the selected group of American physicians studied by Robert Hudson was twenty-four at midcentury.[47] At the newly opened medical school of the University of Michigan, which set higher admission standards than most, the entering class of 1850 ranged in age from eighteen to thirty-one, with most of them over twenty-three.[48] Fragmentary data on European universities in this era suggest a similar maturing of the medical student body. At Tübingen, for example, the average age of a

44. Mary Putnam Jacobi, "Woman in Medicine," in *Woman's Work in America*, ed. Annie Nathan Meyer (New York: Holt, 1891), 162.

45. *Olive Branch*, January 17, 1852, in New England Female Medical College Scrapbook, Countway Library, Harvard Medical School.

46. John J. Heagerty, *Four Centuries of Medical History in Canada*, 2 vols. (Toronto: Macmillan, 1928), 2:67.

47. Hudson, "Patterns of Medical Education," 50, table 4.

48. Student Register, 1850–71, Michigan University Medical School Records, Box 135, Bentley Historical Library, University of Michigan.

medical graduate in the 1850s and 1860s was now twenty-four, and one in ten was older than thirty-five.[49]

Although older than earlier students, the medical student of the middle decades of the century still suffered from the reputation of being immature, unruly, quarrelsome, and ungovernable. "Steeplechasing in the dissecting room, cheating on the Latin examination, flirting with the barmaid, gin-and-water until three o'clock in the morning," reads one account, were still "the stereotypical activities of the British student of medicine."[50]

A chain of incidents in London and elsewhere seemed to confirm the popular image of medical students as violent and disorderly. When Guy's Hospital students were excluded from an operating theater at St. Thomas's Hospital in 1836, for example, they assaulted the doorkeeper "violently" and nearly threw him over a high balustrade before smashing down a heavy oaken door to enter the auditorium.[51] A typical incident at Edinburgh in 1845 involved the throwing of snowballs in chemistry class, which led to the suspension ("rustication") of four students.[52] An unspecified series of "extreme measures" was threatened against gambling and drinking by students at Manchester in 1855.[53] At the University of London, the records of the medical faculty in the 1850s are full of accounts of "ill-timed frolics" in the hospital, dragging large bathtubs through the wards, fighting with boxing gloves in the laboratory, "disfiguring the walls" of lecture rooms, engaging in "riotous conduct" and mass drunkenness, and using "most unbecoming language."[54]

In the medical schools of North America, the public image of the student of medicine was scarcely better. Frederick Waite explained the rowdy reputation of students in Cleveland at midcentury as resulting, at least in part, from popular attitudes toward dissection. "The public considered every medical student," he wrote, "as a potential body-snatcher, and put them in a social class that was taboo," which then caused the students "to try to live up to this reputation."[55] Whether accurate or not, the characterization of medical students as drunken, immature, and irreverent persisted well into the second half of the nineteenth century. A par-

49. Grossman, "Medizinische Promotionen in Tübingen," 71–72.

50. M. Jeanne Peterson, *The Medical Profession in Mid-Victorian London* (Berkeley and Los Angeles: University of California Press, 1978), 40.

51. *London Times*, December 22, 1836, clipping in folder "Students, Lecturers, Curricula," St. Thomas Medical School, Greater London Record Office, HI/ST/K/o/27.

52. Minutes of Senatus, March 13, 1845, University of Edinburgh Archive.

53. Minutes of meetings of Lecturers, February 28, 1855, Manchester Royal School of Medicine and Surgery, Manchester Collection, F4fxviii (copy), Rylands Library, University of Manchester.

54. Minutes of Medical Faculty, 1853–57, College Record Office, University College London.

55. Frederick C. Waite, "A Century and a Quarter of Medical Education in Cleveland," unpublished manuscript, 1938, Cleveland Health Historical Sciences Library.

ticularly harsh attack on them appeared in a Philadelphia newspaper of 1856, describing local students, probably southerners, as "the roughest we ever saw . . . hair as long as that of a savage . . . sword canes, dirk knives, revolvers, attire very unfashionably made, hard swearing, hard drinking, coarse language, tobacco quids, and pools of tobacco spittle . . . medical students are a contemned, despised, disrespected class."[56] Although such descriptions can scarcely have applied to the majority of American and British students, their constant repetition made them very hard to overcome.

In Europe, by contrast, the concern about student behavior was much more likely to lie in their activist politics. In the conservative and often repressive atmosphere of the post-Napoleonic years, continental students were often viewed suspiciously for their association with liberal or radical causes. In both France and Germany, medical students were thought to be particularly zealous and aggressive in seeking an outlet for their beliefs. It was the "turbulent and seditious" medical students of Paris, explained an English observer, who had brought about the closing of the medical school and the purging of its faculty in the 1820s.[57] Student disturbances in Paris and Montpellier and at the provincial medical schools were reported regularly throughout the 1830s and 1840s, especially during and after the uprisings of 1830 and 1848.[58]

Similar unrest was reported in the German states. A number of medical students were under suspicion, and some were arrested during the widespread disorders following the murder of the conservative writer August von Kotzenbue in 1819; a half-dozen professors and students at the University of Bonn were investigated during the 1820s because of their political associations; eleven medical students were arrested in Munich in 1833 for their "ultraliberalism"; and Berlin authorities kept a careful watch on the political participation of all students, a disproportionate number of whom were studying medicine, throughout the 1840s and 1850s.[59]

A number of professors and students sought refuge from German repression in the new liberal university in Zurich (1833), where such political dissidents as Schönlein, Henle, Carl Ludwig, and Karl Ewald Hasse

56. *Philadelphia City Item*, n.d., quoted in *Medical and Surgical Reporter* 1 (1856): 139–40.

57. Royal Commission, *Evidence, Oral and Documentary, taken and received by the Commissioners appointed by His Majesty George IV, July 23d, 1826; and re-appointed by His Majesty William IV, October 12th, 1830, for visiting the Universities of Scotland,* 4 vols. (London: His Majesty's Stationery Office, 1837), 1:351.

58. Files on "Student Disorders," Archives nationales, F17 4451 and AJ16 6685.

59. See "Verhaftungen und Untersuchungen gegen den stud. med. Carl Franz Joseph Bader in Berlin," GSPK, 77, Tit. 21, Lit. B, Nr. 1, Merseburg; "Die Untersuchung gegen einige Professoren und andere Personnen der Universität Bonn wegen geheimen politischen Verbindungen," 2 vols., 1820–25, GSPK, 76 Va, Sekt. 3, Tit. IV, Nr. 5; "Universität, Aufsicht auf Studieriende," 1832–47, Bayerisches Hauptstaatsarchiv, MInn 45820, Munich; "Die Beteiligung von Professoren und Lehrern an politischen Umtreiben," 1849–65, GSPK, 76, I, Sekt. 24, Nr. 7.

found "a peaceful island in a stormy ocean."[60] After his imprisonment in 1851, the liberal democrat Abraham Jacobi followed a different route to the United States.[61]

The daily routine of life at schools of medicine, for all the roughhousing and political activism, was scarcely glamorous by any standard. For the vast majority of students, life was an endless and demanding round of crowded lectures, scrambling for places during the hurried tours by teachers through the wards, long and often painful hours in the anatomy room, late nights of bookish study, little social diversion, and moments of loneliness and introspection. "I was never so busy in my life," wrote the Michigan student James Lamb to his wife in 1853, "how I would like to be with you this evening, but . . . I must be satisfied with my books for companions. . . . You can scarcely form any idea of how much there is to learn. . . . I fear that [the time] will be gone before I have learned half enough."[62] Farther west, on completing his medical course, the Illinois student Samuel Willard wrote home that "I get woefully discouraged at times . . . the feeling of responsibility sometimes weighs me down awefully [*sic*] and I feel as if I wanted to run away if I could honorably."[63]

The daily routine at Louisville about 1850 was described by one student as consisting of six hours of lectures, two hours of dissection, and constant scurrying upstairs and downstairs to find favorable classroom seats, especially for clinical lectures. When the janitor unlocked the door, he wrote, "in we burst, leaping downwards over the backs of the seats . . . to the bottom, where the Professor stood . . . [at] a revolving table . . . on which lay the corpse he was demonstrating . . . or a dead body to operate on—or some times a living patient who underwent an operation before the class." In the dissecting room, each group consisted of six students "dressed with black cambric aprons . . . & a black cap generally—; the dead body lay on a narrow table . . . they sat around the body on tall stools—; some dissecting, & some reading aloud from the Anatomy."[64]

A Changing Curriculum

Although it varied greatly from school to school and from country to country, the program of study now almost certainly included lectures and perhaps demonstrations in the newer sciences; traditional classes in the

60. Elaine Schwöbel-Schrafl, *Was verdankt die medizinische Fakultät Zürich ihren ausländischen Dozenten? 1833 bis 1863* (Zurich: Juris Druck & Verlag, 1985), 47.

61. Abraham Jacobi, "Memoiren aus Preussischen Gefaengnissen," *Aufsätze, Vorträge und Reden*, 2 vols. (New York: Stettiner, Lambert, 1893), 1:1–46.

62. James Lamb to Sarah Lamb (transcript), January 15, 1853, James Lamb Papers, Bentley Historical Library, University of Michigan.

63. Quoted in John K. Crellin, "American Medical Education: For Teachers or Students?" in *History of Medical Education*, ed. Teizo Ogawa (Tokyo: Saikon, 1983), 6.

64. Manuscript autobiography of Charles H. Hentz, 103–4, copy in Kornhauser Library Historical Collections, University of Louisville.

institutes of medicine, surgery, medical practice, pharmacy, therapeutics, and obstetrics; and some provision for clinical or hospital instruction. The time spent in acquiring a medical degree in a university was now five years in the Hapsburg domains, four years in France, the German states, and the Scottish schools, whereas degrees in the United States were awarded after two courses of study and three years of preceptorship.

The principal differences from fifty years earlier were the longer periods of study, the increasing authority of the scientific subjects, and the rising proportion of a student's time spent in practical activity. Even in the United States, where clinical facilities were limited, the expectation, even though imperfectly realized, was that students would spend far more time with a preceptor or in a hospital than in the classroom. For those in large cities and who could afford them there were always the private schools. The head of one such school likened them to the French *écoles de perfectionment*. Medical education, he advised students in 1857, "should not commence within the walls of the College" or be confined to them.[65]

In Britain as well, reliance on private or "cramming" courses outside the medical school, or on a traditional apprenticeship, continued strong at midcentury. The apprentice's experience in the 1850s, according to a British source, was "not very different" from that of earlier generations, except that specific provision was now made to release him for two periods of study in a medical school during his five years of service.[66] A typical contract for a three-year term of private teaching in the United States around 1850 contained similar provisions for allowing the student "to attend the Lectures in any Medical Institution for four or eight months."[67]

If there were a universal complaint among students of medicine about their education, regardless of country, it was the desire to see even more practical training given within the walls or under the supervision of the school of medicine. The students themselves were often an important force in seeking to unite clinical experience with classroom theory. Even in the hospital schools of London, noted worldwide for their practical emphasis, students were frequently critical of the few opportunities for organized, hands-on experience at the bedside. When University College London opened without a hospital, for example, the students protested vehemently that a substitute arrangement with Middlesex Hospital was "utterly inadequate."[68] Faculty member Charles Bell, who opposed a separate hospital and hoped that all hospitals in the metropolis would be-

65. Edward Parrish, *Summer Medical Teaching in Philadelphia: An Introductory Lecture* (Philadelphia: Merrihew & Thompson, 1857), 3, 19.

66. J. S. Beveridge, "The Medical Apprenticeship," 1854, manuscript, University of Edinburgh Archive.

67. See the contract of Lyman W. Trask and Amaziah Moore in Frederick C. Waite, "A Contract for Private Medical Teaching in Northern Ohio in 1846," *Ohio State Medical Journal* 33 (1937): 545–47.

68. Resolution adopted by medical students of the University of London, October 30, 1829, college correspondence, file 3337B, University College London Archive.

come the "clinical schools" of the university, warned his colleagues of "the agitated state of the Medical Students."[69]

Accounts of students' protests and complaints about clinical teaching, or the lack thereof, appeared regularly in London journals throughout the 1830s and 1840s. "Irregular attendance [by teachers], broken engagements, imperfect lectures," reads a *Lancet* editorial of 1842 about student concerns in London, "and, in several of the hospitals, an entire absence of books containing records of the cases."[70] At the Westminster Hospital School, a group of students complained to the board of governors in 1845, "as a duty we owe to ourselves as Pupils," about the poor surgical teaching at the hospital and the surgeon's "total want of Surgical knowledge and ability."[71] Enterprising students at Guy's formed their own "Clinical Society" to record and discuss cases in a systematic way in order to "cultivate a spirit of inquiry." So great was its success that a hospital board member commented admiringly in 1839 that "Few Persons ever thought, the Pupils had sufficient perseverance to raise the Society to the state, in which it now exists, without the assistance of any Medical Authority." For the students at Guy's, who were now assigned by their colleagues to particular cases and duties, it meant, in the words of one student, an end to the "wandering from bed to bed thro' all the wards" and a means of "fixing upon [a] proper method by which he should enter upon, or direct, his labours."[72]

"Too much lecturing and not enough sickbed experience" ran the common refrain among students everywhere. In Glasgow, Scottish students, urging the "great advantages to be derived from instruction conveyed at the bedside," pleaded with the university senate in 1851 to establish permanent teaching positions in clinical medicine and surgery.[73] The faculty at Berlin complained in 1840 "that the students were against theoretical lectures and preferred to watch operations and to participate in clinical lectures."[74] Parisian students, it was widely reported, were discontented with the balance between lectures and practical teaching in their studies. "The French," claimed a German visitor in 1844, "realize the lack of [practical] education" in their system.[75] In the case of Ameri-

69. Charles Bell to Council, November 6, 1829, University College London Archive.

70. *Lancet* 1 (1842): 266.

71. Minutes, medical committee, November 15, 1845, Westminster Hospital, Greater London Record Office, H2/wh. The committee, of which the offending surgeon was a member, voted that the students were "not competent" to make such a judgment.

72. General Reports of the Clinical Society, October 12, 1839, Wills Medical Library, Guy's Hospital.

73. Senate Records, May 1, 1851, University of Glasgow Archive.

74. Hans H. Simmer, "Principles and Problems of Medical Undergraduate Education in Germany During the Nineteenth and Early Twentieth Centuries," in *The History of Medical Education*, ed. C. D. O'Malley (Berkeley and Los Angeles: University of California Press, 1970), 181.

75. Hugo Sonnenkalb, *Die medicinische Facultät zu Paris* (Leipzig, 1844), 38.

can schools, the concern of students was chronic and constant to find a means of learning practical medicine.

The clinical instruction offered in American hospitals at midcentury, principally in the eastern cities, was almost entirely in the form of lectures in large amphitheaters, where a patient was presented and discussed as part of a scheduled operation or medical procedure. Quite often, the clinical presentation was entirely uncoordinated with the teaching taking place in the classroom.[76] Smaller schools, such as the Willoughby Medical College in Ohio, made extravagant claims for their college clinics, where, it was announced at Willoughby, each student would be "personally instructed in percussion, auscultation, etc."[77]

No American teacher had as yet any firm control over the clinical or hospital environment in which he taught. The instruction given by a preceptor was likewise unrelated to the daily teaching in a medical school. It is small wonder that so many students under these conditions longed for some kind of systematic introduction to the practice of medicine. Like the physicians who wrote the 1848 report of the American Medical Association on medical teaching, students viewed as "defective and erroneous, every system of medical instruction which does not rest on the basis of practical demonstration and clinical teaching."[78]

Here and there, a few American schools did attempt for short periods to unite hospital instruction with classroom teaching. The New York Medical College, for example, founded in 1850, claimed to specialize in the "bedside teaching" of students, in addition to providing academic instruction. The German exile Abraham Jacobi, who taught there, credited the school with being the first in his adopted country to provide regular clinical teaching that was related to instruction in the classroom.[79]

In New Orleans, Erasmus Fenner, an admirer of Robert Graves, sought in 1856 to create a system of clinical teaching at the Charity Hospital that would be "very much like that pursued in Germany, where [students are] taught better than anywhere in the world." Seven of the professors at the New Orleans School of Medicine, he said, "have entire control of wards in the Hospital."[80] In the northern cities he had visited, he charged, ef-

76. Dale C. Smith, "The Emergence of Organized Clinical Instruction in the Nineteenth Century American Cities of Boston, New York and Philadelphia" (Ph.D. diss., University of Minnesota, 1979), 158.

77. *Announcement Concerning the Opening of the School and Courses of Lectures, Willoughby Medical College of Columbus, 1847*, reprinted in Ohio State University College of Medicine, *A Collection of Source Material Covering a Century of Medical Progress, 1834–1934* (Blanchester, OH: Brown, 1934), 78.

78. "Report of the Committee on Medical Education," *Transactions of the American Medical Association* 1 (1848): 246.

79. Abraham Jacobi, "The New York Medical College, 1782–1906," *Annals of Medical History* 1 (1918): 370–71.

80. Erasmus D. Fenner, "Introductory Lecture delivered at the Opening of the New Orleans School of Medicine," *New Orleans Medical News and Hospital Gazette* 3 (1856): 599.

forts to bring clinical training into the orbit of the medical school were extremely weak. Massachusetts General Hospital in Boston, for example, "although well endowed" presented "but a limited field for medical observation," whereas New York's Bellevue Hospital, he found, was "closed against lecturers and students" altogether.[81]

Finally, at the University of Michigan, a little-noticed effort was made in 1857 to establish systematic clinical training for students in nearby Detroit. Professors were to lead "deliberate walks through the wards" and to give "thorough instruction at the bed-side of the sick" for a period of twelve weeks. These practical experiences, furthermore, were to be tied to "systematic lectures to the whole clinical class on practical subjects . . . illustrated by the cases which have been seen."[82] The plan, said Professor Zina Pitcher, an important figure in national reform efforts, divided students who had completed their theoretical courses into small sections— "as in Austria and Prussia"—to let them "examine patients, keep case records, and discuss particular cases with their teacher at the bedside."[83] Later, Michigan built its own hospital under faculty control.

The growing emphasis on science and theory in the medical curriculum, especially in Germany, was often seen by students as a further threat to their practical training. Nearly every medical school was now offering courses in physiology, organic chemistry, pathological anatomy, and other new subjects, and in Germany, research institutes and laboratory courses for students were being inaugurated in a number of fields. Courses in using the microscope were available to students in every medical school in the German states by the middle of the century.[84] An analysis of the medical school catalogs of 1850 reveals a flood of new and specialized offerings, such as the physiology of metabolism and the "physiology of blood" at Heidelberg, "microscopical examination of tissues" and "experimental physiology" at Munich, and histology, comparative physiology, and experimental studies on the effects of drugs on animals at Berlin.[85]

---

81. Erasmus D. Fenner, "Letters from the North," *New Orleans Medical and Surgical Journal* 3 (1846): 198–202.

82. Alonzo B. Palmer, "Reform in the Medical Schools—Clinical Instruction at Detroit," *Peninsular Journal of Medicine, and the Collateral Sciences* 4 (1857): 603–4.

83. Zina Pitcher, "On Clinical Instruction," *Peninsular Journal of Medicine and the Collateral Sciences* 5 (1858): 393–400.

84. Konrad Kläss, "Die Einführung besonderer Kurse für Mikroskopie und physikalische Diagnostik (Perkussion und Auskultation) in dem medizinischen Unterricht an deutschen Universitäten im 19.Jahrhundert" (med. diss., University of Göttingen, 1971), 14, table.

85. *Anzeige der Vorlesungen, welche im Winterhalbjahr 1850–51 auf der Grossherzöglich Badischen Ruprecht-Carolinischen Universität zu Heidelberg gehalten werden sollen* (Heidelberg: C. F. Winter, 1850), 8; *Verzeichnis der Vorlesungen an der Königlichen Ludwig-Maximilians-Universität zu München im Sommer-Semester 1850* (Munich: Weiss, 1850), 10–12; *Verzeichnis der Vorlesungen, welche von der Friedrich-Wilhelms-Universität zu Berlin im Winterhalbjahre vom October 1850 bis zum 5. April 1851 gehalten werden* (Berlin, 1850), 3–6.

The physiological point of view in medicine was rapidly gaining ground in central Europe, even though it was generally resisted by medical educators in western Europe and America. Unless the period of study were further lengthened, it was often argued, students would be unable to spend enough time on the practical essentials of their craft. How necessary, or even useful, asked many students and their teachers, were the new scientific studies for the ordinary practice of medicine? Of what practical help were they when confronting a crisis at the bedside? James Syme of Edinburgh spoke for many in 1863 when he charged that the academic curriculum was already so crowded with the new sciences that students had "neither time nor freedom of mind . . . for due attention to any sort of practical study."[86] Regarding the study of physiology, a teacher at St. Bartholomew's Hospital complained that it helped no one "to become good practitioners . . . [and] the majority are hindered by it." Students, he said, had "hundreds and hundreds of lectures . . . inflicted upon them without mercy."[87] In the United States, too, in 1850, science was as yet seen to be "very much on the margins" of students' interests.[88]

The growing number of offerings open to or required of students created confusion regarding the best order of studies. Should students be required—or at least be guided more than in the past—to follow a particular sequence of courses in order to enhance the possibilities of learning? Should some subjects be required of all students and others made optional? Were there not some courses and experiences that were essential to their preparation in medicine? Was it necessary to extend further the length of terms or the whole period of study in order to accommodate all the courses that were needed? And how much control should teachers exert over the attendance of pupils in their classes? These questions were hotly debated in every country and sometimes in every faculty in the middle of the nineteenth century.

In France, as had been true since the Revolution, requirements for the medical degree, which in turn brought the right to practice, continued to be set by the state, and the sequence of courses to be taken, except for some electives, was more inflexible than in any other country. The German pattern of studies, on the other hand, was shaped by the differing requirements for a degree in medicine and for a license to practice. The state examinations for licensure made demands that were often quite different from the requirements for a medical degree. German students, who were free to follow their own preferences in selecting courses, dif-

86. James Syme, "Observations on Medical Education," *Edinburgh Medical Journal* 9 (1864): 583.

87. P. M. Latham, "A Word or Two on Medical Education: and a Hint or Two for Those who think it needs Reforming," *British Medical Journal* 1 (1864): 141–42.

88. John Harley Warner, "The Fall and Rise of Professional Mystery: Epistemology, Authority and the Emergence of Laboratory Medicine in Nineteenth-Century America," in *The Laboratory Revolution in Medicine*, ed. Andrew Cunningham and Perry Williams (Cambridge: Cambridge University Press, 1992), 129.

fered widely in their choices and the order in which they took them. In German practice, it was the student's responsibility to prepare himself at his own pace and in his own way for the *Staatsexamen* (state licensing examination). Some professors, however, insisting that the "academic freedom" of students should not apply to those studying medicine, contended that they often made poor choices and failed to take courses in a logical order. The stakes were too high in medicine, it was argued, to permit such liberty.

Many German faculties compromised by announcing a "suggested curriculum" that began with the fundamental sciences, proceeded to pathology and general medical and surgical lectures, and concluded with up to two years of clinical study.[89] But variations among universities were widespread, and students deviated frequently from the suggested order.

If students enjoyed so much freedom in their studies, how then could teachers control attendance in their classes? Almost no German or French professors resorted to frequently testing their students and taking attendance, as their British and American counterparts did. In the latter schools, rules for students were strict and examinations constant. At Edinburgh and Glasgow, for example, in order to combat absenteeism, the medical faculties voted to "ascertain, at least twenty times in a six months course . . . the actual attendance of pupils," and the University of London faculty required teachers to examine pupils "every fifth lecture at least."[90] Similarly, in the United States, J. L. Cabell, chairman of the American Medical Association's Committee on Education, urged in 1851 that "searching examinations . . . be given each day, on the lectures of the preceding day."[91]

An ordered sequence of courses, on the other hand, was scarcely possible under the conditions that existed in British and especially American medical schools. "It is impossible," wrote John Abercrombie in 1838 about the circumstances in Edinburgh, "to require a regular order of

89. At Heidelberg in 1854, for example, the "study plan" listed specific courses for each of the eight semesters of study: Term 1: physics, inorganic chemistry, dissection; Term 2: botany, organic chemistry, practical chemistry, zoology; Term 3: special pathology, materia medica, dissection, histology; Term 4: medical botany, pathology, medical diagnosis and pathological anatomy, beginning medical clinic; Term 5: surgery and bandaging, obstetrics, pharmaceutical chemistry, medical and surgical clinics; Term 6: medical, obstetrical, ophthalmological, and women's and children's diseases clinics; Term 7: policlinic, legal medicine, hygiene, psychiatry; Term 8: clinics. Akten der medizinischen Fakultät, III, 4a, 97, 30–31, University of Heidelberg Archive.

90. "Notice to Lecturers and Students," Surgeons Hall, Edinburgh, November 29, 1836, medical faculty correspondence, miscellaneous file, University College of London Archive; Minutes, Medical Faculty, University of Glasgow, October 31, 1856, University of Glasgow Archive; Minutes, Medical Faculty, November 23, 1837, paleography room, University of London Library. The wording of the rule on attendance taking is from the University of Edinburgh; an identical rule was approved by the Glasgow faculty.

91. J. L. Cabell, "Report of the Committee on Medical Education," *Transactions of the American Medical Association* 7 (1851): 62.

courses."[92] In the United States, except for a few of the non-degree-granting schools (especially the Boylston Medical School in Boston), the practice of repeating many of the same courses in the second term of study as were taken in the first continued until late in the century.[93] The reformer Daniel Drake, admitting that "it would [not] be practicable to class our students . . . into juniors and seniors, and have lectures adopted to each division," nevertheless urged students to concentrate on theoretical subjects in the first year and reserve the more practical studies for the second.[94]

Some evidence suggests that a number of American students did in fact try to arrange their studies in this order. Not all students repeated mindlessly the same courses over two consecutive years. Abner Webb, a typical student of the mid-1840s in Cleveland, for example, took chemistry, anatomy, materia medica, general pathology, and the theory and practice of medicine in his first term and special anatomy (pathological anatomy?), obstetrics, and surgery, in addition to repeating the lectures in chemistry and materia medica, in the second.[95]

In addition to the swiftly changing curriculum at midcentury, British and American students continued to face such familiar problems as finding an opportunity to dissect bodies and to practice midwifery. Both anatomy and midwifery, contrary to a half-century before, were now deemed not only desirable but essential for the doctor entering general practice. Victorian sensitivities about man-midwifery and cutting of the human body in anatomy classes, however, continued to plague students and teachers. In Europe, the German states and France had passed liberal laws governing the use of unclaimed bodies for teaching purposes by 1850, and obstetrical clinics were available to medical students and midwives on both sides of the Rhine. British and especially American students, however, sometimes finished their studies without having performed a complete dissection or made a pelvic examination or seen a woman in labor.[96] A student contracting with an Ohio preceptor in 1846, for example, was barred specifically by a provision of his contract from accompanying his mentor "to cases of Midwifery and Diseases of Women of a delicate nature."[97]

92. John Abercrombie to J. A. Clark, October 15, 1838, Royal College of Physicians of Edinburgh.

93. On grading in the private schools, see Smith, "Emergence of Organized Clinical Instruction," 203.

94. Daniel Drake, "Medical Colleges," *Western Journal of the Medical and Physical Sciences* 5 (1831): 11–12.

95. S. Camp, "Abner Webb, Jr.: A Doctor, 1821–1874," typescript, Cleveland Historical Sciences Library.

96. See the comments by J. C. Reeve, Class of 1849, in Minutes, Western Reserve University Medical Alumni Association, June 12, 1901, p. 134, Cleveland Historical Sciences Library.

97. Contract of Lyman W. Trask and Amaziah Moore, in Waite, "Contract for Private Medical Teaching," 546.

In Britain, the Anatomy Law of 1832 had eased somewhat the problem of securing bodies, but many of the smaller schools continued to report a chronic shortage. Although St. Bartholomew's Hospital School in London could lay claim to forty-six bodies from workhouses and twenty-two from the hospital itself during a four-month period in 1833, the faculty at Leeds, as late as 1864, was still lamenting the shortage of bodies and paying the master of the local workhouse £5 annually "in consideration of his readiness to promote the supply of subjects for dissection."[98] Students at Leeds complained about the "most unwholesome atmosphere" in the anatomy room, and the faculty, agreeing, told the governing council that the small size of the room "does not allow more than one body to be dissected at a time."[99]

For American students, the situation was worse because of the absence of effective legislation to make bodies available to schools of medicine. Nearly every school was dependent at midcentury, in greater or lesser degree, on the resourcefulness of students, demonstrators, or hired agents in locating unguarded bodies in local graveyards. The bodies of slaves or free African Americans were especially vulnerable to exhumation. No school of this era was without its "horror stories" of nightly raids on cemeteries, a provoked and outraged citizenry, and violent attacks on the offending parties. As late as the 1870s, an Ann Arbor student excitedly wrote his mother about a classmate's exploits "out west" in bringing the bodies of two slain gunmen back to Michigan for dissection.[100]

The daily life of students of all countries at midcentury was remarkably similar. Lectures now consumed from four to six hours of every day, often including Saturdays; clinics and dissections, depending on the school and country, occupied from two to four hours; and the students spent the rest of the time studying in their rooms. In the German universities, it was not unusual for a student to sit in lectures or clinics for six to eight hours a day, including some courses that he was repeating; a French student was required to register for a minimum of four courses each term, including daily lectures, clinics, and hospital visits of varying length; London hospital classes were scheduled from nine o'clock in the morning to eight o'clock at night, but absenteeism was rife and classes were poorly attended; and a probably typical student at the University of Michigan wrote in 1863 that he got up at daylight, studied until eight o'clock, dissected for three hours, listened to four lectures, and then went home to

98. Record of Bodies Dissected, 1832–33, manuscript, St. Bartholomew's Hospital Archive; Minutes of Council, Leeds School of Medicine, July 2, 1864, Leeds University Archive.

99. Minutes of Council, Leeds School of Medicine, July 17, 1863, Leeds University Archive.

100. Charles Tufts to mother, October 1, 1876, Bentley Historical Library, University of Michigan.

study.[101] Such strong pressures on the time of the student—when added to youthfulness, social isolation, and the anxieties of beginning a practice—may help explain the bizarre behavior of some students when at leisure.

Beyond the Classroom

Life outside the classroom or clinic was described by almost every student as dull and monotonous. Few had time for social diversions, though exceptions were not unknown. "Every theatre except the lecture-theatre," reads an account of London students in the 1860s, "is generally forbidden fruit to a reading man."[102] Amenities for students in the school of medicine itself were few and far between. At Liverpool, where students enjoyed the use of a library and reading room, they were required to leave if a teacher wished to use it.[103] At a number of schools, particularly in London, students formed their own societies or clubs that were partly social and partly professional. Some of the London societies joined together into a citywide "union" or "Junior Medical Society of London."[104] American schools, too, were the site of similar societies.

In France, students were forbidden by law to form any association "without having obtained the permission of the local authorities and giving notice to the dean," but purely social organizations and those aimed at medical purposes were normally approved without difficulty.[105] The German student, especially if he were from a well-to-do family, was likely to join one of the famous fraternities (*corps*), which offered a strenuous social life of comradely activity, drinking, dueling, and nationalistic politics, in which medical students often took part. In contrast with Britain and America, writes Konrad Jarausch, "both curricular and extracurricular activities were remarkably [unregulated] in Germany."[106]

Parental fears of city attractions for the young student were exploited by the provincial schools, especially in Britain and America. Such schools, argued the Manchester physician John Davis in 1837, "afford all the advantages of domestic society, and all the advantages of parental superin-

---

101. Simmer, "Principles and Problems," 180; Amédée Amette, *Guide générale de l'étudiant en médecine* (Paris: Victor Masson, 1874), 11–13; Albert Smith, *The London Medical Student* (London: Routledge, Warne, & Routledge, 1861), 2; Stillman Smith to cousin, December 6, 1863, Stillman Smith Papers, Bentley Historical Library, University of Michigan.

102. R. Temple Wright, *Medical Students of the Period* (Edinburgh and London: William Blackwood, 1867), 114.

103. Henry A. Ormerod, *The Early History of the Liverpool Medical School from 1834 to 1877* (Liverpool: C. Tilling, 1954), 40.

104. Wright, *Medical Students*, 113.

105. Amette, *Guide*, sec. 146.

106. Konrad H. Jarausch, *Students, Society, and Politics in Imperial Germany: The Rise of Academic Illiberalism* (Princeton, NJ: Princeton University Press, 1982), 240.

tendance." To go to London, he warned, "has often been like the blight that affects the opening bud."[107] A Bristol professor observed that it was "a most cruel thing to force young men into a . . . residence in the modern Babylon [that is, London]."[108] In America, even the country medical school in tiny Willoughby, Ohio, assured its clientele that the village where it was located "is entirely free from those temptations to vice and dissipation which are always present in considerable towns."[109]

Those students who did live in cities were urged by their families to seek board with one of the professors or at least a cooperative living arrangement with other students. Lodging at the home of professors, however, was more common at rural schools than those in cities. A number of London students did share lodgings that featured a large sitting room with separate bedrooms, but most sought their own quarters if they could afford it.[110]

A new development in student housing, encouraged by James Paget at St. Bartholomew's Hospital, was the use of hospital-owned houses to accommodate students. The hospital approved in 1842 the inauguration of a "collegiate establishment" of six dwellings to house thirty students.[111] Modeled after the residential colleges of Oxford and Cambridge, the new venture put great emphasis on suitable furnishings, dining halls, low costs, and student discipline. Paget became the first "warden" and established a program of tutoring and guidance for the houses. By 1849, he could report that the number of pupils "enticed" to the school had doubled since the creation of the program.[112] Not only those in the residences but other students as well were invited to seek guidance and assistance from the warden. Gradually, Paget wrote in his memoirs, "it became the duty of the Warden to advise nearly all students as to their course of study."[113]

Other schools followed the St. Bartholomew's pattern. King's College, for example, announcing in 1850 the services of a "resident medical tutor . . . to superintend the studies and conduct of medical students," explained that the tutor would meet with groups of fifteen students three times weekly and give "advice to each student as to his plan of reading and note-taking."[114]

107. John Davis, *The Annual Address delivered . . . on Opening the Session of the Royal School of Medicine and Surgery, Pine Street* (Manchester: Love and Barton, 1837), 22–23.

108. Clipping from Bristol medical publication, no name or date, c. 1848, in Minutes of Council, Leeds School of Medicine, August 5, 1848, Leeds University Archive.

109. *Annual Announcement of the Willoughby Medical College, Session of 1845–46*, 5.

110. Wright, *Medical Students*, 128–29.

111. Minutes, General Court, October 11, 1842, St. Bartholomew's Hospital Archive.

112. Ibid., November 1, 1849.

113. Stephen Paget, ed., *Memoirs and Letters of Sir James Paget* (London: Longmans, Green, 1902), 125.

114. King's College, London, *Calendar for 1850–51* (London: John W. Parker, 1850), 121.

The costs of board and lodging, as well as for instruction, were a worry to many students. Compared with that a half-century earlier, attendance at medical school was considerably more expensive. The period of study, after all, was generally much longer; the expense of individual courses had risen nearly everywhere; more books and equipment were needed; and charges for rooms and meals were generally higher than in their fathers' or grandfathers' day. Making ends meet, as evident in the surviving letters and diaries of the period, was a particular concern of those from less affluent families in both Europe and America. "My expenses at the college will be about 25 dollars, a little more than I expected," David Rankin wrote to his wife from Ann Arbor (Michigan) in 1862, "if I had known every thing I would have gone to Cincinnatti [sic]."[115] By "going into a club" with three other students, Rankin was able to rent a room for fifty cents a week, which included cooking privileges, and he kept the cost of food to seventy cents a week.[116] At the University of Vienna, according to a contemporary guidebook, two of every three students were classified as "needy," held scholarships of some sort, or were forced to attend lectures without credit as auditors.[117]

The reform of medical costs became a battle cry of those students who participated in the German uprisings of 1848. The Prussian official Joseph Hermann Schmidt, however, responded unsympathetically that "whoever lacks sufficient money and contacts . . . may as well stay away from [medical] study."[118] In France, the records of all medical schools during these years contain applications for study that included requests for the waiving of tuition charges because of need.[119]

The cost of medical education in France was reputedly the lowest in Europe. According to an estimate of 1847, four years of study at a degree-granting school required the relatively modest payment of 1,100 francs (roughly U.S.$200 at the time) for instruction, but the expense of a room in the Latin Quarter of Paris could be as much as 40 francs a month and a like amount for meals.[120] An American student in Paris, according to a contemporary guidebook, could expect to spend $50 a month, or about $600 for a year of instruction.[121] To become a second-class *officier de santé*, on the other hand, a student paid only 700 francs for instruction over a three-year period, and living costs in the provinces

115. David Rankin to wife, October 23, 1862, David Rankin Papers, Bentley Historical Library, University of Michigan.

116. Ibid., October 27, 1862, January 16, 1863.

117. Wilhelm Herzig, *Das medicinische Wien: Wegweiser für Aerzte und Naturforscher* (Vienna: Wilhelm Braumüller, 1848), 14–15.

118. Joseph Hermann Schmidt, *Die Reform der Medicinal-Verfassung Preussens* (Berlin, 1846), 106.

119. See "Demandes d'inscription," Archives nationales, AJ[16] 6375.

120. Amette, *Guide*, 18; Léonard, *Vie quotidienne*, 29.

121. L. J. Frazee, *The Medical Student in Europe* (Maysville, KY: Richard H. Collins, 1849), 117.

were lower.[122] Across the Rhine, the minimal cost of a degree in medicine, including living expenses, was computed to be in the range of 3,000 thaler (or $2,000 in current dollars).[123] Many German and Viennese students were able to obtain waivers of professors' fees and some other costs.

In London, according to an estimate by Jeanne Peterson, the expenses of an apprenticeship, lecture fees, books, and room and board for a student on a "minimum budget" in 1860 were about £250 (about $1,200 in current dollars), whereas an education in the provinces could be had for about 20 percent less.[124] A survey of St. Bartholomew students in 1843 showed that most paid 9 to 16 shillings per week for rent, 2 to 4 shillings for coal, and 9 to 15 pence per day for dinner.[125] A recent estimate of average (as opposed to minimal) expenses at midcentury puts the total costs of medical study in London at between £500 and £1,000, the highest cost for becoming a doctor in the Western world.[126] An effort by St. Bartholomew's to get other London schools to raise minimal charges for instruction still higher to 100 guineas in 1858, though well received by some of the schools, was unsuccessful.[127]

Schooling in America, by contrast, was cheaper than anywhere in Europe. Even in New York, according to the surgeon John Watson, who was familiar with charges in Britain, the same hospital privileges that cost several hundred dollars a year in London could be had for "I almost blush to name it, the amount of eight dollars annually!"[128] For the country as a whole, according to the studies of William Frederick Norwood, the total expense of a medical education, including apprenticeship, course fees, room and board, ranged from $200 to $400. "At most rural schools," he writes, "everything except clothing was obtainable for under $150."[129] In Columbus, Ohio, the Starling Medical College advertised its charges for a single session in 1849, inclusive of room and board, at $92 to $100.[130]

Expenses at some city schools in America, however, especially if full advantage were taken of summer courses and other opportunities for educa-

122. Amette, *Guide*, 33.

123. Friedrich Graevell, *Uber die Reform der Medicinal-Verfassung Preussens: Ein kritischer Uberblick* (Leipzig, 1847), 72.

124. Peterson, *Medical Profession*, 74, table 7.

125. Minutes, General Court, March 9, 1843, St. Bartholomew's Hospital Archive.

126. Paul K. Underhill, "Science, Professionalism and the Development of Medical Education in England: An Historical Sociology" (Ph.D. diss., University of Edinburgh, 1987), 219. Another estimate of £650 to educate a general practitioner in 1858 is in "Medical Education," *Westminster Review* 70 (1858): 141–42.

127. Minutes, medical college, May 8, 1858, St. Bartholomew's Hospital Archive.

128. John Watson, *A Lecture on Practical Education in Medicine, and on the Course of Instruction at the N.Y. Hospital* (New York: J. & H. G. Langley, 1846), 18.

129. William F. Norwood, *Medical Education in the United States Before the Civil War* (Philadelphia: University of Pennsylvania Press, 1944), 393–94.

130. Starling Medical College, *Catalogue of the Officers and Students for the Session of 1849–50* (Columbus, OH: Scott & Bascom, 1850), 15.

tion outside the medical school, could run as high as $1,000.[131] Provision was made by most schools for a few poor students, but the vast majority of Americans studying medicine were forced to raise the entire cost themselves.

Studying medicine at midcentury had become an increasingly burdensome enterprise. Whether in America or Europe, it was costly; entailed a commitment of three, four, or more years of one's life; required a preparatory education of growing length; demanded some knowledge of the natural sciences; and was becoming increasingly regulated by public and professional authority. Just ahead was a pedagogical revolution in medical teaching—the rise and spread of laboratory teaching—that would add still further to the burdens of future students of medicine.

---

131. "Students' Expenses," *Medical and Surgical Reporter* 1 (1858): 26.

9

The Spread of Laboratory
Teaching, 1850–1870

"I still see the narrow, long hallway in the university building," reminisced Albert von Kölliker,

> where Henle, for lack of another room for demonstrations, showed
> us and explained the simplest things, so awe inspiring in their nov-
> elty, with scarcely five or six microscopes: epithelia, skin scales, cilia
> cells, blood corpuscles, pus cells, semen, then teased-out prepara-
> tions from muscles, ligaments, nerves, sections from cartilage, cuts of
> bones, etc.

Something of the excitement and sense of adventure conveyed to students by the early use of the microscope in teaching is reflected in Kölliker's words and those of other students of the 1830s and 1840s. But at
that time, few students anywhere had had direct, personal experience in
the use of the microscope or other laboratory instruments, and indeed
not many teachers believed that such experience was important to the education of the average student of medicine. New improvements in the
microscope in the late 1830s had made it feasible to consider using the
instrument for teaching purposes, but what were its pedagogical advantages? Of what value was it at the bedside if a physician were skillful in
using the microscope and could do simple chemical tests? No one questioned the advantages afforded by the new chemistry and physics to those
who used them in research in a special workplace, now called the *laboratory*, but the "belief that practical experience [in a laboratory] was impor-

tant for all students, not merely for a small elite" constituted the real pedagogical revolution in the teaching of medicine.[1]

Like the earlier shift to clinical teaching, the transition to laboratory teaching, including the use of the microscope, came slowly and sporadically, had roots in the immediate past, was justified by its practical uses, and was shaped by a variety of educational and political circumstances in each country. Just as some contemporaries as well as later admirers reified the French achievement in clinical teaching because of the simultaneous scientific advances and superb opportunities opened to students in the Paris hospitals, so the remarkable pedagogical opening and research achievements of the German laboratory were extravagantly admired by visitors and later writers alike. In both cases, it was the massive scale of the pedagogical change that left the deepest impression on all who witnessed it. "A third-rate poverty-stricken German university," intoned Thomas Henry Huxley a few years later, "turns out more [scientific teaching and research] each year than our fine and wealthy foundations elaborate in ten."[2]

Why Germany?

How did it happen? Why did the concept of the teaching laboratory find so congenial and fertile a soil in the German university and not in the schools of France and Britain? It was in Paris, after all, that an "environment favorable to the development of the laboratory sciences" first developed in such places as the Academy of Medicine.[3] Indeed, some of the most important medical discoveries of the first half of the nineteenth century were credited to François Magendie, Claude Bernard, and their coworkers in the laboratories of the Collège de France. But in France, as well as in Britain and America, as outlined in earlier chapters, the events of half a century had pushed the formal teaching of medicine further and further away from both the traditional university and the specialized institutions of science.

As opposed to scientific study, medicine was now pursued on both sides of the English Channel as a predominantly professional activity best

1. Arleen M. Tuchman, "From the Lecture to the Laboratory: The Institutionalization of Scientific Medicine at the University of Heidelberg," in *The Investigative Enterprise: Experimental Physiology in Nineteenth-Century Medicine*, ed. William Coleman and Frederic L. Holmes (Berkeley and Los Angeles: University of California Press, 1988), 74–75. The quotation from Kölliker, cited by Tuchman, is from Albert von Kölliker, *Erinnerungen aus meinem Leben* (Leipzig, 1899), 8.

2. Cited in Gerald B. Webb and Desmond Powell, *Henry Sewall, Physiologist and Physician* (Baltimore: Johns Hopkins University Press, 1946), 47.

3. John E. Lesch, "The Paris Academy of Medicine and Experimental Science, 1820–1848," in *The Investigative Enterprise: Physiology in Nineteenth-Century Medicine*, ed. William Coleman and Frederic L. Holmes (Berkeley and Los Angeles: University of California Press, 1988), 101.

carried out in the wards of a large hospital. The eighteenth-century universities of Britain, notably Edinburgh, that had offered both theoretical and practical training in medicine were now in relative decline, and the university faculties of France—disbanded in 1792 and regrouped as regional centers of specialized study in law, medicine, or theology or as examining bodies in letters and science for *lycée* graduates and teachers—played almost no role, except for the medical faculties, in the education of physicians.[4] In England, by midcentury, according to a royal commission, Oxford "had ceased altogether to be a school of Medicine."[5] Similarly in the United States, medical teaching was even further separated from collegiate programs in science than it had been at the beginning of the century.

During these same years, by contrast, the German university was becoming a powerful state institution and the dominant site of medical study, having squeezed out the many practical schools of medicine. Whereas the French student, wrote the historian Heinrich von Sybel, went to a professional school of medicine "where faculties deliver a finished product for the profession" and the English student, if he went to Oxford, studied at best in "an advanced high school of general education," the German student attended a comprehensive university that borrowed from both traditions, giving him "as deep an exposure as possible to science and scholarship."[6] This disjunction of scientific and literary learning from training in medicine outside Germany, relatively unimportant during the long heyday of clinical teaching, was now becoming a severe handicap as a knowledge of the methods of experimental science and their applications to medicine were being integrated into the medical curriculum.

In Germany, humanistic scholars, scientists, and physicians alike, by reason of their common home in the university, had worked since the beginning of the century to build comprehensive institutions of learning. After the defeat of their armies by Napoleon, writes Joseph Ben-David, "the Germans could find comfort only in the unprecedented flowering of [their] national philosophy and literature." Rejecting any suggestion that they follow the French example of breaking up their faculties into *grand écoles* or specialized practical schools, German intellectuals and officials, admitting the need for reform, sought instead to make universities more useful and their faculties of arts and sciences, in particular, to be the equivalent of the prestigious French academies.[7]

4. Peter Lundgreen, "The Organization of Science and Technology in France: A German Perspective," in *The Organization of Science and Technology in France, 1808–1914*, ed. Robert Fox and George Weisz (Cambridge: Cambridge University Press, 1980), 311.

5. "Extracts from Report of Her Majesty's Commissioners . . . Universities and Colleges of Oxford, 1852," in *The Universities in the Nineteenth Century*, ed. Michael Sanderson (London: Routledge & Kegan Paul, 1975), 93.

6. Heinrich von Sybel, *Vorträge und Aufsätze* (Berlin: A. Hofmann, 1875), 45–46.

7. Joseph Ben-David, *The Scientist's Role in Society: A Comparative Study* (Englewood Cliffs, NJ: Prentice-Hall, 1971), 112.

After the Napoleonic era, the successor German states aimed at educational improvements at all levels in an effort to stimulate the skills and capacities needed to revive their shaken cultural identity and to encourage the growth of manufacturing, trade, and transportation. An interest in science, technology, and better methods of measurement and investigation, in particular, was encouraged as never before. The public school system in Prussia, for example, reorganized as a two-tiered system of classical and scientific study in 1812 and put increased emphasis on physics and other sciences as well as on modern languages and other practical subjects. Some teachers, too, began to introduce students to practical exercises in science that foreshadowed the laboratory instruction of students.[8] Lawmakers in Baden likewise decreed new courses in natural history, science, and mathematics for secondary students, arguing in part, as Arleen Tuchman explained, "that an education in those skills [was] necessary for improving the economy."[9]

In contrast with Britain and France, the educational authorities of Germany, building on the swelling number of better-prepared students, now demanded a higher level of scientific readiness and educational ability in their universities and medical classes. This made possible, in turn, the introduction of more advanced work in science in the universities. Furthermore, the German faculties, long encouraged to combine teaching with research, enjoyed a high degree of public and financial support that went well beyond that of other nations. Initially in humanistic and historical studies and then in science, medicine, and the law, a reorientation of the teacher's job from "the training of practitioners to the education of scholars and research workers" was taking place in Prussia and beyond.[10]

The resulting competition among universities for outstanding professors and promising students became an important obligation of the state. The entire universe of German-speaking universities, twenty-eight in all, became a bidding pool for academic talent to bring students, renown, and financial support to a favored institution. Appointments in science and medicine, in particular, grew prodigiously, especially in the years after 1830. To read the files of a typical educational ministry in Germany of these years is to be reminded of how early the stratagems and etiquette of academic negotiation for a talented scholar were fixed firmly in place.

The huge Prussian file of letters and memoranda on the appointment of a single physiologist at Königsberg in the late 1840s, for example—a competition that at times pitted Hermann von Helmholtz against Emil

---

8. Kathryn M. Olesko, "Physics Instruction in Prussian Secondary Schools Before 1859," in *Science in Germany: The Intersection of Institutional and Intellectual Issues*, vol. 5, ed. Kathryn M. Olesko (*Osiris*, 1989), 95–108.

9. Arleen Tuchman, "Experimental Physiology, Medical Reform, and the Politics of Education at the University of Heidelberg: A Case Study," *Bulletin of the History of Medicine* 61 (1987): 205.

10. R. Steven Turner, "The Growth of Professorial Research in Prussia, 1818 to 1848—Causes and Context," *Historical Studies in the Physical Sciences* 3 (1971): 138.

DuBois-Reymond and Ernst von Brücke and involved Johannes Müller, Carl Ludwig, and other leading figures—is a marvel of academic intrigue, deferential demands, offers and counteroffers, and governmental politics. Writing about Ludwig, whose politics were thought to be suspect, the physiologist Alfred Volkmann defended his earlier involvement in demonstrations in Hesse as youthful indiscretions and assured the minister that Ludwig now understood that "only the hegemony of Prussia" could halt "the anarchy and threatening communism" of the times.[11] In arguing his own fitness for the position, Brücke, while declaring his eagerness to go to Königsberg, where he would "stimulate the spirit of the young toward a high and glorious science," confided that he needed more money, since he was going to be married and his finances were "threatening in the highest degree."[12] To the beneficial effects of such competition for talent, the Göttingen professor Walter Perry ascribed in 1846 "the astonishing activity and industry which prevail in the universities."[13]

It was thus many of the same factors that had hindered medical pedagogy in Germany earlier in the century—the struggle to maintain a foothold for professional study in the university, the tension between classroom and clinic, the small size of the numerous and widely distributed medical schools, the strict and varying regulations of individual states, and a reputation for theoretical speculation over purely practical study—that now seemed to give an important advantage to German medical teaching. Far from representing a sharp break from the past, however, the pedagogical developments of midcentury were the outcome of these long decades of struggle over the place of professional studies in the university and of the insistence by German authorities on the need for a large measure of public utility in academic work.

Largely unplanned, often dependent on historical circumstance and the chance role of personality, the new laboratory teaching—as had been true of the development of the clinic—was accepted unevenly, even in Germany, and so had to overcome the massive inertia of established ways and vested interests. Only gradually, over a period of half a century, did science as a process of discovering new knowledge in universities become in Germany so specialized and highly favored an occupation. By 1850, a vigorously competitive academic system had grown slowly out of the political and social conditions of a disunited, prosperous, ambitious, and prideful nation. Most important of all, only in that country at midcentury was medical education almost exclusively in the hands of university professors rather than medical practitioners.[14]

11. Emil DuBois-Reymond to minister, April 22, 1849, GSPK, Merseburg, 76 Va, Sekt. 11, T.T. IV, Nr. 13.
12. Ernst Brücke to minister, August 14, 1847, ibid.
13. Walter C. Perry, *German University Education: The Professors and Students of Germany*, 2nd ed. (London: Longman, Brown, Green, and Longmans, 1846), 12.
14. Paul K. Underhill, "Science, Professionalism and the Development of Medical Education in England: An Historical Sociology" (Ph.D. diss., University of Edinburgh, 1987), 524.

The Laboratory as an Extension of Practical Teaching

The first teaching laboratories in German medical schools were inevitably justified by their contribution to the practical skills of students and the nation. Building on the successful example of the teaching clinic, medical educators now similarly described experience in a laboratory as adding to the student's store of practical knowledge in medicine. "A personal familiarity with the objects of research, the sharpening of the senses and the actual handling of instruments should be seen as principal tasks of instruction," declared the Tübingen clinician Wilhelm Griesinger in 1848.[15] For more than a century, after all, the teaching of anatomy had been carried out in specially equipped rooms, where learning by doing through dissection of the human body was held to be the foundation stone of all medical knowledge. Medical botany was likewise taught practically by the use of botanical gardens. Why should medical students not learn the chemical makeup of basic body fluids and of medicinal substances or the dynamic functioning of the body's parts in the same way?

If simple "experiments" and the use of animals were required to understand better the working of the body in health and disease, then a practicable method had to be devised to bring students to a place where these could be taught, just as students were brought earlier for similar reasons to the hospital clinic or the ward. "Practical work in the sciences," advised the pharmacologist Philipp Phoebus in 1849, "sharpens the senses and understanding" of the future physician, gives him "practice in making judgments and drawing conclusions," and "develops his powers of observation more acutely than in almost any other activity." Furthermore, it enabled him to do individual tests and investigations "that will prove helpful in practice," such as examining body fluids and wastes, testing the quality of drugs, looking for poisonous substances in the blood, or understanding the acoustical basis of hearing problems.[16]

The value of the laboratory to the teacher as a place for research and uncovering new knowledge was downplayed in favor of its importance in teaching students. The early institutes for physiological teaching at Breslau, Berlin, and Bonn, for example, were alike in the case made for teaching students as their principal raison d'être. The creation of autonomous organizations, complete with auditoriums, laboratories, and preparation rooms, it was argued, "would support physiological lectures and would offer students hands-on experience in experimentation and observation."[17]

---

15. Wilhelm Griesinger, "Referat über das medicinische Unterrichts—und Prüfungswesen in Württemberg" [1848], *Gesammelte Abhandlungen* 2 (1872): 151.

16. Philipp Phoebus, *Uber die Naturwissenschaften als Gegenstand des Studiums, des Unterrichts und der Prüfung* (Nordhausen: Adolph Büchting, 1849), 2–9, 34–35.

17. Richard L. Kremer, "Building Institutes for Physiology in Prussia, 1836–1846," in *The Laboratory Revolution in Medicine*, ed. Andrew Cunningham and Perry Williams (Cambridge: Cambridge University Press, 1992), 101.

Students were essential to the case for scientific laboratories. "Without the enrollment of numerous medical students," in the judgment of William Coleman and Frederic Holmes, "the [research] institute as we know it would not have received the generous public support that came its way."[18] By the 1840s in the state of Baden, the spread of practical laboratory education to the average or "less gifted" student, encouraged by Henle, was a principal objective of both the state and the medical school.[19] Indeed, all the new medical institutes spreading across Germany by 1850 "were designed to impart laboratory training to the man of average talent intended for a career in routine medical practice."[20]

The leaders of German medicine also saw laboratory teaching as a means of narrowing the growing divide between medical theory and practice. "There are cases where the split between science and practical medicine is so great," Virchow told the Society for Scientific Medicine in Berlin in 1846, "that it is said of the academic physician that he can do nothing, and of the practitioner that he knows nothing." Through learning the methods of science in the laboratory, he pointed out, the student was learning a universal language and the uses of experiment that were "accessible to the whole world."[21] By creating a separate institute and laboratory for pathology in Berlin, Virchow wrote after being appointed to a chair there, the Prussian government was taking a large step in bridging "the huge chasm" between teaching the theory and the practice of medicine.[22]

Other influential teachers stressed the practical applications of their scientific work. In the small university at Giessen, Justus von Liebig, aware of the practical teaching being done in the innovative pharmacy institute at Erfurt, announced in 1827 his intention to teach "experimental chemistry" to supplement the theoretical lectures and experience in apothecaries' shops of students of pharmacy.[23] Most of the students who flocked to Giessen over the next quarter-century, including a sizable number of Americans, were attracted by the many practical applications of Liebig's experimental work in chemistry to such fields as pharmacy, agriculture, sanitation, manufacturing, and education, as well as medicine.[24] In 1851,

18. *The Investigative Enterprise*, 11.

19. Ibid., 90–91.

20. Timothy Lenoir, "Laboratories, Medicine and Public Life in Germany, 1830–1849," in *The Laboratory Revolution in Medicine*, ed. Andrew Cunningham and Perry Williams (Cambridge: Cambridge University Press, 1992), 15.

21. Rudolph Virchow, "Uber die Standpunkte in der wissenschaftlichen Medicin," *Archiv für Pathologische Anatomie und Physiologie* 1 (1847): 5, 17.

22. Virchow to minister, May 22, 1856, GSPK, Merseburg, 76 Va, Sekt. 2, Tit. IV, Nr. 40.

23. Frederic L. Holmes, "The Complementarity of Teaching and Research in Liebig's Laboratory," in *Science in Germany: The Intersection of Institutional and Intellectual Issues*, vol. 5, ed. Kathryn M. Olesko (*Osiris*, 1989), 127–28.

24. See, for example, Margaret W. Rossiter, *The Emergence of Agricultural Science: Justus Liebig and the Americans, 1840–1880* (New Haven, CT: Yale University Press, 1975).

the American Benjamin Silliman, visiting Liebig's "working laboratory," found some twenty to thirty students in "actual labor" on specific projects surrounded by "chemical vessels and reagents, and . . . the disorder which necessarily attends on numerous operations in which many persons are engaged."[25] The state of Baden, influenced by Liebig's successful joining together of scientific teaching and useful research, gave generous support to a new chemical institute at Heidelberg to be headed by Robert Bunsen.[26]

Even though the practical benefits of the laboratory teaching of chemistry to soil analysis or to industrial processes might be self-evident, what were the practical uses of a laboratory to teach so theoretical a subject as physiology? What could be done in such a workplace that would affect the physician's ability to understand the illness or heal the suffering of a patient? Many contemporary teachers of medicine, especially in places where medical training had become intensely practical, questioned the launching of such expensive ventures as physiological laboratories when they produced as yet so little of value to medicine. Later historians, too, enjoying a longer perspective, have echoed these concerns and searched, often in vain, for some explanation of why "scientific medicine," as epitomized by physiology, developed so prodigiously before it showed much in the way of therapeutic results. In fact, the average student of medicine, even in Germany, found before the 1860s relatively little practical use for the laboratory training he received.

What was always held forth by those making the case for laboratory training in science for medical students was the skill they gained in using laboratory instruments and the huge potential of scientific medicine for the future. Neither the clinic alone nor any number of didactic lectures or textbooks, it was frequently asserted, could lead medicine out of the therapeutic doldrums in which it had long found itself. "After working my way through all the medical men's old rubbish for six years as a student," Ludwig wrote to DuBois-Reymond in 1849, "I proceeded . . . to study the natural sciences."[27]

It was the harnessing of physiology and other laboratory sciences to the work of the clinic, with all that this promised for the future, that evoked the greatest enthusiasm among teachers of medicine. Some saw in physiological experimentation the means of ending the decades of "therapeutic nihilism" engendered by Parisian and Viennese clinical teaching. "The direct utility to practical medicine of pathological physiology linked with experimental pharmacology," writes one scholar, "was to be the watchword of those seeking to . . . displace clinicians from their pre-eminent

25. Benjamin Silliman, *Visit to Europe in 1851*, 2 vols. (New York: Putnam, 1854), 2:293–94.

26. Tuchman, "Experimental Physiology," 206.

27. Ludwig to DuBois-Reymond, June 14, 1849, in *Two Great Scientists of the Nineteenth Century: Correspondence of Emil DuBois-Reymond and Carl Ludwig*, ed. Paul F. Cranefield (Baltimore: Johns Hopkins University Press, 1982), 39.

position in the republic of medicine."[28] By 1866, according to a contemporary survey, sixteen of the German universities had already created independent institutes of pharmacology with the mission to teach and investigate the healing properties of drugs.[29]

New diagnostic instruments created as by-products of physical, chemical, or physiological research were also seen to have a clinical usefulness. When Helmholtz devised an instrument to view better the structure of the eye, for example, or when Wunderlich demonstrated the practicality of using a thermometer to measure changes in body heat, it suggested to many that further such practical uses would flow from the experimental study of normal bodily processes. In basing medical study on demonstrated facts and testable hypotheses, Wunderlich declared, the old easy faith in "irrational medical recipes and the efficacy of useless substances" would be replaced by experimentally derived and scientifically demonstrable therapies.[30] The only proper study of disease, he argued, was as a deviation from the normal functioning of the body, and the latter could be understood only through experimental physiology, whereas the effective treatment of disease could come only through a science-based pharmacology. By 1877, Virchow was proclaiming that all "therapeutic doctrine has [now] become biological and thereby experimental science."[31]

The Spread of Laboratory Teaching, 1850–1870

Wherever the laboratory was adopted to teach medical students, the justification given for the large expense was to teach them practical skills and the use of instruments. The laboratory sessions in Germany were called *übungen*, or practical exercises, and in Britain and America the first ventures in laboratory teaching were invariably described as courses in "practical chemistry" or "practical physiology." At the school of science in Lille, Louis Pasteur likewise told an assembly in 1855 that it was the teaching of practical skills to students in the laboratory that represented "the hope of the faculty."[32]

The first practical classes, however, were frequently large, giving the student little direct contact with a teacher and little coordination with

28. Underhill, "Science, Professionalism and the Development of Medical Education in England," 529.

29. Edith Heischkel, "Schauplätze pharmakologischer Forschung und Lehre im Jahre 1866," *Medizinhistorisches Journal* 1 (1966): 113.

30. Carl Wunderlich and Wilhelm Roser, "Uber die Mängel der heutigen deutschen Medicin und über die Nothwendigkeit einer entschieden wissenschaftlichen Richtung in derselben," *Archiv für physiologische Heilkunde* 1 (1842): ii.

31. Rudolf Virchow, *Disease, Life and Man: Selected Essays*, ed. L. J. Rather (Stanford, CA: Stanford University Press, 1958), 10.

32. Nicole Hulin, "L'organisation de l'enseignement scientifique au milieu du XIXe siècle," *Revue du palais de la découverte* 13 (1985): 59.

classroom instruction. Some of the criticisms directed at the teaching clinic earlier—that it was overcrowded, impersonal, and unrelated to other teaching—were now used to describe the teaching of students in German laboratories. When a student in a laboratory did show unusual skill or aptitude in experimentation or research, he was frequently separated from the rest of the class and invited to work in the professor's own laboratory. "Herr Doktor," Johannes Müller reportedly would address a student in his laboratory of 150 students, "why don't you join me upstairs in my *Kabinet?* You will be able to work much better there away from all this confusion."[33] Thus began an early informal system of training advanced students in the techniques of experimentation and research while preserving at the same time the institute's reason for teaching practical skills to large numbers of medical students.

By the late 1850s, the laboratory instruction of students, especially in chemistry and physiology, had spread widely but unevenly across the German academic world. Physiology, by this time, was an important and independent subject in nearly every university; institutes for research and teaching in pathological anatomy, however, were found as yet in only a third of the German-speaking universities; and only one chair had been created in physiological chemistry.[34] Expenditures by state governments for medical and scientific installations had jumped in Baden from 15,000 to 183,000 florins between 1848 and 1860 and in Bavaria from 650 to 100,000 florins.[35] In Prussia, the capital outlays and operating costs for medical and scientific instruction were rising even more spectacularly.[36] Some of the older facilities, such as those for anatomical study, were systematically rebuilt or replaced.[37] By 1860, the total expenditure in the German states for university science was more than four times that of England.[38]

In the meantime, a number of the German states moved to require lab-

33. From *Münchener medizinische Wochenschrift* 81 (1934): 62, quoted in Timothy Lenoir, "Science for the Clinic: Science Policy and the Formation of Carl Ludwig's Institute in Leipzig," in *The Investigative Enterprise: Experimental Physiology in Nineteenth-Century Medicine*, ed. William Coleman and Frederic L. Holmes (Berkeley and Los Angeles: University of California Press, 1988), 146.

34. Christiane Borschel, "Das physiologische Institut der Universität Göttingen 1840 bis zur Gegenwart" (med. diss., University of Göttingen, 1987), 98; Irmgard Hort, "Die pathologischen Institute der deutschsprachigen Universitäten (1850–1914)" (med. diss., University of Cologne, 1987), 63–64; Hans-Heinz Eulner, *Die Entwicklung der medizinischen Spezialfächer an den Universitäten des deutschen Sprachgebietes* (Stuttgart: Ferdinand Enke, 1970), 93.

35. Horst W. Kupka, "Die Ausgaben der süddeutschen Länder für die medizinischen und naturwissenschaftlichen Hochschul-Einrichtungen, 1848–1914" (med. diss., University of Bonn, 1970), 136–37, 156–57.

36. Frank R. Pfetsch, *Zur Entwicklung der Wissenschaftspolitik in Deutschland, 1750–1914* (Berlin: Duncker & Humblot, 1974), 53–54.

37. Wilhelm Lexis, *Die deutschen Universitäten*, 2 vols. (Berlin: A. Asher, 1893), 2:192.

38. Pfetsch, *Entwicklung der Wissenschaftspolitik*, 339.

oratory study in physiology, physics, chemistry, and anatomy as part of the medical curriculum. Bavaria passed legislation in 1858, for example, that made mandatory an examination in these subjects after "at least one year" of medical study, and Prussia instituted a similar requirement (the *tentamen physicum*) in 1861.[39]

The Teaching Laboratory in France

As the laboratory movement spread across the medical world of Germany, it began simultaneously to gain its first footholds in other nations. In France, teaching laboratories, long a part of the small facilities for research in such Parisian centers as the Ecole normale, the Collège de France, and the Ecole polytechnique, were now found increasingly in such provincial cities as Strasbourg, Lille, and Cannes. These institutions, however, were quite different from those in Germany, as they had little or no connection with the routine teaching of medical students. Here there were as yet no "numerous medical students" or "generous public support" of the kind that made laboratory teaching so favored across the Rhine. Even at the best of the French facilities, moreover, teachers had at their disposal, in the words of an assistant to Louis Pasteur, "only the premises and funds allocated to their chair. . . . When they wanted to work . . . they set themselves up as best they could in the quiet corner of a lecture room, always ready to clear away their apparatus at lecture times."[40] None of the renowned figures in French laboratory medicine at midcentury—Magendie, Bernard, Pasteur—held an appointment in a faculty of medicine.

The need for change, recognized by a government commission in 1837 and in a highly critical report by the chemist Jean-Baptiste Dumas in 1840, had not found much recognition in governmental and educational circles. The minister of education, Hippolyte Fortoul, dismissed the growing concern about developments beyond the Rhine in 1852, arguing that French supremacy in science was assured because of its universal appeal and "the suitability of French as the language of science."[41] A year-long debate in the mid-1850s among members of the Academy of Medicine on the usefulness of the microscope in clinical medicine ended

39. Acta des Königlich akademisches Senats, das Studium der Medicin, G.I. 96, University of Munich Archive; Claudia Huerkamp, *Der Aufstieg der Ärzte im 19.Jahrhundert* (Göttingen: Vandenhoeck & Ruprecht, 1985), 102.

40. E. Duclaux, "Le laboratoire de M. Pasteur," in *Le centenaire de l'école normale,* quoted in Robert Fox, "Scientific Enterprise and the Patronage of Research in France, 1800–70," *Minerva* 11 (1973): 459.

41. Hippolyte Fortoul, "Discours, 12 August 1852," Fortoul Papers, Archives nationales, 246 AP 19, cited in Harry W. Paul, *The Sorcerer's Apprentice: The French Scientist's Image of German Science, 1840–1919* (Gainesville: University Presses of Florida, 1972), 6–7.

without resolution.[42] In 1857, Armand Trousseau, the professor of clinical medicine at the Paris school, told students that they needed to know only enough chemistry and physics "to understand the application of these sciences to medicine" and that he would "profoundly deplore" any extension of study time in the "auxiliary sciences." "Gentlemen," he told them, "let us have a little less science and a little more art."[43]

Not until the 1860s did the interest in laboratory teaching for medical students attract much critical attention from policymakers in Paris. Fueled in part by the growing threat of a powerful, unified state led by Prussia across the Rhine, a flurry of governmental and private investigations of laboratories and medical schools in Germany was undertaken, and efforts were begun to stimulate greater scientific study in France. For the first time a few French students were leaving their own country to seek further training beyond the Rhine. Their number was very small, however, in comparison with those from Britain and America. A French medical traveler, returning from Germany in 1860, praised what he had seen, especially the "teaching methods" and research institutes in the schools of medicine, but was nonetheless sensitive to any suggestion that he wanted to "Germanize" French teaching. France, he said, must choose "only those institutions that are in keeping with our customs and our national genius."[44] This was a typically cautious reaction to a rival system that Frenchmen saw as at once admirable and threatening to their national pride.

In 1863, the dean of the Paris faculty of medicine, about to make changes at his own school, sent the pathologist and clinician Sigismond Jaccoud to study the German system of teaching medicine. What he found, Jaccoud reported, was "a true intellectual revolution" in teaching that had taken place with "surprising rapidity." He was especially struck, he said, by the decentralized character of medical training in Germany, contrasting it with the high degree of concentration of students and authority in Paris. But all the schools, he noted, were alike in their commitment to experimental physiology and pathology as the twin bases in science for effective medical teaching. Students he found to be performing scientific experiments for themselves as well as playing an active role in caring for clinic patients. It was this eminently practical nature of German instruction in both the clinic and the laboratory that impressed him most.[45]

42. Ann LaBerge and Mordechai Feingold, eds., *French Medical Culture in the Nineteenth Century* (Amsterdam: Rodopi, 1994), 3.

43. Quoted in Charles Coury, "The Teaching of Medicine in France from the Beginning of the Seventeenth Century," in *The History of Medical Education*, ed. C. D. O'Malley (Berkeley and Los Angeles: University of California Press, 1970), 158.

44. Dr. Gallavardin, *Voyage médical en Allemagne* (Paris: J. B. Baillière, 1860), 164.

45. Sigismond Jaccoud, *De l'organisation des facultés de médecine en Allemagne* (Paris: Adrien Delahye, 1864), 4–25.

The minister of education, Victor Duruy, moved cautiously in the early 1860s to reform the curriculum. The number of subjects taught was increased and fledgling instructors, called *agregés*, were given new teaching responsibilities. All students of medicine, not just externs and interns, were now required to spend some time in a teaching clinic. Laboratory teaching, however, despite the increased interest, remained the exception in French medical schools and not the rule.[46]

By the mid-1860s, demands for more opportunities for research and better facilities for teaching in France were reported in the medical and popular press. The immense prestige of Bernard and now Pasteur contributed to the belief that science must somehow be made a larger part of French medical pedagogy. Following a visit to Germany in 1866, the young surgeon Léon Le Fort called for the complete decentralization of scientific teaching and a single standard of medical education, as in Germany, in order to stimulate both teaching and research.[47] The well-known chemist and Alsatian Adolf Wurtz, overwhelmed by the magnificent new laboratories at Bonn, complained about the meager outlays for science in Paris and contrasted conditions in the French capital with plans he had seen for yet another building in Bonn costing two million francs. French medical teaching, he said, needed similar laboratories, more professors, and a greater number of clinical teachers in order to compete.[48]

"For thirty years," warned Pasteur in 1868, "France has slept in the shadow of its old trophies [while] Germany has been covered by vast and rich laboratories. Every day sees a new one."[49] It was little wonder, then, that French scientists increasingly saw their rivals' system as a kind of "sorcerer's apprentice" that seemed to pour money madly into its institutions of science.[50]

Even in the secondary schools of medicine the sentiment for change was building. In Lyon, the director of the school—dispatched in 1868 by municipal authorities to survey conditions in Germany—reported that the students there were "no longer condemned to take all [their] education in lessons and books," as in France, but now had "another, more nourishing source, the laboratory." German superiority, he told the council of Lyon, was due entirely to its "system of practical teaching." The continu-

46. George Weisz, "Reform and Conflict in French Medical Education, 1870–1914," in *The Organization of Science and Technology in France, 1808–1914*, ed. Robert Fox and George Weisz (Cambridge: Cambridge University Press, 1980), 63–64.

47. Léon Le Fort, *La liberté de la pratique et la liberté de l'enseignement de la médecine* (Paris: Victor Masson, 1866), 23, 28–31.

48. Adolf Wurtz to minister of education, April 8, 1868, Archives nationales, F[17] 4020, cited in Paul, *Sorcerer's Apprentice*, 8.

49. Louis Pasteur, "Le budget de la science," *Revue des cours scientifique de la France et de l'etranger* 9 (1868): 137. Another important contemporary critique of conditions in France vis-à-vis Germany is in Paul Lorain, *De la réforme des études médicales par les laboratoires* (Paris, 1868).

50. Paul, *Sorcerer's Apprentice*.

ing portrayal of the natural sciences in France as merely "auxiliary" to clinical medicine, he stated in a further report, must be ended in favor of a recognition that scientific study was now "fundamental" to medicine. The "precise research" of the laboratory, he insisted, "must be integrated into clinical observations."[51] Although the extent of actual change in the two decades before 1870 in this and other schools was modest, the readiness for change was clearly growing and was quickly exploited in the revolutionary conditions that prevailed after the French defeat of 1870.

Anglo-American Teaching and the Laboratory

The reception of laboratory teaching in Anglo-America was as resistant to change as it was in France. Only in the older universities of England and Scotland, after all, whose programs had steadily lost ground to the practical schools of London and the provinces, did the potential even exist to combine scientific and practical teaching in the same way as in the German universities. British and American medical teachers, furthermore, though they were as impressed as those of France by the growing reputation of medical science in Germany, were less motivated by a sense of the urgent need to change and were far less fearful of the national consequences of scientific weakness.

During the 1840s, Britons had outnumbered all others in their eagerness to absorb what was happening in the practical teaching of German science. By 1856, fifty-nine of them had gone to Giessen alone to study chemistry under Liebig. One of them, A. W. Hofmann, founded the first systematic teaching laboratory in Britain at the Royal College of Chemistry.[52] By 1848 some of the leading scientists of the nation—Charles Lyell, Charles Babbage, and David Brewster—were calling on Oxford and Cambridge to make drastic changes in their teaching of science and to introduce Germanic methods into Britain.[53]

But the obstacles to decisive change in Great Britain were in some ways more formidable than in France. More than 80 percent of all physicians being educated in Britain at midcentury were trained without any contact with a university or a strong preparatory school. The English universities were strongly committed to an older humanistic and classical view of education that paid little heed to the reputed need for "practical" training in the sciences. And a national revulsion at vivisection discouraged the kind of experimentation now routinely carried out by students and teachers on the continent.[54]

51. Alexandre Glénard, *Rapport pour l'année scolaire 1867–68, Ecole préparatoire de médecine et de pharmacie* (Lyons: Vingtrinier, 1868), 7; ibid., 1868–69, 17–20.

52. Rainald von Gizycki, "Centre and Periphery in the International Scientific Community: Germany, France and Great Britain in the 19th Century," *Minerva* 11 (1973): 483.

53. Ibid., 486.

54. Gerald L. Geison, "Social and Institutional Factors in the Stagnancy of English Physiology, 1840–1870," *Bulletin of the History of Medicine* 46 (1972): 35–45.

The average English medical practitioner, observed the Erlangen professor J. M. Leupoldt in 1853, completes a "scanty general education," spends a number of years with a "similarly educated apothecary or surgeon," then "attends one or another medical course in a hospital or medical school," and finally passes "a not particularly difficult examination given by a group of apothecaries or surgeons." There is nothing, he said, that is "comprehensive," "thorough," or "scientific" about it.[55]

In English eyes, experimental science was of dubious value at best to the practitioner, and consequently courses requiring laboratory experience or even demonstrations were rare. In 1868, William Gull of Guy's Hospital could praise the gains in scientific understanding of medicine yet warn at the same time of the need to protect medical study "against assaults on the side of science . . . lest we betray it by accepting a too chemical or physical limit to our thought."[56] The study of physiology was still firmly joined to anatomy in the practical hospital schools, and all the teachers were normally clinicians with little training in science. "Physiology," wrote DuBois-Reymond to Ludwig on his return to Germany from Great Britain in 1852, "does not exist in England."[57] Such skilled microscopists as Robert Bentley Todd at King's College and William Sharpey at University College did offer students careful demonstrations and some experience in the use of the microscope, but their teaching did not provide for a laboratory of the German type.

The "peculiarities" of British medical education, according to historian Gerald Geison, became "more apparent and even more exaggerated" after 1840 as more and more changes were made on the Continent. Laboratory instruction in physics and chemistry—crucial to scientific and medical development in Germany and increasingly so in France—was not available anywhere in a British medical school until the late 1860s. Independent chairs or laboratories in physiology were likewise virtually unknown until 1870.[58] In words reminiscent of those of Pasteur, Thomas Henry Huxley complained that "nothing but what is absolutely practical will go down in England. . . . A man of science in these times is like an Esau who sells his birthright for a mess of pottage."[59]

But Huxley was painting too dark a picture. German teachers, too, had been forced to use practical stratagems to introduce laboratory science into the medical curriculum. They, too, had encountered resistance and political obstacles. In Britain, furthermore, the General Medical Council, whose members included some of the foremost champions of change,

55. J. M. Leupoldt, *Uber ärztliche Bildung und Bildungsanstalten* (Frankfurt am Main: Heyder & Zimmer, 1853), 29–30.

56. Cited in Kenneth D. Keele, *The Evolution of Clinical Methods in Medicine* (Springfield, IL: Thomas, 1963), 104.

57. DuBois-Reymond to Ludwig, August 2, 1852, in *Two Great Scientists*, 73.

58. Geison, "Social and Institutional Factors," 46–52.

59. Leonard Huxley, ed., *Life and Letters of Thomas Henry Huxley*, 2 vols. (London: Macmillan, 1900), 1:66.

was moving cautiously toward a larger role for science in the curriculum. In 1864, it announced that it would "view favorably any effort to prosecute study of the natural sciences."[60] Five years later, it gave support to laboratory courses in chemistry, which were "so necessary for good medical training," and to the teaching of microscopy in courses on physiology. In an appendix to the council's report, Benjamin Brodie urged that chemistry be taught at all schools for "a year at least in a laboratory."[61] Even though the requirements for medical practice remained focused on traditional classroom and clinical courses, the pressures were clearly building for change.

The greatest interest in the new pedagogy before 1870 was found in Edinburgh and London. At University College in London, George Harley, an assistant to William Sharpey, was teaching a course in practical physiology and histology to students as early as 1857. He told the dean in that year that it was "requisite to demonstrate each physiological fact of importance by direct experiment," which required a considerable outlay of money for apparatus and materials. The expense, he claimed, "will prevent my class ever becoming a large one," since the practical method of teaching could be used with only "a very limited number of pupils." Essentially, Harley saw it as his responsibility to demonstrate to students "every fact which the student had heard fully explained by Dr. Sharpey."[62]

The practical classes at University College remained small (Harley had only twelve pupils in 1857) and were weakly supported in comparison with those of Germany, but a beginning had been made, and more practical classes were added during the 1860s. By 1870 the college was devoting a special section of its catalog to "departments for practical study," which included a physiological laboratory taught by John Burdon Sanderson, in which microscopes and "other requisite apparatus" were available, as well as a practical anatomy room and a "spacious laboratory" in chemistry for "senior pupils."[63]

A similar evolution was taking place in Edinburgh, where John Hughes Bennett had been teaching a class in "practical physiology" since 1862. Within three years of beginning the course, students were being examined for degrees in physiology "by means of the Microscope [and] by practical Demonstration of apparatus used for Physiological researches."[64] In its organization, which was most like that of the German

60. General Medical Council, *Report of the Committee on Professional Education (1864)* (London: General Medical Council, 1864), 5.

61. General Medical Council, *Report of the Committee on Professional Education (1869)* (London: General Medical Council, 1869), xi, xvii, 17.

62. George Harley to Dean Jenner, March 11, 1857, Faculty of Medicine correspondence, file 243–61, University College London Archive.

63. University College, London, *Calendar, session MDCCCLXX-LXXI* (London, 1870), 83–85.

64. Minutes of medical faculty, June 28, 1865, University of Edinburgh Archive.

universities, the University of Edinburgh provided an environment for the scientific development of medicine that, however unappreciated by contemporaries, made it the most congenial in Britain until at least 1870.[65]

Here and there, other medical schools offered limited opportunities for laboratory work by the end of the 1860s. Some students in Manchester had access to the laboratories at Owens College, where H. E. Roscoe was building "the biggest and very probably the best school of chemistry in the country."[66] A physiological laboratory had been started at Kings College in London, where William Rutherford was "committed to the development of physiology as the basis of an education in medical science."[67] More modest efforts were under way at Guy's, St. Bartholomew's, and St. Thomas's.

The medical school in Liverpool, too, appointed a demonstrator of histology in 1869 "in connection with the Lectures in Physiology" as part of an effort "to extend in every way, the various practical classes."[68] Even Anderson's Medical School in Glasgow announced an evening class on "Practical Chemistry in the Laboratory" in the fall of 1870.[69] At Oxford and Cambridge, courses and scholarships in natural science were increasingly open to students of medicine. The Regius Professor of Medicine at Oxford, Henry Acland, had taken the lead in building a scientific museum to house laboratories and museums that would help restore the university's reputation for scientific work.[70]

Reformers, of course, belittled these efforts as insignificant, and historians have generally followed their lead. The controversial Huxley, for example, ignoring the groundswell of support for the reform of medical teaching in Britain, told London students in 1870 that British teaching was hopelessly behind that of the Continent and that physiology was still taught "as if it were a mere matter of books and of hearsay."[71] Like William Henry Welch in America a decade or two later, Huxley championed the cause of pedagogical reform as if he and his associates were writ-

65. Geison, "Social and Institutional Factors," 56–57. An anecdotal account of the beginnings of British physiology by Michael Foster, "Reminiscences of a Physiologist," can be found in *Colorado Medical Journal* 6 (1900): 419–29.

66. D. S. L. Cardwell, "The Development of Scientific Research in Modern Universities: A Comparative Study of Motives and Opportunities," in *Scientific Change*, ed. A. C. Crombie (New York: Basic Books, 1963), 669.

67. Steven W. Sturdy, "A Co-ordinated Whole: The Life and Work of John Scott Haldane" (Ph.D. diss., University of Edinburgh, 1987), 80.

68. Minutes, Liverpool Royal Infirmary Medical School, December 11, 1869, University of Liverpool Archive.

69. Records, Anderson's University Medical School, session 1870–71, University of Glasgow Archive.

70. Charles Newman, *The Evolution of Medical Education in the Nineteenth Century* (Oxford: Oxford University Press, 1957), 279.

71. Thomas H. Huxley, "On Medical Education," in Thomas H. Huxley, *Critiques and Addresses of Thomas Henry Huxley* (New York: D. Appleton, 1887), 61.

ing on a *tabula rasa* bereft of any hopeful signs of changes. The judgment of Burdon Sanderson in 1871—that "so much has been already accomplished affords encouragement [that] a dozen years of good work would place us again side by side with Germany"—though overoptimistic, was probably closer to the mark than the somber pronouncements of Huxley and the reformers.[72]

And what about America? To those who glimpsed the pedagogical revolution occurring in Germany after 1850, the future of laboratory instruction in medicine in their own country must have seemed as remote as it did in Britain. "We have nothing in America like these laboratory courses," Welch wrote from Strasbourg as late as 1876; "in New York physiology is taught only by lectures, here there is an excellent physiological laboratory where one can do all the experiments and study the subject practically."[73] By this time, Americans had been coming for a quarter-century in ever larger numbers to the medical schools and clinics of central Europe.

Almost all of them had gone to the clinical centers of Vienna and Berlin, just as their predecessors had gone to Paris, to learn practical methods of diagnosis and treatment in the growing specialties.[74] Inevitably, many became aware of the growing use of the laboratory in German pedagogy, though few had direct personal experience in it. Some sensed the pedagogical importance of the shift toward natural science even as they enrolled in numerous private courses to learn the practical applications of laboratory study. "It has been more than I expected," wrote Henry Ingersoll Bowditch of his experience in Vienna in 1859. "I have learned much, not perhaps in particular facts as in more enlightened general views of [matters] about which I knew little or nothing before."[75] The Detroit surgeon Theodore McGraw, returning from a lengthy sojourn in Germany in the early 1860s, was likewise struck by the contrast with teaching methods at home and lamented that more American schools did not follow the example of the University of Michigan in requiring a laboratory course (in chemistry) for graduation in medicine.[76]

By the end of the Civil War in 1865, a steady stream of Americans were arriving in Vienna and other German cities to join, in the words of John

72. J. Burdon Sanderson, "Physiological Laboratories in Great Britain," *Nature* 3 (1871): 189.

73. William H. Welch to sister, June 18, 1876, Welch Papers, Alan M. Chesney Medical Archives, Johns Hopkins University.

74. Thomas N. Bonner, *American Doctors and German Universities: A Chapter in International Intellectual Relations, 1870–1914* (Lincoln: University of Nebraska Press, Landmark edition, 1987), 71–73.

75. Letter of May 30, 1859, in *Life and Correspondence of Henry Ingersoll Bowditch*, 2 vols. (Boston: Houghton Mifflin, 1902), 1:316.

76. Theodore A. McGraw, "The Medical Schools of the Last Half-Century," *Journal of the Michigan State Medical Society* 14 (1915): 516.

Collins Warren, the "colony of American students already there."[77] Warren himself, while enrolling in a number of private, how-to courses in obstetrics, dermatology, auscultation, and laryngoscopy, also enlisted in a laboratory course in pathological anatomy.[78]

The early reaction of Americans such as Warren to their study in Germany reflected the realities at home. Their interest was overwhelmingly clinical and focused on the advantages of Vienna and Berlin. The pioneer American ophthalmologists Hasket Derby and Edward L. Holmes, for example, wrote enthusiastically in the early 1860s of their impressions of the popular Viennese clinics, the easy access to hospital wards, and the unprecedented opportunities for students to gain hands-on experience, but neither made any reference to the laboratory instruction of students.[79] American medical schools of these years operated under the same constraints that held back the inauguration of scientific courses and laboratory instruction in Britain: their overwhelmingly professional purpose, their divorce from the natural science departments of universities or liberal arts colleges, the reliance on busy practitioners for teaching, and their dependence on student fees.

In both countries, the resistance to change was also linked to serious doubts about the utility of laboratory instruction for medical practice. German arguments about the practical uses of such instruction for both the student and the state carried less weight in the competitive, laissez-faire, educationally divided world of Anglo-America. Neither country was yet able to demand a thorough educational or scientific preparation for medicine. Indeed, so low were the standards for admission to medical school in the United States, declared the AMA Committee on Education in 1858, that even the existing didactic courses in physiology, albeit "beautiful" and "so important," would be ten times more valuable if students only had the educational background and time to digest them.[80]

Physiology was taught in both Britain and America largely by means of formal lectures supplemented by demonstrations that gave students an opportunity to see for themselves. As in Britain, courses in microscopy in the United States and Canada, in which students learned the use of the instrument in studying anatomy and physiology, were not uncommon. At the rural school in Woodstock, Vermont, for example, several achromatic microscopes were being used for teaching as early as 1849 in order that "*all* the students will be enabled to become familiar with most of the

---

77. John Collins Warren to mother, October 16, 1867, Warren Papers, Massachusetts Historical Society.

78. John Collins Warren to J. M. Warren, October 8, 1866, ibid.

79. Hasket Derby, "Medical Advantages of Vienna for American Students," *Boston Medical and Surgical Journal* 63 (1860): 51–53; Edward L. Holmes, "Clinical Instruction in the Hospitals of Vienna," *Boston Medical and Surgical Journal* 67 (1863): 520–23.

80. James R. Wood, "Report of the Special Committee on Medical Education," *Transactions of the American Medical Association* 11 (1858): 559–60.

elementary structures and several of the leading physiological phenom-ena."[81]

Few educators, however, believed that it was practicable or even useful in American conditions to allow students to perform experiments them-selves. "In this country," explained the surgeon Henry Bigelow in 1871,

> the teacher . . . has no more right to employ the time of the ignorant student . . . in the pleasant and seductive paths of laboratory experi-mentation, because some of these may one day lead to Pathology or Therapeutics, than a guardian has to invest the money of his ward in stocks or securities of equally uncertain prospective value.[82]

The research by the few teachers who undertook experimental work was carried out at their own expense in their office or workplace at home. Those Americans who had worked in the laboratories of such men as Claude Bernard, notably John Dalton and Weir Mitchell, were more prone then others to use experiments and even vivisection in their class-rooms but were no more likely than their British counterparts were to see laboratory instruction as a practicable option for an American medical school.[83]

How was it, then, that in both Britain and North America the tide began to turn in favor of laboratory and scientific teaching during the decade of the 1870s? In France, too, the first important steps were taken to create new universities, loosen the highly centralized structure of med-ical education, reunite scientific and professional education in medicine, and build teaching laboratories on the model of their Germanic rivals. What common impulse underlay the nearly simultaneous move to strengthen the scientific foundations of medicine in such disparate politi-cal environments as France's Third Republic, post–Civil War America, a united imperial Germany, and a Victorian Britain at the zenith of its po-litical and economic power? It is this watershed of the 1870s—and the ensuing fight for the curriculum—that is the subject of the next chapter.

81. Frederick C. Waite, *The Story of a Country Medical College* (Montpellier: Vermont Historical Society, 1945), 114. Emphasis is in original.

82. Henry J. Bigelow, "Medical Education in America," *Proceedings of the Massachusetts Medical Society* 11 (1874): 219–20.

83. Robert G. Frank Jr., "American Physiologists in German Laboratories, 1865–1914," in *Physiology in the American Context, 1850–1940*, ed. Gerald L. Geison (Bethesda, MD: American Philosophical Society, 1987), 13–15.

10

The Laboratory Versus the Clinic: The Fight for the Curriculum, 1870–1890

What was most compelling in the case for science in medicine after 1870 were the stunning achievements in laboratory medicine by that time. During the preceding decades, the work of laboratory scientists, especially in France and Germany, had brought a far more sophisticated understanding of the physical and chemical makeup and functioning of the human body and had produced a host of new tests, instruments, and techniques that were being increasingly used to study the sick patient. The role of bacteria in fermentation and then in wound pus had been demonstrated in the years preceding 1870, and they were now claimed to be responsible for a number of specific diseases. These discoveries, in turn, stimulated a great burst of energy in surgery, eventually gave a new and more certain basis to public health work, infused new optimism into the search for pharmacological remedies, and opened up new possibilities of protection against illness through deliberate immunization. Virtually no subject in the medical curriculum was untouched by the changes in medical knowledge, as dozens of new courses were created to teach the new viewpoints in disease.

The new viewpoints were deemed necessary for students to master, even though they had as yet little impact on therapy. Contrary to some later critics, medicine has always been more than the simple application of "cures" to human ailments. For thousands of years as well as in our own time, the understanding of disease, its origins and causes, its transmission, and its prevention, prognosis, and palliation have been principal reasons for consulting a physician. In the years around 1870, in particular, science made enormous gains in understanding ancient afflictions and was gaining in ways to control, alleviate, and, in a few cases, to cure them. Was science important to medicine in these years, despite the slow pace of therapeutic change? Indeed it was, even if much of ordinary medical practice, especially the healing of many illnesses, was not immediately affected by what students learned.

The Axis of the 1870s

The rapid-fire developments of these years created a vision of an experimentally based, irresistible medical science that would soon sweep all doubts before it. No longer did it seem necessary to justify laboratory training and scientific study by their practical uses alone, since the possibilities for improving medicine and hence human life seemed obvious and unlimited. Physicians in every country began to talk openly of medicine as a "science," relishing the new authority that came with a term normally reserved for such exact sciences as mathematics and astronomy.

The enthusiasm was infectious. In the entire transatlantic world, not only in Germany, came a new hope for medicine's future. At Guy's Hospital in London, students talked in 1872 of the possibilities of their doing "original research" and solemnly resolved that more scientific study was indispensable to "those, who, of all, should be Men of Science—the Students of Medicine."[1] In far-off Kansas, the practically trained physicians of that state agreed the same year that "the scientific method of the present age is different . . . [it] collects all the facts . . . illustrates if practicable by actual experiment, discusses the laws of phenomena . . . until all the facts crystallize."[2] In Wichita, a group of doctors met daily for two hours, each bringing his own microscope, to study and discuss pathological specimens.[3]

This enthusiasm for the possibilities of science in medicine coincided in time with a vast increase in the industrializing countries' wealth and a sharp rise in the demand for well-trained physicians. The heavy cost of laboratory training no longer seemed so onerous a burden in relation to its benefits as it once did. Educational levels were climbing, too, in all the major countries, and it was now practicable to consider higher levels of preparation, especially in science, for medical study.

A number of political crises in the transatlantic nations contributed to the sense of urgency and hence to the need to reconsider old patterns and institutions, much as the revolutionary disturbances of the late eighteenth century had been a fertile seedbed for educational reform. France,

1. *Guy's Hospital Gazette*, December 7, 1872, p. 41, and January 24, 1874, p. 129.
2. *Transactions of the Fifth Annual Meeting of the Kansas Academy of Science* 1 (1872): 3.
3. D. Basham, "Some Observations on the Early Medical History of Wichita," *Medical Bulletin* (Wichita) 6 (1936): 8.

overwhelmed and embittered by a humiliating defeat at the hands of Prussia in 1870, was desperately searching for ways to rebuild its educational and scientific strength. It was the German university, declared Louis Pasteur, Ernest Renan, and others, that had won the war against France.[4] Germany itself—now united, increasingly industrialized, and facing an uncertain future—moved to create an imperial structure of control that, among other changes, included physicians' study, their qualifications to practice, and the creation of a new model university in conquered Strasbourg. In the United States, the long and devastating Civil War and a major transformation of the economy produced opportunities to reconstruct the country along national lines. By the end of the 1870s, a wave of social and institutional change was sweeping over higher education in America with profound implications for training in medicine.

The German University at Its Zenith

In its organization, spirit, faculties, and scientific output, the German university reached the apogee of its influence in the 1870s. Here were teachers—Waldeyer, His, and Kölliker in anatomy; Ludwig, DuBois-Reymond, Brücke, and Pflüger in physiology; Hoppe-Seyler, Voit, and Kühne in biochemistry; Virchow, Recklinghausen, Cohnheim, Weigert, and Klebs in pathology; Frerichs, Traube, Wunderlich, and Kussmaul in medicine; Volkmann, Langenbeck, Kocher, and Billroth in surgery; and Graefe, Arlt, Hebra, Politzer, and Meynert in the specialties—who were unequaled in their reputation for original investigation and medical teaching.

Foreign visitors carried back glowing accounts of the way in which German faculties filled important vacancies by encouraging widespread applications for each post and then nominating several of the best-qualified persons, often on the basis of their research accomplishments, before the state authorities made a final choice. Visitors were struck, too, by the rigorous, comprehensive theoretical and practical medical examinations and by the faculty's unwonted autonomy in educational affairs. "In a word," marveled the Harvard surgeon Henry Bigelow in 1871,

> a medical school virtually appointed and carried on by medical men . . . a system of guaranteeing to the soundest teacher the widest reputation and the largest classes . . . and holding out as its final prize, a permanent tenure of its highest offices . . . such are the elements of the great success of modern German medical education.[5]

---

4. Theodore Zeldin, *France, 1848–1945*, 2 vols. (Oxford: Clarendon Press, 1977), 2:320.

5. Henry J. Bigelow, *Medical Education in America* (Cambridge, MA: Welch, Bigelow, 1871), 67–75. This paragraph is adapted from my *American Doctors and German Universities: A Chapter in International Intellectual Relations, 1870–1914* (Lincoln: University of Nebraska Press, Landmark edition, 1987), 14–15.

Bismarck's triumph in unifying the German states into a single *Reich* brought the end of differing state requirements for the educational preparation of physicians. New national standards of medical education and practice, modeled principally after Prussia's regime and putting new emphasis on scientific study, replaced the regulations of the individual states. According to a statute of 1869—enacted after the defeat of Austria and the formation of the North German Confederation—the minimal requirements for taking the state examination in medicine throughout Germany were now a diploma (*abitur*) from a classical secondary school (*gymnasium*), four years of medical study in a university including two semesters in medical and surgical clinics, and the independent delivery of four infants.

The national examination for licensing now included a section on the basic medical sciences; written and clinical tests of a student's knowledge of medicine, surgery, ophthalmology, obstetrics, and gynecology; and a final oral interview. The examination in basic science, given to four students at a time, involved the answering of extemporaneous questions, the preparation of pathological specimens, a practical exercise in histology and physiology, and a demonstration of the use of the microscope in examining anatomical and physiological specimens.

For the clinical subjects, the student was assigned the care of six patients (two each in medicine, surgery, and gynecology) for a period of eight days, during which he was quizzed about his diagnoses, recommended treatments and prescriptions, and knowledge of surgical procedures. Dissection of a cadaver or a part of one was also required, whereas demonstrations of surgical operations on a corpse were "recommended." In obstetrics, the student was given responsibility for one birth during the examination period and was required to demonstrate delivery procedures on an anatomical model.[6] In no other country were such uniformly high standards for practice found before the twentieth century.

In 1872 came a dramatic, if insensitive, demonstration of the power of German scientific medicine in the opening of an imperial university in the former French medical center of Strasbourg. The new medical school, inaugurated with great fanfare as a showcase of German superiority, was given immense resources, especially in science, and was placed along with the university under the direct supervision of Chancellor Otto von Bismarck. Local residents were informed by authorities that existing French schools in medicine and other fields—contemptuously referred to by German authorities as *Fachschulen*, or trade schools—were to be disbanded and absorbed into the new university.[7] Advice by the Alsatian clinician and German admirer Charles Schuetzenberger that in order to be successful, the medical school, like the university, must not be patterned

---

6. *Reglemente für die Prüfung der Ärzte und Zahnärzte vom 25.September 1869* (Berlin: August Hirschwald, 1869).

7. "Gesetzblatt für Elsass-Lothringen, 28 April 1872," GSPK, Merseburg, 2.2.l., Nr. 21693.

directly on the German model was ignored. Indeed, the new institution's very raison d'être was "the expectation that it would contribute to the Germanization of the captured provinces of Alsace and Lorraine."[8]

German efforts to recruit members of the previous French faculty were largely unsuccessful. Only four medical teachers joined the German faculty, and they did not include Schuetzenberger, Victor Stoeber, or the well-known surgeon Eugène Boeckel.[9] The new medical faculty, formally appointed by the kaiser himself, represented the cream of German medical science. To teach pathology, Friedrich von Recklinghausen was lured from Würzburg, Wilhelm Waldeyer from Breslau in anatomy, Felix Hoppe-Seyler from Tübingen in physiology, and Oswald Schmiedeberg from Dorpat in pharmacology.[10] "I find it to be pretty generally acknowledged," William Henry Welch wrote from the city in 1876, "that for scientific medicine Strassburg is now better than any other German university."[11]

But however great its renown as the world's premier site for learning scientific medicine and its attraction for foreign visitors like Welch, the school failed to win over the local population, as Schuetzenberger had predicted. Not only did the great bulk of the French faculty leave Strasbourg for the new French medical school in Nancy, but also only a quarter of the new student body traced its origins to Alsace or Lorraine.[12] Clearly, the national rivalries at Strasbourg as elsewhere proved to be important factors in the shaping of modern medical education.

Reappraising Medical Training in France

More even than in Germany, the 1870s was a time of fundamental reappraisal and striking rethinking of medical teaching by educators and government officials in France. A new school of medicine, the first since the Napoleonic era, was created at Nancy to replace the lost faculty at Strasbourg, and major reforms were made in national policy toward science and medicine. The new republican government stressed especially the need to strengthen "practical work" in science at all levels and to open scientific careers for those doing original research.[13] In medicine, nearly all reformers now agreed in principle on the need to unite science and

8. John E. Craig, "A Mission for German Learning: The University of Strasbourg and Alsatian Society, 1870–1918" (Ph.D. diss., Stanford University, 1963), 4, 90–92.

9. Ibid., 250.

10. *Verzeichnis der Vorlesungen welche an der Universität Strassburg im Sommersemester 1872 von 1. Mai bis zum 15. August gehalten werden* (Strasbourg: Hertz, 1872), 1–3. See also official correspondence in GSPK, Merseburg, 2.2.1, Nr. 21693 (1871–82).

11. William H. Welch to sister, May 15, 1876, Welch Papers, Alan M. Chesney Medical Archives, Johns Hopkins University.

12. Craig, "Mission for German Learning," 343, table 4.

13. Georg Weisz, "Reform and Conflict in French Medical Education, 1870–1914," in *The Organization of Science and Technology in France, 1808–1914*, ed. Robert Fox and Georg Weisz (Cambridge: Cambridge University Press, 1980), 69.

practical teaching and thus to end the long-standing division between the clinic and the laboratory in France. Criticisms of hospital-based teaching and its isolation from the rest of medical instruction grew swiftly during the decade.[14]

The failure to develop in France the wide variety of clinical specialties being offered in the German universities came under especially withering attack. This was attributed to the effects of the *concours* and the separation of hospital teaching from that of the medical school. French methods of recruiting and appointing teachers were under constant scrutiny and compared unfavorably with the German system, in which, wrote Léon Le Fort, "the professorship is a career." In France, by contrast, "one cannot live in Paris or in the provinces on the salaries paid professors alone."[15]

Faculty and governmental plans for change came hard on the heels of the French defeat. A commission created by the Paris medical faculty in 1871 reported on the widespread dissatisfaction with the methods of selecting faculty members begun during the last imperial regime."[16] The following year, the National Assembly authorized the creation of laboratories in the faculty-run clinics of Paris's principal hospitals.[17] Administrators at the Hôtel-Dieu promptly sent the dean a request for 6,790 francs for personnel and a long list of laboratory requirements, including four microscopes, a spectroscope, two balances, a laboratory table, eight thermometers, and sundry other needs.[18] Debates broke out in Lyon and other cities where new facilities were being planned, over whether future clinics should be located at the site of the medical school, as in Germany, or whether the medical school and its laboratories should be moved close to the hospital.[19] From every medical faculty came mounting demands for more laboratories and more facilities for research.

An important governmental commission headed by the medical reformer Paul Bert, himself a member of the National Assembly and a strong advocate of science, recommended successfully in 1874 that the secondary schools in Lyon and Bordeaux be converted at last into full-fledged medical faculties. Citing the lack of attention given students and their "deplorable isolation" from professors in large auditoriums and clinics, the commission called for more teachers in all schools, more personal contacts with students, and the increased use of demonstrations and labo-

14. See, for example, the discussion of criticisms in the French press in *Lyon médical* 19 (1875): 573–76.

15. Léon Le Fort, *Etude sur l'organisation de la médecine en France et à l'étranger* (Paris: Germer Baillière, 1874), 72.

16. Rapport sur la réforme des études médicales, February 10, 1871, 6, 11, Archives nationales, AJ[16] 6357.

17. Germaine Picard, "La réglementation des études médicales en France: Son évolution de la révolution à nos jours" (med. diss., University of Paris, 1967), 29.

18. Letter of December 14, 1872, Archives nationales, AJ[16] 6555.

19. *Lyon médical* 12 (1873): 73.

ratories. It approved the combining of faculties of medicine and pharmacy into "mixed" faculties at Lyon and Bordeaux, as had already been done in Nancy.

In choosing Lyon and Bordeaux as the sites of an expanded teaching enterprise in medicine, Bert emphasized the importance of their strong faculties in science and veterinary medicine and their large hospital resources. Both cities, furthermore, had pledged large sums of money for the construction and start-up costs of the new ventures.[20] The city of Lille, passed over by the Bert Commission, pleaded the cause of "northern students" who could not afford a costly education at the nearest school in Paris and expressed fears of the "seductions" that endangered students in the French capital. With the strong support of the Catholic Church and the threat of forming an independent Catholic school of medicine, the city gained the approval of the National Assembly in 1875 to build a third new faculty of medicine.[21]

The Ministry of Public Instruction and Culture was as much disturbed by the loss of French hegemony in clinical medicine as by the nation's slowness in developing teaching laboratories. Inspector General E. Chauffard headed a commission in 1875 that urged an immediate reorganization of the clinics of the Paris School of Medicine, in order to force the creation of clinical courses in the specialties, as was common in Germany and Britain. If the faculty did not cooperate, he warned, the hospitals would be encouraged to offer still more of their own courses and thus make "the present deplorable situation" still worse.

Courses in such specialized subjects as pediatrics, dermatology, syphilitic diseases, ophthalmology, and nervous disorders—because of the faculty's resistance to subdividing the large medical and surgical clinics— had grown up independently in the hospitals as "free" offerings outside the official curriculum. The hospital doctors teaching these courses, said the commission, should be eligible to become professors (*professeurs de clinique complémentaire*), without having to pass through the rigid steps normally required of those holding academic appointments.[22]

Some limited accommodation to the proposal was made by the faculty, but the separation of the two groups of teachers—those with faculty appointments and those employed by the hospital, each observing a different set of rules, teaching separate courses, and given very different emoluments and recognition—continued into the twentieth century.

Not until 1878 was practical work in the laboratory made compulsory for all medical students. The new curriculum, still four years in length, required a *baccalaureat* (diploma) from an approved secondary school in

20. Paul Bert, Rapport sur la création de nouvelles facultés de médecine presenté à l'Assemblée nationale (Paris: Delagrave, 1874), 9, 106, 117–18, 121–29, Archives nationales, AJ[16] 6357.

21. See letter and printed statement by M. Cazese, Archives nationales, AJ[16] 6685.

22. E. Chauffard, Rapport sur la réorganisation des cours complémentaire de la faculté de médecine de Paris, 1875, Archives nationales, AJ[16] 6356.

both science and letters; an initial year of work in physics, chemistry, and natural history at the medical school; laboratory work in physiology, pathology, anatomy, and histology; and the usual clinics in medicine, surgery, and obstetrics. Examinations on both classroom and laboratory instruction were now to be given at five intervals spaced over the entire course of study.[23]

By the end of the 1870s, the cumulative changes in French medical education were substantial: three new medical schools, a national budget for medical training that had been substantially raised, a considerably larger number of faculty members, better remuneration for teachers, expanded facilities, more provision for professorial research, and laboratories growing, in the words of George Weisz, "at [a] most spectacular rate."[24] "Our medical teaching," declared Chauffard in a public article in 1878, "has emerged from a long period of torpor and semi-inertia." Unlike German teaching, however, he continued, "French medicine, even that which is devoted to experiment, remains essentially clinical . . . we love less the studies of the isolated laboratory, detached from the history of disease and its therapy; we focus [instead] on the recognition of lesions and of morbid actions."[25] By identifying the clinic as the core and purpose of French medical teaching and thereby distinguishing it from the German emphasis on science, Chauffard struck a chord that resounded again and again in the future, notably in the observations on French teaching of the historian Theodor Puschmann in 1889, the foundation executive Abraham Flexner in 1912, and the medical dean Willard Rappleye in 1930.

A watershed had been reached in French medical education, although dissatisfaction remained high in many quarters. Complaints remained frequent throughout the 1870s and beyond that the new laboratories were poorly equipped, salaries were too low, and the *concours* system of choosing faculty members gave too much encouragement to "memorization of anatomical detail and rhetorical ability."[26] In addition, the extended use of the *cours complémentaires* in the hospitals, though an improvement, proved to be inadequate to solve the problem of specialized clinical teaching in France. Resentment remained high at the concentration of teaching, academic distinction, and research in Paris. The author of an American guidebook summarized a common judgment among visitors on Parisian teaching when he described it as "so much less satisfactory than in Germany," "rather didactic" in character, and largely passive, since "students take no active part in the clinic." The lectures given at the

23. Décret portant règlement d'administration publique déterminant les conditions d'études exigées, des aspirans au grade de docteur en médecine, June 20, 1878, Archives nationales, AJ[16] 6356.

24. Weisz, "Reform and Conflict," 69–77.

25. E. Chauffard, "De la situation de l'enseignement médical en France," *Revue des deux mondes*, 1878, pp. 165–66.

26. Weisz, "Reform and Conflict," 77.

medical school, he added, were "either unillustrated or are illustrated by drawings and models."[27]

The 1870s in Great Britain

In Britain and America, no less than on the Continent, the decade of the 1870s was the most significant period of change since early in the century. The fulcrum of action, different from that of France or Germany, was not the power of the state but instead was an independent and voluntary effort. In Britain, wrote the American John Shaw Billings in 1878, "all that the government undertakes is to publish an authentic list of qualified practitioners, and to define the minimum of qualifications which should entitle a physician to be recorded on this list."[28] Although this understated the efforts of the General Medical Council to bring about change, the council itself was to a large degree the representative of private interests. Of its twenty-three members in 1879, only six were appointed by the Crown, nine represented the medical corporations, and eight were from the universities of Great Britain and Ireland.[29]

By this time, the council—claiming such reform-minded members as James Syme, George Paget, Henry Acland, Robert Christison, and William Sharpey—had achieved some limited success in bringing cooperation among the regulatory bodies in the form of conjoint examinations and had issued guidelines on minimal requirements in natural science for licensure. The conduct of joint examinations by the licensing groups, long sought by reformers in Britain, was finally agreed to in both England and Scotland in the 1880s and became the most common route to licensure by the end of the century. The *conjoint examination*, as it was called, was often the only avenue open to women excluded from the universities to qualify as medical practitioners.

The council also urged now a definite order of medical studies, ranging from courses in preparatory science to clinical teaching. A number of the examining bodies had made laboratory courses in chemistry and physics, as well as those in physiology and pathology, compulsory for future students.[30]

27. Henry Hun, *A Guide to American Medical Students in Europe* (New York: William Wood, 1883), 97, 99.

28. John Shaw Billings, "Higher Medical Education," *American Journal of the Medical Sciences* 76 (1878): 184.

29. House of Commons, Select Committee on Medical Act, *Special Report from the Select Committee, together with the Proceedings of the Committee, Minutes of Evidence, Appendix, and Index* (London: House of Commons, 1879), 1–2.

30. D. R. Haldane, General Medical Council, to Board of Medical Studies, Cambridge, November 11, 1880, University of Cambridge Archive; June Jones, "Science, Utility and the 'Second City of the Empire': The Sciences and Especially the Medical Sciences at Liverpool University, 1881–1925" (Ph.D. diss., University of Manchester, 1989), 149–50.

The Royal College of Surgeons, for example, beginning in 1870, required all candidates to attend "a practical course of general anatomy and physiology," in which "the learners themselves shall individually be engaged in the necessary experiments, manipulations, &c." This sweeping requirement, quickly adopted by the University of London, "may have been," in the words of one careful student, "the single most important factor in the transformation of late Victorian physiology."[31] For both Britain and Germany, students of medicine were the principal target of efforts to create a market for the new laboratory courses in physiology and other fields. That such an action, forcing a large majority of future practitioners to work in the laboratory, was taken by such a practical, professional body as the College of Surgeons is yet further testimony of the immense power of the scientific ideal by 1870.

In order to promote work in laboratory science, the hard-pressed medical schools of the English provinces sought union with the burgeoning regional universities in the manufacturing and commercial centers of the Midlands and northern England. These civic universities, principally modeling themselves after the University of London and the universities of Germany, emphasized from the outset the scientific and technological subjects and also cooperation with local industry. Some of these universities, such as those in Leeds and Birmingham, initially attempted to exclude the humanities altogether from the curriculum.[32] By the end of the 1870s, schools of science and technology were flourishing in Manchester, Newcastle, Leeds, Bristol, Sheffield, Birmingham, and Liverpool, making the period, according to Michael Sanderson, "arguably the most active of the whole century in university development."[33]

In 1870, in Manchester, the Royal Medical School was joined to one of these schools, Owens College, and three years later a full-time appointment in physiology urged by Thomas Huxley was made.[34] The person appointed to the post, Arthur Gangee, had ambitions to "emulate the example of continental Europe, especially Leipzig—and in England ... University College London and the University of Cambridge." Gangee had serious problems attracting advanced students and financing his teaching laboratory, however.[35] In 1881, for example, he complained

31. Gerald L. Geison, *Michael Foster and the Cambridge School of Physiology: The Scientific Enterprise in Late Victorian Society* (Princeton, NJ: Princeton University Press, 1978), 151.

32. Peter Alter, *The Reluctant Patron: Science and the State in Britain, 1850–1920* (Oxford: Berg, 1987), 28–29.

33. Michael Sanderson, *The Universities in the Nineteenth Century* (London: Routledge & Kegan Paul, 1975), 142–43.

34. Jones, "Science, Utility and the 'Second City'," 150; see also the references to T. H. Huxley in Reports to the Court of Governors and Minutes of the Court of the Owens College, manuscript, Manchester Collection, F4li, Rylands Library, University of Manchester.

35. Arthur Gangee, *Studies from the Physiological Laboratory at Owens College* (Cambridge: Cambridge University Press, 1877), 1. The references to Cambridge and University College London are discussed in the pages ahead.

about "the difficulties in conducting practical work in physiology" at Manchester and the lack of financial support, to which the university's senate responded by suggesting a special student fee for using a microscope.[36]

Meanwhile at Leeds, the teaching of chemistry to medical students was transferred to the Yorkshire College of Science in 1875, followed by the shift of botany and then comparative anatomy to the college three years later. A similar arrangement was made in Sheffield, in which the Royal Infirmary Medical School was amalgamated into the new University College in that city.[37]

At all these schools the administrators scrambled to strengthen their offerings in science. At Leeds, for example, the governing council resolved in 1871 to allocate £60 for microscopes and £20 for apparatus, after beating back an amendment to require students to furnish their own microscopes. The following year, a full-time lecturer on pathology was appointed to replace "the present desultory way of teaching Pathological Anatomy." In 1875 the professor of physiology at the school reported that his workroom could be converted, "with certain alterations," into "a convenient room for the teaching of practical physiology."[38] Similarly, the medical school in Liverpool raised enough money from private sources to erect two new chemistry laboratories and an "urgently required Physiological laboratory."[39]

Everywhere after 1870 the laboratory study of physiology, crucial to medicine's claim to scientific status, began to make gains. At Cambridge, Oxford, Edinburgh, and London, as well as in the new regional universities, steps were taken to build laboratories, appoint full-time teachers, and reorient medical education around a core of scientific study. Even the practical schools attached to hospitals provided a modicum of laboratory instruction. In many places, the teacher of physiology became the first full-time teacher in the medical school.[40]

Students of William Sharpey at the University College of London, notably Michael Foster, John Burdon Sanderson, and Edward Shäfer, were now able to find the opportunities they sought. All of them found opportunities to establish physiological laboratories or institutes at which medical students could be taught and research could be undertaken. As in

36. Senate Minutes, Owens Extension College, February 14, 1874 and March 12, 1881, University Archive, Manchester.

37. Jones, "Science, Utility and the 'Second City'," 150–51.

38. Leeds School of Medicine, Minutes of Council, July 22, 1871, June 22, 1872, July 29, 1875, University of Leeds Archive.

39. Henry A. Ormerod, *The Early History of the Liverpool Medical School from 1834 to 1877* (Liverpool: C. Tinling, 1954), 48–49.

40. Stella V. F. Butler, "Science and the Education of Doctors in the Nineteenth Century: A Study of British Medical Schools with Particular Reference to the Development and Uses of Physiology" (Ph.D. diss., University of Manchester, 1981), 67–68.

Germany, the pedagogical purpose of the new laboratories was "to train future practitioners in scientific method."[41]

Laboratory science in medical education was thus gaining a foothold in Britain as it simultaneously was in other countries. If the hold was so far less powerful in Britain (and America) than it was on the European continent, it was nevertheless firm and became increasingly so toward the end of the century. An "intellectual revolution," said Michael Foster in 1878, was under way, and educators must find a way to control "the advancing flood of knowledge."[42]

Foster's own work at Cambridge, where he began teaching in 1870, benefited from the support of sympathetic colleagues—"the revolution of the dons"—who favored the new outlook on experimental science. Many of them admired as much as Foster did the scientific and medical achievements of Germany. Three years after his arrival at Cambridge, he announced a "practical course" in anatomy and physiology in which students would spend three times as much time in the laboratory as listening to lectures. The announcement, in the words of one authority, "marks the beginning of a new epoch in the teaching of biology in the English universities."[43] For the rest of his career Foster expended most of his energy in teaching such elementary courses, and former students were put in charge of advanced instruction. Enrollment in his courses in elementary physiology rose steadily from twenty at the beginning to more than one hundred in 1882.[44]

By 1878 Foster was calling for the establishment of a full medical school at Cambridge that would not train "ordinary practitioners," as London did, but "send into the world the best trained and most able doctors possible."[45] Such "best-trained" doctors, it was clear, would be university graduates steeped in the uses of science and the laboratory, much like the graduates of the "new university . . . now taking shape in Baltimore," described by John Shaw Billings that same year in an American publication.[46]

Foster's work at the University of London, after his departure for Cambridge, was taken over by John Burdon Sanderson, who had already acquired a reputation for scientific investigation. Soon after his appointment, he notified the authorities of University College that the growing enrollment in practical physiology made necessary a large increase in laboratory space. "It is obvious that a system of teaching of which it is the fundamental principle that the student should himself perform the exer-

41. Ibid., 160.

42. Michael Foster, *On Medical Education at Cambridge* (London: Macmillan, 1878), 4.

43. Geison, *Michael Foster*, 117. I am indebted to Geison's account for much of this paragraph.

44. Ibid., 173, table 1.

45. Foster, *Medical Education*, 20.

46. Billings, "Higher Medical Education," 189.

cises," he wrote, required *"that each student should have his own place for working*—his own stool and table."[47] A new laboratory was promptly constructed that could accommodate fifty students. Around Sanderson's growing reputation as a teacher and researcher, University College built a cadre of laboratory investigators and students in the 1870s and 1880s. In 1883, however, Sanderson left for Oxford where he attempted, with less success than at London or Cambridge, to build a teaching and research program in physiology.

Elsewhere in London, William Rutherford was named professor of physiology at King's College in 1869 and proceeded to stimulate course work in practical physiology. While on a trip to laboratories in Europe in the summer of 1870, he wrote reminders in his notebook to "do this experiment before my class" (at Paul Bert's laboratory in Paris) and "get this made. It is quite simple" (of Ludwig's sphygmograph in Leipzig).[48] Apparently Rutherford did rely heavily on demonstrations in his own laboratory teaching, reporting in 1871 that "full-scale student participation in the experimental work" was as yet "impracticable and undesirable."[49]

In the hospital schools of London, where the teaching continued to be professionally oriented, the changes were less sweeping (as in America's practical schools), but accommodations were nevertheless made to the new requirements of the College of Surgeons. Increasingly, the hospitals themselves broke with tradition to furnish all or part of the monies needed to build laboratories and other facilities.

The Scottish universities, long cognizant of the importance of theoretical teaching, also moved to meet the changing requirements in science being pressed on them by the General Medical Council and by their determination to keep up with their English rivals. The earlier openness of the Scottish system to students of varying backgrounds gave way to more stringent demands on students to come to the university better prepared and to order their studies more carefully after their arrival. A new degree in science, together with an independent science faculty, was introduced at Glasgow in 1871. More provision was made, too, for laboratories and the financial support of professors' research at all the Scottish schools.

In Edinburgh, major new medical facilities were begun in 1877.[50] William Rutherford, who saw physiology as the foundation stone for all training in medicine, had come to Edinburgh three years earlier to replace the aging John Hughes Bennett. Under Rutherford's leadership, laboratory courses in physiology were expanded, and new laboratories in anatomy, pathology, and pharmacology were opened by the early 1880s. All these new studies were justified by "a rhetoric of scientific reform"

47. John Burdon Sanderson to Council, University College, April 1872, copy in William Sharpey Papers, Archive, University College of London. Emphasis in original.
48. Notebook, 1870, William Rutherford Papers, University of Edinburgh Archive.
49. *Lancet*, 1871, p. 707.
50. Butler, "Science and the Education of Doctors," 95–103.

that promised "a new rational basis for medical practice."[51] For many, Edinburgh remained an attractive site for the scientific teaching of medicine.

America in the 1870s

On the other side of the Atlantic, none of the transforming events in Britain or in Germany went unnoticed. More and more of the Americans who went abroad were now venturing beyond Vienna and other clinical centers to experience working in a laboratory. Although they were only a small proportion of those seeking training abroad, scores of Americans spent several months or more in a German laboratory. A number of them, including Welch, John J. Abel, and Franklin Mall, were still considering working in clinical medicine when they went abroad but discovered while there the exciting world of laboratories and opportunities for scientific work.

As Welch wrote to Mall's biographer, "Mall went to Germany for clinical work, as so many young American doctors were accustomed to do and without any particular interest in science. It was his contact with [Wilhelm] His and especially with Ludwig which opened his eyes to the sciences of anatomy and physiology."[52] Like Henry P. Bowditch, Welch, Charles Minot, Russell Chittenden, and others, Mall became a zealous advocate of the scientific basis of medicine and an apostle of inductive laboratory teaching. By the end of his stay in Germany, Mall was confiding to his sister in almost religious terms that he had "changed ideas materially as regards the objects of life. I think it is a sin to seek pleasure only . . . the highest mark should be usefulness . . . . My aim is to make scientific medicine a life work."[53]

The nation to which these men returned in the 1870s was dramatically different from the divided agricultural country of the antebellum years. Social and institutional changes were being instituted across American higher education. The acceleration of industrial reorganization after the Civil War strengthened the demand for technical and scientific education. Large fortunes were accumulating that were sometimes used to promote existing colleges or to create new universities. Sixty new colleges sprang up after the passage of the Land-Grant Act of 1862 to offer broad technical and scientific training and instruction in agriculture. New student populations, new subjects, and new demands for professional training pushed hard on the doors of the traditional American college. In a single

51. Steven W. Sturdy, "A Co-ordinated Whole: The Life and Work of John Scott Haldane" (Ph.D. diss., University of Edinburgh, 1987), 83.

52. Florence R. Sabin, *Franklin Paine Mall: The Story of a Mind* (Baltimore: Johns Hopkins University Press, 1934), 29.

53. Ibid., 64.

generation, the long pent-up drive for reform broke through the wall of resistance to create a new type of American university at Cornell, Harvard, Johns Hopkins, Michigan, Yale, Wisconsin, and Chicago. It was this transformation of the nation's system of higher education after 1870, along with the concurrent growth of secondary education and medical philanthropy—as Kenneth Ludmerer emphasized—that created the institutional framework within which the long sought-for reforms in medical education could occur.[54]

It would be a mistake, however, to play down the importance of the long years of preparation for change. For half a century, voices had been raised, ever louder, in favor of longer periods of study, better preparation, more academic training, new courses in science, and higher standards of practice. No more than the advent of clinical training in France or the laboratory movement in Germany did the changes in American medical study spring anew at a given moment in time. As they were in other nations and at other times, the developments of these years were subsequently described chiefly by the remarkable men who themselves struggled to gain a foothold in the shifting grounds of medical education and to shape career opportunities for themselves. If read critically in the context of their time, the reports by the American Medical Association before 1870 were unusually progressive documents reflecting a readiness for change despite discouraging conditions in an important part of the medical profession.

When change did come, as it did in the 1870s, it benefited greatly from the very looseness and chaotic conditions in education that prevailed. Here were no established royal corporations as in Britain to hold back change, no powerful clerical interests as in France to protect the status of rural doctors, and no professorial mandarate as in Germany to put a brake on further curricular experimentation.

Once committed to the process of change, the American profession and its academic leaders faced only the daunting task of pushing its program through the maze of American federalism. Yet even here, once the barriers to cooperation across sectarian medical boundaries were breached in the 1870s, a number of the states—Kentucky, Missouri, Louisiana, Kansas, Illinois—began to pass laws similar to the British registration statutes of twenty years before. The Illinois law of 1877, for example, which was seen by contemporaries as the most advanced of the period, was the first to give state examiners the power to reject diplomas that did not meet its minimal standards, thereby causing 40 percent of the state's practitioners, according to a subsequent report, to leave the state.[55]

After so many years of fruitless effort to find a common medical standard, the decade of the 1870s was a time of both deep pessimism about

54. Kenneth M. Ludmerer, *Learning to Heal: The Development of American Medical Education* (New York: Basic Books, 1985), 38–46, 191–206.

55. Thomas N. Bonner, *Medicine in Chicago, 1850–1950: A Chapter in the Social and Scientific Development of a City*, 2nd ed. (Urbana: University of Illinois Press, 1991), 234.

further change and a fresh hopefulness based on the new developments. The Civil War, which had closed southern schools and brought a shortage of teachers and students to the north, was followed by the establishment of more freestanding medical schools that threatened to postpone still further the day of effective regulation. Twenty-one new schools were added to the number of regular schools between 1867 and 1877, making a total of forty-four, while twenty-nine schools of homeopathy, eclectic, and botanic medicine were open to students in 1877. Many of these schools, it should be said, were small and accounted for only a small percentage of medical graduates. Still, as late as 1900, five hundred students were graduating each year from the homeopathic and eclectic schools. By that time, five thousand Americans were graduating from all the schools of medicine, more than from the schools of Britain, Germany, and France combined.[56]

Discouraged proponents of reform voiced new levels of frustration and discontent. "What is the value of a medical degree?" asked a Kansas journal in 1868, and answered its own question: "Nothing–absolutely *nothing*!"[57] In New Orleans, the professor of physiology Stanford Chaillé wrote in 1874 that although his twenty years of professional experience had "increased my conviction of the importance of improvement . . . it has destroyed my hope that I might live to see it."[58] William Pepper, a reform-minded administrator at the University of Pennsylvania, described the still growing competition among medical colleges as "suicidal" and blamed the government for its failure to act.[59] And William Welch, returning from Germany in 1878, wrote his sister that a friend he had made abroad was thinking of returning to Europe for "there is no use of attempting to do anything here," and he added: "I do think that the condition of medical education here is simply horrible."[60]

Although the impatience of such critics was understandable, it seriously understated the changes already under way. By the time that Welch wrote, new efforts to unite the medical colleges in a common effort had been undertaken. Apprenticeship teaching was everywhere in sharp decline. In Chicago, a three-year graded term, as noted earlier, had been introduced at N. S. Davis's school, which was then adopted by Harvard and Pennsylvania. The state of Illinois had begun its program of medical registration by this time. New or enlarged teaching hospitals had been

---

56. *Medical News* 16 (1895): 22; Irving S. Cutter, "The School of Medicine," in *Higher Education in America*, ed. Raymond A. Kent (Boston: Ginn, 1930), 344, table VI.

57. *Leavenworth Medical Herald*, 1 (1868): 576. Emphasis in original.

58. Stanford E. Chaillé, "The Medical Colleges, the Medical Profession, and the Public," *New Orleans Medical and Surgical Journal* 11 (1874): 822.

59. William Pepper, *Higher Medical Education, The True Interest of the Public and the Profession: Two Addresses delivered before the Medical Department of the University of Pennsylvania on October 1, 1877, and October 2, 1893* (Philadelphia: Lippincott, 1894), 24, 30. The remarks cited are from his 1877 address.

60. Quoted in Simon Flexner and James T. Flexner, *William Henry Welch and the Heroic Age of American Medicine* (New York: Dover, 1941), 113.

opened in New York, Philadelphia, and Ann Arbor. In Baltimore the Johns Hopkins University had been given a faculty experienced in German methods of teaching and research. Michigan had extended its laboratory teaching and was now offering a doctorate in chemistry. And Charles Eliot had brought a whirlwind of change to the Harvard Medical School.

"The whole system of medical education in this country," Eliot declared in 1870, "needs thorough reformation. The course of professional instruction should be a progressive one covering 3 years: the Winter Session and the Summer Session should be combined; and the student should give his attendance at lectures and recitations, at hospitals and laboratories during the whole year."[61] Unlike earlier critics, Eliot acted to overcome the dependence on student fees that fueled the destructive competition, and he followed the earlier example of Michigan in making faculty salaries a university responsibility. The planned medical school in Baltimore, too, according to John Shaw Billings, would make instruction "entirely independent of students" so that it could "afford to consult their welfare instead of their wishes."[62]

Both Harvard and Hopkins planned a "first class physiological laboratory," to use Billings's term, in order to build a core of scientific teaching at the heart of the medical curriculum. A medical diploma from a good university, Billings asserted, should guarantee not only a well-educated physician but also one who "has learned to think and investigate for himself, and is therefore prepared to undertake . . . the study of some of the many problems still awaiting solution."[63] Similarly, the chemist Eliot expressed the same pedagogical insistence at Harvard on laboratory experience, especially in physiology, as a discipline for scientific, problem-solving thinking in the medical student. "The powers of observation, the inductive faculty, the sober imagination," he said in terms reminiscent of the earlier German arguments, were best cultivated in the laboratory.[64] New laboratories were constructed for physiologist Henry P. Bowditch; the number of workplaces in chemistry for Harvard students was increased to a hundred; and students were forced to spend some time in these and other laboratories.[65] As in Germany, little was said about the research uses of these laboratories, whereas much was made of their importance for medical study.

Besides Harvard and the school being planned in Baltimore, teaching laboratories in physiology and histology were organized at Pennsylvania

61. Charles W. Eliot, *Annual Report of the President of Harvard College, 1869–70* (Boston, 1870), 26.

62. Johns Hopkins Hospital, *Five Essays relating to the Construction, Organization & Management of Hospitals* (New York: William Wood, 1875), 3.

63. Ibid., 3–4.

64. "Inaugural Address," *Charles W. Eliot: The Man and His Beliefs*, ed. William A. Neilson, 2 vols. (New York: Harper, 1926), 1:6.

65. Kenneth M. Ludmerer, "Reform at Harvard Medical School, 1869–1909," *Bulletin of the History of Medicine* 55 (1981): 348.

and Michigan in 1874 and 1877, respectively.[66] At Yale as early as the
mid-1870s, Russell Chittenden was urging that the laboratory work in
physiological chemistry be incorporated into the medical curriculum.[67] At
the University of California, the progressive educator Daniel Coit Gilman
was outlining many of the ideas—the importance of scientific study to
physicians, the need for better premedical preparation, longer terms of
study, and the place of medical education in a university—that he later
carried to the Johns Hopkins School of Medicine.[68]

Although laboratory instruction in medicine, as it was in Britain, was
far from universal and scores of American schools were as yet untouched
by the change, a corner had been turned in the quest for more science in
medical study. By 1883 the aging Oliver Wendell Holmes, long numbered among the opponents of the new developments, was telling a centennial gathering at Harvard that medical study "begins with chemistry,
anatomy, physiology, and thus prepares its students for study at the bedside and in the operating-room."[69]

The Fight for the Curriculum

The years following the advent of laboratory teaching, especially after
1870, are sometimes described as the period of the relentless advance of
scientific training in medicine, culminating in the conquest of the clinic
itself by the methods of the laboratory. But this was not actually the case
in any country. Everywhere the enormous time and expense demanded
by the laboratory, together with skepticism about claims for its utility,
brought resistance from clinicians, educators, and students alike. Understandably, those whose self-interest was adversely affected by the growth
of the laboratory, notably the clinicians, were slow to surrender their
claims to a dominant place in the curriculum.

Even in Germany, the vaunted system of medical training that had won
world renown for its practical work in the clinic and then in the laboratory was in serious conflict by the 1870s. The very success of laboratory
medicine in Germany in bringing science into the curriculum brought

66. John Harley Warner, "Physiology," in *The Education of American Physicians: Historical Essays*, ed. Ronald L. Numbers (Berkeley and Los Angeles: University of California
Press, 1980), 63. For a full account of the development of physiology at Michigan, see Horace W. Davenport, "Physiology, 1850–1923: The View from Michigan," supplement to
The Physiologist 25 (1982): v–63.

67. Russell H. Chittenden, *The Development of Physiological Chemistry in the United
States*(New York: Chemical Catalog Company, 1930), 33–34.

68. Gert H. Brieger, "The California Origins of the Johns Hopkins Medical School,"
Bulletin of the History of Medicine 51 (1977): 346–50.

69. Oliver W. Holmes, "Endowment of the Harvard Medical School," in *The New Century and the New Building of the Harvard Medical School, 1783–1883* (Cambridge, MA:
Wilson, 1884), 52.

with it a steady erosion of traditional clinical teaching. "Many of the German medical leaders," in the words of a modern critic, "were attempting to reduce clinical medicine to the principles of inanimate science, physics, chemistry and mathematics," on the assumption "that all patients with a given set of measurements are alike."[70]

Conflict in Germany

The new view of medical education, corresponding to the changed outlook, gained ground steadily in Germany after 1870. Teaching in the laboratories in Germany was seen as more than a helpful adjunct to practical training at the bedside and increasingly as the principal component of a physician's training.[71] The German-trained Charles Minot, acknowledging that "I am not a physician and have never had any interest in becoming one," expressed the new German ideology of medical science when he declared in 1881 that conventional medical training "warps the mind" of the student and prevented him from seeing medicine as "only the practical application of the laws of biology."[72] His American colleague, the acerbic Franklin Mall, went further in describing the coming of science to the medical curriculum as bringing an end to "the production of shoemaker-physicians."[73]

Concerns grew swiftly in Germany that the practical instruction of the student in the clinic, long the mainstay of the nation's high reputation for medical teaching, was in jeopardy. Many clinicians and practitioners feared and resented what they saw as inordinate attention to what were now called the *basic medical sciences.* A new breed of scientifically oriented clinical teachers, led by Theodor von Frerichs of Berlin, seemed to belittle the old bedside teaching of students as the relic of a prescientific past. When building a large auditorium for 250 students in 1859, Frerichs announced that "real progress in medicine will come only at the hands of those physicians who never stray from the pathway of strict scientific research."[74] A brilliant researcher and investigator, Frerichs "had

70. Stewart Wolf, foreword to Mark D. Altschule, *Essays on the Rise and Decline of Bedside Medicine* (Bangor, PA: Totts Gap Medical Research Laboratories, 1989), vii.

71. Johanna Bleker, "Medical Students—To the Bed-side or to the Laboratory? The Emergence of Laboratory-training in German Medical Education, 1870–1900," *Clio Medica* 21 (1987–88): 36.

72. Charles S. Minot, "A Grave Defect in Our Medical Education," *Boston Medical and Surgical Journal* 105 (1881): 565.

73. Franklin P. Mall, "The Value of Research in the Medical School," *Michigan Alumnus,* 1904, 395–96.

74. Quoted in Claudia Huerkamp, *Der Aufstieg der Ärzte im 19.Jahrhundert: Vom gelehrten Stand zum professionellen Experten: Das Beispiel Preussens* (Göttingen: Vandenhoeck & Ruprecht, 1985), 97.

no interest in the individual student," according to Bernard Naunyn, who had sat in his classes.[75]

Students now spent less time in the wards and received less hands-on experience in the diagnosis and treatment of patients. "Our clinical instruction," warned Adolf Gusserow in 1879, "is in danger of falling back into its old demonstrative mode."[76] In Berlin, according to historian Johanna Bleker, "more than two hundred students each semester attended the so-called practical part of the lectures in clinical medicine. That is to say that as far as practical skills were concerned there was no clinical education at all."[77]

Medical enrollments in Germany tripled between 1870 and 1890, causing a huge increase in the size of clinical lectures, so that students lost even the benefit of viewing a well-conducted demonstration at close hand. Candidates for medical licensure spent 52 percent less time with patients during their examinations in 1901 than they had in 1869.[78] In Göttingen, where practical bedside instruction for every student had long been a strong feature of its appeal, the director of the medical clinic, Wilhelm Ebstein, announced in 1889 that he no longer saw any reason to bring students into the sickroom. He preferred, he said, the more efficient lecture-demonstration to be held in the auditorium.[79] The increased use of clinical laboratories attached to basic science departments also represented a further "triumph of the experimental ideal."[80]

Nowhere were the twin pressures on the curriculum of advancing enrollment and the demand for increased laboratory teaching more keenly felt than in the medical school of Vienna. Here was an early warning signal of the emerging conflict between laboratory and clinical teaching that resounded throughout the transatlantic world. As early as 1867, the ophthalmologist Eduard Jaeger pointed to the dangers of the "one-sided theoretical direction of our studies" that left "the young physician at the sickbed without help or advice." He painted a grim picture of the growing isolation of students from clinical teachers as hundreds of students fought for places in the lecture halls, some of them having waited two

---

75. Bernard Naunyn, *Erinnerungen, Gedanken und Meinungen* (Munich: Bergmann, 1925), 128.

76. Adolf Gusserow, *Zur Geschichte und Methode des klinischen Unterrichts* (Berlin: Gustav Lange, 1879), 26.

77. Bleker, "Medical Students," 26.

78. Dieter Irrgang, "Aspekte der Ausbildung des Mediziners im deutschsprachigen Kulturraum zwischen 1872 und 1901 anhand von Selbstzeugnissen deutscher Ärzte" (med. diss., University of Bonn, 1989), 24.

79. Wilhelm Ebstein, "Uber die Entwicklung des klinischen Unterrichts an der Göttinger Hochschule und über die heutigen Aufgaben der medizinischen Klinik," *Klinisches Jahrbuch* 1 (1889): 97.

80. Paul K. Underhill, "Science, Professionalism and the Development of Medical Education in England: An Historical Sociology" (Ph.D. diss., University of Edinburgh, 1987), 531.

hours to get a front-row seat.[81] Two years later, the Viennese students themselves published a pamphlet on "the crimes of the University of Vienna" in permitting nine hundred students to register for an anatomy course and nearly six hundred in a course in chemistry.[82]

Teaching at the bedside, the classical achievement of Viennese teachers, was now all but impossible. By 1872, clinicians were forced to abandon altogether "the intimacy and closeness of bedside teaching" in favor of the lecture room.[83] The surgeon Theodor Billroth, deploring the "monstrous" enrollments in Vienna, urged students to flee the city for smaller universities during the clinical semesters.[84] "The more or less openly expressed opinion," he wrote in 1876, "is that the study of the natural sciences (including physiology) is stressed far too much and at the expense of the student's professional medical training."[85] His colleague J. Dumreicher called it "wrong-headed and illogical" that all students should be forced to take courses "in the spirit and methods of research." It was impracticable in any case, he added, to try "to make microscopists, histologists and researchers" out of a class of 150 students. Of the thirty-seven classes recommended to medical students at Vienna, according to his analysis, not fewer than thirty-three were taught by lectures, demonstrations, and "reminiscences" alone.[86]

Throughout Germany similar complaints were commonplace by the 1870s. In 1874, the noted Munich clinician Hugo von Ziemssen deplored the decline of the "German method" of clinical training that had given individual responsibility to students. The *Hauptvorlesung*, or grand lecture, was now used by all the prominent teachers to enable them to teach the growing number of students and also to make time for their own research. Contacts between professors and students grew more distant and impersonal. In the large clinical classes, few of the *Praktikanten* (students who were assigned to join the professor in examining the patient before the class) now had more than a fleeting chance to observe and learn at the bedside. "In a word," said Ziemssen, "the clinical student sees the sick too little, he does not get close to them, he does not learn . . . how a diagnosis is made, how one follows the course of an ill-

81. Eduard Jaeger, *Ein freies Wort über medicinische Unterrichts und Prüfungsnormen* (Leipzig: Otto Wigand, 1867), 21, 80.

82. *Der medicinische Unterricht an der Wiener Hochschule und seine Gebrechen, von einigen Studenten* (Vienna: G. J. Manz, 1869), 6–8.

83. Helmut Wyklicky and Manfred Skopec, "The Development of Clinical Instruction in Vienna," in *History of Medical Education*, ed. Teizo Ogawa (Tokyo: Saikon, 1983), 143.

84. Theodor Billroth, *Aphorismen zum "Lehren und Lernen der medicinischen Wissenschaften,"* 2nd ed. (Vienna: Carl Gerold's Sohn, 1886), 51.

85. Theodor Billroth, *The Medical Sciences in the German Universities*, trans. from German (New York: Macmillan, 1924), 44. The original German edition was published in 1876.

86. J. Dumreicher, *Über die Nothwendigkeit von Reformen des Unterrichtes an den Medicinischen Facultäten Osterreichs* (Vienna: Alfred Hölder, 1878), 6–7, 15.

ness ... [or] how a treatment is finally carried out."[87] A few years later, Adolf von Strümpell was complaining that "students listen to lectures from eight to ten hours a day. From morning to night their time is taken up with classes; they rush out of one lecture hall into another hearing a huge mass of facts and theories put forward."[88] His complaint was reminiscent of those made by students in France and Anglo-America a half-century before.

Clinical education in Germany, in fact, was entering a prolonged period of crisis. To meet the converging pressures to accommodate the new specialized courses and the swift growth of enrollment, as well as to preserve a modicum of clinical experience, educators resorted to such expedients as providing longer hours of instruction, holding classes on Saturday as late as 6 p.m., lengthening the period of study, and encouraging students (as in Anglo-America) to use vacation time and the year after graduation to gain firsthand experience with patients. Pressures were growing in Germany, too, to add a fifth year, consisting of hospital experience, to the requirements for a medical license, since all too often now the student left medical school with almost no practical education.

The students strongly criticized the shift to large clinical lectures and the gradual abandonment of bedside instruction. Only in the smaller German universities was the old system able to survive. Students at Berlin in the 1870s, such as Ferdinand Hüppe and Ismar Boas, questioned the usefulness of the huge classes and regretted not having any contact with patients. "Without question," recalled Boas, preclinical studies were generally remote from students' interests and unconnected with the meager clinical study they received, so that most students now had only "a purely passive role" in their own educations.[89] At Breslau, on the other hand, instruction in the clinic was still given "in small groups under personal direction" as late as 1892.[90] Students at other small schools, such as Heidelberg, Dorpat, and Zurich, reported similar favorable circumstances. The difference between Heidelberg and Tübingen, for example, was "that the student in Heidelberg was [still] able to act on his own responsibility as a practicing physician," whereas in Tübingen he was "more spectator ... than actual practitioner."[91]

Carl Wunderlich's clinic at Leipzig was often praised by students for the important role it gave to *Praktikanten* and advanced students. At Erlangen, too, the student Gustav Hauser thought his clinical experience "deeper and more personal" than he would later find at Munich, citing instances when the whole class at Erlangen had come forward to hear the

87. Hugo von Ziemssen, "Uber den klinischen Unterricht in Deutschland," *Deutsches Archiv für klinische Medicin* 13 (1874): 13.

88. Adolf von Strümpell, *Uber den medizinisch–klinischen Unterricht: Erfahrungen und Vorschläge* (Leipzig and Erlangen: Deichert, 1901), 11.

89. Irrgang, "Aspekte der Ausbildung des Mediziners," 70–71.

90. Ibid., 71.

91. Ibid., 78.

heart sounds of a patient being examined.[92] Some professors with large classes like those of Frerichs responded to the growing criticism by boldly asserting the superiority of the demonstrative lecture. "How much better is teaching in today's auditorium," declared Friedrich Mosler of Greifswald, "than in earlier days when teacher and students crowded around a bed in a tiny sickroom!"[93]

Foreign visitors noticed and commented on the dwindling importance of bedside teaching in Germany. John Shaw Billings, for example, expressed his conviction in 1876 that for all their weaknesses, the English medical schools were better for beginning students than those of Germany were. Too much emphasis, he asserted, was being placed in Germany on instilling at the beginning of study the spirit of science and the importance of experimental work, causing the student "to think that his highest aim should be to do some experiment which no one has done before."[94] Eight years later, in a letter to a Canadian journal, William Osler commented in reference to Ludwig's famous institute in Leipzig that "the work which shall advance the science, which brings renown to the professor and to the university . . . occupies the chief time of the Director . . . [while] the teaching function . . . is apt to be neglected in the more seductive pursuit of the 'bauble reputation.'"[95]

By 1893 Harvard instructor Charles Withington was describing German medical education as "generally admirable," even though "the average student gets probably less from it than he would from trying to unravel a few obscure cases for himself." The life of a student in Germany was spent, he remarked, "not so much [at] the bed-side as on the lecture bench," where "he is made the subject of a constant intellectual gavage, in which if you will allow the figure, the pabulum is of the best quality . . . but is so thoroughly predigested that very little work is left for his own intellectual powers."[96]

In a strange reversal of roles, German critics now praised the English system of practical education and sometimes urged the adoption in Germany of its system of clerks and dressers. Articles began to appear in medical journals in the 1880s contrasting the large number of English students who received practical experience as ward clerks and surgical dressers with the smaller number of "assistant physicians" who obtained similar training in German hospitals. In one report, for example, the clinical teaching at St. Bartholomew's Hospital in London was compared favorably with that of the surgical clinic in Berlin. According to this com-

92. Ibid., 79, 83.

93. Friedrich Mosler, "Uber den Unterricht in der medizinischen Klinik zu Greifswald," *Klinisches Jahrbuch* 1 (1889): 117.

94. Fielding H. Garrison, *John Shaw Billings* (New York: Putnam, 1915), 198.

95. Harvey Cushing, *The Life of Sir William Osler* (New York: Oxford University Press, 1940), 218.

96. Charles F. Withington, "Medical Teaching in Germany," *Boston Medical and Surgical Journal* 129 (1893): 586–87.

parison, London dressers were given a chance to examine patients themselves, apply bandages, and do small procedures. In three-month rotations, nearly a hundred students at St. Bartholomew's got such experience each year, whereas in Berlin only a handful of students got similar training, and most left the clinic without ever doing even a case history.[97]

The medical historian Theodor Puschmann argued in 1886 that it was "not sufficient to call students to the sickbed several times during a semester." Instead, he urged the creation of "arrangements similar to those of Clerks and Dressers in the English hospitals."[98] In the same year, Billroth raised the question of whether in the crisis facing German medical education, it would not be wise to build practical schools like those in England.[99] And the author of a four-part series on medical education in a Berlin journal of 1893 referred to the voices now "increasingly heard that the present education of physicians no longer meets contemporary needs" and that changes must be made "to create a more practical education . . . [as in] England." A "nearly ideal medical education," he opined, could be given "if it were possible to unite the English clerk system with the German clinical lecture."[100] Many English and American reformers were coming to the same conclusion.

Outside Germany, the struggle for control of the curriculum was even more fiercely fought. In Germany, after all, the conflict between clinician and laboratory scientist was muted by the nearly universal acceptance of the scientific ideal and the pedagogical tradition of accommodating scientific and practical studies under the same roof. Even such clinicians as Frerichs and Ziemssen thought of themselves as full-time scientists engaged in scholarly research, whereas elsewhere, especially in Britain and America, the clinician was almost always a full-time practitioner with no thought of a career in science or education.

Without such traditions of full-time scientific teaching and curricular accommodation to science, laboratory medicine in these countries necessarily had to enter the curriculum from the outside, aided by reform-minded professional and university leaders, as it did in the United States and Britain, or in France by the action of a government concerned about the national threat posed by Germany. In other words, France, Britain, and America could not look for reform, as Germany could, to an established professoriate in medicine that was already inclined to view science as a positive force for change.

97. Undated reprint from *Arztliches Vereinsblatt* [1893], in GSPK, Merseburg, 76 Va, Sekt. 1, Tit. VII, Nr. 67.

98. Theodor Puschmann, *Betrachtungen über unser medicinisches Unterrichtswesen* (Vienna: Georg Szelinski, 1886), 13.

99. Billroth, *Aphorismen*, 33.

100. W. Nagel, "Über das medicinische Studium in England in Vergleich mit Deutschland," *Berliner klinische Wochenschrift* 30 (1893): 858, 932.

The Clinic Versus the Laboratory in Great Britain

Instead, west of the Rhine in both France and the English-speaking countries, resistance to the increased expense of laboratories and to the reduction in time spent by students in lecture halls and clinics was often formidable. The union of teaching and research, furthermore, so firmly rooted in the German medical school, was slow to take hold in nations with no strong tradition of faculty research. Quite differently from those in Germany, the early laboratory teachers were often regarded by entrenched clinicians as inferior. Even those who lauded the important role of laboratory medicine in new discoveries were frequently skeptical of its utility in ordinary medical training. "When you enter my wards," the eccentric clinician Samuel Gee told his students at St. Bartholomew's in 1888, "your first duty is to forget all your physiology. Physiology is an experimental science—and a very good thing no doubt in its proper place. Medicine is not a science, but an empirical art."[101]

Skepticism of the utility of laboratory teaching for most medical students was deep and abiding among the practitioner-teachers of Britain and America. The "tenacious clinical culture" of Great Britain, as one student termed it, often discouraged efforts to make a larger place for experimental science in the curriculum.[102] Whereas university teachers at Cambridge, Edinburgh, or London might enjoy the support of like-minded colleagues in other fields, the more numerous hospital teachers, isolated from close contact with academic science, lived and taught in an environment that was essentially hostile to demands for change. The high costs of laboratory education, the dependence of the teaching enterprise on student fees and private practice, and the orientation of the hospital toward patient service all contributed to a reluctance to make any but the most necessary changes.

Student pressures, always important to a freestanding or proprietary school, were sometimes decisive in bringing change. At St. Mary's Hospital Medical School, a full-time appointment in physiology was finally made in 1884 after two years of student agitation.[103] A deputation of students to the governing board at London Hospital the same year made an urgent appeal for "further teaching in the Microscopical portion of Pathology" and requested the appointment of "one or more demonstrators."[104] Meanwhile, students at Guy's were urging the consolidation of the twelve independent medical schools of London. No one school, read

---

101. Cited by Kenneth D. Keele, *The Evolution of Clinical Methods in Medicine* (London: Pitman, 1963), 105.

102. Underhill, "Science, Professionalism and the Development of Medical Education," 494.

103. Zachary Cope, *The History of St. Mary's Hospital Medical School* (London: William Heinemann, 1954), 81.

104. London Hospital Medical College, Minutes of College Board, February 26, 1884, London Hospital Archive.

a student editorial, could possibly offer a full scientific education under these circumstances, with the result that even so important a subject as physiology suffered from "a great lack of experimental teaching," and students were forced to read in books about "experiments which they have never seen."[105]

Even at the universities in Britain, laboratory scientists faced greater obstacles than did their colleagues in France or especially Germany. At Edinburgh, for example, most surgical teachers ignored John Hughes Bennett's plea to teach the uses of histology in the diagnosis of tumors.[106] Glasgow surgeons were likewise "singularly reluctant . . . to modify their procedures in order to make pathological diagnosis an integral part of their clinical practice."[107] Oxford traditionalists were largely successful in preventing Burdon Sanderson from building additional programs in laboratory science to supplement his work in the physiological laboratory. "He was in a minority," writes a recent student, "in believing that physiology had the potential to alter medical practise."[108] Even Michael Foster, the most successful creator of a teaching laboratory in Britain, was frequently opposed at Cambridge by such clinicians as George Paget, who dissented "emphatically" from Foster's plan to defer clinical study until after a thorough period of scientific preparation.[109]

Resistance to Laboratory Science in America

In the practical schools of North America, for many of the same reasons, the few teachers who had had laboratory training in Germany, along with their allies, faced formidable resistance to major redirection of the curriculum.[110] Although important steps were taken in the 1870s to introduce laboratory science into the curriculum, the further spread of the lab-

---

105. *Guy's Hospital Gazette* 7 (1875): 1.

106. Sturdy, "A Co-ordinated Whole," 83.

107. L. S. Jacyna, "The Laboratory and the Clinic: The Impact of Pathology on Surgical Diagnosis in the Glasgow Western Infirmary, 1875–1910," *Bulletin of the History of Medicine* 62 (1988): 396. Jacyna concludes that "the tradition of the integrity and autonomy of clinical medicine . . . proved remarkably resistant to the newer laboratory science" (p. 405).

108. From a paper by Terrie M. Romano, "John Burdon Sanderson and the Oxford School of Physiology," presented at the annual meeting of the American Association for the History of Medicine, May 2, 1992. I am indebted to Dr. Romano for sending me a copy of her paper.

109. Report of the Special Board for Medicine, Proposed for Confirmation by the Senate, November 12, 1883, University of Cambridge Archive, CUR 28.4.2.

110. The best accounts of the development of laboratory science in American medical schools can be found in Ludmerer, *Learning to Heal*; William G. Rothstein, *American Medical Schools and the Practice of Medicine: A History* (New York: Oxford University Press, 1987); Gerald L. Geison, ed., *Physiology in the American Context, 1850–1940* (Bethesda, MD: American Physiological Society, 1987); and W. Bruce Fye, *The Development of American Physiology: Scientific Medicine in the Nineteenth Century* (Baltimore: Johns Hopkins University Press, 1987).

oratory as a teaching method seemed to many clinicians "a dangerous will-o-the-wisp."[111] While admitting the pedagogical value of learning by direct observation the ways in which the animal body carried out its functions, they often severely questioned the need for endless repetition of experiments by the students themselves.

Of what use was such training to the physician in actual practice, compared with more time spent in the clinic or hospital? The aging Alfred Stillé, about to leave his chair at Pennsylvania in 1883, stated that he was greatly concerned about the growing emphasis on experimental science for students, fearing that it was weakening their commitment to bedside observation and "empirical facts."[112] As late as 1902, the author of a widely read book of advice for physicians was urging students and practitioners alike to be wary of the claims made for science, telling them to ask themselves before accepting any new procedure or theory: "What is its use to me?"[113]

Although by 1880, courses in physiology and other sciences, including study in the laboratory, had been instituted in a number of schools, it was generally not until the end of the century that students were required to take them. Enrollments, in fact, were modest in comparison with those of the popular clinical courses. Although many believed that such courses were important to explaining how disease affected healthy tissues and cells, they were thought to be of little help in teaching the would-be physician what to do at the bedside. More than in continental Europe, American and British teachers continued to emphasize the uniqueness of each patient's illness. Treatment must rest, it was believed, not on scientific laws that might or might not apply to a particular illness but on centuries of accumulated experience. The medical practitioner, noted the respected clinician Austin Flint in 1883, "does not deal with facts and laws having the exactness of those pertaining to physics."[114]

The early praise of German methods of teaching, especially by those with laboratory training abroad, was now countered by critics who questioned their value to the average practitioner. "Germany is appealed to as the medical Utopia," said a speaker at the American Medical Association meeting of 1872, "where perfection in the system of medical education has been attained . . . they have hospitals on the grandest scale; their laboratories are the most ample and the best furnished." But what, he asked "in a spirit of perfect candor," had it all amounted to?

111. Charles E. Rosenberg, "The Therapeutic Revolution," in *The Therapeutic Revolution: Essays in the Social History of American Medicine,* ed. Morris J. Vogel and Charles E. Rosenberg (Philadelphia: University of Pennsylvania Press, 1979), 20.

112. Alfred Stillé, "An Address delivered to the Medical Class of the University of Pennsylvania, on withdrawing from his Chair," *Medical News* 44 (1884): 433.

113. D. W. Cathell and William T. Cathell, *Book on the Physician Himself, and Things that concern his Reputation and Success,* 11th ed. (Philadelphia: Davis, 1902), 109.

114. Quoted in John Harley Warner, "Ideals of Science and Their Discontents in Late Nineteenth-Century American Medicine," *Isis* 82 (1991): 467.

The practice of physic in Germany—is it, at this time, little more than a meditation on death? Have not placebos taken the place of remedies in their hospitals? Standing idly by while disease is running its course . . . waiting to see whether nature will win or not . . . the physician seems intent mainly on tracing its ravages in the cadaver. . . . To this ghastly complexion, it may be, American medicine must come at last, but I am sure no philanthropist can be impatient to see the day.[115]

The French Clinic and the "Auxiliary" Sciences

In France during these same years, laboratory teaching stood midway between Germany and the English-speaking countries in its impact on the medical curriculum. Laboratory courses in France were more widespread and usually better financed than those in either Britain or America, but they still lagged behind those of Germany. Always they were designed to be "auxiliary" to the powerful clinical core of French teaching. There was far less talk than in Germany of medicine's becoming a science in which clinical judgment might be progressively less important.

Tensions between clinicians and laboratory teachers in France nevertheless rose as the proportion of laboratory courses in the curriculum began to climb. "For many doctors," one authority wrote, "the new emphasis on 'science' was inexplicable since medical schools were supposed to train practitioners." As they were in Germany, the students were concerned about the overcrowding of clinics as the emphasis shifted to scientific study. The dean of the new school at Lille complained in 1889 that "the faculties are unanimous in declaring that clinical studies have declined . . . [because of] the heavy extension given to the study of the sciences."[116]

After 1890

By 1890, then, it was far from clear how large a place in the curriculum that the science and laboratory courses would occupy in the future. In every country, turmoil and uncertainty marked the boundary between scientific teaching and the clinic. Even in Germany, a vigorous counterattack was being mounted against the dominance of natural science in the training of doctors. Contrary to some opinions, the further march of experimental science was so far neither inevitable nor unstoppable. When Welch pronounced in 1892 that "the current has set irresistibly in the

---

115. *Medical Record* 7 (1872): 172.
116. Weisz, "Reform and Conflict in French Medical Education," 80.

right direction," he was as much encouraging his fellow crusaders as stating a historical certainty.[117]

A review of the curriculum struggles of these years in Europe and America as revealed in faculty records, medical journals, and contemporary writings suggests other possible outcomes. Expressions of angry doubt and serious reservations about the impact of science on medical education were growing louder in 1890, not softer. For many educators, the decline of clinical teaching was a far greater concern than the slowness in accepting science in medicine. The practical teaching of medicine outside universities was expanding, not declining, in both Britain and America. And the teaching of medicine in universities, central to the German pedagogical triumph, was gaining ground only slowly elsewhere, accounting for a very small proportion of medical teaching in Anglo-America, and was still unrealized in France. What Kenneth Ludmerer wrote about the 1870s and 1880s in America—that "the fate of modern medical education remained highly uncertain"—was equally true of the other transatlantic nations.[118]

It was the developments after 1890 that largely explain the final success of the laboratory revolution and the triumph of university teaching in medicine in the twentieth century. Not least in importance were the spectacular achievements in the closing years of the century, of the new laboratory science of bacteriology in diagnosing and controlling disease. Now, for the first time in human history, medicine was able to determine with a high degree of exactness the origins of dozens of ancient afflictions and to promise the ultimate conquest of many of them. Medical doctors were no longer competing on equal terms with irregular practitioners in the treatment of disease, and surgical successes in antiseptic and aseptic practices were obvious for everyone to see.

At the same time, the growing public consciousness of the promise and utility of scientific medicine stimulated governments, university leaders, and philanthropists to intervene more forcefully in the support and regulation of medical study. The impact of rising living standards, new programs of social welfare, higher levels of education, and the chance role of personality at critical junctures gave further direction to medical education. By the early twentieth century, the major pedagogical question was no longer the place of science and the laboratory in medical training but how the clinic could be made more scientific and more accessible to the student in training.

117. William Henry Welch, "The Advancement of Medical Education," in William Henry Welch, *Papers and Addresses*, 3 vols. (Baltimore: Johns Hopkins University Press, 1920), 3:44. The quotation is from an address to the Harvard Medical School Association in June 1892.
118. Ludmerer, *Learning to Heal*, 62.

11

Toward a University Standard of Medical Education, 1890–1920

In the waning years of the nineteenth century, despite (or perhaps because of) the inroads of laboratory science, uncertainty still hung heavy over the future shape of the medical curriculum. Although currents of change now flowed freely through the medical schools and conditions of study were shifting in every country, agreement was far from universal on such primary questions as the place of science and the laboratory in medical study, how clinical medicine should best be taught, the best way to prepare for medical study, the order of studies, minimal requirements for practice, and the importance of postgraduate study. "Perturbations and violent readjustments," an American professor told his audience in 1897, marked the life of every medical school in this "remarkable epoch in the history of medicine."[1]

Similar to the era of change a century before, students were again confronted with bewildering choices. Old questions long thought settled rose in new form. Did the practical study of medicine belong in a university at all? Was bedside instruction still needed by every student in training, or was the superbly conducted clinical demonstration not as good or even better? Should students perform experiments themselves in laboratories so as to understand the real meaning of science and its promise for medicine, or was it a waste of valuable time for the vast majority?

1. J. C. Wilson, "Modern Medical Education: Address of the President," *Bulletin of the American Academy of Medicine* 3 (1897): 4, 6.

And what about the university—now the home of advanced science, original research work, and the scientific laboratory—was it to be the only site to learn the medicine of the future? What about the still numerous hospital and independent schools, the mainstay of teaching in Anglo-America in 1890—did they still have a place in the teaching of medicine?

The Persistence of National Differences

Amidst the often clamorous debates on these and other questions, the teaching enterprise was still shaped by strong national cultural differences. In the final years of the century, the Western world was experiencing a new sense of national identity and pride that ran through developments in science and medicine as well as politics. The strident nationalism and industrial–scientific strength of a united Germany, evident to physicians studying there, thoroughly frightened many in the rest of Europe. Leaders in France, in particular, looking to the scientific and industrial foundations of their own national power, moved closer in both scientific and diplomatic relations to their ancient foe, Great Britain.

Statesmen in Britain, whose economic and military might and educational system were seen to be declining vis-à-vis Germany, sought a new rapprochement with the United States, showing new interest in that nation's educational and scientific achievements. And in the United States, emerging from long decades of preoccupation with internal growth and national issues, leaders began to look outside its borders with a new sense of the nation's industrial power and scientific potential. It was against this shifting backdrop of world events that much that now happened in higher education and medicine took place.

Only in imperial Germany, where the acceptance of the laboratory and science's role in medicine was widespread, were the universities firmly in place as the dominant site of medical instruction. In the twenty-one universities of the new *Reich*, now excluding the schools of Austria and Switzerland, the number of students in medicine had climbed by 1890 to nearly nine thousand, compared with seven thousand in the sixteen secondary schools and seven universities of France and a somewhat smaller number spread over the thirty-five medical schools of all kinds in the United Kingdom.[2] In England, proclaimed a Liverpool editor in 1898,

2. W. Lexis, *Die deutschen Universitäten*, 2 vols. (Berlin: A. Asher, 1893), 1:120–21; Georg Heinemann, "Die Studierenden der Medizin in Deutschland am Anfang des 20.Jahrhunderts," *Klinisches Jahrbuch* 10 (1903): 223–24; Rapport sur le programme sommaire de réforme des études médicales, manuscript, 1893, Léon Le Fort, rapporteur, Archives nationales, AJ16 6357, 35, 42–43; George Weisz, *The Emergence of Modern Universities in France, 1863–1914* (Princeton, NJ: Princeton University Press, 1983), 49, table 1.6; Walter Rivington, *The Medical Profession* (Dublin: Fannin, 1879), 256–59.

with some exaggeration, "nine-tenths of the study of medicine" was still "prosecuted at schools unconnected with any university."[3]

At the same time, medical enrollment in the United States and Canada, thanks to a spurt in the number of nonuniversity schools, was rising more swiftly than in Europe. According to figures compiled by the Illinois State Board of Health, a total of 148 medical schools of diverse nature (all but 13 in the United States) accounted for sixteen thousand students engaged in medical study in 1890. Of this number, two thousand were enrolled in the 24 schools of homeopathy, eclectic and physiomedicine, all of them in the United States, and only a handful as yet studied in a university school of medicine.[4]

The power of the state to determine the shape of medical studies was still incomparably greater in Europe than in either Britain or America. After the final consolidation of imperial power in Berlin in 1883, the new German *Reich*—influenced by ministerial and professional concerns about overcrowding in medical ranks and by increasing pressures on the curriculum—lengthened the period of medical study for all students to nine semesters. Pressures were building, too, for an additional "practical year" to replace the dwindling amount of time devoted to bedside experience in the curriculum. Representatives of the nation's physicians, meeting in annual "physicians' day" conventions in 1890 and 1891, urged Berlin to require a fifth year of experience "as an assistant in a hospital" before allowing a physician to practice.[5] By 1893 the government was sending a confidential proposal to university faculties that, among other changes, suggested such an additional year.[6] After eight more years of intensive discussion and debate, marked by charges that further lengthening of study would make medicine "a monopoly of the well-to-do," the government decreed the additional hospital year in 1901.[7]

In France, the long-standing concentration of decision making over medical education in Paris continued unabated, although new attacks on centralized control were mounted by physicians' organizations and provincial schools of medicine. The medical faculty at Montpellier, for example, responding in 1881 to a request from the Ministry of Education for suggestions to attract teachers and students to the provinces, deplored

3. Cited in June Jones, "Science, Utility and the `Second City of the Empire': The Sciences and Especially the Medical Sciences at Liverpool University, 1881–1925" (Ph.D. diss., University of Manchester, 1989), 185.

4. Illinois State Board of Health, *Medical Education, Medical Colleges and the Regulation of the Practice of Medicine in the United States and Canada, 1765–1891* (Springfield: H. W. Rokker, 1891), xxiv–xxv.

5. *Die Organization des medicinischen Unterrichts: Sonderdruck aus den Verhandlungen der XIX.deutschen Arztetage zu Weimar am 22. und 23.Juni 1891* (Leipzig: Ackermann & Glaser, 1892), 4.

6. Grundzüge für die Neugestaltung der medizinischen Prüfungen: Vertrauliche Mitteilung, August 21, 1893, manuscript, GSPK, Merseburg, 76 Va, Sekt 1, Tit. VII, Nr. 67.

7. *Die gesetzlichen Bestimmungen über die ärztlichen Prüfungen für das Deutsche Reich vom 28 Mai 1901* (Berlin: August Hirschwald, 1918), 24.

in words taken from a speech by the minister himself "the terribly dangerous absorption of France by Paris from which France suffers and Paris suffers too." The government, charged the Montpellier physicians, "is creating an official science imposed at a time when everyone is proclaiming that free discussion and free science are the absolute conditions of progress."[8] The distinctive national system of the *concours,* in which teaching and study appointments in the hospitals were administered from Paris, was widely scorned by critics as creating a medical caste system with Parisian physicians at the top. In 1892, in response to the growing pressures from unionlike organizations of physicians (*syndicats*), the government finally moved to abolish the *officiers de santé,* assigning new responsibility at the same time to secondary and preparatory schools to teach advanced courses in medicine.

France thus achieved the "single portal" to medicine that Germany had pioneered some forty years before. The following year, after decades of irresolution, the government also instituted a preparatory year of study in the sciences for medical students—called *P.C.N.* for *certificat d'études physiques, chemiques, et naturelles*—to be taught in the schools of science throughout the country rather than in medical schools. The change, proclaimed Louis Liard, the director of higher education, only recognized the fact that medicine was now "an experimental science" requiring an understanding of its method before beginning study.[9] The action by Paris was unpopular, however, and was strongly resisted by secondary medical faculties, who called it "undemocratic" for barring the "intelligent but poor" from medicine by adding further to the students' study time and expense.[10]

Beyond the continent of Europe, the free-enterprise structure of medical learning in Britain and America, though beginning to yield to professional and public pressures, was still largely intact at the century's end. Asked by a parliamentary commission about the governance of London's hospital schools in 1879, John Simon, a longtime medical official in the government, responded in words equally applicable to America's schools that they were "entirely private adventure schools."[11] The major feature of medical education in England, wrote the author of a prize-winning

8. Faculté de médecine de Montpellier, rapport redigé en réponse à la circulaire ministerielle du 23 décembre 1881 relative aux concours d'aggregation, Archives nationales, AJ[16] 6685.

9. Louis Liard, "La nouvelle réglementation des études médicales," *Revue des deux mondes,* October 15, 1894, pp. 810, 813.

10. See the letters from medical deans in Rouen, Angers, Rennes, Nantes, Montpellier, Amiens, Dijon, and Clermont-Ferrand written to the ministry in June and July 1893, in Archives nationales, AJ[16] 6357.

11. House of Commons, Select Committee on Medical Act, *Special Report . . . together with the Proceedings of the Committee, Minutes of Evidence, Appendix, and Index* (London: House of Commons, 1879), 67.

essay, was "the existence of a number of medical schools, independent, and in competition with each other, entirely uncontrolled by the State, but owing allegiance to the nineteen Licensing Corporations."[12]

The General Medical Council, whose "recommendations" now carried increasing weight, was still dependent on persuasion and example to get its way with the fractious corporations. In 1879, for example, the council had begun to push hard to force medical candidates to complete courses in physics, chemistry, and biology before entering medical school, but a measure of success came only after Cambridge and other licensing bodies agreed to the change.[13] As late as 1903, a physician member of Parliament was calling for the abolition of the council because it strongly backed a fifth year of medical study and was urging the establishment of laboratories in bacteriology and physiology at every medical school.[14]

In the United States, where government had played the smallest part in medical education of any of the nations under study, by the end of the century, a number of the states were beginning to establish licensing boards with modest powers. By 1890, thirty-two states had rudimentary legislation on their books which was limited, in most cases, to requiring practitioners to register their diplomas with county or state authorities. Some states, notably Alabama, Minnesota, New Jersey, the Carolinas, and Virginia, were examining all candidates for licensure and rejecting a small proportion of them.[15]

The efforts in America to increase control over the education of physicians by state boards of registration were bitterly resisted by smaller and less affluent schools. In Missouri, for example, a move in 1891 to define a medical college "in good standing" to mean one offering three years of instruction went down to defeat at the hands of opponents who argued that it "would work a hardship upon 'the poor young man'—it would be class legislation, therefore undemocratic."[16] None but the most ardent reformer held out much hope that the federal government might intervene as in Europe. Reform, if it were to come, must emerge as in Britain from the voluntary efforts of medical educators themselves and their allies in the profession, as well as from the new leadership in universities.

Baffled by the workings of the American federal system and the widespread defeatism regarding the chances for reform, foreign critics could not understand why the national government seemed so powerless to act in so important a matter. "If you fall sick in the United States," wrote a

---

12. Rivington, *Medical Profession*, 271.

13. See D. R. Haldane, General Medical Council, to Board of Medical Studies, Cambridge, November 11, 1880, and the discussion in the Cambridge Board, Archive, Cambridge University.

14. Robert Farquharson, "Suggestions on Medical Education and Reform," *British Medical Journal* 2 (1903): 595.

15. Illinois State Board of Health, *Medical Education*, v–vii, xx–xxi.

16. "Defeat of the Obligatory Three Years' Course Bill in Missouri," *Medical News* 58 (1891): 505–6.

French scholar in 1894 after describing the great freedom to practice medicine, "God help you if you fall into the hands of an American physician."[17] After spending several months visiting medical schools, a German visitor asked his readers to try to conceive of a system of medical colleges whose only requirements were an easily obtained charter, a house, and six "self-appointed" professors.[18] Even William Osler, addressing a Canadian audience in 1885, asked: "How is it that such a shrewd practical people as those in the United States should have drifted into such a loose, slipshod way of conducting medical schools?"[19]

The Systems at the Fin de Siècle

Differences among the several nations also persisted in the amounts of premedical education required, the length of medical study, the makeup of the curriculum, and the order of studies followed. In 1890, if a British student was not a university graduate, he was forced to pass examinations in Greek, Latin, English, and mathematics before commencing his medical study, but in the United States a majority of medical schools still demanded little of their entering students.[20] An American survey in that year revealed that twenty-three schools had no obligatory entrance requirements at all and that only thirteen required a reading knowledge of Latin.[21] Eight schools, including Pennsylvania, Cornell, Yale, and Wisconsin, had organized their own preparatory courses for medical students.[22] Canadian schools, by contrast, had largely achieved uniform standards of admission, causing Americans, according to the study's author, "a humiliating sense of inferiority."[23] The situation changed rapidly after the turn of the century, however, and by 1910 twenty-two schools in the United States were demanding two or more years of college preparation before admitting a student.[24]

17. Octave Laurent, *Les universités des Etats-Unis et du Canada* (Brussels: H. Lamertin, 1894), 138.

18. Johannes Odontius, *Student, "College" und Arzt in den Vereinigten Staaten von Nord-Amerika* (Stuttgart: Union Deutsche Verlagsgesellschaft, 1890), 10.

19. Harvey Cushing, *The Life of Sir William Osler* (New York: Oxford University Press, 1940), 261.

20. "Medical Education in the United Kingdom," *Edinburgh Medical Journal* 2 (1897): iii–vi. See also Charles B. Keetley, *The Student's and Junior Practitioner's Guide to the Medical Profession*, 2nd ed. (London: Ballière, Tindall, and Cox, 1885).

21. J. E. Emerson, "The Requirements for Preliminary Education in the Medical Schools of the United States and Canada," *Journal of the American Medical Association* 14 (1890): 272.

22. Illinois State Board of Health, *Medical Education*, xi.

23. Emerson, "Requirements for Preliminary Education," 272.

24. Abraham Flexner, *Medical Education in the United States and Canada: A Report to the Carnegie Foundation for the Advancement of Teaching* (New York: Carnegie Foundation for the Advancement of Teaching, Bulletin no. 4, 1910), 28.

On the European continent, by contrast, a diploma from a classical secondary school had long been a sine qua non for admission to medical school. In both France and Germany, movements to broaden admissions policies to include graduates of more scientifically and modern-oriented secondary schools were strongly opposed by physicians' organizations and medical faculties. French professors of medicine, writes George Weisz, "fought a bitter defensive action" against any weakening of traditional requirements for entering the profession. "In every faculty [but] especially those of medicine," resistance was strong to any "lowering of standards and swamping France's elite with the half-educated."[25]

In Germany the battle to open the medical schools to graduates of the *Realschulen*, or modern schools emphasizing natural science and modern languages, was prolonged and acrimonious. For half a century the issue was fought out in medical schools, medical societies, and governmental ministries. As early as 1853, the author of a book on medical education had warned that the spread of such schools and the acceptance of their graduates by medical faculties could lead only to the transformation of university schools of medicine into "technical trade schools" like those of France.[26] In 1869, five of the nine medical faculties of Prussia voted down a proposal to admit *Realschule* graduates.[27] A decade later, an overwhelming majority of Germany's physicians, concerned about their standing relative to other professions to which only classical graduates were admitted, voted to reject the idea of opening wider the gateway to medicine.[28] In asserting the superiority of the humanistic high school, the faculty at Bonn claimed that *Realschule* graduates "devote themselves for the most part to the practical life [and] the acquiring of material goods."[29]

The issue pitted some of the most famous medical names of the day against one another. The surgeon Billroth, for example, passionately urged the retention of a classical preparation for medicine, including Latin and Greek, as "indispensable" to the culture of a medical man, and Virchow insisted no less urgently that the day of the classical languages was over and that it was now "the experimental natural sciences," especially physics and chemistry, that were "indispensable" to a student's preparation for medicine.[30] Not until 1900 was the issue settled by an

---

25. Weisz, *Emergence of Modern Universities*, 232, 234.

26. J. M. Leupoldt, *Uber ärztliche Bildung und Bildungsanstalten* (Frankfurt am Main: Heyder and Zimmer, 1853), 24–26.

27. Theodor Puschmann, *Geschichte des medicinischen Unterrichtes von den ältesten Zeiten bis zur Gegenwart* (Leipzig, 1889), 497.

28. *Deutsche medizinische Wochenschrift* 5 (1879): 115.

29. Draft of letter by dean to Ministry of Education, January 4, 1879, University of Bonn Archive, MF 4003.

30. Theodor Billroth, *Aphorismen zum "Lehren und Lernen der medicinischen Wissenschaften,"* 2nd ed. (Vienna: Carl Gerold's Sohn, 1886), 3; Rudolf Virchow, *Lernen und Forschen* (Berlin: August Hirschwald, 1892), 14–24.

edict from Wilhelm II, himself a disgruntled humanistic graduate, in favor of opening the universities to both kinds of graduates.

Other differences continued to separate the national systems of training doctors. Britain and Europe moved to require five or more years of study, including hospital experience, and all the major nations reached that goal by 1909, but the United States edged only slowly toward a longer period of obligatory study. In 1895, even though the three-year graded course had become nearly universal, only a third of all students were enrolled in schools requiring four years of training.[31] By the early twentieth century, however, virtually all American schools were offering a four-year program, and the length of the school year had reached thirty-two weeks.[32]

The order of studies also continued to vary widely from country to country, from the early and continuing French emphasis on the clinic, starting with the first year, to the heavy German concentration on the basic medical sciences for more than half the period of study, to the loosely structured British hospital program where "it is left to [the students'] sweet will and discretion" to arrange their study, to the now graded and flexible American curriculum that—according to the chairman of the new National Conference of State Medical Boards in 1903—was in urgent need of being "systematized and unified."[33]

Medical observers were often struck by the quite different experience of students in one country from another. Inevitably, such observers saw the teaching in other nations through the lens of their own experience at home. Osler, for example, was most impressed in Paris by the "one advantage" that French students had over all others in the centrality of the hospital to their training. "To the hospitals of Great Britain and Germany," he wrote in 1905, "the medical student is admitted as a right; in the United States he is too often only tolerated and not always admitted to the wards," but in Paris "the hospital is his home." For the French student, "the hospital is everything; the medical school is—well, quite a secondary consideration."[34]

To the Viennese historian of medicine, Theodor Puschmann, on the other hand, French medical teaching, despite providing excellent clinical training to some, suffered by comparison with Germany from a number of "lamentable defects," especially the "minute regulations from Paris,"

31. "Medical Education in America," *Medical and Surgical Reporter* 73 (1895): 495. This article is an abstract from *New Science Review*, October 1895.

32. "Professor" Tilmann, "Über amerikanische Aerzte und ihre Ausbildung," *Deutsche Arzte-Zeitung*, July 1, 1901, 9.

33. Rivington, *Medical Profession*, 263; *Medical Education in London: Being a Guide to the Schools of the University of London in the Faculty of Medicine, with Notes on the General Facilities for Clinical Study and Research in the Metropolis* (London: Ash, 1908), 18–19; N. R. Coleman, "Remarks upon Medical Instruction—A Plea for Greater Uniformity," *New York Medical Journal and Philadelphia Medical Journal* 78 (1903): 205–6.

34. William Osler, "Impressions of Paris," *Journal of the American Medical Association* 52 (1905): 771.

the postponement of serious study of medical science to the second year, and (as the French themselves complained) the limited field from which professors were selected. British schools, too, he found lacking and permeated by a "keen sense of the practical applicability of acquired knowledge," whereas degrees granted in American schools were often "in the same category as those amiable but meaningless distinctions . . . conferred upon people dancing the cotillion."[35]

The French critic of higher education René Cruchet, who found much to praise in German science and the autonomy of its universities, insisted nevertheless that the total experience of students and "the learning of practical medicine" were far better at home.[36] English and American travelers, for their part, wavered in their assessment of German medical teaching between strong admiration for the courses in laboratory science, lacking at home, and disparagement of clinical instruction in the larger universities. "Dispensary attendance and bedside instruction, which hold such an important position in England and America," wrote the American Eugene St. Jacques in 1909, "are in Germany almost if not altogether neglected."[37]

Universities, Laboratory Science, and Medicine

Striking as these differences were, more significant at the turn of the century was the common impulse to build a more comprehensive framework than the hospital alone for teaching scientific medicine. In the comprehensive university, so enormously successful in Germany, many found the best way to bring together the studies of the laboratory with those of the clinic. The hospital school of medicine, long dominant in France and Britain, became harder to defend as the best place to prepare for an increasingly scientific medicine.

For the first time in a century, the university reemerged as the favored site of medical instruction. Beginning in the 1870s, more and more nations created new universities or reorganized older ones in an effort to match Germany's achievements. By 1920, the university teaching of medicine had become the standard in much of Europe and was almost unchallenged as a goal in the United States and, to a lesser extent, in Britain. This fusion of laboratory medicine with the clinic in a university setting proved to be the key development in the shaping of twentieth-century medical education.

35. Theodor Puschmann, *A History of Medical Education* (New York: Hafner, 1966), 513, 534–52.

36. René Cruchet, La médecine dans les universités allemandes (Bordeaux: G. Guinovilhou, 1902), 34–35.

37. Eugene St. Jacques, "Medical Education in France and Germany," *Medical Record* 15 (1909): 265.

The swiftness of the transformation surprised many. "During the past fifteen years," Dean William Hunter of Charing Cross Hospital told a royal commission in 1911, "a great change has occurred. The chief feature of English medical education . . . has been the increasing demand for a university, as distinguished from a non-university medical education."[38] In North America, the changeover was even more dramatic. In regard to Canada, the editor of the *Canadian Medical Association Journal* wrote in the year of Hunter's testimony that "medical education is now wholly in the hands of the universities."[39] And in the United States, the president of the new Carnegie Foundation for the Advancement of Teaching declared categorically that "the historical and right home of the medical school in America is the university." By 1910, according to his figures, 82 of 150 American schools were already "connected with actual colleges or universities."[40]

In France, where the rebuilding of the universities had begun in 1875, the end of the rank of officier and the advent of the P.C.N., together with the regrouping of separate faculties into fifteen universities in 1896, brought medical education once more into the orbit of the university. The growth of university science in these years in France, according to historian Harry Paul, was nothing less than "astounding."[41]

The success of the university model signaled the final acceptance of laboratory science as the foundation stone of all medical teaching. Survival of such competing training grounds as the proprietary school in America, the hospital in England, and the programs for training *officiers* in France rested at bottom on the belief that they provided all the essentials needed to practice medicine. As late as 1890, the case could still be made, though more weakly than a decade before, that it was enough for a student to hear lectures on medical science, to see demonstrations of scientific and clinical phenomena, to practice dissection, and to learn to treat patients in a clinic or hospital. But in the closing years of the century, the fundamental importance of scientific understanding to medicine gained wholesale acceptance.

It was the revolution in bacteriology, as suggested at the end of the last chapter, that finally forced laboratory and scientific study to the forefront in medical education after 1890. Achievements in that field gave reformers everywhere "a persuasive argument for placing greater emphasis on

---

38. Royal Commission on University Education in London, *Reports*, 5 vols. (London: His Majesty's Stationery Office, 1910–12), 5:114, appendix.

39. *Canadian Medical Association Journal* 1 (1911): 1091.

40. Henry S. Pritchett, "The Obligations of the University to Medical Education," *Journal of the American Medical Association* 4 (1910): 1109–10. These remarks were delivered some months before the release of Abraham Flexner's famous report.

41. Harry W. Paul, *From Knowledge to Power: The Rise of the Science Empire in France, 1860–1939* (Cambridge: Cambridge University Press, 1985), 3.

science in the medical curriculum."[42] More than any previous scientific discoveries, the causative role of bacteria in specific diseases was important to practitioners and clinicians, who were still heavily burdened by the frightful struggle against communicable disease. "From Listerian antisepsis ... through pathogenic specificity ... to the new serum and chemotherapeutic regimes of the 1890s and 1900s," asserts Russell Maulitz, "physicians came to embrace a constellation of concepts and techniques associated with bacteriology."[43]

In every country, the new therapeutic optimism about scientific medicine inspired those working to bring more laboratory study, more research, and a university setting to the study of medicine. The French medical establishment, heretofore hesitant about embracing "Pasteurism," reversed itself in the face of the new practical uses of bacteriology, especially the introduction of an effective antitoxin for diphtheria in 1894.[44] In Britain, similarly, "the advent of bacteriology ... substantially transform[ed] the climate in which the general public, long justifiably skeptical of medical men's professional claims, evaluated medical care and therapeutic practices."[45] A "profound shift" in favor of the laboratory in the medical teaching of Canada has also been attributed to "the electric effect of a series of breakthroughs in medical science."[46] And the American Frank Billings, addressing the American Medical Association in 1903, warned that "the private—the proprietary—medical school ... must go," for a knowledge of germ theory, preventive inoculation, and Listerism was now "indispensable" to medical practice.

Although "not every student ... can become an experimenter," Billings explained,

> every physician must be so educated that he may intelligently apply the knowledge furnished him by experimental medicine in the cure

42. W. Bruce Fye, "Growth of American Physiology, 1850–1900," in *Physiology in the American Context, 1850–1940*, ed. Gerald L. Geison (Bethesda, MD: American Physiological Society, 1987), 57.

43. Russell C. Maulitz, "'Physician versus Bacteriologist': The Ideology of Science in Clinical Medicine," in *The Therapeutic Revolution: Essays in the Social History of American Medicine*, ed. Morris J. Vogel and Charles E. Rosenberg (Philadelphia: University of Pennsylvania Press, 1979), 92. For a measured recent interpretation of the impact of science on medicine in these years, see W. F. Bynum, *Science and the Practice of Medicine in the Nineteenth Century* (Cambridge: Cambridge University Press, 1994).

44. Bruno Latour, *Les microbes: Guerre et paix, suivi de irréductions* (Paris: Métailié, 1984), 142–50. See also Evelyn B. Ackerman, *Health Care in the Parisian Countryside, 1800–1914* (New Brunswick, NJ: Rutgers University Press, 1990), 94–107.

45. Paul K. Underhill, "Science, Professionalism and the Development of Medical Education in England: An Historical Sociology" (Ph.D. diss., University of Edinburgh, 1987), 600.

46. R. D. Gidney and W. P. J. Millar, "The Reorientation of Medical Education in Late Nineteenth-Century Ontario: The Proprietary Medical Schools and the Founding of the Faculty of Medicine at the University of Toronto," *Journal of the History of Medicine and Allied Sciences* 49 (1994): 62.

of such diseases as can be cured. He will no longer juggle with the life of his patient by an attempt to cure with drugs or otherwise, where no help is possible.[47]

A university education, declared the 1901 report of the AMA on medical education, "guarantees that the knowledge which the student gets shall look toward science, and not stop with mere information."[48]

Medical Education and the American University

Nowhere was the transfer of medical teaching to the university swifter or more surprising than in the United States. As late as 1880 only a handful of American medical schools could lay claim to being connected at all to a university, and few universities in the European sense even existed. Yet two decades later Billings could declare flatly in his AMA address that "in the future medicine must be taught in . . . universities."[49] European observers quickly noticed the remarkable transformation. The Munich teacher and internist, Friedrich von Müller, for example, struck on his 1907 trip to America by the high quality of university teaching and the practical methods of laboratory instruction, applauded the opportunities given ordinary students to carry out experiments themselves in the laboratory. Such opportunities did not come in Germany, he said, until the postgraduate years. "How much more solidly," he wrote, "must these self-made observations impress themselves upon the memory."[50] The ophthalmologist Julius Herschberg, likewise impressed by "the amount, quality, and newness" of laboratory equipment in the universities, declared that in this respect "an ocean separates us from America."[51] Similar observations came from other visitors before World War I.[52]

The advance of the university as the home of medical teaching in the United States, as demonstrated in the work of Kenneth Ludmerer, was due to a combination of favorable circumstances.[53] The idea of a research university itself, virtually unknown before the Civil War, had spread across the country in the 1870s and 1880s. The new type of university

47. Frank Billings, "Medical Education in the United States," *Journal of the American Medical Association* 40 (1903): 1273, 1275.

48. "Medical Education," *Journal of the American Medical Association* 37 (1901): 766.

49. Billings, "Medical Education," 1276.

50. Friedrich von Müller, "Amerikanische Reiseeindrücke," *Münchner medizinische Wochenschrift* 54 (1907): 2390.

51. Julius Hirschberg, "Meine dritte Amerika-Fahrt," *Medizinische Klinik* 1 (1905): 1195.

52. See Thomas N. Bonner, "The Tide Begins to Turn: German Doctors in America Before 1914," in Thomas N. Bonner, *American Doctors and German Universities: A Chapter in International Intellectual Relations, 1870–1914* (Lincoln: University of Nebraska Press, Landmark edition, 1987), 139–56.

53. Kenneth M. Ludmerer, *Learning to Heal: The Development of American Medical Education* (New York: Basic Books, 1985), esp. 29–46, 102–22, 191–206.

offered opportunities for careers to those returned from lengthy study in Germany, who became their principal beneficiaries and supporters. Newly made fortunes were put to use in supporting the universities and particularly their work in science and medicine. Nor can the chance role of personality be discounted in such instances as that of Welch and Osler at Johns Hopkins or of Arthur Dean Bevan in the American Medical Association. The heretofore chaotic state of educating physicians in America, long the target of reformers, proved also to be an unexpected advantage in creating a favorable environment for change. Innovation was possible without the rearguard action of the "monopolies of academic power" of Europe, as Ben-David called them.[54]

Where did the creators of the American pattern of university education in medicine find their inspiration?[55] Clearly they were most influenced by the German example and the experience of those who had worked in a German laboratory. But the German model, it is important to note, was transformed in important ways as it made its way across the Atlantic. A number of features of the German university system, notably the research-oriented institute, the private teacher or *dozent*, the great power of the professors, and the freedom of students to select their own courses were found impracticable or undesirable in the American environment.

More important, American educators did not adopt the German practice of deferring major clinical experience to the year of internship after graduation but followed instead the more congenial British example, made popular by Osler at the Johns Hopkins Hospital, of appointing students as clinical clerks and dressers in the last years of medical school. In doing this, they created a fusion between scientific and clinical teaching at the undergraduate level that resembled that in the German university of a half-century before. The example of the Johns Hopkins University and Hospital, created between 1889 and 1893, was justly acclaimed as a model for the new scientific medicine in America.

What further distinguished the emerging American model of university medical education was its emphasis on laboratory instruction and later clinical experience—quite different from that of Germany or Britain—for the run-of-the-mill student of medicine. Müller was struck during his American stay, he reported, by the large number of laboratory courses open to students, the mountains of equipment and supplies they used, and the enormous expense that such preparation entailed. One university alone, he told his German audience enviously, used four thousand frogs in a single year for teaching.[56] By 1916 Welch was claiming with justifica-

54. Joseph Ben-David, "The Universities and the Growth of Science in Germany and the United States," *Minerva* 7 (1968): 19.

55. The discussion in this and the next paragraphs follows my "The German Model of Training Physicians in the United States, 1870–1914: How Closely Was It Followed?" *Bulletin of the History of Medicine* 64 (1990): 18–34.

56. Müller, "Reiseeindrücke," 2389–90.

tion that "we lay . . . greater emphasis upon the teaching of undergraduate medical students in the laboratory than is done elsewhere."[57]

What was being fashioned out of the intersection of German, British, and American practice was a system more individualized, more equalitarian, and far more expensive than anything yet seen in Europe. The costs of the new teaching, said Billings in his 1903 address, were "appalling," but its success guaranteed that the future physician "would be, in truth, a member of a learned profession." And from an educational point of view, he would rank as an equal with the scholar in philosophy, law, and theology.[58] The entire profession would benefit from the change. Thus did organized medicine make common cause with academic scientists and foundation leaders to advance the new education in medicine.

The educational pioneers at Hopkins and elsewhere tirelessly preached the pedagogical doctrine that only close personal teaching of the kind they had experienced as researchers in German laboratories was suited to the teaching of beginning medical students in America. They ignored altogether the popular didactic lecture before hundreds of students that had become the staple of German medical teaching. "Only the knowledge that comes to students from personal laboratory experience," stated Welch in a dozen public addresses, "is real and living, and not that which comes from mere observation of external appearances, or from reading or being told about things, or, still less, merely thinking about them."[59] "Knowledge lives in the laboratory," declared Charles Minot, and "when it is dead, we bury it decently in a book."[60] At the University of Minnesota, C. M. Jackson followed the injunction: "Never tell a student anything he can observe for himself; never draw a conclusion or solve a problem which he can be led to reason for himself; and never do anything for him that he can do for himself."[61]

By 1910, so great was the shift to independent learning for the normal medical student at leading colleges that Abraham Flexner could declare in his famous report: "The student no longer merely watches, listens, memorizes; he *does*. His own activities in the laboratory and in the clinic are the main factors in his instruction and discipline."[62]

That so radical and expensive a pedagogy could take root in the America of the turn of the century was a remarkable turn of events. It moved

---

57. William Henry Welch, "Medical Education," in William Henry Welch, *Papers and Addresses*, 3 vols. (Baltimore: Johns Hopkins University Press, 1920), 3:126–27.

58. Billings, "Medical Education," 1273–75.

59. Welch, "The Evolution of Modern Scientific Laboratories," in *Papers and Addresses*, 3:208.

60. Cited by Richard M. Pearce, "The Experimental Method: Its Influence on the Teaching of Medicine," in *Medical Research and Education*, ed. J. McKeen Cattell (New York: Science Press, 1913), 92.

61. C. M. Jackson, "On the Improvement of Medical Teaching, in *Medical Education and Research*, ed. J. McKeen Cattell (New York: Science Press, 1913), 371.

62. Flexner, *Medical Education*, 53. Emphasis in original.

sharply away from what was happening in the overcrowded medical schools of London, Paris, and Berlin. It did not simply copy the German system but turned it upside down, so that beginning students got the kind of attention reserved for advanced students and graduates in Germany. At first, it was believed that so expensive a system could be undertaken at only a few well-endowed universities with highly selected student bodies. "The Medical Schools in Boston, New York, Philadelphia, Baltimore, and the West," John Shaw Billings told a Johns Hopkins audience in 1877, "are educating practitioners . . . what I propose is, that the field shall be left perfectly clear to them, and that we undertake to do what they cannot do."[63] But the ambitious and influential leaders at such universities as Harvard, Yale, Pennsylvania, Michigan, and then others were not content to allow a few schools to become the premier medical training centers of the nation. "Once a single institution had committed itself to research and graduate education," writes Ben-David, "the elite colleges had no choice but to follow suit."[64]

Schools of the second and third rank likewise rallied to raise their standards and reputations. Not all, of course, were able or willing to follow the German–Hopkins example. The German model, sharply recast at Hopkins and other elite schools, was further transformed as it made its way into the majority of schools. Some schools disappeared quickly in the face of the growing demands made by state and professional licensing bodies; others fought vainly to preserve something of the older practical orientation of American medical schools; and still others were able to survive by minimal but timely accretions to staff and facilities. In Chicago, for example, the three oldest medical schools all became affiliated with universities in the 1890s; all made some provision for laboratory instruction by full-time teachers; and all were able to withstand Flexner's characterization of Chicago as "the plague spot of the country" in his 1910 report.[65] The schools that survived, then, moved closer to universities, constructed at least minimal teaching laboratories, and made some full-time appointments, but they still were a far cry from the richly supported institution in Baltimore.

The special-purpose schools for women and blacks, like the irregular schools that had flourished since the early years of the century, all faced extinction in the light of these events. All of them were dependent on student fees for their support, and few were able to arrange a liaison with a sheltering university. Pressures became intense to extend the period of study, screen applicants more carefully, equip laboratories, and appoint

63. John Shaw Billings, "Two Papers by John Shaw Billings on Medical Education," *Bulletin of the Institute of the History of Medicine* 6 (1938): 321.

64. Joseph Ben-David, *Centers of Learning: Britain, France, Germany, United States: An Essay* (New York: McGraw-Hill, 1977), 61.

65. Thomas N. Bonner, *Medicine in Chicago, 1850–1950: A Chapter in the Social and Scientific Development of a City*, 2nd ed. (Urbana: University of Illinois Press, 1991), 108–17.

full-time teachers in the scientific subjects. The advance of coeducation, holding the promise of an end to discrimination against women, added to the problems of the single-sex schools. In the case of the irregular schools, the teaching of homeopathic and eclectic medicine became increasingly difficult to reconcile with the growing acceptance of science by all schools as the basis of medical teaching. "While traditional medicine tended to divide physicians," writes William Rothstein, "scientific medicine tended to unify them."[66] One by one, the special and irregular schools began to close their doors. By 1920, only one women's school, three black schools, five homeopathic schools, and one eclectic school remained from the fifty-five such schools in 1900.[67]

The Goal of University Teaching in Britain

In Great Britain, the goal of university teaching in medicine, though widely acknowledged, was much more difficult to attain than in the United States. The power of the royal colleges and sometimes the old universities was often ranged against the forces of change. As late as 1905, the United Kingdom had fewer universities than any other major Western country.[68] Only a fraction of British practitioners had medical degrees, since unlike the United States, only a university could grant them. Except for a handful of degrees granted by the established English universities, those seeking degrees were still dependent on the Scottish universities and to a lesser extent on the University of London. The latter school, according to a contemporary account, "can be looked upon as a university . . . in name only. She examines, it is true, but she performs none of the other functions of a University. She tests, but she does not teach."[69]

In the Midlands, a degree-granting university centered in Manchester but embracing schools in Leeds and Liverpool—calling itself the "Victoria University"—was created in 1881 to serve "the hard-working middle classes, from among whose ranks the representatives of medicine are almost wholly recruited."[70] By 1896 this multicampus university, according

66. William G. Rothstein, *American Physicians in the Nineteenth Century: From Sects to Science* (Baltimore: Johns Hopkins University Press, 1972), 323.

67. Thomas N. Bonner, *To the Ends of the Earth: Women's Search for Education in Medicine* (Cambridge, MA: Harvard University Press, 1992), 149–55; Todd L. Savitt, "Abraham Flexner and the Black Medical Schools," in *Beyond Flexner: Medical Education in the Twentieth Century*, ed. Barbara Barzansky and Norman Gevitz (New York: Greenwood Press, 1991), 67, table 5.1; Rothstein, *American Physicians in the Nineteenth Century*, 287, table XV.1.

68. Peter Alter, *The Reluctant Patron: Science and the State in Britain, 1850–1920* (Oxford: Berg, 1987), 26.

69. John E. Morgan, *The Victoria University: Why Are There No Medical Degrees?* (Manchester: J. E. Cornish, 1881), 9, 13.

70. Ibid., 19.

to a Manchester estimate, was awarding three times as many degrees in medicine as were the universities of London, Oxford, and Cambridge combined.[71]

But the separate schools of medicine within Victoria University, each with its varying strengths and interests, continued to follow a largely independent path and to quarrel over one another's inadequacies. "Liverpool College," wrote the editor of a medical student publication in Manchester in 1901, "is a weak and ill-nourished infant . . . supported by the vigorous and virile College of Manchester."[72] The following year the authorities at Manchester made a strong argument for separate universities "on the model of the great universities of Scotland, Germany, France, and America."[73] After further debate, Parliament finally authorized in 1904 the establishment of degree-granting universities in each of the cities.

In the meantime, the twelve hospital schools of London, all located within five miles of one another, came under increasing pressure to combine their resources, especially in the basic medical sciences. The costs of education, as elsewhere, were mounting swiftly while enrollment in many of the schools was dropping by the end of the century. Efforts to agree on raising tuition fees among the schools foundered on the sharp differences among them. As late as 1906, most of the hospitals had no clear responsibility or even a separate budget for their programs in medical teaching.[74] Many administrators, besieged by constant demands for new courses, more teachers and equipment, and the expansion of laboratories, despaired of keeping pace with the growing need. At the London Hospital, if the medical school were to survive, the need for housing for students was becoming "urgent and pressing."[75]

Why, it was asked more and more often, should the twelve schools not combine their teaching of introductory science at the University of London and leave clinical training to be carried out in the separate hospitals? The university, argued critics, should be turned from an examining into a teaching institution. Numerous plans were devised, but conflicting interests continued to slow progress. A royal commission of 1889 reported in favor of combining the teaching and research programs of University College and King's College into a reorganized University of London. Opposition was strong, however, from the royal colleges and from pow-

---

71. Minute book, Medical Section of Senate, Owens College, November 1896, University Archive, University of Manchester.

72. *Manchester Medical Students' Gazette* 1 (1901): 126.

73. *The Case for the Establishment of independent Universities of Manchester, Liverpool, and Yorkshire* (Manchester: Sherratt & Hughes, 1902), 21.

74. Report of King Edward's Hospital Fund, 1905, in "Financial Relations Between the Hospital and Medical School, Guy's Hospital," December 18, 1906, Greater London Record Office, H9/QY/A87/1.

75. Minutes, London Hospital Medical College, January 15, 1880, London Hospital Archive.

erful clinicians who feared the growing emphasis on science and the loss of their own control over teaching. A resolution by the Guy's faculty in 1891, for example, was directed against "any scheme . . . under which a preponderating influence would be given to University and King's College in determining the curricula."[76] The Royal College of Physicians was likewise alarmed by the possible effects of such a change on its role in examining. "The College should not take part in a university," said one member at a 1892 meeting, "in which its influence is not paramount as regards medicine."[77] In 1898, when Parliament did finally empower the University of London to incorporate other institutions as "constituent schools," old jealousies prevented them from easily yielding control over their teaching programs.

In 1910, when Abraham Flexner, fresh from his study of American medical education, arrived as an observer in London, medical education was in serious turmoil. British tardiness in adopting the university approach to medicine and in building teaching laboratories was disturbing to influential educators. William Osler, having recently come to Britain as the Regius Professor of Medicine at Oxford, sharply criticized the neglect of laboratory studies in an address at the London Hospital.[78] Both Flexner and Osler, along with Friedrich von Müller of Munich, were invited to give testimony before a royal commission on university education in London headed by Lord Haldane. All three strongly urged the restructuring of medical education in London into a university pattern.

Flexner's strong statement, based on his admiration for the Johns Hopkins School of Medicine, became the point of departure for the hearings. "Medical education in London," he told the commission, "is not fully modern . . . even the fundamental branches are not as yet entirely emancipated or fully developed." He criticized particularly the lack of close interaction between courses in medical science and those in the clinic of the kind now common at Johns Hopkins and other American universities, as well as in Germany. What London and Great Britain needed, he pointed out, was a university model that would "break the existing level of mediocrity." Asked by Lord Haldane whether the ideal model could be found in Baltimore, Flexner replied simply, "Yes."[79] Flexner's support of a plan to make university professors responsible for clinical teaching in the hospitals was vigorously seconded by Osler, who urged the establishment of "hospital units" similar to those in Germany and Baltimore. "We need an invasion of the hospitals by the universities," said Osler.[80]

76. Minutes of School Meetings, Guy's Hospital, June 12, 1891, Wills Library, Guy's Hospital.
77. Suggestions Towards the Formation of the Medical Faculty in a New University of London, June 1892, Royal College of Physicians of London.
78. Cushing, *Life of Sir William Osler*, 876.
79. Royal Commission, *Reports*, 3:2–6.
80. Reported in *Journal of the American Medical Association* 58 (1912): 582.

Much of the testimony before the commission, however, strongly opposed the German–Hopkins university model. The former president of the Royal College of Surgeons, Henry Morris, warned that in Britain the university professor "is not so universally looked upon as the highest pinnacle of intellectual ambition or social glory. . . . German training is very theoretical and scientific and not a preparation fitting a man to go into practise."[81] Almost all who appeared before the commission urged its members not to sacrifice the great strength of the English system of clerks and dressers, which the dean of the London School of Medicine for Women termed "the soul of the English system of training medical students."[82]

The commission's subsequent report largely endorsed Flexner's and Osler's recommendations while emphasizing the importance of retaining the clerkship system under professorial direction. "The main features of the [report]," explained Haldane in 1913, "are a recognition of the great strides being made in university education by the United States and Germany."[83]

Science, the Clinic, and Flexner

The rapid spread of the university as the principal site of medical teaching, though ensuring a key place to science in the education of physicians, raised new tensions between clinicians and scientists. The fight in London over the Flexner plan was but a skirmish in a larger conflict between university reformers and hospital clinicians over control and balance in the curriculum. The happy coming together of the English clerkship and the German laboratory at Baltimore, thanks to the opportunity to build anew and the emollient personalities of Osler and Welch, had set a new goal for Anglo-American educators but concealed a number of unresolved frictions. Because the outcome of the conflict between scientists and clinicians is known, it is often portrayed as foreordained and those who opposed change as shortsighted and selfish. But the final shape of the new curriculum, as contemporaries were well aware, was not yet settled in 1910, and the precise place of science in the professional education of physicians still remained to be worked out.

By 1910 few questioned the need for serious scientific preparation in the beginning period of medical study. Rather, at stake was how much science was needed, how it should be taught, and who should teach it. Should the study of the medical sciences be completed before commencing clinical work, as in Germany, or should it be introduced simultaneously with hospital training, as in France? If laboratory training were essential to becoming a doctor, as most now believed, did it require the students to carry out extensive experiments themselves?

What was the real purpose of the laboratory experience for the average practitioner? Was it to learn scientific method as a critical tool to be used at the bedside and in interpreting laboratory results, or did it go beyond that to acquiring "the spirit of research," as the anatomist Franklin Mall demanded?[84] What was the future of the classroom lecture in medical science, so important to German pedagogy, in which it was augmented by carefully prepared demonstrations and some opportunity for students to see for themselves? How far would the radical strictures against lecturing by such reformers as Mall carry American teaching away from contemporary pedagogical practice in Germany? And what about teaching the individual branches of medical science, such as physiology and pharmacology—did each of them now require a full-time university expert trained in research and investigation?

By its nature, a university was biased in favor of theoretical learning, as opposed to practical study. In Germany, the continuing advance of medical science, as described in Chapter 10, had largely forced the practical studies at the bedside out of the university into an additional year at the hospital. But the newly made universities of France, Britain, and North America, which had only recently become a major site of medical study, grew out of a different historical experience, in which practical study was the *summum bonum* of a medical education. The British and French clinical tradition, moreover, which had carried over to North America, made the sudden shift to a heavily academic and theoretical education for physicians seem highly improbable.

The approach taken to reform in America, noted Lewellys Barker, medical chief at the Johns Hopkins Hospital, in a speech in 1911, "has been . . . successful for having avoided utopian attempts; it has been satisfied with a gradual, though steady, stride toward attainable ideals."[85] What was needed in America, in the view of Arthur Dean Bevan, the longtime chairman of the AMA's Council on Medical Education, was a common standard that was both "high and yet practical." To Bevan— who did more than any other person to shape the emerging balance between scientific and clinical education—an "American standard" meant a high school education and a thorough grounding in physics, chemistry, and biology at the college level; two years of largely laboratory work in the medical sciences; two years of clinical study; and a year of internship in a hospital. But no more than in Britain, in his judgment, should a college degree be required for entrance into medicine. In the medical

84. Franklin P. Mall, "The Value of Research in the Medical School," *Michigan Alumnus* 8 (1904): 396.

85. Lewellys F. Barker, "Some Tendencies in Medical Education in the United States," *Medical Review of Reviews* 57 (1911): 614.

school, he added, "we should insist upon a close association and cooperation between the departments of the laboratory and clinical years."[86] This formulation of an American goal for medical education, supported by organized physicians and university reformers and embodying both German scientific and British clinical practice, became the rallying point for proponents of change in both America and Britain.

Many clinicians continued to resist the growing place of scientific teaching in the curriculum. Still part-time teachers in the universities outside Germany, they viewed with alarm the power of full-time scientific colleagues to shape the curriculum and limit the time spent in clinical study. Professors of basic medical science such as Mall looked for opportunities to displace the old style of clinical teacher with the science-based and laboratory-oriented instructor they had seen in Germany. "It falls to us," wrote Mall to Minot in 1911, "to demand of the last two years of medicine what [is] demanded of the first two."[87] At Harvard the tension between scientists and clinicians became so great around 1910, in the recollection of a former student, that "there was limited communication between them." The clinical teachers "brushed off the preclinical sciences as mere laboratory men who knew but little of medicine, and the scientists looked upon the practice of medicine as largely unscientific guesswork."[88]

In Britain likewise, leading practitioners "routinely invoked science as the foundation of medicine" but "prescribed for science only a limited role in clinical practice." They "resisted the wholesale conversion of bedside practice into a science—any science."[89] French doctors, too, joined students in the first decade of the century in challenging the new emphasis on science in the reorganized universities and demanding an education that was more "practical, longer, and centered in the hospital."[90] Clinical teaching in France, charged a Nantes clinician in 1907, had become "absolutely defective." What was "indispensable" to the teaching of medicine, he said, was not "sumptuous buildings, luxurious laboratories, and eminent scientists" but training at the bedside in a hospital.[91]

Particularly disputed was the usefulness to students of hands-on experimental work in the laboratory. In his 1910 study of American medical

86. Arthur D. Bevan, "Medical Education in the United States: The Need for a Uniform Standard," *Journal of the American Medical Association* 51 (1908): 568–70.

87. Cited in Florence R. Sabin, *Franklin Paine Mall: The Story of a Mind* (Baltimore: Johns Hopkins University Press, 1934), 261.

88. James H. Means, "Experiences and Opinions of a Full-Time Medical Teacher," *Perspectives in Biology and Medicine* 2 (1959): 132–33.

89. Christopher Lawrence, "Incommunicable Knowledge: Science, Technology and the Clinical Art in Britain, 1850–1914," *Journal of Contemporary History* 20 (1985): 504–5.

90. George Weisz, "Reform and Conflict in French Medical Education, 1870–1914," in *The Organization of Science and Technology in France, 1808–1914*, ed. Robert Fox and George Weisz (Cambridge: Cambridge University Press, 1980), 90.

91. E. Bureau, "Modifications à apporter à l'enseignement clinique dans les facultés et écoles de médecine," *Gazette médicale de Nantes* 25 (1907): 821, 824.

schools, Flexner criticized those "conservative medical educators" who saw laboratory science and medical practice as incompatible. What the student learned by doing experiments in the laboratory, he insisted, was the relationship between theory and fact, as "his mind flies like a shuttle between reasonable hypothesis and observed fact." As a practitioner, the doctor faced the same problems as in performing experiments. "Only powers of observation trained in actual experiment," Flexner asserted, enabled him to move from working hypothesis to diagnosis. "The progress of science and the . . . intelligent practice of medicine employ . . . the same technique . . . [They are] one in spirit, method, and object."[92]

For others, however, the case for experimental laboratory study in the undergraduate medical class had not been proved. Richard Cabot of Harvard, himself deeply committed to making diagnosis more scientific, nevertheless claimed that not more than 10 percent of the basic medical science of the early years of medical school was ever used in the first years of practice.[93] In Britain, James Mackenzie sharply criticized Flexner for his "doctrinaire" approach to medical teaching and for ignoring the practical interests of students and practitioners. "It is scarcely realized," he told the Royal Medical Society in 1917, "how crude and limited are all physiological experiments" and how little was scientifically known about the effects of drugs on the human body. Academic teachers of medicine, warmly praised by Flexner, were "obsessed by something they called scientific methods," but as narrow specialists they had little to teach students of what was needed to practice medicine.[94]

University reformers insisted that clinical medicine itself must be made more scientific. How could so much time spent in clinical study be otherwise justified in the scientific atmosphere of a university? Some American and British teachers sought to emulate the example of German clinicians like Ziemssen, Frerichs, and Bernard Naunyn in bringing laboratory experience directly into clinical teaching. Frerichs had joined with Ernst von Leyden in 1880 to found a journal devoted exclusively to clinical science. In the German clinics, new technological innovations, such as the gastric tube and the pocket thermometer, were familiar to students and were being put to regular use in practice and research. Advances in bacteriology, too, were taught in the clinic as important to the physician's ability to understand and treat disease.[95]

92. Flexner, *Medical Education in the United States*, 54–56.

93. R. C. Cabot to Henry Christian, March 1, 1914, Harvard Medical School Archives, Countway Library, cited in T. Andrews Dodds, "Richard Cabot: Medical Reformer During the Progressive Era (1890–1920)," *Annals of Internal Medicine* 119 (1993): 419.

94. James Mackenzie, "The Aim of Medical Education," *Edinburgh Medical Journal* 20 (1918): 32–33, 42–43, 46.

95. Russell C. Maulitz, "'Physician Versus Bacteriologist': The Ideology of Science in Clinical Medicine," in *The Therapeutic Revolution: Essays in the Social History of American Medicine*, ed. Morris J. Vogel and Charles E. Rosenberg (Philadelphia: University of Pennsylvania Press, 1979), 94–95.

Ziemssen had persuaded the authorities to build a laboratory in the new university hospital in Munich, with departments of physiology, pathology, and chemistry. Clinical medicine, he told his students, was a natural science focused on the diagnosis and treatment of disease. German clinics, observed Osler in 1884, were now "clinical laboratories utilized for the scientific study and treatment of disease."[96] The German clinician, unlike his British or American counterpart, stated Flexner in his 1912 report on medical education in Europe, was a research scientist, a full-time university professor, someone who devoted his life to the natural history of disease. "In a soundly organized university," he told his readers, "there is no distinction in kind between the professors of the fundamental or theoretical branches . . . and the professors of the clinical or practical branches." Both must have their research laboratories where basic problems of disease could be investigated by chemical and biological methods.[97]

But in the English-speaking countries, Flexner reported, clinical teaching was still the province of local practitioners. The conditions that made clinical instruction in Germany a respectable profession—full-time appointments, laboratories attached to clinics, and university control of hospitals—scarcely existed in the Britain or North America of 1910, and "clinical medicine droops in consequence."[98] Even at Harvard and other leading institutions, the faculty had as yet no effective control over its affiliated hospitals.[99] A teaching hospital of the type familiar in Europe for more than a century still seemed a long way off. As for clinical research and investigation, they were as yet extremely rare among clinical teachers in Britain and America.

Many clinicians outside Germany claimed that bringing research and laboratory work to the clinic would lead to the loss of traditional bedside skills. Others were concerned about their loss of economic and professional independence if scientifically trained clinicians began to invade departments of medicine. The very concept of clinical science in America was "a radical one at the turn of the century."[100] In Britain, where laboratory science had a "peculiarly difficult passage" into the curriculum, clinical teaching was still thought to require "the ineffable wisdom and experience that came only with advanced years, a classical education and the bearing of a gentleman."[101]

Among those who figured prominently in the reinterpretation of clinical study as a science in Britain were Clifford Allbutt and Ernest Starling

96. Cushing, *Life of Osler*, 225.

97. Abraham Flexner, *Medical Education in Europe* (New York: Carnegie Foundation for the Advancement of Teaching, Bulletin no. 6, 1912), 145, 161.

98. Flexner, Medical *Education in the United States*, 101.

99. Kenneth M. Ludmerer, "Reform at Harvard Medical School, 1869–1909," *Bulletin of the History of Medicine* 55 (1981): 356–57.

100. A. McGehee Harvey, *Science at the Bedside: Clinical Research in American Medicine, 1905–1945* (Baltimore: Johns Hopkins University Press, 1981), 19–30, 115.

101. Lawrence, "Incommunicable Knowledge," 510.

while in America Graham Lusk, Samuel Meltzer, and Lewellys Barker played similar roles. Starling had advocated for some time a fusion of basic medical science with the work of the London clinics by means of "clinical units" of the kind supported by Flexner and Osler. Allbutt, for his part, was urging the appointment of full-time professors and the building of scientific laboratories in the hospitals to "irrigate the profession from the sponge of pure science."[102]

In the United States, the German-trained Lusk wrote in 1909 that the development of American medicine "can come only through men who have a knowledge of medical chemistry, physiology, pharmacology and pathology."[103] No clinical teacher in America, he said, could be compared with a Friedrich von Müller or other German clinicians.[104] At the Johns Hopkins Hospital, Barker, having just returned from an extended stay at Müller's clinic in Munich, expanded the work of the clinical laboratories begun by Osler. "It is just as necessary for physicians and surgeons to have their own laboratories," he proclaimed in 1908, "as it is for aniline dye manufacturers to have chemical laboratories attached to their plants."[105]

But the acceptance of laboratory study in the clinic was as slow and halting as its introduction into the preclinical years had been. In his studies of medical education, Flexner attributed the continued superiority of German medical education to the historic contiguity of scientific departments to the medical clinics in every German university. In Britain and France, as well as in the United States, by contrast, "a consistently organized and motivated university school of medicine"—except for Johns Hopkins—"does not exist."[106] For all the popularity of clinical teaching in France and Britain, he wrote, it was a strength that "scientific medicine refuses to recognize."[107] Although both countries, along with the United States, had made giant strides in organizing and equipping laboratories, they were still physically remote and unintegrated into the teaching of medicine. Not in France or Britain or America was teaching in the hospitals under the sway of medical faculties. "The university spirit," he observed, "is missing in the clinical half of the . . . medical school."[108]

102. Clifford Allbutt, "BMA Address," *British Medical Journal* 2 (1920): 8.

103. Eugene F. DuBois, "Graham Lusk, 1866–1932," *Ergebnisse der Physiologie und experimentellen Pharmakologie* 25 (1933): 10.

104. Graham Lusk, "Medical Education: A Plea for the Development of Leaders," *Journal of the American Medical Association* 52 (1909): 1229. For Müller's influence on American clinical medicine, see Thomas N. Bonner, "Friedrich von Müller of Munich and the Growth of Clinical Science in America, 1902–14," *Journal of the History of Medicine and Allied Sciences* 45 (1990): 556–69.

105. Lewellys F. Barker, "Medical Laboratories: Their Relations to Medical Practise and to Medical Discovery," *Science* 27 (1908): 607.

106. Flexner, *Medical Education in Europe*, 15.

107. Ibid., 230–31.

108. Abraham Flexner, "The German Side of Medical Education," *Atlantic Monthly* 112 (1913): 660–61.

Even in Germany, for all its achievements in medical teaching, Flexner saw weaknesses in the overcrowded curriculum and the overemphasis on didactic lectures and clinical demonstrations in the large classes. "Pedagogically considered," he said in 1912, "the German practice is surely mistaken . . . the most brilliant demonstration is . . . less educative than a more or less bungled experiment executed by the student with his own hands."[109] The great strength of the emerging American system of medical education, he believed with Bevan and others, lay in the attention given to the individual student in both the clinical training borrowed from England and the laboratory instruction taken from Germany.

The power of Flexner's argument, buttressed by the revolutionary changes under way in American medicine and the millions given by the Rockefeller Foundation to support his views, affected scores of medical educators on both sides of the Atlantic. More than forty thousand copies of his reports on medical education in Europe and North America were distributed across America, Britain, and the European continent.[110] The heart of Flexner's conviction about medical study lay in the belief that experimental science had made the union between science and medicine both inevitable and irreversible. Inductive teaching in medicine and science—"learning by doing"—was the key to a pedagogical revolution that was sweeping over the medical schools.[111] The fledgling physician must himself see, feel, hear, and test in the laboratory, in the clinic, and at the bedside. Only in a university that joined investigative science to practical training, such as Johns Hopkins, could a modern physician be educated. There could no longer be two types of medical schools, he argued, one for medical scientists and one for ordinary practitioners, if the aim of medical education were the production of "alert, systematic, thorough, critically open-minded" doctors.[112] Medicine as science could not be separated from medicine as useful human service.[113]

Flexner saw the appointment of full-time professors as the only way to create teaching clinics in America comparable to those of Germany. Although American educators had "no slight cause for satisfaction" in the "race of laboratory men" now teaching full time in the schools of medicine, he wrote in 1910, "on the clinical side the outlook is less reassuring."[114] Working closely with Welch and Mall, he offered Johns Hopkins University an opportunity in 1911 to make full-time appointments in clinical medicine. Clinical professors, according to the plan, would see patients in the university hospital, but the fees collected would go to de-

109. Flexner, *Medical Education in Europe*, 84.
110. Howard J. Savage to Abraham Flexner, July 18, 1924, Flexner Papers, Library of Congress.
111. Ludmerer, *Learning to Heal*, 64–65.
112. Flexner, *Medical Education in the United States*, 56.
113. This paragraph follows my argument in "Abraham Flexner as Critic of British and Continental Medical Education," *Medical History* 33 (1989): 476–77.
114. Flexner, *Medical Education in the United States*, 105.

partmental uses and not to the professor. Such appointments would open careers to scientifically minded clinicians who would otherwise have to enter what Meltzer had called the "bewitching graveyard" of medical practice.[115]

Even though private consulting by clinical teachers was common in Germany, Flexner insisted that any compromise with the greed of private practice in America would leave the busy practitioner in charge of educational and hospital policies. "The clinicians," he wrote to his wife in regard to the University of Michigan, "are the problem. They are a mercenary lot. . . . The laboratory men are heroes—men of ideals who have stood up to their jobs for sheer love of science!"[116] What Flexner sought in behalf of the Rockefeller Foundation in his flinty, drawn-out negotiations with Johns Hopkins and later with Washington University, Yale, Vanderbilt, Rochester, Iowa, and other universities was the creation of an informal national standard subsidized by private philanthropy to bring clinical teaching abreast of that in Germany. His persistence and drive helped move "a disjointed collection of institutionally weak medical schools, universities, and hospitals [to] a fundamentally related national system."[117] The philanthropic foundation he served thus played in some ways the role played by governments in Europe.

For many clinicians, full-time appointments were the last straw in the destruction of traditional clinical medicine. Osler wrote from Oxford warning that "pure laboratory men"—he was undoubtedly referring to Mall and probably Welch—were misleading Johns Hopkins officials. He cited the London testimony of Friedrich von Müller—"who represents the most advanced thought in medicine in Germany"—in which Müller had attacked the full-time system as "directly prejudicial to the teacher and to the school."[118] Other critics asserted that American conditions made it impossible to recruit full-time teachers and scientists in clinical medicine in as sufficient number as in Germany. Still others were convinced that clinical teaching would suffer, not benefit, if it lost touch with its professional roots. Many were fearful, too, of the impact of restrictions on income on their own futures. But Flexner continued to push doggedly for his plan. In explaining why German clinical consulting was less of a danger than in America, he argued that "their scientific ideals [are] more

115. S. J. Meltzer, "The Science of Clinical Medicine: What It Ought to Be and the Men to Uphold It, *Journal of the American Medical Association*, 53 (1909): 512.

116. Abraham Flexner to his wife, December 6, 1920, Flexner Papers, Library of Congress.

117. Steven C. Wheatley, *The Politics of Philanthropy: Abraham Flexner and Medical Education* (Madison: University of Wisconsin Press, 1988), ix. See also, for a reappraisal of Flexner's role, Thomas N. Bonner, "Abraham Flexner and the Historians," *Journal of the History of Medicine and Allied Sciences* 45 (1990): 3–10.

118. Cited in Alan M. Chesney, *The Johns Hopkins Hospital and the Johns Hopkins University School of Medicine*, 3 vols. (Baltimore: Johns Hopkins University Press, 1943–63), 3:181.

potent [and] men have been less readily led away from science to money."[119] By 1912 he was suggesting that even in Germany "the tendency to exploit university clinical positions may ... require to be checked."[120]

As Flexner continued his campaign for full-time clinical positions in America and Britain into the postwar years, opposition mounted. The concept of "geographical full-time," a practice similar to that in Germany calling for a limited private practice within a full-time commitment to teaching and research, became more and more popular as an alternative to Flexner's stringent proposal. By the middle of the 1920s, when his influence began to wane, most universities in America and Britain came to favor the appointment of career-minded clinicians whose primary interests lay in instruction and investigation, with less said about excluding them altogether from income from private practice.

The War and Medical Education, 1914–1920

When the guns sounded in 1914, medical education in the transatlantic world had clearly changed from that of a quarter-century before. A number of broad similarities on both sides of the Atlantic were now apparent in the striving for a university standard of medical education, the nearly universal requirement of a thorough liberal and scientific preparation before beginning study, and the important role played by experimental science in educating doctors. Nearly all now insisted on at least a year of clinical experience before beginning practice, and the growing use of the clerkship or internship was widely seen as the capstone of a medical education.

Important national differences remained in such matters as the role taken by the state, the length of formal study, the balance between scientific and clinical courses, and the amount of hands-on training provided to students. Particularly striking were such differences as the persistence of the hospital medical school without close university connections in Britain; the growing crisis over the teaching of ordinary medical students in Germany; the still unbridged divide between hospital and medical school in France; and the equalitarian yet highly selective nature of the emerging system in the United States. The American medical school was becoming smaller and more student oriented at the very time that European schools were growing in size and complaints of impersonality by students becoming more frequent.

The war itself brought new attention to concerns over the readiness of medical graduates for practice. Demands for skilled practitioners on the battlefield and at home highlighted weaknesses in clinical preparation in

---

119. Ibid., 3:301.
120. Flexner, *Medical Education in Europe*, 148.

all the warring nations. Courses of study were cut short by the acute needs; practical medicine and surgery were understandably given more prominence; and standards were lowered in the search for qualified applicants. The German minister for educational affairs complained in 1915 of graduates' inability to handle medical and surgical cases in battle, their overspecialization, and their lack of practical experience. "Medical education must not neglect its practical side," warned the editor of Germany's leading medical journal at the end of the war. "Medicine is a profession whose real achievement rests on the practical application of scientific results." For all the advances of scientific method in medicine, he told his readers, "it cannot be denied that observation of the sick person has been subjugated in favor of the laboratory."[121]

The war provided a dramatic reminder to other countries, too, of the clinical and observational roots of medical practice. In Great Britain, James Mackenzie told the Edinburgh Pathological Club in 1917 that "an uneasy sense" had fallen over the medical world that "a profound misconception of what clinical medicine really is" had taken root. The medicine of the postwar world, he said, "cannot be pursued on the lines that may suit other sciences." Students must always have the opportunity to study symptoms as well as laboratory results and to follow closely the course of a disease in a living patient.[122]

By 1920 the zeal for more science in medical training, especially in the form of laboratory exercises, had clearly run its course. A correspondent in London for the *New York Medical Journal* described the growing belief there "that too much attention is paid nowadays to bacteriology to the neglect of clinical medicine."[123] The chief adviser to the British Ministry of Health, George Newman, pushed hard at the war's end for shortening the curriculum and creating clinical units in the hospitals, where "a clinical professor [is in] control of wards and an out-patient department."[124] Among American physicians who graduated between 1915 and 1922, complaints were rife of "redundant laboratory work" and the failure of teachers to concentrate on basic scientific concepts "that would give them understanding of the sciences themselves." The argument that performing extensive laboratory experiments instilled a problem-solving, scientific spirit in students was challenged more and more by those who saw such exercises "as a set of tedious and detailed techniques often unrelated to the concepts involved and inappropriate to clinical problems."[125]

121. J. Schwalbe, *Zur Neuordnung des medizinischen Studiums* (Berlin: Georg Thieme, 1918), 10–11.

122. James Mackenzie, "The Aim of Medical Education," *Edinburgh Medical Journal* 20 (1918): 32–33, 38.

123. "London Letter," *New York Medical Journal* 112 (1920): 460.

124. George Newman, *Some Notes on Medical Education in England* (London: His Majesty's Stationery Office, 1918), 26.

125. William G. Rothstein, *American Medical Schools and the Practice of Medicine: A History* (New York: Oxford University Press, 1987), 155–56.

The war impoverished much of European medicine as it impoverished so much of European life. Germany, in particular, suffered a profound and bitter demoralization. Its economy was staggering; its universities were on the verge of bankruptcy; its science was suspect; and its reputation was tarnished by the hatreds of war. "The plight of the sciences is deplorable," wrote Flexner after a postwar visit; "the whole university edifice is being disintegrated through poverty. If the work of destruction is not halted, the finest intellectual organ ever created will be lost to civilization."[126] France and Britain likewise faced overwhelming problems of reconstruction and reorganization after 1918. Although it revived briefly after the war, the prewar traffic in postgraduate education between America and Europe, especially Germany, would never again be the same. "It was only gradually," wrote the Chicago surgeon Max Thorek, "that we began to realize, with disappointed nostalgia mixed with a certain pride, that the war had written *Finis* to a chapter of medical history . . . . The capital of the medical and surgical world was moving westward across the Atlantic."[127]

126. Abraham Flexner to his wife, March 28, 1922, Flexner Papers, Library of Congress.

127. Max Thorek, *A Surgeon's World* (Philadelphia: Lippincott, 1943), 215–16.

12

Changing Student Populations in the Late Nineteenth and Early Twentieth Century

By the turn of the twentieth century, the drive to make medicine more scientific and comprehensive and to limit its ranks to the well prepared had had a profound effect on student populations. Almost universally, students were now older, better educated, more schooled in science, less rowdy, and able to spend larger amounts of time and money in study than their counterparts in 1850 had been. Their ranks, now including a growing number of women, were also likely to include fewer representatives of working- and lower-middle-class families, especially in Britain and America, than a half-century before.

Changing Expectations and Rising Costs

Nations still differed, sometimes sharply, in their openness to students from different social classes. The relative openness of the German universities to the broad middle classes, as well as their inclusion of a small representation of "peasantry and artisans," wrote Lord Bryce in 1885, was a sharp contrast with "the English failure to reach and serve all classes." The burgeoning German enrollments, he noted, were owing to "a growing disposition on the part of mercantile men, and what may be called the lower professional class, to give their sons a university education." More students by far from the farm and working classes of Germany, which accounted for nearly 14 percent of medical enrollment, he observed, were able to get an advanced education than were such students in England.[1]

A historic transformation in the social makeup of universities, according to historian Konrad Jarausch—from "traditional elite" to a "modern middle-class system"—was taking place in the latter nineteenth century.[2] In France, rising standards in education, together with the abolition of the rank of *officiers de santé*—which for a century had opened medical training to the less affluent—were forcing medical education into a middle-class mold. In the United States, the steeply rising requirements in medicine, along with the closing of the least expensive schools, narrowed the social differences among medical students and brought sharp complaints from the less advantaged.[3]

The costs of medical education in some countries threatened to drive all but the most thriving of the middle classes from a chance to learn medicine. "The study of medicine," wrote a concerned German professor in 1896, "is becoming a monopoly of the wealthy."[4] The total cost of a medical education in Germany, according to a report that same year, was now about 12,000 marks (roughly $2,700), a very large sum for this period.[5] Perhaps a fifth of the students received some support in the form of partial scholarships and free meals (*Freitisch*). Costs in Paris, it has been estimated, were similar but were somewhat lower in the French provinces.[6] In both countries, only a dwindling number of families could afford the rising levels of expense.

High as these costs were, a London student visiting the continent in 1908 found them "absurdly low" in comparison with those in the British capital.[7] The total expenses of a British medical education for five years of study in these years ranged from $3,700 to $4,600 in London to somewhat less in the provincial schools.[8] In the United States, despite mounting costs and lengthening periods of study, the average expenditures were still the lowest in the Western world. "No one making a careful study," pointed out the Illinois official John Rauch in 1891, "can fail to be struck

1. James Bryce, Introduction to Johannes Conrad, *The German Universities for the Last Fifty Years*, trans. from German (Glasgow: David Bryce, 1885), xvii–xviii, 69.

2. Konrad Jarausch, "The Social Transformation of the University: The Case of Prussia 1865–1914," *Journal of Social History* 12 (1979): 628.

3. Robert P. Hudson, "Patterns of Medical Education in Nineteenth Century America" (master's thesis, Johns Hopkins University, 1966), 194.

4. O. Mankiewicz, "Zum Entwurf einer neuen Prüfungsordnung," *Deutsche medizinische Wochenschrift* 22 (1896): 553.

5. "Cost of Medical Education in Germany," *British Medical Journal* 2 (1896): 675. See also W. Lexis, *Die deutschen Universitäten*, 2 vols. (Berlin: A. Asher, 1893), 1:187.

6. Pierre Darmon, *La vie quotidienne du médecin parisien en 1900* (Paris: Hachette, 1988), 31–34.

7. "Notes of a roving Guy's Man," *Guy's Hospital Gazette* 22 (1908): 131.

8. Stella V. F. Butler, "Science and the Education of Doctors in the Nineteenth Century: A Study of British Medical Schools with Particular Reference to the Development and Uses of Physiology" (Ph.D. diss., University of Manchester, 1981), 300, appendix II.

with the cheapness of the American degree."[9] An Ann Arbor (Michigan) student who kept an "exact record" of his expenses in 1896 put his expenditures at $584 for one of his three years of study.[10] It was possible to learn medicine for still less, especially in the cheaper schools. A German immigrant named George Dohrmann, who enrolled in an evening medical school in Chicago, reported to his parents in 1897 that he was paying only $145 a year for all his academic expenses and only a little more than that for his board and room.[11]

In both America and Britain, the evening schools of medicine, always few in number, which served working students such as Dohrmann, began to weaken and disappear. These "sundown institutions," remarked Frank Billings in 1903, had "enabled the clerk, the streetcar conductor, the janitor, and others employed during the day to obtain a medical degree."[12] In the United Kingdom, beginning in the late 1880s, the actions of licensing bodies to deny recognition to such schools met with strong denunciation. It was an injustice, said a spokesman for a large evening medical school in Dublin, to make distinctions on the basis of the time of day when study was done rather than by examination and thereby deny opportunity "to men who in the face of the greatest difficulties exhibit untiring energy in their efforts to enter the profession of Medicine."[13]

In American cities even after 1900, a few opportunities for evening medical study still existed. Chicago alone was responsible for three such colleges in 1907. At the Harvey Medical College, Dohrmann wrote that he attended classes from seven to ten o'clock each night, except on Sundays, although after a strenuous day of work he found "little time to study." The situation in the school, which enrolled a hundred students, was "somewhat different than in Germany. There the medical students are fine gentlemen, while we here are nothing but work horses."[14] By the early twentieth century, such schools were under mounting pressure from the licensing authorities and the Council on Medical Education of the American Medical Association to close, and none survived the savage descriptions of their inadequacies in the Flexner Report of 1910.[15]

9. Illinois State Board of Health, *Medical Education, Medical Colleges and the Regulation of the Practice of Medicine in the United States and Canada, 1765–1891* (Springfield: H. W. Rokker, 1891), xxii.

10. H. Winnett Orr, "A Medical Student of the 1890s and of the University of Michigan Class of 1899," manuscript, Bentley Historical Library, University of Michigan.

11. George Dohrmann III, "Medical Education in the United States as Seen by a German Immigrant: The Letters of George Dohrmann, 1897 to 1901," *Journal of the History of Medicine and Allied Sciences* 33 (1978): 480.

12. Frank Billings, "Medical Education in the United States," *Journal of the American Medical Association* 40 (1903): 1272.

13. John W. Moore, "Medical Education and Examinations in 1887," *Dublin Journal of the Medical Sciences* 85 (1888): 45.

14. Dohrmann, "Medical Education in the United States," 479–81.

15. Abraham Flexner, *Medical Education in the United States and Canada: A Report to the Carnegie Foundation for the Advancement of Teaching* (New York: Carnegie Foundation for the Advancement of Teaching, Bulletin no. 4, 1910), 211–17.

The segregated schools of medicine for freed blacks created after the Civil War likewise found it difficult to survive in an era of escalating costs and rising standards of accreditation. In all, fourteen such schools had been founded before 1900, of which only the hard-pressed Howard University Department of Medicine and Meharry Medical College remained at the very end of the reform era.[16] Some of them, notably Howard, which had offered evening programs for working blacks, were forced to discontinue them. As an alternative, students were sometimes allowed to finish their spring term early so that they "could take summer jobs on Pullman cars in order to earn enough as porters to finish next year's education."[17] Flexner's evaluations of these black schools have been described as "harsh," "frank," "chiding," "sarcastic," and "biting," although they were scarcely more so than his descriptions of other schools.[18]

In the mainstream medical schools, only a handful of African Americans gained entrance before 1920. At the University of Pennsylvania, the first black medical student was reportedly told to sit behind a screen and, after refusing to do so, was forced to sit alone on a bench during lectures.[19] Discrimination was the general practice, too, after graduation, especially in medical societies and hospitals. At the 1870 convention of the AMA, N. S. Davis had led an effort to bar membership to a medical society that enrolled black physicians in the District of Columbia. "It is a fact worthy of note," read a protesting memorial from black physicians to Congress, "that this is the only country and the only profession in which such a distinction is made."[20] A visiting German doctor expressed the opinion in 1901 that "the Negro problem throws a question" concerning medical life in the United States and described the efforts at separate education as "extraordinarily bad."[21]

The Limited Admission of Women to Medicine

The medical school at Howard recognized early the connection between the struggle of women and that of blacks to gain equality in education. Alumni of the school attacked discrimination against women in 1873 "as

16. Todd L. Savitt, "Abraham Flexner and the Black Medical Schools," in *Beyond Flexner: Medical Education in the Twentieth Century*, ed. Barbara Barzansky and Norman Gevitz (Westport, CT: Greenwood Press, 1992), 67, table 5.1.

17. M. O. Bousfield, "An Account of Physicians of Color in the United States," *Bulletin of the History of Medicine* 17 (1945): 71.

18. Savitt, "Abraham Flexner and the Black Medical Schools," 71–72.

19. Herbert M. Morais, *The History of the Negro in Medicine* (New York: Publishers Co., 1967), 80.

20. Ibid., 39.

21. "Professor" Tillman, "Uber amerikanische Arzte und ihre Ausbildung," *Deutsche Arzte-Zeitung*, July 1, 1901, p. 9.

being unmanly and unworthy of the [medical] profession."[22] At this time, only a few universities in Europe and America were open to women. At the University of Zurich, beginning in 1864, and in Paris, starting in 1867, women had been admitted into university schools of medicine for the first time. For the next half-century the medical schools of these cities, joined by other Swiss universities, admitted a stream of women from all over Europe, especially Russia, and from the English-speaking countries. The migration was heaviest from those countries that were slowest to give women equal treatment in medical education—Russia, Germany, Austria, Britain, and, at a distance, the United States. The creation of separate women's schools in Russia (1872) and Great Britain (1874), following the American example, failed to halt the exodus of women from these countries to foreign schools. These schools for women in Europe, like those of America, were justified largely by the need of women for practitioners of their own sex.

Medical coeducation continued to be resisted everywhere outside Switzerland and France. In Germany, for example, medical schools remained closed to women until 1900 (in Prussia until 1908), whereas the leading British and American universities, with few exceptions, barred them until World War I. By this time, according to my estimate, at least ten thousand women had left their homelands to study abroad.[23]

In Europe, however, once women were finally admitted to the government schools of medicine, their enrollment rose steadily in the early years of the twentieth century, whereas change in Britain and North America remained slow and halting. Nowhere was the doctrine of "separate but equal" education in medicine so stoutly defended, even by women, as it was in the English-speaking countries. Separate education was made possible in both America and Britain by the relative ease with which private colleges could be chartered in comparison with those in continental Europe. National differences in political ideology thus played as an important part in shaping the course of women's medical education as they did other aspects of medical training. When coeducation in medicine was finally tried at the University of Michigan in 1870, it was described for many years as an "experiment," and few schools moved to follow its example. The battle for coeducation here, unlike that in Europe, was fought in dozens of states and scores of medical colleges before a measure of success was finally achieved.

A deep ambiguity about women's special traits and fitness for medicine slowed the movement for change. On the one hand, the women's medical movement in Britain and America insisted on broadened and equal opportunities for women in medical study, but on the other, it acknowl-

---

22. Morais, *History*, 43.

23. This account, including the next several paragraphs, follows my *To the Ends of the Earth: Women's Search for Education in Medicine* (Cambridge, MA: Harvard University Press, 1992).

edged that women were different from men and that special arrangements for their education might be necessary. As late as 1881, a survey of American women physicians concluded that a majority preferred not to receive all their instruction in mixed classes, "even though this might prove necessary for a first-rate education."[24] The argument for a special place in medicine for women was readily translated into a justification of special schools for them and their exclusion from other schools. These separate schools, in turn, suffered from their isolation from the mainstream of medicine. The resulting stigma of inferiority, writes one authority, "was internalized if not perpetuated by women doctors themselves."[25]

The fight for medical coeducation in Britain and America, then, was especially hard fought. Not until 1894 did coeducation finally overtake separatism in American medical schools, and as late as 1910 a fifth of all women were still studying in separate schools. Gradually, in the United States and Canada, the women's schools closed their doors, but in Great Britain, where the old English universities and the London schools of medicine still banned coeducation, they remained a principal avenue to medical study for women into the 1920s.

Quite unexpectedly, World War I gave a boost to the medical education of women. The universal need for doctors, along with the declining numbers of men in medical school, stimulated efforts to encourage women to enter the schools of medicine. In Britain, Germany, and Russia, women reached new levels of acceptance in medicine amidst the terrible devastation of the war. At the staid University of Marburg, German women made up 30 percent of all medical students by 1917; in the British medical school at Manchester, the number of women students shot up by 400 percent between 1914 and 1918; and in revolutionary Russia, the previously tightly controlled medical courses for women at St. Petersburg were opened to a flood of 1,426 new students, most of them women, in 1918.

By war's end more than ten thousand women were studying medicine in these three countries alone. Coeducation in the medical schools of Britain and North America, on the other hand, made less sweeping gains. Three of the London hospital schools were opened temporarily to women, and a dozen schools in Canada and the United States—including McGill, Yale, and Pennsylvania—brought women into their medical classes for the first time. The "ill wind of war," wrote the editor of the *Medical Woman's Journal*, "brought much good to medical women in

24. Emily F. Pope, Emma L. Call, and Augusta Pope, *The Practice of Medicine by Women in the United States* (Boston: Wright & Potter, 1881), 1, 10.

25. Regina M. Morantz-Sanchez, "Women Physicians, Coeducation, and the Struggle for Professional Standards in Nineteenth-Century Medical Education," paper presented at Berkshire Conference on the History of Women, August 1978, pp. 3–7.

that it opened so many schools to women students and so many hospitals to women internes."[26]

Anti-Semitism and Medical Study

Among the women who persevered the hardest to get a medical education in the face of unimaginable odds in the years before the war were the Russian Jews. Spurred by liberal doctrines of women's equality, encouraged by their comrades in the intelligentsia, and confronted by a bar to academic study and a near-feudal structure of social relationships in Russia, these women somehow "developed an inner spirit of freedom," writes one scholar, that made them "confident of their equality with men and their ability to be doctors, lawyers, mathematics, chemists."[27] Russian women made up 70 to 80 percent of all those women who studied medicine in coeducational schools abroad before 1914 and fought hard for the few places open to them at home.

Their presence in western Europe, along with that of male Jewish colleagues and the growth of native Jewish student populations, sparked a wave of anti-Semitism in France, Switzerland, and Germany. In Lyon, for example, students demonstrated in 1896 against the influx of foreigners, especially women, charging that they were crowding French students out of clinics and classes, preempting favored places, and offering unwelcome competition in the concours for the few positions in the hospitals.[28] Even more threatening to many was the great number of foreigners in Paris, where some five thousand students and doctors, many of them Jews, vied for entrance into the limited facilities for study.[29] Swiss students were likewise upset by the aggressive competition of Russian women for favorable laboratory and classroom places. They attacked the clannishness of the Russian women, their dress and manners, and their interest in radical politics. "Hyenas of the Revolution" and "seductresses of youth" the Bern press called them, describing their student communities as an "underworld of sickly, half-educated, and uncontrolled creatures."[30]

The most savage response to the foreign students came in the German

---

26. *Medical Woman's Journal* 35 (1928): 291.

27. Ruth A. Dudgeon, "Women and Higher Education in Russia, 1855–1905" (Ph.D. diss., George Washington University, 1975), 388–90. See also the discussion of the reasons for Russian women's greater zeal in seeking medical education in Bonner, *To the Ends of the Earth*, 81–100.

28. L. Bard, "De l'admission en France des étudiants et des médecins étrangers," *Lyon médical* 82 (1896): 371–78, 406–14.

29. See, for example, Rapport de la commission chargée d'examiner la proposition de M. le Professeur Debove relative à l'admission des étrangers à la faculté de médecine de Paris, Archives nationales, AJ[16] 6496.

30. Marianna Progin and Werner Seitz, "Das Frauenstudium an der Universität Bern," 47, manuscript, 1980, Historical Seminar, University of Bern.

universities, where anti-Semitism had been on the rise since the 1880s. From university after university came reports in the early years of the new century of student demonstrations, harshly worded petitions, and occasionally ugly incidents. A petition from students at Jena, for example, called on university authorities in 1905 to restrict further enrollment of Russian Jews, whose "aggressive manner" and "offensive conduct" aggravated the overcrowding in classrooms, and to give preference to German students.[31] At Heidelberg, Russian students pleaded with the entire student body to understand their predicament and to cease the attacks on them.[32]

More serious was a strike called by clinical students at Halle in 1912, where foreigners made up a third of the student body. It subsequently spread to Giessen and other universities. Over the objections of the medical faculty, the state authorities yielded to the students' demands and imposed harsh new limits on foreign students.[33] Commenting on the Halle strike, one newspaper, the *Nationalzeitung*, warned against the "blind chauvinism of the students."[34]

Jewish groups complained bitterly of the wave of anti-Semitism in the universities. The Society of German Jews (Verband der deutschen Juden) charged that fewer Jews were reaching the rank of full professor in 1910 than in 1875 and that they comprised only 2.5 percent of all such appointments. In the case of medicine, only one Jewish full professor had been named since 1884.[35]

The Student Experience

By the turn of the century, student life had clearly become much more serious. Although medical students in Britain and America were still occasionally described as "rough, tough, and boisterous," an American journalist wrote in 1896 that "the modern type has none of these characteristics, and is probably better behaved than the average of any other body of men or boys."[36] An Oxford professor recalled a few years later that "the time when any outbreak of rowdyism in London more than usually disgraceful was sure to be attributed . . . to medical students" but that this

31. Clipping in "Studentenschaft und soziale Bewegungen, 1895–1915," GSPK, Merseburg, 77, CB, S, Nr. 10.

32. "An die Heidelberger Studentschaft," *Akten der medizinischen Facultät*, III, 4a, 168, p. 59, University of Heidelberg Archive.

33. Clippings, especially from *Tägliche Rundschau* (Berlin), in GSPK, Merseburg, 76 Va, Sekt 1, Tit VII, Nr. 67, Ad hib D.

34. *Nationalzeitung*, December 19, 1912.

35. Bernhard Breslauer, *Die Zurücksetzung der Juden an den Universitäten Deutschlands* (Berlin: Verband der deutschen Juden, 1911), 532–33.

36. A. L. Benedict, "The Life of a Medical Student," *Lippincott's Monthly Magazine* 58 (1896): 394.

was now "a matter of the past." The change was due, he and others believed, to the infusion of older, more settled university graduates into the student body.[37] Many of those now studying medicine, it was widely noticed, were not only older but also had previously attended a college where they had put behind them the rowdy antics of youth released from parental supervision. The new breed of medical student, remarked Osler in 1905, was no longer given to "taverns and sack and wine."[38]

Not only were the students older, but they also studied longer. By the end of the century, the average age at graduation of the American physicians that Hudson studied had risen to nearly twenty-six years.[39] "Nearly if not quite half our medical students," said the journalist cited earlier, "are over thirty, and the presence of men of fifty excites no comment."[40] Many of these, of course, were part-time students or those beginning a second career. Americans in any case, observed the *Medical News*, were entering practice "from one to three years beyond that of students in foreign countries."[41]

But although the students in Europe and Britain might sometimes be younger at graduation, they frequently spent long years in preparing for licensing examinations. In regard to Glasgow students qualifying for a license in 1906, for example, one in five had spent six years or more since first registering at a medical school.[42] Figures from the General Medical Council for the same year reveal that the mean length of study for licensing for all of Great Britain and Ireland was six years and eleven months.[43]

A French report of 1893 showed similarly that three-fourths of all students in Paris were taking more than six years to complete their studies—which in France entitled them to practice—whereas 38 percent studied for more than eight years, and an astounding 15 percent spent more than eleven years before taking their final examinations.[44] It was not uncommon for a student to take five or six years to prepare for the *concours* alone, which then gave him (and very occasionally her) four years of valuable experience in a hospital as an intern before beginning to practice.[45] Comparable data for the state examinations in Germany are not readily available, but the studies by Wilhelm Lexis indicate that the average age

37. Reported in "The Behavior of Medical Students," *New York Medical Journal* 80 (1904): 265.

38. William Osler, "The Student Life," *Aequanimatas with other Addresses to Medical Students, Nurses and Practitioners of Medicine,* 3rd ed. (Philadelphia: Blakiston, 1932), 403.

39. Hudson, "Patterns of Medical Education," 50.

40. Benedict, "Life of a Medical Student," 395.

41. "Higher Medical Education," *Medical News* 66 (1895): 23.

42. Minutes, Medical Faculty, October 4, 1908, University of Glasgow Archive.

43. Felix Semon, "English and German Education: A Parallel," *Medical Review of Reviews* 13 (1907): 1204.

44. Rapport sur le programme sommaire de réforme des études médicales, manuscript, 1893, Léon Le Fort, rapporteur, Archives nationales, AJ[16] 6357.

45. Henri Huchard, *La réforme de l'enseignement médical et des concours de médecine* (Paris: O. Berthier, 1890), 16.

of medical students in 1890 was twenty-four, indicating that graduates were twenty-six or more and still had to pass their licensing examinations.[46]

What was the daily life of a student in these changing circumstances? The American journalist mentioned earlier portrayed a typical student at the end of the century as spending eight hours a day, including Saturdays and part of Sundays, in classes or clinics and then dissecting for two hours each night. Most worked in a laboratory from two to three hours each afternoon, "with the microscope on one day, with test-tubes, retorts, and beakers on another, again learning something of the pharmacist's art, or investigating the phenomena of the lower forms of life." Attendance at clinics, which were held three times a week, was "allowed during the first year and advised during the next" but became "of the highest importance" in the third and final year. Seniors were "turned into the wards of a hospital" for several hours each week, where they were "allowed to examine patients, to note the treatment, perhaps to assist in bathing, cupping, [and] giving electricity."[47]

Access to Patients and Clinics

Not all students had easy access to the wards of a hospital, however. American students at the turn of the century still depended heavily on the hospitals' goodwill for experience with patients. The system of clinical clerks introduced in 1896 at the Johns Hopkins Hospital, which made students directly responsible for caring for patients under faculty supervision—much like the German schools a half-century earlier—advanced only slowly beyond Baltimore. By 1910 no more than a dozen colleges in America had adopted some form of the clerkship system.

Faculty members in other schools at this time had almost no control over the use of hospital beds for assigning responsibility for patients to individual students. In the first decade of the century, writes Ludmerer, "very few medical students could be found actively caring for patients."[48] Complaints were frequent. Despite the "unbounded hospital and dispensary facilities" in Detroit, wrote the student editor of a Detroit Medical College publication, "half of the time [we] never get near a bedside."[49] At Harvard, James Means found the teaching of clinical medicine in 1909 to be "dreadful" and patient contact to be "tenuous" after the hands-on laboratory training of the first two years.[50] A student in New York asked

---

46. W. Lexis, *Die deutschen Universitäten*, 2 vols. (Berlin: A. Asher, 1893), 1:138, table V.

47. Benedict, "Life of a Medical Student," 391–92.

48. Kenneth M. Ludmerer, "The Plight of Clinical Teaching in America," *Bulletin of the History of Medicine* 57 (1983): 218.

49. *The Leucocyte* 6 (1899): 17. This publication is in the Walter P. Reuther Archive for Labor and Urban History, Wayne State University, Detroit.

50. James H. Means, "Experiences and Opinions of a Full-Time Medical Teacher," *Perspectives in Biology and Medicine* 2 (1959): 133.

why students could not at least "do some of the work left entirely to the nurses, such as the taking of temperatures, the counting of pulses, the tubbing of typhoid cases, perhaps, and the like."[51]

Students found that clinical teaching was still largely through lectures and recitations. Means recalled that three and sometimes four lectures were held each afternoon, at which patients were rarely present. In the mornings, students were divided into sections to visit wards and outpatient clinics. "We were taken as if on a Cook's tour by an instructor who showed us interesting patients and quizzed us on them a bit, but we were actually observers, not participants."[52] But by the early years of the century, teaching in small sections in the wards had become the rule, although some students reported that the only benefit of the smaller sections was that "lectures are now delivered to an audience of twenty to thirty students instead of to two hundred men gathered in a lecture hall."[53]

In the hands of a skilled and dedicated teacher, however, such as George Dock at Michigan, teaching in the smaller groups could be very effective. Dock divided his classes into sections of five or six students, all of whom were given some responsibility for patients until they were discharged, sometimes with follow-up visits at home. Students took histories, examined patients, made daily visits, and suggested a diagnosis and plan of treatment. "What do you think has been going on in your patient since you saw him before?" reads a stenographic record of Dock's questioning of one student. "I have examined the records," was the reply, "and have seen no development." "Did you examine him in the ward?" Dock gently led the student.

> Don't you think that would have been a better place? In the laboratory you have only second-hand information, so that you are leaning on some other man and the other man may be a cripple. You can learn a good deal more by seeing your patient for two minutes than by turning over the leaves of a record.[54]

It was small wonder that on his 1907 visit to America, such teaching caused Friedrich von Müller to describe it as a vast improvement over the large clinical lectures in Germany.[55]

Teaching conditions for American students improved generally after 1910. The growing power of medical schools and organized medicine, the increased licensing requirements, the new philanthropic and state

51. Benjamin Michailovsky, "Some Points in Medical Education Considered from the Standpoint of the Student," *Medical Record* 73 (1908): 18.

52. Means, "Experiences and Opinions," 134.

53. Michailovsky, "Some Points in Medical Education," 17.

54. Horace W. Davenport, *Doctor Dock: Teaching and Learning Medicine at the Turn of the Century* (New Brunswick, NJ: Rutgers University Press, 1987), 18.

55. Friedrich von Müller, "Amerikanische Reiseeindrücke," *Münchener medizinische Wochenschrift* 54 (1907): 2391.

support, and the example of Johns Hopkins and others worked together to increase the number of medical teachers and to reduce the size of classes. More and more schools turned to the clerkship system, in which students were given some responsibility for patients, as the best way to impart clinical experience. Some built teaching hospitals or forged stronger relationships with existing ones. Columbia, Harvard, and Washington universities all entered into new teaching relationships in these years with major hospitals—giving them the power to appoint medical staff and to use them to teach students. Hospitals, for their part, were coming to view an affiliation with a medical school as an asset rather than a liability in serving the public. Consequently by 1921, every medical school had some use of a teaching hospital for its faculty and students.[56]

By this time, too, the postgraduate internship had become a fixture in many medical schools. After 1890, the experience of a year or more in a hospital, as a "house officer" or "intern" after graduation to acquire the bedside training so often lacking in medical school had become common. Although not required by most schools of medicine, three of every four graduates in 1914 were taking an internship of some kind before beginning to practice.[57] Although the American practice resembled in some ways the French *internat*, after which it was named, it was much closer to the German "practical year" that followed the completion of medical studies.

No such sweeping change in clinical teaching occurred in Great Britain during the years before World War I. Long accustomed to the clerkship and relatively free access to hospitals, students were far more concerned about the large size of clinical lectures and the impersonality of their relationships with the teaching faculty. British students and graduates traveling abroad invariably commented on the greater informality and closer ties between teachers and students. While the size of medical classes was dropping in America in response to higher standards and increased support, in Britain the large auditorium lecture remained the principal method of teaching clinical subjects. A student publication in London asked sarcastically in 1899: "Why should not opera glasses, on the principle of 'put-a-penny-in-the-slot' be fitted to the back rows of rails?"[58] Students in Manchester staged a debate two years later on a resolution that "systematic lectures ought to be abolished," which carried "amidst prolonged cheering." One speaker claimed that "lectures are really a relic of by-gone ages, when students were few, and books still less numerous."

56. Kenneth M. Ludmerer, "Washington University and the Creation of the Teaching Hospital," *Journal of the American Medical Association* 266 (1991): 1983.

57. Rosemary Stevens, "Graduate Medical Education: A Continuing History," *Journal of Medical Education* 53 (1983): 6–7.

58. *The Gyroscope*, June 9, 1897, p. 70. This was a publication of Guy's students that can be found in the Wills Medical Library, Guy's Hospital.

Of what use was it, he demanded, to give "long lists of symptoms of a disease, when one can get a patient who exhibits all these symptoms?"[59]

On the Continent, the daily routine of students hardly changed in the decade and a half before World War I. In Paris, still the largest medical school in Europe, more than five thousand students crowded into the hospitals, clinics, and amphitheaters spread across the city. Experience in a hospital remained the heart of preparation for medicine, though most had little direct responsibility for patients during their years of study. Students were exposed early to the hospital, saw patients being examined and procedures undertaken, but only on occasion, depending on the professor and the size of the group, were given the opportunity to examine a patient or to take part in managing a case.

It was in the hospital nevertheless that a French student was expected to learn the basic procedures of physical examination and treatment of the sick. Sometimes the early exposure to serious illness brought shock. One student recalled the impression made on him on his third day in medical school when he was asked to "assist" at a major operation for removal of a leg at the hip. Although the operation took only three minutes, he wrote, "the sight of the limb falling like a tree" from the table "impressed me [far] more than an autopsy."[60]

A typical day for a beginning French student around 1900 began with five hours in the hospital, followed by three hours of lectures and library study, several hours of dissection, two hours in a large amphitheater (sometimes holding two thousand students), dinner, and study at home. Students still frequently took private courses to supplement the prescribed curriculum, as they did in Germany, or to gain more personal instruction. Sometimes these courses, too, could be very large. The popular clinician Léon Le Fort, for example, often attracted three hundred students to his private course.

The students' most common criticism of the French hospital system of instruction was the unevenness of its teaching and its inadequacy for many. Even though the mornings spent in the hospital extended over at least four of the five years of study, and a student might make more than five hundred such visits in all, many complained that the time invested was of little value in learning medicine. "The student can present himself every day at the hospital," according to one account, "sign the registration books, and not examine a single patient. Frequently, he attends a service in which the chief does not know his name and never asks a question. He can never have palpated, never auscultated, never diagnosed and never opened an abscess."[61]

The life of a French student, wrote a traveling fellow from Guy's Hos-

59. *Manchester Medical Students Gazette* 1 (1901): 13–14. This publication is located in the Manchester Collection, Rylands Library, University of Manchester.

60. Charles Achard, *Confession d'un vieil homme du siècle* (Paris: Mercure, 1943), 42.

61. Darmon, *Vie quotidienne*, 42–43, 69–70.

pital in 1908, "cannot be as pleasant as that of his London compeer. From the time of matriculation until he is qualified he may never be attached to a hospital . . . must look out for himself, and find out . . . what courses to attend, and what work to do."[62] Only a small elite was ever able to win a coveted position as intern in a hospital. Two of every three students, according to the author of a turn-of-the-century guidebook, left the schools of France without having served as either an extern or an intern and thus "see their first sick persons" when they encountered their first patients.[63]

Students still found time for demonstrations and political action. They contributed to the sense of crisis that hung over French medical education in the years before the war. Together with practicing doctors, now organized into powerful professional groups, they attacked the status quo, especially the weaknesses of clinical training, the overcrowding in the hospitals, the *concours*, and the privileged position of the academic elite. "What of the student poor in money and connections," wrote one critic, "what can he hope from . . . our pseudo-democratic and egalitarian future? Nothing but to be a modest practitioner . . . to whom the hospitals and faculties pitilessly close their doors forever: he has not been an intern."[64]

A common cause of student hostility in France was also the complex and severe system of examinations. Individual professors were singled out for the difficulty and length of their questions, and their homes and offices were sometimes made the sites of demonstrations. In 1905 the whole Latin Quarter exploded in riot when the police chief struck a protesting student at the home of one professor. Fifteen hundred students poured into the streets around the school of medicine, set up barricades, and succeeded in closing the school.[65] Protests and demonstrations continually rocked the schools in the decade before the war. The school in Paris was closed nearly every year between 1905 and 1913. As the profession itself became more militant in these years—demanding an education that was "practical, longer, and centered in the hospitals"—the medical faculties, especially in Paris, felt themselves under siege. At a time when the academic profession of medicine was coming into its own in America, its French counterpart was being bludgeoned by the hostility of students and the outright opposition of practitioners.[66]

62. Arthur F. Hertz, "Aspects of French Medicine," *Guy's Hospital Gazette* 22 (1908): 155.

63. Darmon, *Vie quotidienne*, 61.

64. Lucien Grellety, *Encombrement et dépréciation de la profession médicale* (Macon: Protat, 1893), 22–23.

65. Julien Noir, "Les manifestations des étudiants en médecine," *Progrés médical* 21 (1905): 188.

66. George Weisz, "Reform and Conflict in French Medical Education, 1870–1914," in *The Organization of Science and Technology in France, 1808–1914*, ed. Robert Fox and George Weisz (Cambridge: Cambridge University Press, 1980), 89–94.

According to the same visitor from Guy's, German students had even more trouble than those of France in getting bedside experience. As many as two hundred students could be found attending a typical clinic by 1906, he reported, and "it is obviously impossible . . . to teach at the bedside." As a result, he found that "the theoretical knowledge of the students [is] more developed than the practical."[67] Especially in the larger universities, most practical training was now deferred to the final practical year spent in a hospital.

By this time, observed Flexner in a scathing review of German clinical teaching, "it is [a] case of locking the stable after the horse has strayed. Free run of the hospital for a year furnishes experience, not training." The system of completing all theoretical study before getting practical experience, he asserted, "inverts sound pedagogical order." For most students, the only exposure to patients in undergraduate teaching came during periods of vacation employment in a hospital or by serving as a *Praktikant* in a clinical class. One or two of the *Praktikanten*—who were designated to receive credit in a particular class by "assisting" the professor—might be called down during a class to examine the patient being discussed and to be subjected to questions, but the experience, in the view of most students, had little pedagogical value.

Flexner described a typical experience of a student called to examine an "unusual case" by the professor. First, he said, the student had had no previous preparation for "the part which he is abruptly required to play." Then, standing before an auditorium of classmates and visitors, he paused, embarrassed, overwhelmed by the moment, until he was given a clue. The professor "watches him fumble, and then, almost without knowing it, takes the ball, as indeed he must." In a few minutes, "the *Praktikant* has slunk out of sight," and the practical exercise is over. "It is," Flexner concluded, "a futile device."[68]

As suggested earlier, by 1910 many German teachers admitted that their clinical training was now inferior to that of Britain and France. "The English student grows up in the hospital," wrote Friedrich von Müller, as did the student in France, but the German student now got less hands-on experience than either.[69] "Forty or fifty years ago," he told students in 1912, "clinical teaching [in Germany] . . . was done very differently from today. Then the physician went through the wards with his pupils, who were small in number, examined patients together and followed the daily changes in them." Now the great number of students in the large universities, without a corresponding increase in teachers, had made this impos-

---

67. Arthur F. Hertz, "Aspects of German Medicine," *Guy's Hospital Gazette* 20 (1906): 408–9.

68. Abraham Flexner, *Medical Education in Europe* (New York: Carnegie Foundation for the Advancement of Teaching, Bulletin no. 6, 1912), 172–76.

69. Friedrich von Müller, "Studium der inneren Medizin," *Münchener medizinische Wochenschrift*, 1900, 585.

sible, and so "we have to regard clinical teaching in the auditorium as necessary." At the smaller universities, however, the old form of teaching still persisted, and Müller urged his students to go to one of them during their semesters of clinical study.[70]

The national systems of clinical training had thus come almost full circle since the middle of the last century. The German student of medicine, who once enjoyed more individualized attention and responsibility for patients than any of his contemporaries did, now received his bedside training almost wholly after completing his formal study. The average French or English student, on the other hand, who long had had easy access to a hospital but little responsibility at the bedside, still found some opportunities for practical instruction. And the American student, for whom bedside training had come largely from an apprenticeship in 1850, was beginning to benefit from a new pedagogy that stressed the value of patient responsibility at an early stage of medical training.

70. Friedrich von Müller, *Wie studiert man Medizin?* (Munich: Ernst Reinhardt, 1912), 22–23.

13

Consolidation, Stability, and New Upheavals, 1920–1945

By the end of World War I, the basic structures of undergraduate medical education in both Europe and America were largely in place. Future practitioners on both sides of the Atlantic now began their training with a lengthy preparation in liberal studies, with special attention to physics, chemistry, and biology, then studied for two or more years in laboratory-based courses in the preclinical medical sciences followed by a like period of clinical study, and finally spent at least a year in acquiring practical, hands-on training in a hospital. With few changes, except for the growth of postgraduate education, this basic pattern prevailed everywhere in the interwar years before 1945. In the transatlantic nations, in short, these were years of consolidation of patterns formed well before 1914.

The study of medicine now consumed a minimum of five years beyond the school-leaving or college experience and frequently took six to ten years to complete. Except for the hospital schools of London, nearly every medical school in the Western world was attached to a university. Almost no school of medicine was without its teaching hospital where training students was a primary concern. Governments everywhere played an ever larger role in setting basic requirements and providing financial support of medical education. Physicians' associations became more and more powerful and sometimes dominant in setting standards of education and licensure. And in these postwar years, the practice of medicine became an almost wholly middle-class occupation, exacting high standards of preparation and social expectation and open to only the most exceptional among the less affluent. The costs of study were rising so steeply that it was largely unavailable to the poor, even in the United States.[1]

The Aftermath of War

The national differences of a quarter-century before, though evened out in many particulars, were still discernible in 1920. The war, after all, permitted no major changes in instruction, equipment, or curriculum in Europe, and reform efforts after the war were hampered by the need to restore and rebuild. Flexner, now at the peak of his power and influence in the early 1920s, found no change in the German system that would give "a more practical character to medical education," and he described medical teaching in France as "quite stationary." French educators, he said, continued as they had before the war to put a "premature and excessive emphasis" on the clinical experience, as did the British, but in the latter country, the government was at last taking steps to install "clinical units" under academic leadership in the hospitals of University College, St. Bartholomew's, and St. Thomas's.

These British efforts at change in the direction of the Johns Hopkins program, like others in Europe and America, were given crucial support by the Rockefeller Foundation. Leaders of the foundation backed vigorously the reform agenda of universities and academic physicians as offering the best chance to overcome or control disease and to improve the public's health. Those staffing the new Rockefeller-supported units in London were the first full-time teachers of medicine and surgery in their respective schools. The government in Britain had also moved to create the Medical Research Council in 1913 that was authorized to award fellowships to promising scientific investigators, who might then be expected to become teachers in the medical schools. But all in all, concluded Flexner in 1924, surveying schools across Britain and Europe, "except for the damage done by the war, Western Europe continues to work along the same lines that existed prior to the war."[2]

In America, by contrast, where the war had brought far less disruption and aroused instead a great burst of national energy, he found change "enormously greater than anywhere else." The number of medical schools had been cut almost in half; equipment and facilities were vastly expanded; laboratory courses were normally taught by full-time teachers; and clinical instruction, while still left frequently to busy practitioners, was nonetheless moving toward "a genuinely professional clinical teach-

---

1. Commission on Medical Education, *Medical Education and Related Problems in Europe* (New Haven, CT: Commission on Medical Education, 1930), 175, 191; William G. Rothstein, *American Medical Schools and the Practice of Medicine: A History* (New York: Oxford University Press, 1987), 153.

2. Abraham Flexner, "Medical Education, 1909–1924," *Educational Record*, April 1924, (reprint), 4–6.

ing staff of high quality." The explanation for this transformation, Flexner argued, lay in the great distance that American medical education had had to travel to reach European standards, as well as in the swiftly rising level of support that could not "have been dreamed of a decade ago."[3]

The Rockefeller Foundation, which Flexner represented, led the international efforts to direct these changes. In 1920, for example, apart from the aid being given to American and European schools, it awarded $5 million to improve medical training in Canada, especially at McGill and Toronto universities. By 1928, all eight Canadian schools—none had been closed following Flexner's 1910 report—were rated in the Class A category by the American Medical Association's Council on Medical Education.[4]

Still to be overcome on the American side of the border, in Flexner's view, were the continuing differences that separated the best from the weakest schools and the new uniformity of curricular requirements being imposed by the Council on Medical Education. "What sound reason," Flexner asked the council in 1924, "can be given for requiring the able and the less able, the industrious and the less industrious, to complete practically the same course of instruction in the same period of time?" In comparison with European authorities, American medical school leaders, he charged, took far too paternalistic an interest in the individual student. This made it necessary for the schools to limit their enrollments beyond all reason. What was needed, he insisted, was the abandonment of "the notion that there is only one way in which to train a physician."

While avoiding such "monstrosities" as the medical schools of Vienna, Berlin or Paris, at which practical teaching was "all but impossible," Flexner counseled that America should seek a middle way between the small classes of twenty-five, now common in the United States, and the European lecture hall with its hundreds of students. With all that had been accomplished in America, Flexner told the council in 1924, "we are still near the beginning. . . . It will take us twenty or thirty or forty years to round ourselves out."[5]

Between the Wars

Flexner's advice was not taken. Rather than moving toward the German standard of student freedom, the American medical school became increasingly standardized and inflexible during the interwar years. The

---

3. Ibid., 7.

4. N. Tait McPhedran, "Canadian Medical Schools Before ACMC," *Canadian Medical Association Journal* 148 (1993): 1536. See also McPhedran's *Canadian Medical Schools: Two Centuries of Medical History, 1822 to 1992* (Montreal: Harvest House, 1993), 12–17.

5. Flexner, "Medical Education," 6–18.

number of hours spent by American students in required courses rose steadily in response to the growing body of specialized knowledge believed necessary for every practitioner. Often the curriculum allowed almost no deviation from a prescribed set of courses.

The program of study, after all, was still intended for the vast majority of students who, after a year or so of experience in a hospital, took up the demands of a general practice in medicine and surgery. As courses grew more numerous and specialized, their content became more narrow and the teaching more didactic. Some schools, such as Yale in 1926 and Johns Hopkins a year later, did offer students some choice among electives, but only a few competitors followed their example. Eventually, these schools, too—pressed to prepare students for standardized state examinations—began to reduce the students' choices, and by 1945 almost no medical school offered more than a few hours of electives.[6]

The major characteristics of the North American system of training doctors in the 1920s and 1930s were its controlled size, its uniformly high standards, its lavish expenditures, the balance between preclinical science and clinical study, the growing emphasis on research, and the emergence of a residency system of training teachers and specialists in hospitals. The internship experience after graduation, which had been offered by a number of hospitals before the war, now became commonplace across the country. By 1923 enough hospitals were offering positions to interns to meet the needs of all graduates for a year of hospital training.[7]

The size of the medical teaching enterprise in the United States, which had reached a peak of 162 schools in 1906, plummeted to 76 in 1930, and student enrollment fell in the same period from 25,000 to 21,000, despite a sizable increase in population. Some schools, beginning with Johns Hopkins, had begun restricting enrollments before the war; by 1924 three-quarters of them were limiting the numbers admitted each year. The secretary of the Council on Medical Education, N. P. Colwell, was so concerned that well-qualified students might not win a place in medicine in the postwar years that he urged schools to relax their quotas and "provide space for reasonably large classes."[8] Students in both the United States and Canada were now applying for admission with stronger records of preparation in science and general study than ever before. In 1921, for example, when all but 7 schools demanded at least two years of college study, nearly 45 percent of graduating medical students already

6. John K. Crellin, "American Medical Education: For Teachers or Students?" in *History of Medical Education*, ed. Teizo Ogawa (Tokyo: Saikon, 1983), 14–15.

7. Edward C. Atwater, "'Making Fewer Mistakes': A History of Students and Patients," *Bulletin of the History of Medicine* 57 (1983): 176.

8. N. P. Colwell, "Present Needs of Medical Education," *Journal of the American Medical Association* 82 (1924): 839.

held degrees in the arts and sciences. A visiting British official from the General Medical Council called the proportion "remarkable."[9]

The curriculum in place in American schools in the early 1920s remained largely unchanged for the next three decades. In the first year of study came classes in anatomy, biochemistry, and physiology, in which the students spent as much as half their time in anatomical dissection and doing experiments in chemistry and physiology from a laboratory manual that guided them step by step in their work. Further study in preclinical science in the second year normally included pathology, bacteriology, and pharmacology, as well as an introduction to clinical medicine. The latter course, which emphasized diagnostic techniques, history taking, and use of the stethoscope, was aimed at bridging what a contributor to the *Journal of the American Medical Association* in 1923 described as "the chasm between the fundamental and clinical branches of medicine."[10] In his work in pathology, the student spent long hours looking at diseased organs and tissues under a microscope and attending autopsies in the hospital.

Some schools offered a second-year course in practical laboratory techniques in which a number of procedures, such as urinalysis, stool examination, and blood counts, were carried out. Pharmacology in the 1920s was still "a strange mixture of prescription writing and demonstrations or laboratory exercises in which the effects of drugs on laboratory animals were observed." The final two years of clinical study for all students were "the period in their lives when they worked the longest hours, studied the hardest, learned the most, and were the most exhilarated." Here the student served his or her clinical rotations, learned to perform a normal delivery, and began to prepare for his or her licensing examination.[11]

The most important new direction in medical education of the 1920s in North America was setting the standards for those seeking to qualify themselves as specialists. Postgraduate programs had grown up before and during the war around such leading figures as the surgeon William Halsted at the Johns Hopkins Hospital. The situation had become chaotic, however, and threatened to duplicate the earlier disorder in requirements for general medical practice. Both hospitals and medical schools were offering programs of varying duration and content in a number of specialties.

As early as 1916, the Council on Medical Education began visiting the

9. Norman Walker, "Some Comments on Medical Education, Legislation, and Practice in the United States," *Edinburgh Medical Journal* 26 (1921): 24.

10. J. A. Myers, "Bridging the Chasm Between the Fundamental and Clinical Branches in Medical Schools," *Journal of the American Medical Association* 81 (1923): 599–601.

11. Vernon W. Lippard, *A Half-Century of American Medical Education: 1920–1970* (New York: Josiah Macy, Jr. Foundation, 1974), 8–11. For a contemporary analysis of the curriculum about 1930, see Irving S. Cutter, "The School of Medicine," in *Higher Education in America*, ed. Raymond A. Kent (Boston: Ginn, 1930), 284–347.

sites of postgraduate training and by 1921 was setting preliminary standards for the minimum length and subject content of programs. Two
years later, the American Medical Association approved a set of principles
concerning admissions to postgraduate programs and their curricula, faculty, supervision, and facilities, as well as a list of approved sites. By the
middle of the decade, the council had given its blessing to twenty-two
such programs and to 263 hospital sites that offered residencies or *advanced internships*, as they were then called.[12] Hospitals had thus become
(and would remain) the principal training ground for graduate medical
education. So far, however, the significance of these programs to the total
teaching enterprise, except for the training of teachers, was small, but the
groundwork was being laid for the great expansion in specialty training
that took place after World War II.

In war-weary Europe, there were no such major changes. The postwar
governments, faced with enormous problems of dislocation and the destruction of humans and property during the 1914–18 period, found it
almost impossible to undertake new initiatives or to provide additional
levels of support. The situation was made worse by the large number of
returning veterans who had postponed their entrance to medical study.
Women were frequently displaced in the schools that had recruited them
during the war. In every country, those medical leaders committed to
change tried to revive the prewar agenda of reform, especially the effort
to reduce the huge size of classes and to close the gap between scientific
and clinical teaching in medicine—but with little success. Advocates of
the American system of small-group instruction in the laboratory and
ward ran afoul of rising enrollments, inadequate funding, and entrenched
conservative interests.

British Efforts at Change in the 1920s

In Great Britain, where small amounts of government aid had been given
to the universities since 1908, a campaign was launched after the war to
carry out the recommendations of the earlier Haldane Commission and especially to establish a full-time academic presence in the clinical branches of
medical schools. But the resistance was strong, even in London, where the
first clinical units in hospitals were established. In the hospital schools, with
their deeply entrenched consulting specialists, it was difficult to find scientifically trained clinicians who were willing to sacrifice large incomes from
practice to conduct teaching and research as full-time university professors.

Throughout this period, British hospitals remained "generally unsym-

---

12. Colwell, "Present Needs," 839–40. The best studies of the development of specialization in American and British medicine are those by Rosemary Stevens: *American Medicine and the Public Interest* (New Haven, CT: Yale University Press, 1971); and *Medical
Practice in Modern England: The Impact of Specialization and State Medicine* (New Haven,
CT: Yale University Press, 1966).

pathetic to experimental, academic medicine," in the words of historian John Pickstone and his colleagues, "at least when it encroached on the clinical." In the provinces, it was even more difficult to "transcend the English divide between . . . consultants and . . . medical science."[13] Some of the faculty at Manchester, for example, who wanted to follow the London plan, found "no great enthusiasm" for the idea and observed that "it is regarded as largely experimental."[14] In the entire period before World War II, only thirteen full-time clinical chairs were established in Britain's medical schools.[15]

No one in postwar Britain championed more ardently the university standard of medical education and the need to emulate recent changes in the United States than George Newman, the chief medical officer of both the national Board of Education and the Ministry of Health. Without the huge resources open to Flexner and hampered by a tradition-bound medical establishment, Newman nevertheless proclaimed many of the same objectives for Great Britain. "A University course in medicine," he declared at the end of the war, "demands an effective interrelationship between study in laboratory science and the clinical practice of medicine. Both must take place under the same roof and be conducted by university professors."

In language reminiscent of Flexner, Newman insisted that "the immediate need of English Medicine lies in the application of the findings of the laboratory, for medical knowledge is complete only when it embraces the chemical and pathological as well as the clinical facts of the case." This was happening, he pointed out, in none of the great English hospitals. Like Flexner, he believed that the foundation sciences of chemistry, physics, and biology were best acquired in the premedical years, that the preclinical sciences should be under the direction of trained scientists (whether or not they possessed medical degrees), and that clinical teaching should be in the hands of full-time instructors "who would devote the greater part of their time to teaching and research."[16]

13. John V. Pickstone, Roger J. Cooter, and Caroline C. S. Murphy, "Exploring `Clinical Research'; Academic Medicine and the Clinicians in Early Twentieth Century Britain," paper prepared for the conference "Science in Modern Medicine," at Manchester, April 1985. I am indebted to Prof. Pickstone for his kindness in sending me a copy of this paper.

14. Board of the Faculty of Medicine, Victorian University of Manchester, "Report of the Reconstruction Committee of the Faculty of Medicine on the Advisability of Appointing `Whole-Time' Professors of Medicine, Surgery, and Gynecology," 1920, Manchester Collection, F4L iv (d), Rylands Library, University of Manchester.

15. R. Milnes Walker, *Medical Education in Britain* (London: Nuffield Provincial Hospitals Trust, 1965), 25. According to George Newman, chief medical officer of the Ministry of Health and the Board of Education, eight to twelve "professional units with whole-time staff appointed by the universities" existed in 1932. See "Medical Education in England," *Quarterly Bulletin of the Health Organisation of the League of Nations* 1 (1932): 30.

16. George Newman, *Some Notes on Medical Education in England* (London: His Majesty's Stationery Office, 1918), 26–77. For the influence of Flexner on Newman, a paper, "Sir George Newman and the American Way," by W. F. Bynum is in press. I am grateful to Prof. Bynum for sharing it with me.

By 1923 Newman could report progress toward the first two objectives but continuing resistance to the last. Britain, he declared, was not like America, for it could not

> establish the perfect model . . . start a new organization, full-blown, immaculate and complete. We are not a New World, with new cities, new Universities, new ideals, and without a past. We have a hospital tradition which has more than a thousand years behind it, and the first British Medical School is 400 years old.[17]

Newman claimed nevertheless that by means of various expedients, the teaching of clinical medicine in a scientific context was gradually improving. "How the term `gradually' is understood in Britain," later wrote the historian F. N. L. Poynter, "may be gathered from the fact that it took another world war and a nationalized Health Service to bring about any substantial speeding up of this historical process."[18]

The Continent: Echoes of Old Battles

Changes in medical education on the Continent came with no less difficulty than in Britain. The postwar years, during which so much effort was aimed at repairing and rebuilding programs and reputations, were succeeded by the years of depression and turmoil of the 1930s, when new directions seemed all but impossible. In France as in Germany, the requirements for medical study in the interwar period began with the completion of a strongly classical secondary education, followed by a year of concentrated university study in physics, chemistry, and natural history (P.C.N.). Then came the medical study itself, extending over a period of five years, during which seven demanding examinations were administered at regular intervals.

Students continued to protest, as they had before the war, the lack of personal contact with teachers, especially in the clinics, and the inordinate amount of time needed to prepare for and take the examinations. A petition in 1920, for example, claimed that examinations took a total of twenty-four days to complete and demanded at least two months of preparation.[19] In 1934 a sixth year of hospital training for all students was finally added to the requirements, but many continued to take seven, eight, or even nine years to earn a degree.

French students began their medical instruction, as they had for more than a century, in the hospital with morning clinics that extended over

17. George Newman, *Recent Advances in Medical Education in England* (London: His Majesty's Stationery Office, 1923), 95.

18. F. N. L. Poynter, "Medical Education in England Since 1600," in *The History of Medical Education*, ed C. D. O'Malley (Berkeley and Los Angeles: University of California Press, 1970), 246.

19. File of student petitions, Archives nationales, AJ[16] 6358.

the whole period of study. Afternoons were spent chiefly in laboratories and lectures in the medical sciences. A thesis was still required, as it was generally in Europe, for the medical degree. "The outstanding feature" of French medical training in the late 1920s, concluded an American commission headed by Willard C. Rappleye, "is that [it] is primarily clinical and conducted by the staff of the hospital rather than the faculty of the medical school. [It] is essentially training with a single objective, the production of doctors by practical methods."

Inevitably, wrote Rappleye, "teaching in the medical sciences must be slighted. The students are preoccupied and quite overwhelmed with clinical problems for the understanding of which they have had no preparation." This judgment did not differ from Flexner's evaluation twenty years before or from that of the turn-of-the-century critics in France itself. By 1928 nine university faculties in medicine were in existence, including a school in French Algiers, and fifteen *écoles préparatoires*, which together enrolled nearly twelve thousand students, a third more than the medical schools of Great Britain, a nation slightly larger than France.[20]

Only in Strasbourg, which became a French university once more in 1918, did the teaching of medicine resemble that of Germany or the United States. Here many of the characteristics of the period of German hegemony lingered on in the postwar years. The teaching in Strasbourg was carried out principally by university rather than hospital staff members, and students, unlike those in the rest of France, were barred from clinics until they had finished two years of preclinical study. The hospital was under direct control of the faculty, unlike that of Paris and the other French schools.[21] The laboratory and research facilities surrendered by Germany gave France for the first time, according to Flexner, "a modern medical school plant." It was his hope that the new French university might become "a national experiment station [combining] the practical features of French clinical training with the laboratory features and investigative activities characteristic of the German university organization."[22]

If critics of French medical training focused on the "slighting" of the preclinical sciences and their "wholly subsidiary" relationship to clinical experience, as was the case with the Rappleye Commission, the reverse was true of their impressions of Germany. Although the length of German medical study was extended to eleven semesters in 1927, exclusive of the "practical year," the acquisition of practical skills was pushed even further into the postgraduate years. For Rappleye and his colleagues—as for Flexner, Newman, and others before them—education in Germany was "highly theoretical . . . very little of practical experience is prescribed.

20. Commission on Medical Education, *Medical Education*, 78-82, 163, 188–90. See also the account of French medical education in 1930 by G. Roussy, "Medical Education in France," *Quarterly Bulletin of the Health Organisation of the League of Nations* 1 (1932): 315–61.

21. Commission on Medical Education, *Medical Education*, 94–95.

22. Flexner, "Medical Education," 5.

. . . The senses cannot be trained by demonstrative methods. . . . The required German training is distinctly a passive process."

In the commission's view, most German students "never got an adequate laboratory experience," received only "discontinuous and fragmentary" clinical training, and suffered an "overemphasis on lecturing." As for the professors, they "do not burden their conscience or time with instruction of individual students," which meant that the students were wholly dependent "on their own responsibility."[23]

German critics themselves proclaimed a crisis in medical training. Julius Schwalbe, the longtime editor of the *Deutsche medizinische Wochenschrift*, began a campaign in 1918 to reform medical study in favor of more attention to the diagnostic and therapeutic skills needed by the average practitioner. Citing earlier warnings of the decay of bedside skills, Schwalbe argued that the war had proved them right, that the time had come to shorten and simplify the scientific content of medicine, and that more practical instruction was urgently needed.[24]

His strictures brought widespread comment in the medical and public journals of the 1920s. While many supported his campaign for fundamental change, others attacked any reduction in the time spent in the study of natural science. Still others were troubled by the enormous expense involved in making the sweeping changes that Schwalbe urged and the impracticability of reform under postwar conditions in any case. For their part, many professors decried what they saw as an effort to discredit the success and reputation of German science.

The social critic Karl Kautsky charged in 1919 that medical education, like all university study, had now become a "mass industry" and that the universities were no more than "educational factories." Medicine, he declared, was "no exact science but above all else a practical art" learned best by close observation of the work of "an older, more experienced physician." Success in practice depended on a knowledge of human relationships and an understanding of "individual persons as unique and not identically constructed and reacting representatives of the species Homo Sapiens." The greatest mistake of mass medical education, he explained, was "that the so necessary close contact between teacher and pupil is more and more lost." To remedy the crisis, the great power of the full professors (*Ordinaria*) must be broken, and the teaching must be redistributed among all teachers so as to permit "teaching in small groups at the bedside and in the laboratory."[25]

The most savage attack on German medical education in the postwar years came from the pen of the Karlsruhe psychologist Willy Hellpach. In a lengthy polemic, Hellpach denounced as contradictory a system of edu-

23. Commission on Medical Education, *Medical Education*, 63–72.

24. Julius Schwalbe, *Zur Neuordnung des medizinischen Studiums* (Leipzig: Georg Thieme, 1918), 1–12.

25. Karl Kautsky, "Aerztliche Erziehungsfragen," *Der Kampf* 12 (1919): 421–22.

cating doctors to heal sick people that kept them away from patients for the first two-thirds of their training. The early months of the war had shown the folly of current methods of study as new graduates "stood by in silent helplessness" while nurses, sanitary workers, and Red Cross officers administered to the sick and wounded. The modern graduate in medicine, he charged, had "a great deal of knowledge, but a frightening poverty of practical skills." The clinical lectures given in huge auditoriums in the typical German medical school were worse than useless; they were "too much theater" and too little education.

In their place, he urged a return to the continuous teaching of students at the sickbed, in which Germany had pioneered, starting at the very beginning of clinical education. "The clinical student must be responsible for sick people from the first day" of his clinical study. He should not simply be called before a class to examine a "case" but be given real patients to take care of. Only a radical restructuring of the curriculum, one that integrated preclinical courses with active observation and experience of the "living person," could reverse the failure of German medical training.

It was a "monstrous fiction," Hellpach charged, that medicine was an applied science; the direct usefulness of most scientific courses in everyday practice had been "grotesquely" overestimated. "Whoever educates medical students to think only in physical and chemical terms runs the danger of raising a physician who takes the [human] organism for a retort or a steam pressure gauge or an electric battery."[26] Consciously or not, Hellpach, like Kautsky and other reformers, was calling for medical education to be restructured along the lines of the Anglo-American clerkship.

For all the passion of such reformers, however, the time spent by German medical students in acquiring practical experience actually declined in the 1920s. A German report to the League of Nations in 1932 described the medical student's experience as "a procession of diseases, lecture halls, and professors."[27] Chaotic financial conditions, together with political instability and the undiminished power of the professoriate, stifled the voices of reform.

The student population in medicine in Germany, the largest in Europe and approximating that of the United States, continued to climb and in

26. Willy Hellpach, *Die Neugestaltung des medizinischen Unterrichts* (Berlin: Urban & Schwarzenberg, 1919), 5–6, 26, 36, 53, 67. I am indebted to Prof. Hendrik van den Bussche of the University of Hamburg for calling my attention to Hellpach's work. See Hendrik van den Bussche, "Willy Hellpach und die 'lebendige Unterrichtsmethode,'" in *Medizinische Ausbildung: Festschrift zu Ehren von Dietrich Habeck und Hans E. Renschler*, ed. Thomas Kleinheinrich and Reinhard Lohölter (Munster: Mitteilungsblatt der Gesellschaft für Medizinische Ausbildung, 1990), 4–13.

27. C. Hamel, J. Jadassohn, C. Prausnitz, and M. Taute, "Medical Education in the German Reich," *Quarterly Bulletin of the Health Organisation of the League of Nations* 1 (1932): 177.

1931 reached 21,000 in a population much smaller than America's.[28] The aging Friedrich von Müller, writing in 1934, blamed the chronic overcrowding of medical classes, now a familiar feature of German medical education, for the continuing problems and called for limitations on enrollment as in America and Britain. The gap between academic and practical medicine should not be closed, however, simply by lowering the scientific content of medical instruction. "Today the young German physicians are going in large numbers to America," he wrote, "in order to learn the new ideas in science and practice," and he warned that only heroic efforts at home could stop the trend.[29]

The Hardening of National Differences

By the time Müller wrote, it was clear that the long-standing differences in national systems, despite growing similarities of curriculum and surface appearance, had actually hardened in the postwar years. The traditional openness of the German university to students, its high reputation in research, and the dominant place of natural science in teaching had produced a distinctive method of training physicians that found little room in the undergraduate years for the bedside learning valued so highly elsewhere. The French insistence on the centrality of the clinic, on the other hand, a heritage of the Revolution and the historical separation of the hospital from theoretical study, made difficult the close liaison between academy and hospital sought outside France. The centuries-long British tradition of entrepreneurial education in medicine and the powerful place of the great hospitals and royal corporations placed a heavy brake on efforts in that country to set a university standard for all medical education. And in the United States, the very looseness and lack of organization of nineteenth-century medicine, along with the subsequent creation of universities and great national wealth, enabled reformers to build an individualized, expensive system of training students in the laboratories and clinics of the nation's universities.

To contemporary observers, the systems of training doctors in America, Canada, and Great Britain, though clearly different, continued to seem more alike than akin to those of continental Europe. All three countries, it was frequently pointed out, shared an entrepreneurial and laissez-faire tradition, a common historical background, the same professional language, and an abiding interest in the practical outcomes of education. When filtered through their separate systems, the influence of continental methods of teaching, especially those of Germany, had pro-

28. Fritz K. Ringer, *Education and Society in Modern Europe* (Bloomington: Indiana University Press, 1979), 292, table V.
29. Friedrich von Müller, "Zur Reform des Medizinstudiums," *Münchener medizinische Wochenschrift* 23 (1934): 19–28.

duced a similar mix of training. After surveying schools in all three countries in 1929, Squire Sprigg, the editor of the British journal *Lancet*, reported that he had found "a practical reciprocity" in "the medicine of the English-speaking peoples." Medical courses in all three nations, he wrote, were similar in content; the balance between scientific and clinical study was closer than in either France or Germany; the clerkship was common to all three countries; and the duration of study was roughly equivalent. The differences, notably in the universities' power over medical training and their control of the teaching hospitals, as well as in systems of licensing and examination, were less striking, he insisted, than the features common to all. Most to be envied, said the British editor, was "the riot of expenditures" on medical education in the United States, whereas the British advantage lay in its "greater experience."[30]

Students, Depression, and Political Turmoil

In the years after 1929, a wrenching economic depression and a protracted political crisis, even greater than the dislocations of the 1920s, profoundly upset the lives of doctors and those planning a career in medicine. Not since the era of the French Revolution were so many careers so deeply affected by so long a period of crisis in international politics. "It is not surprising," began a League of Nations report on medical education in 1933, "to find a medical crisis when a crisis exists in all spheres of human activity."[31] Doctors in every country suffered a loss of confidence in the 1930s as the demand for medical services fell and the numbers of patients plummeted, sometimes drastically. Not a few American physicians found themselves on public relief rolls. Those who did not had plenty of work but often could not collect fees for it. For the first time in memory, empty beds outnumbered the number of patients in hospitals in several countries. Nations without a comprehensive system of sickness insurance, notably the United States, experienced new pressures to organize protection along the lines pioneered by Germany and Great Britain. The sense of crisis was nearly universal. "Chins up," a Kansas editor told his colleagues in 1933, "no matter how slow collections are, no matter how scarce money is, your neighbor to the right, to the left, fore and aft, is in the same boat."[32]

Professional groups in France and Germany began to seek a limitation on the numbers admitted to medical school, and their counterparts in Britain and America worked quietly toward the same end. Governments

---

30. Squire Sprigge, "Medical Education in the United States and Canada," special supplement to *Lancet*, January 5, 1929, pp. iii, xxxvi–xl.

31. Etienne Burnet, "Medical Education and the Reform of Medical Studies," *Quarterly Bulletin, Health Organisation of the League of Nations* 2 (1933): 621.

32. *Medical Bulletin* (Sedgwick County, Kansas) 3 (1933): 6–8.

everywhere, faced with appalling needs from every quarter, slackened and sometimes sharply cut appropriations to medical education. Canadian universities, for example, were forced to weigh the elimination of two of the nation's eight medical schools, at Dalhousie and Western University—schools that Flexner had pictured "as bad as anything this side of the line"—but both managed to survive by vigorously recruiting American students at much higher fees than those paid by Canadians.[33] In the United States, the depression "caused severe damage" to medical education as schools laid off faculty members, cut salaries, scrambled for students, and postponed curricular and building changes.[34]

Many students hesitated to enter so unpromising a career, but the alternatives often seemed even worse. Indeed, contrary to a widespread expectation that young people might take up medicine in fewer numbers, the actual impact of the economic crisis, the League of Nations reported, "has been the reverse." Medical enrollment in several of the major nations, at least in the early 1930s, showed a modest increase.[35]

Women's Study Between the Wars

Barriers to study by women and ethnic minorities, however, which had been lowered during the Great War, rose in the postwar years.[36] As the guns were stilled in 1918, the reaction came. Men in the warring nations were given a sympathetic reception as they returned from military service to medical school or training hospital. Competing women were accused throughout the 1920s of "taking the places" of the returned veterans. For example, Lord Knutsford, the chairman of London Hospital's board, announced in 1922 that now that the crisis had passed, his hospital would take no more women students.[37] One by one, the schools and hospitals of London that had admitted women in wartime closed their doors to them.

In Germany, a strong reaction was felt against the huge growth in female medical study during the war. "Women doctors," according to one account, "became at once second-class physicians as soon as the question came up of the distribution of scarce study places."[38] The proportion of

33. McPhedran, "Canadian Medical Schools," 17.

34. Saul Jarcho, "Medical Education in the United States, 1910–1956," *Journal of the Mount Sinai Hospital* 26 (1959): 362.

35. Burnet, "Medical Education," 638.

36. This account of women's medical study between the wars is a much shortened version of that in my *To the Ends of the Earth: Women's Search for Education in Medicine* (Cambridge, MA: Harvard University Press, 1992), 161–67.

37. Untitled newspaper clipping, London, March 22, 1922, Archives and Special Collections on Women in Medicine, Medical College of Pennsylvania, Philadelphia.

38. Christine Eckelmann and Kristin Hoesch, "Arztinnen-Emanzipation durch den Krieg," in *Medizin und Krieg: vom Dilemma der Heilberufe, 1865 bis 1915*, ed. Johanna Bleker and Heinz-Peter Schmiedebach (Berlin: Fischer, 1985), 167.

women in German medical schools dropped 17 percent between 1923 and 1928.[39] In the United States a similar reaction set in. At the University of Pennsylvania, for example, which had only recently begun to admit women, the senior medical class voted in 1920 to oppose continuing the practice, saying that it "disadvantages every student."[40]

By the early 1930s, however, despite the economic depression, the level of women's study in Europe had begun to recover. In Germany, women accounted for one-fifth of all medical enrollment in 1932–33. More than six thousand women were preparing to be doctors, or more than six times the number in the United States.[41] Even in Great Britain, where enrollment by women had lagged, the proportion of women completing medical school was double that of their American counterparts. In the United States, despite the gains made in wartime, figures for the postwar era showed a marked decline in the number of women seeking and gaining admission to medical school. The proportion of women in medical school scarcely rose above 5 percent throughout the 1930s.

What had happened? The most likely explanation for the lag in women's medical education in America was in the weaker role played by government. Even though America and Europe shared the same gender conventions about women's role in medicine, it was the relationship of education to the nation-state that proved to be of greatest significance. The governments in Switzerland and France, as described in earlier chapters, had given women the legal right to study medicine since the 1860s, and much of continental Europe had followed by 1914. Even those states such as Germany, where hostility to women doctors remained high, now easily surpassed the United States and Canada in the numbers of women admitted to medical schools and hospitals.

In the United States, Canada, and Britain, the role of powerful private institutions, unchecked by law or governmental policy, thwarted the advance of medical coeducation. The policies of hundreds of private boards, hospitals, and training institutions in rejecting or limiting women enforced the continuing discrimination against women doctors. Why were so few American women entering medicine? "The reason," explained the surgeon Bertha Van Hoosen in 1930, "is the same as our pioneer great-grandmothers had to face"—that the medical schools and hospitals "simply don't want them."[42] By the 1930s, the American failure in women's education was increasingly evident.[43]

39. Antke Luhn, "Geschichte des Frauenstudiums an der medizinischen Fakultät der Universität Göttingen" (med. diss., University of Göttingen, 1971), 99.

40. *The Pennsylvanian*, February 14, 1920.

41. Luhn, "Geschichte des Frauenstudiums," 99; Elisabeth Burger, "Entwicklung des medizinischen Frauenstudiums" (med. diss., University of Marburg, 1947), 69.

42. Untitled newspaper clipping, 1930, Bertha Van Hoosen Papers, Bentley Library, University of Michigan.

43. For further discussion of the argument presented here, see my *To the Ends of the Earth*, 163–66.

The Great Depression and World War II, bringing upheaval to the lives of all social groups, also profoundly affected women. In many countries, a marked hostility to women's competing for jobs with men emerged in the years of economic chaos. In Germany, the Nazi regime quickly dissolved the existing women's organizations and moved to limit women's access to universities and the professions. The proportion of women in the German universities dropped once more, from 16 percent in 1932 to 11 percent in 1938. In the first year alone of National Socialism, the number of women entering medical school fell from 1,118 to 871.[44] The American Alice Hamilton, after a visit to Germany, wrote in 1934: "German women had a long and hard fight but they had won a fair measure of equality. . . . Now all seems to be lost and suddenly they are set back, perhaps as much as a hundred years."[45]

But Hitler's war, like the war a quarter-century before, stimulated a huge new demand for doctors in Germany and all the belligerent states. The mobilization of civilian populations on an unprecedented scale brought thousands of women into professional and technical careers for the first time. Hundreds of thousands of casualties in the major countries created an enormous demand for physicians and health personnel. By the end of the war, a quarter or more of all the medical students of France, Germany, and Britain were women, and the proportion of women in the Soviet Union reached 80 percent. In the United States, less severely affected by the war, the recruitment of women increased more slowly, reaching a level of 8 percent in 1945.[46] Hospitals, too, began accepting women as interns and residents in ever larger numbers. "Hospitals are hanging out the welcome signs to women physicians these days," reported the *New York Times* in 1942, "fledgling women doctors, once excluded. . .are now being snapped up as fast as the ink dries on their diplomas."[47]

Anti-Semitism in Germany and Elsewhere

The Hitler regime brought devastating change to the lives of Jewish teachers and students, both men and women. The chronic anti-Semitism of the German universities, increasingly overt in the 1920s, prepared the way for the savage onslaughts of the Nazi period. All through the postwar years, German medical students, even more than those of other facul-

44. Ringer, *Education and Society*, 67; Burger, "Entwicklung des medizinischen Frauenstudiums," 68. See also the discussion of medical women under the Nazis in Michael Kater, *Doctors Under Hitler* (Chapel Hill: University of North Carolina Press, 1989), 89–110.

45. Alice Hamilton, "Woman's Place in Germany," *Survey Graphic*, January 1934, p. 26.

46. Mary R. Walsh, *"Doctors Wanted: No Women Need Apply": Sexual Barriers in the Medical Profession, 1835–1975* (New Haven, CT: Yale University Press, 1977), 244–49.

47. *New York Times*, June 21, 1942.

ties, had ranged themselves on the side of the nationalistic and xenophobic currents sweeping through German life. Students in Munich, including a sizable number from medicine, had taken part in Hitler's abortive putsch of 1923, and a large majority of all students participating in public demonstrations in the city identified themselves as supporters of Hitler. In Prussia, three of every four students voted in 1927 against a new student ordinance forbidding the division of students into organizations along racial lines.[48] Medical students, the largest and politically most powerful of all student groups in Germany, barred Jews completely from their national organization throughout the pre-Hitler years.[49] In Erlangen, for example, the local organization of medical students resolved in 1932 to fight "Jews, those of Jewish descent, and non-Germans" studying in the city.[50]

After 1933, the political climate became deadly for Jews, and many dropped out of the universities altogether or left the country. Jewish professors of medicine were systematically hounded from their positions; Jewish student organizations were forcefully disbanded; and leadership in the universities fell more and more to active members of the Nazi Party. Of all those chosen to be rectors of German universities between 1933 and 1945, 59 percent were medical professors.[51] By the middle of the decade, scarcely a Jewish professor or student of medicine continued to study or teach, and worse was still to come.

Discrimination against Jewish medical students and teachers outside Germany and Austria also reflected the destructive prejudices prevailing in various countries. During the years of German aggression, the Nazi regime attempted to extend its racial doctrines to the nations under Hitler's control but had varying degrees of success. Elsewhere, beyond the pale of German influence, restrictions against Jews in medicine, notably in the United States, were largely confined to secret quotas in medical schools and hospitals. The number of Jewish applicants to medical school in America, inspired by what has been called "an almost mystical reverence for medicine," grew by leaps and bounds after World War I.[52] Many were the sons and daughters of immigrants from eastern Europe and Russia, where a majority of the medical students were Jews seeking to escape from the closed communities into which they were born. The

48. Anselm Faust, *Der nationalsozialistische Studentenbund,* 2 vols. (Düsseldorf: Schwann, 1973), 1:25, 32.

49. Bernhard Vieten, *Medizinstudenten in Münster: Universität, Studentenschaft und Medizin, 1905 bis 1945* (Cologne: Pahl-Rugenstein, 1982), 180. I have followed Vieten's pioneering work on German medical students in this period in this and the following paragraph.

50. Ibid., 180.

51. Kater, *Doctors Under Hitler,* 111.

52. Leon Sokoloff, "The Rise and Decline of the Jewish Quota in Medical School Admissions," *Bulletin of the New York Academy of Medicine* 68 (1992): 498. This paragraph follows Sokoloff's fresh and comprehensive account.

burst of new applications from Jews coincided in time with the growing competition for the places available in American medical schools.

Pressure for admission to the remaining places became intense. School after school found ways, both subtle and informal—such as new requirements of photographs or information about the place of birth of parents—to make more "traditional" selections and limit the number of Jews. At Columbia, for example, President Nicholas Murray Butler found an effective way to direct medical school recruitment to areas beyond the mushrooming Jewish population of New York City. The dean of Cornell's medical school in New York, W. S. Ladd, wrote privately in 1940 that "we limit the number of Jews admitted to each class to roughly the proportion of Jews in the population of the state."[53]

Many of those who failed to gain admission flocked to European schools, especially those of Scotland and Switzerland. By 1938, more than five hundred Americans, almost all of them Jews, were studying medicine in Glasgow and Edinburgh alone.[54] In a curious way, they duplicated the journey of the thousands of Russian Jews who had come west rather than east to find opportunity a half-century before.

African Americans and Medical Study

Whereas the number of Jewish students in American medical schools, despite the restrictions, remained comparatively high, the reverse was true of African Americans. The earlier demise of most of the black schools, together with the total exclusion of black students from southern schools and their token admission to only a few northern schools, kept their number very low throughout the interwar period. During the harsh depression years, the number of blacks entering medical school scarcely exceeded seventy per year. In 1938, only 1.6 percent of all medical students were African American, and nine-tenths of these were enrolled in the black schools of Meharry and Howard.[55] Three years later, fewer black students were enrolled in medicine than in 1920. Meharry and Howard themselves faced enormous difficulties in maintaining their precarious hold on accreditation, and for a time Meharry was placed on probation by the Council on Medical Education.

Few accredited hospitals, furthermore, were willing to accept African Americans as interns. Only the Freedmen's Hospital in Washington and one or two others accepted more than an occasional black intern during the interwar period. "We are all your good friends," wrote the director of

53. Ibid., 502.

54. John Duffy, *From Humors to Medical Science: A History of American Medicine*, 2nd ed. (Urbana: University of Illinois Press, 1993), 311.

55. Lippard, *Half-Century of American Medical Education*. See also Ruth M. Raup and Elizabeth A. Williams, "Negro Students in Medical Schools in the United States," *Journal of Medical Education* 39 (1964), esp. 446–49.

one hospital to a black woman graduate of the Woman's Medical College in Philadelphia, "and it is a most unpleasant thing to have to tell you that just because you are colored, we can't arrange to take you comfortably into the hospital."[56] Residencies for study in the specialties for black physicians were even harder to find. Not a single program approved by the American Medical Association accepted blacks in the 1920s, and in the following decade only thirty-one residencies were offered in a small number of approved black hospitals.[57] All in all, no group faced such daunting prospects in medicine as did this interwar generation of African Americans.

War and Medical Study, 1939–1945

With the outbreak of global conflict in 1939 came a series of overwhelming events that affected students and teachers in every country and brought dislocations to all their lives. Young doctors who had decided on medicine in the depths of an economic depression and had scrimped and cut corners to complete their education now found themselves in uniform, often far from home, for much of the next six or seven years. Not untypical perhaps was the career of a young German graduate of 1939, who is known to me, who was inducted into Hitler's legions as they prepared to move into Poland, served as a military surgeon to the troops on the western front and in Italy, was sent to Russia in 1944, and was released from a British prison camp in northern Germany in 1946. Young graduates of other nations likewise spent the first long years of professional life in treating the victims of war under the most trying conditions known to a doctor of medicine.

Those still in medical school found their terms of study cut, vacation periods eliminated, internships reduced in length, and a new emphasis on medical and surgical trauma, in addition to a plethora of infectious and tropical diseases. Deans and faculties of schools that had demanded long years of premedical education were now frequently content with much less. In Britain, the period of medical study was reduced by six months, in Germany by a year, and in the United States doctors were educated in four consecutive terms of nine months each.[58] The effect of the accelerated American program was to graduate more than seven thousand additional doctors between 1942 and 1947. By the end of the war, "students were exhausted . . . instructors were continuously occupied in teaching,

---

56. Herbert M. Morais, *The History of the Negro in Medicine* (New York: Association for the Study of Negro Life and History, 1967), 94. Much of this account follows Morais, pp. 90–100.

57. Ibid., 95.

58. W. Tomaszewski, "Medical Education in Continental Europe and in Great Britain: A Comparison," *University of Edinburgh Journal* 12 (1942–43): 25–26.

and many had excessive loads because colleagues were in the armed forces."[59]

The war marked a seismic shift in the relationship between medical schools and national governments. For the first time in the United States, science and medicine now stood at the center of a new interest by the government in the universities' research prowess. Laboratories in medical schools became an important part of a coordinated effort to control wartime diseases and to devise new means of treating them. Money for research needed in the war, particularly in the United States, was available on a scale hitherto unknown. "The men who put together the wartime research empire," writes the historian Hunter Dupree, "were conscious that they were operating in huge new ways." Medical professors and sometimes students took part in projects of vital national importance to test vaccines, synthesize new drugs, and try experimental procedures for treating battlefield wounds.

It was already clear that both clinical and basic research in medicine would play a different role in the medical schools of the postwar world. "By the time the bombs fell on Hiroshima and Nagasaki," says Dupree, "the entire country was aware that science was a political, economic and social force of the first magnitude."[60]

The world after 1945 would indeed be a different place for medical students and teachers than it had been in previous years. New forces and events pressed down on the historical framework of medical education. Over the next half-century came a massive growth in the research enterprise, an explosion of specialized teaching and postgraduate training, and the final realization of the old dream of full-time instruction in clinical medicine. The teaching of undergraduate medical students, the historic raison d'être of a school of medicine, dwindled in importance in comparison with research, specialty training, and patient care in the great "academic health centers" that succeeded the old medical schools. Close academic ties to the university, long the goal of medical school reformers in every country, were weakened by the new relationships and concerns of health centers and their growing financial independence. The teaching hospital, once seen as an appendix to the school of medicine in the idealized view of 1900, became the site of a flourishing postgraduate industry and the place of choice for a greatly expanded number of patient services.

The close union of undergraduate teaching and patient care in a clinic or hospital, a constant goal of educators since Hufeland and Fourcroy, was more and more preempted by the mushrooming of patient services provided by an academic hospital. Most remarkable was the steady advance of the power of government, especially in Anglo-America, in setting the goals and level of support for medical education. Medical train-

---

59. Jarcho, "Medical Education," 372.
60. A. Hunter Dupree, *Science in the Federal Government* (Cambridge, MA: Belknap Press, 1957), 369.

ing in every country was now largely dependent on the policies of government. And the gateway to medical study itself, which had narrowed in the first half of the century, became somewhat wider after 1950 in all the Western countries, especially for women and, in the United States, African Americans. But all of this is another and complex story, beyond the reach of this one.

14

A Closing Word

Despite all the changes in undergraduate medical education after World War II, especially in its core of scientific training, it actually had shifted only slightly in essential ways by the end of the twentieth century. If a student from an earlier era sat down in the classrooms and clinics of the 1990s—although doubtless overwhelmed by the new knowledge and technology—he or she would still find much that was familiar in the teaching methods, curriculum, conduct of clinics, bedside training, laboratory instruction, and educational preparation of fellow students. "The medicine of 1900," writes William Bynum, "[is] closer to us almost a century later than it was to the medicine of 1790."[1] The historic differences among nations in teaching methods, too, though less striking than in earlier times, were still visible in the characteristic responses of medical educators and students to the social and scientific changes.

Alone among the professions, education for medicine had come to combine a long period of theoretical study with an intensely practical experience in the observation, handling, and treatment of patients. The resulting tension and shifting balance between academic study and clinical training, between theory and practice, between medicine as art and medicine as science, has been the perpetual condition of medical pedagogy since the Enlightenment. That a different balance was struck at different times in different nations because of differing social and political circum-

---

1. W. F. Bynum, *Science and the Practice of Medicine in the Nineteenth Century* (Cambridge: Cambridge University Press, 1994), xi.

stances is the underlying theme of this book. In the first half of this century, if a boundless faith in science and the ultimate rationality of medicine came to dominate nearly everywhere, that faith has been overwhelmed in our own time by postmodern doubts about human progress and the explanatory powers of science. But the pendulum will doubtless swing again.

In any case, for most educators and students, the ideal remains what it has been for most of the period covered in this book—a unity of systematic academic study, especially in the sciences, with hands-on experience to create a physician who thinks critically, can solve problems, possesses a wide knowledge of underlying disease processes, and is skilled at applying what has been learned to real-life situations.

From the Enlightenment to the mid-twentieth century, the basic medical preparation of physicians was shaped, step by step, in a cultural and intellectual environment peculiar to the Western world. The present forms of medical education in the West stem directly from intellectual and entrepreneurial energies unloosed in the latter eighteenth century—ideas about utility, rationality, and human betterment; concepts of practical teaching in a hospital or clinic, of the possibilities of observational and scientific knowledge, of the humanitarian obligations of a modern state. Faith in the promise of science in medicine leaped in the next century, reaching an apogee in imperial Germany. Then, at the end of the nineteenth century, new combinations of practical and scientific learning were devised in a transformed social and educational climate in the United States. Throughout, the changing content of medical education was a vital factor in the growing acceptance by the public of medicine's claim to authority.

Acceptance of that claim sharply reduced the ranks of alternative healers. The division between "scientific" and "practical" doctors, characteristic of the eighteenth and much of the nineteenth century, was all but gone by 1950. Governments that had largely ignored the education of doctors in 1750 were exerting close control everywhere in Europe by 1850 and in Anglo-America a century later. The role of physicians' associations in medical education, which grew rapidly in the nineteenth century, became very powerful in the English-speaking countries. The ranks of students, narrowly confined to the comfortable classes in all countries in the eighteenth century, grew wider in the nineteenth, then narrowed again by 1920, only to broaden once more in our own time. The students themselves came to play a shrinking role in planning and choosing their own course of study, even though their choices of particular programs continued to matter in the twentieth century.

In a celebrated study in 1984, reviewing the state of medical education, the Association of American Medical Colleges called for long-familiar reforms in the teaching of medical undergraduates: fewer lectures, more independent learning, more faculty involvement in basic medical teaching, and greater recognition of the social circumstances in which medicine was practiced. "Perhaps the most important concept emerging from the study," declared the authors, "is that medical students must be prepared to learn throughout their lives."[2] Similar conclusions have been reached in recent years by study groups in Europe. But none of the changes called for, we should add, would have seemed exceptionable to Tissot or Frank in the eighteenth century, to Pinel or Paget in the nineteenth, or to Flexner or Hellpach in the twentieth.

The concerns of our own time about the direction of medical study—the need to "humanize" physicians in an increasingly technological age, the lack of student experience in dealing with normal patients in an ambulatory setting, the estrangement of hospital and medical school, the fear that medical training has become too specialized, the complaint that students learn too much of the science of medicine and too little of its art—only echo the historic tensions recounted in these pages.

To such concerns there have been and will be no final answers, for the teaching of medicine, as argued at the outset, is inescapably embedded in a changing social environment. What students learn in the future and how they learn it, as was true in the past, will be rooted in a particular historical and cultural milieu that varies from nation to nation and from time to time.

2. Association of American Medical Colleges, *Physicians for the Twenty-First Century: The GPEP Report* (Washington, DC: Association of American Medical Colleges, 1984), 34.

Bibliography

Archives and Special Collections

France

Lyon Le musée de la faculté de médecine; les archives municipales de Lyon
Montpellier Archives de la faculté de médecine
Paris Archives nationales
Strasbourg Archives départmentales du Bas-Rhin

Germany (and Austria)

Berlin Universitätsarchiv, Humboldt University; Universitätsbibliothek, Humboldt University (Hochschulschriftensammlung)
Bonn Universitätsarchiv
Göttingen Universitätsarchiv
Heidelberg Universitätsarchiv
Leipzig Universitätsarchiv
Merseburg Geheimes Staatsarchiv, Preussischer Kulturbesitz. This archive has recently been moved to Berlin.
Munich Bayerisches Hauptstaatsarchiv; Universitätsarchiv
Vienna Universitätsarchiv
Würzburg Institut für Hochschulkunde

Great Britain

Cambridge University Archive
Edinburgh Royal College of Physicians of Edinburgh Collections; Scottish Record Office; Edinburgh University Library, Special Collections

Glasgow Royal College of Physicians and Surgeons Collections; University of Glasgow Archives and Business Record Centre; University of Glasgow Library, Special Collections
Leeds Leeds University Archives
Liverpool University of Liverpool Archives
London Greater London Record Office; Guy's Hospital, Wills Medical Library; King's College Archive; London Hospital Archives Centre and Museum; St. Bartholomew's Hospital Archive; University College London, Rare Books and Manuscripts Room, and College Record Office; University of London Library, Paleography Room; Wellcome Institute for the History of Medicine, Western Manuscripts Collection
Manchester University of Manchester, University Archives; Manchester Collection

United States

Ann Arbor, MI Bentley Historical Library, University of Michigan
Baltimore, MD Johns Hopkins University, Alan M. Chesney Archive
Boston, MA Harvard Medical School, Francis Countway Library, Rare Book Room
Chicago, IL Chicago Historical Society; Rush–Presbyterian–St. Luke's Medical Center Archive; University of Chicago: Historical Library and Archives; Society of Medical History of Chicago Collection
Cincinnati, OH Cincinnati Historical Society Archive; University of Cincinnati School of Medicine Archive
Cleveland, OH Cleveland Health Sciences Library; Cleveland Historical Society
Columbus, OH Ohio Historical Society Archive; Ohio State University Archive
Detroit, MI Wayne State University, Walter P. Reuther Archive for Labor and Urban Affairs
Louisville, KY University of Louisville: Kornhauser Health Sciences Library, Historical Collections
New Haven, CT Yale University School of Medicine Historical Library
Philadelphia, PA College of Physicians of Philadelphia Collections; Medical College of Pennsylvania: Archives and Special Collections on Women in Medicine
Washington, DC Library of Congress Manuscript Division

Dissertations and Theses

Amzalac, Jean-Claude. "Réflexions sur l'enseignements de la médecine en France des origines à la révolution." University of Paris, 1967.
Becht, Manfred. "Das Dekanatsbuch der Tübinger medizinischen Fakultät, 1808–1858 (Teil 6: 1829–1833)." University of Tübingen, 1982.
Beese, Martina. "Die medizinischen Promotionen in Tübingen 1750–1799." University of Tübingen, 1977.
Bescher, André. "L'enseignement de la chimie en médecine au début du XIXe siècle." University of Lyon, 1959.
Boecker-Reinartz, Adelheid. "Die Augen-Kliniken der Universitäten des deutschen Sprachgebietes (1769–1914)." University of Cologne, 1990.

Böhmer, Paul. "Die medizinischen Schulen Bambergs in der ersten Hälfte des 19.Jahrhunderts." University of Erlangen–Nuremberg, 1970.

Böhner, Hans. "Die Geschichte des medizinischen Ausbildungs- und Prüfungswesen in Deutschland von etwa 1240n. Chr. bis Heute." University of Cologne, 1962.

Borschel, Christiane. "Das physiologische Institut der Universität Göttingen 1840 bis zur Gegenwart." University of Göttingen, 1987.

Bräuer, Heinrich. "Die Leipziger Hebammenschule und ihr geburtshilflichen Wirken in den Jahren 1810–20." University of Leipzig, 1941.

Broman, Thomas H. "The Transformation of Academic Medicine in Germany, 1780–1820." Princeton University, 1987.

Buchholz, Eckart. "Grossbritannische Reiseeindrücke deutscher und österreichischer Arzte von 1750 bis 1810." University of Frankfurt am Main, 1960.

Burgdorf, Volker. "John Gregory über Lernen und Lehren der Medizin." University of Kiel, 1970.

Busse, Adolf. "Der medizinische Unterricht an der Ludwig-Maximilians-Universität von 1826 bis 1875 im Spiegel der Vorlesungsankündigungen." University of Munich, 1978.

Butler, Stella V. F. "Science and the Education of Doctors in the Nineteenth Century: A Study of British Medical Schools with Particular Reference to the Development and Uses of Physiology." University of Manchester, 1981.

Cangi, Ellen C. "Principles Before Practice: The Reform of Medical Education in Cincinnati Before and After the Flexner Report." University of Cincinnati, 1983.

Cox, Dwayne. "A History of the University of Louisville." University of Kentucky, 1984.

Craig, John E. "A Mission for German Learning: The University of Strasbourg and Alsatian Society, 1870–1918." Stanford University, 1973.

Dominique, Mounier. "Journal du voyage médico–chirurgical de Jean Hunczovcki (1752–1798) en Europe occidentale." University of Rennes, 1968.

Donegan, Jane B. "Midwifery in America, 1760–1860: A Study in Medicine and Morality." Syracuse University, 1972.

Egglmaier, Herbert H. "Das medizinisch–chirurgische Studium in Graz: Ein Beispiel für den Wandel staatlicher Zielvorstellungen im Bildungs- und Medizinalwesen." University of Graz, 1980.

Emsch-Dériaz, Antoinette S. "Towards a Social Conception of Health in the Second Half of the Eighteenth Century: Tissot (1728–1797) and the new Preoccupation with Health and Well-being." University of Rochester, 1983.

Engels, Gerald. "Orthopädische Heilstätten im deutschen Sprachgebiet (1816–1918)." University of Cologne, 1990.

Flicker, Bernard. "Abraham Flexner's Educational Thought and Its Critical Appraisal." New York University, 1963.

Forstmann, Dietrich. "Die medizinisch–chirurgische Lehranstalt zu Greifswald." University of Berlin, 1938.

Geigenmüller, Ursula. "Aussagen über die französische Medizin der Jahre 1820–1847 in Reiseberichten deutscher Arzte." Free University of Berlin, 1985.

Granger, Jean. "Recherches sur l'enseignement de la médecine militaire à Strasbourg au XVIIIe siècle." University of Strasbourg, 1967.

Groopman, Leonard C. "The Internat des Hôpitaux de Paris: The Shaping and Transformation of the French Medical Elite, 1802–1914." Harvard University, 1986.

Gross, Michael. "Function and Structure in Nineteenth Century French Physiology." Princeton University, 1974.

Grossmann, Dieter. "Die medizinischen Promotionen in Tübingen 1850–1869." University of Tübingen, 1976.

Hader, Sigrid. "Geburtshilfe in Frankreich im Spiegel ihrer Einrichtungen." University of Cologne, 1988.

Hannaway, Caroline C. F. "Medicine, Public Welfare and the State in Eighteenth Century France: The Societé Royale de Médecine of Paris (1776–1793)." Johns Hopkins University, 1974.

Hautman, Johannes M. "Die ärztliche Ausbildung im Königreich und im Freistaat Bayern, 1808–1980." Technical University of Munich, 1982.

Hort, Imgard. "Die Pathologischen Institute der deutschsprachigen Universitäten (1850–1914). University of Cologne, 1987.

Huddle, Thomas S. "Science, Practice and the Reform of American Medical Education." University of Illinois at Urbana–Champaign, 1988.

Hudson, Robert P. "Patterns of Medical Education in Nineteenth Century America." Johns Hopkins University, 1966.

Imbault-Huart, Marie-José. "L'école pratique de dissection de Paris de 1750 à 1822 ou l'influence du concept de médecine pratique et de médecine d'observation dans l'enseignement medico–chirurgical au XVIIIème siècle et au debut du XIXème siècle." University of Paris, 1973.

Irrgang, Dieter. "Aspekte der Ausbildung des Mediziners im deutschsprachigen Kulturrahm zwischen 1872 und 1901 anhand von Selbstzeugnissen deutscher Arzte." University of Bonn, 1989.

Jentzch, Gunda. "Zur Geschichte der klinischen Medizin in Göttingen: Das Ernst-August-Hospital 1850–1890." University of Göttingen, 1988.

Jones, June. "Science, Utility, and the `Second City of the Empire': The Sciences and Especially the Medical Sciences at Liverpool University, 1881–1925." University of Manchester, 1989.

Keller, Marita. "Die Geschichte des Tübingen Klinikums im ersten Halbjahrhundert seines Bestehens (1792–1846): Medizinische und soziale Bedingungen seiner Entwicklung." University of Tübingen, 1969.

Kilpatrick, Robert L. "Nature's Schools: The Hunterian Revolution in London Hospital Medicine 1780–1825." Cambridge University, 1988.

Kirschner, Siegbert. "Die Lehrer der Heilkunde der Universität Erlangen 1819–1842 mit Wiedergabe der Vorlesungsverzeichnisse bis 1832." University of Erlangen, 1967.

Kläss, Konrad. "Die Einführung besonderer Kurse für Mikroskopie und physikalische Diagnostik (Perkussion und Auskultation) in dem medizinischen Unterricht an deutschen Universitäten im 19.Jahrhundert." University of Göttingen, 1971.

Kondratas, Ramúnas A. "Joseph Frank (1771–1842) and the Development of Clinical Medicine." Harvard University, 1977.

Kupka, Horst W. "Die Ausgaben der Süddeutschen Länder für die medizinischen und naturwissenschaftlichen Hochschul-Einrichtungen 1848–1914." University of Bonn, 1970.

Landau-Bruckner, Sigrid. "Amerika und seine Medizin im Spiegel historischer Reiseberichte Europäischer Ärzte (1744–1969)." University of Heidelberg, 1973.

Lawrence, Christopher J. "Medicine as Culture: Edinburgh and the Scottish Enlightenment." University College London, 1984.

Lawrence, Susan C. "Science and Medicine at the London Hospitals: The Development of Teaching and Research, 1750–1815." University of Toronto, 1985.

Lehmann, Carlos. "Uber die Medizin an der Academia Ottoniana und Universitas Ottoniano–Fridericiana Bambergensis, 1735–1803." University of Erlangen–Nuremberg, 1967.

Léonard, Jacques. "Les médecins de l'ouest au XIXème siècle." University of Paris IV, 1976.

Lippoth, Siegrun. "Tübinger Medizinstudium vor hundert Jahren: Tatsachen, Bestrebungen, Kritik und Reformvorschläge Tübinger Dozenten im 19ten.Jahrhundert." University of Tübingen, 1970.

Macleod, Marion. "The Role of Science and Technology in the Process of Medical Specialization." University of Edinburgh, 1985.

Maier, Anton E. "Die niederärztliche Ausbildung zu Salzburg im 19.Jahrhundert." University of Erlangen–Nuremberg, n.d.

McRae, Sandra F. "The 'Scientific Spirit' in Medicine at the University of Toronto, 1880–1910." University of Toronto, 1987.

Movrich, Ronald F. "Before the Gates of Excellence: Abraham Flexner and Education, 1866–1918." University of California at Berkeley, 1981.

Niklas, Brigitte. "Das Dekanatsbuch der Tübinger Medizinischen Fakultät, 1808–1858 (Teil 2: 1816–1818)." University of Tübingen, 1985.

Niklas, Edgar. "Das Dekanatsbuch der Tübinger Medizinischen Fakultät, 1808–1858 (Teil 3: 1818–1822)." University of Tübingen, 1985.

O'Hara, Leo J. "An Emerging Profession: Philadelphia Medicine, 1860–1900." University of Pennsylvania, 1976.

Paetzke, Axel. "Die Lehrer der Heilkunde der Universität Erlangen 1792–1918 mit Wiedergabe der Vorlesungsverzeichnisse." University of Erlangen, 1966.

Peschel-Kudernatsch, Uta. "Die medizinischen Promotionen in Tübingen 1800–1814." University of Tübingen, 1985.

Picard, Germaine. "La réglementation des études médicales en France: Son évolution de la révolution a nos jours." University of Paris, 1967.

Pickstone, John V. "The Origins of General Physiology in France with Special Emphasis on the Work of R. J. H. Dutrochet." University of London, 1973.

Reupke, Hansjörg. "Zur Geschichte der Ausübung der Heilkunde durch nichtapprobierte Personen in Hamburg von den Anfängen bis zum Erlass des 'Heilpraktikergesetzes' im Jahre 1939." University of Hamburg, 1986.

Richter, Wolfgang. "Die Geschichte und Entwicklung der Hals-Nasen-Ohrenheilkunde in Göttingen von 1737 bis 1963." University of Göttingen, 1986.

Rieberer, Gabriela. "Das Institut für medizinische Chemie und Hygiene der Universität Göttingen von der Gründung 1833 bis 1955." University of Göttingen, 1990.

Roche, Christian. "L'enseignement médical à Lyon de 1821 à 1877." University of Lyon, 1975.

Rosner, Lisa. "Students and Apprentices: Medical Education at Edinburgh University, 1760–1810." Johns Hopkins University, 1985.

Rüden, Anna D. von. "Medicina Graecensis: Das medizinisch–chirurgische Studium in Graz (1782–1862)." Technical University of Munich, 1978.

Scherg-Zeisner, Christiane. "Die ärztliche Ausbildung an der Königlich-bayerischen Julius-Maximilians-Universität in Würzburg 1814–1872." University of Würzburg, 1973.

Seelig, Rudolf. "Die medizinischen Promotionen in Tübingen 1890–1899." University of Tübingen, 1973.

Siroy, Pascale. "Histoire de la faculté mixte de médecine et de pharmacie de Lyon (Période de 1877 à 1931)." University of Lyon, 1949.

Slama, Wolfgang B. "Die medizinischen Promotionen in Tübingen, 1870–1889." University of Tübingen, 1976.

Smith, Dale C. "The Emergence of Organized Clinical Instruction in the Nineteenth Century American Cities of Boston, New York and Philadelphia." University of Minnesota, 1979.

Steiner, Albert. "Ludwig Choulant und seine 'Anleitung zu dem Studium der Medicin' (1829)." University of Zurich, 1987.

Steudel, Wolf-Ingo. "Die Innovationszeit von Prüfungsfächern in der medizinischen Ausbildung in Deutschland und ihre Bedingtheiten (dargestellt am Verhalten der Administrative): Materialien und Analyzen zur Entwicklung der medizinischen Ausbildung seit 100 Jahren (1869–1969)." University of Kiel, 1973.

Sturdy, Steven W. "A Co-ordinated Whole: The Life and Work of John Scott Haldane." University of Edinburgh, 1987.

Suárez, Eisenhower P. "Der medizinische Unterricht an der Ludwig-Maximilians-Universität zu München von 1875 bis 1925 im Spiegel der Vorlesungsankündigungen." University of Munich, 1979.

Tasche, Wilhelm. "Die Anatomischen Theater und Institute der deutschsprachigen Unterrichtsstätten (1500–1914)." University of Cologne, 1989.

Todorović, Olivier W. "Irische Schulen der Medizin, ihre Lehrer und Hospitäler (1600–1920)." University of Cologne, 1994.

Tuchman, Arleen M. "Science, Medicine and the State: The Institutionalization of Scientific Medicine at the University of Heidelberg." University of Wisconsin at Madison, 1985.

Turner, Roy S. "The Prussian Universities and the Research Imperative, 1806 to 1848." Princeton University, 1973.

Underhill, Paul K. "Science, Professionalism and the Development of Medical Education in England: An Historical Sociology." University of Edinburgh, 1987.

Unger, Werner. "Die Erziehung zum Arzt als Teil ärztlicher Ausbildung in der Medizin der Aufklärung." University of Hannover, 1977.

Vieten, Bernward. "Medizinstudenten in Münster: Universität, Studentenschaft und Medizin." University of Münster, 1979.

Voldman, Danièle. "Les hôpitaux militaires dans l'espace sanitaire français, 1708–1789." University of Paris, n.d.

Wang, Agnès. "L'enseignement de la médecine à Nancy de 1789 à 1822." University of Nancy, 1969.

Webb, Katherine A. "The Development of the Medical Profession in Manchester, 1750– 1860." University of Manchester, 1988.

Wenig, Hans G. "Medizinische Ausbildung im 19.Jahrhundert." University of Bonn, 1969.

Wessling, Mary N. "Medicine and Government in Early Modern Württemberg." University of Michigan, 1988.

Willems, Michael. "Medizinische Universitätskliniken im deutschen Sprachgebeit (1753–1914)." University of Cologne, 1983.

Winkelmann, Heike. "Das akademische Hospital in Göttingen von 1781 bis 1850." University of Göttingen, 1981.

Wiriot, Mireille. "L'enseignement clinique dans les hôpitaux de Paris entre 1794 et 1848." University of Paris, 1970.

Wolff, Christian. "Faculté, écoles de médecine et hôpitaux militaires à Strasbourg sous la révolution et l'empire (1789–1815)." University of Strasbourg, 1986.

Zürcher, Manfred. "Das Dekanatsbuch der Tübinger Medizinischen Fakultät, 1808–1858 (Teil 5: 1826–1829)." University of Tübingen, 1982.

Miscellaneous Unpublished Papers

Bleker, Johanna. "'Der einzig wahre Weg, brauchbare Männer zu bilden'—Der medizinisch–klinische Unterricht an der Berliner Universität, 1810–1850."

Borell, Merriley, Deborah J. Coon, H. Hughes Evans, and Gail Hornstein. "Selective Importation of the 'Exact Method': Experimental Physiology and Psychology in the United States, 1860–1910." Paper presented at the joint meeting of the History of Science Society and the British Society for the History of Science, Manchester, July 13, 1988.

Bynum, W. F. "Sir George Newman and the American Way."

Chaplin, Arnold. "The History of Medical Education in the Universities of Oxford and Cambridge, 1500–1850." Typescript, 1920, Royal College of Physicians of London.

Coury, Charles. "Medical Education in France from the Beginning of the 17th Century to Our Day." Manuscript, 1968, Institut für Geschichte der Medizin, Vienna.

Harvey, Joy. "Faithful to Its Old Traditions: Paris Clinical Medicine from the Late 1840s to the Third Republic."

Heteren, Godelieve van. "Medical Internationalism Under National Flags: The 1867, 1881 and 1890 International Medical Congresses." Paper presented at the joint meeting of the History of Science Society and the British History of Science Society in Manchester, July 13, 1988.

Karenberg, Axel. "Die Kliniken an den Universitäten der deutschen Kleinstaaten (1780–1815)."

Langley, Harold D. "The Navy's School in Philadelphia: An Experiment in 19th Century Professional Education." Paper presented at the annual meeting of American Association for the History of Medicine, Louisville, KY, June 16, 1993.

Lesky, Erna. "Pathology in Austria During the Romantic Period (1800–1848)." Manuscript, Institut für Geschichte der Medizin, Vienna.

Lindemann, Mary. "The Enlightenment Encountered: Medical Practice and Enlightenment in Northern Germany, 1750–1820." Paper presented at the Wellcome Institute for the History of Medicine, London, 1992.

Luyendijk-Elshout, Antonie M. "The Medical World of the Nineteenth Century: Its Impact upon Medical Education."

Marcus, Peter S. "The Fenner System of Medical Education: Clinical Training in Antebellum New Orleans." Paper presented at the annual meeting of the American Association for the History of Medicine, Seattle, April 1992.

Maulitz, Russell C. "Intellectual Migration: The Case of Pathological Anatomy." Paper presented at the joint meeting of the History of Science Society and the British Society for the History of Science, Manchester, July 13, 1988.

Pickstone, John V. "Models of Medicine: Medicine as Model." Paper presented to the British Society for the History of Science, London, May 8, 1991 (revised May 13, 1992).

Pickstone, John V., Roger J. Cooter, and Caroline C. S. Murphy. "Exploring 'Clinical Research'; Academic Medicine and the Clinicians in Early Twentieth Century Britain." Paper presented at the conference "Science in Modern Medicine," Manchester, 1985.

Renschler, Hans E. "Entwicklung der Methodenlehre in der Unterrichtung von Arzten." Paper presented to the second European Congress on Continuing Medical Education, Bad Nauheim, January 19, 1979.

———. "Vermittlung problemorientierter Inhalte des Fachgebietes Chirugie." Paper presented at the tenth Munich Symposium on Academic Surgery, September 20, 1991.

Richet, Gabriel. "Le sens de la responsabilité médicale: Son acquisition par la pédagogie clinique."

Romano, Terrie M. "John Burdon Sanderson and the Oxford School of Physiology." Paper presented at the annual meeting of the American Association for the History of Medicine, Seattle, May 2, 1992.

Rothstein, William. "The Professionalization of Academic Medicine." Paper presented at the annual meeting of the American Historical Association, Cincinnati, December 28, 1988.

Tuchman, Arleen. "Reevaluating Early Nineteenth Century German Medical Education." Paper presented at the annual meeting of American Historical Association, Cincinnati, December 28, 1988.

Warner, John H. "The Medical Migrant's Baggage Unpacked: Anglo-American Construction of the Paris Clinical School." Paper presented at the joint meeting of the History of Science Society and the British History of Science Society, Manchester, July 13, 1988.

———. "Paradigm Lost or Paradise Declining? American Physicians and the 'Dead End' of the Paris Clinical School." Paper presented at the conference "The History of Scientific Medicine in Paris, 1790–1850: A Reinterpretation." Wood Institute for the History of Medicine, College of Physicians of Philadelphia, February 1992.

Medical Journals

American Academy of Medicine Bulletin
American Journal of Clinical Medicine
American Journal of the Medical Sciences

American Medical Association, *Transactions*
American Public Health Association, *Reports and Papers*
Annals of Medical History
Archiv für anatomie, physiologie, und wissenschaftliche medizin
Archives generales de médecine
Archives of Internal Medicine
Association of American Medical Colleges, *Journal*
Association of American Physicians, *Transactions*
Berliner klinische Wochenschrift
Boston Medical and Surgical Journal
British Medical Journal
Bulletin de l'academie de médecine
Bulletin of the History of Medicine
Canadian Medical Association Journal
College of Physicians of Philadelphia, *Transactions*
Congress of American Physicians and Surgeons, *Transactions*
Deutsche medizinische Wochenschrift
Deutsches Archiv für klinische Medizin
Dublin Journal of Medical Science
Edinburgh Medical (and Surgical) Journal
Janus: Archives internationales pour l'histoire de la médecine
Journal of the American Medical Association (JAMA)
Journal of the History of Medicine and Allied Sciences
Johns Hopkins Hospital Bulletin
Lancet
Lyon médical
Medical History
Medical News
Medical Record
Medical Review of Reviews
Medical and Surgical Reporter
Medizin-historisches Journal
Montpellier médical
Münchener medizinische Wochenschrift
New York Medical Journal
Practitioner (London)
Le progrés médical
Public Health Reports
Science
Societe médicale des hôpitaux de Paris
Sudhoffs Archiv

Printed Primary Sources

Abel, John J. "On the Teaching of Pharmacology, Materia Medica, and Therapeutics in Our Medical Schools." *Philadelphia Medical Journal* 6 (1900): 384–90.
Abrams, Albert. "Medical Education in Germany." *Pacific Medical and Surgical Journal* 25 (1883): 505–11.

Achard, Charles. *Confessions d'un vieil homme du siècle*. Paris: Mercure, 1943.

Acland, Henry W. *Medical Education. A Letter Addressed to the Authorities of the Johns Hopkins Hospital and the Johns Hopkins University*. Baltimore: Johns Hopkins University, 1879.

Allbutt, T. Clifford. *On Professional Education with Special Reference to Medicine*. London: Macmillan, 1906.

Almanach général de médecine pour la ville de Paris. Paris, 1853.

Alsima [George Skelton Stephenson]. *Reminiscences of a Student's Life at Edinburgh in the Seventies*. Edinburgh: Oliver and Boyd, 1918.

American Almanac and Repository of Useful Knowledge. Boston: Charles Bowen, 1832.

Amette, Amédée. *Guide général de l'étudiant en médecine*. Paris: Victor Masson, 1847.

Ammon, Friedrich A. *Parallele der französischen und deutschen Chirurgie nach Resultaten einer in den Jahren 1821 und 1822 gemachten Reise*. Leipzig: C. H. F. Hartmann, 1823.

Andrews, T. F. "An Account of the Medical Institutions of Berlin." *American Medical Record* 6 (1823): 471–86.

Anonymous. *An Examination into the Causes of the Declining Reputation of the Medical Faculty of the University of Edinburgh*. Edinburgh: W. Burness, 1834.

———. *Observations on Medical Reform: Illustrating the present Condition of Medical Science, Education, and Practise Throughout Great-Britain and Ireland*. Dublin: M. Keene, 1807.

———. *Observations on the Present System of Medical Education, with a View to Reform*. London: Sherwood, Gilbert, and Piper, 1834.

———. *Practical Remarks on the Measures Proposed for Reform in the Medical Profession*. London: S. Highley, 1841.

———. "Review of Recent Works from German and British Schools of Physiology." *British Foreign Medical Review* 5 (1839): 75–116.

———. *The University of Göttingen at the Beginning of the Year 1835*. London: Robert Boswell, 1836.

Arneth, F. H. *Uber Geburtshülfe und Gynaekologie in Frankreich, Grossbritannien und Irland*. Vienna: Wilhelm Braumüller, 1853.

Arnold, Johann W. *Hodegetik für Medicin-Studirende oder Anleitung zum Studium der Medicin*. Vienna: Karl Gerold, 1832.

Arnold, Matthew. *High Schools & Universities in Germany*. London: Macmillan, 1868.

Ballingall, George. *Remarks on Schools of Instruction for Military and Naval Surgeons*. Edinburgh: Balfour and Jack, 1843.

Barclay, J. *The Medical School of Edinburgh*. Edinburgh, 1819.

Bard, L. "De l'admission en France des étudiants et des médecins étrangers." *Bulletin du Lyon médical* 82 (1896): 371–78, 406–14.

Barker, Lewellys. "Medical Laboratories: Their Relations to Medical Practise and to Medical Discovery." *Science* 27 (1908): 601–11.

———. "The Organization of the Laboratories in the Medical Clinic of the Johns Hopkins Hospital." *Bulletin of the Johns Hopkins Hospital* 18 (1907): 193–98.

———. "Some Tendencies in Medical Education in the United States." *Medical Review of Reviews* 57 (1911): 613–21.

Bartlett, Elisha. *An Essay on the Philosophy of Medical Science*. Philadelphia: Lea & Blanchard, 1844.

Beaunis, H. *L'école du service de santé militaire de Strasbourg et la faculté de médecine de Strasbourg de 1856 à 1870.* Nancy: Berger-Levrault, 1888.

Becher, Wolf. "Aus einer Anleitung für Medizinstudierende." *Deutsche medizinische Wochenschrift* 33 (1907): 67–69, 108–10.

Beck, T. Romeyn. "Statistics of the Medical Colleges of the United States." *Transactions of the Medical Society of the State of New York* 4 (1840): 166–228.

Bedford, Gunning S. *An Address, Introductory to a Course of Lectures Delivered in the Hall of the Medical College of South Carolina.* Charleston: J. S. Burges, 1833.

Benedict, A. L. "The Life of a Medical Student." *Lippincott's Monthly Magazine* 58 (1896): 389–95.

Bennett, J. Hughes. "Observations on Medical Education." *Lancet* 1 (1866): 505–8.

Berlin, University of. *Vorlesungs-Verzeichnis und Index Lectionum der Universität Berlin,* 1810–70.

Berliner medicinische Gesellschaft. "Verhandlung über die Frage der Zulassung der Abiturienten der Realschule erster Ordnung zum Studium der Medicin." *Berliner klinische Wochenschrift* 16 (1879): 143–44, 158–59, 173–74.

Bert, Paul. *Rapport sur la création de nouvelles facultés de médecine.* Paris: Ch. Delagrave, 1874.

Bevan, Arthur Dean. "Medical Education in the United States: The Need for a Uniform Standard." *Journal of the American Medical Association* 51 (1908): 566–71.

Bezel, Ernst, ed. *Johann Jakob Steger, 1798–1857: Beispiel eines Medizinstudenten im frühen 19.Jahrhundert nach den Briefen an seine Eltern.* Zurich: Juris Druck & Verlag, 1981.

Bigelow, Henry J. *Medical Education in America.* Cambridge, MA: Welch, Bigelow, 1871.

Bigelow, Horatio R. "Berlin as a Medical Center—A Guide for American Practitioners and Students." *New England Medical Monthly* 4 (1884–85): 369–82, 411–20, 516–28, 553–59.

Billings, Frank. "Medical Education in the United States." *Journal of the American Medical Association* 40 (1903): 1271–76.

Billings, John Shaw. "Higher Medical Education." *American Journal of the Medical Sciences* 76 (1878): 174–89.

Billroth, Theodor. *Aphorismen Zum "Lehren und Lernen der medicinischen Wissenschaften."* 2nd ed. Vienna: Carl Gerold's Son, 1886.

———. *The Medical Sciences in the German Universities: A Study in the History of Civilization.* New York: Macmillan, 1924. Originally published in German in 1876.

Blanchard, R. *Les universités allemandes.* Paris, 1883.

Boardman, Andrew. *An Essay on the Means of Improving Medical Education.* Philadelphia: Haswell, Barrington, and Haswell, 1840.

Bock, Carl. *Auch ein Votum in Betriff der Medicinalreform in Sachsen.* Leipzig: Reclam, 1846.

Bonn, University of. *Vorlesungen auf der Königlich Preussisch-Rheinischen Universität.* 1818-1914.

Börner, Ernst. *Eine gynaecologische Reise durch Deutschland, England und Frankreich.* Graz: Leuschner & Lubinsky, 1876.

Bowditch, Henry P. "The Medical School of the Future." *Medical News* 76 (1900): 681–90.

Bowditch, Vincent Y. *Life and Correspondence of Henry Ingersoll Bowditch.* 2 vols. Boston: Houghton Mifflin, 1902.

Breslauer, Bernhard. *Die Zurücksetzung der Juden an den Universitäten Deutschlands.* Berlin: Verband der deutschen Juden, 1911.

Broca, Paul. *Correspondance, 1841–1857.* Paris: privately printed, 1886.

———. *Rapport de la commission chargée d'étudier les réformes à introduire dans l'enseignement de la faculté de médecine de Paris.* Paris, 1876.

Brockbank, W., and F. Kenworthy, eds. *The Diary of Richard Kay, 1716–51, of Baldingstone, Near Burg: A Lancashire Doctor.* Manchester: Chetham Society, 1968.

Bruté, S. G. B. *Essai sur l'histoire et les avantages des institutions cliniques.* Paris: Belin, 1803.

Budde, Karl, ed. *Wilhelm Budde's Heidelberger Tagebuch aus den Jahren 1807 und 1808.* Heidelberg: G. Koester, 1920.

Bureau, E. "Modifications à apporter à l'enseignement clinique dans les facultés de médecine." *Gazette médicale de Nantes* 25 (1907): 821–27.

Burnet, Etienne. "Medical Education and the Reform of Medical Studies." *Quarterly Bulletin of the Health Organisation of the League of Nations* 2 (1933): 620–749.

Cabanis, P. J. G. *Coup d'oeil sur les révolutions et sur la réforme de la médecine.* Paris, 1804.

———. "Rapport fait au conseil des cinq-cents, sur l'organisation des écoles de médecine." In *Oeuvres complètes,* vol. 1, 363–402. Paris: Bossanges, 1823.

Cahan, David, ed. *Letters of Hermann von Helmholtz to His Parents: The Medical Education of a German Scientist, 1837–1846.* Stuttgart: Franz Steiner, 1993.

Caldwell, Charles. *Autobiography.* Philadelphia: Lippincott, Grambo, 1855.

Callender, George W. *On the Present System of Medical Education in England.* London: Spottiswoode, 1864.

Calvert, George H. *First Years in Europe.* N.p.: William V. Spencer, 1866.

Carbutt, Edward. *Clinical Lectures in the Manchester Royal Infirmary.* Manchester: Thomas Sowler, 1834.

Caron, Jean Charles. *Demonstration rigoureuse du peu d'utilité de l'école de médecine, du grand avantage que l'on a retiré, et que l'on retirera toujours du réestablissement du collège de chirurgie.* Paris: Pillet, 1818.

———. *Réflexions sur l'exercise de la médecine.* Paris: Clousier, 1804.

Casper, Johann Ludwig. *Charakteristik der französischen Medicin, mit vergleichenden Hinblicken auf die englische.* Leipzig: Brockhaus, 1822.

Castan, A. *Rapport sur les travaux de la faculté de médecine de Montpellier pendant l'année scolaire 1885–1886.* Montpellier: Boehm et fils, 1887.

Cathell, D. W., and William T. Cathell. *Book on the Physician Himself, and Things that concern his Reputation and Success.* Philadelphia: Davis, 1902.

Cattell, J. McKeen, ed. *Medical Research and Education.* New York: Science Press, 1913.

Caullery, Maurice. *Universities and Scientific Life in the United States.* Cambridge, MA: Harvard University Press, 1922.

Chaillé. Stanford E. "The Medical Colleges, the Medical Profession, and the Public." *New Orleans Medical and Surgical Journal* 1 (1874): 818–41.

Chamberlaine, William. *Tyrocinium Medicum; or a Dissertation on the Duties of Youth apprenticed to the Medical Profession*. London: privately printed, 1812.

Chauffard, E. "De la situation de l'enseignement médical en France." *Revue des deux mondes*, 1878, 124–66.

Chew, Samuel. *Lectures on Medical Education, or on the proper Method of Studying Medicine*. Philadelphia: Lindsay & Blakiston, 1864.

Chittenden, Russell H. *The Development of Physiological Chemistry in the United States*. New York: Chemical Catalog, 1930.

Christian, Henry A. "The Concentration Plan of Teaching Medicine." *Bulletin of the American Academy of Medicine* 11 (1910): 705–19.

Christison, Robert. *Graduation Under the Medical and Scottish Universities Act*. Edinburgh: Black, 1861.

Choulant, Ludwig. *Anleitung zu dem Studium der Medicin*. Leipzig: Leopold Voss, 1829.

Clarke, Edward H., Henry J. Bigelow, Samuel D. Gross, T. Gaillard Thomas, and John Shaw Billings. *A Century of Medicine 1776–1876*. Brinklow, MD: Old Hickory Bookshop, 1962. Originally published in 1876.

Coates, Reynell. *Oration on the Defects in the Present System of Medical Instruction in the United States*. Philadelphia: James Kay, Jun. and Brother, 1835.

Colwell, N. P. "Present Needs of Medical Education." *Journal of the American Medical Association* 82 (1924): 838–40.

Commission on Medical Education. *Medical Education and Related Problems in Europe*. New Haven, CT: Commission on Medical Education, 1930.

Conrad, Johannes. *The German Universities for the Last Fifty Years*. Trans. John Hutchinson. Glasgow: Bryce, 1885.

Conradi, Johann Wilhelm Heinrich. *Uber das medicinisch–klinische Institut in dem Akademischen Hospital in Heidelberg*. Heidelberg: Mohr and Winter, 1817.

Conseil Municipal de Lyon. *Organisation de la faculté de médecine et de l'école supérieure de pharmacie*. Lyon: J. Gallet, 1876.

Constancio, Francisco S. *An Appeal to the Gentlemen Studying Medicine at the University of Edinburgh*. Edinburgh: privately printed, 1797.

Cope, Zachary, ed. "Extracts from the Diary of Thomas Laycock Chiefly Written When He Was a Medical Student 1833–5." *Medical History* 9 (1968): 169–76.

Cousin, Victor. *De l'enseignement et de l'exercise de la médecine et de pharmacie*. Paris: J.-B. Baillière, 1850.

Cranefield, Paul F., ed. *Two Great Scientists of the Nineteenth Century: Correspondence of Emil Du Bois-Reymond and Carl Ludwig*. Trans. Sabine Lichtner-Ayed. Baltimore: Johns Hopkins University Press, 1982.

Crittenden, Russell H. *The Development of Physiological Chemistry in the United States*. New York: Chemical Catalog, 1930.

Crosland, Maurice P., ed. *Science in France in the Revolutionary Era Described by Thomas Bugge, Danish Astronomer Royal*. Cambridge, MA: MIT Press, 1969.

Crosse, John Green. *Paris et Montpellier, ou tableau de la médecine dans ces deux écoles*. Paris: J.-B. Baillère, 1820.

———. *Sketches of the Medical Schools of Paris*. London: J. Callow, 1815.

Cruchet, René. *La médecine dans les universités allemandes*. Bordeaux: G. Gounovilhov, 1902.

———. *Les universités allemandes au XXe siècle*. Paris: Armand Colin, 1914.

Cushing, E. W. "Medical Education in Germany." *Boston Medical and Surgical Journal* 113 (1885): 214–16.

Dance, J. B. H. *Guide pour l'étude de la clinique médicale ou prècis de sémiotique*. Paris, 1834.

Davis, John. *The Annual Address delivered on. . .Opening the Session of the Royal School of Medicine and Surgery, Pine Street*. Manchester: Love and Barton, 1837.

Davis, Nathan Smith. *Address on Free Medical Schools*. Chicago, 1849.

———. *Inaugural Address delivered at the Opening of the Medical Department of the Lind University*. Chicago, 1859.

Derby, Hasket. "Medical Advantages of Vienna for American Students." *Boston Medical and Surgical Journal* 63 (1860): 51–53.

D. H. C. A. O. *Einige Gedanken über den gegenwärtigen Zustand der wissenschaftlichen Kultur, hauptsächlich in Beziehung auf akademischen Unterricht*. Sulzbach: J. E. Seidel, 1807.

Diday, P. "Du siège des cliniques par rapport aux écoles de médecine." *Lyon médical* 12 (1873): 73–81.

Doane, George. "Comparative Advantages of Vienna and Paris, as Places for Medical Study." *New Jersey Medical Reporter* 7 (1854): 17–20.

Dodson, John M. "The Elective System in Medical Education." *Bulletin of the American Academy of Medicine* 4 (1899): 331–42.

Dohrmann, George III. "Medical Education in the United States as Seen by a German Immigrant: The Letters of George Dohrmann, 1897 to 1901." *Journal of the History of Medicine and Allied Sciences* 33 (1978): 477–506.

Dolch, Oskar. *Geschichte des deutschen Studenthums von der Gründung der deutschen Universitäten bis zu den deutschen Freiheitskriegen*. Leipzig, 1858.

Domange-Hubert. *Guide général de l'étudiant en médecine*. Paris, 1846.

Drake, Daniel. *An Inaugural Discourse on Medical Education Delivered at the Opening of the Medical College of Ohio*. Cincinnati: Lookes, Palmer and Reynolds, 1820.

———. *An Introductory Discourse, to a Course of Lectures on Clinical Medicine and Pathological Anatomy*. Louisville: Prentice and Weissinger, 1840.

———. *An Introductory Lecture, on the Means of Promoting the Intellectual Improvement of the Students and Physicians of the Valley of the Mississippi*. Louisville: Prentice and Weissinger, 1844.

———. *Practical Essays on Medical Education and the Medical Profession in the United States*. Baltimore: Johns Hopkins University Press, 1952.

———. *Strictures on Some of the Defects and Infirmities of Intellectual and Moral Character, in Students of Medicine: An Introductory Lecture*. Louisville: Prentice and Weissinger, 1847.

Duchanoy, Claude-François, and Jean-Baptiste Jumelin. "Memoire sur la utilité d'une école clinique en médecine." *Observations sur la physique, sur l'histoire naturelle et les arts* 13 (1778) (supplement): 227–86.

Dumreicher, J. von. *Uber die Nothwendigkeit von Reformen des Unterrichtes an den medicinischen Facultäten Osterreichs*. Vienna: Alfred Hölder, 1878.

Duncan, Alexander. *Memorials of the Faculty of Physicians and Surgeons of Glasgow*. Glasgow: Maclehose, 1896.

Dunglison, Robley. *The Medical Student; or, Aids to the Study of Medicine.* Philadelphia: Carey, Lea & Blanchard, 1837.

Dureau, A. "Notes sur l'enseignement et l'exercise de la médecine en Europe." *Gazette hebdomadaire de médecine et de chirurgie* 9 (1872): 110–11, 241–49, 257–66, 481–87, 578–86.

Dwight, Henry E. "The Influence of German Universities upon Our Profession." *Journal of the American Medical Association* 16 (1891): 438–41.

Ebstein, Wilhelm. "Uber die Entwickelung des klinischen Unterrichts an der Göttinger Hochschule und über die heutigen Aufgaben der medizinischen Klinik." *Klinisches Jahrbuch* 1 (1889): 67–99.

Ecker, Alexander. *Für unsere Universität: Ein Mahnwart eines Freiburger Bürgers an seine Mitbürger bei gelegenheit der Eröffnung der neuen deutschen Reichsuniversität Strassburg.* Freiburg: Wagner, 1872.

Ecole de médecine de Strasbourg. *Plan général de l'enseignement.* Strasbourg: F. G. Levrault, an VI (1799).

Ecole de santé de Montpellier. *Programme des cours d'enseignement.* Paris: Imprimerie des sciences et arts, 1796.

L'école de santé de Paris. *De l'état actuel de l'école de santé de Paris.* Paris: Didot Jeuve, 1798.

L'école speciale de médecine de Strasbourg. *Observations sur le rapport fait au nom de la commission d'instruction publique et d'institutions républicaines réunies, par le Citoyen Hardy, membre de conseil des cinq-cents, sur l'organisation des écoles de médecine.* Strasbourg: Philippe Dannbach, 1798.

Edinburgh Pathological Club. "The Edinburgh Medical School: The Curriculum and the General Efficiency of the School." *Edinburgh Medical Journal* 3 (1909): 293–319.

———. "Report of the Edinburgh Pathological Club on the Training of the Student of Medicine." *Edinburgh Medical Journal* 22 (1919): 187–200.

Eliot, Charles W. *Annual Report of the President of Harvard College, 1869–70.* Boston, 1870.

Elliotson, John. *Address, delivered at the Opening of the Medical Session in the University of London, October 1, 1832.* London: Longman, Rees, 1832.

Emerson, J. E. "The Requirements for Preliminary Education in the Medical Schools of the United States and Canada." *Journal of the American Medical Association* 14 (1890): 271–72.

Exner, Sigmund. "Die neue medicinische Rigorosenordnung für Oesterreich." *Die Zeit* (Vienna), no. 275 (1900): 5–7.

Faculté de médecine de Paris. *Programme des questions pour les examens de fin d'année.* Paris: Libraire de la faculté de médecine, 1849.

———. *Rapport sur la réforme des études médicales.* Paris: G. Steinheil, 1893.

———. *Réfutation des calomnies publiées par un anonyme.* Paris: Faculté de médecine, 1816.

———. *Organisation des études en vue du doctorat en médecine.* Paris: Imprimerie administrative centrale, 1934.

Fawdington, Thomas. *A Catalogue descriptive chiefly of the Morbid Preparations contained in the Museum of the Manchester Theatre of Anatomy and Medicine, Marsden Street.* Manchester: Harrison and Crosfield, 1833.

Felschow, Eva-Marie, and Emil Heuser, eds. *Universität und Ministerium: Justus Liebigs Briefwechsel mit Justin von Linde.* Giessen: Ferber, 1992.

Fenner, Erasmus D. "Introductory Lecture delivered at the Opening of the New Orleans School of Medicine." *New Orleans Medical News and Hospital Gazette* 3 (1856): 577–600.

———. "Letters from the North." *New Orleans Medical and Surgical Journal* 3 (1846): 198–202.

Fiaux, Louis. *L'enseignement de la médecine en Allemagne.* Paris: Librairie Germer-Baillière, 1877.

Fischer, C. E. *Medicinische und chirurgische Bemerkungen über London und die englische Heilkunde überhaupt.* Göttingen: Johann Christian Dieterich, 1796.

Ford, John M. T., ed. *A Medical Student at St. Thomas's Hospital, 1801–1802: The Weekes Family Letters.* London: Wellcome Institute for the History of Medicine, supplement to *Medical History,* 1987.

Formey, D. Ludewig. *Uber den gegenwärtigen Zustand der Medicin in Hinsicht auf die Bildung künftiger Arzte.* Berlin: Karl Friedrich Amelang, 1809.

Foster, Michael. *On Medical Education at Cambridge.* London: Macmillan, 1878.

———. "Reminiscences of a Physiologist." *Colorado Medical Journal* 6 (1900): 419–28.

France, University of. *Statut portant réglement général concernant les concours dans les facultés de droit et de médecine.* Paris: Imprimerie royale, 1825.

Frank, Johann Peter. "Akademische Rede über die Priesterärzte." *Wiener Universitäts Taschenbuch,* 1804, i–lx.

———. *Plan d'école clinique ou méthode d'enseigner la pratique de la médecine dans un hôpital academique.* Vienna: Wapples, 1790.

———. *A System of Complete Medical Police.* Ed. Erna Lesky. Baltimore: Johns Hopkins University Press, 1970.

Frank, Joseph. *Reise nach Paris, London, und einem grossen Theile des übrigen Englands und Schottlands.* 2 vols. Vienna: Camesinaische Buchhandlung, 1804.

Frazee, L. J. *The Medical Student in Europe.* Maysville, KY: Richard H. Collins, 1849.

Freiburg, University of. *Studienplan der Studierende der Medizin an der Albert-Ludwigs-Universität zu Freiburg im Breisgau.* Freiburg: Universitäts-Buchdruckerei, 1914.

———. *Die Universität Freiburg nach ihrem Ursprunge, ihrem Zwecke, ihren Mitteln und Studienstiftungsfonds, ihrer Eigenschaft als geistliche Corporation und fromme Stiftung, ihrer Organisation, ihren Instituten und nach den Kirchen—und staatsrechtlichen Garantien ihres Fortbestandes.* Freiburg: Herber'sche Verlagshandlung, 1844.

Freudenberger, Joseph. *Ein Sommersemester in der Klinik des Herrn Professor Dr. von Ziemssen zu München.* Munich: Jos. Ant. Finsterlin, 1883.

Fritze, Friedrich. *Uber die Schwierigkeiten und Annehmlichkeiten des medizinischen und chirurgischen Studiums.* Magdeburg: Faber, 1833.

Gailleton, M. *Rapport sur la création d'une faculté de médecine et d'une école supérieure de pharmacie.* Lyon: Association typographique, 1873.

———. "Rapport sur l'organisation de la faculté de médecine et de l'école supérieure de pharmacie de Lyon." *Lyon médical* 23 (1876): 369–84.

Gallavardin, "Dr." *Voyage médical en Allemagne.* Paris: J.-B. Baillière et fils, 1860.

Gangee, Arthur. *Studies from the Physiological Laboratory at Owens College.* Cambridge: Cambridge University Press, 1877.

Germany. *Die gesetzlichen Bestimmungen über die ärztlichen Prüfungen für das Deutsche Reich von 28 Mai 1901.* Berlin: August Hirschwald, 1918.

Gessner, Johannes. *Johannes Gessners Pariser Tagebuch 1727.* Ed. Urs Boschung. Bern: Hans Huber, 1985.

Gibbons, Henry. *Some defensive Remarks on the Medical Education and Medical Schools of America, and particularly of California.* San Francisco: Bonnard & Daly, 1877.

Gibson, William. *Rambles in Europe in 1839.* Philadelphia: Lea and Blanchard, 1841.

Glénard, M. *Rapport pour l'année scolaire 1867–68.* Lyon: D'Aimé Vingtrinier, 1868.

Glisan, Rodney. *Two Years in Europe.* New York: Putnam, 1887.

Graevell, Friedrich. *Uber die Reform der Medicinal-Verfassung Preussens: Ein kritischer Uberblick.* Leipzig, 1847.

Graves, Robert J. "On Clinical Instruction, with a Comparative Estimate of the Mode in which It is Conducted in the British and Continental Schools." *London Medical Gazette* 10 (1832): 401–6.

———. *Clinical Lectures on the Practice of Medicine.* 2 vols. London: New Sydenham Society, 1884.

Great Britain. General Medical Council. *Reports of the Committee on Professional Education, 1864, 1869.* London, 1864, 1869.

———. House of Commons, Select Committee on Anatomy. *Report.* London: House of Commons, 1828.

———. House of Commons, Select Committee on Medical Act. *Special Report from the Select Committee on Medical Act (1858). . .; Together with the Proceedings of the Committee, Minutes of Evidence, Appendix, and Index.* London: House of Commons, 1879.

———. House of Commons, Select Committee on Medical Education. *Report.* 3 vols. London: House of Commons, 1834.

———. House of Commons, Select Committee on Medical Registration and Medical Law Amendment. *First and Second Reports; Together with the Minutes of Evidence and Appendix.* London: House of Commons, 1848.

———. Medical Acts Commission. *Report of the Royal Commissioners appointed to inquire into the Medical Acts.* London: Her Majesty's Stationery Office, 1882.

———. Royal Commission. *Evidence, Oral and Documentary, Taken and received by the Commissioners appointed by His Majesty George IV, July 23d, 1826; and re-appointed by His Majesty William IV, October 12th, 1830; for visiting the Universities of Scotland.* 4 vols. London: His Majesty's Stationery Office, 1837.

———. Royal Commission. *Report of the Commissioners appointed in pursuance of an Act of Parliament.* London: Her Majesty's Stationery Office, 1840.

———. Royal Commission on University Education in London. *Reports.* 5 vols. London: His Majesty's Stationery Office, 1910–12.

Gregory, [John]. *Answer to Dr James Hamilton, Junior.* Edinburgh, 1793.

Gregory, Samuel. *Letter to Ladies, in Favor of Female Physicians for their own Sex.* Boston: Female Medical Education Society, 1850.

Grellety, Lucien. *Encombrement et dépreciation de la profession médicale.* Macon: Protat, 1893.

Guilaume, M. J., ed. *Procès-verbaux du comité d'instruction publique de la convention nationale.* 6 vols. Paris: Imprimerie nationale, 1891–1904.

Gusserow, Adolph. *Zur Geschichte und Methode des klinischen Unterrichts.* Berlin: Gustav Lange, 1879.

Gwyn, Norman B. "The Letters of a Devoted Father to an Unresponsive Son, Student of Medicine at McGill and London." *Bulletin of the History of Medicine* 7 (1939): 335–51.

Haffter, Carl, ed. *Tagebuch des Zürcher Medizinstudenten Elias Haffter aus dem Jahre 1823.* Zurich: Hans Rohr, 1976.

Hamel, C., J. Jadassohn, C. Prausnitz, and M. Taute. "Medical Education in the German Reich." *Quarterly Bulletin of the Health Organisation of the League of Nations* 1 (1932): 159–207.

Hardwicke, Herbert Junius. *Medical Education and Practise in All Parts of the World.* London: J. & A. Churchill, 1880.

Harrison, Edward. *Remarks on the Ineffective State of the Practise of Physic in Great Britain, with Proposals for Its Future Regulation and Improvement.* London: R. Bickerstaff, 1806.

Hart, James. *German Universities: A Narrative of Personal Experience.* New York: Putnam, 1878.

Hay, John B., ed. *Inaugural Addresses by Lords Rector of the University of Glasgow.* Glasgow: University of Glasgow, 1839.

Hayward, Oliver S., and Elizabeth H. Thompson, eds. *The Journal of William Tully: Medical Student at Dartmouth, 1808–1809.* New York: Science History Publications, 1977.

Hecker, Augustus Friedrich. *Heilkunst auf ihren Wegen zur Gewissheit; oder die Theorien, Systeme und Heilmethoden der Aerzte seit Hippokrates bis auf unsere Zeiten.* 4th ed. Erfurt and Gotha: Hennings'schen Buchhandlung, 1819.

Heidelberg, University of. *Anzeige der Vorlesungen. 1800–1900.*

Heimann, Georg. "Die Studierenden der Medizin in Deutschland am Anfange des 20.Jahrhunderts." *Klinisches Jahrbuch* 10 (1903): 223–44.

Hellpach, Willy. *Die Neugestaltung des medizinischen Unterrichts.* Berlin: Urban & Schwarzenberg, 1919.

Henle, Jacob. "Medizinische Wissenschaft und Empirie." *Zeitschrift für rationelle Medizin* 1 (1844): 1–35.

Hertz, Arthur F. "Aspects of German Medicine." *Guy's Hospital Gazette* 20 (1906): 407–9, 427–29, 465–67, 498.

Herzig, Wilhelm. *Das medicinische Wien: Wegweiser für Aerzte und Naturforscher, vorzugsweise für Fremde.* Vienna: Wilhelm Braumüller, 1848.

Hildenbrand, Johann V. von. *Discours preliminaire sur l'histoire des cliniques.* Trans. A. Gauthier. Paris, 1824.

———. *Médecine pratique.* Paris: Gabon, 1828.

Hille, C. A. *Skizzen, gesammelt auf einer wissenschaftlichen Reise durch Deutschland, Frankreich und England.* Dresden: Arnoldische Buchhandlung, 1849.

Hirschberg, Julius. *Von New York nach San Francisco: Tagebuchblätter.* Leipzig: Veit, 1888.

Hirschel, Bernhard. *Compendium der Geschichte der Medicin von den Urzeiten bis auf die Gegenwart.* Vienna: Wilhelm Braumüller, 1862.

Hoche, Alfred E. *Strassburg und seine Universität: Ein Buch der Erinnerung.* Munich: J. F. Lehmann, 1939.

Hoeffel, Jean. *Aperçu historique sur l'ancienne faculté de médecine de Strasbourg.* Strasbourg: Treuttel and Wurtz, 1872.

Hoffmann, Max. *Neueste Satzungen und Bedingungen für die Erwerbung des Doktorgrades bei den medizinischen Fakultäten der deutschen Universitäten.* Leipzig: Max Hoffmann, 1897.

Hofmann, August W. *The Chemical Laboratories in Course of Erection in the Universities of Bonn and Berlin.* London: Science and Art Department of the Committee of Council on Education, 1866.

Hofmann, Christian Gottlieb. *Erste Nachricht von der Anstalt für arme Kranke zu Altorf im Nürngergischem.* Attorf and Nuremberg: George Peter Monath, 1787.

Holmes, Edward L. "Clinical Instruction in the Hospitals of Vienna." *Boston Medical and Surgical Journal* 67 (1863): 520–23.

Honan, James Henry. *Honan's Handbook to Medical Europe.* Philadelphia: P. Blakiston's Son, 1912.

Horn, Wilhelm. *Reise durch Deutschland, Ungarn, Holland, Italien, Frankreich, Grossbritannien und Irland; in Rücksicht auf medicinische und naturwissenschaftliche Institute, Armenpflege, u.s.w.* 3 vols. Berlin: Th. Chr. Fr. Enslin, 1831.

Horsch, Philipp J. *Uber die Bildung des Arztes als Klinikers und als Staatsdieners.* Würzburg: Joseph Stabel, 1807.

Howell, William H. "Instruction in Physiology in the Medical Schools." *Michigan Alumnus* 6 (1900): 133–50.

Huchard, Henri. *La réforme de l'enseignement médical et des concours de médecine.* Paris: O. Berthier, 1890.

Hufeland, Christoph W. "Nachrichten von der medicinisch–chirurgischen Krankenanstalt zu Jena, nebst einer Vergleichung der klinischen und Hospitalanstalten überhaupt." *Journal der praktischen Heilkunde* 3 (1797): 528–66.

———. *System der practischen Heilkunde.* Jena, 1800.

———. "Zweck und Einrichtung des medicinischen Cursus zu Berlin." *Hufelands Journal* 14 (1802): 5–31.

Hun, Henry. *A Guide to American Medical Students in Europe.* New York: William Wood, 1883.

Hunczovski, Johann. *Medicinische–chirurgische Beobachtungen auf einer Reise durch England und Frankreich besonders über die Spitäler.* Vienna, 1783.

Hunt, Harriot K. *Glimpses and Glances; or Fifty Years Social, including Twenty Years Professional Life.* Boston: John P. Jewett, 1856.

Huxley, Leonard, ed. *Life and Letters of Thomas Henry Huxley.* 2 vols. London: Macmillan, 1900.

Huxley, Thomas Henry. *Critiques and Addresses.* New York: D. Appleton, 1887.

Illinois State Board of Health. *Medical Education, Medical Colleges and the Regulation of the Practice of Medicine in the United States and Canada, 1765–1891.* Springfield: H. W. Rokker, 1891.

Israel, O. "Zur praktischen Ausbildung der Arzte." *Berliner klinische Wochenschrift* 29 (1892): 1291–93.

Jaccoud, Sigismond. *De l'organisation des facultés de médecine en Allemagne.* Paris: Adrien Delahye, 1864.

Jackson, Samuel. *Medical Education.* Philadelphia: T. K. and P. G. Collins, 1853.

Jacobi, Abraham. *Aufsätze, Vorträge und Reden.* 2 vols. New York: Stettiner, Lambert, 1893.

Jaxthal, Eduard J. *Ein freies Wort über medicinische Unterrichts und Prüfungsnormen.* Leipzig: Otto Wigand, 1867.

Johns Hopkins Hospital. *Five Essays relating to the Construction, Organization & Management of Hospitals.* New York: William Wood, 1875.

Johnson, J. *A Guide for Gentlemen Studying Medicine at the University of Edinburgh.* London: Robinson, 1792.

Johnson, Robert W. "Impressions of Vienna as a Medical School." *Philadelphia Medical Times* 11 (1880): 129–38.

Jones, Richard. *Observations on Medical Education, with a View to Legislative Interference.* London: John Murray, 1839.

Jugler, J. H. *Gekrönte Preisschrift über die von den Churfürstlichen Akademie nützlicher Wissenschaften zu Erfurt aufgegebene Frage: Ist es notwendig, u. ist es möglich, beide Theile der Heilkunst, die Medicin u. die Chirurgie, sowohl in ihrer Erlernung als Ausübung wieder zu vereinigen?* Erfurt, 1799.

Kautsky, Karl. "Aerztliche Erzeihungsfragen." *Der Kampf* 12 (1919): 420–24.

Keetley, Charles B. *The Student's and Junior Practitioner's Guide to the Medical Profession.* 2nd ed. London: Ballière, Tindall, and Cox, 1885.

Keyser, Georg A. *Beantwortung der Frage: Wie kann man auf eine leichte Art den Wundärzten, denen das Landvolk anvertrauet ist, und die der leidenden Menschen oft mehr schädlich, als nützlich sind, einen besseren und zweckmässigeren Unterricht beybringen.* Erfurt: Keyser, 1791.

Kilian, H. F. *Die Universitaeten Deutschlands in medicinisch-naturwissenschaftlichen Hinsicht.* Heidelberg, 1828. Reprinted by B. M. Israël, Amsterdam, 1966.

Kind, C. M. "On Medical Education in the German Universities." *Lancet* 1 (1827): 249–57.

King, Henry. "Notes of a Visit to the Medical Institutions of New York." *Dublin Quarterly Journal of Medical Science* 38 (1864): 288–334.

Kopp, Johann H. *Arztliche Bemerkungen, veranlasst durch eine Reise in Deutschland und Frankreich im Frühjahr und Sommer 1824.* Frankfurt am Main: Hermann, 1825.

Kussmaul, Adolf. *Aus meiner Dozentenzeit in Heidelberg.* 3rd and 4th ed. Stuttgart: Adolf Bonz, 1925.

Laennec, R. T. H. *A Treatise on the Diseases of the Chest, in which they are described according to their anatomical Character, and their Diagnosis, established by means of Accoustick Instruments.* Trans. from French with Preface and Notes by John Forbes, M.D. Philadelphia: James Webster, 1823.

Langlebert, Edmond. *Guide pratique et méthodique de l'étudiant en médecine, ou conseils aux éléves sur la direction qu'ils doivent donner à leurs études.* Paris: Jules Masson, 1848.

LaRoche, René. "An Account of the Origin, Progress, and present State of the Medical School of Paris." *American Journal of the Medical Sciences* 8 (1828): 109–24; 9 (1828): 351–88.

Laurent, Octave. *Les universités des deux mondes.* Paris, 1896.

———. *Les universités des Etats-Unis et du Canada et spécialement leurs institutions médicales.* Brussels, 1894.

Lee, Edwin. *Observations on the Principal Medical Institutions and Practise of France, Italy, and Germany.* London: J. Churchill, 1843.

LeFort, Léon. *Etude sur l'organisation de la médecine en France et à l'étranger.* Paris: Germer Baillière, 1874.

———. *La liberté de la pratique et la liberté de l'enseignement de la médecine.* Paris: Victor Masson, 1866.

Leipzig, University of. *Catalogus Lectionum.* 1800–1900.

Leitschuh, F. *Die Vorbilder und Muster der Bamberger ärztlichen Schule.* Bamberg: Schmidt, 1877.

Lentin, Jacob F. *Medizinische Bemerkungen auf einer literärischen Reise durch Deutschland.* Berlin: Heinrich August Rottmann, 1800.

Leo-Wolf, Joseph. "Medical Education in Germany." *American Medical Recorder* 13 (1828): 481–90.

[Lersch, J. H. L.]. *Die rheinische Friedrich-Wilhelms-Universität zu Bonn.* Bonn: Henry & Cohen, 1839.

Leupoldt, J. M. *Uber ärztliche Bildung und Bildungsanstalten.* Frankfurt am Main: Heyder and Zimmer, 1853.

Liard, Louis. "La nouvelle réglementation des études médicales." *Revue des deux mondes,* October 15, 1894, pp. 810–42.

———. *Universités et facultés.* Paris: Gaston Née, 1890.

Lincoln, D. F. "The Medical School of Berlin Compared with that of Vienna." *Boston Medical and Surgical Journal* 9 (1872): 165–67.

Lorain, Paul. *De la réforme des études médicales par les laboratoires.* Paris, 1868.

Lucas, James. *A Candid Inquiry into the Education, Qualifications, and Offices of a Surgeon-Apothecary.* Bath: S. Hazard, 1800.

Lucas-Championnière. *Statistique du personnel médical en France et dans les autres contrées de l'Europe.* Paris: Bureau du *Journal de médecine,* 1845.

Lusk, Graham. "Medical Education: A Plea for the Development of Leaders." *Journal of the American Medical Association* 52 (1909): 1229–30.

Lyon. City Commission. *Création d'une faculté de médecine et d'une école de pharmacie: Rapport de la commission.* Lyon: Ray & Sézanne, 1873.

Mackensen, William F. A. *Letztes Wort über Göttingen und seine Lehrer, 1791.* Göttingen: Vandenhoeck & Ruprecht, 1787.

Mackenzie, James. "The Aim of Medical Education." *Edinburgh Medical Journal* 20 (1918): 31–48.

[MacKenzie, William]. "Sketches of the Medical School of Vienna." *Quarterly Journal of Foreign Medicine and Surgery* 1 (1818–19): 34–53, 171–92.

Macleod, J. J. R. "Medical Education." *Canadian Medical Association Journal* 10 (1920): 638–51.

Maddocks, James, and William Blizard. *Expediency and Utility of Teaching the Several Branches of Physic and Surgery, by Lectures at the London Hospital; and for Erecting Theatres for that Purpose.* London, 1783.

Makittrick, James. *Commentaries on the Principles and Practise of Physic.* London: T. Becket, 1772.

Mall, Franklin P. "The Anatomical Course and Laboratory of the Johns Hopkins University." *Bulletin of the Johns Hopkins Hospital* 7 (1896): 85–99.

———. "On the Teaching of Anatomy." *Anatomical Record* 2 (1908): 313–34.

———. "The Value of Research in the Medical School." *Michigan Alumnus,* May 1904, 395–97.

Mankiewicz, O. "Zum Entwurf einer neuen Prüfungsordnung." *Deutsche medizinische Wochenschrift* 22 (1896): 552–53.

Marburg, University of. *Studienplan der Studenten der Medizin zu Marburg.* Marburg: Universitäts-Buchdruckerei, 1910.

Marcet, Alexander. *Some Remarks on Clinical Lectures, being the Substance of an Introductory Lecture delivered at Guy's Hospital, on the 27th of January 1818.* London: G. Woodfall, 1818.

Marquais, J. Th. *Rapport au roi sur l'état actuel de la médecine en France, et sur la nécessité d'une réforme dans l'étude et l'exercise de cette science.* Paris: privately printed, 1814.

Marshall, William Barrett. *An Essay on Medical Education.* London: Burgess and Hill, 1827.

McArdle, J. S. "Medical Education as It Is and as It Should Be." *Dublin Journal of Medical Science* 98 (1894): 394–403.

McGraw, Theodore A. "The Medical Schools of the Last Half-Century." *Journal of the Michigan State Medical Society* 14 (1915): 514–17.

Means, James H. "Experiences and Opinions of a Full-Time Medical Teacher." *Perspectives in Biology and Medicine* 2 (1959): 127–62.

The Medical Calendar: A Student's Guide to the Medical School. Edinburgh: MacLachlen, 1828.

"Medical Education." *Westminster Review* 70 (1858): 107–63.

Medical Education in London: Being a Guide to the Schools of the University of London in the Faculty of Medicine, with Notes on the General Facilities for Clinical Study and Research in the Metropolis. London: Ash and Co., 1908.

Der medicinische Unterricht an der Wiener Hochschule und seine Gebrechen, von einigen Studenten. Vienna: G. J. Manz, 1869.

Meltzer, Samuel J. "Headship and Organization of Clinical Departments of First-Class Medical Schools." *Science* 40 (1914): 620–28.

———. "The Science of Clinical Medicine: What It Ought to Be and the Men to Uphold It." *Journal of the American Medical Association* 53 (1909): 503–13.

Michaelis, Johann D. *Räsonnement über die protestantische Universitäten in Deutschland.* 4 vols. Frankfurt am Main: Andreä, 1768–76.

Michailovsky, Benjamin. "Some Points in Medical Education Considered from the Standpoint of the Student." *Medical Record* 73 (1908): 15–18.

Ministère de l'instruction publique, des beaux-arts et des cultes. *Enquêtes et documents relatifs à l'enseignement superieur, XXI, état numerique des grades, 1795–1885.* Paris: Imprimerie nationale, 1886.

Minot, Charles S. "A Grave Defect in Our Medical Education." *Boston Medical and Surgical Journal* 105 (1881): 565–67.

Montaux, Nicolas Chambon de. *Moyens de rendre les hôpitaux plus utiles à la nation.* Paris, 1787.

Morgan, John. *A Discourse upon the Institution of Medical Schools in America.* New York: Arno Press, 1975. Reprint of edition published in 1765 by W. Bradford of Philadelphia.

Morgan, John E. *Medical Education at the Universities.* Manchester: J. E. Cornish, 1875.

———. *The Victoria University: Why Are There No Medical Degrees?* Manchester: J. E. Cornish, 1881.

Mosler, Friedrich. "Uber den Unterricht in der medizinischen Klinik zu Greifswald." *Klinisches Jahrbuch* 1 (1889): 110–20.

Mott, Valentine. *Reminiscenses of Medical Teaching and Teachers in New York:*

An Address Introductory to a Course of Lectures at the College of Physicians and Surgeons, New York. New York: Jennings, 1850.

Myers, J. A. "Bridging the Chasm Between the Fundamental and Clinical Branches in Medical Schools." *Journal of the American Medical Association* 81 (1923): 599–601.

Muehry, Adolph. *Observations on the Comparative State of Medicine in France, England, and Germany During a Journey into These Countries in the Year 1835.* Trans. from German by Edward G. Davis. Philadelphia: A. Waldie, 1838.

Müller, Friedrich von. "Amerikanische Reiseeindrücke." *Münchener medizinische Wochenschrift* 59 (1907): 2388–90, 2430–34.

———. *Lebenserinnerungen.* Munich: J. F. Lehmann, 1951.

———. "Medical Education and the Universities." *British Medical Journal,* 1911, pp. 1421–24.

———. *Wie studiert man Medizin?* Munich: Ernst Reinhardt, 1912.

———. *Zur Reform des Medizinstudiums.* Reprinted from *Münchener medizinische Wochenschrift,* 1934, no. 23.

Müller, L. R. "Das Studium der inneren Medicin in Frankreich, England und Deutschland." *Münchener medicinische Wochenschrift* 47 (1900): 584–86.

Munich, University of. *Encyclopädisches Verzeichnis der Lehrvorträge.* 1800–1900.

———. *Studienplan für Mediziner.* 5th ed. Munich: M. Rieger, 1904.

———. *Studienplan für Mediziner.* Munich, 1910.

Nagel, W. "Uber das medicinische Studium in England in Vergleich mit Deutschland." *Berliner klinische Wochenscrift* 30 (1893): 858–59, 882–83, 905–7, 931–32.

Nasse, D. *Vom dem Krankenhause zur Bildung angehender Arzte zu Halle und der damit verbundenen Krankenbesuchs-Anstalt.* Halle: Renger, 1816.

Naunyn, Bernard. *Erinnerungen, Gedanken, und Meinungen.* Munich: J. F. Bergmann, 1925.

Newman, George. "Medical Education in England." *Quarterly Bulletin of the Health Organisation of the League of Nations* 1 (1932): 7–45.

———. *Recent Advances in Medical Education in England.* London: His Majesty's Stationery Office, 1923.

———. *Some Notes on Medical Education in England.* London: His Majesty's Stationery Office, 1918.

Nixon, C. J. "Scientific Teaching in Medicine." *Dublin Journal of Medical Science* 96 (1893): 457–89.

Odontius, Johannes. *Student, "College" und Arzt in den Vereinigten Staaten von Nord-Amerika.* Stuttgart: Union Deutsche Verlagsgesellschaft, 1890.

Ohio State University College of Medicine. *A Collection of Source Material covering a Century of Medical Progress.* Blanchester, OH: Brown, 1934.

Oliver, Henry K., Jr. "The Vienna Hospital." *Boston Medical and Surgical Journal* 57 (1857): 49–58, 71–77.

Orth, Johannes. *Medizinischer Unterricht und ärztliche Praxis.* Wiesbaden: J. F. Bergmann, 1898.

Osler, William. "The Hospital as a College." *Aequanimatas.* New York: Norton, 1963.

———. "Impressions of Paris." *Journal of the American Medical Association* 52 (1905): 771–74.

————. "Vienna After Thirty-Four Years." *Journal of the American Medical Association* 50 (1908): 1523–25.

Otterburg, S. J. *Das medizinische Paris.* Karlsruhe: A. Bielefeld, 1841.

Otto, D. C. *Reise durch die Schweiz, Italien, Frankreich, Grossbritannien und Holland, mit besonderer Rücksicht auf Spitäler, Heilmethoden und den übrigen medizinischen Zustand dieser Länder.* 2 vols. Hamburg: August Campe, 1825.

Paget, James. "What Becomes of Medical Students?" *St. Bartholomew's Hospital Reports* 5 (1869), 238–42.

Paget, Stephen, ed. *Memoirs and Letters of Sir James Paget.* London: Longmans, Green, 1902.

Paine, Martyn. *A Defence of the Medical Profession of the United States.* New York: Samuel S. & William Wood, 1846.

Palmer, Alonzo B. "Reform in the Medical Schools—Clinical Instruction at Detroit." *Peninsular Journal of Medicine* 4 (1857): 601–5.

Parat, P. *Mémoire sur les moyens de perfectionner les études de l'art de guérir.* Lyon, 1791.

Parkinson, James. *The Hospital Pupil; or an Essay intended to Facilitate the Study of Medicine and Surgery in Four Letters.* London: H. D. Symonds, 1800.

Parrish, Edward. *Summer Medical Teaching in Philadelphia: An Introductory Lecture.* Philadelphia: Merrihew & Thompson, 1857.

Pasteur, Louis. "Le budget de la science." *Revue des cours scientifiques de la France et de l'etranger* 5 (1868): 137–39.

Paulsen, Friedrich. *The German Universities and University Study.* New York: Scribner's, 1906.

Peabody, Francis W. "The Physician and the Laboratory." *Boston Medical and Surgical Journal* 187 (1922): 324–28.

Penrose, R. A. F. *Medical Education in the United States.* Philadelphia, 1876.

Pepper, William. *Higher Medical Education, the True Interests of the Public and the Profession: Two Addresses delivered before the Medical Department of the University of Pennsylvania on October 1, 1877 and October 2, 1893.* Philadelphia: Lippincott, 1894.

Perrot, Ernest. "Etudiants d'Allemagne: Notes de voyage d'un étudiant français." *Revue moderne de médecine et de chirurgie,* 1906, pp. 370–82.

Perry, Walter C. *German University Education, or the Professors and Students of Germany.* 2nd ed. London: Layman, Green, 1846.

Peter, Robert. *Thoughts on Medical Education in America: An Introductory Lecture, delivered in the Chapel of Morrison College, to the Medical Students of Transylvania University.* Lexington, KY: Observer & Reporter, 1838.

Pfeufer, Karl von. "Uber den gegenwärtigen Zustand der Medicin." *Annalen der städtischen allgemeinen Krankenhäusern in München* 1 (1878): 395–406.

Phoebus, Philipp. *Uber die Naturwissenschaften als Gegenstand des Studiums, des Unterrichts und der Prüfung angehender Arzte.* Nordhausen: Adolph Büchting, 1849.

Pinel, Philippe. *The Clinical Training of Doctors: An Essay of 1793.* Trans. with an introduction by Dora B. Weiner. Baltimore: Johns Hopkins University Press, 1980.

————. *La médecine clinique rendue plus précise et plus exacte par l'application de l'analyse, ou recueil et résultat d'observations sur les malades aiguës, faites à la salpêtrière.* 3rd ed. Paris: J. A. Brosson, 1815.

Pinet, M. A. *Lois, Décrets, réglements et circulaires concernant les facultés et les écoles préparatoires de médecine.* 2 vols. Paris: Societé anonyme, 1880–82.

Pitcher, Zina. "On Clinical Instruction." *Peninsular Journal of Medicine and the Collateral Sciences* 5 (1858): 393–402.

Placzek, Siegfried. *Die medizinische Wissenschaft in den Vereinigten Staaten.* Leipzig: Georg Thieme, 1894.

Ploucquet, D. *Wilhelm Gottfried. Der Arzt, oder über die Ausbildung, die Studien, Pflichten, Sitten, und die Klugheit des Arztes.* Tübingen: J. G. Cotta, 1797.

Pointe, "le Docteur." *De l'enseignement clinique. Discours prononcé à l'ouverture du cours de clinique médicale.* Lyon: Léon Boitel, 1850.

Pope, Emily F., Emma L. Call, and Augusta Pope. *The Practice of Medicine by Women in the United States.* Boston: Wright & Potter, 1881.

Porter, W. T. "The Teaching of Physiology in Medical Schools." *Boston Medical and Surgical Journal* 139 (1898): 647–52.

Potter, Samuel. "American Versus European Medical Education." *Journal of the American Medical Association* 15 (1890): 81–91.

Prausnitz, W. "Uber das Studium der Medizin und die Einführung des 'Praktischen Jahres' in Oesterreich." *Wiener klinische Wochenschrift* 21 (1918): 134–39.

Pritchett, Henry S. "Progress in Medical Education." *Journal of the American Medical Association* 60 (1913): 743–47.

Puschmann, Theodor. *Betrachtungen über unser medicinisches Unterrichtswesen.* Vienna: Georg Szelinski, 1886.

Putnam, Ruth, ed. *Life and Letters of Mary Putnam Jacobi.* New York: Putnam, 1925.

Quain, Richard. *Observations on Medical Education.* London: Walton and Maberly, 1865.

Ratier, F. S. "Coup d'oeil sur les cliniques médicales de la faculté de médecine et des hôpitaux civils de Paris." *Archives générales de médecine* 13 (1827): 321–34; 15 (1828): 161–85; 16 (1828): 215–32; 17 (1828): 217–54.

Ravoth, "Dr." *Zur Revision und Reformirung der Lehr- und Lernmethode an den Universitäten, hauptsächlich der Medicin. In Hinblick auf der Rückgang der Berliner Universität.* Berlin: Elwin Staude, 1874.

Reed, Boardman, and Ray L. Wilbur. "Should There Be Two Degrees in Medicine?" *Bulletin of the American Academy of Medicine* 12 (1911): 347–55.

Reil, Johann Christian. *Pepiniēren zum Unterricht ärztliches Routiniers als Bedürfnisse des Staats nach seiner Lage wie sie ist.* Halle: Curtschen Buchhandlung, 1804.

Resneck, Samuel. "A Course of Medical Education in New York City in 1828–29: The Journal of Asa Fitch." *Bulletin of the History of Medicine* 42 (1968): 555–65.

Revere, John. *An Introductory Lecture on the Comparative State of the Profession of Medicine, and of Medical Education, in the United States and Europe.* New York: University of the City of New York, 1846–47.

Rivington, Walter. *The Medical Profession: Being an Essay to which was awarded The First Carmichael Prize of £200 by the Council of the Royal College of Surgeons, Ireland.* Dublin: Fannin, 1879.

Roberton, John. *Medical Police: or, the Causes of Disease, with the Means of Prevention; and Rules for Diet, Regimen, etc. adopted particularly to the Cities of London and Edinburgh, and generally to all large Towns.* Edinburgh, 1809.

[Robertson, Henry]. *Blast from the North. In Vindication of the Medical Gradu-*

ates of Edinburgh against the Invidious and Calumnious Aspersions cast upon their Literary and Professional Education, through the Bye Laws of the London College of Physicians. London: Horatio Phillips, 1828.

Robinson, G. Canby. "The Modern Teacher of Internal Medicine." *Old Dominion Journal of Medicine and Surgery* 8 (1909): 382–87.

Rogers, Frank B., ed. *Selected Papers of John Shaw Billings.* Chicago: Medical Library Association, 1965.

Rosenbaum, Julius. *Neun Jahre aus dem Leben eines Privatdocenten: Ein Beitrag zur inneren Geschichte der medicinischen Fakultät zu Halle.* Leipzig: Gebauer, 1847.

Roussy, G. "Medical Education in France." *Quarterly Bulletin of the Health Organisation of the League of Nations* 1 (1932): 315–61.

Roux, Philibert-Joseph. *Relation d'un voyage fait à Londres en 1814; ou parallele de la chirurgie anglaise avec la chirurgie françoise.* Paris, 1815.

Rudolphi, Carl A. *Bemerkungen aus dem Gebiet der Naturgeschichte, Medicin und Thierarzneykunde, auf einer Reise durch einen Theil von Deutschland, Holland und Frankreich.* Berlin: Realschulbuchhandlung, 1805.

Rust, Johann N. *Aufsätze und Abhandlungen aus dem Gebiete der Medicin, Chirurgie und Staatsarzneikunde.* 3 vols. Berlin, 1840.

Rutherford, William. "On Medical Education and Reform: Address to the Medical Graduates of the University of Edinburgh, 22d August 1880." *Edinburgh Medical Journal* 26 (1880): 193–204.

Sanderson, J. Burdon. "Physiological Laboratories in Great Britain." *Nature* 3 (1871): 189.

Schickert, "Dr." *Die militärärztlichen Bildungsanstalten von ihrer Gründung bis zur Gegenwart.* Berlin: Ernst Siegfried Mittler, 1895.

Schmidt, Joseph Hermann. *Die Reform der medicinal-Verfassung Preussens.* Berlin, 1846.

Schütz, Friedrich. *Englisch–französischer Rasirspiegel für Deutschlands Universitäten.* Braunschweig and Leipzig: Comtoir, 1830.

Schützenberger, Charles. *Fragments de philosophie médicale.* Paris: Masson, 1879.

Schwalbe, Julius. *Zur Neuordnung des medizinischen Studiums.* Leipzig: Georg Thieme, 1918.

Semon, Felix. "English and German Education: A Parallel." *Medical Review of Reviews* 13 (1907): 1197–1206.

Sewall, Henry. "Henry Newell Martin." *Johns Hopkins Hospital Bulletin* 22 (1911): 327–33.

Sharpey-Schafer, Edward. "The Position of Physiology in Medicine." *Edinburgh Medical Journal,* 1919 (reprint).

———. "Relationship of Physiology to Medicine and Surgery." *Lancet,* 1927 (reprint).

Siboutie, Poumiès de la. *Souvenirs d'un médecin de Paris.* Paris: Plon-Nourrit, 1910.

Sigismund, R. "Die Reformen des medizinischen Unterrichts in Frankreich nach der Revue des deux Mondes." *Berliner klinische Wochenschrift* 16 (1879): 52–53.

Silliman, Benjamin. *A Visit to Europe in 1851.* 2 vols. New York: Putnam, 1854.

Simon-Bailly, René. *Souvenirs d'un éléve des écoles de santé de Strasbourg et de Paris pendant la révolution.* Strasbourg: Strasbourg médical, 1924.

Smith, Albert. *The London Medical Student.* London: Routledge, Warner & Routledge, 1861.

Société royale de médecine. *Nouveau plan de constitution pour la médecine en France.* Paris, 1790.

Spalteholz, Werner. "Einführung in das Studium der Medizin." *Deutsche medicinische Wochenschrift* 39 (1913): 753–55.

Spilman, C. H. "The Defects in Our Present System of Medical Education." *Transactions of the Kentucky State Medical Society, 1871.* Louisville: Davidson, 1871.

Sprigge, Squire. "Medical Education in the United States and Canada." Special supplement to *Lancet*, January 5, 1929, pp. i–xl.

St. Jacques, Eugene. "Medical Education in France and Germany." *Medical Record* 15 (1909): 264–68.

Stähele, A. *Letter to the Council of the University of London.* London: Hunt and Clarke, 1828.

Starr, Charles S. "Medical Study in Europe." *Medical Annals* 5 (1884): 161–71.

Stern, Carl. "Die soziale Medizin und der Ausbildungsgang der Medizinstudierenden." *Deutsche medizinische Wochenschrift* 34 (1908): 789–90.

Stewart, F. Campbell. *The Hospitals and Surgeons of Paris.* New York: Langley, 1843.

Stieglitz, I. *Uber das Zusammenseyn der Aerzte am Krankenbett, und über ihre Verhältnisse unter sich überhaupt.* Hannover: Gebrüder Hahn, 1798.

Stillé, Alfred. *Medical Education in the United States.* Philadelphia: Isaac Ashmond, 1846.

Stoeber, Victor. *Médecine pratique.* Paris: Gabon, 1828.

———. *De l'organisation médicale en France.* Paris: F. G. Levrault, 1830.

Stokes, William, ed. *Studies in Physiology and Medicine by the Late Robert James Graves, F.R.S.* London: John Churchill, 1863.

Strümpell, Adolf. *Aus dem Leben eines deutschen Klinikers: Erinnerungen und Beobachtungen.* Leipzig: F. C. W. Vogel, 1925.

Syme, James, and G. Owen C. Macness. "Medical Education: Excerpts from Speeches by James Symes and G. Owen C. Macness." *Edinburgh Medical Journal* 4 (1910): 527–40.

[Taplin, William]. *A Dose for the Doctors; or the Aesculapian Labrynth Explored.* 3rd ed. London: G. Kearsley, 1789.

Taylor, Shepherd T. *The Diary of a Medical Student During the Mid-Victorian Period, 1860–1864.* Norwich: Jarrold, 1927.

Tenon, Jacques. *Mémoires sur les hôpitaux de Paris.* Paris: P. H. Pierres, 1788.

Thiery, François. *Voeux d'un patriote sur la médecine en France.* Paris: Garnery, 1789.

Thomas, Henry M. "Some Memories of the Development of the Medical School and of Osler's Advent." *Bulletin of the Johns Hopkins Hospital* 30 (1919): 185–89.

Tilmann, "Professor." "Uber amerikanische Arzte und ihre Ausbildung." *Deutsche Arzte-Zeitung* 13 (1901): 1–20.

Tissot, S. A. D. *Essai sur les moyens de perfectionner les études de médecine.* Basel, 1785.

Tomaszewski, W. "Medical Education in Continental Europe and in Great Britain: A Comparison." *University of Edinburgh Journal* 12 (1942–43): 24–36.

Touche, E. Perrin de la. *L'enseignement médical à Rennes (1800–1896).* Rennes: Oberthur, 1896.

Trélat, Ulysse. "Mémoire historique et critique sur les hôpitaux." *Journal des pro-*

grés des sciences et institutions médicales 11 (1828): 192–227; 13 (1829): 184–211.

Tübingen, University of. *Studienplan für die klinischen Semester an der Universität Tübingen.* Tübingen, 1911.

———. *Studienplan für die Studierenden der Medizin in Tübingen.* Tübingen, 1909.

University of London, Council. *Second Statement by the Council of the University of London explanatory of the Plan of Instruction.* London: John Taylor, 1828.

———. *Statement by the Council of the University of London explanatory of the Nature and Objects of the Institution.* London: Longman, Rees, 1827.

Väidy, T. V. *Plan d'étude, à l'usage des aspirans.* Paris, 1816.

Varrentrapp, Georg. *Tagebuch einer medizinischen Reise nach England, Holland und Belgien.* Frankfurt am Main: Franz Varrentrapp, 1839.

Vienna, University of. *Vorlesungsverzeichnisse.* 1835–1915.

Vietor, Agnes C., ed. *A Woman's Quest: The Life of Marie E. Zakrzewska M.D.* New York: D. Appleton, 1924.

Villiers, Charles. *Coup d'oeil sur les universités.* Cassell, 1808.

Virchow, Rudolf. *Die Gründung der Berliner Universität und der Uebergang aus dem philosophischen in das naturwissenschaftliche Zeitalter.* Berlin: August Hirschwald, 1893.

———. *Lernen und Forschen.* Berlin: Hirschwald, 1892.

———. "Der medicinische Unterricht." *Die medicinische Reform,* September 22, 1848, pp. 77–79.

———. "Uber die Standpunkte in der wissenschiftlichen Medicin." *Archiv für pathologische Anatomie und Physiologie* 1 (1847): 3–19.

Wagner, Wilhelm. *Uber die medizinal-Anstalten und den jetzigen Zustand der Heilkunde in Grossbritannien und Irland.* Berlin: G. Reimer, 1825.

Waldeyer-Hartz, Wilhelm von. *Lebenserinnerungen.* 2nd ed. Bonn: Friedrich Cohen, 1921.

Walther, Fr. von. *Uber klinische Lehranstalten in städtischen Krankenhäusern.* Freiburg: Heider, 1846.

Ware, John. *Discourses on Medical Education and on the Medical Profession.* Boston: James Munroe, 1847.

Watson, John. *A Lecture on Practical Education in Medicine, and on the Course of Instruction at the N.Y. Hospital.* New York: J. & H. G. Langley, 1846.

Wedekind, Georg. *Uber medicinischen Unterricht.* Mainz, 1789.

Weisse, Johann F. *Paris und London für den Arzt, besonders in Rücksicht der öffentlichen Kranken-und Verpflegungs-Anstalten.* St. Petersburg: Akademie der Wissenschaften, 1820.

Welch, William H. "The Evolution of Modern Scientific Laboratories." *Bulletin of the Johns Hopkins Hospital* 7 (1896): 19–24.

———. *Papers and Addresses.* 3 vols. Baltimore: Johns Hopkins University Press, 1920.

Wenzl, J.-Bapt. *Uber den Zustand der Augenheilkunde in Frankreich; nebst kritischen Bemerkungen über denselhen in Deutschland.* Nuremberg: Johann Leonhard Schrag, 1815.

Wetzel, Friedrich G. *Briefe über das Studium der Medizin für Jünglinge, die sich ihr widmen wollen.* Leipzig: C. G. Weigel, 1805.

Whalley, Lawson. "A Vindication of the University of Edinburgh (as a School of Medicine) from the Aspersions of 'a Member of the University of Oxford'." *Edinburgh Medical Journal* 13 (1817): 225–29.

White, William, ed. "Medical Education at McGill in the Seventies: Excerpts from the 'Autobiographie' of the late Paul Zotique Hebert, M.D." *Bulletin of the History of Medicine* 13 (1943): 614–26.

Wiesner, J. *Die Notwendigkeit des naturhistorischen Unterrichtes im medicinischen Studium.* Vienna: Alfred Hölder, 1896.

Wigglesworth, Edward. "Advantages of Foreign Study to American Medical Graduates." *Boston Medical and Surgical Journal* 83 (1870): 289–92.

Wilde, W. R. *Austria: Its Literary, Scientific, and Medical Institutions.* Dublin: William Curry, Jun., 1843.

Withers, Thomas. *A Treatise on the Errors and Defects of Medical Education in which are contained Observations on the Means of Correcting Them.* London: C. Dilly, 1794.

Withington, Charles F. "Medical Teaching in Germany." *Boston Medical and Surgical Journal* 129 (1893): 585–89.

———. *The Relation of Hospitals to Medical Education.* Boston: Cupples, Upham, 1886.

Wood, H. C., Jr. "Medical Education in the United States." *Lippincott's Magazine* 16 (1875): 703–11.

Wright, R. Temple. *Medical Students of the Period: A Few Words in Defence of those much maligned People, with Digressions on Various Topics of Public Interest connected with Medical Science.* Edinburgh: William Blackwood, 1867.

Wunderlich, Carl A. *Wien und Paris: Ein Beitrag zur Geschichte und Beurteilung der gegenwärtigen Heilkunde in Deutschland und Frankreich.* Bern: Hans Huber, 1974. Reprinted from 1841 edition.

Wunderlich, Carl A., and Wilhelm Roser. "Uber die Mängel der heutigen deutschen Medicin und über die Nothwendigkeit einer entschiedenen wissenschaftlichen Richtung in derselben." *Archiv für physiologische Heilkunde* 1 (1842): i–xxx.

Wurtz, Adolphe. "L'enseignement clinique dans les universités allemandes." *Gazette des hôpitaux,* 1869, 197–98, 201–2, 205–7, 209–10, 213–14, 217–18.

———. *Les hautes études pratiques dans les universités allemandes.* Paris: Imprimerie impériale, 1870.

Wurtz, G. E. *Mémoire sur l'établissement des écoles de médecine pratique à former dans les principaux hôpitaux de la France.* Paris, 1784.

Yandell, L. P. "History of the Louisville Medical Institute." *Western Journal of Medicine and Surgery* 11 (1853): 1–26.

Zehender, Wilhelm von. *Uber den Beruf der Frauen zum Studium und zur praktischen Ausbildung der Heilwissenschaft.* Rostock: Stiller, 1875.

Ziegler, Theobald. *Der deutsche Student am Ende des 19.Jahrhunderts.* Stuttgart: G. J. Göschen, 1895.

Ziemssen, Hugo von. "Uber die Aufgaben des klinischen Unterrichts und der klinischen Institute." *Deutsches Archiv für klinische Medicin* 23 (1879): 1–22.

———. "Uber den klinischen Unterricht in Deutschland." *Deutsches Archiv für klinische Medicin* 13 (1874): 1–20.

Secondary Books and Articles

Abel-Smith, Brian. *The Hospitals 1800–1948: A Study in Social Administration in England and Wales.* London: Heinemann, 1964.

Abrahams, Harold J. *The Extinct Medical Schools of Baltimore, Maryland.* Baltimore: Maryland Historical Society, 1969.

———. *Extinct Medical Schools of Nineteenth-Century Philadelphia.* Philadelphia: University of Pennsylvania Press, 1966.

Ackerknecht, Erwin H. "Elisha Bartlett and the Philosophy of the Paris Clinical School." *Bulletin of the History of Medicine* 24 (1950): 43–60.

———. "Medical Education in 19th Century France." *Journal of Medical Education* 32 (1957): 148–53.

———. *Medicine at the Paris Hospital 1794–1848.* Baltimore: Johns Hopkins University Press, 1967.

———. "Typen der medizinischen Ausbildung im 19.Jahrhundert." *Schweizerische medizinische Wochenschrift* 87 (1957): 1361–66.

Ackerman, Evelyn B. *Health Care in the Parisian Countryside, 1800–1914.* New Brunswick, NJ: Rutgers University Press, 1990.

Actes du 110e Congrès national des societés savantes. *Histoire de l'école médicale de Montpellier.* Paris: C. T. H. S., 1985.

Alsop, Gulielma F. *History of the Woman's Medical College, Philadelphia, Pennsylvania.* Philadelphia: Lippincott, 1950.

Alter, Peter. *The Reluctant Patron: Science and the State in Britain, 1850–1920.* Oxford: Berg, 1987.

Altschule, Mark D. *Essays on the Rise and Decline of Bedside Medicine.* Philadelphia: Lea & Febinger, 1989.

Anning, S. T., and W. K. J. Walls. *A History of Leeds School of Medicine: One and a Half Centuries 1831–1981.* Leeds: Leeds University Press, 1982.

Arlt, Ferdinand. *Meine Erlebnisse.* Wiesbaden: J. F. Bergmann, 1887.

Artelt, Walter. *Das Bauprogramm unserer medizinischen Fakultäten, geschichtlich gesehen.* Frankfurt am Main: Vittorio Klostermann, 1963.

Astrow, Alan B. "The French Revolution and the Dilemma of Medical Training." *Biology and Medicine* 33 (1990): 444–56.

Atkins, Harry. *The Dean: Willard C. Rappleye and the Evolution of American Medical Education.* New York: Josiah Macy, Jr. Foundation, 1975.

Atlay, James B. *Sir Henry Wentworth Acland.* London: Smith, Elder, 1903.

Atlee, John L. "The Education of a Physician in Early 19th Century." *Journal of the Lancester County Historical Society* 91 (1987–88): 78–88.

Atwater, Edward C. "'Making Fewer Mistakes': A History of Students and Patients." *Bulletin of the History of Medicine* 57 (1983): 165–87.

———. "'Squeezing Mother Nature': Experimental Physiology in the United States Before 1870." *Bulletin of the History of Medicine* 52 (1978): 313–35.

Bachmann, Wolf. "Die Gründung der ersten Medizinischen Fakultät in Munchen 1823: Aufbruch der empirischen Medizin in Bayern." *Münchener medizinische Wochenschrift* 110 (1968): 2568–73.

Bahnson, Karsten, et al. *Student und Hochschule im 19.Jahrhundert: Studien und Materialen.* Göttingen: Vandenhoeck & Ruprecht, 1975.

Barzansky, Barbara, and Norman Gevitz, eds. *Beyond Flexner: Medical Education in the Twentieth Century.* Westport, CT: Greenwood Press, 1992.

Bayer, Friedrich-Wilhelm. *Reisen deutscher Arzte ins Ausland (1750–1850).* Berlin, 1937.

Beecher, Henry K., and Altschule, Mark D. *Medicine at Harvard: The First Three Hundred Years.* Hanover, NH: University Press of New England, 1977.

Bell, Whitfield J. "Medical Students and Their Examiners in Eighteenth Century America." *Transactions of the College of Physicians of Philadelphia* 21 (1953): 14–24.

Bellot, H. Hale. *University College, London 1816–1926.* London: University of London Press, 1929.

Ben-David, Joseph. *Centers of Learning: Britain, France, Germany, United States.* New York: McGraw-Hill, 1977.

———. "Emergence of National Traditions in the Sociology of Science: The United States and Great Britain." *Sociology of Science, 197–218.* Ed. Jerry Gaston. San Francisco: Jossey-Bass, 1978.

———. *Fundamental Research and the Universities: Some Comments on International Differences.* Paris: Organization for Economic Cooperation and Development, 1969.

———. "Scientific Productivity and Academic Organization in Nineteenth Century Medicine." *Science and Society.* Ed. Norman Kaplan, pp. 39–61. Chicago: Rand McNally, 1965.

———. *The Scientist's Role in Society: A Comparative Study.* Englewood Cliffs, NJ: Prentice-Hall, 1971.

———. "The Universities and the Growth of Science in Germany and the United States." *Minerva* 7 (1968): 1–35.

Benes, Peter, ed. *Medicine and Healing: The Dublin Seminar for New England Folklife, Annual Proceedings 1990.* Boston: Boston University Press, 1992.

Benison, Saul, A. Clifford Barger, and Elin L. Wolfe. *Walter B. Cannon: The Life and Times of a Young Scientist.* Cambridge, MA: Belknap Press, 1987.

Berlant, Jeffrey L. *Profession and Monopoly: A Study of Medicine in the United States and Great Britain.* Berkeley and Los Angeles: University of California Press, 1975.

Bernard, Paul P. "The Limits of Absolutism: Joseph II and the Allgemeine Krankenhaus." *Eighteenth-Century Studies* 9 (1975): 193–215.

Berry, Diana, and Campbell Mackenzie. *Richard Bright, 1789–1858: Physician in an Age of Revolution and Reform.* London: Royal Society of Medicine, 1992.

Bertaut, Jules. "Un étudiant en médecine sous la premier empire." *Histoire de la médecine* 2 (1952): 23–31.

Beukers, H., and J. Moll, eds. *Clinical Teaching, Past and Present.* Vol. 21, *Clio Medica* series, 1987–88. Amsterdam: Rodopi, 1989.

Bezel, Ernst, ed. *Johann Jakob Steger 1798–1857: Beispiel eines Medizinstudiums im frühen 19.Jahrhundert nach den Briefen an seine Eltern.* Zurich: Juris Druck & Verlag, 1981.

Bledstein, Burton J. *The Culture of Professionalism: The Middle Class and the Development of Higher Education in America.* New York: Norton, 1976.

Bleker, Johanna. "Die Idee der Einheit von Theorie und Praxis in der Medizin und ihr Einfluss auf den klinischen Unterricht im 19.Jahrhundert." *Arzt und Krankenhaus* 6 (1982): 232–36.

———. *Die naturhistorische Schule 1825–1845: Ein Beitrag zur Geschichte der klinischen Medizin in Deutschland.* Stuttgart: Gustav Fischer, 1981.

Bleker, Johanna, and Norbert Jachertz. *Medizin im Dritten Reich.* Cologne: Arzte-Verlag, 1989.

Bonner, Thomas N. "Abraham Flexner as Critic of British and Continental Medical Education." *Medical History* 33 (1989): 472–79.

——. *American Doctors and German Universities: A Chapter in International Intellectual Relations 1870–1914*. Lincoln: University of Nebraska Press, Landmark ed., 1987.

——. *To the Ends of the Earth: Women's Search for Education in Medicine*. Cambridge, MA: Harvard University Press, 1992.

——. "The German Model of Training Physicians in the United States, 1870–1914: How Closely Was It Followed?" *Bulletin of the History of Medicine* 64 (1990): 18–34.

——. *Medicine in Chicago, 1850–1950: A Chapter in the Social and Scientific Development of a City*. 2nd ed. Urbana: University of Illinois Press, 1991.

Borscheid, Peter. *Naturwissenschaft, Staat und Industrie in Baden (1848–1914)*. Stuttgart: Ernst Klett, 1976.

Bousfield, M. O. "An Account of Physicians of Color in the United States." *Bulletin of the History of Medicine* 17 (1945): 61–84.

Bower, Alexander. *The History of the University of Edinburgh*. 2 vols. Edinburgh: Oliphant, Waugh and Innes, 1817.

Brand, Jeanne L. *Doctors and the State: The British Medical Profession and Government Action in Public Health, 1870–1912*. Baltimore: Johns Hopkins University Press, 1965.

Bridge, Norman, and John E. Rhodes. *Rush Medical College*. Chicago: Oxford Publishing, 1896.

Brieger, Gert H. "The California Origins of the Johns Hopkins Medical School." *Bulletin of the History of Medicine* 51 (1977): 339–52.

——. "'Fit to Study Medicine': Notes for a History of Pre-Medical Education in America." *Bulletin of the History of Medicine* 57 (1983): 1–21.

——, ed. *Medical America in the Nineteenth Century: Readings from the Literature*. Baltimore: Johns Hopkins University Press, 1971.

Bright, Pamela. *Dr Richard Bright (1789–1858)*. London: Bodley Head, 1983.

Britten, D. J., ed. *The Story of King's College Hospital and Its Medical School*. London: Farrand, 1991.

Brockbank, Edward M. *The Foundation of Provincial Medical Education in England and of the Manchester School in Particular*. Manchester: Manchester University Press, 1936.

Brockliss, Laurence W. B. *French Higher Education in the Seventeenth and Eighteenth Centuries: A Cultural History*. Oxford: Clarendon Press, 1987.

——. "L'enseignement médical et la révolution." *Histoire de l'education* 42 (1989): 79–110.

Broman, Thomas. "University Reform in Medical Thought at the End of the Eighteenth Century." *Osiris* 5 (1989): 36–53.

Brunton, Deborah C. "The Transfer of Medical Education: Teaching at the Edinburgh and Philadelphia Medical Schools." In *Scotland and America in the Age of Enlightenment*. Ed. R. B. Sher and J. R. Smith, pp. 241–58. Princeton, NJ: Princeton University Press, 1990.

Buck, W. D. *Medical Education*. Manchester, NH: John B. Clarke, 1869.

Burrow, James G. *AMA: Voice of American Medicine*. Baltimore: Johns Hopkins University Press, 1963.

——. *Organized Medicine in the Progressive Era: The Move Toward Monopoly*. Baltimore: Johns Hopkins University Press, 1977.

Butler, Stella V. F. "A Transformation in Training: The Formation of University Medical Faculties in Manchester, Leeds, and Liverpool, 1870–84." *Medical History* 30 (1986): 115–32.

Bynum, W. F. *Science and the Practice of Medicine in the Nineteenth Century.* Cambridge: Cambridge University Press, 1994.

Bynum, W. F., and Roy Porter, eds. *William Hunter and the Eighteenth-Century Medical World.* Cambridge: Cambridge University Press, 1985.

Cameron, H. C. *Mr. Guy's Hospital, 1726–1948.* London: Longmans, Green, 1954.

Cannon, W. B. "The Case Method of Teaching Systematic Medicine." *Boston Medical and Surgical Journal* 142 (1900): 31–36, 563–64.

Cardwell, D. S. L. "The Development of Scientific Research in Modern Universities: A Comparative Study of Motives and Opportunities." In *Scientific Change.* Ed. A. C. Crombie, pp. 661–67. New York: Basic Books, 1963.

Carr-Saunders, A. M., and P. A. Wilson. *The Professions.* Oxford: Clarendon Press, 1933.

Carson, Joseph. *A History of the Medical Department of the University of Pennsylvania from Its Foundation in 1765.* Philadelphia: Lindsay and Blakiston, 1869.

Carter, B. Noland. "The Fruition of Halsted's Concept of Surgical Training." *Surgery* 32 (1952): 518–27.

Cash, Philip. "Setting the Stage: Dr. Benjamin Waterhouse's Reception in Boston, 1782–1788." *Journal of the History of Medicine and Allied Sciences* 47 (1992): 5–28.

Castan, A. "Coup d'oeil sur l'histoire de la faculté de médecine de Montpellier." *Montpellier médical* 34 (1875): 489–515.

Chapman, Carleton B. *Order Out of Chaos: John Shaw Billings and America's Coming of Age.* Boston: Boston Medical Library, 1994.

Chesney, Alan M. *The Johns Hopkins Hospital and the Johns Hopkins University School of Medicine.* 3 vols. Baltimore: Johns Hopkins University Press, 1943–63.

Chinard, Gilbert. "The Life of a Parisian Medical Student in the Eighteenth Century." *Bulletin of the History of Medicine* 7 (1939): 374–80.

Chitnis, Anant. "Medical Education in Edinburgh, 1790–1826, and Some Victorian Social Consequences." *Medical History* 17 (1970): 173–85.

Clark, George, and A. M. Cooke. *A History of the Royal College of Physicians of London.* 3 vols. Oxford: Clarendon Press, 1966–72.

Coleman, N. R. "Remarks upon Medical Instruction—A Plea for Greater Uniformity." *New York Medical Journal* 78 (1903): 205–10.

Coleman, William, ed. *French Views of German Science.* New York: Arno Press, 1981.

Coleman, William, and Frederick L. Holmes, eds. *The Investigative Enterprise: Experimental Physiology in Nineteenth-Century Medicine.* Berkeley and Los Angeles: University of California Press, 1988.

Comrie, John D. *History of Scottish Medicine.* 2 vols. London: Wellcome Historical Medical Museum, 1932.

Congrès national des sociétés savantes. *Histoire de l'école médicale de Montpellier: Colloque.* Paris: Comité des travaux historiques et scientifiques, 1985.

Connor, J. T. H. "'A Sort of Felo-de-se': Eclecticism, Related Medical Sects, and Their Decline in Victorian Ontario." *Bulletin of the History of Medicine* 65 (1991): 503–27.

Conze, Werner, ed. *Staat und Gesellschaft im deutschen Vormärz, 1815–1848.* Stuttgart: Ernst Klett, 1962.

Cope, Zachary. *The History of St. Mary's Hospital Medical School.* London: William Heinemann, 1954.

———. "The Influence of the Free Dispensaries upon Medical Education in Britain." *Medical History* 13 (1969): 29–36.

Copeman, W. S. C. "The Evolution of Clinical Method in English Medical Education." *Proceedings of the Royal Society of Medicine* 58 (1965): 887–94.

Corlieu, Auguste. *Centenaire de la faculté de médecine de Paris (1794–1894).* Paris: Imprimerie nationale, 1896.

Corner, George W. *Two Centuries of Medicine: A History of the School of Medicine, University of Pennsylvania.* Philadelphia: Lippincott, 1965.

Coury, Charles. *Enseignement de la médecine en France des origines à nos jours.* Paris: Expansion scientifique françoise, 1968.

Cowen, David L. *Medical Education: The Queen's–Rutgers Experience, 1792–1830.* New Brunswick, NJ: Rutgers Medical School, 1966.

Crawford, Elisabeth. "Competition and Centralization in German and French Science in the Nineteenth and Early Twentieth Centuries: The Theses of Joseph Ben-David." *Minerva* 26 (1988): 618–26.

Crosland, Maurice. "History of Science in a National Context." *British Journal for the History of Science* 10 (1977): 95–113.

———. *Science Under Control: The French Academy of Sciences, 1795–1914.* Cambridge: Cambridge University Press, 1992.

Crosse, V. Mary. *A Surgeon in the Early Nineteenth Century: The Life and Times of John Green Crosse, 1790–1850.* Edinburgh: E & S. Livingstone, 1968.

Cunningham, Andrew, and Roger French, eds. *The Medical Enlightenment of the Eighteenth Century.* Cambridge: Cambridge University Press, 1990.

Cunningham, Andrew, and Perry Williams, eds. *The Laboratory Revolution in Medicine.* Cambridge: Cambridge University Press, 1992.

Cushing, Harvey. *The Life of Sir William Osler.* Oxford: Oxford University Press, 1940.

Cutter, Irving. *The School of Medicine.* Boston: Ginn, 1930.

Darmon, Pierre. *La vie quotidienne du médecin parisien en 1900.* Paris: Hachette, 1988.

Davenport, Horace W. *Doctor Dock: Teaching and Learning Medicine at the Turn of the Century.* New Brunswick, NJ: Rutgers University Press, 1987.

———. *Fifty Years of Medicine at the University of Michigan, 1891–1941.* Ann Arbor: University of Michigan Medical School, 1986.

———. "The Life and Death of Laboratory Teaching of Medical Physiology: A Personal Narrative." *American Journal of Physiology* 263 (1993): 516–23; 265 (1993): 555–71.

———. "Physiology, 1850–1923: The View from Michigan." Supplement to *The Physiologist* 25 (1982): v–63.

Davis, Nathan S. "A Brief History of the Origin of the American Medical Association." *Janus* 2 (1897): 30–37.

———. *Contributions to the History of Medical Education and Medical Institutions in the United States of America 1776–1876.* Washington, DC: U.S. Government Printing Office, 1877.

———. *History of Medical Education and Institutions in the United States.* Chicago: S. C. Griggs, 1851.

Delauney, Paul. "Les médecines, la restauration et la révolution de 1830." *Médecine internationale illustrée*, supplements, January 1931 to May 1932. Sixteen installments.

Delmas, Paul. "Les étapes de l'enseignement clinique à Montpellier." *L'Informateur médical* 5 (1926): 2–6.

Despierres, Gab. *Histoire de l'enseignement médical à Lyon de l'antiguite à nos jours*. Lyon: Edition ACEML, 1984.

―――. "Histoire de la naissance de la faculté de médecine de Lyon; son premier doyen: Louis Lortet." *Conferences d'histoire de la médecine, cycle 81–82*. Lyon: Institut d'histoire de la médecine, Université Claude Bernard, 1982.

―――. "Histoire de la these médicale sous l'ancien régime en France et même à Lyon." *Conferences d'histoire de la médecine, cycle 84–85*. Lyon: Institut d'histoire de la médecine, Université Claude Bernard, 1985.

Diepgen, Paul, and Edith Heischkel. *Die Medizin an der Berliner Charité bis zur Gründung der Universität*. Berlin: Julius Springer, 1935.

Digby, Anne. *Making a Medical Living: Doctors and Patients in the English Market for Medicine, 1720–1911*. Cambridge: Cambridge University Press, 1994.

Dodds, T. Andrew. "Richard Cabot: Medical Reformer During the Progressive Era (1890–1920)." *Annals of Internal Medicine* 119 (1993): 417–22.

Doig, A., J. P. S. Ferguson, I. A. Milne, and R. Passmore. *William Cullen and the Eighteenth Century Medical World: A Bicentenary Exhibition and Symposium Arranged by the Royal College of Physicians at Edinburgh in 1990*. Edinburgh: University of Edinburgh Press, 1993.

Doolin, William. "Dublin's Contribution to Medicine." *Journal of the History of Medicine and Allied Sciences* 2 (1947): 321–26.

Dow, Derek, and Michael Moss. "The Medical Curriculum at Glasgow in the Early Nineteenth Century." *History of Universities* 7 (1988): 227–57.

Dow, Derek, and Kenneth C. Calman, eds. *The Royal Medico–Chirurgical Society of Glasgow: A History, 1814–1989*. Glasgow: Royal Medico–Chirurgical Society, 1989.

Drachman, Virginia G. *Hospital with a Heart: Women Doctors and the Paradox of Separatism at the New England Hospital, 1862–1969*. Ithaca, NY: Cornell University Press, 1984.

Duffy, John. *From Humors to Medical Science: A History of American Medicine*. 2nd ed. Urbana: University of Illinois Press, 1993.

Dulieu, Louis. *La médecine à Montpellier, tome IV: De la première a la troisième république*. Avignon: privately printed, 1988.

―――. "La vie médicale et chirurgicale à Montpellier du 12 août 1792 au 14 frimaire an III." *Revue d'histoire des sciences et de leurs applications* 8 (1955): 38–51, 146–69.

Dupree, A. Hunter. *Science in the Federal Government*. Cambridge, MA: Belknap Press, 1957.

―――. "The Structure of the Government–University Partnership after World War II." *Bulletin of the History of Medicine* 39 (1965): 245–60.

Durand-Fardel, Raymond. *L'internat en médecine et en chirurgie des hôpitaux et hospices civils de Paris: Centenaire de l'internat, 1802–1902*. Paris: G. Steinheil, 1903.

Eisendrath, Daniel N. "The Elective System in Medical Schools." *Medical News* 82 (1903): 489–91.

Elliger, Tilman J. *Die Mediziner-Ausbildung in Osterreich: Analyse eines Studienganges in seinem historischen und sozialen Kontext*. Munich: Profil, 1986

Ellis, Jack D. *The Physician-Legislators of France: Medicine and Politics in the Early Third Republic 1870–1914*. Cambridge: Cambridge University Press, 1990.

Ellis, John. *LHMC 1785–1985: The Story of the London Hospital Medical College.* London: London Hospital Medical Club, 1986.

———. "Medical Education in the UK and Europe." In *Oxford Companion to Medicine.* Ed. J. N. Walton et al., pp. 714–32. New York: Oxford University Press, 1986.

Emsch-Dériaz, Antoinette. "L'enseignement clinique au XVIIIe siècle: L'example de Tissot." *Canadian Bulletin of Medical History* 4 (1987): 145–64.

———. *Tissot: Physician of the Enlightenment.* New York: Peter Lang, 1992.

Estes, J. Worth, and David M. Goodman. *The Changing Humors of Portsmouth: The Medical Biography of an American Town, 1623–1983.* Boston: Francis A. Countway Library of Medicine, 1986.

Eulenburg, Franz. *Die Frequenz der deutschen Universitäten von ihrer Gründung bis zur Gegenwart.* Leipzig: B. G. Teubner, 1904.

Eulner, Hans-Heinz. *Die Entwicklung der medizinischen Spezialfächer an den Universitäten des deutschen Sprachgebietes.* Stuttgart: Ferdinand Enke, 1970.

———. "Historische Aspekte zu aktuellen Fragen des Medizinstudiums." *Medizinhistorisches Journal* 3 (1968): 186–94.

Farmer, Harold E. "An Account of the Earliest Colored Gentlemen in Medical Science in the United States." *Bulletin of the History of Medicine* 8 (1940): 599–618.

Faure, Olivier. *Genèse de l'hôpital moderne: Les hospices civils de Lyon de 1802–1845.* Lyon: Editions de CNRSL presses universitaire de Lyon, 1982.

Faust, Anselm. *Der nationalsozialistische Studentenbund.* 2 vols. Düsseldorf: Schwann, 1973.

Felter, Harvey W. *History of the Eclectic Medical Institute of Cincinnati, Ohio.* Cincinnati: Alumnae Association of the Eclectic Medical Institute, 1902.

Ferland, Jean-Jacques. *Les grandes questions de la pédagogie médicale: Perspective nord-americaine.* Quebec: Les presses de l'Université Laval, 1987.

Fiddes, Edward. *Chapters in the History of Owens College and of Manchester University 1851–1914.* Manchester: Manchester University Press, 1937.

Finot, André. *Les facultés de médecine de province avant la révolution.* Paris, 1958.

Fischer, Alfons. *Geschichte des deutschen Gesundheitswesen.* 2 vols. Berlin: Hildesheim, 1965.

Fissell, Mary E. *Patients, Power, and the Poor in Eighteenth-Century Bristol.* Cambridge: Cambridge University Press, 1991.

Fitz, Reginald. "The Surprising Career of Peter la Terrière, Bachelor in Medicine." *Annals of Medical History* 3 (1941): 395–417.

Fleming, Donald. *William H. Welch and the Rise of Modern Medicine.* Boston: Little, Brown, 1954.

Flexner, Abraham. "The German Side of Medical Education." *Atlantic Monthly* 112 (1913): 654–62.

———. *Medical Education: A Comparative Study.* New York: Macmillan, 1925.

———. "Medical Education, 1905–1924." *Educational Record*, April 1924, pp. 3–17.

———. *Medical Education in Europe.* New York: Carnegie Foundation for the Advancement of Teaching, Bulletin no. 6, 1912.

———. *Medical Education in the United States and Canada.* New York: Carnegie Foundation for the Advancement of Teaching, Bulletin no. 4, 1910.

Flexner, Simon. *The Evolution and Organization of the University Clinic.* Oxford: Clarendon Press, 1939.

Flexner, Simon, and James T. Flexner. *William Henry Welch and the Heroic Age of American Medicine.* New York: Dover, 1966.

Forster, Robert, and Orest Ranum, eds. *Medicine and Society in France: Selections from the Annales Economies, Sociétés, Civilisations.* Vol. 6. Trans. Elborg Forster and Patricia M. Ranum. Baltimore: Johns Hopkins University Press, 1980.

Fossard, Jacques. *Histoire polymorphe de l'internat en médecine et chirurgie des hôpitaux et hospices civils de Paris.* 2 vols. Grenoble: C. P. B. F., 1982.

Foucault, Michel. *The Birth of the Clinic: An Archaeology of Medical Perception.* Trans. A. M. Sheridan Smith. New York: Pantheon Books, 1973.

———, et al. *Les machines à guerir.* Paris: Institut de l'environnement, 1975.

Fox, Daniel M. "Abraham Flexner's Unpublished Report: Foundations and Medical Education, 1909–1928." *Bulletin of the History of Medicine* 4 (1980): 475–96.

Fox, Robert. "Scientific Enterprise and the Patronage of Research in France 1800–70." *Minerva* 11 (1972): 442–73.

Fox, Robert, and George Weisz, eds. *The Organization of Science and Technology in France 1808–1914.* Cambridge: Cambridge University Press, 1980.

Frank, Robert G., Jr. "Science, Medicine and the Universities of Early Modern England: Background and Sources." *History of Science* 11 (1973): 194–216, 339–69.

Freidson, Eliot. *Profession of Medicine.* New York: Dodd, Mead, 1970.

French, Roger, and Andrew Wear, eds. *British Medicine in an Age of Reform.* London: Routledge, 1991.

Frijhoff, Willem. "L'école de chirurgie de Paris et les Pays-Bas: Analyse d'un recrutement, 1752–1791." *LIAS* (Maarsen/Holland) 17 (1990): 185–239.

Froggatt, Peter. "The People's Choice: The Medical Schools of Belfast 'Inst' (1835–1849) and the Catholic University (1855–1908) Compared." *Journal of the Irish Colleges of Physicians and Surgeons* 20 (1991): 49–59.

Fye, W. Bruce. *The Development of American Physiology: Scientific Medicine in the Nineteenth Century.* Baltimore: Johns Hopkins University Press, 1987.

———. "The Origin of the Full-Time Faculty System." *Journal of the American Medical Association* 265 (1991): 1555–62.

Gabriel, Richard A., and Karen S. Metz. *A History of Military Medicine.* 2 vols. Westport, CT: Greenwood Press, 1992.

Gardiner, Charles F. "Getting a Medical Education in New York City in the Eighteen-Seventies." *Academy Bookman* 8 (1955): 3–12.

Garrison, Fielding H. *John Shaw Billings.* New York: Putnam, 1915.

Gaston, J. McFadden. "Rudimentary Preparation Compared with Higher Education for Specialties in Medicine and Surgery." *Bulletin of the American Academy of Medicine* 2 (1895): 1–15.

Geison, Gerald L. *Michael Foster and the Cambridge School of Physiology: The Scientific Enterprise in Late Victorian Society.* Princeton, NJ: Princeton University Press, 1978.

———. "Social and Institutional Factors in the Stagnancy of English Physiology, 1840–1870." *Bulletin of the History of Medicine* 46 (1972): 30–58.

———, ed. *Physiology in the American Context 1850–1940.* Bethesda, MD: American Physiological Society, 1987.

————, ed. *Professions and the French State, 1700–1900.* Philadelphia: University of Pennsylvania Press, 1984.

Gelfand, Toby. "A Confrontation over Clinical Instruction at the Hôtel-Dieu of Paris During the French Revolution." *Journal of the History of Medical and Allied Sciences* 28 (1973): 268–82.

————. "Gestation of the Clinic." *Medical History* 25 (1981): 169–80.

————. "The 'Paris Manner' of Dissection: Student Anatomical Dissection in Early Eighteenth-Century Paris." *Bulletin of the History of Medicine* 46 (1972): 99–130.

————. *Professionalizing Modern Medicine: Paris Surgeons and Medical Science and Institutions in the 18th Century.* Westport, CT: Greenwood Press, 1980.

Gélis, Jacques. *La sage-femme ou le médecin: Une nouvelle conception de la vie.* Paris: Fayard, 1988.

Geoffrey, Daniel. "La vie d'un étudiant en médecine à Nantes en 1820." *Archives médicales de l'ouest* 14 (1982): 279–80.

Geyer-Kordesch, Johanna. "Court Physicians and State Regulation in Eighteenth-Century Prussia: The Emergence of Medical Science and the Demystification of the Body." In *Medicine at the Courts of Europe, 1500–1837.* Ed. Vivian Nutton, pp. 155–81. London: Routledge, 1990.

Geyer-Kordesch, Johanna, and Mark Weatherall, with Harmke Kaminga. *The History of Medicine in Cambridge: Education, Science, and the Healing Arts.* Cambridge: School of Clinical Medicine, 1990.

Gidney, R. D., and W. P. J. Millar. "The Reorientation of Medical Education in Late Nineteenth-Century Ontario: The Proprietary Medical Schools and the Founding of the Faculty in Medicine at the University of Toronto." *Journal of the History of Medicine and Allied Sciences* 49 (1994): 52–78.

Gizycki, Rainald von. "Centre and Periphery in the International Scientific Community: Germany, France and Great Britain in the 19th Century." *Minerva* 11 (1973): 474–94.

Goodrich, James T. "The Colonial American Medical Student: 1750–1776." *Connecticut Medicine* 40 (1976): 829–44.

Goubert, Jean-Pierre, ed. *La médicalisation de la societé française, 1770–1830.* Special issue of *Historical Reflections/Reflexions historiques,* spring and summer, 1982, p. 9.

Gougher, Ronald L. "Comparison of English and American Views of the German University, 1840–1865." *History of Education Quarterly* 10 (1969): 95–113.

Grawitz, Paul. *Geschichte der medizinischen Fakultät Greifswald, 1806–1906.* Greifswald: Julius Abel, 1906.

Greenbaum, Louis S. "'Measure of Civilization': The Hospital Thought of Jacques Tenon on the Eve of the French Revolution." *Bulletin of the History of Medicine* 40 (1975): 43–56.

————. "Thomas Jefferson's University of Virginia and the Paris Hospitals on the Eve of the French Revolution." *Medical History* 36 (1992): 306–19.

Griffiths, W. Handsel. "On the Teaching of Materia Medica and Therapeutics." *Practitioner* 13 (1874): 314–18.

Gruber, Georg B. "Frühgeschichte der pathologischen Anatomie in Göttingen." *Sudhoffs Archiv* 39 (1955): 315–33.

Grunwald, Erhard. *Das niedere Medizinalpersonal im Bayern des 19.Jahrhunderts.* Munich: Demeter, 1990.

———. *Studien zum militärärztlichen Ausbildungswesen in Deutschland, 1919–1945.* Munich: Demeter, 1980.

Gubalke, Wolfgang. *Die Hebamme im Wandel der Zeiten.* Hannover: Elwin Staude, 1964.

Guiart, J. "L'enseignement médico–chirurgical à Paris, en 1764, jugé par un étudiant allemand." *Bulletin de la societé française d'histoire de la médecine* 19 (1925): 25–29.

G. T. M. *De l'enseignement clinique dans les écoles de Paris.* Paris: A. Egron, 1818.

Haines, George, IV. *Essays on German Influence upon English Education and Science, 1850–1919.* New London, CT: Connecticut College, 1969.

———. *German Influence upon English Education and Science, 1800–1866.* New London, CT: Connecticut College, 1957.

Haller, John S., Jr. *American Medicine in Transition, 1840–1910.* Urbana: University of Illinois Press, 1981.

———. *Medical Protestants: The Eclectics in American Medicine, 1825–1939.* Carbondale: Southern Illinois University Press, 1994.

Halpern, Sydney A. *American Pediatrics: The Social Dynamics of Professionalism, 1880–1980.* Berkeley and Los Angeles: University of California Press, 1988.

Hamilton, David. *The Healers: A History of Medicine in Scotland.* Edinburgh: Canongate, 1981.

Harig, Georg, ed. *Chirurgische Ausbildung im 18.Jahrhundert. Abhandlung zur Geschichte der Medizin und der Naturwissenschaften, No. 57.* Husum: Matthiesen, 1990.

Harrington, Thomas F. *The Harvard Medical School: A History, Narrative and Documentary.* 3 vols. New York: Lewis Publishing, 1905.

Harte, Negley. *The University of London 1836–1936.* London: Athlone Press, 1986.

Harvey, A. McGehee. "Creators of Clinical Medicine's Scientific Base: Franklin Paine Mall, Lewellys Franklin Barker and Rufus Cole." *Johns Hopkins Medical Journal* 136 (1975): 168–77.

———. "Samuel J. Meltzer: Pioneer Catalyst in the Evolution of Clinical Science in America." *Perspectives in Biology and Medicine* 21 (1978): 431–40.

———. *Science at the Bedside: Clinical Research in American Medicine, 1905–1945.* Baltimore: Johns Hopkins University Press, 1981.

Harvey, A. McGehee, Gert H. Brieger, Susan L. Abrams, and Victor A. McKissick. *A Model of Its Kind: A Centennial History of Medicine at Johns Hopkins.* 2 vols. Baltimore: Johns Hopkins University Press, 1989.

Harwood, Jonathan. *Styles of Scientific Thought: The German Genetic Community, 1900–1933.* Chicago: University of Chicago Press, 1993.

Heagerty, John J. *Four Centuries of Medical History in Canada.* 2 vols. Toronto: Macmillan, 1928.

Heer, Georg. *Marburger Studentenleben 1527 bis 1927.* Marburg: M. G. Elwert, 1927.

Heidenheimer, Arnold J. "Professional Knowledge and State Policy in Comparative Historical Perspective: Law and Medicine in Britain, Germany and the United States." *International Social Science Journal* 122 (1989): 529–53.

Heischkel, Edith. "Die Entwicklung des medizinischen Unterrichts." *Medizinische Welt* 13 (1939): 1238–41, 1267–69.

———. "Schauplätze pharmakologischer Forschung und Lehre im Jahre 1866." *Medizinhistorisches Journal* 1 (1966): 110–17.

Heller, Robert. "Johann Christian Reil's Training Scheme for Medical Auxiliaries." *Medical History* 19 (1975): 321–32.

———. "Officiers de Santé: The Second-Class Doctors of Nineteenth-Century France." *Medical History* 22 (1978): 25–43.

Hermann, Henri. "Histoire de la faculté de médecine." *Revue lyonnaise de médecine*, special issue, 1958, pp. 222–38.

Hildreth, Martha L. *Doctors, Bureaucrats, and Public Health in France, 1888–1902.* New York: Garland, 1987.

Hoepke, Hermann. "Der Streit der Professoren Tiedemann und Henle um den Neubau des Anatomischen Instituts in Heidelberg (1844–1849)." *Heidelberger Jahrbücher* 5 (1961): 114–27.

———. "Studentisches Leben aus Jakob Henles Bonner Zeit." *Heidelberger Jahrbücher* 13 (1969): 23–33.

Holloway, Lisabeth M. "A Chart of Graduating Classes at American Medical Colleges Before 1907." *Watermark: Newsletter of the Association of Librarians in the History of the Health Sciences* 5 (1981): 1–12.

Holloway, S. W. F. "The Apothecaries' Act, 1815: A Reinterpretation." *Medical History* 10 (1966): 107–29, 221–36.

———. "Medical Education in England, 1830–1858: A Sociological Analysis." *History* 49 (1968): 299–324.

Holt, Anna C. "A Medical Student in Boston, 1825–26." *Harvard Library Bulletin* 6 (1952): 176–92, 358–75.

Horine, Emmet F. "Daniel Drake and His Contributions to Education." *Papers of the Bibliographical Society of America* 34 (1940): 303–14.

———. *Daniel Drake (1785–1852): Pioneer Physician of the Midwest.* Philadelphia: University of Pennsylvania Press, 1961.

Horn, David B. *A Short History of the University of Edinburgh, 1556–1889.* Edinburgh: Edinburgh University Press, 1967.

Horvilleur, Alain. *L'enseignement médical à Lyon de 1789 à 1821: Naissance de l'école secondaire de médecine.* Lyon: Bosc, 1965

Howell, Joel D., ed. *Medical Lives and Scientific Medicine at Michigan, 1891–1969.* Ann Arbor: University of Michigan Press, 1993.

Howie, William B. *Medical Education in 18th Century Hospitals.* Scottish Society of the History of Medicine, 1970.

Huard, P., and M. J. Imbault-Huart. "Concepts et réalités de l'éducation et de la profession médico-chirurgicales pendant la révolution." *Journal des savants*, 1973, pp. 126–50.

———. "L'enseignement libre de la médecine à Paris au XIXe siècle." *Revue d'histoire des sciences* 27 (1974): 45–62.

———. "Quelques réflexions sur les origines de la clinique parisienne." *Bulletin de l'academie de médecine* 159 (1975): 583–88.

———. "Structure et fonctionnement de la faculté de médecine de Paris en 1813." *Revue d'histoire des sciences et de leur applications* 28 (1975): 139–68.

Huddle, Thomas S. "Looking Backward: The 1871 Reforms at Harvard Medical School Reconsidered." *Bulletin of the History of Medicine* 65 (1991): 340–65.

Huddle, Thomas S., and Jack Ende. "Osler's Clinical Clerkship: Origins and Interpretations." *Journal of the History of Medicine and Allied Sciences* 49 (1994): 483–503.

Huerkamp, Claudia. *Der Aufstieg der Arzte im 19.Jahrhundert: Vom gelehrten*

Stand zum professionellen Experten. Göttingen: Vandenhoeck & Ruprecht, 1985.

———. "The Making of the Modern Medical Profession, 1800–1914: Prussian Doctors in the Nineteenth Century." In *German Professions, 1800–1950*. Ed. Geoffrey Cocks and Konrad H. Jarausch, pp. 66–84. New York: Oxford University Press, 1990.

Hulin, Nicole. "L'organisation de l'enseignement scientifique au milieu du XIXe siècle: L. Pasteur, témoin et acteur." *Revue du palais de la découverte* 13 (1985): 51–73.

Imbert, Jean. "La crise économique des hôpitaux français sous la révolution." In *Nouvelles frontières des défenses sanitaire et sociales*. Ed. Maurice Guéniot, pp. 23–30. Paris: Université René Descartes, 1990.

———, ed. *La protection sociale sous la révolution française*. Paris: Association pour l'étude de l'histoire de la securité sociale, 1990.

Irons, Ernest E. *The Story of Rush Medical College*. Chicago: Rush Medical College, 1953.

Jacobi, Abraham. "The New York Medical College 1782–1906." *Annals of Medical History* 1 (1918): 368–73.

Jacobson, Timothy C. *Making Medical Doctors: Science and Medicine at Vanderbilt Since Flexner*. Tuscaloosa: University of Alabama Press, 1987.

Jacyna, L. S. "The Laboratory and the Clinic: The Impact of Pathology on Surgical Diagnosis in the Glasgow Western Infirmary." *Bulletin of the History of Medicine* 62 (1988): 384–406.

———. "Au Lit des Malades: A. F. Chomel's Clinic at the Charité, 1828–9." *Medical History* 34 (1989): 420–49.

———. "Medical Science and Moral Science: The Cultural Relations of Physiology in Restoration France." *History of Science* 25 (1987): 111–46.

———. "The Politics of Medicine in Restoration France." *Social History of Medicine* 40 (1987): 84–85.

———, ed. *A Tale of Three Cities: The Correspondence of William Sharpey and Allen Thomson*. London: Wellcome Institute for the History of Medicine, supplement to *Medical History*, 1989.

James, W. W. Keen, ed. *The Memoirs of William Williams Keen*. Doylestown, PA: Keen, 1990.

Jarausch, Konrad H. "The Social Transformation of the University: The Case of Prussia, 1865–1914." *Journal of Social History* 12 (1979): 609–36.

———. *Students, Society, and Politics in Imperial Germany: The Rise of Academic Illiberalism*. Princeton, NJ: Princeton University Press, 1982.

———, ed. *The Transformation of Higher Learning 1860–1930: Expansion, Diversification, Social Opening, and Professionalization in England, Germany, Russia, and the United States*. Chicago: University of Chicago Press, 1983.

Jarcho, Saul. "The Fate of British Traditions in the United States as Shown in Medical Education and in the Care of the Mentally Ill." *Bulletin of the New York Academy of Medicine* 52 (1976): 419–40.

———. "Medical Education in the United States—1910–1956." *Journal of the Mount Sinai Hospital* 26 (1959): 339–85.

Jetter, Dieter. "Die ersten Universitätskliniken westdeutscher Staaten." *Deutsche medizinische Wochenschrift* 87 (1962): 2037–42.

Jewson, N. D. "The Disappearance of the Sick Man from Medical Cosmology, 1770–1870." *Sociology* 10 (1974): 225–44.

Johnson, Charles B. "Getting My Anatomy in the Sixties." *Bulletin of the Society of Medical History of Chicago* 3 (1923): 109–15.

Johnson, Jeffrey A. "Academic Chemistry in Imperial Germany." *Isis* 76 (1985): 500–24.

———. *The Kaiser's Chemists: Science and Modernization in Imperial Germany.* Chapel Hill: University of North Carolina Press, 1990.

Jonas, Steven. *Medical Mystery: The Training of Doctors in the United States.* New York: Norton, 1978.

Jones, Colin. *The Charitable Imperative: Hospitals and Nursing in Ancient Regime and Revolutionary France.* London: Routledge, 1989.

———. "Montpellier Medical Students and the Medicalization of 18th Century France." In *Problems and Methods in the History of Medicine.* Eds. Roy Porter and Andrew Wear, pp. 57–80. London: Croom Helm, 1987.

Jones, David R. *The Origins of Civic Universities: Manchester, Leeds & Liverpool.* London: Routledge, 1988.

Jones, Russell M. "American Doctors and the Parisian Medical World, 1830–1840." *Bulletin of the History of Medicine* 47 (1975): 40–65, 177–204.

———. "American Doctors in Paris, 1820–1861: A Statistical Profile." *Journal of the History of Medicine and Allied Sciences* 25 (1970): 143–57.

———, ed. *The Parisian Education of an American Surgeon: Letters of Jonathan Mason Warren (1832–1835).* Philadelphia: American Philosophical Society, 1978.

Jordan, F. W. *Life of Joseph Jordan, Surgeon, and an Account of the Rise and Progress of Medical Schools in Manchester.* Manchester: Sherratt & Hughes, 1904.

Joseph, Max. *Die deutschen Universitäten im Urteile französischer Gelehrter in der Zeit von 1900–1920.* Berlin: Emil Ebering, 1923.

Juettner, Otto. "Rise of Medical Colleges in the Ohio Valley." *Ohio Historical and Archaeological Quarterly* 22 (1913): 481–91.

Kaiser, Wolfram. "Hallesche Mediziner als Zeitzeugen und Fachchronisten: Aus der Memoiren-Literatur von 7 Jahrzehnten (1848–1918)." *Zeitschrift für die gesamte Innere Medizin* 45 (1990): 84–89.

———. "Vor 200 Jahren: Medizinische Sonderpromotion des 18.Jahrhunderts am halleschen Beispiel." *Zeitschrift für die gesamte Innere Medizin* 46 (1991): 288–95.

Kaiser, Wolfram, and Reinhard Mocek. *Johann Christian Reil.* Leipzig: B. G. Teubner, 1979.

Kaiser, Wolfram, and Arina Völker. "Die Geschichte der halleschen Ars medica Judaica." *Zeitschrift für die gesamte Innere Medizin* 44 (1989): 25–30, 241–46.

Karenberg, Axel. "Lernen am Bett der Schwangeren: Zur Typologie des Entbindungshauses in Deutschland (1728–1840)." *Zentralblatt für Gynäkologie* 113 (1991): 899–912.

———. "Osterreichische und deutsche Einflüsse während der Gründung der ersten Hochschulkliniken in Breslau." *Würzburger medizinhistorische Mitteilungen* 10 (1992): 433–41.

———. "Spitäler in Prag um 1800 als Unterrichtskrankenhäuser." *Arzt und Krankenhaus* 9 (1992): 333–39.

Kästner, Ingrid, and Achim Thom. *575 Jahre Medizinische Fakultät der Universität Leipzig.* Leipzig: Johann Ambrosius Barth, 1990.

Kater, Michael H. *Doctors Under Hitler.* Chapel Hill: University of North Carolina Press, 1989.

Kaufman, Martin. *American Medical Education: The Formative Years, 1765–1910.* Westport, CT: Greenwood Press, 1976.

———. "How Prospective Doctors Spent Their Days: Student Life at the University of Vermont." *Vermont History* 43 (1975): 274–91.

Keel, Othmar. "La problématique institutionelle de la clinique en France et à l'étranger." *Bulletin canadienne d'histoire de médecine* 2 (1985): 183–204; 3 (1985): 1–30.

Keele, Kenneth D. *The Evolution of Clinical Methods in Medicine.* Springfield, IL: Thomas, 1963.

Keller, Richard A. *Geschichte der Universität Heidelberg im ersten Jahrzehnt nach der Reorganisation durch Karl Friedrich (1803–1813).* Heidelberg: Carl Winter, 1913.

Kelly, Thomas. *For Advancement of Learning: The University of Liverpool, 1881–1981.* Liverpool: Liverpool University Press, 1981.

Kett, Joseph F. "American and Canadian Medical Institutions, 1800–1870." *Journal of the History of Medicine and Allied Sciences* 22 (1967): 343–56.

———. *The Formation of the American Medical Profession: The Role of Institutions, 1780–1860.* New Haven, CT: Yale University Press, 1968.

Killian, Hans. *Meister der Chirurgie und die Chirurgenschulen im gesamten deutschen Sprachraum.* 2nd ed. Stuttgart: Georg Thieme, 1980.

King, Lester S. *Transformations in American Medicine from Benjamin Rush to William Osler.* Baltimore: Johns Hopkins University Press, 1991.

Klein, Marc. "Histoire de l'enseignement médical à Strasbourg." In *La faculté dans sa ville.* Strasbourg: Sandoz, 1970.

———. *Regards d'un biologiste: Evolution de l'approche scientifique l'enseignement médical strasbourgeois.* Paris: Herman, 1980.

Kleinheinrich, Thomas, and Reinhard Lohölter, eds. "Festschrift zu Ehren von Dietrich Habeck und Hans E. Renschler." *Medizinische Ausbildung* 7 (1990): 1–122.

Klickstein, Herbert S. "A Short History of the Professorship of Chemistry at the University of Pennsylvania School of Medicine, 1765–1847." *Bulletin of the History of Medicine* 27 (1953): 43–68.

Klimpel, V. "Zur chirurgischen Ausbildung am ehemaligen Dresdner Collegium Medico–Chirurgicum." *Zentralblatt für Chirurgie* 115 (1990): 181–85.

Klostermann, Erich. *Die Rückkehr der Strassburger Dozenten 1918/19 und ihre Aufnahme.* Halle: Max Niemeyer, 1932.

Koch, Hans-Theodor. "Zwei Studienreisen des halleschen Chirurgen Carl Heinrich Dzondi (1770–1835) nach Paris (1821) und nach Holland, England, Schottland und Irland (1822)." *Acta Historische Leopoldina* 2 (1905): 145–61.

Kohler, Robert E. *From Medical Chemistry to Biochemistry: The Making of a Biomedical Discipline.* Cambridge: Cambridge University Press, 1982.

———. *Partners in Science: Foundations and Natural Scientists, 1900–1945.* Chicago: University of Chicago Press, 1991.

Köpke, Rudolf. *Die Gründung der königlichen Friedrich-Wilhelms-Universität zu Berlin.* Berlin: Gustav Schade, 1860.

Kremer, Richard L. "Between Wissenschaft und Praxis: Experimental Medicine and the Prussian State, 1807–1848." In *"Einsamkeit und Freiheit" neu Besichtigt.* Ed. Gert Schubring, pp. 55–70. Stuttgart: Franz Steiner, 1991.

Krobot, Alois. *Zur Geschichte der medizinischen Ausbildung an der Prager Karl-suniversität von 1650 bis 1800.* Zurich: Juris Druck & Verlag, 1985.

Kruta, Vladislav. "J. E. Purkyne's Account of the Origin and Early History of the Institute of Physiology in Breslau (1841)." *Scripta Medica* 39 (1966): 1–16.

Kürz, Ernst G. *Die Freiburger medizinische Fakultät und die Romantik.* Munich: Münchener Beiträge zur Geschichte und Literatur der Naturwissenschaften und Medizin, no. 17, 1929.

LaBerge, Ann, and Mordechai Feingold, eds. *French Medical Culture in the Nineteenth Century.* Amsterdam: *Clio Medica*, 1994.

Lane, Joan. "The Medical Practitioners of Provincial England in 1783." *Medical History* 28 (1984): 353–71.

Latour, Bruno. *Les microbes: Guerre et paix suivi de irréductions.* Paris: A. M. Metailié, 1984.

Lawrence, Christopher. "The Edinburgh Medical School and the End of the 'Old Thing' 1790–1830." *History of Universities* 7 (1988): 259–86.

———. "Incommunicable Knowledge: Science, Technology and the Clinical Art in Britain 1850–1914." *Journal of Contemporary History* 20 (1985): 504–20.

Lawrence, Susan C. "'Desirous of Improvements in Medicine': Pupils and Practitioners in the Medical Societies at Guy's and St. Bartholomew's Hospital, 1795–1815." *Bulletin of the History of Medicine* 59 (1985): 89–104.

———. "Entrepreneurs and Private Enterprise: The Development of Medical Lecturing in London, 1775–1820." *Bulletin of the History of Medicine* 62 (1988): 171–92.

Leisebach, Moritz. *Das medizinisch-chirurgische Institut in Zürich, 1782–1833: Vorläufer der medizinischen Fakultät der Universität Zurich.* Zurich: Hans Rohr, 1982.

Lenel, Otto. *Die Universität Strassburg, 1621–1921.* Freiburg: Julius Boltze, 1921.

Lenoir, Timothy. "The Göttingen School and the Development of Transcendental Naturphilosophie in the Romantic Era." *Studies in the History of Biology* 5 (1981): 111–205.

———. *The Strategy of Life: Teleology and Mechanics in Nineteenth-Century German Biology.* Chicago: University of Chicago Press, 1982.

———. "Teleology Without Regrets: The Transformation of Physiology in Germany 1790–1847." *Studies in the History and Philosophy of Science* 12 (1981): 293–354.

Lenz, Max. *Geschichte der königlichen Friedrich-Wilhelms-Universität zu Berlin.* 2 vols. Halle: Buchhandlung des Waisenhauses, 1910.

Léonard, Jacques. "Les études médicales en France entre 1815 et 1848." *Revue d'histoire moderne et contemporaine* 13 (1966): 87–94.

———. *La médecine entre les savoirs et les pouvoirs.* Paris: Aubier, 1981.

———. *Médecins, malades et societé dans la France du XIX siècle.* Paris: Sciences et situation, 1992.

———. *La vie quotidienne du médecin de province au XIXe siècle.* Paris: Hachette, 1982.

Lesch, John E. *Science and Medicine in France: The Emergence of Experimental Physiology, 1790–1855.* Cambridge, MA: Harvard University Press, 1984.

Lesky, Erna. "Johann Peter Frank als Organisator des medizinischen Unterrichts." *Sudhoffs Archiv* 39 (1955): 1–29.

———. *Die Wiener medizinische Schule im 19. Jahrhundert.* Graz and Cologne: Hermann Böhlaus, 1965.

Levine, Daniel. *Poverty and Society: The Growth of the American Welfare State in International Comparison.* New Brunswick, NJ: Rutgers University Press, 1988.

Lewis, Samuel. "List of the American Graduates in Medicine in the University at Edinburgh." *New England Historical and Genealogical Register* 42 (1888): 159–65.

Lexis, Wilhelm. *Die deutschen Universitäten.* 2 vols. Berlin: A. Asher, 1893.

Lippard, Vernon W. *A Half-Century of American Medical Education: 1920–1970.* New York: Josiah Macy, Jr. Foundation, 1974.

Lobban, R. D. *Edinburgh and the Medical Revolution.* Cambridge: Cambridge University Press, 1980.

Long, Esmond R. *A History of Pathology.* 2nd ed. New York: Dover, 1965.

Loudon, Irvine. "Historical Importance of the Outpatient." *British Medical Journal,* 1978, pp. 974–77.

———. *Medical Care and the General Practitioner, 1750–1850.* Oxford: Clarendon Press, 1986.

———. "The Origins and Growth of the Dispensary Movement in England." *Bulletin of the History of Medicine* 55 (1981): 322–42.

———. "Two Thousand Medical Men in 1847." *Social History of Medicine* 33 (1983): 4–8.

Ludmerer, Kenneth M. *Learning to Heal: The Development of American Medical Education.* New York: Basic Books, 1985.

———. "The Plight of Clinical Teaching in America." *Bulletin of the History of Medicine* 57 (1983): 218–29.

———. "Reform at Harvard Medical School, 1869–1909." *Bulletin of the History of Medicine* 55 (1981): 343–70.

———. "Reform of Medical Education at Washington University." *Journal of the History of Medicine and Allied Sciences* 35 (1980): 149–73.

———. "Washington University and the Creation of the Teaching Hospital." *Journal of the American Medical Association* 266 (1991): 1981–83.

MacCallum, W. G. *William Stewart Halsted, Surgeon.* Baltimore: Johns Hopkins University Press, 1930.

Manton, Jo. *Elizabeth Garrett Anderson.* New York: Dutton, 1965.

Marland, Hilary, ed. *The Art of Midwifery: Early Modern Midwives in Europe.* London: Routledge, 1993.

Mathew, W. M. "The Origins and Occupations of Glasgow Students, 1740–1839." *Past and Present* 33 (1966): 74–94.

Maulitz, Russell C. "Channel Crossing: The Lure of French Pathology for English Medical Students, 1816–36." *Bulletin of the History of Medicine* 55 (1981): 475–96.

———. *Morbid Appearances: The Anatomy of Pathology in the Early Nineteenth Century.* Cambridge: Cambridge University Press, 1987.

Mazumdar, Pauline M. H. "Anatomical Physiology and the Reform of Medical Education: London, 1825–1835." *Bulletin of the History of Medicine* 57 (1983): 230–46.

———. "Anatomy, Physiology, and Surgery: Physiology Teaching in Early Nineteenth-Century London." *Canadian Bulletin of Medical History* 4 (1987): 119–43.

McClelland, Charles E. *The German Experience of Professionalization: Modern Learned Professions and Their Organizations from the Early Nineteenth Century to the Hitler Era.* Cambridge: Cambridge University Press, 1991.

McPhedran, N. Tait. *Canadian Medical Schools: Two Centuries of Medical History, 1822 to 1992*. Montreal: Harvest House, 1993.

Medvei, Victor C., and John L. Thornton, eds. *The Royal Hospital of Saint Bartholomew 1123–1973*. London: St. Bartholomew Hospital, 1974.

Merrington, W. R. *University College Hospital and Its Medical School: A History*. London: Heinemann, 1976.

Miller, Genevieve, William F. Norwood, and George E. Miller. "Medical Education in the American Colonies." *Journal of Medical Education* 31 (1956): 82–94.

———. "Medical Education and the Rise of Hospitals." *Journal of the American Medical Association* 186 (1963): 938–41, 1008–12, 1075–79.

Miller, Henry. "Fifty Years After Flexner." *Lancet* (1966): 648–54.

Miller, Kelly. "The Historic Background of the Negro Physician." *Journal of Negro History* 1 (1916): 99–109.

Milt, Bernhard. "Aus den Lehrjahren eines angehenden Chirurgen des 18.Jahrhunderts." *Vierteljahrschrift der naturforschenden Gesellschaft in Zürich* 99 (1954): 266–71.

Mitchell, Allan. *The Divided Path: The German Influence on Social Reform in France After 1870*. Chapel Hill: University of North Carolina Press, 1991.

Moore, Norman. *The History of St. Bartholomew's Hospital*. 2 vols. London: C. Arthur Pearson, 1918.

———. *The History of the Study of Medicine in the British Isles*. Oxford: Clarendon Press, 1908.

Moore, Thomas E., Jr. "The Early Years of the Harvard Medical School: Its Founding and Curriculum, 1782–1810." *Bulletin of the History of Medicine* 27 (1953): 530–61.

Morais, Herbert M. *The History of the Negro in Medicine*. New York: Association for the Study of Negro Life and History, 1967.

Morantz-Sanchez, Regina M. *Sympathy and Science: Women Physicians in American Medicine*. New York: Oxford University Press, 1985.

Morris, E. W. *A History of the London Hospital*. London: Edward Arnold, 1926.

Murken, Axel H. *Das Bild des deutschen Krankenhauses im 19.Jahrhundert*. Münster: Murken-Altrogge, 1978.

Murphy, Lamar R. *Enter the Physician: The Transformation of Domestic Medicine 1760–1860*. Tuscaloosa: University of Alabama Press, 1991.

Nauck, E. Th. "Uber die anatomischen, chirurgischen und geburtshilflichen Lehranstalten vornehmlich ausserhalb der Universitäten im 16.–19. Jahrhundert. Veruch einer Ubersicht." *Anatomischer Anzeiger* 113 (1963): 193–213; 116 (1965): 202–16.

———. *Zur Geschichte des medizinischen Lehrplans und Unterrichts der Universität Frieburg I. Br.* Freiburg: Universitätsbuchhandlung, 1952.

———. "Die Zahl der Medizinstudenten der deutschen Hochschulen im 14.–18.Jahrhundert." *Sudhoffs Archiv* 38 (1954): 180–85.

Neidhardt, J. P. H. "L'université de Strasbourg et l'enseignement médical de 1870 à 1918." *Conferences d'histoire de la médecine*, cycle 87–88, pp. 47–61. Lyon: Institut d'histoire de la médecine, Université Claude Bernard.

Neilson, William A., ed. *Charles W. Eliot: The Man and His Beliefs*. 2 vols. New York: Harper, 1926.

Neuburger, Max. *British Medicine and the Vienna School: Contacts and Parallels*. London: William Heinemann, 1943.

———, ed. *Die Wiener medizinische Schule im Vormärz*. Vienna: Rikola, 1921.

Newman, Charles. *The Evolution of Medical Education in the Nineteenth Century.* Oxford: Oxford University Press, 1957.

Norwood, William F. "The Beginnings of Medical Education in California." *Bulletin of the History of Medicine* 21 (1947): 760–71.

———. *Medical Education in the United States Before the Civil War.* Philadelphia: University of Pennsylvania Press, 1944.

Numbers, Ronald L., ed. *The Education of American Physicians: Historical Essays.* Berkeley and Los Angeles: University of California Press, 1980.

Numbers, Ronald L., and Todd L. Savitt, eds. *Science and Medicine in the Old South.* Baton Rouge: Louisiana State University Press, 1989.

Nye, Mary Jo. *Science in the Provinces: Scientific Communities and Provincial Leadership in France, 1860–1930.* Berkeley and Los Angeles: University of California Press, 1986.

Ogawa, Teizo, ed. *History of Medical Education.* Tokyo: Saikon, 1983.

O'Hara, Leo J. *An Emerging Profession: Philadelphia Doctors 1860–1900.* New York: Garland Press, 1989.

Olesko, Kathryn M. *Physics as a Calling: Discipline and Practice in the Königsberg Seminar for Physics.* Ithaca, NY: Cornell University Press, 1991.

———, ed. *Science in Germany: The Intersection of Institutional and Intellectual Issues. Osiris,* 2nd series (1989): 5.

Oliviér, Jean. "Un concours à Montpellier en 1812." *Le progrés medical* 6 (1952): 140–42.

O'Malley, C. D., ed. *The History of Medical Education.* Berkeley and Los Angeles: University of California Press, 1970.

Ormerod, Henry A. *The Early History of the Liverpool Medical School from 1834 to 1877.* Liverpool: C. Tinling, 1954.

Ormsby, Lambert H. *Medical History of the Meath Hospital and Couty Dublin Infirmary.* Dublin: Fannin, 1888.

Packard, Francis R. "Early Methods of Medical Education in North America." *Journal of the American Medical Association* 32 (1899): 635–40.

———. *History of Medicine in the United States.* 2 vols. New York: Paul B. Hoeber, 1931.

———. "How London and Edinburgh Influenced Medicine in Philadelphia in the Eighteenth Century." *Annals of Medical History* 4 (1932): 219–44.

———. *Some Account of the Pennsylvania Hospital from Its First Rise to the Beginning of the Year 1938.* Philadelphia: Pennsylvania Hospital, 1938.

Pantel, Johannes, and Axel Bauer. "Die Etablierung der pathologischen Anatomie an der Universität Heidelberg (1823–1876)." *Ruperto Carolla* 42 (1990): 87–100.

———. "Die Institutionalisierung der pathologischen Anatomie im 19. Jahrhundert an den Universitäten Deutschlands, der deutschen Schweiz und Osterreichs." *Gesnerus* 47 (1990): 303–28.

Parascondola, John. *The Development of American Pharmacology: John J. Abel and the Shaping of a Discipline.* Baltimore: Johns Hopkins University Press, 1992.

Parry, Noel, and José Parry. *The Rise of the Medical Profession.* London: Croom Helm, 1976.

Parsons, F. G. *The History of St. Thomas's Hospital.* 3 vols. London: Methuen, 1932–36.

Paton, D. Noël. "The Development of the Edinburgh School of Medicine." *Edinburgh Medical Journal* 40 (1894): 443–49.

Pattison, F. L. M. *Granville Sharp Pattison: Anatomist and Antagonist, 1791–1851*. Tuscaloosa: University of Alabama Press, 1987.

Paul, Harry W. *From Knowledge to Power: The Rise of the Science Empire in France, 1860–1939*. Cambridge: Cambridge University Press, 1985.

———. *The Sorcerer's Apprentice: The French Scientist's Image of German Science 1840–1919*. Gainesville: University of Florida Press, 1972.

Paulsen, Friedrich. *German Education, Past and Present*. London: T. F. Unwin, 1908.

———. *Geschichte des gelehrten Unterrichts auf den deutschen Schulen und Universitäten vom Ausgang des Mittelalters bis zur Gegenwart*. 2 vols. Berlin and Leipzig: Vereinigung wissenschaftlicher Verlagen, 1921.

Payer, Lynn. *Medicine and Culture: Varieties of Treatment in the United States, England, West Germany, and France*. New York: Henry Holt, 1988.

Peitzman, Steven J. "Thoroughly Practical: America's Polyclinic Medical Schools." *Bulletin of the History of Medicine* 54 (1980): 166–87.

Penman, W. Robert. "The Introduction of the Edinburgh Quizzing System into American Medical Education." *Bulletin of the History of Medicine* 52 (1978): 89–95.

Pennington, Carolyn. *The Modernisation of Medical Teaching at Aberdeen in the Nineteenth Century*. Aberdeen: Aberdeen University Press, 1994.

Perkin, Harold. "The Historical Perspective." In *Perspectives on Higher Education*. Ed. Burton R. Clark, pp. 17–55. Berkeley and Los Angeles: University of California Press, 1984.

———. *The Rise of Professional Society: England Since 1880*. London: Routledge, 1989.

Pery, G. *Histoire de la faculté de médecine de Bordeaux et de l'enseignement médical dans cette ville, 1441–1888*. Paris: O. Doin, 1888.

Peterson, M. Jeanne. *The Medical Profession in Mid-Victorian London*. Berkeley and Los Angeles: University of California Press, 1978.

Pfetsch, Frank R. *Zur Entwicklung der Wissenschaftspolitik in Deutschland, 1750–1914*. Berlin: Duncker & Humblot, 1974.

———. *Innovation und Widerstände in der Wissenschaft*. Düsseldorf: Bertelsmann, 1973.

Pickstone, John V. *Medicine and Industrial Society: A History of Hospital Development in Manchester and Its Region, 1752–1946*. Manchester: University of Manchester Press, 1985.

———. "A Profession of Discovery: Physiology in Nineteenth-Century History." *British Journal of the History of Science* 23 (1990): 207–16.

———, ed. *Medical Innovations in Historical Perspective*. New York: St. Martin's Press, 1992.

Pizon, Pierre. "Un étudiant en médecine du premier empire." *La presse médicale* 62 (1954): 1259–61.

Porter, Dorothy, and Roy Porter. *Patient's Progress: Doctors and Doctoring in Eighteenth-Century England*. Stanford, CA: Stanford University Press, 1989.

Porter, Roy. *Health for Sale: Quackery in England 1660–1850*. Manchester: Manchester University Press, 1989.

———, ed. *Patients and Practitioners: Lay Perceptions of Medicine in Pre-Industrial Society*. Cambridge: Cambridge University Press, 1985.

———, ed. *Medicine in the Enlightenment*. Amsterdam: Rodopi, 1995.

Porter, Roy, and Mikulàs Teich, eds. *The Enlightenment in National Context.* Cambridge: Cambridge University Press, 1981.

———, eds. *The Scientific Revolution in National Context.* Cambridge: Cambridge University Press, 1992.

Postell, William D. "F. B. Coleman, A Medical Student of the 1830's." *Bulletin of the History of Medicine* 18 (1945): 179–84.

———. "Medical Education and Medical Schools in Colonial America." *International Record of Medicine* 171 (1958): 364–70.

Poynter, F. N. L. *Medicine and Science in the 1860's.* London: Wellcome Institute for the History of Medicine, 1968.

———, ed. *The Evolution of Medical Education in Britain.* London: Pitman Medical Publishing, 1966.

Probst, Christian. "Johann Peter Frank als Arzt am Krankenbett." *Sudhoffs Archiv* 59 (1975): 20–53.

———. *Der Weg des ärztlichen Erkennens am Krankenbett: Hermann Boerhaave und die ältere Wiener medizinische Schule (1701–1787).* Supplement to *Sudhoffs Archiv,* no. 15. Wiesbaden: Franz Steiner, 1972.

Puschmann, Theodor. "Geschichte des klinischen Unterrichts." *Klinisches Jahrbuch* 1 (1889): 11–66.

———. *A History of Medical Education.* New York: Hafner, 1966. Facsimile of 1891 edition.

———. *Die Medicin in Wien während der letzten 100 Jahre.* Vienna: Moritz Perles, 1884.

Quenu, Jean. *Notre internat.* Paris: Doin, 1971.

Ramsay, Matthew. "Medical Power and Popular Medicine: Illegal Healers in Nineteenth-Century France." *Journal of Social History* 10 (1976–77): 560–87.

———. *Professional and Popular Medicine in France, 1770–1830: The Social World of Medical Practice.* Cambridge: Cambridge University Press, 1988.

Rath, Gernot. *Die Entwicklung des klinischen Unterrichts.* Göttingen: Vandenhoeck & Ruprecht, 1965.

Rather, L. J., ed. *Disease, Life and Man: Selected Essays.* Stanford, CA: Stanford University Press, 1958.

Reader, W. J. *Professional Men: The Rise of the Professional Classes in Nineteenth-Century England.* London: Weidenfeld and Nicolson, 1966.

Rebmann, Georg. *Der Leipziger Student vor hundert Jahren.* Leipzig: J. C. Hinrichs, 1897.

Redslob, Edmond. "Alors que j'était étudiant en médecine à la faculté de médecine allemande de Strasbourg." *Strasbourg médical* 10 (1959): 44–46.

Reingold, Nathan. "National Styles in the Sciences: The United States Case." In *Human Implications of Scientific Advance.* Ed. Eric G. Forbes, pp. 163–73. Edinburgh: University of Edinburgh Press, 1978.

Reiser, Stanley J. *Medicine and the Reign of Technology.* Cambridge: Cambridge University Press, 1978.

Reitzes, Dietrich. *Negroes and Medicine.* Cambridge, MA: Harvard University Press, 1958.

Renschler, Hans E. *Die Praxisphase im Medizinstudium: Die geschichtliche Entwicklung der klinischen Ausbildung mit der Fallmethode.* Berlin: Springer, 1987.

Richardson, Ruth. *Death, Dissection & the Destitute.* London: Routledge & Kegan Paul, 1987.

Riese, Reinhard. *Die Hochschule auf dem Wege zum wissenschaftlichen Grossbetrich: Die Universität Heidelberg und das badische Hochschulwesen, 1860–1914.* Stuttgart: Ernst Klett, 1977.

Riesman, David. "Clinical Teaching in America, with Some Remarks on Early Medical Schools." *Transactions and Studies of the College of Physicians of Philadelphia* 7 (1939–40): 89–110.

———. "The Dublin Medical School and Its Influence upon Medicine in America." *Annals of Medical History* 4 (1922): 86–96.

Ringer, Fritz K. *The Decline of the German Mandarins: The German Academic Community, 1890–1933.* Cambridge, MA: Harvard University Press, 1969.

———. *Education and Society in Modern Europe.* Bloomington: Indiana University Press, 1979.

———. *Fields of Knowledge: French Academic Culture in Comparative Perspective, 1800–1920.* Cambridge: Cambridge University Press, 1992.

Risse, Guenter B. *Hospital Life in Enlightenment Scotland: Care and Teaching at the Royal Infirmary of Edinburgh.* Cambridge: Cambridge University Press, 1986.

Rivett, Geoffrey. *The Development of the London Hospital System, 1823–1982.* London: King Edward's Hospital Fund, 1986.

Riznick, Barnes. "The Professional Lives of Early Nineteenth-Century New England Doctors." *Journal of the History of Medicine and Allied Sciences* 19 (1964): 1–16.

Roger, Henri. *Entre deux siècles: Souvenirs d'un vieux biologiste.* Paris: L'Expansion scientifique française, 1947.

Rolleston, Humphrey D. *The Cambridge Medical School: A Biographical History.* Cambridge: Cambridge University Press, 1932.

Rook, Arthur, ed. *Cambridge and Its Contribution to Medicine.* London: Wellcome Institute of the History of Medicine, 1971.

Rosen, George. "Cameralism and the Concept of Medical Police." *Bulletin of the History of Medicine* 27 (1952): 21–42.

———. "The Fate of the Concept of Medical Police, 1780–1890." *Centaurus* 5 (1957): 97–113.

Rosenberg, Charles E. *The Care of Strangers: The Rise of America's Hospital System.* New York: Basic Books, 1987.

———, ed. *The Origins of Specialization in American Medicine.* New York: Garland Press, 1989.

Rosner, Lisa. "Eighteenth-Century Medical Education and the Didactic Model of Experiment." In *The Literary Structure of Scientific Argument: Historical Studies.* Ed. Peter Dear, pp. 182–94. Philadelphia: University of Pennsylvania Press, 1991.

———. *Medical Education and the Age of Improvement: Edinburgh Students and Apprentices, 1760–1826.* Edinburgh: University of Edinburgh Press, 1991.

———. "Thistle on the Delaware: Edinburgh Medical Education and Philadelphia Practice, 1800–1825." *Social History of Medicine* 5 (1992): 19–42.

Rossiter, Margaret W. *The Emergence of Agricultural Science: Justus Liebig and the Americans, 1840–1880.* New Haven, CT: Yale University Press, 1975.

Rössler, Hellmuth, and Günther Franz, eds. *Universität und Gelehrtenstand, 1400–1800.* Limburg/Lahn: C. A. Starke, 1970.

Roth, Gottfried, ed. *Vom Baderlehrling zum Wundarzt: Carl Rabl, ein Mediziner im Biedermeier.* Vienna: Oberösterreichischer Landesverlag, n.d.

Rothblatt, Sheldon, and Björn Wittrock, eds. *The European and American University Since 1800: Historical and Sociological Essays.* Cambridge: Cambridge University Press, 1993.

Rothschuh, Karl E. *History of Physiology.* Huntington, NY: Robert E. Krieger, 1973.

Rothstein, William G. *American Medical Schools and the Practice of Medicine: A History.* New York: Oxford University Press, 1987.

———. *American Physicians in the Nineteenth Century: From Sects to Science.* Baltimore: Johns Hopkins University Press, 1972.

Sabin, Florence R. *Franklin Paine Mall: The Story of a Mind.* Baltimore: Johns Hopkins University Press, 1934.

Sander, Sabine. *Handwerkschirurgen: Sozialgeschichte einer verdrängten Berufsgruppe.* Göttingen: Vandenhoeck & Ruprecht, 1989.

Sanderson, Michael. *The Universities in the Nineteenth Century.* London: Routledge & Kegan Paul, 1975.

Savitt, Todd L. *Medicine and Slavery: The Diseases and Health Care of Blacks in Antebellum Virginia.* Chicago: University of Chicago Press, 1978.

Schickert, "Dr." *Die militärärztlichen Bildungsanstalten von ihrer Gründung bis zur Gegenwart.* Berlin: Ernst Siegfried Mittler, 1895.

Schipperges, Heinrich, Eduard Seidler, and Paul U. Unschuld, eds. *Krankheit, Heilkunst, Heilung.* Munich: Karl Alber, 1978.

Schmitt, Franz J. *Anfänge und Entwicklung der Hebammenkunst, des geburtshilflichen Lehrstuhles und der Universitäts-Frauenklinik in Würzburg.* Würzburg: Gebrüder Memminger, 1934.

Schmiz, Karl. *Die medizinische Fakultät der Universität Bonn 1818–1918.* Bonn: R. Marcus and E. Weber, 1920.

Schneck, Peter. "Die Gehurtshilfe und Gynäkologie als Lehrgegenstand in der ärztlichen Ausbildung während des 19.Jahrhunderts." *Zentralblatt für Gynäkologie* 108 (1986): 1324–29.

Schöler, Walter. *Geschichte des naturwissenschaftlichen Unterrichts im 17. bis 19.Jahrhundert.* Berlin: Walter de Gruyter, 1970.

Schumacher, Joseph, ed. *Melemata: Festschrift für Werner Leibbrand zum siebzigsten Geburtstag.* Mannheim: Grossdruckerei, 1967.

Schwöbel-Schrafl, Elaine. *Was verdankt die medizinische Fakultät Zürich ihren ausländischen Dozenten? 1833 bis 1863.* Zurich: Juris Druck & Verlag, 1985.

Seidler, Eduard. "Entwicklung naturwissenschaftlichen Denkens in der Medizin zur Zeit der Heidelberger Romantik." *Sudhoffs Archiv für Geschichte der Medizin* 47 (1963): 47–53.

———. *Die medizinische Fakultät der Albert-Ludwigs-Universität Freiburg im Breslau: Grundlagen und Entwicklungen.* Berlin: Springer, 1991.

———. "Wie wird man Arzt? Historische Grundformen der medizinischen Ausbildung." *Jahrbuch des Instituts für Geschichte der Medizin,* 1984, pp. 28–41.

Shafer, Henry Burnell. *The American Medical Profession 1783 to 1850.* New York: Columbia University Press, 1936.

Shryock, Richard H. *The Development of Modern Medicine: An Interpretation of the Social and Scientific Factors Involved.* New York: Knopf, 1947.

―――. "European Backgrounds of American Medical Education (1600–1900)." *Journal of the American Medical Association* 194 (1965): 709–14.

―――. *Medicine and Society in America 1660–1860.* New York: New York University Press, 1960.

―――. *The Unique Influence of the Johns Hopkins University on American Medicine.* Copenhagen: Ejnar Munksgaard, 1953.

Singer, Charles, and S. W. F. Holloway. "Early Medical Education in England in Relation to the Pre-History of London University." *Medical History* 4 (1960): 1–17.

Smeaton, W. A. *Fourcroy: Chemist and Revolutionary, 1755–1809.* Cambridge: privately printed, 1962.

Sokoloff, Leon. "The Rise and Decline of the Jewish Quota in Medical School Admissions." *Bulletin of the New York Academy of Medicine* 68 (1992): 497–518.

Sournia, Jean-Charles. *La médecine révolutionnaire, 1789–1799.* Paris: Editions Payot, 1989.

Spencer, Herbert R. *The History of British Midwifery from 1650 to 1800.* London: John Bale, 1927.

Staum, Martin S. *Cabanis: Enlightenment and Medical Philosophy in the French Revolution.* Princeton, NJ: Princeton University Press, 1980.

Starr, Paul. *The Social Transformation of American Medicine.* New York: Basic Books, 1982.

Steiner, Albert. *Ludwig Choulant und seine "Anleitung zu dem Studium der Medicin" (1829).* Zurich: Juris Druck & Verlag, 1987.

Stephens, Michael D., and Gordon W. Roderick. "American and English Attitudes to Scientific Education During the Nineteenth-Century." *Annals of Science* 30 (1933): 435–56.

Steudel, Johannes. *Die Frühzeit der Bonner medizinischen Fakultät.* Bonn: University of Bonn, 1944.

―――. "Medizinische Ausbildung in Deutschland 1600–1850." In *Et Multum et Multa: Festgabe für Kurt Lindner.* Ed. Sigrid Schwenk, Gunnar Tilander, and Carl Arnold Willemsen, pp. 394–420. Berlin: Walter de Gruyter, 1971.

Stevens, Rosemary. *American Medicine and the Public Interest.* New Haven, CT: Yale University Press, 1971.

―――. *Medical Practice in Modern England: The Impact of Specialization and State Medicine.* New Haven, CT: Yale University Press, 1966.

―――. *In Sickness and in Wealth: American Hospitals in the Twentieth Century.* New York: Basic Books, 1989.

Sticker, Georg. "Wunderlich, Roser, Griesinger: 'Die drei Schwäbischen Reformatoren der Medizin'." *Sudhoffs Archiv für Geschichte der Medizin und der Naturwissenschaften* 32 (1940–41): 217–73; 33 (1940–41): 1–53.

Stookey, Byron. *A History of Colonial Medical Education in the Province of New York, with Its Subsequent Development (1767–1830).* Springfield, IL: Thomas, 1962.

Struthers, John. "Historical Sketch of the Edinburgh Anatomical School." *Edinburgh Medical Journal* 12 (1866): 289–315, 431–57, 539–59.

Stübler, Eberhard. *Geschichte der medizinischen Fakultät der Universität Heidelberg, 1386–1925.* Heidelberg: Universitätsbuchhandlung, 1926.

Stürzbecher, Manfred. "Zur Geschichte der Ausbildung von Wundärzten in Berlin in der 1.Hälfte des 19.Jahrhunderts." *Forschungen und Fortschritte* 33 (1959): 141–47.

Summerville, James. *Educating Black Doctors: A History of Meharry Medical College.* Tuscaloosa: University of Alabama Press, 1983.

Sussman, George D. "The Glut of Doctors in Mid-Nineteenth-Century France." *Comparative Studies in Society and History* 19 (1977): 287–304.

Sybel, Heinrich von. *Vorträge und Aufsätze.* Berlin: A. Hofmann & Co., 1875.

Tansey, E. M. "'. . .the science least adequately studied in England': Physiology and the George Henry Lewes Studentship, 1879–1939." *Journal of the History of Medicine and Allied Sciences* 47 (1992): 163–85.

Taton, René, ed. *Enseignement et diffusion des sciences en France au XVIIIe siècle.* Paris: Hermann, 1964.

Taylor, David. *The Godless Students of Gower Street.* London: University College London Union, 1968.

Taylor, D. W. "The Life and Teaching of William Sharpey, (1802–1880): `Father of Modern Physiology' in Britain." *Medical History* 15 (1971): 126–53, 241–59.

Taylor, Selwyn. *Robert Graves: The Golden Years of Irish Medicine.* London: Royal Society of Medicine, 1989.

Temkin, Owsei. "The Role of Surgery in the Rise of Modern Medical Thought." *Bulletin of the History of Medicine* 25 (1951): 248–59.

Thielen, Jack E. "The Medical Student of 1852." *Bulletin of the History of Medicine* 27 (1953): 428–43.

Thompson, Ralph L. *Glimpses of Medical Europe.* Philadelphia: Lippincott, 1908.

Thompson, Stewart C. "The Great Windmill Street School." *Bulletin of the History of Medicine* 12 (1942): 377–91.

Thomson, Elizabeth H. "Thomas Bond, 1713–84: First Professor of Clinical Medicine in the American Colonies." *Journal of Medical Education* 33 (1958): 614–24.

Thwing, Charles F. *The American and the German University.* New York: Macmillan, 1928.

Tröhler, Ulrich. "250 Jahre Göttinger Medizin: Begründung-Folgen-Folgerungen." *Göttinger Universitätsschriften* 13 (1988): 9–36.

Tuchman, Arleen. "Experimental Physiology, Medical Reform, and the Politics of Education at the University of Heidelberg: A Case Study." *Bulletin of the History of Medicine* 61 (1987): 203–15.

———. *Science, Medicine, and the State in Germany: The Case of Baden, 1815–1871.* New York: Oxford University Press, 1993.

Turner, A. Logan. *Story of a Great Hospital: The Royal Infirmary of Edinburgh, 1729–1929.* Edinburgh: James Thin, 1979.

Turner, R. Steven. "The Great Transition and the Social Patterns of German Science." *Minerva* 25 (1987): 56–76.

———. "The Growth of Professorial Research in Prussia, 1818 to 1848—Causes and Context." *Historical Studies in the Physical Sciences* 3 (1971): 137–82.

Uhl, Felix. *Amerikanische Medizin von Europäern Beurteilt.* Zurich: Ferdinand Berger, 1959.

Ulrich, Laurel T. *A Midwife's Tale: The Life of Martha Ballard. Based on Her Diary, 1785–1812.* New York: Knopf, 1990.

Vaultier, Roger. "La vie des étudiants en médecine à travers les ages." *Presse médical* 62 (1954): 431–32.

Vaughan, Victor C. *A Doctor's Memories.* Indianapolis: Bobbs-Merrill, 1926.

Veleut, "Dr." *140 ans de réformes: L'évolution de l'enseignement des sciences medico-pharmaceutiques en France, 1794–1934.* Poitiers: Societé française d'imprimerie et de librairie, 1934.

Vess, David M. "The Collapse and Revival of Medical Education in France: A Consequence of Revolution and War, 1789–1795." *History of Education Quarterly* 7 (1967): 71–92.

———. *Medical Revolution in France 1789–1796.* Gainesville: University Presses of Florida, 1975.

Vevier, Charles, ed. *Flexner: 75 Years Later: A Current Commentary on Medical Education.* Lanham, MD: University Press of America, 1987.

Vieten, Bernhard. *Medizinstudenten in Münster: Universität, Studentenschaft und Medizin, 1905 bis 1945.* Cologne: Pahl-Rugenstein, 1982.

Vogel, Morris J. *The Invention of the American Hospital: Boston, 1870–1930.* Chicago: University of Chicago Press, 1980.

Vogel, Morris J., and Charles E. Rosenberg, eds. *The Therapeutic Revolution: Essays in the Social History of American Medicine.* Philadelphia: University of Pennsylvania Press, 1979.

Waddington, Ivan. *The Medical Profession in the Industrial Revolution.* Dublin: Gill and Macmillan, 1984.

———. "The Role of the Hospital in the Development of Modern Medicine: A Sociological Approach." *Sociology* 7 (1973): 211–24.

Wagner, Wilhelm. *Uber die medizinal-Anstalten und den jetzigen Zustand der Heilkunde in Grossbritannien und Irland.* Berlin: G. Reimer, 1825.

Waite, Frederick C. "American Sectarian Medical Colleges Before the Civil War." *Bulletin of the History of Medicine* 19 (1946): 148–66.

———. "Grave Robbing in New England." *Medical Library Association Bulletin* 33 (1945): 272–87.

———. "Medical Degrees Conferred in the American Colonies and in the United States in the Eighteenth Century." *Annals of Medical History* 9 (1937): 314–20.

———. *The Story of a Country Medical College: A History of the Clinical School of Medicine and the Vermont Medical College, Woodstock Vermont, 1827–1856.* Montpelier: Vermont Historical Society, 1945.

Walker, R. Milnes. *Medical Education in Britain.* London: Nuffield Provincial Hospitals Trust, 1965.

Walsh, Mary R. *"Doctors Wanted: No Women Need Apply": Sexual Barriers in the Medical Profession, 1875–1975.* New Haven, CT: Yale University Press, 1977.

Warner, John H. "The Fall and Rise of Professional Mystery: Epistemology, Authority and the Emergence of Laboratory Medicine in Nineteenth-Century America." In *The Laboratory Revolution in Medicine.* Ed. Andrew Cunningham and Perry Williams, pp. 110–41. Cambridge: Cambridge University Press, 1992.

———. "Ideals of Science and Their Discontents in Late Nineteenth-Century American Medicine." *Isis* 82 (1991): 454–74.

———. "Remembering Paris: Memory and the American Disciples of French Medicine in the Nineteenth Century." *Bulletin of the History of Medicine* 65 (1991): 301–25.

——. "Science in Medicine." In *Historical Writing on American Science*. Eds. Sally G. Kohlstedt and Margaret W. Rossiter. *Osiris* 1 (1985): 37–58.

——. "The Selective Transport of Medical Knowledge: Antebellum American Physicians and Parisian Medical Therapeutics." *Bulletin of the History of Medicine* 59 (1985): 213–31.

——. *The Therapeutic Perspective: Medical Practice, Knowledge, and Identity in America, 1820–1885*. Cambridge, MA: Harvard University Press, 1986.

Wartman, William B., ed. *Medical Teaching in Western Civilization*. Chicago: Yearbook Medical Publishers, 1961.

Webb, Gerald B., and Desmond Powell. *Henry Sewall: Physiologist and Physician*. Baltimore: Johns Hopkins University Press, 1946.

Weindling, Paul. "The Rockefeller Foundation and German Biomedical Sciences, 1920–40: From Educational Philanthropy to International Science Policy." In *Science, Politics and the Public Good*. Ed. Nicolaas A. Rupke, pp. 119–40. London: Macmillan, 1988.

Weiner, Dora B. *The Citizen-Patient in Revolutionary and Imperial Paris*. Baltimore: Johns Hopkins University Press, 1993.

Weisser, Ursula. "'Kurzer Unterricht für angehende der Arzneygelehrt beflissene': Gegenstandskatalog der Erlanger medizinischen Fakultät aus dem Jahre 1770." *Münchener medizinische Wochenschrift* 126 (1984): 1445–48.

Weisz, George. "Constructing the Medical Elite in France: The Creation of the Royal Academy of Medecine, 1814–20." *Medical History* 30 (1986): 419–43.

——. *The Emergence of Modern Universities in France, 1863–1914*. Princeton, NJ: Princeton University Press, 1983.

——. "The Medical Elite in France in the Early Nineteenth Century." *Minerva* 25 (1987): 150–70.

——. "The Politics of Medical Professionalization in France, 1845–1848." *Journal of Social History* 12 (1978): 3–30.

Wheatley, Steven C. "Abraham Flexner and the Politics of Educational Reform." *History of Higher Education Annual* 8 (1988): 45–57.

——. *The Politics of Philanthropy: Abraham Flexner and Medical Education*. Madison: University of Wisconsin Press, 1988.

White, Brenda M. "Medical Police, Politics and Police: The Fate of John Roberton." *Medical History* 27 (1983): 407–22.

Wickersheimer, Ernest. "Une institution oubliée: Le collège des étudians en médecine de la rue Saint-Victor." *Bulletin de la societé française d'histoire de la médecine* 5 (1906): 345–53.

Wilks, Samuel, and G. T. Bettany. *A Biographical History of Guy's Hospital*. London: Ward, Lock, 1892.

Wilson, J. Gordon. "The Influence of Edinburgh on American Medicine in the 18th Century." *Proceedings of the Institute of Medicine of Chicago* 7 (1929): 129–38.

Winau, Rolf. *Medizin in Berlin*. Berlin: Walter de Gruyter, 1987.

Winstanley, D. A. *Early Victorian Cambridge*. Cambridge: Cambridge University Press, 1940.

Woodward, John, and David Richards, eds. *Health Care and Popular Medicine in Nineteenth Century England: Essays in the Social History of Medicine*. London: Croom Helm, 1977.

Wright-St. Clair, Rex E. *Doctors Monro: A Medical Saga*. London: Wellcome Historical Medical Library, 1964.

Wrigley, E. A. *Continuity, Chance and Change: The Character of the Industrial Revolution in England*. Cambridge: Cambridge University Press, 1988.

Youngson, A. J. *The Scientific Revolution in Victorian Medicine*. London: Croom Helm, 1979.

Zimmerman, Leo M. "Surgeons and the Rise of Clinical Teaching in England." *Bulletin of the History of Medicine* 37 (1963): 167–77.

Zloczower, A. *Career Opportunities and the Growth of Scientific Discovery in 19th Century Germany*. New York: Arno Press, 1981.

Index